Magaret O. Oliphant

Chronicles of Carlingford

Magaret O. Oliphant

Chronicles of Carlingford

ISBN/EAN: 9783743306110

Manufactured in Europe, USA, Canada, Australia, Japa

Cover: Foto ©ninafisch / pixelio.de

Manufactured and distributed by brebook publishing software (www.brebook.com)

Magaret O. Oliphant

Chronicles of Carlingford

CHRONICLES OF CARLINGFORD

by

Margaret O. Oliphant

VOL. 3

Miss Marjoribanks

Chronicles of Carlingford.

MISS MARJORIBANKS.

CHAPTER I.

Miss Marjoribanks lost her mother when she was only fifteen, and when, to add to the misfortune, she was absent at school, and could not have it in her power to soothe her dear mamma's last moments, as she herself said. Words are sometimes very poor exponents of such an event: but it happens now and then, on the other hand, that a plain intimation expresses too much, and suggests emotion and suffering which, in reality, have but little, if any, existence. Mrs Marjoribanks, poor lady, had been an invalid for many years; she had grown a little peevish in her loneliness, not feeling herself of much account in this world. There are some rare natures that are content to acquiesce in the general neglect, and forget themselves when they find themselves forgotten; but it is unfortunately much more usual to take the plan adopted by Mrs Marjoribanks, who devoted all her powers, during the last ten years of her life, to the solacement and care of that poor self which other people neglected. The consequence was, that when she disappeared from her sofa—except for the mere physical fact that she was no longer there—no one, except her maid, whose occupation was gone, could have found out much difference. Her husband, it is true, who had, somewhere, hidden deep in some secret corner of his physical organisation, the remains of a heart, experienced a certain sentiment of sadness when he re-entered the house from which she had gone away for ever. But Dr Marjoribanks was too busy a man to waste his feelings on a mere sentiment. His daughter, however, was only fifteen, and had floods of tears at her command, as was natural at that age. All the way home she revolved the situation in her mind, which was considerably enlightened by novels and popular philosophy—for the lady at the head of Miss Marjoribanks's school was a devoted admirer of 'Friends in Council,' and was fond of bestowing that work as a prize, with pencil-marks on the margin—so that Lucilla's mind had been cultivated, and was brim-full of the best of sentiments. She made up her mind on her journey to a great many virtuous resolutions; for, in such a case as hers, it was evidently the duty of an only child to devote herself to her father's comfort, and become the sunshine of his life, as so many young persons of her age have been known to become in literature. Miss Marjoribanks had a lively mind, and was capable of grasping all the circumstances of the situation at a glance. Thus, between the outbreaks of her tears for her mother, it became apparent to her that she must sacrifice her own feelings, and make a cheerful home for papa, and that a great many changes would be necessary in the household—changes which went so far as even to extend to the furniture. Miss Marjoribanks sketched to herself, as she lay back in the corner of the railway carriage, with her veil down, how she would wind herself up to the duty of presiding at her papa's dinner-parties, and charming everybody by her good-humour and brightness, and devotion to his comfort; and how, when it was all over, she would withdraw and cry her eyes out in her own room, and be found in the morning languid and worn-out, but always heroical, ready to go down-stairs and assist at dear papa's breakfast, and keep up her smiles for him till he had gone out to his patients. Altogether the picture was a very pretty one; and, considering that a great many young ladies in deep mourning put force upon their feelings in novels, and maintain a smile for the benefit of the unobservant male creatures of whom they have the charge, the idea was not at all extravagant, considering that Miss Marjoribanks was but fifteen. She was not, however, exactly the kind of figure for this *mise en scène*. When her schoolfellows talked of her to their friends—for Lucilla was already an important personage at Mount Pleasant—the most common description they gave of her was, that she was "a large girl;" and there was great truth in the adjective. She was not to be described as a tall girl—which conveys an altogether different idea—but she was large in all particulars, full and well-developed, with somewhat large features, not at all pretty as yet, though it was known in Mount Pleasant that somebody had said that such a face might ripen into beauty, and become "grandiose," for anything anybody could tell. Miss Marjoribanks was not vain; but the word had taken possession of her imagination, as was natural, and solaced her much when she made the painful discovery that her gloves were half a number larger, and her shoes a hairbreadth broader, than those of any of her companions; but the hands and the feet were both perfectly well shaped; and being at the same time well clothed and plump, were much more presentable and pleasant to look upon than the lean rudimentary school-girl hands with which they were surrounded. To add to these excellences, Lucilla had a mass of hair which, if it could but have been cleared a little in its tint, would have been golden, though at present it was nothing more than tawny, and curly to exasperation. She wore it in large thick curls, which did not, however, float or wave, or do any of the graceful things which curls ought to do; for it had this aggravating quality, that it would not grow long, but would grow ridiculously, unmanageably thick, to the admiration of her companions, but to her own despair, for there was no knowing what to do with those short but ponderous locks. These were the external characteristics of the girl who was going home to be a comfort to her widowed father, and meant to sacrifice herself to his happiness. In the course of her rapid journey she had already settled upon everything that had to be done; or rather, to speak more truly, had rehearsed everything, according to the habit already acquired by a quick mind, a good deal occupied with itself. First, she meant to fall into her father's arms—forgetting, with that singular facility for overlooking the peculiarities of others which belongs to such a character, that Dr Marjoribanks was very little given to embracing, and that a hasty kiss on her forehead was the warmest caress he had ever given his daughter—and then to rush up to the chamber of death and weep over dear mamma. "And to think I was not there to soothe her last moments!" Lucilla said to herself, with a sob, and with feelings sufficiently real in their way. After this, the devoted daughter made up her mind to come down-stairs again, pale as death, but self-controlled, and devote herself to papa. Perhaps, if great emotion should make him tearless, as such cases had been known, Miss Marjoribanks would steal into his arms unawares, and so surprise him into weeping. All this went briskly through her mind, undeterred by the reflection that tears were as much out of the Doctor's way as embraces; and in this mood she sped swiftly along in the inspiration of her first sorrow, as she imagined, but in reality to suffer her first disappointment, which was of a less soothing character than that mild and manageable grief.

When Miss Marjoribanks reached home her mother had been dead for twenty-four hours; and her father was not at the door to receive her as she had expected, but by the bedside of a patient in extremity, who could not consent to go out of the world without the Doctor. This was a sad reversal of her intentions, but Lucilla was not the woman to be disconcerted. She carried out the second part of her programme without either interference or sympathy, except from Mrs Marjoribanks's maid, who had some hopes from the moment of her arrival. "I can't abear to think as I'm to be parted from you all, miss," sobbed the faithful attendant. "I've lost the best missus as ever was, and I shouldn't mind going after her. Whenever any one gets a good friend in this world, they're the first to be took away," said the weeping handmaiden, who naturally saw her own loss in the most vivid light. "Ah, Ellis," cried Miss Marjoribanks, reposing her sorrow in the arms of this anxious attendant, "we must try to be a comfort to poor papa!"

With this end Lucilla made herself very troublesome to the sober-minded Doctor during those few dim days before the faint and daily lessening shadow of poor Mrs Marjoribanks was removed altogether from the house. When that sad ceremony had taken place, and the Doctor returned, serious enough, heaven knows, to the great house, where the faded helpless woman, who had notwithstanding been his love and his bride in other days, lay no longer on the familiar sofa, the crisis arrived which Miss Marjoribanks had rehearsed so often, but after quite a different fashion. The widower was tearless, indeed, but not from excess of emotion. On the contrary, a painful heaviness possessed him when he became aware how little real sorrow was in his mind, and how small an actual loss was this loss of his wife, which bulked before the world as an event of just as much magnitude as the loss, for example, which poor Mr Lake, the drawing-master, was at the same moment suffering. It was even sad, in another point of view, to think of a human creature passing out of the world, and leaving so little trace that she had ever been there. As for the pretty creature whom Dr Marjoribanks had married, she had vanished into thin air years and years ago. These thoughts were heavy enough—perhaps even more overwhelming than that grief which develops love to its highest point of intensity. But such were not precisely the kind of reflections which could be solaced by paternal *attendrissement* over a weeping and devoted daughter. It was May, and the weather was warm for the season; but Lucilla had caused the fire to be lighted in the large gloomy library where Dr Marjoribanks always sat in the evenings, with the idea that it would be a "comfort" to him; and, for the same reason, she had ordered tea to be served there, instead of the dinner, for which her father, as she imagined, could have little appetite. When the Doctor went in to his favourite seclusion, tired and heated and sad—for even on the day of his wife's funeral the favourite doctor of Carlingford had patients to think of—the very heaviness of his thoughts gave warmth to his indignation. He had longed for the quiet and the coolness and the solitude of his library, apart from everybody; and when he found it radiant with firelight, tea set on the table, and Lucilla crying by the fire, in her new crape, the effect upon a temper by no means perfect may be imagined. The unfortunate man threw both the windows wide open and rang the bell violently, and gave instant orders for the removal of the unnecessary fire and the tea-service. "Let me know when dinner is ready," he said, in a voice like thunder; "and if Miss Marjoribanks wants a fire, let it be lighted in the drawing-room." Lucilla was so much taken by surprise by this sudden overthrow of her programme, that she submitted, as a girl of much less spirit might have done, and suffered herself and her fire and her tea-things to be dismissed up-stairs, where she wept still more at sight of dear mamma's sofa, and where Ellis came to mingle her tears with those of her young mistress, and to beg dear Miss Lucilla, for the sake of her precious 'elth and her dear papa, to be persuaded to take some tea. On the whole, master stood lessened in the eyes of all the household by his ability to eat his dinner, and his resentment at having his habitudes disturbed. "Them men would eat and drink if we was all in our graves," said the indignant cook, who indeed had a real grievance; and the outraged sentiment of the kitchen was avenged by a bad and hasty dinner, which the Doctor, though generally "very particular," swallowed without remark. About an hour afterwards he went up-stairs to the drawing-room, where Miss Marjoribanks was waiting for him, much less at ease than she had expected to be. Though he gave a little sigh at the sight of his wife's sofa, he did not hesitate to sit down upon it, and even to draw it a little out of its position, which, as Lucilla described afterwards, was like a knife going into her heart. Though, indeed, she had herself decided already, in the intervals of her tears, that the drawing-room furniture had got very faded and shabby, and that it would be very expedient to have it renewed for the new reign of youth and energy which was about to commence. As for the Doctor, though Miss Marjoribanks thought him insensible, his heart was heavy enough. His wife had gone out of the world without leaving the least mark of her existence, except in that large girl, whose spirits and forces were unbounded, but whose discretion at the present moment did not seem much greater than her mother's. Instead of thinking of her as a comfort, the Doctor felt himself called upon to face a new and unexpected embarrassment. It would have been a satisfaction to him just then to have been left to himself, and permitted to work on quietly at his profession, and to write his papers for the 'Lancet,' and to see his friends now and then when he chose; for Dr Marjoribanks was not a man who had any great need of sympathy by nature, or who was at all addicted to demonstrations of feeling; consequently, he drew his wife's sofa a little further from the fire, and took his seat on it soberly, quite unaware that, by so doing, he was putting a knife into his daughter's heart.

"I hope you have had something to eat, Lucilla," he said; "don't get into that foolish habit of flying to tea as a man flies to a dram. It's a more innocent stimulant, but it's the same kind of intention. I am not so much against a fire; it has always a kind of cheerful look."

"Oh, papa," cried his daughter, with a flood of indignant tears, "you can't suppose I want anything to look cheerful this dreadful day."

"I am far from blaming you, my dear," said the Doctor; "it is natural you should cry. I am sorry I did not write for my sister to come, who would have taken care of you; but I dislike strangers in the house at such a time. However, I hope, Lucilla, you will soon feel yourself able to return to school; occupation is always the best remedy, and you will have your friends and companions——"

"Papa!" cried Miss Marjoribanks; and then she summoned courage, and rushed up to him, and threw herself and her clouds of crape on the carpet at his side (and it may here be mentioned that Lucilla had seized the opportunity to have her mourning made *long*, which had been the desire of her heart, baffled by mamma and governess for at least a year). "Papa!" she exclaimed with fervour, raising to him her tear-stained face, and clasping her fair plump hands, "oh,' don't send me away! I was only a silly girl the other day, but *this* has made me a woman. Though I can never, never hope to take dear mamma's place, and be—all—that she was to you, still I feel I can be a comfort to you if you will let me. You shall not see me cry any more," cried Lucilla with energy, rubbing away her tears. "I will never give way to my feelings. I will ask for no companions—nor—nor anything. As for pleasure, that is all over. Oh, papa, you shall never see me regret anything, or wish for anything. I will give up everything in the world to be a comfort to you!"

This address, which was utterly unexpected, drove Dr Marjoribanks to despair. He said, "Get up, Lucilla;" but the devoted daughter knew better than to get up. She hid her face in her hands, and rested her hands upon her mother's sofa, where the Doctor was sitting; and the sobs of that emotion which she meant to control henceforward, echoed through the room. "It is only for this once—I can—cannot help it," she cried. When her father found that he could neither soothe her, nor succeed in raising her, he got up himself, which was the only thing left to him, and began to walk about the room with hasty steps. Her mother, too, had possessed this dangerous faculty of tears; and it was not wonderful if the soberminded Doctor, roused for the first time to consider his little girl as a creature possessed of individual character, should recognise, with a thrill of dismay, the appearance of the same qualities which had wearied his life out, and brought his youthful affections to an untimely end. Lucilla was, it is true, as different from her mother as summer from winter; but Dr Marjoribanks had no means of knowing that his daughter was only doing her duty by him in his widowhood, according to a programme of filial devotion resolved upon, in accordance with the best models, some days before.

Accordingly, when her sobs had ceased, her father returned and raised her up not unkindly, and placed her in her chair. In doing so, the Doctor put his finger by instinct upon Lucilla's pulse, which was sufficiently calm and well regulated to reassure the most anxious parent. And then a furtive momentary smile gleamed for a single instant round the corners of his mouth.

"It is very good of you to propose sacrificing yourself for me," he said; "and if you would sacrifice your excitement in the mean time, and listen to me quietly, it would really be something—but you are only fifteen, Lucilla, and I have no wish to take you from school just now; wait till I have done. Your poor mother is gone, and it is very natural you should cry; but you were a good child to her on the whole, which will be a comfort to you. We did everything that could be thought of to prolong her days, and, when that was impossible, to lessen what she had to suffer; and we have every reason to hope," said the Doctor, as indeed he was accustomed to say in the exercise of his profession to mourning relatives, "that she's far better off now than if she had been with us. When that is said, I don't know that there is anything more to add. I am not fond of sacrifices, either one way or another; and I've a great objection to any one making a sacrifice for me——"

"But, oh papa, it would be no sacrifice," said Lucilla, "if you would only let me be a comfort to you!"

"That is just where it is, my dear," said the steady Doctor; "I have been used to be left a great deal to myself; and I am not prepared to say that the responsibility of having you here without a mother to take care of you, and all your lessons interrupted, would not neutralise any comfort you might be. You see," said Dr Marjoribanks, trying to soften matters a little, "a man is what his habits make him; and I have been used to be left a great deal to myself. It answers in some cases, but I doubt if it would answer with me."

And then there was a pause, in which Lucilla wept and stifled her tears in her handkerchief, with a warmer flood of vexation and disappointment than even her natural grief had produced. "Of course, papa, if I can't be any comfort——I will—go back to school," she sobbed, with a touch of sullenness which did not escape the Doctor's ear.

"Yes, my dear, you will certainly go back to school," said the peremptory father; "I never had any doubt on that subject. You can stay over Sunday and rest yourself. Monday or Tuesday will be time enough to go back to Mount Pleasant; and now you had better ring the bell, and get somebody to bring you something—or I'll see to that when I go down-stairs. It's getting late, and this has been a fatiguing day. I'll send you up some negus, and I think you had better go to bed."

And with these commonplace words, Dr Marjoribanks withdrew in calm possession of the field. As for Lucilla, she obeyed him, and betook herself to her own room, and swallowed her negus with a sense, not only of defeat, but of disappointment and mortification which was very unpleasant. To go back again and be an ordinary school-girl, after the pomp of woe in which she had come away, was naturally a painful thought; she who had ordered her mourning to be made long, and contemplated new furniture in the drawing-room, and expected to be mistress of her father's house, not to speak of the still dearer privilege of being a comfort to him; and now, after all, her active mind was to be condemned over again to verbs and chromatic scales, though she felt within herself capacities so much more extended. Miss Marjoribanks did not by any means learn by this defeat to take the characters of the other *personæ* in her little drama into consideration, when she rehearsed her pet scenes hereafter—for that is a knowledge slowly acquired—but she was wise enough to know when resistance was futile; and like most people of lively imagination, she had a power of submitting to circumstances when it became impossible to change them. Thus she consented to postpone her reign, if not with a good grace, yet still without foolish resistance, and retired with the full honours of war. She had already re-arranged all the details, and settled upon all the means possible of preparing herself for what she called the charge of the establishment when her final emancipation took place, before she returned to school. "Papa thought me too young," she said, when she reached Mount Pleasant, "though it was dreadful to come away and leave him alone with only the servants; but, dear Miss Martha, you will let me learn all about political economy and things, to help me manage everything; for now that dear mamma is gone, there is nobody but me to be a comfort to papa."

And by this means Miss Marjoribanks managed to influence the excellent woman who believed in 'Friends in Council,' and to direct the future tenor of her own education; while, at least, in that one moment of opportunity, she had achieved long dresses, which was a visible mark of womanhood, and a step which could not be retraced.

CHAPTER II.

Dr Marjoribanks was so far from feeling the lack of his daughter's powers of consolation, that he kept her at Mount Pleasant for three years longer, during which time it is to be supposed he managed to be comfortable after a benighted fashion —good enough for a man of fifty, who had come to an end of his illusions. To be sure, there were in the world, and even in Carlingford, kind women, who would not have objected to take charge of the Doctor and his "establishment," and be a comfort to him; but, on the whole, it was undeniable that he managed tolerably well in external matters, and gave very good men's dinners, and kept everything in perfect order, so far as it went. Naturally the fairer part of existence was left out altogether in that grim, though well-ordered, house; but then he was only a man and a doctor, and knew no better; and while the feminine part of Grange Lane regarded him with natural pity, not only for what he lacked, but for a still more sad defect, his total want of perception on the subject, their husbands and fathers rather liked to dine with the Doctor, and brought home accounts of sauces which were enough to drive any woman to despair. Some of the ladies of Grange Lane—Mrs Chiley, for example, who was fond of good living herself, and liked, as she said, "a little variety"—laid siege to the Doctor, and did their best to coax his receipts out of him; but Dr Marjoribanks knew better than that. He gave all the credit to his cook, like a man of sense; and as that functionary was known in Carlingford to be utterly regardless and unprincipled in respect to gravy-beef, and the materials for "stock," or "consommé," as some people called it, society was disinclined to exert its ordinary arts to seduce so great an artiste from the kitchen of her indulgent master. And then there were other ladies who took a different tone. "Dr Marjoribanks, poor man, has nothing but his table to take up his mind," said Mrs Centum, who had six children; "I never heard that the heart could be nourished upon sauces, for my part; and for a man who has his children's future to think of, I must say I am surprised at you, Mr Centum." As for young Mrs Woodburn, her reply was still more decisive, though milder in its tone. "Poor cook! I am so sorry for her," said the gentle young matron. "You know you always like something for breakfast, Charles; and then there is the children's dinner, and our lunch, and the servants' dinner, so that the poor thing is worn out before she comes to what *you* call the great event of the day; and you know how angry you were when I asked for a kitchen-maid for her, poor soul." The consequence of all this was, that Dr Marjoribanks remained unrivalled in Grange Lane in this respect at least. When rumours arose in Carlingford of a possible second marriage for the Doctor—and such rumours naturally arose three or four times in the course of the three years—the men of Grange Lane said, "Heaven forbid!" "No wife in the world could replace Nancy," said Colonel Chiley, after that fervent aspiration, "and none could put up with her;" while, on the other side, there were curious speculations afloat as to the effect upon the house, and especially the table, of the daughter's return. When a young woman comes to be eighteen it is difficult to keep her at school; and though the Doctor had staved off the danger for the moment, by sending Lucilla off along with one of her schoolfellows, whose family was going abroad, to make orthodox acquaintance with all the Swiss mountains, and all the Italian capitals, still that was plainly an expedient for the moment; and a new mistress to the house, which had got along so well without any mistress, was inevitable. So that it cannot be denied Miss Marjoribanks's advent was regarded in Carlingford with as much interest and curiosity as she could have wished. For it was already known that the Doctor's daughter was not a mild young lady, easy to be controlled; but, on the contrary, had all the energy and determination to have her own way, which naturally belonged to a girl who possessed a considerable chin, and a mouth which could shut, and tightly curling tawny tresses, which were still more determined than she was to be arranged only according to their inclination. It was even vaguely reported that some passages-of-arms had occurred between Miss Majoribanks and the redoubtable Nancy during the short and uncertain opportunities which were afforded by holidays; and the community, accordingly, regarded as an affair of almost municipal importance Lucilla's final return home.

As for the young lady herself, though she was at school, she was conscious of having had a career not without importance, even during these three years of pupilage. Since the day when she began to read political economy with Miss Martha Blount, who, though the second sister, was the directing spirit of the establishment, Lucilla had exercised a certain influence upon the school itself which was very satisfactory. Perhaps her course might be a little deficient in grace, but grace, after all, is but a secondary quality; and, at all events, Miss Marjoribanks went straight forward, leaving an unquestionable wake behind her, and running down with indifference the little skiffs in her way. She was possessed by nature of that kind of egotism, or rather egoism, which is predestined to impress itself, by its perfect reality and good faith, upon the surrounding world. There are people who talk of themselves, and think of themselves, as it were, under protest, and with depreciation, not actually able to convince themselves that anybody cares; but Lucilla, for her part, had the calmest and most profound conviction that, when she discussed her own doings and plans and clevernesses, she was bringing forward the subject most interesting to her audience as well as to herself. Such a conviction is never without its fruits. To be sure, there were always one or two independent spirits who revolted; but for the crowd, it soon became impressed with a profound belief in the creed which Miss Marjoribanks supported so firmly. This conviction of the importance and value of her own proceedings made Lucilla, as she grew older, a copious and amusing conversationalist—a rank which few people who are indifferent to, or do not believe in, themselves can attain to. One thing she had made up her mind to as soon as she should return home, and that was to revolutionise society in Carlingford. On the whole, she was pleased with the success of the Doctor's dinners, though a little piqued to think that they owed nothing to herself; but Lucilla, whose instinct of government was of the true despotic order, and who had no objection to stoop, if by that means she could conquer, had no such designs against Nancy as were attributed to her by the expectant audience in Carlingford. On the contrary, she was quite as much disposed as her father was to take Nancy for prime-minister; for Miss Marjoribanks, though too much occupied with herself to divine the characteristic points of other people, had a sensible and thorough belief in those superficial general truths which most minds acquiesce in, without taking the trouble to believe. She knew, for example, that there was a great difference between the brilliant society of London, or of Paris, which appears in books, where women have generally the best of it, and can rule in their own right; and even the very best society of a country town, where husbands are very commonly unmanageable, and have a great deal more of their own way in respect to the houses they will or will not go to, than is good for that inferior branch of the human family. Miss Marjoribanks had the good sense to see and appreciate these details; and she knew that a good dinner was a great attraction to a man, and that, in Carlingford at least, when these refractory mortals were secured, the wives and daughters would necessarily follow. Besides, as is not uncommon with women who are clever women, and aware of the fact, Miss Marjoribanks preferred the society of men, and rather liked to say so. With all these intentions in her mind, it may be imagined that she received coolly enough the invitation of her friend to join in the grand tour, and the ready consent given by her father when he heard of it. But even the grand tour was a tool which Lucilla saw how to make use of. Nowadays, when people go everywhere, an untravelled woman would find it so much the harder to keep up the *rôle* of a leader of society to which she had devoted herself; and she felt to the depth of her heart the endless advantage to her future conversation of the experiences to be acquired in Switzerland and Italy. But she rejected with scorn the insinuation of other accidents that might occur on the way.

"You will never come back again, Lucilla," said one of her companions; "you will marry some enchanting Italian with a beautiful black beard, and a voice like an angel; and he'll sing serenades to you, and do all sorts of things: oh, how I wish I was you!"

"That may be," said Miss Marjoribanks, "but I shall never marry an Italian, my dear. I don't think I shall marry anybody for a long time. I want to amuse myself. I wonder, by the way, if it would improve my voice to take lessons in Italy. Did I ever tell you of the Italian nobleman that was so very attentive to me that Christmas I spent at Sissy Vernon's? He was very handsome. I suppose they really are all very handsome—except, of course, the Italian masters; but I did not pay any attention to him. My object, dear, and you know it, is to return home as well educated as possible, to be a comfort to dear papa."

"Yes, dear Lucilla," said the sympathetic girl, "and it is so good of you; but do tell me about the Italian nobleman—what did he look like—and what did he say?"

"Oh, as for what he said, that is quite a different matter," said Lucilla; "but it is not what they say, but the way they say it, that is the fun. I did not give him the least encouragement. As for that, I think, a girl can always stop a man when she does not care for him. It depends on whether you intend him to commit himself or not," Miss Marjoribanks continued, and fixed her eyes meditatively, but intently, upon her friend's face.

"Whether I intend?—oh goodness, Lucilla! how can you speak so? as if I ever intended anything," said her companion, confused, yet flattered, by the possibility; to which the elder sage answered calmly, with all the composure in the world—

"No, I never supposed you did; I was thinking of myself," said Lucilla, as if, indeed, that was the only reasonable subject of thought. "You know I have seen a good deal of the world, one way and another, with going to spend the holidays, and I could tell you quantities of things. It is quite astonishing how much experience one gets. When I was at Midhurst, at Easter, there was my cousin Tom, who was quite ridiculous; I declare he nearly brought things to an explanation, Fanny—which, of course, of all things in the world I most wanted to avoid."

"Oh, but why, Lucilla?" cried Fanny, full of delight and wonder; "I do so want to know what they say when they make——explanations, as you call them. Oh, do tell me, Lucilla, why?"

"My dear," said Miss Marjoribanks, "a cousin of my own! and only twenty-one, and reading for the bar! In the first place, my aunt would never have forgiven me, and I am very fond of my aunt. It's so nice to like all one's relations. I know some girls who can't bear theirs. And then a boy not much older than myself, with nothing but what his mother pleases! Fortunately he did not just say the words, so I escaped that time; but, of course, I could understand perfectly what he meant."

"But, oh, Lucilla, tell me the words," cried the persistent questioner; "do, there's a darling! I am quite sure you have heard them—and I should so like to know exactly what they say;—do they go down on their knees?—or do they try to take your hand as they always do in novels?—or what do they do?—Oh, Lucilla, tell me, there's a dear!"

"Nonsense," said Lucilla; "I only want you to understand that I am not likely to fall into any danger of that sort. My only ambition, Fanny, as I have told you often, is to go home to Carlingford and be a comfort to dear papa."

"Yes," said Fanny, kissing her devoted companion, "and it is so good of you, dear; but then you cannot go on all your life being a comfort to dear papa," said the intelligent girl, bethinking herself, and looking again with some curiosity in Lucilla's face.

"We must leave that to Providence," said Miss Marjoribanks, with a sense of paying a compliment to Providence in intrusting it with such a responsibility. "I have always been guided for the best hitherto," she continued, with an innocent and unintentional profanity, which sounded solemn to her equally innocent companion, "and I don't doubt I shall be so till the end." From which it will be perceived that Miss Marjoribanks was of the numerous class of religionists who keep up civilities with heaven, and pay all the proper attentions, and show their respect for the divine government in a manner befitting persons who know the value of their own approbation. The conversation dropped at this point; for Lucilla was too important a person to be left to the undivided possession of an inquisitive innocent like Fanny Middleton, who was only sixteen, and had never had even a flirtation in her own person. There were no Carlingford girls at Mount Pleasant, except poor little Rose Lake, the drawing-master's second daughter, who had been received on Dr Marjoribanks's recommendation, and who heard the little children their geography and reading, and gave them little lessons in drawing, by way of paying for her own education; but then Rose was entirely out of Miss Marjoribanks's way, and could never count for anything in her designs for the future. The girls at Mount Pleasant were good girls on the whole, and were rather improved by the influence of Lucilla, who was extremely good-natured, and, so long as her superiority was duly acknowledged, was ready to do anything for anybody—so that Rose Lake was not at all badly off in her inferior position. She could be made useful too, which was a great point in her favour; and Miss Marjoribanks, who possessed by nature some of the finest qualities of a ruler, instinctively understood and appreciated the instruments that came to her hand. As for Rose, she had been brought up at the School of Design in Carlingford, of which, under the supervision of the authorities who, in those days, inhabited Marlborough House, Mr Lake was the master. Rose was the pride of the school in the peaceable days before her mother died; she did not know much else, poor child, except novels, but her copies "from the round" filled her father with admiration, and her design for a Honiton-lace flounce, a spirited composition of dragons' tails and the striking plant called teazle, which flourishes in the neighbourhood of Carlingford (for Mr Lake had leanings towards Preraphaelitism), was thought by the best judges to show a wonderful amount of feeling for art, and just missed being selected for the prize. A girl with such a talent was naturally much appreciated in Mount Pleasant. She made the most charming design for Miss Marjoribanks's handkerchief—"Lucilla," in Gothic characters, enclosed in a wreath of forget-me-nots, skilfully combined with thistle-leaves, which Rose took great pains to explain were so much better adapted to ornamentation than foliage of a less distinct character ; and the young draughtswoman was so charmed by Lucilla's enthusiastic admiration, that she volunteered to work the design in the cambric, which was a much more serious matter. This was on the eve of Miss Marjoribanks's final departure from school. She was to spend a year abroad, to the envy of all whom she left behind ; but for herself, Lucilla was not elated. She thought it very probable that she would ascend Mont Blanc as far as the Grands Mulets at least, and, of course, in spring, go up Vesuvius, having got through the Carnival and Miserere and all the balls in Rome ; but none of these things moved her out of her usual composure. She took it all in the way of business, as she had taken her French and her German and her singing and her political economy. As she stepped into the steamboat at Dover which was to convey her to scenes so new, Lucilla felt more and more that she who held the reorganisation of society in Carlingford in her hands was a woman with a mission. She was going abroad as the heir-apparent went to America and the Holy Land, to complete her education, and fit herself, by an examination of the peculiarities of other nations, for an illustrious and glorious reign at home.

CHAPTER III.

It may be well to seize the opportunity of Miss Marjoribanks's travels, through which it is unnecessary to follow her, as they have nothing particular to do with the legitimate history of her great undertaking, to explain a little the state of affairs in Carlingford before this distinguished revolutionary began her labours. It is something like going back into the prehistoric period—those ages of the flint, which only ingenious quarrymen and learned geologists can elucidate—to recall the social condition of the town before Miss Marjoribanks began her Thursday evenings, before St Roque's Chapel was built or thought of, while Mr Bury, the Evangelical Rector, was still in full activity, and before old Mr Tufton, at Salem Chapel (who sometimes drank tea at the Rectory, and thus had a kind of clandestine entrance into the dim outskirts of that chaos which was then called society), had his first "stroke." From this latter circumstance alone the entirely disorganised condition of affairs will be visible at a glance. It is true, Mr Vincent, who succeeded Mr Tufton, was received by Lady Western, in days when public opinion had made great advances; but then Lady Western was the most good-natured creature in the world, and gave an invitation, when it happened to come into her head, without the least regard for the consequences; and, after all, Mr Vincent was very nice-looking and clever, and quite presentable. Fortunately, however, the period to which we allude was prior to the entrance of Lady Western into Grange Lane. She was a very pretty woman, and knew how to look like a lady of fashion, which is always of importance; but she was terribly inconsequent, as Miss Marjoribanks said, and her introductions were not in the least to be depended upon. She was indeed quite capable of inviting a family of retired drapers to meet the best people in Grange Lane, for no better reason than to gratify her *protégés*, which, of course, was a proceeding calculated to strike at the roots of all society. Fortunately for Carlingford, its reorganisation was in abler hands. Affairs were in an utterly chaotic state at the period when this record commences. There was nothing which could be properly called a centre in the entire town. To be sure, Grange Lane was inhabited, as at present, by the best families in Carlingford; but then, without organisation, what good does it do to have a number of people together? For example, Mr Bury was utterly unqualified to take any lead. Mrs Bury had been dead a long time, and the daughters were married, and the Rector's maiden sister, who lived with him, was entirely of his own way of thinking, and asked people to tea-parties, which were like Methodists' class-meetings, and where Mr Tufton was to be met with, and sometimes other Dissenters, to whom the Rector gave what he called the right hand of fellowship. But he never gave anything else to society, except weak tea and thin bread-and-butter, which was fare, the ladies said, which the gentlemen did not relish. "I never can induce Charles to go out to tea," said young Mrs Woodburn, piteously; "he won't, and there is an end of it. After dinner he thinks of nothing but an easy-chair and the papers; and, my dear Miss Bury, what can I do?"

B

"It is a great pity, my dear, that your husband's carelessness should deprive you of the benefit of Christian conversation; but, to be sure, it is your duty to stay with him, and I hope it will be made up to you at home," Miss Bury would say. As for the Rector, his favourites were devoted to him; and as he always saw enough of familiar faces at his sister's tea-parties, he took no account of the defaulters. Then there was Dr Marjoribanks, who gave only dinners, to which naturally, as there was no lady in the house, ladies could not be invited, and who, besides, was rather a drawback than a benefit to society, since he made the men quite intolerable, and filled them with such expectations, in the way of cookery, that they never were properly content with a good family dinner after. Then the ladies, from whom something might justly have been expected in the way of making society pleasant—such as Mrs Centum and Mrs Woodburn, for example, who had everything they could desire, and the most liberal housekeeping allowances—were either incapacitated by circumstances (which was a polite term in use at Carlingford, and meant babies) or by character. Mrs Woodburn liked nothing so well as to sit by the fire and read novels, and "take off" her neighbours, when any one called on her; and, of course, the lady who was her audience on one occasion, left with the comfortable conviction that next time she would be the victim; a circumstance which, indeed, did not make the offender unpopular—for there were very few people in Carlingford who could be amusing, even at the expense of their neighbours—but made it quite impossible that she should ever do anything in the way of knitting people together, and making a harmonious whole out of the scraps and fragments of society. As for Mrs Chiley, she was old, and had not energy enough for such an undertaking; and, besides, she had no children, and disliked bustle and trouble, and was of opinion that the Colonel never enjoyed his dinner if he had more than four people to help him to eat it; and, in short, you might have gone over Grange Lane, house by house, finding a great deal of capital material, but without encountering a single individual capable of making anything out of it. Such was the lamentable condition, at the moment this history commences, of society in Carlingford.

And yet nobody could say that there were not very good elements to make society with. When you add to a man capable of giving excellent dinners, like Dr Marjoribanks, another man like young Mr Cavendish, Mrs Woodburn's brother, who was a wit and a man of fashion, and belonged to one of the best clubs in town, and brought down gossip with the bloom on it to Grange Lane; and when you join to Mrs Centum, who was always so good and so much out of temper that it was safe to calculate on something amusing from her, the languid but trenchant humour of Mrs Woodburn—not to speak of their husbands, who were perfectly available for the background, and all the nephews and cousins and grandchildren, who constantly paid visits to old Mr Western and Colonel Chiley; and the Browns, when they were at home, with their floating suite of admirers; and the young ladies who sang, and the young ladies who sketched, and the men who went out with the hounds, when business permitted them; and the people who came about the town when there was an election; and the barristers who made the circuit; and the gay people who came to the races; not to speak of the varying chances of curates, who could talk or play the piano, with which Mr Bury favoured his parishioners —for he changed his curates very often; and the occasional visits of the lesser county people, and the country clergymen; —it will be plainly apparent that all that was wanting to Carlingford was a master-hand to blend these different elements. There had even been a few feeble preliminary attempts at this great work, which had failed, as such attempts always fail when they are premature, and when the real agent of the change is already on the way; but preparations and presentiments had taken vague possession of the mind of the town, as has always been observed to be the case before a great revolution, or when a man destined to put his mark on his generation, as the newspapers say, is about to appear. To be sure, it was not a man this time, but Miss Marjoribanks; but the atmosphere thrilled and trembled to the advent of the new luminary all the same.

Yet, at the same time, the world of Carlingford had not the least idea of the real quarter from which the sovereign intelligence which was to develop it from chaos into order and harmony was, *effectivement*, to come. Some people had hoped in Mrs Woodburn before she fell into her present languor of appearance and expression; and a great many people hoped in Mr Cavendish's wife, if he married, as he was said to intend to do; for this gentleman, who was in the habit of describing himself, no doubt very truthfully, as one of the Cavendishes, was a person of great consideration in Grange Lane; and some hoped in a new Rector, for it was apparent that Mr Bury could not last very long. Thus, with the ordinary shortsightedness of the human species, Carlingford blinded itself, and turned its eyes in every direction in the world rather than in that of the Swiss mountains, which were being climbed at that moment by a large and blooming young woman, with tawny short curls and alert decided movements; so little do we know what momentous issues may hang upon the most possible accident! Had that energetic traveller slipped but an inch further upon the *mer de glace*—had she taken that other step which she was with difficulty persuaded not to take on the Wengern Alp—there would have been an end of all the hopes of social importance for Carlingford. But the good fairies took care of Lucilla and her mission, and saved her from the precipice and the crevasses; and instinctively the air at home got note of what was coming, and whispered the news mysteriously through the keyholes. "Miss Marjoribanks is coming home," the unsuspecting male public said to itself as it returned from Dr Marjoribanks's dinners, with a certain distressing, but mistaken presentiment, that these delights were to come to an end; and the ladies repeated the same piece of news, conjoining with it benevolent intimations of their intention to call upon her, and make the poor thing feel herself at home. "Perhaps she may be amusing," Mrs Woodburn was good enough to add; but these words meant only that perhaps Lucilla, who was coming to set them all right, was worthy of being placed in the satirist's collection along with Mrs Centum and Mrs Chiley. Thus, while the town ripened more and more for her great mission, and the ignorant human creatures, who were to be her subjects, showed their usual blindness and ignorance, the time drew nearer and nearer for Miss Marjoribanks's return.

CHAPTER IV.

"My daughter is coming home, Nancy," said Dr Marjoribanks. "You will have to make preparations for her immediately. So far as I can make out from this letter, she will arrive to-morrow by the half-past five train."

"Well, sir," said Nancy, with the tone of a woman who makes the best of a misfortune, "it ain't every young lady as would have the sense to fix an hour like that. Ladies is terrible tiresome in that way; they'll come in the middle o' the day, when a body don't know in the world what to have for them; or they'll come at night, when a body's tired, and ain't got the heart to go into a supper. There was always a deal of sense in Miss Lucilla, when she hadn't got nothing in her head."

"Just so," said Dr Majoribanks, who was rather relieved to have got through the announcement so easily. "You will see that her room is ready, and everything comfortable; and, of course, to-morrow she and I will dine alone."

"Yes, sir," said Nancy; but this assent was not given in the decisive tone of a woman whose audience was over; and then she was seized with a desire to arrange in a more satisfactory manner the cold beef on the sideboard. When she had secured this little interval for thought, she returned again to the table, where her master ate his breakfast, with a presentiment. "If you please, sir," said Nancy, "not to give you no vexation nor trouble, which every one knows as it has been the aim o' my life to spare you, as has so much on your mind. But it's best to settle afore commencing, and then we needn't have no heart-burning. If you please, am I to take my orders of Miss Lucilla, or of you, as I've always been used to? In the missus's time," said Nancy, with modest confidence, "as was a good missus, and never gave no trouble as long as she had her soup and her jelly comfortable, it was always you as said what there was to be for dinner. I don't make no objection to doing up a nice little luncheon for Miss Lucilla, and giving a little more thought now and again to the sweets; but it ain't my part to tell you, sir, as a lady's taste, and more special a young lady's, ain't to be expected to be the same as yours and mine as has been cultivated like. I'm not one as likes contention," continued the domestic oracle, "but I couldn't abear to see a good master put upon; and if it should be as Miss Lucilla sets her mind upon messes as ain't got no taste in them, and milk-puddings and stuff, like the most of the ladies, I'd just like to know out of your own mouth, afore the commencement, what I'm to do?"

Dr Marjoribanks was so moved by this appeal that he laid down his knife and contemplated the alarming future with some dismay. "It is to be hoped Miss Lucilla will know better," he said. "She has a great deal of good sense, and it is to be hoped that she will be wise enough to consult the tastes of the house."

But the Doctor was not to be let off so easily. "As you say, sir, everything's to be hoped," said Nancy, steadily; "but there's a-many ladies as don't seem to me to have got no taste to their mouths; and it ain't as if it was a thing that could be left to hopes. Supposin' as it comes to that, sir, what am I to do?"

"Well," said the Doctor, who was himself a little puzzled, "you know Miss Lucilla is nineteen, Nancy, and my only child, and the natural mistress of the house."

"Sir," said Nancy, austerely, "them is things as it ain't needful to name; that ain't the question as I was asking. Supposin' as things come to such a point, what am I to do?"

"Bless me! it's half-past nine," said the Doctor, "and I have an appointment. You can come just as usual when we are at breakfast, that will be the best way," he said as he went out at the door, and chuckled a little to himself when he felt he had escaped. "Lucilla is her mother's daughter, it is true," he said to himself when he had got into the safe seclusion of his brougham, with a degree of doubt in his tone which was startling, to say the least of it, from the lips of a medical man; "but she is my child all the same," he added, briskly, with returning confidence; and in this conviction there was something which reassured the Doctor. He rubbed his hands as he bowled along to his appointment, and thought within himself that if she turned out a girl of spirit, as he expected, it would be good fun to see Lucilla's struggle with Nancy for the veritable reins of government. If Dr Marjoribanks had entertained any positive apprehensions that his dinners would be spoiled in consequence, his amusement would have come to an abrupt conclusion; but he trusted entirely in Nancy and a little in Lucilla, and suffered his long upper-lip to relax at the thought without much fear.

Her father had not returned from the labours of his long day when Lucilla arrived, but he made his last visits on foot in order to be able to send the brougham for her, which was a great thing for the Doctor to do. There was, indeed, a mutual respect between the two, who were not necessary to each other's comfort, it is true, as such near relations sometimes are; but who, at the same time, except on the sole occasion of Mrs Marjoribanks's death, had never misunderstood each other, as sometimes happens. This time Miss Marjoribanks was rather pleased, on the whole, that the Doctor did not come to meet her. At other times she had been a visitor; now she had come into her kingdom, and had no desire to be received like a guest. A sense of coming home, warmer than she remembered to have felt before, came into Lucilla's active mind as she stepped into the brougham. Not that the words bore any special tender meaning, notwithstanding that it was the desire of her heart, well known to all her friends, to live henceforward as a comfort to dear papa, but that now at last she was coming into her kingdom, and entering the domain in which she intended her will to be law. After living for a year with friends whose arrangements (much inferior to those which she could have made had she had the power) she had to acquiesce in, and whose domestic economy could only be criticised up to a certain point, it was naturally a pleasure to Miss Marjoribanks to feel that now at length she was emancipated, and at liberty to exercise her faculty. There were times during the past year when Lucilla had with difficulty restrained herself from snatching the reins out of the hands of her hosts, and showing them how to manage. But, impatient as she was, she had to restrain herself and make the best of it. Now all that bondage was over. She felt like a young king entering in secret a capital which awaits him with acclamations. Before she presented herself to the rejoicing public, there were arrangements to be made and things to be done; and Miss Marjoribanks gave a rapid glance at the shops in George Street as she drove past, and decided which of them she meant to honour with her patronage. When she entered the garden it was with the same rapid glance of reorganising genius that she cast her eyes around it; and still more decided was the look with which she regarded her own room, where she was guided by the new housemaid, who did not know Miss Lucilla. Nancy, who knew no better (being, like most gifted persons, a woman of one idea), had established her young mistress in the little chamber which had been Lucilla's when she was a child; but Miss Marjoribanks, who had no sentimental notions about white dimity, shook her head at the frigid little apartment, where, however, she was not at all sorry to be placed at present; for if Dr Marjoribanks had been a man of the *prevenant* class, disposed to make all the preparations possible for his daughter, and arrange elegant surprises for her, he would have thoroughly disgusted Lucilla, who was bent on making all the necessary improvements in her own person. When she went down to the drawing-room to await her father, Miss Marjoribanks's look of disapprobation was mingled with so much satisfaction and content in herself that it was pleasant to behold. She shook her head and shrugged her shoulders as she paused in the centre of the large faded room, where there was no light but that of the fire, which burned brightly, and kept up a lively play of glimmer and shadow in the tall glass over the fireplace, and even twinkled dimly in the three long windows, where the curtains hung stiff and solemn in their daylight form. It was not an uncomfortable sort of big, dull, faded, respectable drawing-room; and if there had been a family in it, with recollections attached to every old ottoman and easy-chair, no doubt it would have been charming; but it was only a waste and howling wilderness to Lucilla. When she had walked from one end to the other, and verified all the plans she had already long ago conceived for the embellishment of this inner court and centre of her kingdom, Lucilla walked with her unhesitating step to the fire, and took a match and lighted all the candles in the large old-fashioned candlesticks, which had been flickering in grotesque shadows all over the roof. This proceeding threw a flood of light on the subject of her considerations, and gave Miss Marjoribanks an idea, in passing, about the best mode of lighting, which she afterwards acted upon with great success. She was standing in this flood of light, regarding everything around her with the eye of an enlightened critic and reformer, when Dr Marjoribanks came in. Perhaps there arose in the soul of the Doctor a momentary thought that the startling amount of *eclairage* which he witnessed was scarcely necessary, for it is certain that he gave a momentary glance at the candles as he went up to greet his daughter; but he was far too well-bred a man to suggest such an idea at the moment. On the contrary, he kissed her with a sentiment of real pleasure, and owned to himself that, if she was not a fool, and could keep to her own department, it might be rather agreeable on the whole to have a woman in the house. The sentiment was not enthusiastic, and neither were the words of his salutation—"Well, Lucilla; so this is you!" said the moderate and unexcited father. "Yes, papa, it is me," said Miss Marjoribanks, "and very glad to get home;" and so the two sat down and discussed the journey—whether she had been cold, and what state the railway was in—till the Doctor bethought himself that he had to prepare for dinner. "Nancy is always very punctual, and I am sure you are hungry," he said; "so I'll go up-stairs, with your permission, Lucilla, and change my coat;" and with this the actual arrival terminated, and the new reign began.

But it was only next morning that the young sovereign gave any intimation of her future policy. She had naturally a great deal to tell that first night; and though it was exclusively herself, and her own adventures and achievements, which Miss Marjoribanks related, the occasion of her return made that sufficiently natural; and the Doctor was not altogether superior to the natural prejudice which makes a man interested, even when they are not in themselves particularly interesting, in the doings of his children. She succeeded in doing what is certainly one of the first duties of a woman—she amused her father. He followed her to the drawing-room for a marvel, and took a cup of tea, though it was against his principles; and, on the whole, Lucilla had the satisfaction of feeling that she had made a conquest of the Doctor, which, of course, was the grand and most essential preliminary. In the little interval which he spent over his claret, Miss Marjoribanks had succeeded in effecting another fundamental duty of woman—she had, as she herself expressed it, harmonised the rooms, by the simple method of re-arranging half the chairs and covering the tables with trifles of her own—a proceeding which converted the apartment from an abstract English drawing-room of the old school into Miss Marjoribanks's drawing-room, an individual spot of ground revealing something of the character of its mistress. The Doctor himself was so moved by this, that he looked vaguely round when he came in, as if a little doubtful where he was—but that might only be the effect of the sparkling mass of candles on the mantelpiece, which he was too well-bred to remark upon the first night. But it was only in the morning that Lucilla unfolded her standard. She was down to breakfast, ready to pour out the coffee, before the Doctor had left his room. He found her, to his intense amazement, seated at the foot of the table, in the place which he usually occupied himself, before the urn and the coffee-pot. Dr Marjoribanks hesitated for one momentous instant, stricken dumb by this unparalleled audacity; but so great was the effect of his daughter's courage and steadiness, that after that moment of fate he accepted the seat by the side where everything was arranged for him, and to which Lucilla invited him sweetly, though not without a touch of mental perturbation. The moment he had seated himself, the Doctor's eyes were opened to the importance of the step he had taken. "I am afraid I have taken your seat, papa," said Miss Marjoribanks, with ingenuous sweetness. "But then I should have had to move the urn, and all the things, and I thought you would not mind." The Doctor said nothing but "Humph!" and even that in an under-tone; but he became aware all the same that he had abdicated, without knowing it, and that the reins of state had been smilingly withdrawn from his unconscious hands.

When Nancy made her appearance the fact became still more apparent, though still in the sweetest way. "It is so dreadful to think papa should have been bothered with all these things so long," said Miss Marjoribanks. "After this I am sure you and I, Nancy, can arrange it all without giving him the trouble. Perhaps this morning, papa, as I am a stranger, you will say if there is anything you would like, and then I shall have time to talk it all over with Nancy, and find out what is best,"—and Lucilla smiled so sweetly upon her two amazed subjects that the humour of the situation caught the fancy of the Doctor, who had a keen perception of the ridiculous.

He laughed out, much to Nancy's consternation, who was standing by in open-eyed dismay. "Very well, Lucilla," he said; "you shall try what you can do. I daresay Nancy will be glad to have me back again before long; but in the mean time I am quite content that you should try," and he went off laughing to his brougham, but came back again before Lucilla could take Nancy in hand, who was an antagonist more formidable. "I forgot to tell you," said the Doctor, "that Tom Marjoribanks is coming on Circuit, and that I have asked him to stay here, as a matter of course. I suppose he'll arrive tomorrow. Good-bye till the evening."

This, though Dr Marjoribanks did not in the least intend it, struck Lucilla like a Parthian arrow, and brought her down for the moment. "Tom Marjoribanks!" she ejaculated in a kind of horror. "Of all people in the world, and at this moment!" but when she saw the open eyes and rising colour of Nancy the young dictator recovered herself—for a conqueror in the first moment of his victory has need to be wary. She called Nancy to her in her most affectionate tones as she finished her breakfast. "I sent papa away," said Miss Marjoribanks, "because I wanted to have a good talk with you, Nancy. I want to tell you my object in life. It is to be a comfort to papa. Ever since poor mamma died that is what I have been thinking of; and now I have come home, and I have made up my mind that he is not to be troubled about anything. I know what a good, faithful, valuable woman you are, I assure you. You need not think me a foolish girl who is not able to appreciate you. The dinner was charming last night, Nancy," said Lucilla, with much feeling; "and I never saw anything more beautifully cooked than papa's cutlets to-day."

"Miss Lucilla, I may say as I am very glad I have pleased you," said Nancy, who was not quite conquered as yet. She stood very stiffly upright by the table, and maintained her integrity. "Master *is* particular, I don't deny," continued the prime minister, who felt herself dethroned. "I've always done my best to go in with his little fancies, and I don't mean to say as it isn't right and natural as you should be the missis. But I ain't used to have ado with ladies, and that's the truth. Ladies is stingy in a-many things as is the soul of a good dinner to them as knows. I may be valleyable or not, it ain't for me to say; but I'm not one as can always be kept to a set figger in my gravy-beef, and my bacon, and them sorts of things. As for the butter, I don't know as I could give nobody an idea. I ain't one as likes changes, but I can't abide to be kept to a set figger; and that's the chief thing, Miss Lucilla, as I've got to say."

"And quite reasonable too," said Miss Marjoribanks; "you and I will work perfectly well together, Nancy. I am sure we have both the same meaning; and I hope you don't think I am less concerned about dear papa than about the gravy-beef. He must have been very desolate, with no one to talk to, though he has been so good and kind and self-sacrificing in leaving me to get every advantage; but I mean to make it up to him, now I've come home."

"Yes, miss," said Nancy, somewhat mystified; "not but what master has had his little parties now and again, to cheer him up a bit; and I make bold to say, miss, as I have heard compliments, which it was Thomas that brought 'em downstairs, as might go nigh to turn a body's head, if it was vanity as I was thinking of; but I ain't one as thinks of anything but the comfort of the family," said Nancy, yielding in spite of herself to follow the leadings of the higher will in presence of which she found herself, "and I'm always one as does my best, Miss Lucilla, if I ain't worried nor kept to a set figger with my gravy-beef."

"I have heard of papa's dinners," said Lucilla, graciously, "and I don't mean to let down your reputation, Nancy. Now, we are two women to manage everything, we ought to do still better. I have two or three things in my head that I will tell you after; but in the mean time I want you to know that the object of my life is to be a comfort to poor papa; and now let us think what we had better have for dinner," said the new sovereign. Nancy was so totally unprepared for this manner of dethronement, that she gave in like her master. She followed Miss Marjoribanks humbly into those details in which Lucilla speedily proved herself a woman of original mind, and powers quite equal to her undertaking. The Doctor's formidable housekeeper conducted her young mistress down-stairs afterwards, and showed her everything with the meekness of a saint. Lucilla had won a second victory still more exhilarating and satisfactory than the first; for, to be sure, it is no great credit to a woman of nineteen to make a man of any age throw down his arms; but to conquer a woman is a different matter, and Lucilla was thoroughly sensible of the difference. Now, indeed, she could feel with a sense of reality that her foundations were laid.

Miss Marjoribanks had enough of occupation for that day, and for many days. But her mind was a little distracted by her father's parting intelligence, and she had, besides, a natural desire to view the country she had come to conquer. When she had made a careful supervision of the house, and shifted her own quarters into the pleasantest of the two best bedrooms, and concluded that the little bare dimity chamber she had occupied the previous night was quite good enough for Tom Marjoribanks, Lucilla put on her hat and went out to make a little *reconnaissance*. She walked down to the spot where St Roque's now stands, on her own side of Grange Lane, and up on the other side into George Street, surveying all the capabilities of the place with a rapid but penetrating glance. Dr Marjoribanks's house could not have been better placed as a strategic position, commanding as it did all Grange Lane, of which it was, so to speak, the key, and yet affording a base of communication with the profaner public, which Miss Marjoribanks was wise enough to know a leader of society should never ignore completely; for, indeed, one of the great advantages of that brilliant position is, that it gives a woman a right to be arbitrary, and to select her materials according to her judgment. It was more from a disinclination to repeat herself than any other motive that Lucilla, when she had concluded this preliminary survey, went up into Grove Street, meaning to return home that way. At that hour in the morning the sun was shining on the little gardens on the north side of the street, which was the plebeian side; and as it was the end of October, and by no means warm, Lucilla was glad to cross over and continue her walk by the side of those little enclosures where the straggling chrysanthemums propped each other up, and the cheerful Michaelmas daisies made the best of it in the sunshine that remained to them. Miss Marjoribanks had nearly reached Salem Chapel, which pushed itself forward amid the cosy little line of houses, pondering in her mind the unexpected hindrance which was about to be placed in her triumphant path, in the shape of Tom Marjoribanks, when that singular piece of good fortune occurred to her which had so much effect upon her career in Carlingford. Such happy accidents rarely happen, except to great generals or heroes of romance ; and it would have been, perhaps, a presumption on the part of Lucilla to place herself conspicuously in either of these categories. The fact is, however, that at this eventful moment she was walking along under the shade of her pretty parasol, not expecting anything, but absorbed in many thoughts, and a little cast down in her expectations of success by a consciousness that this unlucky cousin would insist upon making love to her, and perhaps even, as she herself expressed it, *saying the words* which it had taken all her skill to prevent him from saying before. Not that we would have any one believe that love-making in the abstract was disagreeable to Miss Marjoribanks ; but she was only nineteen, well off and good-looking, and with plenty of time for all that ; and at the present moment she had other matters of more importance in hand. It was while occupied with these reflections, and within three doors of Salem Chapel, in front of a little garden where a great deal of mignonette had run to seed, and where the Michaelmas daisies had taken full possession, that Lucilla was roused suddenly out of her musings. The surprise was so great that she stopped short and stood still before the house in the extremity of her astonishment and delight. Who could it be that possessed that voice which Miss Marjoribanks felt by instinct was the very one thing wanting—a round, full, delicious contralto, precisely adapted to supplement without supplanting her own high-pitched and much-cultivated organ ? She stopped short before the door and made a rapid observation even in the first moment of her surprise. The house was not exactly like the other humble houses in Grove Street. Two little blank squares hung in the centre of each of the lower windows, revealed to Lucilla's educated eye the existence of so much "feeling" for art as can be satisfied with a transparent porcelain version of a famous Madonna ; and she could even catch a glimpse, through the curtains of the best room—which, contrary to the wont of humble gentility in Carlingford, were well drawn back, and allowed the light to enter fully—of the glimmer of gilt picture-frames. And in the little garden in front, half-buried among the mignonette, were some remains of plaster-casts, originally placed there for ornament, but long since cast down by rain and neglect. Lucilla made her observations with the promptitude of an accomplished warrior, and before the second bar of the melody indoors was finished, had knocked very energetically. "Is Miss Lake at home?" she asked, with confidence, of the little maid-servant who opened the door to her. And it was thus that Lucilla made her first bold step out of the limits of Grange Lane for the good of society, and secured at once several important personal advantages, and the great charm of those Thursday evenings which made so entire a revolution in the taste and ideas of Carlingford.

CHAPTER V.

MISS MARJORIBANKS did not leave the contralto any time to recover from her surprise; she went up to her direct where she stood, with her song arrested on her lips, as she had risen hastily from the piano. "Is it Rose?" said Lucilla, going forward with the most eager cordiality, and holding out both her hands; though, to be sure, she knew very well it was not Rose, who was about half the height of the singer, and was known to everybody in Mount Pleasant to be utterly innocent of a voice.

"No," said Miss Lake, who was much astonished and startled and offended, as was unfortunately rather her custom. She was a young woman without any of those instincts of politeness, which make some people pleasant in spite of themselves; and she added nothing to soften this abrupt negative, but drew her hands away from the stranger and stood bolt upright, looking at her, with a burning blush, caused by temper much more than by embarrassment, on her face.

"Then," said Lucilla, dropping lightly into the most comfortable chair she could get sight of in the bare little parlour, "it is Barbara—and that is a great deal better; Rose is a good little thing, but—she is different, you know. It is so odd you should not remember me; I thought everybody knew me in Carlingford. You know I have been a long time away, and now I have come home for good. Your voice is just the very thing to go with mine: was it not a lucky thing that I should have passed just at the right moment? I don't know how it is, but somehow these lucky chances *always* happen to me. I am Lucilla Marjoribanks, you know."

"Indeed!" said Barbara, who had not the least intention of being civil, "I did not recognise you in the least."

"Yes, I remember you were always shortsighted a little," said Miss Marjoribanks, calmly. "I should so like if we could try a duet. I have been having lessons in Italy, you know, and I am sure I could give you a few hints. I always like, when I can, to be of use. Tell me what songs you have that we could sing together. You know, my dear, it is not as if I was asking you for mere amusement to myself; my grand object in life is to be a comfort to papa——"

"Do you mean Dr Marjoribanks?" said the uncivil Barbara. "I am sure he does not care in the least for music. I think you must be making a mistake——"

"Oh no," said Lucilla, "I never make mistakes. I don't mean to sing *to* him, you know; but you are just the very person I wanted. As for the ridiculous idea some people have that nobody can be called on who does not live in Grange Lane, I assure you I mean to make an end of that. Of course I cannot commence just all in a moment. But it would always be an advantage to practise a little together. I like to know exactly how far one can calculate upon everybody; then one can tell, without fear of breaking down, just what one may venture to do."

"I don't understand in the least," said Barbara, whose pride was up in arms. "Perhaps you think I am a professional singer?"

"My dear, a professional singer spoils everything," said Miss Marjoribanks; "it changes the character of an evening altogether. There are so few people who understand that. When you have professional singers, you have to give yourself up to music; and that is not my view in the least. My great aim, as all my friends are aware, is to be a comfort to dear papa."

"I wish you would not talk in riddles," said Lucilla's amazed and indignant companion, in her round rich contralto. "I suppose you really are Miss Marjoribanks. I have always heard that Miss Marjoribanks was a little——"

"There!" said Lucilla, triumphantly; "really it is almost like a recitativo to hear you speak. I am so glad. What have you got there? Oh, to be sure, it's *that* duet out of the Trovatore. Do let us try it; there is nobody here, and everything is so convenient—and you know it would never do to risk a breakdown. Will you play the accompaniment, or shall I?" said Miss Marjoribanks, taking off her gloves. As for the drawing-master's daughter, she stood aghast, lost in such sudden bewilderment and perplexity that she could find no words to reply. She was not in the least amiable or yielding by nature; but Lucilla took it so much as a matter of course that Barbara could not find a word to say; and before she could be sure that it was real, Miss Marjoribanks had seated herself at the piano. Barbara was so obstinate that she would not sing the first part, which ought to have been hers; but she was not clever enough for her antagonist. Lucilla sang her part by herself gallantly; and when it came to Barbara's turn the second time, Miss Marjoribanks essayed the second in a false voice, which drove the contralto off her guard; and then the magnificent volume of sound flowed forth, grand enough to have filled Lucilla with envy if she had not been sustained by that sublime confidence in herself which is the first necessity to a woman with a mission. She paused a moment in the accompaniment to clap her hands after that strophe was accomplished, and then resumed with energy. For, to be sure, she knew by instinct what sort of clay the people were made of by whom she had to work, and gave them their reward with that liberality and discrimination which is the glory of enlightened despotism. Miss Marjoribanks was naturally elated when she had performed this important and successful *tour*. She got up from the piano, and closed it in her open, imperial way. "I do not want to tire you, you know," she said; "that will do for to-day. I told you your voice was the very thing to go with mine. Give my love to Rose when she comes in, but don't bring her with you when you come to me. She is a good little thing—but then she is different, you know," said the bland Lucilla; and she held out her hand to her captive graciously, and gathered up her parasol, which she had left on her chair. Barbara Lake let her visitor go after this, with a sense that she had fallen asleep, and had dreamt it all; but, after all, there was something in the visit which was not disagreeable when she came to think it over. The drawing-master was poor, and he had a quantity of children, as was natural, and Barbara had never forgiven her mother for dying just at the moment when she had a chance of seeing a little of what she called the world. At that time Mr Lake and his portfolio of drawings were asked out frequently to tea; and when he had pupils in the family, some kind people asked him to bring one of his daughters with him—so that Barbara, who was ambitious, had beheld herself for a month or two almost on the threshold of Grange Lane. And it was at this moment of all others, just at the same time as Mrs Marjoribanks finished her pale career, that poor Mrs Lake thought fit to die, to the injury of her daughter's prospects and the destruction of her hopes. Naturally Barbara had never quite forgiven that injury. It was this sense of having been ill-used which made her so resolute about sending Rose to Mount Pleasant, though the poor little girl did not in the least want to go, and was very happy helping her papa at the School of Design. But Barbara saw no reason why Rose should be happy, while she herself had to resign her inclinations and look after a set of odious children. To be sure, it was a little hard upon a young woman of a proper ambition, who knew she was handsome, to fall back into housekeeping, and consent to remain unseen and unheard; for Barbara was also aware that she had a remarkable voice. In these circumstances, it may be imagined that, after the first movement of a passionate temper was over, when she had taken breath, and had time to consider this sudden and extraordinary visit, a glimmer of hope and interest penetrated into the bosom of the gloomy girl. She was two years older than Miss Marjoribanks, and as different in "style" as she was in voice. She was not stout as yet, though it is the nature of a contralto to be stout; but she was tall, with all due opportunity for that development which might come later. And then Barbara possessed a kind of beauty, the beauty of a passionate and somewhat sullen brunette, dark and glowing, with straight black eyebrows, very dark and very straight, which gave, oddly enough, a suggestion of oblique vision to her eyes; but her eyes were not in the least oblique, and looked at you straight from under that black line of shadow with no doubtful expression. She was shy in a kind of way, as was natural to a young woman who had never seen any society, and felt herself, on the whole, injured and unappreciated. But no two things could be more different than this shyness which made Barbara look you straight in the face with a kind of scared defiance, and the sweet shyness that pleaded for kind treatment in the soft eyes of little Rose, who was plain, and had the oddest longing to make people comfortable, and please them in her way, which, to be sure, was not always successful. Barbara sat down on the stool before the piano, which Miss Marjoribanks had been so obliging as to close, and thought it all over with growing excitement. No doubt it was a little puzzling to make out how the discovery of a fine contralto, and the possibility of getting up unlimited duets, could further Lucilla in the great aim of her life, which was to be a comfort to her dear papa. But Barbara was like a young soldier of fortune, ready to take a great deal for granted, and to swallow much that was mysterious in the programme of the adventurous general who might lead her on to glory. In half an hour her dreams had gone so far that she saw herself receiving in Miss Marjoribanks's drawing-room the homage, not only of Grange Lane, but even of the county families, who would be attracted by rumours of her wonderful performance; and Barbara was, to her own consciousness, walking up the middle aisle of Carlingford Church in a veil of real Brussels, before little Mr Lake came in, hungry and good-tempered, from his round. To be sure, she had not concluded who was to be the bridegroom; but that was one of those matters of detail which could not be precisely concluded on till the time.

Such was the immediate result, so far as this secondary personage was concerned, of Lucilla's masterly impromptu; and it is needless to say that the accomplished warrior, who had her wits always about her, and had made, while engaged in a simple reconnaissance, so brilliant and successful a capture, withdrew from the scene still more entirely satisfied with herself. Nothing, indeed, could have come more opportunely for Lucilla, who possessed in perfection that faculty of throwing herself into the future, and anticipating the difficulties of a position, which is so valuable to all who aspire to be leaders of mankind. With a prudence which Dr Marjoribanks himself would have acknowledged to be remarkable "in a person of her age and sex," Lucilla had already foreseen that to amuse her guests entirely in her own person, would be at once impracticable and "bad style." The first objection might have been got over, for Miss Marjoribanks had a soul above the ordinary limits of possibility, but the second was unanswerable. This discovery, however, satisfied all the necessities of the position. Lucilla, who was liberal, as genius ought always to be, was perfectly willing that all the young ladies in Carlingford should sing their little songs while she was entertaining her guests; and then at the right moment, when her ruling mind saw it was necessary, would occur the duet—the one duet which would be the great feature of the evening. Thus it will be seen that another quality of the highest order developed itself during Miss Marjoribanks's deliberations; for, to tell the truth, she set a good deal of store by her voice, and had been used to applause, and had tasted the sweetness of individual success. This, however, she was willing to sacrifice for the enhanced and magnificent effect which she felt could be produced by the combination of the two voices; and the sacrifice was one which a weaker woman would have been incapable of making. She went home past Salem Chapel by the little lane which makes a line of communication between the end of Grove Street and the beginning of Grange Lane, with a sentiment of satisfaction worthy the greatness of her mission. Dr Marjoribanks never came home to lunch, and indeed had a contempt for that feminine indulgence; which, to be sure, might be accounted for by the fact, that about that time in the day the Doctor very often found himself to be passing close by one or other of the houses in the neighbourhood which had a reputation for good sherry or madeira, such as exists no more. Lucilla, accordingly, had her lunch alone, served to her with respectful care by Nancy, who was still under the impression of the interview of the morning; and it occurred to Miss Marjoribanks, as she sat at table alone, that this was an opportunity too valuable to be left unimproved; for, to be sure, there are few things more pleasant than a little impromptu luncheon-party, where everybody comes without being expected, fresh from the outside world, and ready to tell all that is going on; though, on the other hand, it was a little doubtful how it might work in Carlingford, where the men had generally something to do, and where the married ladies took their luncheon when the children had their dinner, and presided at the nursery meal. And as for a party of young ladies, even supposing they had the courage to come, with no more solid admixture of the more important members of society, Lucilla, to tell the truth, had no particular taste for that. Miss Marjoribanks reflected as she ate—and indeed, thanks to her perfect health and her agreeable morning walk, Lucilla had a very pretty appetite, and enjoyed her meal in a way that would have been most satisfactory to her many friends—that it must be by way of making his visit, which was aggravating under all circumstances, more aggravating still, that Tom Marjoribanks had decided to come now, of all times in the world. "If he had waited till things were organised, he might have been of a little use," Lucilla said to herself; "for at least he could have brought some of the men that come on circuit, and that would have made a little novelty; but, of course, just now it would never do to make a rush at people, and invite them all at once." After a moment's consideration, however, Miss Marjoribanks, with her usual candour, reflected that it was not in Tom Marjoribanks's power to change the time of the Carlingford assizes, and that, accordingly, he was not to be blamed in this particular at least. "Of course *it* is not his fault," she added, to herself; "but it is astonishing how things happen with some men always at the wrong moment; and it is *so* like Tom." These reflections were interrupted by the arrival of visitors, whom Miss Marjoribanks received with her usual grace. The first was old Mrs Chiley, who kissed Lucilla, and wanted to know how she had enjoyed herself on the Continent, and if she had brought many pretty things home. "My dear, you have grown ever so much since the last time I saw you," the old lady said in her grandmotherly way, "and stout with it, which is such a comfort with a tall girl; and then your poor dear mamma was so delicate. I have always been a little anxious about you on that account, Lucilla; and I am so glad, my dear, to see you looking so strong."

"Dear Mrs Chiley," said Miss Marjoribanks, who perhaps in her heart was not quite so gratified by this compliment as the old lady intended, "the great aim of my life is to be a comfort to dear papa."

Mrs Chiley was very much moved by this filial piety, and she told Lucilla that story about the Colonel's niece, Susan, who was such a good daughter, and had refused three excellent offers, to devote herself to her father and mother, with which the public in Grange Lane were tolerably acquainted. "And one of them was a baronet, my dear," said Mrs Chiley. Miss Marjoribanks did not make any decided response, for she felt that it would be dangerous to commit herself to such a height of self-abnegation as that; but the old lady was quite pleased to hear of her travels and adventures instead; and stayed so long that Mrs Centum and Mrs Woodburn, who happened to arrive at the same moment, found her still there. Mrs Chiley was a little afraid of Mrs Woodburn, and she took her leave hastily, with another kiss; and Lucilla found herself face to face with the only two women who could attempt a rival enterprise to her own in Carlingford. As for Mrs Woodburn, she had settled herself in an easy-chair by the fire, and was fully prepared to take notes. To be sure, Lucilla was the very person to fall victim to her arts; for that confidence in herself which, in one point of view, gave grandeur to the character of Miss Marjoribanks, gave her also a certain *naïveté* and openness which the most simple rustic could not have surpassed.

"I am sure by her face she has been telling you about my niece Susan," said the mimic, assuming Mrs Chiley's tone, and almost her appearance, for the moment, "and that one of them was a baronet, my dear. I always know from her looks what she has been saying; and 'the Colonel was much as usual, but suffering a little from the cold, as he always does in this climate.' She must be a good soul, for she always has her favourite little speeches written in her face."

"I am sure I don't know," said Miss Marjoribanks, who felt it was her duty to make an example; "there has always been one thing remarked of me all my life, that I never have had a great sense of humour. I know it is singular, but when one has a defect, it is always so much better to confess it. I always get on very well with anything else, but I never had any sense of humour, you know; and I am very fond of Mrs Chiley. She has always had a fancy for me from the time I was born; and she has such nice manners. But then, it is so odd I should have no sense of humour," said Lucilla, addressing herself to Mrs Centum, who was sitting on the sofa by her. "Don't you think it is very odd?"

"I am sure it is very nice," said Mrs Centum. "I hate people that laugh at everything. I don't see much to laugh at myself, I am sure, in this distracting world; any one who has a lot of children and servants like me to look after, finds very little to laugh at." And she seized the opportunity to enter upon domestic circumstances. Mrs Woodburn did not answer a word. She made a most dashing murderous sketch of Lucilla, but that did the future ruler of Carlingford very little harm; and then, by the evening, it was known through all Grange Lane that Miss Marjoribanks had snubbed the caricaturist who kept all the good people in terror of their lives. Snubbed her absolutely, and took the words out of her very mouth, was the report that flew through Grange Lane; and it may be imagined how Lucilla's prestige rose in consequence, and how much people began to expect of Miss Marjoribanks, who had performed such a feat almost on the first day of her return home.

CHAPTER VI.

Tom Marjoribanks arrived that night, according to the Doctor's expectation. He arrived, with that curious want of adaptation to the circumstances which characterised the young man, at an hour which put Nancy entirely out, and upset the equanimity of the kitchen for twenty-four hours at least. He came, if any one can conceive of such an instance of carelessness, by the nine o'clock train, just as they had finished putting to rights down-stairs. After this, Miss Marjoribanks's conclusion, that the fact of the Carlingford assizes occurring a day or two after her arrival, when as yet she was not fully prepared to take advantage of them, was *so* like Tom, may be partially understood. And of course he was furiously hungry, and could have managed perfectly to be in time for dinner if he had not missed the train at Didcot Junction, by some wonderful blunder of the railway people, which never could have occurred but for his unlucky presence among the passengers. Lucilla took Thomas apart, and sent him down-stairs with the most conciliatory message. "Tell Nancy not to put herself about, but to send up something cold—the cold pie, or anything she can find handy. Tell her I am *so* vexed, but it is just like Mr Tom; and he never knows what he is eating," said Miss Marjoribanks. As for Nancy, this sweetness did not subdue her in the least. She said, " I'll thank Miss Lucilla to mind her own business. The cold pie is for master's breakfast. I ain't such a goose as not to know what to send up-stairs, and that Tummas can tell her if he likes." In the mean time the Doctor was in the drawing-room, much against his will, with the two young people, spinning about the room, and looking at Lucilla's books and knickknacks on the tables by way of covering his impatience. He wanted to carry off Tom, who was rather a favourite, to his own den down-stairs, where the young man's supper was to be served ; but, at the same time, Dr Marjoribanks could not deny that Lucilla had a right to the greetings and homage of her cousin. He could not help thinking, on the whole, as he looked at the two, what a much more sensible arrangement it would have been if he had had the boy, instead of his sister, who had been a widow for ever so long, and no doubt had spoiled her son, as women always do ; and then Lucilla might have passed under the sway of Mrs Marjoribanks, who no doubt would have known how to manage her. Thus the Doctor mused, with that sense of mild amazement at the blunders of Providence, which so many people experience, and without any idea that Mrs Marjoribanks would have found a task a great deal beyond her powers in the management of Lucilla. As for Tom, he was horribly hungry, having found, as was to be expected, no possible means of lunching at Didcot; but, at the same time, he was exhilarated by Lucilla's smile, and delighted to think of having a week at least to spend in her society. " I don't think I ever saw you looking so well," he was saying; " and you know my opinion generally on that subject." To which Lucilla responded in a way to wither all the germs of sentiment in the bud.

" What subject?" she said; " my looks? I am sure they can't be interesting to you. You are as hungry as ever you can be, and I can see it in your eyes. Papa, he is famishing, and I don't think he can contain himself any longer. Do take him down-stairs, and let him have something to eat. For myself," Lucilla continued, in a lower tone, " it is my duty that keeps me up. You know it has always been the object of my life to be a comfort to papa."

" Come along, Tom," said the Doctor. " Don't waste your time philandering when your supper is ready." And Dr Marjoribanks led the way down-stairs, leaving Tom, who followed him, in a state of great curiosity to know what secret oppression it might be under which his cousin was supported by her duty. Naturally his thoughts reverted to a possible rival— some one whom the sensible Doctor would have nothing to say to; and his very ears grew red with excitement at this idea. But, notwithstanding, he ate a very satisfactory meal in the library, where he had to answer all sorts of questions. Tom had his tray at the end of the table, and the Doctor, who had, according to his hospitable old-fashioned habit, taken a glass of claret to "keep him company," sat in his easy-chair between the fire and the table, and sipped his wine, and admired its colour and purity in the light, and watched with satisfaction the excellent meal his nephew was making. He asked him all about his prospects, and what he was doing, which Tom replied to with the frankest confidence. He was not very fond of work, nor were his abilities anything out of the common; but at the present moment Tom saw no reason why he should not gain the Woolsack in time; and Dr Marjoribanks gave something like a sigh as he listened, and wondered much what Providence could be thinking of not to give *him* the boy.

Lucilla meantime was very much occupied up-stairs. She had the new housemaid up nominally to give her instructions about Mr Tom's room, but really to take the covers off the chairs, and see how they looked when the room was lighted up; but the progress of decay had gone too far to stand that trial. After all, the chintz, though none of the freshest, was the best. When the gentlemen came up-stairs, which Tom, to the Doctor's disgust, insisted on doing, Lucilla was found in the act of pacing the room—pacing, not in the sentimental sense of making a little promenade up and down, but in the homely practical signification, with a view of measuring, that she might form an idea how much carpet was required. Lucilla was tall enough to go through this process without any great drawback in point of grace—the long step giving rather a tragedy-queen effect to her handsome but substantial person and long, sweeping dress. She stopped short, however, when she saw them, and withdrew to the sofa, on which she had established her throne; and there was a little air of conscious pathos on her face as she sat down, which impressed her companions. As for Tom, he instinctively felt that it must have something to do with that mystery under which Lucilla was supported by her duty; and the irrelevant young man conceived immediately a violent desire to knock the fellow down; whereas there was no fellow at all in the case, unless it might be Mr Holden, the upholsterer, whose visits Miss Marjoribanks would have received with greater enthusiasm at this moment than those of the most eligible eldest son in England. And then she gave a little pathetic sigh.

"What were you doing, Lucilla?" said her father,—"rehearsing Lady Macbeth, I suppose. At least you looked exactly like it when we came into the room."

"No, papa," said Lucilla, sweetly; "I was only measuring to see how much carpet we should want; and that, you know, and Tom's coming, made me think of old times. You are so much down-stairs in the library that you don't feel it; but a lady has to spend her life in the drawing-room—and then I always was so domestic. It does not matter what is outside, I always find my pleasure at home. I cannot help if it has a little effect on my spirits now and then," said Miss Marjoribanks, looking down upon her handkerchief, "to be always surrounded with things that have such associations———"

"What associations?" said the amazed Doctor. To be sure, he had not forgotten his wife; but it was four years ago, and he had got used to her absence from her favourite sofa; and, on the whole, in that particular, had acquiesced in the arrangements of Providence. "Really, Lucilla, I don't know what you mean."

"No, papa," said Miss Marjoribanks, with resignation. "I know you don't, and that is what makes it so sad. But talking of new carpets, you know, I had such an adventure to-day that I must tell you—quite one of *my* adventures—the very luckiest thing. It happened when I was out walking; I heard a voice out of a house in Grove Street, just the *very* thing to go with my voice. That is not a thing that happens every day," said Lucilla, "for all the masters have always told me that my voice was something quite by itself. When I heard it, though it was in Grove Street, and all the people about, I could have danced for joy."

"It was a man's voice, I suppose," suggested Tom Marjoribanks, in gloomy tones; and the Doctor added, in his cynical way—

"It's a wonderful advantage to be so pleased about trifles. What number was it? For my part, I have not many patients in Grove Street," said Dr Marjoribanks. "I would find a voice to suit you in another quarter, if I were you."

"Dear papa, it's such a pity that you don't understand," said Lucilla, compassionately. "It turned out to be Barbara Lake; for, of course, I went in directly, and found out. I never heard a voice that went so well with mine." If Miss Marjoribanks did not go into raptures over the contralto on its own merits, it was not from any jealousy, of which, indeed, she was incapable, but simply because its adaptation to her own seemed to her by far its most interesting quality, and indeed almost the sole claim it had to consideration from the world.

"Barbara Lake?" said the Doctor. "There's something in that. If you can do her any good, or get her teaching or anything—I have a regard for poor Lake, poor little fellow! He's kept up wonderfully since his wife died; and nobody expected it of him," Dr Marjoribanks continued, with a momentary dreary recollection of the time when the poor woman took farewell of her children, which indeed was the next day after that on which his own wife, who had nobody in particular to take farewell of, faded out of her useless life.

"Yes," said Lucilla, "I mean her to come here and sing with me; but, then, one needs to organise a little first. I am nineteen—how long is it since you were married, papa?"

"Two-and-twenty years," said the Doctor, abruptly. He

did not observe the strangeness of the question, because he had been thinking for the moment of his wife, and perhaps his face was a trifle graver than usual, though neither of his young companions thought of remarking it. To be sure he was not a young man even when he married; but, on the whole, perhaps something more than this perfect comfort and respectability, and those nice little dinners, had seemed to shine on his horizon when he brought home his incapable bride.

"Two-and-twenty years!" exclaimed Lucilla. "I don't mind talking before Tom, for he is one of the family. The things are all the same as they were when mamma came home, though, I am sure, nobody would believe it. I think it is going against Providence, for my part. Nothing was ever intended to last so long, except the things the Jews, poor souls! wore in the desert, perhaps. Papa, if you have no objection, I should like to choose the colours myself. There is a great deal in choosing colours that go well with one's complexion. People think of that for their dresses, but not for their rooms, which are of so much more importance. I should have liked blue, but blue gets so soon tawdry. I think," said Miss Marjoribanks, rising and looking at herself seriously in the glass, "that I have enough complexion at present to venture upon a pale spring green."

This little calculation, which a timid young woman would have taken care to do by herself, Lucilla did publicly, with her usual discrimination. The Doctor, who had looked a little grim at first, could not but laugh when he saw the sober look of care and thought with which Miss Marjoribanks examined her capabilities in the glass. It was not so much the action itself that amused her father, as the consummate ability of the young revolutionary. Dr Marjoribanks was Scotch, and had a respect for "talent" in every development, as is natural to his nation. He did not even give his daughter that credit for sincerity which she deserved, but set it all to the score of her genius, which was complimentary, certainly, in one point of view; but the fact was that Lucilla was perfectly sincere, and that she did what was natural to her under guidance of her genius, so as always to be in good fortune, just as Tom Marjoribanks, under the guidance of his, brought discredit even upon those eternal ordinances of English government which fixed the time of the Carlingford assizes. Lucilla was quite in earnest in thinking that the colour of the drawing-room was an important matter, and that a woman of sense had very good reason for suiting it to her complexion—an idea which accordingly she proceeded to develop and explain.

"For one can change one's dress," said Miss Marjoribanks, "as often as one likes—at least as often, you know, as one has dresses to change; but the furniture remains the same. I am always a perfect guy, whatever I wear, when I sit against a red curtain. You men say that a woman always knows when she's good-looking, but I am happy to say *I* know when I look a guy. What I mean is a delicate pale-green, papa. For my part, I think it wears just as well as any other colour; and all the painters say it is the very thing for pictures. The carpet, of course, would be a darker shade; and as for the chairs, it is not at all necessary to keep to one colour. Both red and violet go beautifully with green, you know. I am sure Mr Holden and I could settle all about it without giving you any trouble."

"Who told you, Lucilla," said the Doctor, "that I meant to refurnish the house?" He was even a little angry at her boldness, but at the same time he was so much amused and pleased in his heart to have so clever a daughter, that all the tones that could produce terror were softened out of his voice. "I never heard that was a sort of thing that a man had to do for his daughter," said Dr Marjoribanks; "and I would like to know what I should do with all that finery when you get married—as I suppose you will by-and-by—and leave me alone in the house?"

"Ah, that is the important question," said Tom. As usual, it was Tom's luck; but then, when there did happen to be a moment when he ought to be silent, the unfortunate fellow could not help but speak.

"Perhaps I may marry some time," said Miss Marjoribanks, with composure; "it would be foolish, you know, to make any engagements; but that will depend greatly upon how you behave, and how Carlingford behaves, papa. I give myself ten years here, if you should be very good. By twenty-nine I shall be going off a little, and perhaps it may be tiring, for anything I can tell. Ten years is a long time, and naturally, in the mean time, I want to look as well as possible. Stop a minute; I forgot to put down the number of paces for the length. Tom, please to do it over again for me; of course, your steps are a great deal longer than mine."

"Tom is tired," said the Doctor; "and there are no new carpets coming out of my pockets. Besides, he's going to bed, and I'm going down-stairs to the library. We may as well bid you good-night."

These words, however, were addressed to deaf ears. Tom, as was natural, had started immediately to obey Lucilla, as he was in duty bound; and the old Doctor looked on with a little amazement and a little amusement, recognising, with something of the surprise which that discovery always gives to fathers and mothers, that his visitor cared twenty times more for what Lucilla said than for anything that his superior wisdom could suggest. He would have gone off and left them as a couple of young fools, if it had not occurred to him all at once, that since this sort of thing had begun, the last person in the world that he would choose to see dancing attendance on his daughter was Tom Marjoribanks. Oddly enough, though he had just been finding fault with Providence for not giving him a son instead of a daughter, he was not at all delighted nor grateful when Providence put before him this simple method of providing himself with the son he wanted. He took a great deal too much interest in Tom Marjoribanks to let him do anything so foolish; and as for Lucilla, the idea that, after all her accomplishments, and her expensive education, and her year on the Continent, she should marry a man who had nothing, disgusted the Doctor. He kept his seat accordingly, though he was horribly bored by the drawing-room and its claims, and wanted very much to return to the library, and get into his slippers and his dressing-gown. It was rather a pretty picture, on the whole, which he was regarding. Lucilla, perhaps with a view to this discussion, had put on green ribbons on the white dress which she always wore in the evening, and her tawny curls and fresh complexion carried off triumphantly that difficult colour. Perhaps a critical observer might have said that her figure was a little too developed and substantial for those vestal robes; but then Miss Marjoribanks was young, and could bear it. She was standing by, not far from the fire, on the other side from the Doctor, looking on anxiously, while Tom measured the room with his long steps. "I never said you were to stride," said Lucilla; "take moderate steps, and don't be so silly. I was doing it myself famously if you had not come in and interrupted me. It is frightful to belong to a family where the men are so stupid," said Miss Marjoribanks, with a sigh of real distress; for, to be sure, the unlucky Tom immediately bethought himself to take small steps like those of a lady, which all but threw him on his well-formed though meaningless nose. Lucilla shook her head with an exasperated look, and contracted her lips with disdain, as he passed her on his ill-omened career. Of course he came right up against the little table on which she had with her own hand arranged a bouquet of geraniums and mignonette. "It is what he always does," she said to the Doctor, calmly, as Tom arrived at that climax of his fate; and the look with which she accompanied these words, as she rang the bell smartly and promptly, mollified the Doctor's heart.

"I can tell you the size of the room, if that is all you want," said Dr Marjoribanks. "I suppose you mean to give parties, and drive me out of my senses with dancing and singing.—No, Lucilla, you must wait till you get married—that will never do for me."

"Dear papa," said Lucilla, sweetly, "it is so dreadful to hear you say *parties*. Everybody knows that the only thing I care for in life is to be a comfort to you; and as for dancing, I saw at once that was out of the question. Dancing is all very well," said Miss Marjoribanks, thoughtfully; "but it implies quantities of young people—and young people can never make what *I* call society. It is *Evenings* I mean to have, papa. I am sure you want to go down-stairs, and I suppose Tom would think it civil to sit with me, though he is tired; so I will show you a good example, and Thomas can pick up the table and the flowers at his leisure. Good-night, papa," said Lucilla, giving him her round fresh cheek to kiss. She went out of the room with a certain triumph, feeling that she had fully signified her intentions, which is always an important matter; and shook hands in a condescending way with Tom, who had broken his shins in a headlong rush to open the door. She looked at him with an expression of mild despair, and shook her head again as she accorded him that sign of amity. "If you only would look a little where you are going," said Miss Marjoribanks;—perhaps she meant the words to convey an allegorical as well as a positive meaning, as so many people have been found out to do—and then she pursued her peaceful way up-stairs. As for the Doctor, he went off to his library rubbing his hands, glad to be released, and laughing softly at his nephew's abashed looks. "She knows how to put *him* down at least," the Doctor said to himself, well pleased; and he was so much amused by his daughter's superiority to the vulgar festivity of parties, that he almost gave in to the idea of refurnishing the drawing-room to suit Lucilla's complexion. He rubbed his hands once more over the fire, and indulged in a little laugh all by himself over that original idea. "So it is Evenings she means to have?" said the Doctor; and to be sure, nothing could be more faded than the curtains, and there were bits of the carpet in which the pattern was scarcely discernible. So that, on the whole, up to this point there seemed to be a reasonable prospect that Lucilla would have everything her own way.

CHAPTER VII.

Miss Marjoribanks had so many things to think of next morning that she found her cousin, who was rather difficult to get rid of, much in her way: naturally the young man was briefless, and came on circuit for the name of the thing, and was quite disposed to dawdle the first morning, and attach himself to the active footsteps of Lucilla; and for her part, she had things to occupy her so very much more important. For one thing, one of Dr Marjoribanks's little dinner-parties was to take place that evening, which would be the first under the new *régime*, and was naturally a matter of some anxiety to all parties. "I shall go down and ask Mrs Chiley to come with the Colonel," said Lucilla. "I have always meant to do that. We can't have a full dinner-party, you know, as long as the house is so shabby; but I am sure Mrs Chiley will come to take care of me."

"To take care of you!—in your father's house! Do you think they'll bite?" said the Doctor, grimly; but as for Lucilla, she was quite prepared for that.

"I must have a chaperone, you know," she said. "I don't say it is not quite absurd; but then, at first, I always make it a point to give in to the prejudices of society. That is how I have always been so successful," said the experienced Lucilla. "I never went in the face of anybody's prejudices. Afterwards, you know, when one is known——"

The Doctor laughed, but at the same time he sighed. There was nothing to be said against Mrs Chiley, who had, on the whole, as women go, a very superior training, and knew what a good dinner was; but it was the beginning of the revolution of which Dr Marjoribanks, vaguely oppressed with the idea of new paper, new curtains, and all that was involved in the entrance of Mr Holden the upholsterer into the house, did not see the end. He acquiesced, of course, since there was nothing else for it; but it must be confessed that the spectre of Mrs Chiley sitting at his right hand clouded over for the Doctor the pleasant anticipation of the evening. If it had been possible to put her at the head of the table beside Lucilla, whom she was to come to take care of, he could have borne it better—and to be sure it would have been a great deal more reasonable; but then that was absolutely out of the question, and the Doctor gave in with a sigh. Thus it was that he began to realise the more serious result of that semi-abdication into which he had been beguiled. The female element, so long peacefully ignored and kept at a distance, had come in again in triumph and taken possession, and the Doctor knew too well by the experience of a long life what a restless and troublesome element it was. He had begun to feel that it had ceased to be precisely amusing as he took his place in his brougham. It was good sport to see Lucilla make an end of Tom, and put her bridle upon the stiff neck of Nancy; but when it came to changing the character of the Doctor's dinners, his intellect naturally got more obtuse, and he did not see the joke.

As for Tom, he had to be disposed of summarily. "Do go away," Miss Marjoribanks said, in her straightforward way. "You can come back to luncheon if you like;—that is to say, if you can pick up anybody that is very amusing, you may bring him here about half-past one, and if any of my friends have come to call by that time, I will give you lunch; but it must be somebody very amusing, or I will have nothing to say to you," said Lucilla. And with this dismissal Tom Marjoribanks departed, not more content than the Doctor; for, to be sure, the last thing in the world which the poor fellow thought of was to bring somebody who was very amusing, to injure his chances with Lucilla. Tom, like most other people, was utterly incapable of fathoming the grand conception which inspired Miss Marjoribanks. When she told him that it was the object of her life to be a comfort to papa, he believed it to a certain extent; but it never occurred to him that that filial devotion, though beautiful to contemplate, would preserve Lucilla's heart from the ordinary dangers of youth, or that she was at all in earnest in postponing all matrimonial intentions until she was nine-and-twenty, and had begun to "go off" a little. So he went away disconsolate enough, wavering between his instinct of obedience and his desire of being in Lucilla's company, and a desperate determination never to be the means of injuring himself by presenting to her anybody who was very amusing. All Miss Marjoribanks's *monde*, as it happened, was a little out of humour that day. She had gone on so far triumphantly that it had now come to be necessary that she should receive a little check in her victorious career.

When Tom was disposed of, Miss Marjoribanks put on her hat and went down Grange Lane to carry her invitation to Mrs Chiley, who naturally was very much pleased to come. "But, my dear, you must tell me what to put on," the old lady said. "I don't think I have had anything new since you were home last. I have heard so much about Dr Marjoribanks's dinners that I feel a little excited, as if I was going to be made a freemason or something. There is my brown, you know, that I wear at home when we have anybody—and my black velvet; and then there is my French grey that I got for Mary Chiley's marriage."

"Dear Mrs Chiley," said Lucilla, "it doesn't matter in the least what you wear; there are only to be gentlemen, you know, and one never dresses for gentlemen. You must keep that beautiful black velvet for another time."

"Well, my dear," said Mrs Chiley, "*I* am long past that sort of thing—but the men think, you know, that it is always for them we dress."

"Yes," said Miss Marjoribanks, "their vanity is something dreadful—but it is one of my principles *never* to dress unless there are ladies. A white frock, high in the neck," said Lucilla, with sweet simplicity—"as for anything else, it would be bad style."

Mrs Chiley gave her young visitor a very cordial kiss when she went away. "The sense she has!" said the old lady; but at the same time the Colonel's wife was so old-fashioned that this contemptuous way of treating "The Gentlemen" puzzled her unprogressive intelligence. She thought it was superhuman virtue on Lucilla's part, nearly incredible, and yet established by proofs so incontestable that it would be a shame to doubt it; and she felt ashamed of herself—she who might have been a grandmother, had such been the will of Providence—for lingering five minutes undecided between her two best caps. "I daresay Lucilla does not spend so much time on such vanity, and she only nineteen," said the penitent old lady. As for Miss Marjoribanks, she returned up Grange Lane with a mind at ease, and that consciousness of superior endowments which gives amiability and expansion even to the countenance. She did not give any money to the beggar who at that period infested Grange Lane with her six children, for that was contrary to those principles of political economy which she had studied with such success at Mount Pleasant; but she stopped and asked her name, and where she lived, and promised to inquire into her case. "If you are honest and want to work, I will try to find you something to do," said Miss Marjoribanks; which, to be sure, was a threat appalling enough to keep her free from any further molestation on the part of that interesting family. But Lucilla, to do her justice, felt it equally natural that beneficence should issue from her in this manner as in that other mode of feeding the hungry which she was willing to adopt at half-past one, and had solemnly engaged herself to fulfil at seven o'clock. She went up after that to Mr Holden's, and had a most interesting conversation, and found among his stores a delicious damask, softly, spiritually green, of which, to his great astonishment, she tried the effect in one of the great mirrors which ornamented the shop. "It is just the tint I want," Lucilla said, when she had applied that unusual test; and she left the fashionable upholsterer of Carlingford in a state of some uncertainty whether it was curtains or dresses that Miss Marjoribanks meant to have made.

Perhaps this confusion arose from the fact that Lucilla's mind was occupied in discussing the question whether she should not go round by Grove Street, and try that duet again with Barbara, and invite her to Grange Lane in the evening to electrify the little company; or whether, in case this latter idea might not be practicable, she should bring Barbara with her to lunch by way of occupying Tom Marjoribanks. Lucilla stood at Mr Holden's door for five seconds at least balancing the matter; but finally she gave her curls a little shake, and took a quick step forward, and without any more deliberation returned towards Grange Lane; for, on the whole, it was better not to burst in full triumph all at once upon her constituency, and exhaust her forces at the beginning. If she condescended to sing something herself, it would indeed be a greater honour than her father's dinner-party, in strict justice, was entitled to; and as for the second question, though Miss Marjoribanks was too happy in the confidence of her own powers to fear any rivals, and though her cousin's devotion bored her, still she felt doubtful how far it was good policy to produce Barbara at luncheon for the purpose of occupying Tom. Other people might see her besides Tom, and her own grand *coup* might be forestalled for anything she could tell; and then Tom had some title to consideration on his own merits, though he was the unlucky member of the family. He might even, if he were so far left to himself (though Miss Marjoribanks smiled at the idea) fall in love with Barbara; or, what was more likely, driven to despair by Lucilla's indifference, he might *pretend* to fall in love; and Lucilla reflected, that if anything happened, she could never forgive herself. This was the point she had arrived at when she shook her tawny curls and set out suddenly on her return home.

It was now nearly one o'clock, and it was quite possible that Tom, as well as herself, might be on the way to Grange Lane; but Lucilla, who, as she said, made a point of never going against the prejudices of society, made up her mind to remain sweetly unconscious of the hour of luncheon, unless some lady came to keep her company. But then Miss Marjoribanks was always lucky, as she said. A quarter of an hour before Tom applied for admission, Miss Bury came to pay Lucilla a visit. She had been visiting in her district all the morning, and was very easily persuaded to repose herself a little; and then, naturally, she was anxious about her young friend's spiritual condition, and the effect upon her mind of a year's residence abroad. She was asking whether Lucilla had not seen something soul-degrading and dishonouring to religion in all the mummeries of Popery; and Miss Marjoribanks, who was perfectly orthodox, had replied to the question in the most satisfactory manner; when Tom made his appearance, looking rather sheepish and reluctant, and followed by the "somebody amusing" whom Lucilla had commissioned him to bring. He had struggled against his fate, poor fellow! but when it happens to be a man's instinct to do what he is told, he can no more resist it than if it was a criminal impulse. Tom entered with his amusing companion, who had been chosen with care, and was very uninviting to look at; and by-and-by Miss Bury, with the most puzzled looks, found herself listening to gossip about the theatres and all kinds of profane subjects. "I think they are going to hang that fellow that killed the tailor," said the amusing man; "that will stir you up a little in Carlingford, I should suppose. It is as good as a play for a country town. Of course, there will be a party that will get up a memorial, and prove that a man so kind-hearted never existed out of paradise; and there will be another party who will prove him to be insane; and then at the end all the blackguards within a hundred miles will crowd into Carlingford, and the fellow will be hanged, as he deserves to be; but I assure you it's a famous amusement for a country town."

"Sir," said Miss Bury, with a tremulous voice, for her feelings had overcome her, "when you speak of amusement, does it ever occur to you what will become of his miserable soul?"

"I assure you, wretches of that description have no souls," said the young barrister, "or else, of course, I would not permit myself to speak so freely. It is a conclusion I have come to not rashly, but after many opportunities of observing," the young man went on with solemnity; "on the whole, my opinion is, that this is the great difference between one portion of mankind and the other: that description of being, you may take my word for it, has no soul."

"I never take anybody's word for what is so plainly stated in the Holy Scriptures," said Miss Bury; "I never heard any one utter such a terrible idea. I am sure I don't want to defend a—a murderer," cried the Rector's sister, with agitation; "but I have heard of persons in that unfortunate position coming to a heavenly frame of mind, and giving every evidence of being truly converted. The law may take their lives, but it is an awful thing—a truly dreadful thing," said Miss Bury, trembling all over, "to try to take away their soul."

"Oh, nonsense, Lucilla. By Jove! he does not mean that, you know," said Tom, interposing to relieve his friend.

"Do you believe in Jove, Mr Thomas Marjoribanks?" said Miss Bury, looking him in an alarming manner full in the face.

The unfortunate Tom grew red and then he grew green under this question and that awful look. "No, Miss Bury, I can't say I do," he answered, humbly; and the amusing man was so much less brotherly than Tom that he burst into unsympathetic laughter. As for Lucilla, it was the first real check she had sustained in the beginning of her career. There could not have been a more unfortunate *contretemps*, and there is no telling how disastrous the effect might have been, had not her courage and coolness, not to say her orthodoxy, been equal to the occasion. She gave her cousin a look which was still more terrible than Miss Bury's, and then she took affairs into her own hands.

"It is dreadful sometimes to see what straits people are put to, to keep up the conversation," said Lucilla; "Tom in particular, for I think he has a pleasure in talking nonsense. But you must not suppose I am of that opinion. I remember quite well there was a dreadful man once here in jail for something, and Mr Bury made him the most beautiful character! Every creature has a soul. I am sure we say so in the Creed every day of our lives, and especially in that long creed where so many people perish everlastingly. So far from laughing, it is quite dreadful to think of it," said Lucilla. "It is one of my principles never to laugh about anything that has to do with religion. I always think it my duty to speak with respect. It has such a bad effect upon some minds. Miss Bury, if you will not take anything more, I think we had better go up-stairs."

To think that Tom, whose luck, as usual, had betrayed him to such an unlooked-for extent, should have been on the point of following to the drawing-room, was more than Miss Marjoribanks could comprehend; but fortunately his companion had more sense, and took his leave, taking his conductor with him. Miss Bury went up-stairs in silence, sighing heavily from time to time. The good woman was troubled in her spirit at the evident depravity of the young men with whom circumstances had constrained her to sit down at table, and she was sadly afraid that such companionship must have a debasing effect upon the mind of that lamb of the flock who was now standing before her. Miss Bury bethought herself of Dr Marjoribanks's profane jokes, and the indifference he had shown to many things in which it was his duty to have interested himself, and she could not but look with tender pity in her young friend's face.

"Poor dear," said Miss Bury, "it is dreadful indeed if this is the sort of society you are subjected to. I could recommend to Dr Marjoribanks a most admirable woman, a true Christian, who would take charge of things and be your companion, Lucilla. It is not at all nice for you, at your age, to be obliged to receive young men like these alone."

"I had you!" said Lucilla, taking both Miss Bury's hands. "I felt it was such a blessing. I would not have let Tom stay for luncheon if you had not been there; and now I am so glad, because it has shown me the danger of letting him bring people. I am quite sure it was a special providence that made you think of coming here to-day."

"Well, my dear," said Miss Bury, who was naturally mollified by this statement of the question, "I am very glad to have been of use to you. If there is anything I desire in this life, it is to be useful to my fellow-creatures, and to do my work while it is called day. I should not think the time lost, my dear Lucilla, if I could only hope that I had impressed upon your mind that an account must be given of every careless word——"

"Oh, yes," said Lucilla, "that is *so* true; and besides, it is quite against my principles. I make it a point never to speak of anything about religion except with the greatest respect; and I am quite sure it was a special providence that I had *you*."

Miss Bury took her farewell very affectionately, not to say effusively, after this, with her heart melting over the ingenuous young creature who was so thankful for her protection; but at the same time she left Miss Marjoribanks a prey to the horrible sensation of having made a failure. To be sure, there was time to recover herself in the evening, which was, so to speak, her first formal appearance before the public of Carlingford. Tom was so ill-advised as to come in when she was having her cup of tea before dinner to fortify her for her exertions; and the reception he met with may be left to the imagination. But, after all, there was little satisfaction in demolishing Tom; and then Lucilla had known from the beginning that the success of her undertaking depended entirely on herself.

CHAPTER VIII.

THE evening passed off in a way which, if Miss Marjoribanks had been an ordinary woman, would have altogether obliterated from her mind all recollection of the failure at lunch. To speak first of the most important particular, the dinner was perfect. As for the benighted men who had doubted Lucilla, they were covered with shame, and, at the same time, with delight. If there had been a fault in Dr Marjoribanks's table under the ancient *régime*, it lay in a certain want of variety, and occasional over-abundance, which wounded the feelings of young Mr Cavendish, who was a person of refinement. To-night, as that accomplished critic remarked, there was a certain air of feminine grace diffused over everything—and an amount of doubt and expectation, unknown to the composed feastings of old, gave interest to the meal. As for the Doctor, he found Mrs Chiley, at his right hand, not so great a bore as he expected. She was a woman capable of appreciating the triumphs of art that were set before her; and had indeed been trained to as high a pitch of culture in this respect as perhaps is possible to the female intelligence; and then her pride and delight in being admitted to a participation in those sacred mysteries was beyond expression. "My dear Lucilla, I feel exactly as if I was going to be made a freemason; and as if your dear good papa had to blindfold me, and make me swear all sorts of things before he took me down-stairs," she said, as they sat together waiting for the commencement of the ceremony; and when the two ladies returned to the drawing-room, Mrs Chiley took Lucilla in her arms and gave her a kiss, as the only way of expressing adequately her enthusiasm. "My love," said the Colonel's wife, "I never realised before what it was to have a genius. You should be very thankful to Providence for giving you such a gift. I have given dinners all my life—that is, all my married life, my dear, which comes to almost the same thing, for I was only a baby—but I never could come up to anything like that," said Mrs Chiley, with tears in her eyes. As for Miss Marjoribanks, she was so satisfied with her success that she felt at liberty to tranquillise her old friend.

"I am sure you always give very nice dinners," she said; "and then, you know, the Colonel has his favourite dishes—whereas, I must say for papa, he is very reasonable for a man. I am so glad you are pleased. It is very kind of you to say it is genius, but I don't pretend to anything but paying great attention and studying the combinations. There is nothing one cannot manage if one only takes the trouble. Come here to this nice easy-chair—it is so comfortable. It is so nice to have a little moment to ourselves before they come up-stairs."

"That is what I always say," said Mrs Chiley; "but there are not many girls so sensible as you, Lucilla. I hear them all saying it is so much better French fashion. Of course, I am an old woman, and like things in the old style."

"I don't think it is because I am more sensible," said Miss Marjoribanks, with modesty. "I don't pretend to be better than other people. It is because I have thought it all over, you know—and then I went through a course of political economy when I was at Mount Pleasant," Lucilla said, tranquilly, with an air of having explained the whole matter, which much impressed her hearer. "But for all that, something dreadful happened to-day. Tom brought in one of his friends with him, you know, and Miss Bury was here, and they talked —I want to tell you, in case she should say something, and then you will know what to believe. I never felt so dreadfully ashamed in my life—they talked——"

"My dear! not anything improper, I hope," cried the old lady, in dismay.

"Oh, no," said Lucilla; "but they began laughing about some people having no souls, you know—as if there could be anybody without a soul—and poor Miss Bury nearly fainted. You may think what a dreadful thing it was for me."

"My dear child, if that was all," said Mrs Chiley, reassured —"as for everybody having a soul, I am sure I cannot say. You never were in India, to be sure; but Miss Bury should have known better than to faint at a young man's talk, and frighten you, my poor dear. She ought to be ashamed of herself, at her age. Do you think Tom has turned out clever?" the old lady continued, not without a little *finesse*, and watching Lucilla with a curious eye.

"Not in the very least," said Miss Marjoribanks, calmly; "he is just as awkward as he used to be. It is dreadful to have him here just now, when I have so many things to do— and then he would follow me about everywhere if I would let him. A cousin of that sort is always in the way."

"I am always afraid of a cousin, for my part," said Mrs Chiley; "and talking of that, what do you think of Mr Cavendish, Lucilla? He is very nice in himself, and he has a nice property; and some people say he has a very good chance to be member for Carlingford when there is an election. I think that is just what would suit you."

"I could not see him for the lamp," said Lucilla; "it was right between us, you know—but it is no use talking of that sort of thing just now. Of course, if I had liked, I never need have come home at all," Miss Marjoribanks added, with composure; "and, now I have come home, I have got other things to think of. If papa is good, I will not think of leaving him for ten years."

"Oh yes; I have heard girls say that before," said Mrs Chiley; "but they always changed their minds. You would not like to be an old maid, Lucilla; and in ten years——"

"I should have begun to go off a little, no doubt," said Miss Marjoribanks. "No, I can't say I wish to be an old maid. Can they be coming up-stairs already, do you think? Oh, it is Tom, I suppose," said Lucilla, with a little indignation. But when *They* did make their appearance, which was at a tolerably early period—for a return to the drawing-room was quite a novelty for Dr Marjoribanks's friends, and tempted them accordingly—Miss Marjoribanks was quite ready to receive them. And just before ten o'clock, when Mrs Chiley began to think of going home, Lucilla, without being asked, and without indeed a word of preface, suddenly went to the piano, and before anybody knew, had commenced to sing. She was a great deal too sensible to go into high art on this occasion, or to electrify her father's friends with her newly-acquired Italian, or even with German, as some young ladies do. She sang them a ballad out of one of those treasures of resuscitated ballads which the new generation had then begun to dig out of the bowels of the earth. There was not, to tell the truth, a great deal of music in it, which proved Lucilla's disinterestedness. "I only sang it to amuse you," she said, when all the world crowded to the piano; and for that night she was not to be persuaded to further exertions. Thus Miss Marjoribanks proved to her little public that power of subordinating her personal tastes and even her vanity to her great object, which more than anything else demonstrates a mind made to rule. "I hope next time you will be more charitable, and not tantalise us in this way," Mr Cavendish said, as he took his leave; and Lucilla retired from the scene of her triumph, conscious of having achieved entire success in her first appearance in Carlingford. She laid her head upon her pillow with that sweet sense of an approving conscience which accompanies the footsteps of the benefactors of their kind. But even Miss Marjoribanks's satisfaction was not without its drawbacks. She could not get out of her mind that unhappy abortive luncheon and all its horrors; not to speak of the possibility of her religious principles being impugned, which was dreadful in itself ("for people can stand a man being sceptical, you know," Miss Marjoribanks justly observed, "but everybody knows how unbecoming it is in a woman—and me who have such a respect for religion!"), there remained the still more alarming chance that Miss Bury, who was so narrow-minded, might see something improper in the presence of the two young men at Lucilla's maidenly table; for, to be sure, the Rector's sister was altogether incapable of grasping the idea that young men, like old men and the other less interesting members of the human family, were simple material for Miss Marjoribanks's genius, out of which she had a great result to produce. This was the dread that overshadowed the mind of Lucilla as she composed herself to rest after her fatigues. When she slept the sleep of the innocent, it still pursued her into her dreams. She dreamed that she stood at the altar by the side of the member for Carlingford, and that Mr Bury, with inflexible cruelty, insisted upon marrying her to Tom Marjoribanks instead; and then the scene changed, and instead of receiving the salutations of Mr Cavendish as M.P. for the borough, it was the amusing man, in the character of the defeated candidate, who grinned and nodded at her, and said from the hustings that he never would forget the luncheon that had been his first introduction to Carlingford. Such was the nightmare that pursued Lucilla even into the sphere of dreams.

When such a presentiment takes possession of a well-balanced mind like that of Miss Marjoribanks, it may be accepted as certain that something is likely to follow. Lucilla did her best to disarm fate, not only by the sweetest submission and dutifulness to the Doctor and his wishes, but by a severe disregard of Tom, which drove that unhappy young man nearly desperate. Far from saying anything about luncheon, she even ignored his presence at breakfast, and remained calmly unconscious of his empty cup, until he had to ask for some coffee in an injured and pathetic voice, which amused Dr Marjoribanks beyond description. But even this did not prove sufficient to propitiate the Fates. When They were gone—and it may be well to say that Lucilla used this pronoun to signify *the gentlemen*, in greater or smaller number as it might happen—and she had finished all her arrangements, Miss Marjoribanks decided upon going to Grove Street to pay Barbara Lake a visit, and practise some duets, which was certainly as innocent an occupation for her leisure as could have been desired. She was putting on her hat with this object when the bell in the garden rang solemnly, and Lucilla, whose curiosity conquered her good manners for the moment, hastening to the window, saw Mr Bury himself enter the garden, accompanied by a black figure in deep and shabby mourning. All the tremors of the night rushed back upon her mind at the sight. She felt that the moment had arrived for a trial of her courage very different from the exertions which had hitherto sufficed her. Nothing but the most solemn intentions could have supported the Rector in that severe pose of his figure and features, every line in which revealed an intention of being "faithful;" and the accompanying mute in black, whose office the culprit could not divine, had a veil over her face, and wore a widow's dress. Miss Marjoribanks, it is true, was not a woman to be discouraged by appearances, but she felt her heart beat as she collected all her powers to meet this mysterious assault. She took off her hat with an instinctive certainty that, for this morning at least, the duet was impracticable, when she heard Mr Bury's steady step ascending the stairs; but, notwithstanding, it was with a perfectly cheerful politeness that she bade him welcome when he came into the room. "It is so good of you to come," Lucilla said; "you that have so much to do. I scarcely could believe it when I saw you come in: I thought it must be for papa."

"I did hope to find Dr Marjoribanks," said the Rector, "but as he is not at home, I thought it best to come to you. This is Mrs Mortimer," said Mr Bury, taking the chair Lucilla had indicated with a certain want of observance of his companion which betrayed to the keen perceptions of Miss Marjoribanks that she was a dependant of some kind or other. The Rector was a very good man, but he was Evangelical, and had a large female circle who admired and swore by him; and, consequently, he felt it in a manner natural that he should take his seat first, and the place that belonged to him as the principal person present; and then, to be sure, his mission here was for Mrs Mortimer's as well as Miss Marjoribanks's "good." After this introduction, the figure in black put up its veil, and revealed a deprecating woman, with a faint sort of pleading smile on her face. Probably she was making believe to smile at the position in which she found herself; but anyhow she took her seat humbly on another chair at a little distance, and waited, as Lucilla did, for the next golden words that it might please the Rector to say.

"My sister told me what happened yesterday," said Mr Bury. "She is very sorry for you, Miss Marjoribanks. It is sad for you to be left alone so young, and without a mother, and exposed to—to temptations which it is difficult to withstand at your age. Indeed, at all ages, we have great occasion to pray not to be led into temptation; for the heart of man is terribly deceitful. After hearing what she had to say, I thought it best to come up at once this morning and talk to Dr Marjoribanks. I am sure his natural good sense will teach him that you ought not to be left alone in the house."

"I do not see how papa can help it," said Lucilla. "I am sure it is very sad for him as well; but since dear mamma died there has been nobody but me to be a comfort to him. I think he begins to look a little cheerful now," Miss Marjoribanks continued, with beautiful simplicity, looking her adversary in the face. "Everybody knows that to be a comfort to him is the object of my life."

"That is a very good feeling," said the Rector, "but it does not do to depend too much upon our feelings. You are too young to be placed in a position of so much responsibility, and open to so much temptation. I was deeply grieved for Dr Marjoribanks when his partner in life was taken from him; but my dear Miss Lucilla, now you have come home, who stand so much in need of a mother's care, we must try to find some one to fill her place."

Lucilla uttered a scream of genuine alarm and dismay; and then she came to herself, and saw the force of her position. She had it in her power to turn the tables on the Rector, and she did not hesitate, as a weaker woman might have done, out of consideration for anybody's feelings. "Do you mean you have found some one for him to marry?" she asked, with a look of artless surprise, bending her earnest gaze on Mr Bury's face.

As for the Rector, he looked at Lucilla aghast, like a man caught in a trap. "Of course not, of course not," he stammered, after his first pause of consternation; and then he had to stop again to take breath. Lucilla kept up the air of amazement and consternation which had come naturally at the first, and had her eyes fixed on him, leaning forward with all the eager anxiety natural to the circumstances, and the unfortunate clergyman reddened from the edge of his white cravat to the roots of his grey hair. He was almost as sensitive to the idea of having proposed something improper as his sister could have been, though indeed, at the worst, there would have been nothing improper in it had Dr Marjoribanks made up his mind to another wife.

"It is very dreadful for me that am so young to go against *you*," said Lucilla; "but if it is *that*, I cannot be expected to take any part in it—it would not be natural. It is the great object of my life to be a comfort to papa; but if that is what you mean, I could not give in to it. I am sure Miss Bury would understand me," said Miss Marjoribanks; and she looked so nearly on the point of tears, that the Rector's anxious disclaimer found words for itself.

"Nothing of the kind, my dear Miss Lucilla—nothing of the kind," cried Mr Bury; "such an idea never came into my mind. I cannot imagine how I could have said anything — I can't fancy what put such an idea——Mrs Mortimer, you are not going away?"

Lucilla had already seen with the corner of her eye that the victim had started violently, and that her heavy veil had fallen over her face—but she had not taken any notice, for there are cases in which it is absolutely necessary to have a victim. By this time, however, the poor woman had risen in her nervous undecided way.

"I had better go—I am sure I had better go," she said, hurriedly, clasping together a pair of helpless hands, as if they could find a little strength in union. "Miss Marjoribanks will understand you better, and you will perhaps understand Miss Marjoribanks——"

"Oh, sit down, sit down," said Mr Bury, who was not tolerant of feelings. "Perhaps I expressed myself badly. What I meant to say was, that Mrs Mortimer, who has been a little unfortunate in circumstances—sit down, pray—had by a singular providence just applied to me when my sister returned home yesterday. These things do not happen by chance, Lucilla. We are taken care of when we are not thinking of it. Mrs Mortimer is a Christian lady for whom I have the greatest respect. A situation to take the superintendence of the domestic affairs, and to have charge of you, would be just what would suit her. It must be a great anxiety to the Doctor to leave you alone, and without any control, at your age. You may think the liberty is pleasant at first, but if you had a Christian friend to watch over and take care of you——What is the matter?" said the Rector, in great alarm. It was only that the poor widow who was to have charge of Lucilla, according to his benevolent intention, looked so like fainting, that Miss Marjoribanks jumped up from her chair and rang the bell hastily. It was not Lucilla's way to lose time about anything; she took the poor woman by the shoulders and all but lifted her to the sofa, where she was lying down with her bonnet off when the Rector came to his senses. To describe the feelings with which Mr Bury contemplated this little *entr'acte*, which was not in his programme, would be beyond our powers. He went off humbly and opened the window when he was told to do so, and tried to find the eau-de-cologne on the table; while Thomas rushed down-stairs for water at a pace very unlike his usual steady rate of progress. As for Lucilla, she stood by the side of her patient quite self-possessed, while the Rector looked so foolish. "She will be all right directly," Miss Marjoribanks was saying; "luckily she never went right off. When you don't go right off, lying down is everything. If there had been any one to run and get some water she would have got over it; but luckily I saw it in time." What possible answer Mr Bury could make to this, or how he could go on with his address in sight of the strange turn things had taken, it would have been hard to say. Fortunately for the moment he did not attempt it, but walked about in dismay, and put himself in the draught (with his rheumatism), and felt dreadfully vexed and angry with Mrs Mortimer, who, for her part, now she had done with fainting, manifested an inclination to cry, for which Mr Bury in his heart could have whipped her, had that mode of discipline been permitted in the Church of England. Lucilla was merciful, but she could not help taking a little advantage of her victory. She gave the sufferer a glass of water, and the eau-de-cologne to keep her from a relapse, and whispered to her to lie quiet; and then she came back and took her seat, and begged the Rector not to stand in the draught.

"I don't think she is strong," said Miss Marjoribanks, confidentially, when she had wiled the disconcerted clergyman back to her side, " her colour changes so; she never would be able for what there is to do here, even if papa would consent to think of it. For my part I am sure I should be glad of a little assistance," said Lucilla, " but I never like to give false hopes, and I don't think papa would consent;—she looks nice if she was not so weak, poor thing!—and there are such quantities of things to be done here: but if you wish it, Mr Bury, I will speak to papa," said Miss Marjoribanks, lifting her eyes, which were so open and straightforward, to the Rector's face.

To tell the truth, he did not in the least know what to say, and the chances are he would not have been half so vexed and angry, nor felt in so unchristian a disposition with the poor woman on the sofa, had he meant to do her harm instead of good. "Yes, I should be glad if you would mention it to Dr Marjoribanks," he said, without very well knowing what he said; and got up to shake hands with Lucilla, and then recollected that he could not leave his *protégée* behind him, and hesitated, and did not know what to do. He was really grateful, without being aware of it, to Miss Marjoribanks, when once again she came to his aid.

"Please, leave her a little," said Lucilla, "and I can make acquaintance with her, you know, in case papa should be disposed to think of it;—she must lie still till it quite wears off. I would ask you to stay to lunch if I was not afraid of wasting your precious time——"

Mr Bury gave a little gasp of indignation, but he did not say anything. On the whole, even though smarting under the indignity of being asked to lunch, as his sister had been, when probably there might be a repetition of the scene of yesterday, he was glad to get safely out of the house, even at the risk of abandoning his enterprise. As for a woman in want of a situation, who had so little common sense as to faint at such a critical moment, the Rector was disposed to wash his hands of her; for Mr Bury, "like them all," as Lucilla said, was horribly frightened by a faint when he saw one, and afterwards pretended to disbelieve in it, and called it one of the things which a little self-command could always prevent. When he was gone Miss Marjoribanks felt the full importance of her victory; and then, though she had not hesitated to sacrifice this poor woman when it was necessary to have a victim, that moment was over, and she had no pleasure in being cruel; on the contrary, she went and sat by her patient, and talked, and was very kind to her; and after a while heard all her story, and was more comforting than the Rector could have been for his life.

"I knew it would hurt your feelings," Miss Marjoribanks said, candidly, "but I could not do anything else—and you know it was Mr Bury's fault; but I am sure if I can be of any use to you——" It was thus that Lucilla added, without knowing it, another complication to her fortunes; but then, to be sure, clearsighted as she was, she could not see into the future, nor know what was to follow. She told the Doctor in the evening with the greatest faithfulness, and described how Mr Bury looked, and that she had said she did not think papa would be disposed to think of it; and Dr Marjoribanks was so much entertained that he came up-stairs to hear the end, and took a cup of tea. It was the third night in succession that the Doctor had taken this step, though it was against his principles; and thus it will be seen that good came out of evil in a beautifully distinct and appropriate way.

CHAPTER IX.

IT was not till Miss Marjoribanks had surmounted to a certain extent the vexation caused her by her unlucky confidence in Tom, that that unhappy young man took the step which Lucilla had so long dreaded, but which she trusted to her own genius to hinder him from carrying into execution. Miss Marjoribanks had extricated herself so triumphantly from the consequences of that unhappy commencement of her very charming luncheon-parties, that she had begun to forget the culpability of her cousin. She had defeated the Rector in his benevolent intentions, and she had taken up his *protégée* just at the moment when Mr Bury was most disgusted with the unfortunate woman's weakness. Poor Mrs Mortimer, to be sure, had fainted, or been near fainting, at the most inopportune moment, and it was only natural that the Rector should be annoyed; but as for Lucilla, who was always prompt in her actions, and whose good-nature and liberality were undoubted, she found her opportunity in the failure of Mr Bury's scheme. After the Rector had gone away, Miss Marjoribanks herself conducted the widow home; and by this time Mrs Mortimer's prospects were beginning to brighten under the active and efficient patronage of her new friend. This being the case, Lucilla's good-humour was perfectly restored, and she had forgiven Tom his maladroitness. "He cannot help it, you know," she said privately to old Mrs Chiley: "I suppose some people are born to do ridiculous things." And it was indeed as if he had intended to give a practical illustration of the truth of this conclusion that Tom chose the particular moment he did for driving Miss Marjoribanks to the extremity of her patience. The upholsterers were in the house, and indeed had just finished putting up the pictures on the new paper in the drawing-room (which was green, as Lucilla had determined it should be, of the most delicate tint, and looked, as she flattered herself, exactly like silk hangings); and Mr Holden himself waited with a certain complaisance for Miss Marjoribanks's opinion of the effect. He had no doubt on the subject himself; but he was naturally impressed, as most people were, with that confidence in Lucilla's judgment which so much facilitates the operations of those persons who are born to greatness. It was precisely at this moment that his evil genius persuaded Tom Marjoribanks to interrupt Thomas, who was carrying Mr Holden's message to his young mistress, and to shut the library door upon the external world. Lucilla had taken refuge in the library during the renovation of the drawing-room; and she was aware that this was Tom's last day at Carlingford, and had no intention of being unkind to him. To tell the truth, she had at the bottom of her heart a certain regard and impulse of protection and patronage towards Tom, of which something might have come had the unlucky fellow known how to manage. But, at the same time, Miss Marjoribanks was aware that things must be approaching a crisis upstairs, and was listening intently to the movements overhead, and wondering why she was not sent for. This was the moment of all others at which Tom thought fit to claim a hearing; and the state of Lucilla's feelings may be easily imagined when she saw him plant himself by her side, with his face alternately red and white, and all the signs of a desperate resolution in his countenance. For the first time in her life a certain despair took possession of Miss Marjoribanks's mind. The sounds had suddenly ceased up-stairs, as if the artists there were making a pause to contemplate the effect of their completed work—which indeed was precisely the case—and at the same time nobody came to call her, important though the occasion was. She made a last effort to emancipate herself before it was too late.

"Ring, please, Tom," she said; "I want to know if they have finished up-stairs. I am so sorry you are going away; but you know it is one of my principles never to neglect my duty. I am sure they must be waiting for me—if you would only be kind enough to ring."

"Lucilla," said Tom, "you know I would do anything in the world you liked to tell me; but don't ask me to ring just now: I am going to leave you, and there is something I must say to you, Lucilla," said the young man, with agitation. Miss Marjoribanks was seated near the window, and she had a moral certainty that if any of the Browns happened to be in that ridiculous glass-house where they did their photography, they must have a perfectly good view of her, with Tom in the background, who had placed himself so as to shut her into the recess of the window. This, coupled with the evidence of her senses that the workmen up-stairs had ceased their work, and that a slow footstep traversing the floor now and then was all that was audible, drove Lucilla to despair.

"Yes," she said, temporising a little, which was the only thing she could do, "I am sure I am very sorry; but then, you know, with the house in such a condition! Next time you come I shall be able to enjoy your society," said the designing young woman; "but at present I am *so* busy. It is one of my principles, you know, that things are never rightly done if the lady of the house does not pay proper attention. They are sure to make some dreadful mistake up-stairs if I don't look after them. I shall see you again before you go."

"Lucilla, don't be so cruel!" cried the unlucky Tom, and he caught her hand though they were at the window; "do stop a moment and listen to me. Lucilla! what does it matter about furniture and things when a man's heart is bursting?" cried the unfortunate lover; and just at that moment Miss Marjoribanks could see that the curtain was drawn aside a little—ever so little

—in the glass-house. She sat down again with a sigh, and drew her hand away, and prepared herself to meet her fate with heroism at least.

"What in the world can you have been doing?" said Lucilla, innocently; "you used always to tell me, I know, when you got into any difficulty; and I am sure if I can be of any use to you, Tom——. But as for furniture and things, they matter a great deal, I assure you, to people's happiness; and then, you know, it is the object of my life to be a comfort to dear papa."

When she said this, Miss Marjoribanks settled herself again in the recess of the window, so that the Miss Browns could command a full view if they chose; for Lucilla's courage was of the highest order, and nothing, except, perhaps, a strategical necessity of profound importance, would have moved her to retreat before an enemy. As for Tom, he was bewildered, to start with, by this solemn repetition of her great purpose.

"I know how good you are, Lucilla," he said, with humility; "but then my uncle, you know—I don't think he is a man to appreciate——. Oh, Lucilla! why should you go and sacrifice to him the happiness of your life?"

"Tom," said Miss Marjoribanks, with some solemnity, "I wish you would not talk to me of happiness. I have always been brought up to believe that duty was happiness; and everybody has known for a long time what was the object of my life. As for poor papa, it is the worse for him if he does not understand; but that does not make any difference to my duty," said the devoted daughter. She gave a little sigh as she spoke, the sigh of a great soul, whose motives must always remain to some extent unappreciated; and the sight of her resignation and beautiful perseverance overwhelmed her unlucky suitor; for indeed, up to this moment, Lucilla still entertained the hope of preventing Tom from, as she herself described it, "saying the very words," which, to be sure, are awkward words to hear and to say.

"Lucilla, when you are so good to my uncle, you ought to have a little pity on me," said Tom, driven to the deepest despondency. "How do you think I can bear it, to see you getting everything done here, as if you meant to stay all your life —when you know I love you?" said the unfortunate young man; "when you know I have always been so fond of you, Lucilla, and always looked forward to the time——; and now it is very hard to see you care so little for me."

"Tom," said Miss Marjoribanks, with indignant surprise,

"how *can* you say I care little for you? you know I was always very fond of you, on the contrary. I am sure I always stood your friend at home, whatever happened, and never said a word when you broke that pretty little pearl ring I was so fond of, and tore the scarf my aunt gave me. I wonder, for my part, how you can be so unkind as to say so. We have always been the very best friends in the world," said Lucilla, with an air of injury. "I always said at school I liked you the best of all my cousins; and I am very fond of all my cousins." Miss Marjoribanks concluded, after a little pause, "It is so unkind to tell me that I don't care for *you*."

Poor Tom groaned within himself as he listened. He did not know what to answer to Lucilla's aggrieved yet frank confession. Naturally it would have been much less displeasing to Tom to understand that she hated him, and never desired to see him any more. But Miss Marjoribanks was far from entertaining any such unchristian sentiments. She even began to forget her anxiety about what was going on up-stairs in that delightful sense of power and abundant resources with which she was mastering the present difficulty. She reflected in herself that though it was excessively annoying to be thus occupied at such a moment, still it was nearly as important to make an end of Tom as to see that the pictures were hung rightly; for, to be sure, it was always easy to return to the latter subject. Accordingly, she drew her chair a little nearer to the window, and regarded Tom with a calm gaze of benevolent interest which was in perfect accordance with the sentiments she had just expressed; a look in which a little gentle reproach was mingled. "I have always been like a sister to you," said Lucilla; "how can you be so unkind as to say I don't care?"

As for the unhappy Tom, he got up, as was natural, and took a little walk in front of the table, as a young man in trouble is apt to do. "You know very well that is not what I mean, Lucilla," he said, disconsolately. "It is you who are unkind. I don't know why it is that ladies are so cruel; I am not such a snob as to persecute anybody. But what is the good of pretending not to know what I mean?"

"Tom, listen!" cried Miss Marjoribanks, rising in her turn; "I feel sure they must have finished. There is Mr Holden going through the garden. And everybody knows that hanging pictures is just the thing of all others that requires a person of taste. If they have spoiled the room, it will be all your fault."

"Oh, for heaven's sake never mind the room!" said Tom.

"I never thought you would have trifled with a man, Lucilla. You know quite well what I mean; you know it isn't a—a new thing," said the lover, beginning to stammer and get confused. "You know that is what I have been thinking of all along, as soon as ever I had anything to live on. I love you, Lucilla; you know I love you! how can you trifle with me so?"

"It is you who are trifling," said Miss Marjoribanks, "especially when you know I have really something of importance to do. You can come up-stairs with me if you like. Of course we all love each other. What is the good of being relations otherwise?" said Lucilla, calmly; "it is such a natural thing, you know. I suppose it is because you are going away that you are so affectionate to-day. It is very nice of you, I am sure; but, Tom, I feel quite certain you have not packed your things," Miss Marjoribanks added, in an admonitory tone. "Come along with me up-stairs."

And by this time Lucilla's curiosity was beginning again to get the upper hand. If she only could have escaped, it would have been impossible for her cousin to have renewed the conversation; and luckily he was to leave Carlingford the same evening; but then a man is always an inconsequent creature, and not to be calculated on. This time, instead of obeying as usual, Tom—having, as Miss Marjoribanks afterwards described (but only in the strictest confidence), "worked himself up to it"—set himself directly in her way, and seized upon both her hands.

"Lucilla," cried the unlucky fellow, "is it possible that you really have misunderstood me all this time? Do you mean to say that you don't know? Oh, Lucilla, listen just five minutes. It isn't because I am your cousin. I wish to heaven I was not your cousin, but some one you had never seen before. I mean I want you to consent to—to—to—marry me, Lucilla. That is what I mean. I am called to the bar, and I can work for you, and make a reputation. Lucilla, listen to what I have got to say."

Miss Marjoribanks left her hands in his with a calmness which froze poor Tom's heart in his breast. She did not even take the trouble to draw them away. "Have you gone out of your senses, Tom " she asked, in her sensible way; and she lifted her eyes to the face of the poor young fellow who was in love, with an inquiring look, as if she felt a little anxious about him. "If you have any feeling as if fever was coming on," said Lucilla, "I think you should go up-stairs and lie down a little till papa comes in. I heard there had been some cases down about the canal. I hope it is not the assizes that have been too much for you." When Miss Marjoribanks said this, she herself took fast hold of Tom's hands with a motherly grasp to feel if they were hot, and looked into his eyes with a certain serious inspection, which, under the circumstances, poor fellow! was enough to drive him out of the little rationality he had left.

Tom was so far carried away by his frenzy, that he gave her a little shake in his impatience. "You are trying to drive me mad, Lucilla!" cried the young man. "I have got no fever. It is only you who are driving me out of my senses. This time you must hear me. I will not let you go till you have given me an answer. I am called to the bar, and I have begun my Career," said Tom, making a pause for breath. "I knew you would have laughed at me when I was depending on my mother; but now all that is over, Lucilla. I have loved you as long as I can remember; and I always thought—that you— cared for me a little. If you will have me, there is nothing I could not do," said Tom, who thoroughly believed what he was saying; "and if you will not have me, I will not answer for the consequences. If I go off to India, or if I go to the bad——"

"Tom," said Lucilla, solemnly, and this time she drew away her hands, "if you ever want to get married, I think the very best thing you can do is to go to India. As for marrying just now at your age, you know you might as well jump into the sea. You need not be vexed," said Miss Marjoribanks, in her motherly way. "I would not speak so if I was not your best friend. As for marrying me, you know it is ridiculous. I have not the least intention of marrying anybody. If I had thought of that, I need never have come home at all. As for your going to the bad, I am not afraid of that. If I were to let you carry on with such a ridiculous idea, I should never forgive myself. It would be just as sensible to go into a lunatic asylum at once. It is very lucky for you that you said this to *me*," Lucilla went on, "and not to one of the girls that think it great fun to be married. And if I were you, Tom, I would go and pack my things. You know you are always too late; and don't jump on your portmanteau and make such a dreadful noise if it won't shut, but ring the bell for Thomas. You know we are to dine at half-past five to-day, to give you time for the train."

These were the last words Tom Marjoribanks heard as Lucilla left the room. She ran up to the drawing-room without losing a minute, and burst in upon the vacant place where Mr Holden had stood so long waiting for her. To be sure, Miss Marjoribanks's forebodings were so far fulfilled that the St Cecilia, which she meant to have over the piano, was hung quite in the other corner of the room, by reason of being just the same size as another picture at the opposite angle, which the workmen, sternly symmetrical, thought it necessary to "match." But, after all, that was a trifling defect. She stood in the middle of the room, and surveyed the walls, well pleased, with a heart which kept beating very steadily in her bosom. On the whole, perhaps, she was not sorry to have had it out with Tom. So far as he was personally concerned, Miss Marjoribanks, being a physician's daughter, had great faith in the *vis medicatrix*, and was not afraid for her cousin's health or his morals, as a less experienced woman might have been. If she was angry with anybody, it was with herself, who had not taken sufficient precautions to avoid the explanation. "But, after all, everything is for the best," Lucilla said to herself, with that beautiful confidence which is common to people who have things their own way; and she devoted her mind to the St Cecilia, and paid no more attention to Tom. It was not till more than an hour after that a succession of dreadful thumps were not only heard but felt throughout the house. It was Tom, but he was not doing any harm to himself. He was not blowing out his brains or knocking his head against the wall. He was only jumping on his portmanteau, notwithstanding that Lucilla had warned him against such a proceeding—and in his state of mind the jumps were naturally more frantic than usual. When Lucilla heard it, she rang the bell, and told Thomas to go and help Mr Tom with his packing; from which it will be seen that Miss Marjoribanks bore no grudge against her cousin, but was disposed to send him forth in friendship and peace.

CHAPTER X.

It was nearly six weeks after this before all Miss Marjoribanks's arrangements were completed, and she was able with satisfaction to herself to begin her campaign. It was just before Christmas, at the time above all others when society has need of a ruling spirit. For example, Mrs Chiley expected the Colonel's niece, Mary Chiley, who had been married about six months before, and who was not fond of her husband's friends, and at the same time had no home of her own to go to, being an orphan. The Colonel had invited the young couple by way of doing a kind thing, but he grumbled a little at the necessity, and had never liked the fellow, he said—and then what were two old people to do to amuse them? Then Mrs Centum had her two eldest boys home from school, and was driven out of her senses by the noise and the racket, as she confided to her visitors. "It is all very well to make pretty pictures about Christmas," said the exasperated mother, "but I should like to know how one can enjoy anything with such a commotion going on. I get up every morning with a headache, I assure you; and then Mr Centum expects me to be cheerful when he comes in to dinner; men are *so* unreasonable. I should like to know what *they* would do if they had what we have to go through: to look after all the servants—and they are always out of their senses at Christmas—and to see that the children don't have too much pudding, and to support all the noise. The holidays are the hardest work a poor woman can have," she concluded, with a sigh; and when it is taken into consideration that this particular Christmas was a wet Christmas, without any frost or possibility of amusement out of doors, English matrons in general will not refuse their sympathy to Mrs Centum. Mrs Woodburn perhaps was equally to be pitied in a different way. She had to receive several members of her husband's family, who were, like Miss Marjoribanks, without any sense of humour, and who stared, and did not in the least understand her when she "took off" any of her neighbours; not to say that some of them were Low-Church, and thought the practice sinful. Under these circumstances it will be readily believed that the commencement of Lucilla's operations was looked upon with great interest in Carlingford. It was so opportune that society forgot its usual instincts of criticism, and forgave Miss Marjoribanks for being more enlightened and enterprising than her neighbours; and then most people were very anxious to see the drawing-room, now it had been restored.

This was a privilege, however, not accorded to the crowd. Mrs Chiley had seen it under a vow of secrecy, and Mr Cavendish owned to having made a run up-stairs one evening after one of Dr Marjoribanks's little dinners, when the other *convives* were in the library, where Lucilla had erected her temporary throne. But this clandestine inspection met with the failure it deserved, for there was no light in the room except the moonlight, which made three white blotches on the carpet where the windows were, burying everything else in the profoundest darkness; and the spy knocked his foot against something which reduced him to sudden and well-merited agony. As for Mrs Chiley, she was discretion itself, and would say nothing even to her niece. "I mean to work her a footstool in waterlilies, my dear, like the one I did for you when you were married," the old lady said; and that was the only light she would throw on the subject. "My opinion is that it must be in crimson," Mrs Woodburn said, when she heard this, "for I know your aunt's water-lilies. When I see them growing, I always think of you. It would be quite like Lucilla Marjoribanks to have it in crimson—for it is a cheerful colour, you know, and quite different from the old furniture; and that would always be a comfort to her dear papa." From this it will be seen that the curiosity of Carlingford was excited to a lively extent. Many people even went so far as to give the Browns a sitting in their glass-house, with the hope of having a peep at the colour of the hangings at least. But Miss Marjoribanks was too sensible a woman to leave her virgin drawing-room exposed to the sun when there was any, and to the photographers, who were perhaps more dangerous. "I think it is blue, for my part," said Miss Brown, who had got into the habit of rising early in hopes of finding the Doctor's household off its guard. "Lucilla was always a great one for blue; she thinks it is becoming to her complexion;" which, indeed, as the readers of this history are aware, was a matter of fact. As for Miss Marjoribanks, she did her best to keep up this agreeable mystery. "For my part, I am fond of neutral tints," she herself said, when she was questioned on the subject; "anybody who knows me can easily guess my taste. I should have been born a Quaker, you know, I do so like the drabs and greys, and all those soft colours. You can have as much red and green as you like abroad, where the sun is strong, but here it would be bad style," said Lucilla; from which the most simple-minded of her auditors drew the natural conclusion. Thus all the world contemplated with excitement the first Thursday which was to open this enchanted chamber to their admiring eyes. "Don't expect any regular invitation," Miss Marjoribanks said. "I hope you will all come, or as many of you as can. Papa has always some men to dinner with him that day, you know, and it is so dreadfully slow for me with a heap of men. That is why I fixed on Thursday. I want you to come every week, so it would be absurd to send an invitation; and remember it is not a party, only an Evening," said Lucilla. "I shall wear a white frock high, as I always do. Now be sure you come."

"But we can't all go in high white frocks," said Mrs Chiley's niece, Mary, who, if her *trousseau* had been subtracted from the joys of marriage, would not, poor soul! have found very much left. This intimation dismayed the bride a little; for, to be sure, she had decided which dress she was to wear before Lucilla spoke.

"But, my dear, you are married," said Miss Marjoribanks; "that makes it quite different: come in that pretty pink that is so becoming. I don't want to have any dowdies, for my part; and don't forget that I shall expect you all at nine o'clock."

When she had said this, Miss Marjoribanks proceeded on her way, sowing invitations and gratification round her. She asked the youngest Miss Brown to bring her music, in recognition of her ancient claims as the songstress of society in Carlingford; for Lucilla had all that regard for constituted rights which is so necessary to a revolutionary of the highest class. She had no desire to shock anybody's prejudices or wound anybody's feelings. "And she has a nice little voice," Lucilla said to herself, with the most friendly and tolerant feelings. Thus Miss Marjoribanks prepared to establish her kingdom with a benevolence which was almost Utopian, not upon the ruins of other thrones, but with the goodwill and co-operation of the lesser powers, who were, to be sure, too feeble to resist her advance, but whose rights she was quite ready to recognise, and even to promote, in her own way.

At the same time it is necessary here to indicate a certain vague and not disagreeable danger, which appeared to some experienced persons to shadow Lucilla's conquering way. Mr Cavendish, who was a young man of refinement, not to say that he had a very nice property, had begun to pay attention to Miss Marjoribanks in what Mrs Chiley thought quite a marked manner. To be sure, he could not pretend to the honour of taking her in to dinner, which was not his place, being a young man; but he did what was next best, and manœuvred to get the place on her left hand, which, in a party composed chiefly of men, was not difficult to manage. For, to tell the truth, most of the gentlemen present were at that special moment more interested in the dinner than in Lucilla. And after dinner it was Mr Cavendish who was the first to leave the room; and to hear the two talking about all the places they had been to, and all the people they had met, was as good as a play, Mrs Chiley said. Mr Cavendish confided to Lucilla his opinions upon things in general, and accepted the reproofs which she administered (for Miss Marjoribanks was quite unquestionable in her orthodoxy, and thought it a duty, as she said, always to speak with respect of religion) when his sentiments were too speculative, and said, " How charming is divine philosophy!" so as, for the moment, to dazzle Lucilla herself, who thought it a very pretty compliment. He came to her assistance when she made tea, and generally fulfilled all the duties which are expected of a man who is paying attention to a young lady. Old Mrs Chiley watched the nascent regard with her kind old grandmotherly eyes. She calculated over in her own mind the details of his possessions, so far as the public was aware of them, and found them on the whole satisfactory. He had a nice property, and then he was a very nice, indeed an unexceptionable young man; and to add to this, it had been agreed between Colonel Chiley and Mr Centum, and several other of the leading people in Carlingford, that he was the most likely man to represent the borough when old Mr Chiltern, who was always threatening to retire, fulfilled his promise. Mr Cavendish had a very handsome house a little out of town, where a lady would be next thing to a county lady—indeed, quite a county lady, if her husband was the Member for Carlingford.

All these thoughts passed through Mrs Chiley's mind, and, as was natural, in the precious moments after dinner, were suggested in occasional words of meaning to the understanding ear of Miss Marjoribanks. "My dear Lucilla, it is just the position that would suit you—with your talents!" the old lady said; and Lucilla did not say No. To be sure, she had not at the present moment the least inclination to get married, as she truly said; it would, indeed, to tell the truth, disturb her plans considerably; but still, if such was the intention of Providence, and if it was to the Member for Carlingford, Lucilla felt that it was still credible that everything might be for the best.

"But it is a great deal too soon to think of anything of that sort," Miss Marjoribanks would reply.. "If I had thought of that, I need never have come home at all; and especially when papa has been so good about everything." Yet for all that she was not ungracious to Mr Cavendish when he came in first as usual. To marry a man in his position would not, after all, be deranging her plans to any serious extent. Indeed, it would, if his hopes were realised, constitute Lucilla a kind of queen in Carlingford, and she could not but feel that, under these circumstances, it might be a kind of duty to reconsider her resolution. And thus the time passed while the drawing-room was undergoing renovation. Mr Cavendish had been much tantalised, as he said, by the absence of the piano, which prevented them from having any music, and Lucilla had even been tempted into a few snatches of song, which, to tell the truth, some of the gentlemen present, especially the Doctor himself and Colonel Chiley, being old-fashioned, preferred without the accompaniment. And thus it was, under the most brilliant auspices, and with the full confidence of all her future constituency, that Miss Marjoribanks superintended the arrangement of the drawing-room on that momentous Thursday, which was to be the real beginning of her great work in Carlingford.

"My dear, you must leave yourself entirely in my hands," Lucilla said to Barbara Lake on the morning of that eventful day. "Don't get impatient. I daresay you don't know many people, and it may be a little slow for you at first; but everybody has to put up with that, you know, for a beginning. And, by the by, what are you going to wear?"

"I have not thought about it," said Barbara, who had the painful pride of poverty, aggravated much by a sense that the comforts of other people were an injury to her. Poor soul! she had been thinking of little else for at least a week past; and then she had not very much choice in her wardrobe; but her disposition was one which rejected sympathy, and she thought it would look best to pretend to be indifferent. At the same time, she said this with a dull colour on her cheeks, the colour of irritation; and she could not help asking herself why Lucilla, who was not so handsome as she was, had the power to array herself in gorgeous apparel, while she, Barbara, had nothing but a white frock. There are differences even in white frocks, though the masculine mind may be unaware of them. Barbara's muslin had been washed six times, and had a very different air from the vestal robes of her patroness. To be sure, Lucilla was not taken in, in the least, by her companion's look of indifference, and would even have been delighted to bestow a pretty dress upon Barbara, if that had been a possible thing to do.

"There will be no dress," said Miss Marjoribanks, with

solemnity. "I have insisted upon that. You know it is not a party, it is only an Evening. A white frock, *high*—that is all I mean to wear; and mind you don't lose patience. I shall keep my eye on you; and after the first, I feel sure you will enjoy yourself. Good-bye for the present." When she had uttered these encouraging words, Miss Marjoribanks went away to pursue her preparations, and Barbara proceeded to get out her dress and examine it. It was as important to her as all the complicated paraphernalia of the evening's arrangements were to Lucilla. It is true that there were greater interests involved in the case of the leader; but then Barbara was the soldier of fortune who had to open the oyster with her sword, and she was feeling the point of it metaphorically while she pulled out the breadths of her white dress, and tried to think that they would not look limp at night; and what her sentiments lost in breadth, as compared with Lucilla's, they gained in intensity, for—for anything she could tell—her life might change colour by means of this Thursday Evening; and such, indeed, was her hope. Barbara prepared for her first appearance in Grange Lane, with a mind wound up to any degree of daring. It did not occur to her that she required to keep faith with Miss Marjoribanks in anything except the duet. As regarded other matters, Barbara was quite unscrupulous, for at the bottom she could not but feel that any one who was kind to her was taking an unwarrantable liberty. What right had Lucilla Marjoribanks to be kind to her? as if she was not as good as Lucilla any day! and though it might be worth her while to take advantage of it for the moment, it was still an insult, in its way, to be avenged if an opportunity ever should arise.

The evening came, as evenings do come, quite indifferently whether people are glad or sorry; and it was with a calmness which the other ladies regarded as next to miraculous, that Miss Marjoribanks took Colonel Chiley's arm to go to the dining-room. We say the other ladies, for on this great occasion Mrs Centum and Mrs Woodburn were both among the dinner-guests. "To see her eat her dinner as if she had nothing on her mind!" Mrs Centum said in amazement: "as for me, though nobody can blame me if anything goes wrong, I could enjoy nothing for thinking of it. And I must say I was disappointed with the dinner," she added, with a certain air of satisfaction, in Mrs Woodburn's ear. It was when they were going up-stairs, and Lucilla was behind with Mrs Chiley. "The fuss the men have always made about these dinners! and except for a few made dishes that were really nothing, you know, I can't say *I* saw anything particular in it. And as for Lucilla, I can't think she has any feeling," said the banker's wife.

"Oh, my dear, it is because you don't understand," said Mrs Woodburn. "She is kept up, you know, by a sense of duty. It is all because she has set her heart on being a comfort to her dear papa!"

Such, it is true, were the comments that were made upon the public-spirited young woman who was doing so much for Carlingford; but then Lucilla only shared the fate of all the great benefactors of the world. An hour later the glories of the furniture were veiled and hidden by the robes of a radiant flood of society, embracing all that was most fair and all that was most distinguished in Carlingford. No doubt there was a world of heterogeneous elements; but then if there had not been difficulties where would have been the use of Miss Marjoribanks's genius? Mr Bury and his sister, who had been unconsciously mollified by the admirable dinner provided for them down-stairs, found some stray lambs in the assembly who were in need of them, and thus had the double satisfaction of combining pleasure with duty; and though there were several people in the room whose lives were a burden to them in consequence of Mrs Woodburn's remarkable gift, even they found it impossible not to be amused by an occasional representation of an absent individual, or by the dashing sketch of Lucilla, which she gave at intervals in her corner, amid the smothered laughter of the audience, who were half ashamed of themselves. "She is never ill-tempered, you know," the persons who felt themselves threatened in their turn said to each other with a certain piteous resignation; and oddly enough it was in general the most insignificant people about who were afraid of Mrs Woodburn. It is needless to say that such a dread never entered the serene intelligence of Miss Marjoribanks, who believed in herself with a reasonable and steady faith. As for old Mrs Chiley, who had so many funny little ways, and whom the mimic executed to perfection, she also was quite calm on the subject. "You know there is nothing to take off in me," the old lady would say; "I always was a simple body: and then I am old enough to be all your grandmothers, my dear;" which was a saying calculated, as Miss Marjoribanks justly observed, to melt a heart of stone.

Then the Miss Browns had brought their photographs, in which most people in Grange Lane were caricatured hideously, but with such a charming equality that the most *exigeant* forgave the wrong to himself in laughing at his neighbours. Miss Brown had brought her music too, and sang her feeble little strain to the applause of her immediate neighbours, and to the delight of those who were at a distance, and who could talk louder and flirt more openly under cover of the music; and there were other young ladies who had also come prepared with a little roll of songs or "pieces." Lucilla, with her finger as it were upon the pulse of the company, let them all exhibit their powers with that enlightened impartiality which we have already remarked in her. When Mr Cavendish came to her in his ingratiating way, and asked her how she could possibly let all the sparrows chirp like that when the nightingale was present, Miss Marjoribanks proved herself proof to the flattery. She said, "Do go away, like a good man, and make yourself agreeable. There are so few men, you know, who can flirt in Carlingford. I have always reckoned upon you as such a valuable assistant. It is always an advantage to have a man who flirts," said Miss Marjoribanks. This was a sentiment perhaps too large and enlightened, in the truest sense of the word, to meet, as it ought to have done, with the applause of her audience. Most of the persons immediately surrounding her thought, indeed, that it was a mere *bon-mot* to which Lucilla had given utterance, and laughed accordingly; but it is needless to explain that these were persons quite unable to understand her genius.

All this time she was keeping her eyes upon a figure in the corner of a sofa, which looked as if it was glued there, and kept staring defiance at the world in general from under black and level brows. Lucilla, it is true, had introduced Barbara Lake in the most flattering way to Mrs Chiley, and to some of the young ladies present; but then she was a stranger, and an intruder into those regions of the blest, and she could not help feeling so. If her present companions had not whispered among themselves, "Miss Lake! what Miss Lake? Good gracious! Lake the drawing-master's daughter!" she herself would still have reminded herself of her humble paternity. Barbara sat as if she could not move from that corner, looking out upon everybody with scared eyes, which expressed nothing but defiance, and in her own mind making the reflections of bitter poverty upon the airy pretty figures round her, in all the variations of that costume which Miss Marjoribanks had announced as the standard of dress for the evening. Barbara's muslin, six times washed, was not more different from the spotless lightness of all the draperies round her, than was her air of fright, and at the same time of defiance, from the gay babble and pleasant looks of the group which, by a chance combination, she seemed to form part of. She began to say to herself that she had much better go away, and that there never could be anything in common between those frivolous creatures and herself, a poor man's daughter; and she began to get dreadfully exasperated with Lucilla, who had beguiled her into this scene, to make game of her, as poor Barbara said; though, so far from making game of her, nobody took much notice, after the first unsuccessful attempt at conversation, of the unfortunate young woman. It was when she was in this unhappy humour that her eye fell upon Mr Cavendish, who was in the act of making the appeal to Lucilla which we have already recorded. Barbara had never as yet had a lover, but she had read an unlimited number of novels, which came to nearly the same thing, and she saw at a glance that this was somebody who resembled the indispensable hero. She looked at him with a certain fierce interest, and remembered at that instant how often in books it is the humble heroine, behind backs, whom all the young ladies snub, who wins the hero at the last. And then Miss Marjoribanks, though she sent him away, smiled benignantly upon him. The colour flushed to Barbara's cheeks, and her eyes, which had grown dull and fixed between fright and spite, took sudden expression under her straight brows. An intention, which was not so much an intention as an instinct, suddenly sprang into life within her; and, without knowing, she drew a long breath of eagerness and impotence. He was standing quite near by this time, doing his duty according to Miss Marjoribanks's orders, and flirting with all his might; and Barbara looked at him as a hungry schoolboy might be supposed to look at a tempting apple just out of his reach. How was she to get at this suitor of Lucilla's? It would have given her so pure a delight to tear down the golden apple, and tread on it, and trample it to nothing; and then it came into her head that it might be good to eat as well.

It was at this moment that Miss Marjoribanks, who was in six places at once, suddenly touched Barbara's shoulder. "Come with me a minute; I want to show you something," she said loud out. Barbara, on her side, looked round with a crimson countenance, feeling that her secret thoughts must be written in her guilty eyes. But then these were eyes which could be utterly destitute of expression when they pleased, though their owner, at present just at the beginning of her experience, was not quite aware of the fact. She stumbled to her feet with the awkward motion natural to that form of shyness which her temper and her temperament united to produce in her. She did all but put her foot through Miss Brown's delicate skirt, and she had neither the natural disposition nor the acquired grace which can carry off one of those trifling offences against society. Nevertheless, as she stood beside Lucilla at the piano, the company in general owned a little thrill of curiosity. Who was she? A girl with splendid black hair, with brows as level as if they had been made with a line, with intense eyes which looked a little oblique under that straight bar of shadow. Her dress was limp, but she was not such a figure as could be passed over even at an evening party; and then her face was a little flushed, and her eyes lit up with excitement. She seemed to survey everybody with that defiant look which was chiefly awkwardness and temper, but which looked like pride when she was standing up at her full height, and in a conspicuous position, where everybody could see her. Most people concluded she was an Italian whom Lucilla had picked up somewhere in her travels. As for Mr Cavendish, he stopped short altogether in the occupation which Miss Marjoribanks had allotted to him, and drew close to the piano. He thought he had seen the face somewhere under a shabby bonnet in some by-street of Carlingford, and he was even sufficiently learned in female apparel to observe the limpness of her dress.

This preface of curiosity had all been foreseen by Miss Marjoribanks, and she paused a moment, under pretence of selecting her music, to take the full advantage of it; for Lucilla, like most persons of elevated aims, was content to sacrifice herself to the success of her work; and then all at once, before the Carlingford people knew what they were doing, the two voices rose, bursting upon the astonished community like a sudden revelation. For it must be remembered that nobody in Carlingford, except the members of Dr Marjoribanks's dinner-party, had ever heard Lucilla sing, much less her companion; and the account which these gentlemen had carried home to their wives had been generally pooh-poohed and put down. "Mr Centum never listens to a note if he can help it," said the banker's wife, "and how could he know whether she had a nice voice or not?" which, indeed, was a powerful argument. But this evening there could be no mistake about it. The words were arrested on the very lips of the talkers; Mrs Woodburn paused in the midst of doing Lucilla, and, as we have before said, Mr Cavendish broke a flirtation clean off at its most interesting moment.

It is impossible to record what they sang, for those events, as everybody is aware, happened a good many years ago, and the chances are that the present generation has altogether forgotten the duet which made so extraordinary an impression on the inhabitants of Grange Lane. The applause with which the performance was received reached the length of a perfect ovation. Barbara, for her part, who was not conscious of having ever been applauded before, flushed into splendid crimson, and shone out from under her straight eyebrows, intoxicated into absolute beauty. As for Miss Marjoribanks, she took it more calmly. Lucilla had the advantage of knowing what she could do, and accordingly she was not surprised when people found it remarkable. She consented, on urgent persuasion, to repeat the last verse of the duet, but when that was over, was smilingly obdurate. "Almost everybody can sing," said Miss Marjoribanks, with a magnificent depreciation of her own gift. "Perhaps Miss Brown will sing us something; but as for me, you know, I am the mistress of the house."

Lucilla went away as she spoke to attend to her guests, but she left Barbara still crimson and splendid, triumphing over her limp dress and all her disadvantages, by the piano. Fortunately, for that evening Barbara's pride and her shyness prevented her from yielding to the repeated demands addressed to her by the admiring audience. She said to Mr Cavendish, with a disloyalty which that gentleman thought piquant, that "Miss Marjoribanks would not be pleased;" and the future Member for Carlingford thought he could not do better than obey the injunctions of the mistress of the feast by a little flirtation with the gifted unknown. To be sure, Barbara was not gifted in talk, and she was still defiant and contradictory; but then her eyes were blazing with excitement under her level eyebrows, and she was as willing to be flirted with as if she had known a great deal better. And then Mr Cavendish had a weakness for a contralto. While this little by-play was going on, Lucilla was moving about, the centre of a perfect tumult of applause. No more complete success could be imagined than that of this first Thursday Evening, which was remarkable in the records of Carlingford; and yet perhaps Miss Marjoribanks, like other conquerors, was destined to build her victory upon sacrifice. She did not feel any alarm at the present moment; but even if she had, that would have made no difference to Lucilla's proceedings. She was not the woman to shrink from a sacrifice when it was for the promotion of the great object of her life;

and that, as everybody knew who knew Miss Marjoribanks, was to be a comfort to her dear papa.

CHAPTER XI.

"You have never told us who your unknown was," said Mr Cavendish. "I suppose she is professional. Carlingford could not possibly possess two such voices in private life."

"Oh, I don't know about two such voices," said Miss Marjoribanks; "her voice suits mine, you know. It is always a great thing to find two voices that suit. I never would choose to have professional singers, for my part. You have to give yourself up to music when you do such a thing, and that is not my idea of society. I am very fond of music," said Lucilla— "excessively fond of it; but then everybody is not of my opinion—and one has to take so many things into consideration. For people who give one party in the year it does very well— but then I hate parties: the only pleasure in society is when one's friends come to see one without any ado."

"In white frocks, *high*," said Mrs Woodburn, who could not help assuming Lucilla's manner for the moment, even while addressing herself; but as the possibility of such a *lèse-majesté* did not even occur to Miss Marjoribanks, she accepted the observation in good faith.

"Yes; I hate a grand toilette when it is only a meeting of friends," she said—"for the girls, you know; of course you married ladies can always do what you like. You have your husbands to please," said Lucilla. And this was a little hard upon her satirist, for, to tell the truth, that was a particular of domestic duty to which Mrs Woodburn did not much devote herself, according to the opinion of Grange Lane.

"But about the contralto," said Mr Cavendish, who had come to call on Miss Marjoribanks under his sister's wing, and desired above all things to keep the peace between the two ladies, as indeed is a man's duty under such circumstances. "You are always statesmanlike in your views; but I cannot understand why you let poor little Molly Brown carry on her chirping when you had such an astonishing force in reserve. She must have been covered with confusion, the poor little soul."

"Nothing of the sort," said Mrs Woodburn, pursuing her favourite occupation as usual. "She only said, 'Goodness me! how high Lucilla goes! Do you like that dreadfully high music?' and made little eyebrows." To be sure, the mimic made Miss Brown's eyebrows, and spoke in her voice, so that even Lucilla found it a little difficult to keep her gravity. But then Miss Marjoribanks was defended by her mission, and she felt in her heart that, representing public interest as she did, it was her duty to avoid all complicity in any attack upon an individual; and consequently, to a certain extent, it was her duty also to put Mrs Woodburn down.

"Molly Brown has a very nice little voice," said Lucilla, with most disheartening gravity. "I like to hear her sing, for my part—the only thing is that she wants cultivation a little. It doesn't matter much, you know, whether or not you have a voice to begin with. It is cultivation that is the thing," said Miss Marjoribanks, deliberately. "I hope you *really* thought it was a pleasant evening. Of course everybody said so to me; but then one can never put any faith in that. I have said it myself ever so many times when I am sure I did not mean it. For myself, I don't give any importance to the first evening. Anybody can do a thing once, you know; the second and the third, and so on—that is the real test. But I hope you thought it pleasant so far as it went."

"It was a great deal more than pleasant," said Mr Cavendish; "and as for your conception of social politics, it is masterly," the future M.P. added, in a tone which struck Lucilla as very significant; not that she cared particularly about Mr Cavendish's meaning, but still, when a young man who intends to go into Parliament congratulates a young lady upon her statesmanlike views, and her conception of politics, it must be confessed that it looks a little particular; and then, if that was what he meant, it was no doubt Lucilla's duty to make up her mind.

"Oh, you know, I went through a course of political economy at Mount Pleasant," she said, with a laugh. "One of the Miss Blounts was dreadfully strong-minded. I wonder, for my part, that she did not make me literary; but fortunately I escaped that."

"Heaven be praised!" said Mr Cavendish. "I think you ought to be Prime-minister. That contralto of yours is charming raw material; but if I were you I would put her through an elementary course. She knows how to sing, but she does not know how to move; and as for talking, she seems to expect to be insulted. If you make a pretty-behaved young lady out of that, you will beat Adam Smith."

"Oh, I don't know much about Adam Smith," said Miss Marjoribanks. "I think Miss Martha thought him rather old-fashioned. As for poor Barbara, she is only a little shy, but that will soon wear off. I don't see what need she has to talk —or to move either, for that matter. I thought she did very well indeed for a girl who never goes into society. Was it not clever of me to find her out the very first day I was in Carlingford? It has always been so difficult to find a voice that went perfectly with mine."

"For my part, I think it was a great deal more than clever," said Mr Cavendish; for Mrs Woodburn, finding herself unappreciated, was silent and making notes. "It was a stroke of genius. So her name is Barbara? I wonder if it would be indiscreet to ask where Mademoiselle Barbara comes from, or if she belongs to anybody, or lives anywhere. My own impression is that you mean to keep her shut up in a box all the week through, and produce her only on the Thursday evenings. I have a weakness for a fine contralto. If she had been existing in an ordinary habitation like other people in Carlingford, I should have heard her, or heard of her. It is clear to me that you keep her shut up in a box."

"Exactly," said Lucilla. "I don't mean to tell you anything about her. You may be sure, now I have found her out, I mean to keep her for myself. Her box is quite a pretty one, like what Gulliver had somewhere. It is just time for lunch, and you are both going to stay, I hope; and there is poor Mary Chiley and her husband coming through the garden. What a pity it is he is such a goose!"

"Yes; but you know she never would take her uncle's advice, my dear," said the incorrigible mimic, putting on Mrs Chiley's face; "and being an orphan, what could anybody do? And then she does not get on with *his* family. By the way," Mrs Woodburn said, falling into her natural tone, if indeed she could be said to have a natural tone—"I wonder if anybody ever does get on with her husband's family?" The question was one which was a little grave to herself at the moment; and this was the reason why she returned to her identity—for there was no telling how long the Woodburns, who had come for Christmas, meant to stay. "I shall be quite interested to watch *you*, Lucilla, when it comes to be your turn, and see how you manage," she went on, with a keen look at Miss Marjoribanks; and Mr Cavendish laughed. He too looked at her, and Lucilla felt herself in rather a delicate position: not that she was agitated, as might have been the case had the future M.P. for Carlingford "engaged her affections," as she herself would have said. Fortunately these young affections were quite free as yet; but nevertheless Miss Marjoribanks felt that the question was a serious one, as coming from the sister of a gentleman who was undeniably paying her attention. She did not in the least wish to alarm a leading member of a family into which it was possible she might enter; and then at the same time she intended to reserve fully all her individual rights.

"I always make it a point never to shock anybody's prejudices," said Miss Marjoribanks. "I should do just the same with *them* as with other people; all you have to do is to show from the first that you mean to be good friends with everybody. But then I am so lucky: I can *always* get on with people," said Lucilla, rising to greet the two unfortunates who had come to Colonel Chiley's to spend a merry Christmas, and who did not know what to do with themselves. And then they all went down-stairs and lunched together very pleasantly. As for Mr Cavendish, he was "quite devoted," as poor Mary Chiley said, with a touch of envy. To be sure, her *trousseau* was still in its full glory; but yet life under the conditions of marriage was not nearly such fun as it had been when she was a young lady, and had some one paying attention to her: and she rather grudged Lucilla that climax of existence, notwithstanding her own superior standing and dignity as a married lady. And Mrs Woodburn too awoke from her study of the stupid young husband to remark upon her brother's behaviour: she had not seen the two together so often as Mrs Chiley had done, and consequently this was the first time that the thought had occurred to her. She too had been born "one of the Cavendishes," as it was common to say in Carlingford, with a certain imposing yet vague grandeur—and she was a little shocked, like any good sister, at the first idea. She watched Lucilla's movements and looks with a quite different kind of attention after this idea struck her, and made a rapid private calculation as to who Dr Marjoribanks's connections were, and what he would be likely to give his daughter; so that it is evident that Lucilla did not deceive herself, but that Mr Cavendish's attentions must have been marked indeed.

This was the little cloud which arose, as we have said, no

bigger than a man's hand, over Miss Marjoribanks's prosperous way. When the luncheon was over and they had all gone, Lucilla took a few minutes to think it over before she went out. It was not that she was unduly flattered by Mr Cavendish's attentions, as might have happened to an inexperienced young woman; for Lucilla, with her attractions and genius, had not reached the mature age of nineteen without receiving the natural homage of mankind on several clearly-defined occasions. But then the present case had various features peculiar to itself, which prevented Lucilla from crushing it in the bud, as she had meant to do with her cousin's ill-fated passion. She had to consider, in the first place, her mission in Carlingford, which was more important than anything else; but though Miss Marjoribanks had vowed herself to the reorganisation of society in her native town, she had not by any means vowed that it was absolutely as Miss Marjoribanks that she was to accomplish that renovation. And then there was something in the very idea of being M.P. for Carlingford which moved the mind of Lucilla. It was a perfectly ideal position for a woman of her views, and seemed to offer the very field that was necessary for her ambition. This was the reason, of all others, which made her less careful to prevent Mr Cavendish from "saying the words" than she had been with Tom. To be sure, it would be a trial to leave the drawing-room after it had just been furnished so entirely to her liking—not to say to her complexion; but still it was a sacrifice which might be made. It was in this way that Miss Marjoribanks prepared herself for the possible modifications which circumstances might impose. She did not make any rash resolution to resist a change which, on the whole, might possibly be "for the best," but prepared herself to take everything into consideration, and possibly to draw from it a superior good: in short, she looked upon the matter as a superior mind, trained in sound principles of political economy, might be expected to look upon the possible vicissitudes of fortune, with an enlightened regard to the uses of all things, and to the comparative values on either side.

Barbara Lake, as it happened, was out walking at the very moment when Miss Marjoribanks sat down to consider this question. She had gone to the School of Design to meet Rose, with an amiability very unusual in her. Rose had made such progress, after leaving Mount Pleasant, under her father's care, and by the help of that fine feeling for art which has been mentioned in the earlier part of this history, that the charge of the female pupils in the School of Design had been confided to her, with a tiny little salary, which served Mr Lake as an excuse for keeping his favourite little daughter with him. Nothing could be supposed more unlike Barbara than her younger sister, who just came up to her shoulder, and was twice as serviceable and active and "nice," according to the testimony of all the children. Barbara had led her father a hard life, poor man! the time that Rose was at Mount Pleasant; but now that his assistant had come back again, the poor drawing-master had recovered all his old spirits. She was just coming out of the School of Design, with her portfolio under her arm, when Barbara met her. There were not many pupils, it is true, but still there were enough to worry poor Rose, who was not an imposing personage, and who was daily wounded by the discovery that after all there are but a limited number of persons in this world, especially in the poorer classes of the community, and under the age of sixteen, who have a feeling for art. It was utterly inconceivable to the young teacher how her girls could be so clever as to find out each a different way of putting the sublime features of the Belveder Apollo out of drawing, and she was still revolving this difficult problem when her sister joined her. Barbara, for her part, was occupied with thoughts of a hero much more interesting than he of Olympus. She was flushed and eager, and looking very handsome under her shabby bonnet; and her anxiety to have a confidant was so great that she made a dart at Rose, and grasped her by the arm under which she was carrying her portfolio, to the great discomposure of the young artist. She asked, with a little anxiety, "What is the matter? is there anything wrong at home?" and made a rapid movement to get to the other side.

"Oh, Rose," said Barbara, panting with haste and agitation, "only fancy; I have just seen him. I met him right in front of Masters's, and he took off his hat to me. I feel in such a way—I can scarcely speak."

"Met—who?" said Rose—for she was imperfect in her grammar, like most people in a moment of emergency; and, besides, she shared to some extent Miss Marjoribanks's reluctance to shock the prejudices of society, and was disturbed by the idea that somebody might pass and see Barbara in her present state of excitement, and perhaps attribute it to its true cause.

"Oh you stupid little thing!" said Barbara, giving her "a shake" by her disengaged arm. "I tell you, *him!*—the gentleman I met at Lucilla Marjoribanks's. He looked as if he was quite delighted to see me again; and I am sure he turned round to see where I was going. He couldn't speak to me, you know, the first time; though indeed I shouldn't be the least surprised if he had followed—at a distance, you know, only to see where I live," said Barbara, turning round and searching into the distance with her eager eyes. But there was nobody to be seen in the street, except some of Rose's pupils lingering along in the sunshine, and very probably exchanging similar confidences. Barbara turned back again with a touch of disappointment. "I am quite sure he will find out before long; and don't forget I said so," she added, with a little nod of her head.

"I don't see what it matters if he found out directly," said Rose. "Papa would not let anybody come to our house that he did not approve of; and then, you know, he will never have anything to say to people who are patronising. I don't want to hear any more about your fine gentleman. If you were worried as I am, you would think much more of getting home than of anybody bowing to you in the street. One of the gentlemen from Marlborough House once took off his hat to me," said Rose, with a certain solemnity. "Of course I was pleased; but then I knew it was my design he was thinking of—my Honiton flounce, you know. I suppose this other one must have thought you had a pretty voice."

This time, however, it was an angry shake that Barbara gave to her sister. "I wish you would not be such a goose," she said; "who cares about your Honiton flounce? He took off his hat because—because he admired me, I suppose—and then it was a great deal more than just taking off his hat. He gave me such a look! Papa has no sense, though I suppose you will blaze up when I say so. He ought to think of us a little. As for patronising, I should soon change that, I can tell you. But then papa thinks of nothing but paying his bills and keeping out of debt, as he says—as if everybody was not in debt; and how do you suppose we are ever to get settled in life? It would be far more sensible to spend a little more, and go into society a little, and do us justice. Only think all that that old Doctor is doing for Lucilla; and there are four of us when the little ones grow up," said Barbara, in a tone of injury. "I should like to know what papa is thinking of? If mamma had not died when she did——"

"It was not poor mamma's fault," said Rose. "I daresay

she would have lived if she could for all our sakes. But then you have always taken a false view of our position, Barbara. We are a family of *artists*," said the little mistress of the School of Design. She had pretty eyes, very dewy and clear, and they woke up under the excitement of this proud claim. "When papa is appreciated as he deserves, and when Willie has *made a name*," said Rose, with modest confidence, "things will be different. But the true strength of our position is that we are a family of artists. We are everybody's equal, and we are nobody's equal. We have a rank of our own. If you would only remember this, you would not grudge anything to Lucilla Marjoribanks; and then I am sure she has been very kind to you."

"Oh, bother," said the unfeeling Barbara. "You do nothing but encourage papa with your nonsense. And I should like to know what right Lucilla Marjoribanks has to be kind to me? If I am not as good as she, it is a very strange thing. I should never take the trouble to think about *him* if it was not that Lucilla believes he is paying her attention—that is the great fun. It would be delicious to take him from her, and make game of her and her kindness. Goodness! there he is again. I felt sure that he would try to find out the house."

And Barbara crimsoned higher than ever, and held Rose fast by the arm, and called her attention by the most visible and indeed tangible signs to the elegant apparition, like any other underbred young woman. As for Rose, she was a little gentlewoman born, and had a horror unspeakable of her sister's bad manners. When Mr Cavendish made a movement as if to address Barbara, it was the pretty grey eyes of Rose lifted to his face with a look of straightforward surprise and inquiry which made him retire so hastily. He took off his hat again more respectfully than before, and pursued his walk along Grove Street, as if he had no ulterior intention in visiting that humble part of the town. As for Barbara, she held Rose faster than ever, and almost pinched her arm to make her listen. "I knew he was trying to find out the house," she said, in an exultant whisper. "And Lucilla thinks he is paying her attention!" For the fact was, that when Miss Marjoribanks took to being kind to Barbara, she conferred upon the contralto at the same moment a palpable injury and grievance, which was what the drawing-master's daughter had been looking for, for several years of her life. And naturally Lucilla, who was at this moment thinking it all over under the soft green shadows from her new hangings, was deprived of the light which might have been thrown on her reflections, had she seen what was going on in Grove Street. The conditions of humanity are such that even a woman of genius cannot altogether overstep them. And Lucilla still continued to think that Mr Cavendish was paying her attention, which, indeed, was also the general opinion in Grange Lane.

CHAPTER XII.

THE second of her Thursday evenings found Miss Marjoribanks, though secure, perhaps more anxious than on the former occasion. The charm of the first novelty was gone, and Lucilla did not feel quite sure that her subjects had the good sense to recognise all the benefits which she was going to confer upon them. "It is the second time that counts," she said in confidence to Mrs Chiley. "Last Thursday they wanted to see the drawing-room, and they wanted to know what sort of thing it was to be. Dear Mrs Chiley, it is to-night that is the test," said Lucilla, giving a nervous pressure to her old friend's hand; at least a pressure that would have betokened the existence of nerves in any one else but Miss Marjoribanks, whose magnificent organisation was beyond any suspicion of such weakness. But, nevertheless, Mrs Chiley, who watched her with grandmotherly interest, was comforted to perceive that Lucilla, as on the former occasion, had strength of mind to eat her dinner. "She wants a little support, poor dear," the old lady said in her heart; for she was a kinder critic than the younger matrons, who felt instinctively that Miss Marjoribanks was doing what they ought to have done. She took her favourite's arm in hers as they went up-stairs, and gave Mr Cavendish a kindly nod as he opened the door for them. "He will come and give you his assistance as soon as ever he can get away from the gentlemen," said Mrs Chiley, in her consolatory tone; "but, good gracious, Lucilla, what is the matter?" The cause of this exclamation was a universal hum and rustle as of many dresses and many voices; and, to tell the truth, when Miss Marjoribanks and her companion reached the top of the stairs, they found themselves lost in a laughing crowd, which had taken refuge on the landing. "There is no room, Lucilla. Lucilla, everybody in Carlingford is here. Do make a little room for us in the drawing-room," cried this overplus of society. If there was an enviable woman in Carlingford at that moment, it certainly was Miss Marjoribanks, standing on the top of her own stairs, scarcely able to penetrate through the throng of her guests. Her self-possession did not forsake her at this supreme moment. She grasped Mrs Chiley once again with a little significant gesture which pleased the old lady, for she could not but feel that she was Lucilla's only *confidante* in her brilliant but perilous undertaking. "*They* will not be able to get in when they come upstairs," said Miss Marjoribanks; and whether the faint inflection in her voice meant exultation or disappointment, her old friend could not tell.

But the scene changed when the rightful sovereign entered the gay but disorganised dominion where her subjects attended her. Before any one knew how it was done, Miss Marjoribanks had re-established order, and, what was still more important, made room. She said, "You girls have no business to get into corners. The corners are for the people that can talk. It is one of my principles always to flirt in the middle of the company," said Lucilla; and again, as happened so often, ignorant people laughed and thought it a *bon mot*. But it is needless to inform the more intelligent persons who understand Miss Marjoribanks, that it was by no means a *bon mot*, but expressed Lucilla's convictions with the utmost sincerity.

Thus it happened that the second Thursday was more brilliant and infinitely more gratifying than the first had been. For one thing, she felt sure that it was not to see the new furniture, nor to criticise this new sort of entertainment, but with the sincerest intention of enjoying themselves, that all the people had come; and there are moments when the egotism of the public conveys the highest compliment that can be paid to the great minds which take in hand to rule and to amuse it. The only drawback was, that Barbara Lake did not show the same modesty and reticence as on the former occasion. Far from being sensibly silent, which she had been so prudent as to be on Miss Marjoribanks's first Thursday, she forgot herself so far as to occupy a great deal of Mr Cavendish's valuable time, which he might have employed much more usefully. She not only sang by herself when he asked her, having brought some music with her unseen by Lucilla, but she kept her seat upon the stool before the piano ever so long afterwards, detaining him, and, as Miss Marjoribanks had very little doubt, making an exhibition of herself: for Barbara, having received one good gift from nature, had been refused the other, and could not talk. When Lucilla, arrested in the midst of her many occupations, heard her *protégée's* voice rising alone, she stopped quite short with an anxiety which it was touching to behold. It was not the jealousy of a rival cantatrice which inspired Miss Marjoribanks's countenance, but the far broader and grander anxiety of an accomplished statesman, who sees a rash and untrained hand meddling with his most delicate machinery. Lucilla ignored everything for the moment—her own voice, and Mr Cavendish's attentions, and every merely secondary and personal emotion. All these details were swallowed up in the fear that Barbara would not acquit herself as it was necessary for the credit of the house that she should acquit herself; that she should not sing well enough, or that she should sing too much. Once more Miss Marjoribanks put her finger upon the pulse of the community as she and they listened together. Fortunately, things went so far well that Barbara sang her very best, and kept up her *prestige:* but it was different in the second particular; for, unluckily, the contralto knew a great many songs, and showed no inclination to stop. Nothing remained for it but a bold *coup*, which Lucilla executed with all her natural coolness and success.

"My dear Barbara," she said, putting her hands on the singer's shoulders as she finished her strain, "that is enough for to-night. Mr Cavendish will take you down-stairs and get you a cup of tea; for you know there is no room to-night to serve it up-stairs." Thus Miss Marjoribanks proved herself capable of preferring her great work to her personal sentiments, which is generally considered next to impossible for a woman. She did what perhaps nobody else in the room was capable of doing: she sent away the gentleman who was paying attention to her, in company with the girl who was paying attention to him; and at that moment, as was usual when she was excited, Barbara was splendid, with her crimson cheeks, and the eyes blazing out from under her level eyebrows. This Miss Marjoribanks did, not in ignorance, but with a perfect sense of what she was about. It was the only way of preventing her Evening from losing its distinctive character. It was the Lamp of sacrifice which Lucilla had now to employ, and she proved herself capable of the exertion. But it would be hopeless to attempt to describe the indignation of old Mrs Chiley, or the unmitigated amazement of the company in general, which was conscious at the same time that Mr Cavendish was paying attention to Miss Marjoribanks, and that he had been flirting in an inexcusable manner with Miss Lake. "My dear, I would have nothing to do with that bold girl," Mrs Chiley said in Lucilla's ear. "I will go down and look after them if you like. A girl like that always leads the gentlemen astray, you know. I never liked the looks of her. Let me go down-stairs and look after them, my dear. I am sure I want a cup of tea."

"You shall have a cup of tea, dear Mrs Chiley," said Miss Marjoribanks—"some of them will bring you one; but I can't let you take any trouble about Barbara. She had to be stopped, you know, or she would have turned us into a musical party; and as for Mr Cavendish, he is the best assistant I have. There are so few men in Carlingford who can flirt," said Lucilla, regretfully. Her eyes fell as she spoke upon young Osmond Brown, who was actually at that moment talking to Mr Bury's curate, with a disregard of his social duties painful to contemplate. Poor Osmond started when he met Miss Marjoribanks's reproachful eye.

"But then I don't know how," said the disconcerted youth, —and he blushed, poor boy, being only eighteen, and not much more than a schoolboy. As for Lucilla, who had no intention of putting up with that sort of thing, she sent off the curate summarily for Mrs Chiley's cup of tea.

"I did not mean you, my dear Osy," she said, in her motherly tone. "When you are a little older we shall see what you can do; but you are not at all disagreeable for a boy," she added encouragingly, and took Osmond's arm as she made her progress down the room with an indulgence worthy of her maturer years; and even Mrs Centum and Mrs Woodburn and the Miss Browns, who were, in a manner, Lucilla's natural rivals, could not but be impressed with this evidence of her powers. They were like the Tuscan chivalry in the ballad, who could scarce forbear a cheer at the sight of their opponent's prowess. Perhaps nothing that she could have done would have so clearly demonstrated the superiority of her genius to her female audience as that bold step of stopping the music, which began to be too much, by sending off the singer down-stairs under charge of Mr Cavendish. To be sure the men did not even find out what it was that awoke the ladies' attention; but then, in delicate matters of social politics, one never expects to be understood by *them*.

Barbara Lake, as was to be expected, took a very long time over her cup of tea; and even when she returned up-stairs she made another pause on the landing, which was still kept possession of by a lively stream of young people coming and going. Barbara had very little experience, and she was weak enough to believe that Mr Cavendish lingered there to have a little more of her society all to himself; but to tell the truth, his sentiments were of a very different description. For by this time it must be owned that Barbara's admirer began to feel a little ashamed of himself. He could not but be conscious of Lucilla's magnanimity; and, at the same time, he was very well aware that his return with his present companion would be watched and noted and made the subject of comment a great deal more amusing than agreeable. When he did take Barbara in at last, it was with a discomfited air which tickled the spectators beyond measure. And as his evil luck would have it, notwithstanding the long pause he had made on the landing, to watch his opportunity of entering unobserved, Miss Marjoribanks was the first to encounter the returning couple. They met full in the face, a few paces from the door—exactly, as Mrs Chiley said, as if it had been Mr and Mrs Cavendish on their wedding visit, and the lady of the house had gone to meet them. As for the unfortunate gentleman, he could not have looked more utterly disconcerted and guilty if he had been convicted of putting the spoons in his pocket, or of having designs upon the silver tea-service. He found a seat for his companion with all the haste possible; and instead of lingering by her side, as she had anticipated, made off on the instant, and hid himself like a criminal in the dark depths of a group of men who were talking together near the door. These were men who were hopeless, and good for nothing but to talk to each other, and whom Miss Marjoribanks tolerated in her drawing-room partly because their wives, with an excusable weakness, insisted on bringing them, and partly because they made a foil to the brighter part of the company, and served as a butt when anybody wanted to be witty. As for Lucilla, she made no effort to recall the truant from the ranks of the Incurables. It was the only vengeance she took upon his desertion. When he came to take leave of her, she was standing with her hand in that of Mrs Chiley, who was also going away. "I confess I was a little nervous this evening," Miss Marjoribanks was saying. "You know it is always the second that is the test. But I think, on the whole, it has gone off very well. Mr Cavendish, you promised to tell me the truth; for you know I have great confidence in your judgment. Tell me sincerely, do you think it has been a pleasant evening?" Lucilla said, with a beautiful earnestness, looking him in the face.

The guilty individual to whom this question was addressed felt disposed to sink into the earth, if the earth, in the shape of Mr Holden's beautiful new carpet, would but have opened to receive him; but, after all, that was perhaps not a thing to be desired under the circumstances. Mr Cavendish, however, was a man of resources, and not disposed to give up the contest without striking a blow in his own defence.

"Not so pleasant as last Thursday," he said. "I am not fit to be a lady's adviser, for I am too sincere; but I incline to think it is the third that is the test," said the future M.P.; and Lucilla made him, as Mrs Chiley remarked, the most beautiful curtsy; but then nothing could be more delightful than the manner in which that dear girl behaved through the whole affair.

"If everybody would only help me as you do!" said Miss Marjoribanks. "Good-night; I am so sorry you have not enjoyed yourself. But then it is such a consolation to meet with people that are sincere. And I think, on the whole, it has gone off very well for the second," said Lucilla, "though I say it that should not say it." The fact was, it had gone off so well that the house could hardly be cleared of the amiable and satisfied guests. A series of the most enthusiastic compliments were paid to Lucilla as she stood in state in the middle of the room, and bade everybody good-bye. "Next Thursday," she said, with the benevolent grace of an acknowledged sovereign. And when they were all gone, Miss Marjoribanks's reflections, as she stood alone in the centre of her domains, were of a nature very different from the usual reflections which the giver of a feast is supposed to make when all is over. But then, as everybody is aware, it was not a selfish desire for personal pleasure, nor any scheme of worldly ambition, which moved the mind of Lucilla. With such motives it is only natural that the conclusion, "All is vanity," should occur to the weary entertainer in the midst of his withered flowers and extinguished lights. Such ideas had nothing in common with the enlightened conceptions of Miss Marjoribanks. Perhaps it would be false to say that she had suffered in the course of this second Thursday, or that a superior intelligence like Lucilla's could permit itself to feel any jealousy of Barbara Lake; but it would be vain to deny that she had been *surprised*. And any one who knows Miss Marjoribanks will acknowledge that a great deal was implied in that confession. But then she had triumphed over the weakness, and triumphantly proved that her estimate of the importance of her work went far beyond the influence of mere personal feeling. In these circumstances Lucilla could contemplate her withered flowers with perfect calmness, without any thought that all was vanity. But then the fact was, Miss Marjoribanks was accomplishing a great public duty, and at the same time had the unspeakable consolation of knowing that she had proved herself a comfort to her dear papa. The Doctor, it is true, after looking on for a little with a half-amused consciousness that his own assistance was totally unnecessary, had gradually veered into a corner, and from thence had finally managed to escape downstairs to his beloved library. But then the sense of security and tranquillity with which he established himself at the fire, undisturbed by the gay storm that raged outside, gave a certain charm to his retirement. He rubbed his hands and listened, as a man listens to the wind howling out-of-doors, when he is in shelter and comfort. So that, after all, Lucilla's sensation of having accomplished her filial duties in the most effective manner was to a certain extent justified, while at the same time it is quite certain that nobody missed Dr Marjoribanks from the pleasant assembly up-stairs.

CHAPTER XIII.

It was thus that the reign of Miss Marjoribanks became gradually established and confirmed in Carlingford. It would be unnecessary to enter into detail, or to redouble instances of that singular genius which made itself so fully felt to the farthest limits of society, and which even indeed extended those limits miraculously beyond the magic circle of Grange Lane. Lucilla's powers beguiled not only the Powells and Sir John Richmond's family, who were, as everybody knows, fully entitled to be called county people, and came only on the Thursdays when there was moonlight to light them home, which was not so much to be wondered at, since county society in those parts was unusually heavy at that period; but even, what was more extraordinary, Miss Marjoribanks made a lodgment in the enemy's country on the other side, and made a capture, of all people in the world, of John Brown, who lived in his father's big old house at the *town* end of George Street, and had always laughed in his cynical way at the pretensions of Grange Lane. But then Lucilla had, as all the ladies admitted, an influence over "the gentlemen," of which, as was natural, they were slightly contemptuous, even if perhaps envious, to some extent, of the gift. For everybody knows that it requires very little to satisfy the gentlemen, if a woman will only give her mind to it. As for Miss Marjoribanks herself, she confessed frankly that she did her best to please Them. "For you know, after all, in Carlingford, one is obliged to take them into consideration," she said, with a natural apology. "So many of you poor dear people have to go where they like, and see the people they want you to see," Miss Marjoribanks added, fluttering her maiden plumes with a certain disdainful pity in the very eyes of Mrs Centum and Mrs Woodburn, who were well aware, both of them, at the bottom of their hearts, that but for Dr Marjoribanks's dinners, their selfish mates would find infinite objections to the Thursday evening, which was now an institution in Carlingford. And Lucilla knew it just as well as they did, which gave a certain sense of condescension and superiority to her frankness. "I never pretend I don't try to please them," Miss Marjoribanks said; and the matrons found themselves worsted as usual; for, to be sure, it was not for *Them*, but for the good of the community in general, that Lucilla exerted herself so successfully.

Nothing, indeed, could have proved more completely the disinterested character of Miss Marjoribanks's proceedings than her behaviour in respect to Mr Cavendish. After the bold and decisive action taken by Lucilla on the first occasion when the flirtation between him and Barbara Lake became apparent, the misguided young man returned to a better frame of mind; perhaps out of admiration for her magnanimity, perhaps attracted by her indifference, as is the known and ascertained weakness of the gentlemen. And perhaps also Mr Cavendish was ashamed of himself, as, in Mrs Chiley's opinion at least, he had so much reason to be. Anyhow, whatever the cause, he behaved himself with the profoundest decorum for several weeks in succession, and treated the contralto with such overwhelming politeness as reduced poor Barbara out of her momentary exultation into the depths of humiliation and despair. Mr Cavendish was Lucilla's right hand for that short but virtuous period, and fully justified Miss Marjoribanks's opinion, which was founded at once upon reflection and experience, that to have a man who can flirt is next thing to indispensable to a leader of society; that is to say, if he is under efficient discipline, and capable of carrying out a grand conception. Everything went on delightfully so long as this interval lasted, and Lucilla herself did not disdain to recompense her faithful assistant by bestowing upon him various little privileges, such as naturally appertain to a subject whose place is on the steps of the throne. She took him into her confidence, and made him to a certain extent a party to her large and philanthropic projects, and even now and then accepted a suggestion from him with that true candour and modesty which so often accompany administrative genius. While this continued, kind old Mrs Chiley kept caressing them both in her old-womanly way. She even went so far as to call Mr Cavendish "my dear," as if he had been a grandson of her own, and took her afternoon drive in her little brougham past his house with a genial sense of prospective property through Lucilla, which was wonderfully pleasant. To be sure there was not very much known in Carlingford about his connections; but then everybody was aware that he was one of the Cavendishes, and the people who are not content with that must be hard indeed to please. As for Mrs Woodburn, she, it was true, continued to "take off" Miss Marjoribanks; but then, as Mrs Chiley justly remarked, she was a woman who would take off the Archbishop of Canterbury or the Virgin Mary, if she had the opportunity; and there was no fear but Lucilla, if once married, would soon bring her to her senses; and then Mr Chiltern grew more and more feeble, and was scarcely once in a fortnight in his place in Parliament, which was a sacrifice of the interests of the borough dreadful to contemplate. And thus it was in the interests of Lucilla, notwithstanding that ladies are not eligible for election under such circumstances, that Mrs Chiley carried on a quiet little canvass for the future M.P.

All this lasted, alas! only too short a time. After a while the level eyebrows and flashing eyes and magnificent voice of Barbara Lake began to reassert their ancient power. Whatever may be the predisposition of the Cavendishes in general, this particular member of the race was unable to resist these influences. Barbara had managed to persuade Rose to persuade her father that it was necessary for her to have a new dress; and Mr Lake was more persuadable than usual, being naturally pleased to be complimented, when he went to give his lessons, on his daughter's beautiful voice. "Her talent has taken another development from *ours*," he said, with his little air of dignity, "but still she has the artist temperament. All my children have been brought up to love the beautiful;" and this argument had, of course, all the more effect upon him when repeated by his favourite daughter. "And then Barbara has such a noble head," said Rose; "when nobody is looking at her she always makes a fine composition. To be sure, when she is observed she gets awkward, and puts herself out of drawing; but that is not to be wondered at. I don't want her to be fine, or to imitate the Grange Lane people; but then, you know, papa, you always say that we have a rank of our own, being a family of artists," said Rose, holding up her little head with a pretty arrogance which delighted the father both in a paternal and a professional point of view. "If one could only have made a study of her at that moment," he said to himself, regretfully; and he consented to Barbara's dress.

As for the contralto, whose sentiments were very different from those of her father and sister, she watched over the making of the robe thus procured with a certain jealous care which nobody unacquainted with the habits of a family of artists could understand. Barbara's talent was not sufficiently developed to permit of her making it herself; but she knew already by sad experience that Rose's views of what was picturesque in costume were peculiar, and not always successful. And then it was only a new dress to Rose, whereas to Barbara it was a supreme effort of passion and ambition and jealousy and wounded *amour propre*. Mr Cavendish had paid a great deal of attention to her, and she had naturally entertained dreams of the wildest and most magnificent character—of riding in her carriage, as she would herself have said, and dressing as nobody else dressed in Carlingford, and becoming the great lady of the town, and eclipsing utterly Lucilla Marjoribanks, who had been so impertinent as to patronise her. Such had been Barbara's delicious dreams for a whole fortnight; and then Mr Cavendish, who had taken her up, put her down again, and went away from her side, and delivered himself over, heart and soul, to the service of Lucilla. Barbara had no intellect to speak of, but she had what she called a heart—that is to say, a vital centre of inclinations and passions, all of which were set in motion by that intense force of self-regard which belongs to some of the lower organisations. Thus she arrayed herself, not in simple muslin, but in all the power of fascination which a strong will and fixed purpose can add to beauty. And in her excitement and with the sense she had that this was her opportunity, and that advancement and grandeur depended upon the result of her night's work, her level eyebrows, and flushing cheeks, and black intense eyes, rose almost into positive beauty. There was nobody in the room to compare with her when she stood up to sing on that memorable evening. The Miss Browns, for example, were very pretty, especially Lydia, who was afterwards married to young Richmond, Sir John's eldest son; and they were much *nicer* girls, and far more engaging than Barbara Lake, who was not even a lady, Mrs Chiley said. But then her determination, though it was a poor enough thing in itself, gave a certain glow and passion to her coarser beauty.

When she stood up to sing, the whole room was struck with her appearance. She had her new dress on, and though it was only white muslin like other people's, it gave her the air of a priestess inspired by some approaching crisis, and sweeping forward upon the victim who was ready to be sacrificed. And yet the victim that night was far from being ready for the sacrifice. On the contrary, he had been thinking it all over, and had concluded that prudence and every other reasonable sentiment were on the other side, and that in many ways it would be a very good thing for him if he could persuade Miss Marjoribanks to preside over and share his fortunes. He had made up his mind to this with all the more certainty that he was a man habitually prone to run off after everything that attracted him, in direct opposition to prudence—an inclination which he shared with his sister, who, as everybody knew, had ruined poor Mr Woodburn's fortunes by "taking off," before his very face, the only rich uncle in the Woodburn family. Mr Cavendish, with this wise resolution in his mind, stood up in the very path of the contralto as she followed Miss Marjoribanks to the piano, and, confident in his determination, even allowed himself to meet her eye—which was rash, to say the least of it. Barbara flashed upon him as she passed a blaze of intense oblique lightning from under her level brows—or perhaps it was only that straight black line which made it look oblique—and then went on to her place. The result was such as might have been anticipated from the character of the man. Barbara was in richer voice than ever before, and all but obliterated even Lucilla, though she too was singing her best; and thus poor Mr Cavendish again fell into the snare. That very night the flirtation, which had already created so much talk, was resumed with more energy than ever; and Barbara took Miss Marjoribanks's place at the piano, and sang song after song in a kind of intoxication of triumph. This, to be sure, was visible only to a small portion of the guests who crowded

Lucilla's drawing-room. But the result was soon so visible that all Carlingford became aware of it. The hero wavered so much that the excitement was kept up for many weeks; but still from the first nobody could have any reasonable doubt as to how it was to end.

And it was while this process of seduction was going on that the character of Miss Marjoribanks revealed itself in all its native grandeur. Lucilla had various kind friends round her to advise her, and especially old Mrs Chiley, whose indignation went beyond all bounds. "My dear, I would never let her enter my door again—never!" cried the old lady; "I told you long ago I never could bear her looks—you know I warned you, Lucilla. As for her singing, what does it matter? You have a much prettier voice than she has: everybody knows that a soprano is perfect by itself, but a contralto is only a *second*," Mrs Chiley said, with mingled wrath and satisfaction; "and, my dear, I should never let her enter my house again, if it was me."

"Dear Mrs Chiley," said Lucilla, who was now, as usual, equal to the occasion, "it is so nice of you to be vexed. You know I would do anything to please you;—but, after all, there are thousands and thousands of gentlemen, and it is not so easy to find a voice that goes with mine. All my masters always said it was a quite peculiar second I wanted; and suppose Barbara is foolish, that is not to say I should forget *my* duties," Miss Marjoribanks added, with a certain solemnity; "and then, you know, she has no mother to keep her right."

"And neither have you, my poor dear," said Mrs Chiley, kissing her *protégée*. As for Lucilla, she accepted the kiss, but repressed the enthusiasm of partisanship with which her cause was being maintained.

"I have *you*," she said, with artless gratitude; "and then I am different," added Lucilla. Nothing but modesty of the most delicate description could have expressed the fact with such a fine reticence. No doubt Miss Marjoribanks was different; and she proved her superiority, if anybody could have doubted it, by the most beautiful behaviour. She took no more notice of the unprincipled flirtation thus set agoing under her very eyes, than if Mr Cavendish and Barbara Lake had been two figures in gingerbread. So far as anybody knew, not even a flying female shaft from Lucilla's bow, one of those dainty projectiles which the best of women cast forth by times, had ever been directed against the ungrateful young person who

had made so unprincipled a use of her admittance into Grange
Lane; and the faithless gallant had not even the gratification
of feeling that Lucilla was "cool" to him. Whether this singular self-denial cost Miss Marjoribanks any acute sufferings,
nobody could tell, but Mrs Chiley still marked with satisfaction
that Lucilla, poor dear, was able to eat her dinner, of which
she had so much need to support her strength; and after she
had eaten her dinner Miss Marjoribanks would go up-stairs and
show herself just as usual. She was in perfect voice, and
neither lost her colour, nor grew thin, nor showed any of those
external signs of a disappointment in love with which most
people are familiar. "It might have been different, you know,
if my affections had been engaged," she said to her sole and
sympathising counsellor; and Mrs Chiley, who had had a great
deal of experience in girls, became more and more of opinion
that such sense was all but superhuman.

Meantime the tide of public opinion ran very high in Carlingford against Mr Cavendish, who had been so popular a
little while before. If it had been one of the Miss Browns, or
a niece of the Colonel's, or indeed anybody in Grange Lane,
people might have passed over it—but one of Mr Lake the
drawing-master's daughters! The only person indifferent was
Mrs Woodburn, who ought to have known better; but then
she was thoughtless, like her brother, and liked it all the better,
on the whole, that he should transfer those attentions which
he had been paying to Miss Marjoribanks, and which in that
quarter must have come to something, to a little harmless
amusement with Barbara, who, after all, was very handsome,
and had by times a little air of obdurate stupidity which capti-
vated the mimic. As for anything coming of *that*, Mrs Woodburn rejected the idea with a simplicity which was perfectly
consistent with her insight into other people's weaknesses.
She could put on Barbara's stolid defiant look, and even make
her eyebrows square, and give something of an oblique gleam
to her eyes, with the most perfect skill and mastery of the
character, and at the same time be just as stolid as Barbara in
respect to what was going on at her very hand, and to the consequences which must follow. She did not want her brother
to marry Miss Marjoribanks, and yet she could not have said a
word against so unexceptionable a match; and accordingly it
was quite a satisfaction to her to see him turned aside in so
perfectly legitimate a manner. She added to her repertory a
sketch of Barbara at the moment when, yielding to Mr Caven-

dish's entreaties, she seated herself at the piano "for just one song;" and being perfectly successful in the representation, Mrs Woodburn took no further care about the matter. To be sure, the hero was sufficiently experienced in such matters to know how to get out of it when it should be the proper time.

Thus the affair progressed which was to have far more serious consequences than these thoughtless persons dreamed of. Barbara ascended again to the heights of exultation and enchantment. Perhaps she was even a little in love; for, after all, she was young, and grateful to the man who thus distinguished her from the world. Yet, on the whole, it is to be feared that his house and his position in society, and the prospect of unlimited millinery, were more to her than Mr Cavendish. All these details were not perhaps contemplated by himself as he devoted himself to the handsome contralto. He had not begun to dream, as Barbara had done for a long time, of the wedding breakfast and the orange blossoms, or even of furnishing a new drawing-room handsomer than Miss Marjoribanks's, and giving parties which should be real parties and not mere Thursdays. None of these imaginations occupied Mr Cavendish as he followed Barbara's glowing cheeks and flashing eyes to his undoing. But then if he did not mean it she meant it; and, after all, there are occasions in which the woman's determination is the more important of the two. So that, taking everything into consideration, there can be no doubt that it was very fortunate that Lucilla's affections were not engaged. She behaved as nobody else in Carlingford was capable of behaving, and very few people anywhere, according to Mrs Chiley's admiring belief. It was not for a vulgar antagonist like Barbara Lake to touch Lucilla. The way in which she asked her to lunch and went on practising duets with her was angelical—it brought the tears to Mrs Chiley's eyes; and as for the domestic traitor whom Miss Marjoribanks thus contrived to warm in her magnanimous bosom, she was sometimes so full of spite and disappointment that she could neither eat her lunch nor go on with her singing. For, to be sure, the dearest climax of her triumph was wanting so long as Lucilla took no notice; and so far from taking any notice, Miss Marjoribanks was sweeter and more friendly than usual in her serene unconsciousness. "I am so afraid you have caught cold," Lucilla would say; "if you don't feel clear in your lower notes, we can pass over this passage, you know, for to-day. You must see papa before you go away, and he will order you something; but, my dear Barbara, you must take care." And then Barbara could have eaten her fingers instead of the gloves which she kept biting in her vexation. For, to tell the truth, if Miss Marjoribanks was not jealous, the victory was but half a victory after all.

CHAPTER XIV.

It was thus that Miss Marjoribanks went through all the preliminary stages, and succeeded finally in making a triumph out of what would certainly have been a defeat, and a humbling defeat, for anybody else. She was much too sensible to deceive herself on the subject, or not to be aware that to have a gentleman who was paying attention to her withdrawn from her side in this open manner in the sight of all the world, was as trying an accident as can happen to a woman. Fortunately, as Lucilla said, her affections were not engaged; but then, apart from the affections, there are other sentiments which demand consideration. Everybody in Carlingford knew that Mr Cavendish had been paying her a great deal of attention, and the situation was one which required the most delicate skill to get through it successfully. Besides, Miss Marjoribanks's circumstances were all the more difficult, since up to this moment she had been perfectly sincere and natural in all her proceedings. Policy had been constantly inspired and backed by nature in the measures Lucilla had taken for the organisation and welfare of her kingdom, and even what people took for the cleverest calculation was in reality a succession of happy instincts, by means of which, with the sovereignty of true genius, Miss Marjoribanks managed to please everybody by having her own way. A little victory is almost necessary to begin with, and it is a poor nature that does not expand under the stimulus of victory; but now the young reformer had come to the second stage. For, to be sure, that sort of thing cannot last for ever; and this Lucilla, with the natural prevision of a ruling mind, had foreseen from the beginning. The shape in which she had feared defeat, if a nature so full of resources could ever be said to fear, was that of a breakdown, when all the world was looking to her for amusement, or the sudden appearance of a rival entertainer in Carlingford with superior powers: though the last was but a dim and improbable danger, the first was quite possible, and might have arrived at any moment. Miss Marjoribanks was much too sensible not to have foreseen this danger in all its shapes, and even in a kind of a way to have provided against it. But Providence, which had always taken care of her, as Lucilla piously concluded, had spared her the trial in that form. Up to this moment it had always providentially happened that all the principal people in Carlingford were quite well and disengaged on the "evening." To be sure, the ladies had headaches, and the married gentlemen now and then were out of temper in Grange Lane as in other less favoured places; but these social accidents had been mercifully averted on Thursdays, perhaps by means of some special celestial agency, perhaps only through that good-luck which had been born with Lucilla. Not in this vulgar and likely manner was the trial of her strength to come.

But when she was at the height of her success, and full in the eye of the world, and knew that everybody was remarking her, and that, from the sauces for which the Doctor's table was once so famed, but which even Colonel Chiley no longer thought of identifying as Dr Marjoribanks's, to the fashion of the *high* white frock in which Lucilla had taught the young ladies of Carlingford to appear of an evening, she was being imitated on every hand,—at that moment, when an ordinary person would have had her head turned, and gone wild with too much success, Miss Marjoribanks suddenly saw her dragon approaching her. Just then, when she could not put on a new ribbon, or do her hair in a different style, without all Carlingford knowing of it—at that epoch of intoxication and triumph the danger came, sudden, appalling, and unlooked for. If Lucilla was staggered by the encounter, she never showed it, but met the difficulty like a woman of mettle, and scorned to flinch. It had come to be summer weather when the final day arrived upon which Mr Cavendish forgot himself altogether, and went over to the insidious enemy whom Miss Marjoribanks had been nourishing in her bosom. Fifty eyes were upon Lucilla watching her conduct at that critical moment—fifty ears were on the strain to divine her sentiments in her voice, and to catch some intonation at least which should betray her consciousness of what was going on.

But if Miss Marjoribanks's biographer has fitly discharged his duty, the readers of this history will have no difficulty in divining that the curiosity of the spectators got no satisfaction from Lucilla. Many people even supposed she had not remarked anything, her composure was so perfect. No growing red or growing pale, no harsh notes in her voice, nor evidence of distracted attention, betrayed that her mind was elsewhere while she was attending to her guests; and yet, to be sure, she saw, just as other people did, that Barbara, all flushed and crimson, with her eyes blazing under their sullen brows, stood in a glow of triumph at the open window, with Mr Cavendish in devoted attendance—a captive at her chariot-wheels. Matters had been progressing to this point for some time; but yet the two culprits had never before showed themselves so lost to all sense of propriety. Instead of fainting or getting pale, or showing any other symptoms of violent despite, Lucilla went upon her airy way, indirectly approaching this point of interest. She went up and chatted with them, and ordered Mr Cavendish to find a chair for Barbara. "What can you be thinking of to let her stand so near the window? If she were to catch cold and lose her voice, what should we all do?" said Lucilla; and she established the two in the most commodious corner before she left them. "Take care she does not go back again into the draught," were her parting words, and even the culprits themselves could do nothing but stare at each other with consternation and shame.

This was all the notice Lucilla took of what was going on. If she was affronted, or if she was wounded, nobody found it out; and when Mrs Chiley offered the tribute of her indignation and sympathy, it has already been recorded how her young friend responded to her. "Fortunately my affections never were engaged," Lucilla said, and no doubt that was a great advantage; but then, as we have said, there are other things besides affections to be taken into account when the woman whom you have been kind to snaps up the man who has been paying attention to you, not only before your eyes, but before the eyes of all the world. The result of her masterly conduct on this occasion was that her defeat became, as we have said, a triumph for Miss Marjoribanks. To be sure, it is to be hoped that, in the sweets of their mutual regard, the two criminals found compensation for the disapproval of the spectators; but nothing could be more marked than the way in which Carlingford turned its cold shoulder on its early favourite. "I never imagined Cavendish was such a fool," Mr Centum said, who was a man of few words; "if he likes that style of philandering, it is nothing to me, but he need not make an idiot of himself." As for Mr Woodburn, he, as was natural, inflicted vicarious punishment upon his wife. "It must be all your fault," he growled, when he was taking her home, and had her at his mercy, with that logic peculiar to a married man; "you ought to tell him he's making an ass of himself. Why the deuce do you let him go on with that tomfoolery? He'll lose all his chances in life, and then, I hope, you'll be satisfied. You women can never see an inch before your own noses!" cried the uncivil husband; which, it must be confessed, was rather hard upon poor Mrs Woodburn, who had nothing to do with it, and had indeed calculated upon perfecting her sketch of Barbara in the quietness of the walk home; for as everybody lived in Grange Lane, carriages were not necessary for Miss Marjoribanks's guests. They flitted out and in, in the moonlight, with pretty scarfs thrown over their heads and laced handkerchiefs tied under their chins, and made Grange Lane between the two straight lines of garden-wall like a scene in a masquerade.

While Mr Cavendish was thus suffering by deputy the contempt of his former admirers, Lucilla, by herself in the abandoned drawing-room, was thinking over the evening with a severe but on the whole satisfactory self-examination. After the first shock, which she had encountered with so much courage, Miss Marjoribanks was rather grateful than otherwise to Providence, which had brought the necessary trial upon her in this form. If it had been a breakdown and humiliating failure instead, how different would her sensations have been! and Lucilla was quite conscious that such a thing might have occurred. It might have occurred to her, as it had done to so many people, to see Thursday come round with a failure of all that made Thursday agreeable. Lady Richmond might have had her influenza that day, and little Henry Centum his sudden attack, which had kept his mother in conversation ever since, and Mrs Woodburn one of her bad headaches; and as for the Miss Browns, there was nothing in the world but Lucilla's habitual good fortune which prevented them from having blacked their fingers with their photography to such an extent as to make them perfectly unpresentable. Or, to turn to another chapter of accidents, the last duet, which Barbara had insisted upon singing without proper practice, might have broken down utterly. None of these things had happened, and Lucilla drew a long breath of gratitude as she thought how fortunate she had been in all these particulars. To be sure, it was necessary to have a trial of one kind or other; and the modest but intense gratification of having stood the test, diffused itself like a balm through her bosom. No doubt she would have felt, like most people, a certain pleasure in snubbing Barbara; but then there is, on the other hand, a sweetness in sacrificing such impulses to the sacred sense of duty and the high aims of genius which is still more attractive to a well-regulated mind. Miss Marjoribanks herself put out the candles, and went to her own room with that feeling of having acquitted herself satisfactorily which many people think to be the highest gratification of which the mind is capable. After all, it was by no means certain that Mr Cavendish would be M.P. for Carlingford. Mr Chiltern might live for twenty years, or he even might get better, which was more unlikely; or supposing him to be comfortably disposed of, nobody could say with any certainty that some man unknown at present in Carlingford might not start up all of a sudden and gain the most sweet voices of the shopkeepers, who were the majority of the community, and quite outnumbered Grange Lane. It was thus that Lucilla consoled herself as she went meditative but undaunted to her maiden rest.

While all this was going on, Dr Marjoribanks remained an amused spectator, and chuckled a little quietly, without saying anything to anybody, over the turn affairs had taken. The Doctor knew all about everybody in Carlingford, and he had never been an enthusiast in favour of Mrs Woodburn's brother, notwithstanding that the young man had been received so warmly into society as one of the Cavendishes. Perhaps Dr Marjoribanks being Scotch, and having a turn for genealogy, found the description a little vague; but at all events there can be no doubt that he laughed to himself as he retired from the scene of his daughter's trial. The Doctor possibly thought, in a professional point of view, that a little discipline of this description would be useful to Lucilla. Perhaps he thought it would be good for her to find out that—though she had managed to slip the reins out of his hands, and get the control of affairs with a skill which amused the Doctor, and made him a little proud of her abilities, even though he was himself the victim—she could not go on always unchecked in her triumphant career, but must endure like other people an occasional defeat. No doubt, had Lucilla been really worsted, paternal feeling would have interposed, and Dr Marjoribanks would to some extent have suffered in her suffering; but then the case was different, and nobody required, as it turned out, to suffer for Lucilla. The Doctor was pleased she had shown so much spirit, and pleased to see how entirely she had discomfited her antagonists, and turned the tables upon the "young puppy," in whom he had no confidence; and withal Dr Marjoribanks chuckled a little in his secret heart over the event itself, and concluded that it would do Lucilla good. She had vanquished Nancy, and by a skilful jerk taken the reins out of his own experienced hands. He was aware that he had been on the whole very wisely governed since his abdication, but yet he was not sorry that the young conqueror should feel herself human; so that nobody except Mrs Chiley felt that mingled rage and disappointment with which Barbara Lake had hoped to inspire Lucilla's bosom; and Mrs Chiley, so to speak, had nothing to do with it. As for Barbara herself, she returned home in a state of mingled spite and exultation and disgust, which filled her sister with amazement.

"She is such an actor, you know," Barbara said; "she never will give in to let you know how she is feeling—not if she can help it; but for all that she must have felt it. Nobody could help feeling it, though she carried it off so well. I knew how it would be, as soon as I had on a dress that was fit to be seen."

"What is it that she could not help feeling?" said Rose. "I suppose it is Lucilla you mean?"

"I should like to know what right she had to be kind to me," cried Barbara, all glowing in her sullen but excited beauty; "and invite me there, and introduce me in her grand way, as if she was any better than I am! And then to look at all her India muslins; but I knew it would be different as soon as I had a decent dress," said the contralto, rising up to contemplate herself in the little mirror over the mantelpiece.

This conversation took place in Mr Lake's little parlour, where Rose had been waiting for her sister, and where Barbara's white dress made an unusual radiance in the dim and partially-lighted room. Rose herself was all shrouded up in her morning dress, with her pretty round arms and shoulders lost to the common view. She had been amusing herself as she waited by working at a corner of that great design which was to win the prize on a later occasion. Readers of this history who have studied the earlier chapters will remember that Rose's tastes in ornamentation were very clearly defined for so young a person. Instead of losing herself in vague garlands of impossible flowers, the young artist clung with the tenacity of first love to the thistle leaf, which had been the foundation of her early triumphs. Her mind was full of it even while she received and listened to Barbara; whether to treat it in a national point of view, bringing in the rose and shamrock, which was a perfectly allowable proceeding, though perhaps not original—or whether she should yield to the "sweet feeling" which had been so conspicuous in her flounce, in the opinion of the Marlborough-House gentlemen—or whether, on the contrary, she should handle the subject in a boldly naturalistic way, and use her spikes with freedom,—was a question which occupied at that moment all Rose's faculties. Even while she asked Barbara what the subject was on which Lucilla might be supposed to be excited, she was within herself thinking out this difficult idea—all the more difficult, perhaps, considering the nature of the subject, since the design in this case was not for a flounce, in which broad handling is practicable, but for a veil.

"I wish you would not talk in that foolish way," said Rose; "nobody need be any better than you, as you say. To be sure, we don't live in Grange Lane, nor keep a carriage; but I wish you would recollect that these are only accidental circumstances. As for dress, I don't see that you require it; our position is so clearly defined; we are a family of——"

"Oh, for goodness gracious sake, do be quiet with your family of artists!" cried Barbara. "Speak for yourself, if you please. I am not an artist, and never will be, I can tell you. There are better places to live in than Grange Lane; and as for keeping a carriage, I would never call a little bit of a brougham a carriage, if it was me. Lucilla made believe to take no notice, but she did not deceive me with that. She was as disappointed as ever she could be—I daresay now she's sitting crying over it. I never would have cared one straw if I had not wanted to serve Lucilla out!" cried the contralto, with energy. She was still standing before the glass pulling her black hair about into new combinations, and studying the effect; and as for Rose, she too looked up, and, seeing her sister's face reflected in the glass, made the discovery that there was something like grimace in the countenance, and paused in the midst of her meditations with her pencil in her hand.

"Don't put yourself out of drawing," said Rose; "I wish you would not do that so often. When the facial angle is disturbed to that extent—— But about Lucilla, I think you are excessively ungrateful. Gratitude is not a servile sentiment," said the little Preraphaelite, with a rising colour. "It is a slavish sort of idea to think any one has done you an injury by being kind to you. If that is the sort of thing you are going to talk of, I think you had better go to bed."

"Then I will, and I shan't tell you anything," said Barbara, angrily—"you are so poor-spirited. For my part, do you think I'd ever have gone to help Lucilla and sing for her, and all that sort of thing, if it had not been to better myself? Nor I wouldn't have thought of *him* just at first, if it hadn't been to spite *her*. And I've done it too. I'd just like to look in at her room window and see what she's about. I daresay she is crying her eyes out, for all her looking as if she took no notice. I know better than to think she doesn't care. And, Rose, he's such a dear," said Barbara, with a laugh of excitement. To be sure, what she wanted was to be Mrs Cavendish, and to have a handsome house and a great many nice dresses; but at the same time she was young, and Mr Cavendish was good-looking, and she was a little in love, in her way, as well.

"I don't want to hear any more about it," said Rose, who was so much moved as to forget even her design. "I can't think how it is you have no sense of honour, and you one of the Lakes. I would not be a traitor for a dozen Mr Cavendishes!" cried Rose, in the force of her indignation. "He must be a cheat, since you are a traitor. If he was a true man he would have found you out."

"You had better be quiet, Rose," said Barbara; "you may be sure I shall never do anything for you after we are married, if you talk like that; and then you'll be sorry enough."

"After you are married! has he asked you to marry him?" cried Rose. She pushed away her design with both her hands in the vehemence of her feelings, and regarded her sister with eyes which blazed, but which were totally different in their blazing from those which burned under Barbara's level eyebrows. It was too plain a question to have a plain answer. Barbara only lighted her candle in reply, and smiled and shook her head.

"You don't suppose I am going to answer after your insulting ways," she said, taking up her candle; and she swept out of the room in her white dress with a sense of pleasure in leaving this grand point unsettled. To be sure, Mr Cavendish had not yet asked that important question; but then the future was all before them, and the way clear. As for Rose, she clenched her little fists with a gesture that would have been too forcible for any one who was not an artist, and a member of a family of artists. "To think she should be one of us, and not to know what honour means," said Rose; "and as for this man, he must be a cheat himself, or he would find her out."

This was how Mr Cavendish's defection from Lucilla took place; and at the same time it is a satisfaction to know that the event was received by everybody very much as little Rose Lake received it. And as for Miss Marjoribanks, if Barbara could have had the malicious satisfaction of looking in at the window, she would have been mortified to find that right-minded young woman sleeping the sleep of the just and innocent, and enjoying repose as profound and agreeable as if there had been no Mr Cavendish in the world, not to speak of Carlingford;—which, to be sure, was a result to be greatly attributed to Lucilla's perfect health, and entire satisfaction with herself.

CHAPTER XV.

This event was of far too much importance in the limited world of Grange Lane to pass over without some of the many commentaries which were going on upon the subject coming to the ears of Miss Marjoribanks, who was the person principally concerned. As for the Doctor, as we have already said, he was so far lost to a sense of his paternal duties as to chuckle a little within himself over the accident that had happened to Lucilla. It had done her no harm, and Dr Marjoribanks permitted himself to regard the occurrence in a professional point of view, as supplying a little alterative which he could scarcely administer himself; for it is well known that physicians are seldom successful in the treatment of their own families. He was more jocose than usual at breakfast for some days following, and, on the morning of the next Thursday, asked if everybody was to come as usual, with a significance which did not escape the young mistress of the house.

"You know best, papa," she said, cheerfully, as she poured him out his coffee: "if there is anybody who is ill and can't come, it must be your fault—but I did not hear that any one was ill."

"Nor I," said the Doctor, with a quiet laugh; and he could not help thinking it would be good sport to see Cavendish come into the drawing-room all by himself without any support, and make his appearance before Miss Marjoribanks, and do his best to be agreeable, with an awful consciousness of his bad behaviour, and nobody sufficiently benevolent to help him out. The Doctor thought it would serve him right, but yet he was not sufficiently irritated nor sufficiently sympathetic to lose any of the humour of the situation; and it was with a little zest, as for something especially piquant, that he looked forward to the evening. As for Miss Marjoribanks, she too recognised the importance of the occasion. She resolved to produce that evening a new *plat*, which had occupied a corner of her busy mind for some time past. It was a crisis which called for a new step in advance. She sat down by the window after breakfast with various novel combinations floating in her creative brain; and while she was revolving these ideas in her mind, Nancy came in with more than her usual briskness. It is true that Lucilla had her household well in hand, and possessed the faculty of government to a remarkable extent; but still, under the best of circumstances, it was a serious business to propose a new dish to Nancy. Dr Marjoribanks's factotum was a woman of genius in her way, and by no means unenlightened or an enemy of progress; but then she had a weakness common to many persons of superior intelligence and decided character. When there was anything new to be introduced, Nancy liked to be herself the godmother of the interesting novelty; for, to be sure, it was her place, and Miss Lucilla, though she was very clever, was not to be expected to understand what came in best with the other dishes for a dinner. "I ain't one as goes just upon fish and flesh and fowl, like some as call themselves cooks," Nancy said. "If I have a failing, it's for things as suits. When it's brown, make it brown, and don't be mean about the gravy-beef—that's my principle; and when it ain't brown, mind what you're a-doing of—and don't go and throw a heap of entrys and things at a gentleman's head without no 'armony. I always says to Miss Lucilla as 'armony's the thing; and when I've set it all straight in my mind, I ain't one as likes to be put out," Nancy would add, with a gleam of her eye which betokened mischief. Miss Marjoribanks was much too sensible not to be aware of this peculiarity; and accordingly she cleared her throat with something as near nervousness as was possible to Lucilla before she opened her lips to propose the innovation. Miss Marjoribanks, as a general rule, did not show much nervousness in her dealings with her prime minister, any more than in her demeanour towards the less important members of society; and consequently Nancy remarked the momentary timidity, and a flash of sympathy and indignation took the place of her usual impulse of defiance.

"I heard as master said, there was some gentleman as wasn't a-coming," said Nancy. "Not as one makes no difference in a dinner; but I allays likes to know. I don't like no waste, for my part. I ain't one as calk'lates too close, but if there's one thing as I hates like poison, it's waste. I said as I would ask, for Thomas ain't as correct as could be wished. Is it one less than usual, Miss Lucilla?" said Nancy; and it was Lucilla's fault if she did not understand the profound and indignant sympathy in Nancy's voice.

"Oh, no; it is just the usual number," said Miss Marjoribanks. "It was only a joke of papa's—they are all just as usual——" And here Lucilla paused. She was thinking of the dish she wanted, but Nancy thought she was thinking of Mr Cavendish, who had treated her so badly. She studied the countenance of her young mistress with the interest of a woman who has had her experiences, and knows how little *They* are to be depended upon. Nancy murmured "Poor dear!" under her breath, almost without knowing it, and then a brilliant inspiration came to her mind. Few people have the gift of interfering successfully in such cases, but then to offer consolation is a Christian duty, especially when one has the confidence that to give consolation is in one's power.

"Miss Lucilla, I would say as you've been doing too much, if anybody was to ask me," said Nancy, moved by this generous impulse—"all them practisings and things. They're well enough for young ladies as ain't got nothing else to do; but you as has such a deal in your hands—— If there was any little thing as you could fancy for dinner," said Nancy, in her most bland accents; "I've set it all down as I thought would be nicest, allays if you approves, Miss Lucilla; but if there was any little thing as you could fancy——" "Poor dear, it's all as we can do," she murmured to herself. The faithless could not be brought back again; but Ariadne might at least have any little thing she could fancy for dinner, which, indeed, is a very general treatment of such a case on the part of perplexed sympathisers who do not know what to say.

Lucilla was so excited for the moment by this unusual evidence of her own good fortune, that she had almost spoiled all by sitting straight up and entering with her usual energy into the discussion—but instinct saved Miss Marjoribanks from this mistake. She lost no time in taking advantage of the opportunity, and instead of having a fight with Nancy, and getting a reluctant consent, and still more reluctant execution of the novelty, Lucilla felt that she was doing that excellent woman a favour by naming her new dish. Nancy approved so thoroughly as to be enthusiastic. "I always said as she had a deal of sense," she said afterwards, triumphantly. "There ain't one young lady in a hundred as knows what's good for her, like Miss Lucilla." But notwithstanding this fervent declaration of approval, Nancy, softened as she was, could not but linger, when all was concluded, to give a little advice.

"I wouldn't worrit myself with all them practisings, Miss Lucilla, if I was you," said her faithful retainer. "They're a deal too much for you. I've took the liberty, when all was cleaned up, to go on the stair and listen a bit, and there ain't nothing to equal it when you're a-singing by yourself. I don't think nothing of them duets—and as for that bold-faced brazen thing——"

"Oh, Nancy, hush!" said Lucilla; "Miss Lake has a beautiful voice. If she does not look quite like a lady, it is not her fault, poor thing. She has no mamma to set her right, you know. She is the best assistant I have—she and Mr Cavendish," said Lucilla, sweetly; and she gave Nancy a look which moved the faithful servant almost to tears, though she was not addicted to that weakness. Nancy retired with the most enthusiastic determination to exert herself to the utmost for the preparation of the little dish which Lucilla fancied. "But I wouldn't worrit about them duets," she said again, as she left the room. "I wouldn't, not if I was you, Miss Lucilla, asking pardon for the liberty: as for having no mamma, you have no mamma yourself, and you the young lady as is most thought upon in Carlingford, and as different from that brazen-faced thing, with her red cheeks——"

"Hush, oh hush, Nancy," Lucilla said, as she sank back in her chair; but Miss Marjoribanks, after all, was only human, and she was not so distressed by these unpolished epithets as she might or perhaps ought to have been. "Poor Barbara! I wish she could only look a little bit like a lady," she said to herself; and so proceeded with her preparations for the evening. She had all her plans matured, and she felt quite comfortable about that evening which all her friends were thinking would be rather trying to Lucilla. To tell the truth, when a thing became rather trying, Lucilla's spirits rose. Mr Cavendish's desertion was perhaps, on the whole, more than compensated for by the exhilaration of a difficulty to be encountered. She too began to forecast, like her father, the possibilities of the evening, and to think of Mr Cavendish coming in to dinner when there was nobody to support him, and not even a crowd of people to retire among. Would he run the risk of coming, under the circumstances? or, if he came, would he prostrate himself as he had done on a previous occasion, and return to his allegiance? This question roused Lucilla to a degree of energy unusual even to her who was always energetic. It was then that the brilliant idea struck her of adjourning to the garden in the evening—a practice which was received with such enthusiasm in Carlingford, where the gardens were so pretty. She put on her hat directly and went down-stairs, and called the gardener to consult him about it; and it was thus that she was employed when Mrs Chiley rang the bell at the garden-gate. If it had been anybody else in Carlingford, Lucilla would have led her back again to the house, and said nothing about the subject of her conference with the gardener; for it is always best, as all judicious persons are aware, not to forestall these little arrangements which make so agreeable a surprise at the moment; but then Mrs Chiley was Miss Marjoribanks's special confidant. The old lady had her face full of business that bright morning. She listened to what her young friend proposed, but without hearing it, and said, "Oh yes, my dear, I am sure it will be charming," without the very least notion what it was she applauded. "Let us go in and sit down a moment, for I have something to say to you, Lucilla," Mrs Chiley said; and when they had reached the drawing-room and shut the door, the Colonel's wife gave her favourite a kiss, and looked anxiously in her face. "You have not been to see me since Monday," said Mrs Chiley. "I am sure you are not well, or you could not have stayed away so long; but if you did not feel equal to going out, why did not you send for me, Lucilla, my poor dear?" Though Miss Marjoribanks's thoughts at that moment were full of the garden, and not in the least occupied with those more troublesome matters which procured for her Mrs Chiley's sympathy, she placed the kind old lady in the most easy chair, and sat down by her, as Mrs Chiley liked to see a young creature do. Lucilla's affairs were too important to be trusted to a young *confidante* of her own age; but even a person of acknowledged genius like Miss Marjoribanks is the better of some one to whom she can open up her breast.

"Dear Mrs Chiley," said Lucilla, "I am quite well, and I meant to have come to see you to-day."

"My poor dear!" said Mrs Chiley again. "You say you are

quite well, for you have such a spirit; but I can see what you have been going through. I don't understand how you can keep on, and do so much. But it was not *that* that brought me here. There is some one coming to Carlingford that I want you to meet, Lucilla. He is a relation of Mary Chiley's husband, and as she does not get on very well with them, you know, I think it is our duty to be civil. And they say he is a very nice man; and young—enough," said Mrs Chiley, with a look of some anxiety, pausing to see the effect produced upon Lucilla by her words.

Miss Marjoribanks had not, as she once confessed, a very vivid sense of humour, but she laughed a little, in spite of herself, at the old lady's anxious look. "Don't be sorry for me," she said; "I told you that fortunately my affections were not engaged. I don't want any new gentleman introduced to me. If *that* was what I was thinking of, I never need have come home," Lucilla said, with a little dignity; and yet, to be sure, she was naturally curious to know who the new man, who was very nice and young—enough, could be; for such apparitions were not too plentiful in Carlingford; and it did not seem in reason that an individual of this interesting description could come out of Colonel Chiley's house.

"My dear, he is a clergyman," said Mrs Chiley, putting her hand on Miss Marjoribanks's arm, and speaking in a half whisper; "and you know a nice clergyman is always nice, and you need not think of him as a young man unless you like. He has a nice property, and he is Rector of Basing, which is a very good living, and Archdeacon of Stanmore. He has come here to hold a visitation, you know; and they say that if Carlingford was made into a bishopric, he is almost sure to be the first bishop; and you know a bishop, or even an archdeacon, has a very nice position. I want to be civil to him for Mary Chiley's sake, who is not on such terms as we could wish with her husband's friends; and then I suppose he will have to be a great deal in Carlingford, and I should like him to form a good impression. I want you and your dear good papa to come and meet him; and then after that—but one thing is enough at a time," the old lady said, breaking off with a nod and a smile. She too had brought her bit of consolation to Lucilla; and it was a kind of consolation which, when administered at the right moment, is sometimes of sovereign efficacy, as Mrs Chiley was aware.

"I am sure papa will be very happy," said Lucilla; "and,

indeed, if you like, I shall be very glad to ask him here. If he is a friend of yours, that is quite enough for me. It is very nice to know a nice clergyman; but as for being a young man, I can't see how that matters. If I had been thinking of *that*, I need never—but I should think papa would like to meet him; and you know it is the object of my life to please papa."

"Yes, my poor dear," said the Colonel's wife, "and he would be hard-hearted indeed if he was not pleased; but still we must consider you too a little, Lucilla. You do everything for other people, and you never think of yourself. But I like to see you with nice people round you, for my part," Mrs Chiley added—"really nice people, and not these poor-spirited, ungrateful——"

"Hush, hush!" said Lucilla; "I don't know such nice people anywhere as there are in Carlingford. Some people are never pleased with their neighbours, but I always get on so well with everybody. It is my good luck, you know; and so long as I have you, dear Mrs Chiley——"

"Ah, Lucilla!" said the old lady, "that is very kind of you—and you could not have anybody that is fonder of you than I am; but still I am an old woman, old enough to be your grandmother, my dear—and we have your future interests to think of. As for all the vexations you have had, I think I could find it in my heart to turn that ungrateful creature to the door. Don't let her come here any more. I like your voice a great deal better when you are singing by yourself—and I am sure the Archdeacon would be of my opinion," said Mrs Chiley, with a confidence which was beautiful to behold. It was true she had not seen her new hero as yet, but that only left her so much more free to take the good of him and his probable sentiments; for to persons of frank and simple imagination a very little foundation of fact is enough to build upon.

"Dear Mrs Chiley, it is so nice of you to be vexed," said Lucilla, who thought it as well not to enter into any further argument. "Papa will be delighted, I am sure, and I can come in the evening. The Colonel likes to have only six people, and you will be three to start with, so there can't be any room for me at dinner; and you know I don't mind about dinner. I shall come in the evening and make tea for you—and if you think he would like to come next Thursday——" said Lucilla, graciously. This was how it was eventually settled. Mrs Chiley went home again through Grange Lane in the sunshine, with that little old-womanish hobble which Mrs Woodburn executed with such precision, perfectly satisfied with her success, and indulging herself in some pleasant visions. To be sure, a nice clergyman is always nice to know, even though nothing more was to come of it; and a new man in the field of such distinguished pretensions, would be Lucilla's best defence against any sort of mortification. As for Miss Marjoribanks herself, she was thinking a great deal more of the new details for the approaching evening than of anything else more distant, and consequently less important; but, on the whole, she was by no means displeased to hear of the Archdeacon. In such a work as hers, a skilful leader is always on the outlook for auxiliaries; and there are circumstances in which a nice clergyman is almost as useful to the lady of the house as a man who can flirt. To be sure, now and then there occurs a rare example in which both these qualities are united in one person; but even in the most modest point of view, if he was not stupid or obstinately Low-Church, there was nothing to despise in the apparition of the Archdeacon thus suddenly blown to her very door. While she had the seats placed in the garden (not too visibly, but shrouded among the shrubs and round the trunks of the trees), and chose the spot for a little illumination, which was not to be universal, like a tea-garden, but concentrated in one spot under the big lime-tree, Lucilla permitted herself to speculate a little about this unknown hero. She did not so much ask herself if he would be dark or fair, according to the usage of young ladies, as whether he would be High or Broad. But, however, that question, like various others, was still hidden in the surrounding darkness.

This was how Mrs Chiley did her best to cheer up Lucilla in the discouragement from which she supposed her young friend to be suffering. It was perhaps a loftier expedient in one way than Nancy's desire that she should have something she would fancy for dinner; but then there could not be any doubt as to the kindness which prompted both suggestions; and, after all, it is not what people do for you, but the spirit in which they do it, which should be taken into consideration, as Lucilla most justly observed.

CHAPTER XVI.

THAT evening was one which all the people in Grange Lane had unanimously concluded would be rather hard upon Miss Marjoribanks. To be sure, when a crisis arrives there is always a certain excitement which keeps one up; but afterwards, when the excitement is over, then is the time when it becomes really trying. There was naturally, under these circumstances, a larger assemblage than usual to watch the progress of the little drama, and how Lucilla would behave; for, after all, society would be excessively tame if it were not for these personal complications, which are always arising, and which are so much better than a play. As for the Doctor himself, the portion of the evening's entertainment which particularly amused him was that which preceded all the rest—the reception given by Lucilla to her guests at dinner, and especially to the culprit, who came in quite alone, and found nobody to stand up for him. Mr Cavendish, who felt to the full the difficulty of his position, and, to tell the truth, was a little ashamed of himself, came late, in order to abridge his trial as much as possible; but Lucilla's habitual good-fortune was not confined only to her own necessities, but seemed to involve everybody opposed to her in a ceaseless ill-luck, which was very edifying to the spectators. Mr Cavendish was so late that the other guests had formed into groups round the room, leaving a great open space and avenue of approach to the lady of the house in the middle; and the audience, thus arranged, was very impatient and unfavourable to the lingerer who kept them waiting for their dinner. When he came in at last, instead of doing anything to help him, everybody ceased talking and looked on in stern silence as the wretched culprit walked all the length of the room up to Lucilla through the unoccupied space which exposed him so unmercifully on every side. They all stopped in the middle of what they were saying, and fixed stony eyes on him, as the dead sailors did on the Ancient Mariner. He had a very good spirit, but still there are circumstances which take the courage out of a man. To be sure, Miss Marjoribanks, when he reached her at last, received Mr Cavendish with the utmost grace and cordiality; but it is easy to imagine what must have been the feelings of the unfortunate hero. The Balaclava charge itself, in the face of all the guns, could have been nothing to the sensation of walking through that horrible naked space, through a crowd of reproachful men who were waiting for dinner; and it was only after it was all over, and Mr Cavendish had safely arrived at Miss Marjoribanks's side, and was being set at his ease, poor wretch, by her incomparable sweetness, that the Doctor, with a certain grim smile on his countenance, came and shook hands with his unfortunate guest.

"You are late," Dr Marjoribanks said, taking out the great watch by which all the pulses of Grange Lane considered it their duty to keep time, and which marked five minutes after seven, as everybody could see. It was ten minutes after seven by the pretty French clock on the mantelpiece, and at least twenty by the lowering countenances of Dr Marjoribanks's guests. Mr Cavendish made the best of his unhappy position, and threw himself upon Lucilla's charity, who was the only one who had any compassion upon him; for to see Mrs Chiley's forbidding countenance no one could have believed that she had ever called him "my dear." "Dinner is on the table, papa," Miss Marjoribanks said, with a little reassuring nod to the culprit who had made her his refuge; and she got up and shook out her white draperies with a charitable commotion for which her faithless admirer blessed her in his heart.

But the place at her left hand was not left vacant for Mr Cavendish; he had not the spirit to claim it, even had he had the time; and the consequence was that he found himself next to his brother-in-law at table, which was indeed a hard fate. As for Lucilla, nobody had ever seen her in better spirits or looks; she was quite radiant when the famous dish made its appearance which Nancy had elaborated to please her, and told the story of its introduction to her two next neighbours, in a half whisper, to their immense amusement. "When the servants are gone I will tell you what we are laughing at," she breathed across the table to Mrs Chiley, who was "more than delighted," as she said, to see her dear Lucilla keeping up so well; and when the dessert was put upon the table, and Thomas had finally disappeared, Miss Marjoribanks kept her promise. "I could not think how I was to get her to consent," Lucilla said, "but you know she thought I was in low spirits, the dear old soul, and that it would be a comfort to me." Though there was often a great deal of fun at Dr Marjoribanks's table, nothing was ever heard there to compare with the laughter that greeted Lucilla's narrative. Everybody was so entirely aware of the supposed cause of the low spirits, and indeed was so conscious of having speculated, like Nancy, upon Miss Marjoribanks's probable demeanour at this trying moment, that the laughter was not mere laughter, but conveyed, at the same time, a confession of guilt and a storm of applause and admiration. As for Mr Cavendish, it was alarming to look at him in the terrible paroxysm of confusion and shame which he tried to shield under the universal amusement. Miss Marjoribanks left the dining-room that evening with the soothing conviction that she had administered punishment of the most annihilating kind, without for a moment diverging from the perfect sweetness and amiability with which it was her duty to treat all her father's guests. It was so complete and perfect that there was not another word to be said either on one side or the other; and yet Lucilla had not in the least committed herself, or condescended from her maiden dignity. As for Dr Marjoribanks, if he had chuckled over it before, in anticipation, it may be supposed how he enjoyed now this perfect vindication of his daughter's capacity for taking care of herself. The sound of the victory was even heard up-stairs, where the young ladies at the open windows were asking each other, with a little envy, what the men could be laughing at. There was, as we have said, a larger assembly than usual that night. For one thing, it was moonlight, and all the people from the country were there; and then public curiosity was profoundly concerned as to how Lucilla was to conduct herself on so trying an occasion. The laughter even jarred on the sensitive feelings of some people who thought, where a young girl's happiness was concerned, that it was too serious a matter to be laughed at; but then Miss Marjoribanks was not a person who could be classed with ordinary young girls, in the general acceptation of the word.

It was when things were at this crisis, and all eyes were directed to Lucilla, and a certain expectation was diffused through the company, that Miss Marjoribanks made that proposal of adjourning to the garden, which was received with so much applause. Lucilla's instinct, or rather her genius, had warned her that something out of the ordinary course of proceedings would be expected from her on that special occasion. She could not get up and make a speech to her excited and curious audience, neither could she, *apropos* of nothing, tell over again the story which had been received with such applause down-stairs; and yet something was wanting. The ordinary routine did not satisfy Lucilla's constituency, who had come with the laudable intention of observing her on a trying occasion, and watching how she got through it. "The air is so delicious to-night that I had some seats placed in the garden," Miss Marjoribanks said, "and if you all like we will sing to you up here, and give you as much music as ever you please. You know I never would consent to be too musical when everybody was in one room. It does not matter so much, when there are a *suite;* but then papa, you know, is only a professional man, and I have but one drawing-room," said Lucilla, with sweet humility. It was Lady Richmond to whom she was addressing herself at the moment, who was a lady who liked to be the great lady of the party. "It is only in summer that we can be a little like you fine people, who have as many rooms as you please. When you are at a little distance we will sing to you all the evening, if you like."

"But, my dear, are you sure you feel able for so much exertion?" said Lady Richmond, who was one of those people who did not think a young girl's happiness a thing to be trifled with; and she looked with what she described afterwards as a very searching expression in Miss Marjoribanks's face.

"Dear Lady Richmond, I hope I am always able for my duty," said that gentle martyr. "Papa would be wretched if he did not think we were all enjoying ourselves; and you know it is the object of my life to be a comfort to papa."

This was what the searching expression in Lady Richmond's eyes elicited from Lucilla. The sentiment was perhaps a little different from that which she had conveyed to her delighted auditors in the dining-room, but at the same time it was equally true; for everybody in Carlingford was aware of the grand object of Miss Marjoribanks's existence. Lady Richmond went down to the garden at the head of a bevy of ladies, and seated herself under the drawing-room windows, and placed a chair beside her own for Mrs Chiley. "I am afraid that dear girl is keeping up too well," Lady Richmond said; "I never saw such fortitude. All the young people say she does not feel it; but as soon as I fixed my eyes on her I saw the difference. You can always find out what a girl's feelings are when you look into her eyes."

"Yes," said Mrs Chiley, with a little doubt, for she had been shaken in her convictions by the universal laughter, though she was a little mystified herself by Lucilla's anecdote; and then she had never been gifted with eyes like Lady Richmond's, which looked people through and through. "She goes through a great deal, and it never seems to do her any harm," the old lady said, with a little hesitation. "It is such a comfort that she has a good constitution, especially as her mother was so delicate; and then Lucilla has such a spirit——"

"But one may try a good constitution too far," said Lady Richmond; "and I am certain she is full of feeling. It is sure to come out when she sings, and that is why I came to this seat. I should not like to lose a note. And do tell me who is that horrid flirting disagreeable girl?" added the county lady, drawing her chair a little closer. By this time the garden was full of pretty figures and pleasant voices, and under the lime-tree there was a glimmer of yellow light from the lamps, and on the other side the moon was coming up steady like a ball of silver over the dark outlines of Carlingford; and even the two voices which swelled forth up-stairs in the fullest accord, betraying nothing of the personal sentiments of their owners, were not more agreeable to hear than the rustle and murmur of sound which rose all over Dr Marjoribanks's smooth lawn and pretty shrubbery. Here and there a group of the older people sat, like Lady Richmond and Mrs Chiley, listening with all their might; and all about them were clusters of girls and their natural attendants, arrested in their progress, and standing still breathless, "just for this bar," as young people pause in their walks and talks to listen to a chance nightingale. And, to be sure, whenever anybody was tired of the music, there were quantities of corners to retire into, not to speak of that bright spot full of yellow light under the lime-tree.

"Nobody but Lucilla ever could have thought of anything so delicious," was what everybody said. And then the two singers up-stairs gave so much scope to curiosity. "Do you think they are all by themselves?" Lydia Brown was heard to ask, with a little natural anxiety; and the livelier imaginations among the party set to work at once to invent impossible tortures which the soprano might inflict on the contralto. But, to tell the truth, the two singers were by no means alone. Half the gentlemen of the dinner-party, who were past the sentimental age, and did not care about moonlight, had gone up-stairs according to their use and wont, and remained there, finding, to their great satisfaction, room to move about, and comfortable chairs to sit down in. They sat and chatted in the corners in great content and good-humour, while Lucilla and Barbara executed the most charming duets. Now and then old Colonel Chiley paused to put his two hands softly together and cry "Brava!" but on the whole the gentlemen were not much disturbed by the music. And then there were a few ladies, who were subject to neuralgia, or apt to take bad colds in the head, who preferred being up-stairs. So that if Lucilla had meant to pinch or maltreat her rival, circumstances would have made it impossible. Miss Marjoribanks did nothing to Barbara, except incite her to sing her very best; but no doubt she was the means of inflicting considerable pain on Mr Cavendish, who stood at a little distance, and looked and listened to both, and perhaps had inward doubts as to the wisdom of his choice. Such was the arrangement of the personages of the social drama, and it was in this way that everybody was occupied, when an event occurred which at a later period awoke much excitement in Carlingford, and had no small influence upon the future fate of some of the individuals whose history is here recorded.

Everything was as calm and cheerful and agreeable as if Carlingford had been a social paradise, and Miss Marjoribanks's drawing-room the seventh heaven of terrestial harmony. The sky itself was not more peaceful, nor gave less indication of any tempest than did the tranquil atmosphere below, where all the people knew each other, and everybody was friendly. Lucilla had just risen from the piano, and there was a little pause, in which cheers were audible from the garden, and Colonel Chiley, in the midst of his conversation, patted his two hands together; and it was just at that moment that the drawing-room door opened, and Thomas came in, followed by a gentleman. The gentleman was a stranger, whom Miss Marjoribanks had never seen before, and she made a step forward, as was her duty as mistress of the house. But when she had made that one step, Lucilla suddenly stood still, arrested by something more urgent than the arrival of a stranger. Mr Cavendish, too, had been standing with his face to the door, and had seen the new arrival. He was directly in front of Lucilla, so near her that he could not move without attracting her attention. When Miss Marjoribanks took that step in advance, Mr Cavendish, as if by the same impulse, suddenly, and without saying a word, turned right round like a man who had seen something terrible, at which he dared not take a second look. He was too much absorbed at that moment in his own feelings to know that he was betraying himself to Lucilla, or even to be conscious that she was near him. His face was more than pale; it had a green ghastly look, as of a face from which all the blood had suddenly been withdrawn to reinforce the vital centre in some failing of nature. His under-lip hung down, and two hollows which had never been seen there before appeared in his cheeks. Miss Marjoribanks was so taken by surprise that she stood still, thinking no more of her duties, but regarding in utter dismay and amazement the look of dead stupefied terror which thus appeared so unexpectedly before her. Mr Cavendish had turned right round, turning his back upon a lady to whom he had been talking the minute before. But he was as unconscious of doing so as of the fact that he had presented the spectacle of his miserable surprise and alarm in the most striking way to the one woman present who had a right to entertain a certain grudge against him.

During this moment of unusual inaction on Lucilla's part, the stranger had been led up to Colonel Chiley, and had shaken hands with him, and was entering into some explanations which Miss Marjoribanks divined with her usual quick intelligence; and then the old Colonel roused himself up from his easy-chair, and leaned over to speak to Dr Marjoribanks, and showed symptoms of approaching the lady of the house. All these movements Lucilla followed breathlessly, with a strange consciousness that only her presence of mind stood between her faithless suitor and a real danger. And as if to prove the difference, Barbara Lake chose that moment of all others to show her power, and made an appeal to Mr Cavendish and his taste in music, to which the unhappy man made no response. Miss Marjoribanks saw there was no time to lose. With a fearless hand she threw down a great portfolio of music which happened to be close to her, just at his feet, making a merciful disturbance. And then she turned and made her curtsy, and received the homage of Mr Archdeacon Beverley, who had arrived a day before he was expected, and had come to look after his host, since his host had not been at home to receive him.

"But you have broken your music-stand or something, Lucilla," said the Colonel.

"Oh, no; it is only a portfolio. I can't think what could make me so awkward," said Miss Marjoribanks; "I suppose it was seeing some one come in whom I didn't know." And then the old gentleman, as was his duty, paid the Archdeacon a compliment on having made such a commotion. "We used to have the best of it in our day," said the old soldier; "but now you churchmen are the men." Miss Marjoribanks heard the door open again before this little speech was finished. It was Mr Cavendish, who was going out with a long step, as if he with difficulty kept himself from running; and he never came back again to say good-night, or made any further appearance either out of doors or indoors. It is true that the Archdeacon made himself very agreeable, but then one man never quite makes up for another. Miss Marjoribanks said nothing about it, not even when Mrs Woodburn came up to her with a scared face, and in full possession of her own identity, which of itself was an extraordinary fact, and proved that something had happened; but it would be vain to say that Lucilla was not much excited by this sudden gleam of mystery. It gave the Archdeacon an extraordinary and altogether unexpected attraction; and as for Mr Cavendish, it was utterly inconceivable that a man in society, whom everybody knew about, should give way to such a panic. The question was, What did it mean?

CHAPTER XVII.

The arrival of Mr Archdeacon Beverley in Carlingford was, for many reasons, an event of importance to the town, and especially to society, which was concerned in anything that drew new and pleasant people to Grange Lane. For one thing, it occurred at the time when that first proposal of elevating Carlingford into a bishopric, in order to relieve the present bishop of the district of a part of his immense diocese, had just been mooted; and supposing this conception to be ever carried out, nobody could have been more eligible as first bishop than the Archdeacon, who was in the prime of life, and a very successful clergyman. And then, not to speak of anything so important, his presence was a great attraction to the country clergy, especially as he had come to hold a visitation. Notwithstanding all this, it is impossible to deny that Mrs Chiley, his hostess, and even Miss Marjoribanks herself, regarded the manner of his first appearance with a certain displeasure. If he had only had the good sense to stay at home, and not come to seek his entertainers! To be sure it is awkward to arrive at a house and find that everybody is out; but still, as Mrs Chiley justly observed, the Archdeacon was not a baby, and he might have known better. "Coming to you the very first night, and almost in his travelling things, to take the cream off everything," the old lady said, with tears of vexation in her eyes; "and after that, what have we to show him in Carlingford, Lucilla?" As for Miss Marjoribanks, she was annoyed, but she knew the wealth of her own resources, and she was not in despair, like her old friend. "They never know any better," she said, sympathetically. "Dear Mrs Chiley, there was nothing else to be expected; but, at the same time, I don't think things are so very bad," said Lucilla; for she had naturally a confidence in herself of which even Mrs Chiley's admiring faith fell short.

The Archdeacon himself took it quite cheerfully, as if it was the most natural thing in the world. "I have no doubt it was a very pleasant party, if one could have got the key-note," he said, in his Broad-Church way, as if there was nothing more to be said on the subject, and Lucilla's Thursday was the merest ordinary assembly. For there could be no doubt that he was Broad-Church, even though his antecedents had not proclaimed the fact. He had a way of talking on many subjects which alarmed his hostess. It was not that there was anything objectionable in what he said—for, to be sure, a clergyman and an archdeacon may say a great many things that ordinary people would not like to venture on,—but still it was impossible to tell what it might lead to; for it is not everybody who knows when to stop, as Mr Beverley in his position might be expected to do. It was the custom of good society in Carlingford to give a respectful assent, for example, to Mr Bury's extreme Low-Churchism—as if it were profane, as it certainly was not respectable, to differ from the Rector—and to give him as wide a field as possible for his missionary operations by keeping out of the way. But Mr Beverley had not the least regard for respectability, nor that respect for religion which consists in keeping as clear of it as possible; and the way in which he spoke of Mr Bury's views wounded some people's feelings. Altogether, he was, as Mrs Chiley said, an anxious person to have in the house; for he just as often agreed with the gentlemen in their loose ways of thinking, as with the more correct opinions by which the wives and mothers who had charge of their morality strove hard to keep them in the right way; and that was the reverse of what one naturally expected from a clergyman. He was very nice, and had a nice position; and, under all the circumstances, it was not only a duty to pay attention to him, but a duty from which results of a most agreeable character might spring; but still, though she could not be otherwise than kind, it would be impossible to say that it was out of personal predilection that Mrs Chiley devoted herself to her guest. She admitted frankly

that he was not like what clergymen were in her time. For one
thing, he seemed to think that every silly boy and girl ought to
have an opinion and be consulted, as if they had anything to do
with it—which was just the way to turn their heads, and make
them utterly insupportable. On the whole, perhaps, the old lady
was more charitable to Mary Chiley, and understood better how
it was that she, brought up in sound Church principles, did not
get on so well as might be desired with her husband's family,
after a week of the Archdeacon. And yet he was a delightful
person, and full of information, as everybody admitted; and if
Carlingford should be erected into a bishopric, as would be only
right—and if Mr Beverley should happen to be appointed
bishop, as was highly probable—then it would be a pleasure to
think that one had been kind to him. At the same time, it
must be owned that he showed a great want of tact in coming
to Miss Marjoribanks's Thursday on the night of his arrival,
and thus brushing, as it were, the very cream off his introduction to Grange Lane. And Mrs Chiley still sighed a little over
Mr Cavendish, and thought within herself that it was not his
fault, but that designing, artful creature, who was enough to
lead any man wrong. For it was very clear to the meanest
capacity that nobody could ever call the Archdeacon "my dear,"
as, with all his faults, it had been possible to call Mr Cavendish.
And by this line of thought Mrs Chiley was led to regret Mr
Cavendish, and to wonder what had become of him, and what
family affairs it could be that had taken him so suddenly away.

A great many people in Carlingford were at that moment occupied by the same wonders and regrets. Some people thought
he was frightened to find how far he had gone with *that* Miss
Lake, and had left town for a little to be out of the way; and
some thought he must have been speculating, and have lost
money. To tell the truth, it was very strange that he should
have disappeared so suddenly,—just at the moment, too, when
old Mr Chiltern had one of his bad attacks of bronchitis, which
Dr Marjoribanks himself had admitted might carry him off any
day. Nothing could be more important to the future interests
of young Cavendish than to be on the spot at this critical moment, and yet he had disappeared without telling anybody he
was going, or where he was going, which was on the whole a
perfectly unexplainable proceeding. His very servants, as had
been ascertained by some inquiring mind in the community,
were unaware of his intention up to the very last moment; and
certainly he had not said good-bye to anybody before leaving

Dr Marjoribanks's garden on that Thursday evening. Mr Woodburn, who was not a person of very refined perceptions, was the only man who found his disappearance quite natural. "After making such a deuced ass of himself, by George! what could the fellow do?" said his brother-in-law, who naturally enjoyed the discomfiture of so near a connection; and this was no doubt a providential circumstance for Mrs Woodburn, who was thus saved from the necessity of explaining or accounting for her brother's unexpected disappearance; but it failed to satisfy the general community, who did not think Mr Cavendish likely to give in at the first blow even of so distinguished an antagonist as Miss Marjoribanks. Some of the more charitable inhabitants of Grange Lane concluded that it must be the sudden illness of some relative which had called him away; but then, though he was well known to be one of the Cavendishes, neither he nor his sister ever spoke much of their connections; and, on the whole, public opinion fluctuated between the two first suggestions—which seemed truest to nature at least, whether or not they might be fully corroborated by fact—which were, either that Mr Cavendish had taken fright, as he might very naturally have done, at the advanced state of his relations with Barbara Lake; or that he had speculated, and lost money. In either case his departure would have been natural enough, and need not, perhaps, have been accomplished with quite so much precipitation; but still such a community as that in Grange Lane was in circumstances to comprehend how a young man might take fright, and leave home, either because of losing a lot of money, or getting entangled with a drawing-master's daughter.

The immediate result, so far as society was concerned, was one for which people did not know whether to be most glad or sorry. Mrs Woodburn, who kept half the people in Grange Lane in terror of their lives, seemed to have lost all her inspiration now her brother was away. She did not seem to have the heart to take off anybody, which was quite a serious matter for the amusement of the community. To be sure, some people were thankful, as supposing themselves exempted from caricature; but then, unfortunately, as has been said, the people who were most afraid for Mrs Woodburn were precisely those who were unworthy of her trouble, and had nothing about them to give occupation to her graphic powers. As for Miss Marjoribanks, who had supplied one of the mimic's most effective studies, she was much disturbed by the failure of this element of entertainment. "I have always thought it very strange that

I never had any sense of humour," Lucilla said; "but it would not do, you know, if all the world was like me; and society would be nothing if everybody did not exert themselves to the best of their abilities." There was a mournful intonation in Lucilla's voice as she said this; for, to tell the truth, since Mr Cavendish's departure she had been dreadfully sensible of the utter absence of any man who could flirt. As for Osmond Brown and the other boys of his age, it might be possible to train them, but at the best they were only a provision for the future, and in the mean time Miss Marjoribanks could not but be sensible of her loss. She lamented it with such sincerity that all the world thought her the most perfect actress in existence. "I have nothing to say against any of you," Lucilla would say, contemplating with the eye of an artist the young men of Grange Lane who were her raw material. "I daresay you will all fall in love with somebody sooner or later, and be very happy and good for nothing; but you are no assistance in any way to society. It is Mr Cavendish I am sighing for," said the woman of genius, with the candour of a great mind; and even Mrs Woodburn was beguiled out of her despondency by a study so unparalleled. All this time, however, Lucilla had not forgotten the last look of her faithless admirer as he faced round upon her when Mr Archdeacon Beverley came into the room. She too, like everybody else, wondered innocently why Mr Cavendish had gone away, and when he was coming back again; but she never hinted to any one that the Archdeacon had anything to do with it; for indeed, as she said to herself, she had no positive evidence except that of a look that the Archdeacon *had* anything to do with it. By which it will be seen that Miss Marjoribanks's prudence equalled her other great qualities. It would be wrong to say, however, that her curiosity was not excited, and that in a very lively way; for the vague wonder of the public mind over a strange fact, could never be compared in intensity to the surprise and curiosity excited by something one has actually seen, and which gives one, as it were, a share in the secret,—if indeed there was a secret, which was a matter upon which Lucilla within herself had quite made up her mind.

As for the Archdeacon, the place which he took in society was one quite different from that which had been filled by Mr Cavendish, as, indeed, was natural. He was one of those men who are very strong for the masculine side of Christianity; and when he was with the ladies, he had a sense that he ought to be paid attention to, instead of taking that trouble in his own person. Miss Marjoribanks was not a woman to be blind to the advantages of this situation, but still, as was to be expected, it took her a little time to get used to it, and to make all the use of it which was practicable under the circumstances—which was all the more difficult since she was not in the least "viewy" in her own person, but had been brought up in the old-fashioned orthodox way of having a great respect for religion, and as little to do with it as possible, which was a state of mind largely prevalent in Carlingford. But that was not in the least Mr Beverley's way.

It was when Lucilla's mind was much occupied by this problem that she received a visit quite unexpectedly one morning from little Rose Lake, who had just at that time a great deal on her mind. For it may easily be supposed that Mr Cavendish's sudden departure, which bewildered the general public who had no special interest in the matter, must have had a still more overwhelming effect upon Barbara Lake, who had just been raised to the very highest pinnacle of hope, closely touching upon reality, when all her expectations collapsed and came to nothing in a moment. She would not believe at first that it could be true; and then, when it was no longer possible to resist the absolute certainty of Mr Cavendish's departure, her disappointment found vent in every kind of violence—hysterics, and other manifestations of unreason and self-will. Rose had been obliged to leave the Female School of Design upon her papa's overburdened shoulders, and stay at home to nurse her sister. Perhaps the little artist was not the best person to take care of a sufferer under such circumstances; for she was neither unreasonable nor self-willed to speak of, though perhaps a little opinionative in her way—and could not be brought to think that a whole household should be disturbed and disordered, and a young woman in good health retire to her room, and lose all control of herself, because a young man, with whom she had no acquaintance three months before, had gone out of town unexpectedly. Perhaps it was a want of feeling on the part of the unsympathetic sister. She gave out that Barbara was ill, and kept up a most subdued and anxious countenance down-stairs, for the benefit of the children and the maid-of-all-work, who represented public opinion in Grove Street; but when Rose went into her sister's room, where Barbara kept the blinds down, and had her face swollen with crying, it was with a very stern countenance that her little mentor regarded the invalid. "I do not ask you to have a sense of duty," Rose said, with a certain fine disdain, "but at least you might have a proper pride." This was all she took the trouble to say; but it must be admitted that a great deal more to the same effect might be read in her eyes, which were generally so dewy and soft, but which could flash on occasion. And then as the week drew on towards Thursday, and all her representations proved unavailing to induce Barbara to get up and prepare herself for her usual duties, the scorn and vexation and impatience with which the dutiful little soul met her sister's sullen determination that "she was not able" to fulfil her ordinary engagements, roused Rose up to a great resolution. For her own part she was one of the people who do not understand giving in. "What do you mean by lying there?" she said, pounding Barbara down small and cutting her to pieces with infallible goodsense and logic; "will that do any good? You would try to look better than usual, and sing better than usual, if you had any proper pride. *I* did not fall ill when my flounce was passed over at the exhibition. I made up my mind that very evening about the combination for my veil. I would die rather than give in if I were you."

"Your flounce!" sobbed Barbara—"oh you unfeeling insensible thing!—as if your h-heart had anything to do with—that. I only went to s-spite Lucilla—and I won't go—no more—oh, no more—now he's been and deserted me. You can't understand my feelings—g-go away and leave me alone."

"Barbara," said Rose, with solemnity, "I would forgive you if you would not be mean. I don't understand it in one of *us*. If Mr Cavendish has gone away, it shows that he does not care for you; and you would scorn him, and scorn to show you were thinking of him, if you had any proper pride."

But all the answer Barbara gave was to turn away with a jerk of annoyance the old easy-chair in which she was lying buried, with her hands thrust up into her black hair, and her eyes all red; upon which Rose left her to carry out her own resolution. She was prompt in all her movements, and she wasted no time on reconsideration. She went down into Grange Lane, her little head erect, and her bright eyes regarding the world with that air of frank recognition and acknowledgment which Rose felt she owed as an artist to her fellow-creatures. They were all good subjects more or less, and the consciousness that she could draw them and immortalise them gave her the same sense of confidence in their friendliness, and her own perfect command of the situation, as a young princess might have felt whose rank protected her like an invisible buckler. Rose, too, walked erect and open-eyed, in the confidence of *her* rank, which made her everybody's equal. It was in this frame of mind that she arrived at Dr Marjoribanks's house, and found Lucilla, who was very glad to see her. Miss Marjoribanks was pondering deeply on the Archdeacon at that moment, and her little visitor seemed as one sent by heaven to help her out. For to tell the truth, though Lucilla understood all about Mr Cavendish, and men of his description, and how to manage them, and take full use of their powers, even her commanding intelligence felt the lack of experience in respect to such a case as that of the Archdeacon, who required a different treatment to draw him out. She was thinking it over intently at the moment of Rose's arrival, for Lucilla was not a person to give up the advantages of a novel position because she did not quite understand it. She felt within herself that there was no doubt a great effect might be produced if she could but see how to do it. And it was Thursday morning, and there was no time to lose.

"I came to speak to you about Barbara," said Rose. "She is not fit to come out this morning. I told her it was very ungrateful not to make an effort after you had been so kind; but I am sorry to say she has not a strong sense of duty; and I don't think she would be able to sing or do anything but look stupid. I hope you will not think very badly of her. There are some people who can't help giving in, I suppose," said Rose, with an impatient little sigh.

"And so this is you, you dear little Rose!" said Lucilla, "and I have never seen you before since I came home—and you always were such a pet of mine at Mount Pleasant! I can't think why you never came to see me before; as for me, you know, I never have any time. Poor papa has nobody else to take care of him, and it always was the object of my life to be a comfort to papa."

"Yes," said Rose, who was a straightforward little woman, and not given to compliments. "I have a great deal to do too," she said; "and then all my spare moments I am working at my design. Papa always says that society accepts artists for what they can give, and does not expect them to sacrifice their time," Rose continued, with her little air of dignity. Miss Marjoribanks knew very well that society was utterly unconscious of the existence of the Lake family; but then there is always something imposing in such a perfectly innocent and superb assumption as that to which the young Preraphaelite had just given utterance; and it began to dawn upon Lucilla that here was another imperfectly understood but effective instrument lying ready to her hand.

"I should like to see your design," said Miss Marjoribanks, graciously. "You made such a pretty little wreath for the corner of my handkerchief—don't you remember?—all frogs' legs and things. It looked so sweet in the old satin stitch. What is the matter with poor Barbara? I felt sure she would catch cold and lose her voice. I shall tell papa to go and see her. As for to-night, it will be a dreadful loss to be sure, for I never could find a voice that went so well with mine. But if you are sure she can't come——"

"When people have not a sense of duty," said Rose, with an indignant sigh, "nor any proper pride—— Some are so different. Barbara ought to have been some rich person's daughter, with nothing to do. She would not mind being of no use in the world. It is a kind of temperament I don't understand," continued the little artist. All this, it is true, was novel to Miss Marjoribanks, who had a kind of prejudice in favour of the daughters of rich persons who had nothing to do; but Lucilla's genius was broad and catholic, and did not insist upon comprehending everything. She gave Rose a sudden scrutinising look, and measured her mentally against the gap she had to fill. No doubt it was an experiment, and might fail signally; but then Miss Marjoribanks was always at hand to cover deficiencies, and she had that confidence in herself and her good fortune which is necessary to everybody who greatly dares.

"You must come yourself this evening, you dear old Rose," said Lucilla. "You know I always was fond of you. Oh yes, I know you can't sing like Barbara. But the Archdeacon is coming, who understands about art; and if you would like to bring your design—— My principle has always been, that there should be a little of everything in society," said Miss Marjoribanks. "I daresay you will feel a little strange at first with not knowing the people, but that will soon pass off—and you *must* come."

When she had said this, Lucilla bestowed upon little Rose a friendly schoolfellow kiss, putting her hands upon the little artist's shoulders, and looking her full in the face as she did so. "I am sure you can talk," said Miss Marjoribanks. She did not say "Go away now, and leave me to my arrangements;" but Rose, who was quick-witted, understood that the salute was a dismissal, and she went away accordingly, tingling with pride and excitement and pleasure and a kind of pain. The idea of practically exemplifying, in her own person, the kind of demeanour which society ought to expect from an artist had not occurred to Rose; but destiny having arranged it so, she was not the woman to withdraw from her responsibilities. She said to herself that it would be shabby for her who was known to have opinions on this subject, to shrink from carrying them out; and stimulated her courage by recourse to her principles, as people do who feel themselves bound to lay sacrifices on the altar of duty. Notwithstanding this elevated view of the emergency, it must be admitted that a sudden thought of what she would wear had flushed to Rose's very finger-tips, with a heat and tingle of which the little heroine was ashamed. For it was Thursday morning, and there was not a moment to be lost. However, after the first thrill which this idea had given her, Rose bethought herself once more of her principles, and stilled her beating heart. It was not for her to think of what she was to put on, she who had so often proclaimed the exemption of "a family of artists" from the rules which weigh so hard upon the common world. "We have a rank of our own," she said to herself, but with that tremor which always accompanies the transference of a purely theoretical and even fantastic rule of conduct into practical ground—"We are everybody's equal, and we are nobody's equal—and when papa begins to be appreciated as he ought to be, and Willie has made a Name——" This was always the point at which Rose broke off, falling into reverie that could not be expressed in words; but she had no leisure to remark upon the chance "compositions" in the street, or the effects of light and shade, as she went home. A sudden and heavy responsibility had fallen upon her shoulders, and she would have scorned herself had she deserted her post.

CHAPTER XVIII.

But the anticipations of Rose Lake were trifling matters in comparison with the universal interest and even excitement which attended the Archdeacon's first appearance in Carlingford. What might be called his first public appearance took place at

Dr Marjoribanks's table, although he had previously dined at the Rectory, and also at Sir John Richmond's, besides that there had been somebody to dinner at Colonel Chiley's almost every day; but then there were only county people at Sir John's, and Mr Bury's guests naturally counted for very little in Grange Lane;—indeed, it was confidently reported that the Rector had invited Mr Tufton of Salem Chapel to meet the Archdeacon, and that, but for the Dissenting minister having more sense and knowing his place, that unseemly conjunction would have taken place, to the horror of all right-thinking people. So that Dr Marjoribanks's was in reality the first house where he had any chance of seeing society. It would perhaps be using too strong a word to say that Miss Marjoribanks was anxious about the success of her arrangements for this particular evening; but, at the same time, it must be admitted that the circumstances were such as to justify a little anxiety. Mr Cavendish was gone, who, to do him justice, was always agreeable, and his departure disturbed the habitual party; and Mrs Woodburn had lost all her powers, as it seemed, and sat at Dr Marjoribanks's left hand, looking just like other people, and evidently not to be in the least depended on; and Lucilla was aware that Barbara was not coming, which made, if nothing else, a change in the programme. No music, nobody to do the flirting, nor to supply the dramatic by-play to which Grange Lane had become accustomed; and a new man to be made use of, and to be done honour to, and introduced in society. A young woman of powers inferior to those of Miss Marjoribanks would have sunk under such a weight of responsibility, and there was no doubt that Lucilla was a little excited. She felt that everything depended upon her courage and self-possession. If she but lost her head for a moment and lost command of affairs, everything might have been lost; but then fortunately she knew herself and what she could do, and had a modest confidence that she would not lose her head; and thus she could still eat her dinner with the composure of genius, though it would be wrong to deny that Lucilla was a little pale.

And then, as if all these things had not been enough to discourage the lady of the house, another discordant element was added by the presence of Mr Bury and his sister, whom it had been necessary to ask to meet the Archdeacon. The Rector, though he was very Low-Church, had no particular objections to a good dinner—but he made a principle of talking of that important daily necessity in a disparaging, or at best in a pat-

rousing way, which roused Dr Marjoribanks's temper; and sometimes the Doctor would launch a shaft of medical wit at his spiritual guide, which Mr Bury had no means of parrying. Nor was this the only danger to which the peace of the party was exposed. For the Rector, at the same time, regarded Mr Beverley with a certain critical suspiciousness, such as is seldom to be encountered except among clergymen. He did not know much about his clerical superior, who had only recently been appointed to his archdeaconry; but there was something in his air, his looks and demeanour, which indicated what Mr Bury considered a loose way of thinking. When the Archdeacon made any remark the Rector would pause and look up from his plate to listen to it, with his fork suspended in the air the while —and then he would exchange glances with his sister, who was on the other side of the table. All this, it may be supposed, was a little discomposing for Lucilla, who had the responsibility of everything, and who could now look for no assistance among the ordinary members of her father's party, who were, as a general rule, much more occupied with the dinner than with anything else that was going on. In such a state of affairs, it was a great relief to Miss Marjoribanks when the Archdeacon, who occupied the post of honour by her side, made a lively new beginning in the conversation. It had not to call *flagged* before—not precisely flagged—but still there were indications of approaching exhaustion, such as can always be perceived half-a-mile off by anybody who has any experience in society; and when the Archdeacon took up the ball with all the liveliness of a man who is interested in a special question, it will not be difficult to any lady who has ever been in such circumstances to realise to herself Miss Marjoribanks's sense of gratitude and relief.

"By the by," said Mr Beverley, "I meant to ask if any one knew a man whom I am sure I caught a glimpse of the first day I was in Carlingford. Perhaps it was in the morning after I arrived, to be precise. I can't recollect exactly. If he lives about here, he ought to be known, for he is a very clever amusing sort of fellow. I don't know if Carlingford is more blessed than other country towns with people of that complexion," said the Archdeacon, turning to Lucilla with a smile. His smile, as he paused and turned to Miss Marjoribanks, was such as conveys a kind of challenge when it is addressed to a young lady, and meant to lead to a lively little combat by the way; and yet there was something of keen personal anxiety and animosity in it. As for Lucilla, she was conscious of an immediate thrill of curiosity, but still it was curiosity unmingled with any excitement, and she had no particular objection to respond.

"Everybody is nice in Carlingford," said Miss Marjoribanks; "some people are always finding fault with their neighbours, but I always get on so well with everybody—I suppose it is my luck." This was not precisely an answer to the Archdeacon's question; and there was somebody at the table who could have fallen upon Lucilla and beaten her for putting off the revelation which trembled on the lips of Mr Beverley, and yet would have given anything in the world to silence the Archdeacon, and felt capable of rushing at him like a fury and tearing his tongue out, or suffocating him, to stop the next words that he was going to say. But nobody knew anything about this, or could see into the one heart that had begun to flutter and throb with alarm; for outwardly, all the well-dressed, cheerful people at Dr Marjoribanks's table sat eating their dinner, one precisely like another, as if there had been no such thing as mystery or terror in the world.

"You must not expect me to believe in the perfection of human society," said the Archdeacon, going on in the same strain; "I would much rather pin my faith to the amiable dispositions of one young lady who always finds her neighbours agreeable—and I hope she makes no exception to the rule," said the Broad-Churchman, in a parenthesis, with a smile and a bow—and then he raised his voice a little: "The man I speak of is really a very amusing fellow, and very well got up, and calculated to impose upon ordinary observers. It is quite a curious story; he was a son of a trainer or something of that sort about Newmarket. Old Lord Monmouth took an extraordinary fancy to him, and had him constantly about his place—at one time, indeed, he half brought him up along with his grandson, you know. He always was a handsome fellow, and picked up a little polish; and really, for people not quite used to the real thing, was as nearly like a gentleman——"

"Come, now, I don't put any faith in that," said Mr Woodburn. "I don't pretend to be much of a one for fine company myself, but I know a gentleman when I see him; a snob always overdoes it, you know——"

"I never said this man was a snob," said the Archdeacon, with a refined expression of disgust at the interruption flitting over his features; "on the contrary, if he had only been honest, he would have been really a very nice fellow——"

"My dear sir," said Mr Bury, "excuse me for breaking in—

perhaps I am old-fashioned, but don't you think it's a pity to treat the question of honesty so lightly? A dishonest person has a precious soul to be saved, and may be a most deeply interesting character; but to speak of him as a very nice fellow, is—pardon me—I think it's a pity; especially in mixed society, where it is so important for a clergyman to be guarded in his expressions," said the Rector. When Mr Bury began to speak, everybody else at table ceased talking, and gave serious attention to what was going on, for the prospect of a passage of arms between the two clergymen was an opportunity too captivating to be lost.

"I hope Mr Bury's dishonest friends will pardon me," said the Archdeacon; "I mean no harm to their superior claims. Does anybody know the man here, I wonder? He had changed his name when I knew him, and there is no telling what he may call himself now. I assure you he was a very good-looking fellow—dark, good features, nearly six feet high——"

"Oh please don't say any more," said Miss Marjoribanks, and she could not quite have explained why she interrupted these personal details; "if you tell me what he is like, I shall fancy everybody I meet is him; Mr Centum is dark, and has good features, and is nearly six feet high. Never mind what he is like; you gentlemen can never describe anybody—you always keep to *generals;* tell us what he has done."

Somebody drew a long breath at the table when the Archdeacon obeyed Miss Marjoribanks's injunction. More than one person caught the sound, but even Lucilla's keen eyes could not make out beyond controversy from whom it proceeded. To be sure, Lucilla's mind was in a most curious state of tumult and confusion. She was not one of the people who take a long time to form their conclusions; but the natural conclusion to which she felt inclined to jump in this case was one so monstrous and incredible that Miss Marjoribanks felt her only safeguard in the whirl of possibilities was to reject it altogether, and make up her mind that it was impossible; and then all the correspondences and apparent corroborations began to dance and whirl about her in a bewildering ring till her own brain seemed to spin with them. She was as much afraid lest the Archdeacon by some chance should fall upon a really individual feature which the world in general could identify, as if she had had any real concern in the matter. But then, fortunately, there was not much chance of that; for it was one of Lucilla's principles that men never can describe each other. She listened, however, with such a curious commotion in her mind, that she did not quite make out what he was saying, and only pieced it up in little bits from memory afterwards. Not that it was a very dreadful story. It was not a narrative of robbery or murder, or anything very alarming; but if it could by any possibility turn out that the man of whom Mr Beverley was speaking had ever been received in society in Carlingford, then it would be a dreadful blow to the community, and destroy public confidence for ever in the social leaders. This was what Lucilla was thinking in her sudden turmoil of amazement and apprehension. And all this time there was another person at table who knew all about it twenty times better than Lucilla, and knew what was coming, and had a still more intense terror lest some personal detail might drop from the Archdeacon's lips which the public in general would recognise. Mr Beverley went on with his story with a curious sort of personal keenness in his way of telling it, but never dreaming for a moment that anybody that heard him was disturbed or excited by it. "He has a mark on his face," the Archdeacon said—but here Miss Marjoribanks gave a little cry, and held up both her hands in dismay.

"Don't tell us what marks he has on his face," said Lucilla. "I know that I shall think every man who is dark, and has good features, and is six feet, must be him. I wonder if it could be my cousin Tom; *he* has a little mark on his face—and it would be just like his dreadful luck, poor fellow. Would it be right to give up one's own cousin if it should turn out to be Tom?" said Miss Marjoribanks. The people who were sitting at her end of the table laughed, but there was no laughing in Lucilla's mind. And this fright and panic were poor preparatives for the evening, which had to be got through creditably with so few resources, and with such a total reversal of the ordinary programme. Miss Marjoribanks was still tingling with curiosity and alarm when she rose from the table. If it should really come to pass that an adventurer had been received into the best society of Carlingford, and that the best judges had not been able to discriminate between the false and true, how could any one expect that Grange Lane would continue to confide its most important arrangements to such incompetent hands?

Such was the dreadful question that occupied all Lucilla's thoughts. So far as the adventurer himself was concerned, no doubt he deserved anything that might come upon him; but the judgment which might overtake the careless shepherds who had admitted the wolf into the fold was much more in Miss Marjoribanks's mind than any question of abstract justice. So that it was not entirely with a philanthropical intention that she stopped Mr Beverley and put an end to his dangerous details. Now she came to think of it, she began to remember that *nobody of her acquaintance* had any mark on his face; but still it was best not to inquire too closely. It was thus with a preoccupied mind that she went up to the drawing-room, feeling less in spirits for her work than on any previous occasion. It was the first of the unlucky nights, which every woman of Lucilla's large and public-spirited views must calculate upon as inevitable now and then. There was no moon, and the Richmonds naturally were absent, and so were the Miss Browns, who were staying there on a visit—for it was after the engagement between Lydia[*] and John; and Mr Cavendish was away (though perhaps under the circumstances that was no disadvantage); and Mrs Woodburn was silenced; and even Barbara Lake had failed her patroness.

"You are not in spirits to-night, Lucilla, my poor dear," said Mrs Chiley, as they went up-stairs; and the kind old lady cast a fierce glance at Mrs Woodburn, who was going before them with Miss Bury, as if it could be her fault.

"Dear Mrs Chiley," said Miss Marjoribanks, "I am in perfect spirits; it is only the responsibility, you know. Poor Barbara is ill, and we can't have any music, and what if people should be bored? When one has real friends to stand by one it is different," said Lucilla, with an intonation that was not intended for Mrs Chiley, "and I *always* stand by my friends."

This was the spirit with which Miss Marjoribanks went upstairs. It was a sentiment which pervaded her whole life. Even when she had occasion to be sufficiently displeased with the people who surrounded her, and to feel that her own loyal friendship met with no adequate response, this was the unfailing inspiration of her heart. She did not rush into opposition because any misguided man or woman failed for the moment to appreciate her efforts, and return, as they ought to have been glad to do, her sentiments of kindness. On the contrary, nothing could have been more long-suffering and tolerant and benign than the feelings with which Lucilla regarded the unfortunate persons who mistook or did not appreciate her. She

---

[*] It may be mentioned here that this was an engagement that none of the friends approved of, and that it was the greatest possible comfort to Miss Marjoribanks's mind that she had nothing to do with it—either one way or another, as she said.

knew herself, which, however superior they might be, was something they could not know; and she could afford to be sorry (for their own sakes) for their want of discrimination. If there should happen to be somebody in Grange Lane who had gained admittance into society under false pretences, not even such an offence, grievous as it was, could induce Miss Marjoribanks to condemn the culprit unheard. It was at once her settled resolution, and a peculiarity of her character, to stand by her friends; and whatever might be the thoughts in her own mind, her immediate decision was to shut her ears to every indication of the culprit's personality, and to be blind to every suggestion that could identify him. People who like to discover the alloy which blends with all human motives, may suppose that Lucilla felt her own credit as the leader of society at stake, and would not admit that she had been duped. But this had in reality but a very small share in the matter. Her instinct, even when reason suggested that she should be doubtful of them, was always to side with her own friends; and though there might be persons included in that sacred number who were scarcely worthy of the character, yet Lucilla, like every lofty character, could act but according to her own nature, and could not forsake any one whom she supposed to be thus mysteriously and darkly assailed.

And she had her reward. There are virtues in this world which go without any recompense, but there are other virtues upon which a prompt guerdon is bestowed; and Lucilla possessed this happier development. Whether it was that little speech of hers which touched the mimic's heart, or whether the effect was produced by some other secret influence, it is certain that this was the night on which Mrs Woodburn's talent came to what may be called a sort of apotheosis. She shook off her languor as by a sudden inspiration, and gave such a sketch of the Archdeacon as up to this day is remembered more clearly in Carlingford than the man himself. She took him off to his very face, and he never found it out, though everybody else did, and the house shook with restrained laughter. And as if this was not enough, Rose Lake had come with her portfolio, with some sketches of her brother's (who afterwards became so celebrated) in it, which electrified all the people who were fond of art; and by the side of the young Preraphaelite was Barbara, who had come "to spite Lucilla," and who remained unwittingly to grace her triumph. She stood by herself, all wan and crumpled, all the night, showing her disappointment and rage and jilted state so clearly in her face, as to afford to all the mammas in her neighbourhood a most startling example of the danger of showing your feelings, with which to point a moral to the other young people about. She had come because Rose was coming, and she would not be eclipsed by her younger sister. But nobody took any notice of Barbara on this miserable evening; nobody asked her to sing, or offered her a seat, or even spoke to her, except Lucilla, who in her magnanimity found time to say a word as she passed. She was carelessly dressed, and her hair was hastily arranged, and her eyes were red. She had no desire to look as if she had not been jilted, and had no proper pride, as Rose said; and Mrs Chiley, who was Lucilla's partisan and champion, and who thought poor Barbara deserved it all, seized the opportunity, and delivered a little lecture on the subject to the first group of girls who came in her way.

"A disappointment may happen to any one," said Mrs Chiley; "and so long as they had done nothing unbecoming, nobody could blame them; but, my dears, whatever you do, don't show it like that! It makes me ashamed of my sex. And only look at Lucilla!" said the old lady. Lucilla had the best of it now. Instead of a failure, such as for a moment seemed likely, she had a triumphant success. She, and she only, said a word of kindness to her formerly triumphant rival. She drove her chariot over Barbara, and drew an advantage even from her sullen looks and red eyes. And the only thing that dissatisfied Mrs Chiley in the entire course of the evening was the trustful confidence with which Miss Marjoribanks left the Archdeacon, the (possible) new candidate for her favour, beside the Lakes and their portfolio of drawings. In this, as in all other things, Lucilla could not but follow the dictates of her magnanimous nature. And even her own prospects, as her old friend lamented, were as nothing to her in comparison with the good of society. Experience ought to have taught her better; but then experience rarely does that amount of practical good which is generally attributed to it in the world. Lucilla gave little Rose the fullest opportunity of showing her drawings to the Archdeacon and awakening his curiosity, and even securing his affections, as the jealous observer thought; and everybody knows how little is necessary, if a young woman likes to exert herself, to lead a poor man to his undoing; and Mr Beverley, though an archdeacon, was most probably, in this respect at least, no wiser than other men. This was the painful aspect of the case which Mrs Chiley discussed with her husband when they got home.

"He is not like what clergymen were in our day," said the old lady, "but still he is very nice, and has a nice position, and it would just suit Lucilla; but to think of her going and leaving him with these Lake girls, notwithstanding the lesson she has had! and I have no doubt the little one is just as designing and nasty as the other. If it should come to anything, she has only herself to blame," said Mrs Chiley. As for the Colonel, he took it more calmly, as a gentleman might be expected to do.

"You may trust a parson for that," said the old soldier. "He knows what he is about. You will never find him make such an ass of himself as young Cavendish did." But this only made Mrs Chiley sigh the more.

"Poor Mr Cavendish!" said the old lady. "I will never blame him, poor fellow. It was all that deceitful thing laying her snares for him. For my part I never like to have anything to do with those artist kind of people—they are all adventurers," said the Colonel's wife; and she went to bed with this unchristian persuasion in her mind.

While every one else regarded the matter with, to some extent, a personal bias, the only person who looked at it abstractly, and contemplated not the accidents of an evening, but the work itself, which was progressing in the face of all kinds of social difficulties, was the master-mind which first conceived the grand design of turning the chaotic elements of society in Carlingford into one grand unity. Lucilla was not blind to the dangers that surrounded her, nor indifferent to the partial disappointment she had undergone; but she saw that, in spite of all, her great work was making progress. And when we announce that Miss Marjoribanks herself was satisfied, there remains little more to say.

As for the Archdeacon, he, as was natural, knew nothing about the matter. He said again, with the natural obtuseness which is so general among the gentlemen, that it had been a very pleasant party. "She has a fine clear candid nature," said Mr Beverley, which certainly was better than pronouncing solemnly that she was a good woman, which was what he said of Mrs Chiley and Lady Richmond, in the lump, as it were, without considering how unlike they were to each other. That was all he, being only a man, knew about it. But though Lucilla was satisfied with the events of the evening, it would be vain to deny that there were perturbations in her mind as she laid her head upon her maiden pillow. She said to herself again with profounder fervour, that fortunately her affections had not been engaged; but there were more things than affections to be taken into consideration. Could it be possible that mystery, and perhaps imposture, of one kind or another, had crossed the sacred threshold of Grange Lane; and that people might find out and cast in Lucilla's face the dreadful discovery that a man had been received in *her* house who was not what he appeared to be? When such an idea crossed her mind, Miss Marjoribanks shivered under her satin quilt. Of course she could not change the nature of the fact one way or another; but, at least, it was her duty to act with great circumspection, so that if possible it might not be found out—for Lucilla appreciated fully the difference that exists between wrong and discovery. If any man was imposing upon his neighbours and telling lies about himself, it was his own fault; but if a leader of society were to betray the fact of having received and petted such a person, then the responsibility was on *her* shoulders. And softer thoughts mingled with these prudential considerations—that sweet yet stern resolution to stand by her friends which Miss Marjoribanks had this evening expressed, and that sense of pity for everybody who is unfortunate which asserts itself even in the strongest of female intelligences. On the whole, it was clear that prudence was the great thing required, and a determination not to give too hasty heed to anything, nor to put herself in the wrong by any alarmist policy. Fortunately the respectability of Dr Marjoribanks's house was enough to cover its guests with a shining buckler. Thus Lucilla calmed down her own apprehensions, and succeeded in convincing herself that if the impostor whom the Archdeacon had seen had been really received in Grange Lane, it was so much the worse for the impostor; but that, in the mean time, in the lack of evidence it was much the best thing to take no notice. If there was any one else in Carlingford who regarded that past danger with a livelier horror and a more distinct fear, certainly Miss Marjoribanks had no way of knowing of it; and nobody had been remarked as being in a despondent condition, or, indeed, in anything but the highest spirits, in the course of this Thursday, except the ungrateful creature who had begun all the mischief; and tolerant as Lucilla was, it would have been going beyond the limits of nature to have expected that she could have been profoundly sorry for Barbara Lake.

K

At the same time, poor Barbara, though she was not an elevated character, had gone home in a very sad state of mind. She had taken courage to ask Mrs Woodburn about her brother, and Mrs Woodburn had made the very briefest and rudest response to her question, and had "taken off" her woe-begone looks almost to her very face. And no one had shown the least sympathy for the forsaken one. She had not even been called from her solitude to sing, which might have been something, and it was Rose, as she said to herself, who had attracted all the attention; for, like most selfish people, Barbara, though keenly aware of her own wrongs, had no eyes to perceive that Rose, who had a proud little spirit, was anything but satisfied with the evening's entertainment, to which she had herself so largely contributed. "I feel as if I should never see him more," Barbara said, quite subdued and broken down, with a burst of tears, as the two went home; and poor little Rose, who was soft-hearted, forgot all her disapprobation in sympathy. "Never mind them, dear; they have no feeling. We must cling together all the closer, and try to be everything to each other," Rose said, with eyes which were full, but which would not shed any tears. What was passing through her own mind was, that it was not for herself, but for her portfolio and the talk that arose over it, that Lucilla had asked her; but, at the same time, she said to herself, that all that was nothing in comparison to the wound of the heart under which Barbara was suffering. "Dear, never mind, we will be everything to each other," said poor little romantic Rose; and the elder sister, even in the depths of her dejection, could have given her a good shake for uttering such an absurd sentiment; for a great deal of good it would do to be everything to each other—as if that could ever replace the orange blossoms and the wedding tour, and the carriage and handsome house, which were included in the name of Cavendish! "And he was such a dear!" she said to herself in her own mind, and wept, and made her eyes redder and redder. If Mr Cavendish had known all that was going on in Carlingford that night, the chances are that he would have been most flattered by those tears which Barbara shed for him under the lamps in Grove Street; but then it is to be hoped he would not have been insensible either to the just reticence and self-restraint which, mingling with Miss Marjoribanks's suspicions, prevented her, as she herself said, even in the deepest seclusion of her own thoughts, from naming any name.

CHAPTER XIX.

But Lucilla's good luck and powers of persuasion were such that after a while she even succeeded in convincing little Rose Lake of the perfect reasonableness, and indeed necessity, of sacrificing herself to the public interests of the community. "As for enjoying it," Miss Marjoribanks said, "that is quite a different matter. Now and then perhaps for a minute one enjoys it; but that is not what I am thinking of. One owes something to one's fellow-creatures, you know; and if it made the evening go off well, I should not mind in the least to be hustled up in a corner and contradicted. To be sure, I don't remember that it ever happened to me; but then I have such luck; and I am sure I give you full leave to box the Archdeacon's ears next Thursday; or to tell him he does not know anything in the world about art," said Miss Marjoribanks, thoughtfully, with a new combination rising in her mind.

"Thank you, Lucilla," said Rose, "but I shall not come back again. I am much obliged to you. It does not do for people who have work to do. My time is all I have, and I cannot afford to waste it, especially——"

"Rose," said Miss Marjoribanks, "how are you ever to be an artist if you do not know life? That is just the very reason why you ought to go out into the world; and I don't see, for my part, that it matters whether it is pleasant or not. To practise scales all day long is anything but pleasant, but then one has to do it, you know. I don't blame you," said Lucilla, with tender condescension. "You are a dear little thing, and you don't know any better; but *I* went through Political Economy, and learnt all about that;—you don't think *I* choose it for the pleasure? But you all know what is the object of my life, and I hope I am not one to shrink from my duty," Miss Marjoribanks added. And it was difficult to reply to such a sublime declaration. Little Rose left her friend with the conviction that it was her duty, too, to sacrifice herself for the benefit of society and the advancement of art. Such were the lofty sentiments elicited naturally, as enthusiasm responds to enthusiasm, by Lucilla's self-devotion. Already, although she was not much more than twenty, she had the consoling consciousness that she had wrought a great work in Carlingford; and if Miss Marjoribanks required a little sacrifice from her assistants, she did not shrink from making the same in her own person, as has been shadowed forth in the case of Mr Cavendish, and as will yet, in the course of this history, be still more seriously and even sadly evolved.

Three weeks had passed in this way, making it still more and more visible to Lucilla how much she had lost in losing Mr Cavendish, of whom nothing as yet had been heard, when suddenly, one day, about luncheon-time, at the hour when Miss Marjoribanks was known to be at home, the drawing-room door opened without any warning, and the missing man walked in. It was thus that Lucilla herself described the unexpected apparition, which appeared to her to have dropped from the clouds. She avowed afterwards to Mrs Chiley that his entrance was so utterly unexpected, so noiseless, and without warning, that she felt quite silly, and could not tell in the least how she behaved; though the friends of Miss Marjoribanks, it is to be hoped, are too well acquainted with her promptitude of mind and action to imagine that she in any way compromised herself even under the surprise of the moment. As for Mr Cavendish, he exhibited a certain mixture of timidity and excitement which it was remarkable, and indeed rather flattering for any lady to see, in such an accomplished man of the world. Lucilla was not a person to deceive herself, nor did she want experience in such matters, as has been already shown; but it would be vain to deny that the conviction forced upon her mind by the demeanour of her visitor was that it was a man *about to propose* who thus made his unlooked-for appearance before her. She confessed afterwards to her confidential friend that he had all the signs of it in his looks and manners. "He gave that little nervous cough," Lucilla said, "and pulled his cravat *just so*, and stared into his hat as if he had it all written down there; and looked as They always look," Miss Marjoribanks added, with a touch of natural contempt. Nor was this all the change in Mr Cavendish's appearance. He had managed miraculously in his month's absence to grow the most charming little mustache and beard, which were, to be sure, slightly red, like most people's. It gleamed into Miss Marjoribanks's mind in a moment that people did such things sometimes by way of disguising themselves; but if such had been · Mr Cavendish's intention, it had utterly failed, since he seemed rather more like himself than before, in Lucilla's opinion, and certainly was more likely to attract attention, since beards were not so usual in these days. They met on the very spot where Lucilla had seen him last, with that look of insane terror on his handsome face. And the Archdeacon was still in Carlingford, if it was he who had occasioned such a panic. Mr Cavendish came in as if he had never been absent, as if he had seen Miss Marjoribanks on the previous night, and had no fear of anything in the world but of failing to please her; and Lucilla fortunately saw the nature of the position, and was not to be put out even by such an emergency. Of course, under the circumstances, to accept him was utterly out of the question; but, at the same time, Lucilla did not feel it expedient, without much more distinct information, to put a definitive and cruel negative on Mr Cavendish's hopes. As for Barbara Lake, that was a trifle not worth thinking of; and, notwithstanding that there was something rather unaccountable in his conduct, he was still the probable member for Carlingford, just, as Mrs Chiley so often said, the position which, of all others, she would have chosen for Lucilla; so that Miss Marjoribanks was not prepared, without due consideration, to bring the matter to a final end.

While Lucilla made this rapid summary of affairs and took her stand in her own mind, Mr Cavendish had taken a chair and had opened the conversation. He hoped he had not been entirely forgotten, though a fortnight's absence was a severe tax on anybody's memory——

"A fortnight!" said Miss Marjoribanks; "how happy you must have been while you have been away!—for I assure you a month is a month at Carlingford; and one does not get such ornaments in two weeks," said Lucilla, putting her hand to her chin, which made Mr Cavendish laugh, and look more nervous than ever.

"It is a souvenir of where I have been," he said. "I could imagine I had been gone two years, judging by my own feelings. I am so pleased to see that you remember how long it is. I daresay it looked a little droll running away so, but I dared not trust myself with leavetakings," Mr Cavendish said, with an air of sentiment. "I have been watching over a poor friend of mine on his sickbed. He was once very good to me, and when he sent for me I could not delay or refuse him. I found he had telegraphed for me when I got home the last Thursday evening I was here," he continued, looking Lucilla full in the face with the candour of conscious truth—though, to be sure, when people are stating a simple fact, it is seldom that they take the pains to be so particular. "I started by the night-train, and crossed the Channel while you were all fast asleep. I wonder if any one gave me a thought," continued Mr Cavendish; and it was still more and more impressed upon Lucilla that he had all the signs of a man who had come to propose.

"I cannot say about that night in particular, but I am sure a great many people have given you a thought," said Miss Marjoribanks. "We have all been wondering what had become of you, where you were, and when you were coming back. So far as I am concerned, I have missed you dreadfully," said Lucilla, with her usual openness; and she really thought for a moment that Mr Cavendish in a sudden transport was going down on his knees.

"I scarcely hoped for so much happiness," he said; and though he kept up the tone proper to good society, which might mean sport or earnest according as the occasion required, there was a certain air of gratitude and tenderness in his face which sent Lucilla's active mind a-wondering. "He is thinking of the music-stand," she said to herself, and then went on with what she was saying; for though Miss Marjoribanks had a very good opinion of herself, it had not occurred to her that Mr Cavendish was very deeply in love—with *her*, at all events.

"Ah, yes—not only for the flirting, you know, which of itself is a dreadful loss; but then you were so good in keeping the gentlemen to their duty. I missed you dreadfully—there has been nobody at all to help me," said Lucilla. Her tone was so genuinely plaintive that Mr Cavendish grew more and more moved. He put down his hat, he cleared his throat, he got up and walked to the window—evidently he was getting up his courage for the last step.

"But I heard you had some distinguished strangers here," he said, coming back to his seat without having, as it appeared, made up his mind. "My sister wrote—that is to say, I heard —I really don't remember how I got the news; a dean, or bishop, or something——?"

"Oh yes, Mr Archdeacon Beverley; he came precisely the night you went away," said Lucilla. "Didn't you see him? I thought you stayed till after he came into the room. A nice clergyman is very nice, you know; but, after all, a man who has some experience in society—and we have had no music to speak of since you went away. Poor dear Barbara has had such a bad cold. In short, we have all been at sixes and sevens; and the Archdeacon——"

"Oh, never mind the Archdeacon," said Mr Cavendish, and Miss Marjoribanks felt that he had not winced at the name, though he did glance up at her in spite of himself with a little gleam in his eyes when she mentioned Barbara Lake. Perhaps this was because he knew nothing about the Archdeacon, perhaps because he was prepared to hear the Archdeacon named. Lucilla did not give him all the benefit of the uncertainty, for she began to get a little impatient, and to wonder, if the man had come to propose, as appearances suggested, why he did not do it and get done with it?—which was a very reasonable question. This time, however, it certainly was coming. "I don't like nice clergymen," said Mr Cavendish, "especially not when it is *you* who find them so. If I could really flatter myself that you had missed me——"

"We all did," said Lucilla; "there is no compliment about it; and poor dear Barbara has had such a cold——"

"Ah!" said the unfortunate aspirant; and once more he gave a doubtful glance at Lucilla—decidedly the name of Barbara had more effect upon him than that of the Archdeacon. It seemed to damp his fire and smother the words on his lips, and he had to take another promenade to the window to recover himself. After that, however, he came back evidently wound up and determined; and his eyes, as he returned to Miss Marjoribanks's side, fell upon the music-stand by means of which she had covered his fright and flight (if it was not a mere hallucination on Lucilla's part that he had been frightened and had fled) on the night he left Carlingford. He came back with the air of a man who means to delay and deliberate no more.

"If I could flatter myself that *you* had missed me," he said; "*you*—not any one else—I might have the courage to ask——"

It was at that precise moment of all moments that Mrs Chiley, whom they had not heard coming up-stairs, though she was sufficiently audible, suddenly opened the door. Mr Cavendish, as was natural, broke off in a moment with a face which had turned crimson, and even Lucilla herself felt a little annoyed and put out, when, as in duty bound, she got up to meet and welcome her old friend. One thing was fortunate, as Miss Marjoribanks afterwards reflected, that since it was to be interrupted, it had been interrupted so early, before he could have put himself in any ridiculous attitude, for example; for at such moments it is well known that some men go down upon their knees —or at least such is the ineradicable belief of womankind. If Mr Cavendish had been on his knees—though, to tell the truth, he was not a very likely subject—the position would have been much more embarrassing. But as it was, there was an end. *He* turned back again to the window, biting his glove in the most frantic way, and taking up his hat, while *she*, always mistress of the position, advanced to the new-comer with outstretched hands.

"I know you have come to have lunch with me," said Lucilla. "You are always so nice—just when I wanted you; for, of course, I dared not have asked Mr Cavendish to go downstairs if I had been all alone."

"Mr Cavendish!" cried the old lady, with a little scream. "So he has really come back! I am so glad to see you. I can't tell you how glad I am to see you; and, I declare, with a beard! Oh, you need not blush for what I say. I am old enough to be both your grandmothers, and I am so glad to see you together again!" said Mrs Chiley, with an imprudent effusion of sentiment. And it may be imagined what the effect of this utterance was upon the suitor whose lovemaking (if he was really going to make love) was thus cut short in the bud. He coughed more than ever when he shook hands with the new-comer, and kept fast hold of his hat with that despairing grasp which is common to men in trouble. And then he kept looking at the door, as if he expected some one else to come in, or wanted to escape; and so far from following up his interrupted address by any explanatory or regretful glances, he never even looked at Lucilla, which, to be sure, struck her as odd enough.

"Miss Marjoribanks is very good," he said, "and I am very glad to see you so soon after my return, Mrs Chiley—though, of course, I should have called; but I may have to go away in a day or two; and I am afraid I cannot have the pleasure of staying to lunch."

"Oh, yes, you must stay," said Mrs Chiley; "I want to hear all about it. Go away again in a day or two? If I were Lucilla I would not let you go away. She is queen now in Carlingford, you know;—and then poor old Mr Chiltern is so ill. I hope you won't think of going away. They all say it would be such a pity if anything happened to him while you were away. Tell me where you have been, and what you have been doing all this time. We have missed you so dreadfully. And now you look quite like a military man with that beard."

"I have been nursing a sick friend—on the Continent," said Mr Cavendish; "not very cheerful work. I am sorry about Mr Chiltern, but I cannot help it. I have doubts now whether, even if he were to die, I should offer myself. I couldn't give pledges to all the shopkeepers about my opinions," said the embarrassed man; and as he spoke, he put his hat against his breast like a buckler. "I must not detain you from your lunch. Good-bye, Miss Marjoribanks; I am very sorry I can't stay."

"But, dear me, stop a minute—don't run away from us," said Mrs Chiley. "Come and talk it all over with the Colonel, there is a dear—and don't do anything rash. Good-bye, if you *will* go," said the old lady. She sat with a look of consternation in her face, looking at Miss Marjoribanks, as he made his way down-stairs. "Did I come in at a wrong time, Lucilla?" said Mrs Chiley, in distress. "Have you refused him, my dear? What is the matter? I am so dreadfully afraid I came in at the wrong time."

"Dear Mrs Chiley," said Lucilla, sweetly, "you can never come in at a wrong time; and it is just as well, on the whole, that he didn't—for I was not prepared to give him any answer. I am sure, on the contrary, it was quite providential," Miss Marjoribanks said; but it may be doubted whether Lucilla's mind perfectly corresponded to her words on this occasion, though she was so amiable about it, as Mrs Chiley afterwards said. For even when a woman has not her answer ready, she has always a certain curiosity about a proposal; and then when such a delicate matter is crushed in the bud like this, who can tell if it will ever blossom again, and find full expression? Miss Marjoribanks could not be said to be disappointed, but unquestionably she regretted a little that he had not been permitted to say out his say. As for Mrs Chiley, when she understood all the rights of it, she was afflicted beyond measure, and could not forgive herself for the unlucky part she had played.

"If you had only said you were engaged," the old lady exclaimed, "or not at home—or anything, Lucilla! You know, you need never stand on ceremony with me. No wonder he looked as if he could eat me! Poor fellow! and I daresay he has gone away with his heart full," said Mrs Chiley, with the tenderest sympathy. She could not get over it, nor eat any lunch, nor think of anything else. "Poor dear boy! He need not have been so put out with an old woman like me. He might have known if he had given me the least hint, or even a look, I would have gone away," said the kind old woman. "But you must be all the kinder to him when he comes back, Lucilla. And, my dear, if I were you, I would stay in this afternoon. He is sure to come back, and I would not keep him in pain."

"I don't think he will come back," Lucilla could not help saying; for she had a conviction that nothing more would come of it; but nevertheless she did stay in that afternoon, and received several visits, but saw nothing more of Mr Cavendish. It was rather vexatious, to tell the truth; for to see a man so near the point and not even to have the satisfaction of refusing him, is naturally aggravating to a woman. But Miss Marjoribanks had far too much philosophy as well as good sense to be vexed on that account with Mrs Chiley, who could not forgive herself, and to make up for the consequences of her unlucky visit would have done anything in the world. The old lady herself returned in the afternoon to know the result, and was doubly vexed and distressed to hear he had not come back.

"I ought to be on the Archdeacon's side, Lucilla," she said, with tears in her eyes. "I know I ought, when it was I that brought him here: but I can't help feeling for the other, my dear. He always was so nice—a great deal nicer, to my way of thinking, than Mr Beverley; not to say but that the Archdeacon is very agreeable," Mrs Chiley added, recollecting herself; for in matters of that description a woman of experience is aware that she cannot be too particular about what she says; and supposing that Mr Cavendish did not come back, it would never do to prejudice Lucilla against the other candidate. "I never blamed Mr Cavendish about that Lake girl," the old lady continued. "It was not his fault, poor young man. I know he was always devoted to you in his heart; and to think he should come here the very first place as soon as he returned! I only wish I had had one of my headaches this morning, my dear, to keep me indoors for an old Malaprop. I do indeed, Lucilla. It would have served me right, and I should not have minded the pain."

"But indeed I don't wish anything of the sort," said Miss Marjoribanks. "I would not have the best man in the world at the cost of one of those dreadful headaches of yours. It is so good of you to say so; but you know very well it is not that sort of thing I am thinking of. If I were to go off and marry just now, after all that has been done to the drawing-room and everything, I should feel as if I were swindling papa; and it is the object of my life to be a comfort to *him*."

"Yes, my dear," said Mrs Chiley, "but we must not neglect your own interest for all that. I think it is most likely he will come this evening. He has just come from the Continent, you know, where people do make calls in the evening. I meant to have asked you to come down to us, as we shall be all alone——"

"All alone? Then where is the Archdeacon?" asked Lucilla.

"He has gone out to Sir John's for a day or two, my dear," said Mrs Chiley, and she could not understand the little gleam of intelligence that shot into Lucilla's eye. "He left word with me for you that he would be sure to be back before Thursday, but seeing Mr Cavendish when I came in made me forget all about it. He would be quite distressed, poor man! if he thought I had forgotten to give you his message. I won't ask you now to come down and cheer me up a little, Lucilla. I think poor Mr Cavendish is sure to come this evening, and I will not stand in his way again. But, my dear, you must send me a little note after he has been. Now promise. I shall be quite in suspense all night."

"Dear Mrs Chiley, I don't think he will come," said Miss Marjoribanks. "For my part, I think it was providential your coming to-day—for I am sure I don't know what I should have said to him. And it is so odd the Archdeacon should be away just at this moment. I feel quite sure he will not come to-night."

"There is nothing odd about the Archdeacon," said Mrs Chiley. "It was for to-day he was asked, you know; *that* is simple enough. If you are sure that you prefer the Archdeacon, my dear——" the old lady added, with an anxious look. But Lucilla cut short the inquiry, which was becoming too serious, by bringing her kind visitor a cup of tea.

"I hope you don't think I prefer any of them," said the injured maiden. "If I had been thinking of that sort of thing, you know, I need never have come home. If they would only let one do one's duty in peace and quiet," said Lucilla, with a sigh; and, to tell the truth, both the ladies had occasion on that trying afternoon for the consolation of their cup of tea. But while they were thus refreshing themselves, a conversation of a very different kind, yet affecting the same interests, was being carried on not very far off, under the shelter of a little flowery arbour in another of the embowered gardens of Grange Lane, where the subject was just then being discussed from the other side.

CHAPTER XX.

Mr Woodburn's house, everybody admitted, was one of the nicest in Carlingford; but that was not so visible out of doors as in. He was a great amateur of flowers and fruit, and had his garden lined on each side with greenhouses, which were no doubt very fine in their way, but somewhat spoiled the garden, which had not in the least the homely, luxuriant, old-fashioned look of the other gardens, where, for the most part, the flowers and shrubs grew as if they liked it and were at home—whereas Mr Woodburn's flower-beds were occupied only by tenants-at-will; but at one corner near the house there was a little arbour, so covered up and heaped over with clematis that even the Scotch gardener had not the heart to touch it. The mass was so perfect and yet so light that it was the most perfect hiding-place imaginable; and nobody who had not been in it could have suspected that there was a possibility of getting inside. Here Mrs Woodburn and Mr Cavendish were seated on this particular afternoon; she very eager, animated, and in earnest, he silent and leaning his head on his two hands in a sort of downcast, fallen way. Mrs Woodburn had one of her lively eyes on the garden that nobody might enter unseen, and for this once was "taking off" no one, but was most emphatically and unquestionably herself.

"So you did not do it," she said. "Why didn't you do it? when you knew so much depended upon it! You know I did not wish for it myself, at first. But now since this man has come, and you have got into such a panic, and never will have the courage to face it out——"

"How can I have the courage to face it out?" said Mr Cavendish, with a groan. "It is all very easy for a woman to speak who has only to criticise other people. If you had to do it yourself——"

"Ah, if I only had!" cried the sister. "You may be sure I would not make so much fuss. After all, what is there to do? Take your place in society, which you have worked for and won as honestly as anybody ever won it, and look another man in the face who is not half so clever nor so sensible as you are. Why, what can he say? If I only could do it, you may be sure I should not lose any time."

"Yes," said Mr Cavendish, lifting his head. "To be sure,

you're a mimic—you can assume any part you like; but I am not so clever. I tell you again, the only thing I can do is to go away——"

"Run away, you mean," said Mrs Woodburn. "I should be foolish, indeed, if I were trusting to your cleverness to assume a part. My dear good brother, you would find it impossible to put yourself sufficiently in sympathy with another," cried the mimic, in the Archdeacon's very tone, with a laugh, and at the same time a little snarl of bitter contempt.

"Oh, for heaven's sake, Nelly, no foolery just now," said Mr Cavendish. "I don't understand how you can be so heartless. To mimic a man who has my position, my reputation, my very existence in his hands!"

"Have you murdered anybody?" said Mrs Woodburn, with intense scorn. "Have you robbed anybody? If you have, I can understand all this stuff. He is the very man to mimic, on the contrary. I'd like to let you see him as he was on that famous occasion when he delivered his opinions on art in Lucilla's drawing-room. Look here," said the mimic, putting one hand behind an imaginary coat-tail, and with the other holding up a visionary drawing to the light; but this was more than her audience could bear.

"I think you must have vowed to drive me crazy," cried the exasperated brother. "Put aside for once that confounded vanity of yours—as if a man had always leisure to look at you playing the fool." While he spoke in this unusual way, he got up, as was natural, and took one or two steps across the narrow space which was shut in by those luxuriant heaps of clematis; and Mrs Woodburn, for her part, withdrew her chair out of his way in equal heat and indignation.

"You have always the leisure to play the fool yourselves, you men," she said. "Vanity, indeed! as if it were not simply to show you that one can laugh at him without being stricken with thunder. But leave that if you like. You know quite well if you married Lucilla Marjoribanks that there would be no more about it. There *could* be no more about it. Why, all Grange Lane would be in a sort of way pledged to you. I don't mean to say *I* am attached to Lucilla, but you used to be, or to give yourself out for being. You flirted with her dreadfully in the winter, I remember, when those terrible Woodburns were here," she continued, with a shiver. "If you married Lucilla and got into Parliament, you might laugh at all the archdeacons in the world."

"It is very easy for a woman to talk," said the reluctant wooer again.

"I can tell you something it is not easy to do," cried his sister. "It is frightfully hard for a woman to stand by and see a set of men making a mess of things, and not to dare to say a word till all is spoiled. What is this Archdeacon, I would like to know, or what could he say? If you only would have the least courage, and look him in the face, he would be disabled. As if no one had ever heard of mistaken identity before! And in the mean time go and see Lucilla, and get her consent. I can't do that for you; but I could do a great deal of the rest, if you would only have a little pluck, and not give in like this."

"A *little* pluck, by George!" cried the unfortunate man, and he threw himself down upon his chair. "I am not in love with Lucilla Marjoribanks, and I don't want to marry her," he added, doggedly, and sat beating a tune with his fingers on the table, with but a poorly-assumed air of indifference. As for Mrs Woodburn, she regarded him with a look of contempt.

"Perhaps you will tell me who you are in love with," she said, disdainfully; "but I did not ask to be taken into your confidence in such an interesting way. What I wish to know is, whether you want a wife who will keep your position for you. I am not in the least fond of her, but she is very clever. Whether you want the support of all the best people in Carlingford, and connections that would put *all that* to silence, and a real position of your own which nobody could interfere with,—that is what I want to know, Harry; as for the sentimental part, I am not so much interested about that," said Mrs Woodburn, with a contemptuous smile. She was young still, and she was handsome in her way (for people who liked that style), and it jarred a little on the natural feelings to hear a young wife express herself so disdainfully; but, to be sure, her brother was not unaccustomed to that.

"You said once that Woodburn was necessary to your happiness," he said, with a mixture of scorn and appeal, "though I can't say I saw it, for my part."

"Did I?" she said, with a slight shrug of her shoulders; "I saw what was necessary on another score, as you don't seem to do. When a man has nobody belonging to him, it is connections he ought to try for: and Lucilla has very good connections; and it would be as good as securing the support of Grange Lane. Do it for my sake, Harry, if you won't do it for your own," said Mrs Woodburn, with a change of tone. "If you were to let things be said, and give people an advantage, think what would become of me. Woodburn would not mind so much if somebody else were involved; but oh, Harry! if he should find out *he* had been cheated, and he only——"

"He was not cheated! You were always a great deal too good for him, Nelly," said Mr Cavendish, touched at last at an effectual point; "and as for *his* friends and family, and all that——"

"Oh, please, don't speak of them," said Mrs Woodburn, with a shudder; "but there are only two of us in the world; and, Harry, for my sake——"

At this appeal Mr Cavendish got up again, and began to pace the little arbour, two steps to the wall, and two steps back again. "I told you I had almost done it, when that confounded old woman came in," he said: "that could not be called my fault?"

"And she said she was both your grandmothers," said the mimic, with a slightly hysterical laugh, in Mrs Chiley's voice. "I know how she did it. She can't be there still, you know—go now and try."

"Let alone a little; don't hurry a fellow," said her brother, somewhat sullenly; "a man can't move himself up to the point of proposing twice in one day."

"Then promise that you will do it to-morrow," said Mrs Woodburn. "I shall have to go in, for there is somebody coming. Harry, before I go, promise that you will do it to-morrow, for my sake."

"Oh, bother!" said Mr Cavendish; and it was all the answer he deigned to give before Mrs Woodburn was called away, notwithstanding the adjuration she addressed to him. It was then getting late, too late, even had he been disposed for such an exertion, to try his fortunes again that day, and Lucilla's allusion had given him a great longing to see Barbara once more before his sacrifice was accomplished. Not that it was such a great sacrifice, after all. For Mr Cavendish was quite aware that Miss Marjoribanks was a far more suitable match for him than Barbara Lake, and he was not even disposed to offer himself and his name and fortune, such as they were, to the drawing-master's daughter. But, to tell the truth, he was not a person of fixed and settled sentiments, as he ought to have been in order to triumph, as his sister desired, over the difficulties of his position. Perhaps Mrs Woodburn herself would have done just the same, had it been she from whom action was demanded. But she was capable of much more spirited and determined conduct in theory, as was natural, and thought she could have done a great deal better, as so many women do.

Mr Cavendish lounged about the garden a little, with his hands in his pockets, and then strayed out quite accidentally, and in the same unpremeditating mood made his way to Grove Street. He meant nothing by it, and did not even inquire of himself where he was going, but only strolled out to take the air a little. And it was better to go up to the higher parts of the town than to linger here about Grange Lane, where all the people he knew might pass, and stop to talk and ask him where he had been, and worry his life out. And surely he had had enough of bother for one day. By this time it was getting dark, and it was very pleasant in Grove Street, where most of the good people had just watered their little gardens, and brought out the sweetness of the mignonette. Mr Cavendish was not sentimental, but still the hour was not without its influence; and when he looked at the lights that began to appear in the parlour-windows, and breathed in the odours from the little gardens, it is not to be denied that he asked himself for a moment what was the good of going through all this bother and vexation, and whether love in a cottage, with a little garden full of mignonette and a tolerable amount of comfort within, was not, after all, a great deal more reasonable than it looked at first sight? This, however, it must be allowed, was no conclusion arrived at on sufficient premises, and with the calmness that befitted such an important argument, but the mere suggestion, by the way, of an impatient, undecided mind, that did always what at the moment it found most agreeable to do, and reflected afterwards, when the moment of repentance, not of reflection, had arrived.

He had paused by instinct under a lamp not yet lighted, which was almost opposite Mr Lake's house; and it was not his fault if he saw at the upper window a figure looking out, like Mariana, and sighing, "He cometh not." Naturally the figure was concerned to find out who he was, and *he* was anxious to find out who was the figure. And, on the whole, it was in a very innocent manner that this entirely natural curiosity was satisfied. First the window was opened a little—a very little, just enough to change the air—and Mr Cavendish down below heard the voice of Barbara singing softly up above, which settled the matter as to her identity. As to *his*, Barbara had never, from the first moment she perceived him, had any doubt of that. Her heart leaped back, as she thought, to its right place when she first caught sight of that blessed apparition; and with her heart came the orange-flowers, and the wedding breakfast, and the veil of real Brussels for which Barbara had so much wept. She tried to sing something that would convey hope and assurance to her timid lover, according to romantic precedent; but her mind was far from being a prompt one, as has been said. Thus it was all in the most natural way that it came about. When Mr Cavendish felt quite sure who it was, he took off his hat, which was only civil, and made a step or two forward; and then Barbara took the extreme step of going down to the door. No doubt it was an extreme step. Nothing but a great public aim, like that of Miss Marjoribanks, could have justified such a measure; but then Barbara, if she had not a great public, had at least a decided personal purpose, and obeyed the impulse of that mingled inclination towards another and determination to have her own way, which in such a mind calls itself passion, and which sometimes, by sheer force of will, succeeds better than either genius or calculation. She went down to the door, all palpitating with renewed hope, and, at the same time, with the dread that he might escape her in the moment which was necessary for her passage down-stairs. But when she opened the door, and appeared with her cheeks glowing, and her eyes blazing, and her heart thumping in her breast, in the midst of that quiet twilight, the object of her hopes was still there. He had even advanced a little, with an instinctive sense of her approach; and thus they met, the street being comparatively quiet just then, and the mignonette perfuming the air. To be sure, the poetry of the situation was of a homely order, for it was under a lamp-post instead of a tree that the lover had placed himself; and it was not the dew, but the watering, that had brought out the odour of the mignonette; but then neither of the two were very poetical personages, and the accessories did perfectly well for them.

"Is it you, Mr Cavendish? Goodness! I could not think who it was," cried Barbara, out of breath.

"Yes, it is I. I thought, if I had an opportunity, I would ask how you were—before I go away again," said the imprudent man. He did not want to commit himself, but at the same time he was disposed to take the benefit of his position as a hero on the eve of departure. "I heard you had been ill."

L

"Oh, no—not ill," said Barbara; and then she added, taking breath, "I am quite well now. Won't you come in?"

This was the perfectly simple and natural manner in which it occurred. There was nobody in, and Barbara did not see, any more than her lover did, why she should sacrifice any of her advantages. They were, on the whole, quite well matched, and stood in need of no special protection on either side. Though naturally Barbara, who felt by this time as if she could almost see the pattern of the real Brussels, had a much more serious object in view than Mr Cavendish, who went in only because it was a pleasant thing to do at the moment, and offered him a little refuge from himself and his deliberations, and the decision which it was so necessary to come to. Thus it happened that when Mr Lake and Rose came in from the evening walk they had been taking together, they found, to their great amazement, Barbara in the little parlour, singing to Mr Cavendish, who had forgotten all about Grange Lane, and his dangers, and his hopes of better fortune, and was quite as much contented with the mellow contralto that delighted his ears, and the blazing scarlet bloom, and black level brows that pleased his eyes, as anybody could have desired. To be sure, he had not even yet given a thought to the wedding breakfast, which was all arranged already in the mind of the enchantress who thus held him in thrall; but perhaps that may be best accounted for by referring it to one of those indefinable peculiarities of difference that exist between the mind of woman and that of man.

When Mr Lake and his daughter came in from their walk, and their talk about Willie, and about art, and about the "effects" and "bits" which Rose and her father mutually pointed out to each other, to find this unexpected conjunction in the parlour, their surprise, and indeed consternation, may be imagined. But it was only in the mind of Rose that the latter sentiment existed. As for Mr Lake, he had long made up his mind how, as he said, "a man of superior position" ought to be received when he made his appearance in an artist's house. Perhaps, to tell the truth, he forgot for the moment that his visitor was young, and his daughter very handsome, and that it was to visit Barbara and not himself that Mr Cavendish had come. The little drawing-master would not suffer himself to be seduced by thoughts which were apart from the subject from carrying out his principles. When Mr Cavendish rose up confused, with a look of being caught and found out, Mr Lake held out his hand to him with perfect suavity—"I have the pleasure of knowing you only by sight," said the innocent father, "but I am very glad to make your acquaintance in my own house;" and as this was said with the conscious dignity of a man who knows that his house is not just an ordinary house, but one that naturally the patrician portion of the community, if they only knew it, would be glad to seek admittance to, the consequence was that Mr Cavendish felt only the more and more confused.

"I happened to be passing," he explained faintly, "and having heard that Miss Lake, whom I have had the pleasure of meeting——"

"I assure you," said the drawing-master, "that I hail with satisfaction the appearance of a gentleman whose intelligence I have heard so much of. We artists are a little limited, to be sure; for life, you know, is short, and art is long, as the poet says; and our own occupation requires so much of our thoughts. But still we are sympathetic, Mr Cavendish. We can understand other subjects of study, though we cannot share them. Yes, Barbara has been a little poorly—but she does not look as if there was much the matter with her to-night. Ask for the lamp, Rose," said Mr Lake, with a little grandeur. There was no light in the room except the candles at the piano, which lighted that corner and left the rest of the apartment, small as it was, in comparative shade. There was something magnificent in the idea of adding the lamp to that illumination; but then it is true that, as Mr Lake himself said, "every artist is a prodigal in his heart."

Rose had been standing all this time with her hat on, looking at Mr Cavendish like a little Gorgon. What did he want here? How had he been admitted? She scorned to go and interrogate the maid, which involved a kind of infidelity to her sister, but all the same she looked hard at Mr Cavendish with a severity which had on the whole a reassuring effect upon him. For, to tell the truth, the benign reception which he was receiving from Mr Lake, instead of setting the visitor at his ease, made him nervous; for he was not in the least aware of the heroic soul which existed in the drawing-master's limited person. Mr Cavendish thought nothing but that he was being "caught," according to his own vulgar theory. He thought Barbara's father was cringing to him, and playing the usual mean part of an interested parent who means to secure a good match for his daughter. But as for Rose, she evidently, either from jealousy or some other reason, was not in the plot. She stood apart and scowled, as well as she knew how, upon the intruder. "I suppose, papa," said Rose, "Mr Cavendish wished to hear Barbara sing, and she has been singing. She is always very good-natured in that way; but as we have none of us anything particular to do, I don't see what need we have for a lamp."

At this trenchant speech Mr Cavendish rose. He was quite grateful to the little Preraphaelite for her incivility. It made him feel less as if he had committed himself, and more as if he were an intruder, which was the more agreeable suggestion of the two under the present circumstances. "You remind me that I should thank Miss Lake for letting me come in and hear once more her lovely voice," he said. "I am at present only a visitor in Carlingford, and indeed in England—I may have to leave again in a day or two—good-bye. If I am still here, I shall hope to meet you on Thursday." And then he pressed Barbara's hand, who, to tell the truth, was very reluctant to let him go away.

"If you must go——" she said, so low that her father could not hear her, though the vigilant suspicious little Rose caught the sound, and came a step nearer, like a little dragon, as Barbara was disposed to think she was.

"I *must* go," murmured Mr Cavendish; "but I shall see you—we shall meet." He dared not say another word, so alarming were the looks of the small Medusa, whose countenance he could see behind Barbara regarding the parting. As for Mr Lake, he too regarded it with a momentary curiosity. He did not quite understand how it was that his daughter and his visitor could know each other well enough to communicate in this undertone.

"I am sorry to see so little of you," said Mr Lake. "I am afraid it is my little girl's *brusque* way of speaking that hastens your going. I assure you we were quite unoccupied, and would have been very happy—perhaps we may be more fortunate another time;" and with that the drawing-master gave a dignified dismissal to his surprising visitor. It was Rose herself who saw Mr Cavendish to the door, which she opened for him with an utter disregard of his excuses and attempts to do that office for himself. She would not even shake hands, but made him the most majestic curtsy that was ever executed by a personage five feet high, under the influence of which Mr Cavendish went away humbled, and, he could scarcely tell why, ashamed of himself. When Rose came back to the parlour, still with her hat on, she found that Barbara had gone to the window, and was looking out at the edge of the blind—which was all that was wanted to put a climax to her sister's exasperation.

"Papa," said Rose, "I should like to know in your presence, or I should like you to ask Barbara herself, what is the meaning of all that has been going on to-night?"

Mr Lake turned right round at this appeal with an expression of utter amaze and bewilderment, which at another moment would have struck Rose with the profoundest delight as a study; and as for Barbara, without any more ado she burst into a flood of passionate tears.

"Oh, you nasty envious thing! oh, you jealous, disagreeable thing!" sobbed the elder sister; "to send him away and spoil everything with your airs! when he was as near—just as near"—but here Barbara's voice lost itself in her tears.

"My dear, what does this mean?" said Mr Lake.

"It means, papa, that she has encouraged him to come, and invited him in, and been singing to him," cried Rose. "To think she should be one of us, and have no proper pride! If he was fond of her, he would tell her so, and ask your permission; but she is laying herself out to please *him*, and is content that they should all jeer at her in Lucilla's parties, and say she is trying to catch him. I thought I could have died of shame when I saw him here to-night; and compromising you, as if that was why you were so civil. If it were for her good, do you think *I* would ever interfere?" cried Barbara's guardian angel. At this point Rose herself would have liked excessively to cry, if the truth must be told; but Barbara had already appropriated that facile mode of expression, and the little artist scorned to copy. As for Mr Lake, he turned from one to the other of his daughters with unmitigated consternation and dismay.

"It was all your coming in," sobbed Barbara, "if you had only had the sense to see it. *That* was what he meant. If I was singing, it was just to pass the time; I know that was what he came for. And you to send him away with your airs!" cried the injured young woman. All this made up a scene entirely novel to the amazed father, who felt it his duty to put a stop to it, and yet could not tell what to say.

"Girls," he began with a trembling voice, "this is all perfectly new to me. I don't understand. If Mr Cavendish, or—or any one, wishes to pay his addresses to my daughter, it is, of course, his business to apply to me in the first place. Barbara, don't cry. You know how I dislike to hear you cry," said the poor man, gradually losing his head. "Don't make a fuss, Rose; for heaven's sake, girls, can't you say at once what you mean, and don't worry me to death? Ah, if your poor mother had but been spared!" cried the unfortunate widower; and he had five daughters altogether, poor soul!—and it was so easy to drive him out of his senses. At this point Rose intervened, and did what she could to calm matters down. Barbara, still sobbing, retired to her chamber; the boys came in from their cricket, and the little children had to be put to bed; and there was no one to attend to all these matters, in the absence of the eldest sister, except the little mistress of the School of Design, so that naturally all further explanation was postponed for this night.

CHAPTER XXI.

IT was thus that Mr Cavendish, without particularly meaning it, impressed upon two interesting and amiable young women on the same day the conviction that he was about to propose, without in either case realising that expectation. After this last exploit he went home with his head more confused, and his will more undecided, than ever. For he had one of those perverse minds which cling to everything that is forbidden; and the idea that he ought not to have gone near Barbara Lake, and that he ought not to see her again, made him more anxious to seek her out and follow her than he had ever been before. If such a thing had been permissible in England as that a man might marry one wife for his liking and another for his interests, the matter might have been compromised by proposing to them both; and there cannot be a doubt that Lucilla, in such a case, would very soon have triumphed over her handsome, sullen, passionate rival. But then such a way of conciliating a man with himself does not exist in the British Islands, and consequently was not to be thought of. And to be sure, every time he came to think of it, Mr Cavendish saw more and more clearly what a fool he would be to marry Barbara, who was evidently so ready to marry him. The same thing could not with any confidence be predicated of Miss Marjoribanks, though, if she were to accept him, and her father were to consent, nothing could be better for his interests. All this he felt, and yet an unconquerable reluctance kept him back. His history was not quite spotless, and there were chapters in it which he thought it would kill him to have brought before the public of Carlingford; but still he was far from being a bad fellow in his way. And down at the bottom of his heart, out of everybody's sight, and unacknowledged even by himself, there was one little private nook full of gratitude to Lucilla. Though he scarcely knew what was passing at the moment, he knew, when he came to think of it, that she had saved him from the effects of his first panic at the unexpected appearance of Mr Beverley. Perhaps it was partly this consciousness that made him so embarrassed in her presence; and he could not find it in his heart, with this sense of gratitude, to deceive her, and say he loved her, and ask her to marry him. To be sure, if Mr Cavendish had been a very acute observer, he might have felt that Lucilla was quite able to take care of herself in such an emergency, and was at the least a match for him, however seductive he might appear to others; but then, few people are acute observers in a matter so entirely personal to themselves.

He felt furious with himself as he went home, and thought how foolish he had been ever to go near Barbara Lake in the present position of affairs; and yet he could not help feeling that it was more delightful to him to see the colour blaze into her cheeks, and the song rise like a bird from her full crimson lips, and that flush of excitement and triumph come from her eyes, than it could have been in any case to have been admitted to the same degree of intimacy with Lucilla, who was not in the least intoxicated by his presence. Thus the unfortunate man was torn asunder, not so much by love and duty, as by inclination and interest, though the inclination was not strong enough to have allowed of any great sacrifice, nor the interest sufficiently certain to have repaid the exertion. This only made it the more difficult to decide; and in his circumstances, and with the panic that pursued him, he did not feel it possible to adopt the only wise policy that remained to him, and wait.

As Mr Cavendish was thus making his way home, horribly vexed and annoyed with himself, and avoiding Grange Lane as if the plague was in it, Miss Marjoribanks sat in her drawing-room alone, and thought the matter over. Certainly she had not expected him that evening, but still, when she heard ten o'clock strike, and felt that his coming was now absolutely impossible, she was a little—not exactly disappointed, but annoyed at herself for having felt a sort of expectation. Lucilla was not a person to hide her sentiments, or even to conceal a fact which was disagreeable to her *amour propre*. She had too thorough and well-founded a confidence in the natural interest of the world in all belonging to her to do that; so when ten o'clock had done striking, she opened her blotting-book and took one of her pretty sheets of paper, with L^{ucilla} on it in delicate rose-tinted letters, the L very large, and the concluding letters very small, and dashed off her note to Mrs Chiley. The Miss Blounts' at Mount Pleasant had been one of the very first establishments to forsake the handwriting which was all corners, in favour of the bold running hand of the present female generation; and it was accordingly in a very free and strongly-characterised manuscript, black with much ink, that Miss Marjoribanks wrote—

"DEAREST MRS CHILEY,—I never expected him to come, and he has not. I daresay he never meant it. I am so glad. It was Providence that sent you at that particular moment to-day.—Always in haste, with fond love, your most truly affectionate LUCILLA."

And when she had sent Thomas with this note, Miss Marjoribanks felt her mind relieved. Not that it had been much distressed before, but when she had put it in black and white, and concluded upon it, her satisfaction was more complete; and no such troublous thoughts as those which disturbed the hero of this day's transactions—no such wild tears as poured from the eyes of Barbara Lake—interfered with the maidenly composure of Lucilla's meditations. Notwithstanding all that people say to the contrary, there is a power in virtue which makes itself felt in such an emergency. Miss Marjoribanks could turn from Mr Cavendish, who had thus failed to fulfil the demands of his position, to the serene idea of the Archdeacon, with that delightful consciousness of having nothing to reproach herself with, which is balm to a well-regulated mind. She had done her duty, whatever happened. She had not injudiciously discouraged nor encouraged the possible Member for Carlingford; and at the same time she was perfectly free to turn her attention to the possible Bishop; and neither in one case nor the other could anybody say that she had gone a step too far, or committed herself in any way whatsoever. While these consoling reflections were passing through Lucilla's mind, Dr Marjoribanks came up-stairs, as had grown to be his custom lately. Sometimes he took a cup of tea, though it was against his principles, and sometimes he only sat by while his daughter had hers, and amused himself with her chat before he went to bed. He was later than usual to-night, and naturally the tea-tray had disappeared some time before. As for Lucilla, she did not for a moment permit her-own preoccupation to interfere with the discharge of her immediate duty, which was unquestionably to be amusing and agreeable, and a comfort to her dear papa.

"So you had Cavendish here to-day?" said the Doctor. "What brought him here? What has he been doing? Since you and he are on such good terms, I hope he gave you an account of where he has been."

"He has been nursing a sick friend on—the Continent," said Lucilla, with that largeness of geographical expression which is natural to the insular mind. "Who are Mr Cavendish's friends, papa?" added Miss Marjoribanks, with confiding simplicity; and it was beautiful to see how the daughter looked up into her father's face, with that angelic confidence in his knowledge on all subjects which is so rarely to be met with in the present generation. But it was not a question to which the Doctor found it easy to respond.

"Who are his friends?" said Dr Marjoribanks. "He's one of the Cavendishes, they say. We have all heard that. I never knew he had any friends; which is, after all, next best to having very good ones," said the philosophical old Scotchman; and there, as it appeared, he was quite content to let the matter drop.

"I like to know who people belong to, for my part," said Lucilla. "The Archdeacon, for example, one knows all about his friends. It's a great deal nicer, you know, papa. Not that it matters in the least about the Cavendishes——"

"Well, I should have thought not, after the way you made an end of him," said the Doctor. "I hope he doesn't mean to begin that nonsense over again, Lucilla. He is a good fellow enough, and I don't mind asking him to my house; but it is quite a different thing to give him my daughter. He spends too much money, and I can't see what real bottom he has. It may all flare up and come to nothing any day. Nobody can have any certainty with an expensive fellow like that," said Dr Marjoribanks. "There is no telling where he draws his income from ; it isn't from land, and it isn't from business ; and if it's money in the Funds——"

"Dear papa," said Lucilla, "if he had the Bank of England, it would not make any difference to me. I am not going to swindle you, after you have had the drawing-room done up, and everything. I said ten years, and I mean to keep to it,—if nothing very particular happens," Miss Marjoribanks added prudently. "Most likely I shall begin to go off a little in ten years. And all I think of just now is to do my duty, and be a little comfort to you."

Dr Marjoribanks indulged in a faint "humph," under his breath, as he lighted his candle; for, as has been already said, he was not a man to feel so keenly as some men might have felt the enthusiasm of filial devotion which beautified Lucilla's life. But at the same time he had that respect for his daughter's genius, which only experience could have impressed upon him; and he did not venture, or rather he did not think it necessary, to enter into any further explanations. Dr Marjoribanks did not in the least degree share the nervousness of Mr Cavendish, who was afraid of deceiving Lucilla. As for her father, he felt a consoling conviction that she was quite able to conduct her own affairs, and would do him no discredit in any engagements she might form. And at the same time he was amused by the idea that he might be swindled in respect to the drawing-room, if she married at this early moment. He took it for wit, when it was the most solid and sensible reality; but then, fortunately, the points in which he misapprehended her redounded as much to Lucilla's credit, as those in which he seized her meaning clearest, so that on every side there was something gained.

And when Miss Marjoribanks too retired to her maidenly chamber, a sentiment of general content and satisfaction filled her mind. It is true that for the moment she had experienced a natural womanly vexation to see a proposal nipped in the bud. It annoyed her not so much on personal as on general principles; for Lucilla was aware that nothing could be more pernicious to a man than when thus brought to the very point to be thrown back again, and never permitted to produce that delicate bloom of his affections. It was like preventing a rose from putting forth its flowers, a cruelty equally prejudicial to the plant and to the world. But when this pang of wounded philanthropy was over, Miss Marjoribanks felt in her heart that it was Providence that had sent Mrs Chiley at that special moment. There was no telling what embarrassments, what complications she might not have got into, had Mr Cavendish succeeded in unbosoming himself. No doubt Lucilla had a confidence that, whatever difficulties there might have been, she would have extricated herself from them with satisfaction and even *éclat*, but still it was better to avoid the necessity. Thus it was with a serene conviction that "whatever is, is best," that Miss Marjoribanks betook herself to her peaceful slumbers. There are so many people in the world who hold, or are tempted to hold, an entirely different opinion, that it is pleasant to linger over the spectacle of a mind so perfectly well regulated. Very different were the sentiments of Mr Cavendish, who could not sleep for the ghosts that kept tugging at him on every side; and those of Barbara Lake, who felt that for her too the flower of her hero's love had been nipped in the bud. But, to be sure, it is only natural that goodness and self-control should have the best of it sometimes even in this uncertain world.

CHAPTER XXII.

THE Archdeacon returned to Carlingford before Thursday, as he had anticipated; but in the interval Mr Cavendish had not recovered his courage so far as to renew his visit to Miss Marjoribanks, or to face the man who had alarmed him so much. Everybody in Grange Lane remarked at the time how worried poor Mrs Woodburn looked. Her eyes lost their brightness, which some people thought was the only beauty she had, and her nerves and her temper both failed her, no one could tell why. The personal sketches she made at this moment were truculent and bitter to an unheard-of degree. She took off Mr Beverley with a savage force which electrified her audience, and put words into his mouth which everybody admitted were exactly like him, if he could ever be imagined to have fallen into the extraordinary circumstances in which the mimic placed him. In short, Mrs Woodburn made a little drama out of the Archdeacon. Mr Beverley, of course, knew nothing about this, and showed some surprise now and then at the restrained laughter which he heard in the corners; but when anybody spoke of Mrs Woodburn, he showed an instinctive want of confidence. "I have not studied her sufficiently to give an opinion of her," he said, which was certainly the very reverse of her deliverance upon him. To tell the truth, she had rather studied him too much, and gave too keen an edge to his characteristic qualities, as is natural to all literary portraiture, and even went so far that, in the end, people began to ask whether she had any personal spite against him.

"She don't know him," Mr Woodburn said, when he heard some faint echo of this suggestion. "She's clever, and it carries her away, you know. She enters into it so, she don't know how far she is going; but I can answer for it she never saw the Archdeacon before; and Hal isn't here to give her the key-note, as she says. *He* has met everybody, I believe, one place or another," the simple man said, with a little natural pride; for in his heart he was vain of his fashionable brother-in-law. As for Mr Cavendish himself, it began to be understood that he was with a friend who was sick, on the Continent; and soon—for news had a wonderful tendency to increase and grow bigger as it spread in Grange Lane—that his friend was dying, and that a probable large increase of fortune to the popular favourite would be the result, which was an idea that did credit to the imagination of Carlingford. He had disappeared completely once more after the eventful day which we have described, carrying out in the fullest way Lucilla's prediction, but striking Barbara Lake with bitter disappointment. Miss Marjoribanks had a great many things to occupy her, but Barbara had nothing except the humble duty of looking after her little brothers and sisters, and attending to her father's comfort, which had never been occupations particularly to her mind. And then Barbara was aware that, if she neglected her duties, Rose, on her return from the School of Design, would do them, though with a fierce little outbreak of indignation, which the elder sister felt she could bear; and accordingly, she did little else but brood over his sudden disappearance, and spend her time at the window looking for his return.

Lucilla conducted herself, as might have been expected, in a much more rational and dignified manner. She made herself very agreeable to the Archdeacon, who unbended very much, and grew very nice, as Mrs Chiley herself allowed. "But, my dear, I am uneasy about his opinions," the old lady said. He certainly had a very free way of talking, and was ready to discuss *anything*, and was not approved of by Mr Bury. But still he had very good connections and a nice position, and had always a chance of being Bishop of Carlingford; and in marriage it is well known that one never can have everything one wants. So that, on the whole, even Mrs Chiley did not see what difference his opinions made, so far as Lucilla was concerned. When Miss Marjoribanks went down to Colonel Chiley's in the evening and made tea for the old people, like a daughter of the house, Mr Beverley was always disposed to go over to the enemy, as the old Colonel said. No doubt he had enough of Colonel Chiley, who had not received a new idea into his mind since the battle of Waterloo, and did not see what people had to do with such nonsense. And then the Archdeacon would very often walk home with the young visitor. During this time, as was natural, Mr Beverley heard Mr Cavendish's name a hundred times, and regretted, like all the world, that so eminent a member of the Carlingford commonwealth should be absent during his visit; but, at the same time, Lucilla took great care to avoid all personalities, and kept a discreet silence even about the gifts and accomplishments of her almost-lover. Mrs Chiley sighed, poor soul, when she saw how her young friend avoided this subject, and thought sometimes that he was forgotten, sometimes that the poor dear was breaking her heart for him; but it is needless to say that neither of these suppositions was in the least true.

And then it began to be considered rather odd in Carlingford that the Archdeacon should pay such a long visit. Mrs Chiley no doubt was very kind and hospitable, and exceedingly glad to receive such a distinguished clergyman; but when a man has been six weeks in any one's house, and shows no inclination of going, it is natural that people should feel a little surprised. His visitation was over, and he had dined with everybody, and studied the place and its characteristics, and entered into everything that was going on. The only thing, indeed, that he did not seem to think of, was going away. If it had been Mr Cavendish, the chances are that he would have made himself so much one of the family, that his departure would have been felt as a domestic calamity; but the Archdeacon was very different from Mr Cavendish. So long as he was in the house it was impossible to forget either his position or his ways of thinking, or the absence of any real connection between himself and his hosts. He did not combat or contradict anybody, but he would give a faint smile when the Colonel uttered his old-fashioned sentiments, which drove the old soldier frantic. "As if I was not able to form an opinion, by Jove!" Colonel Chiley said; while, on the other hand, the Archdeacon was quite ready to enter into the young people's absurd theories, and discuss the very Bible itself, as if that were a book to be discussed. As for the Rector, he turned his head away when he passed Colonel Chiley's door, and Miss Bury made visits of condolence and sympathy. "You must feel it a great responsibility having Mr Beverley with you," the Rector's sister would say, though naturally without any distinct explanation of her meaning; and then she would look at Mrs Chiley and sigh.

"Oh, I am sure it is a great pleasure," Mrs Chiley answered, not willing to let down the *prestige* of her guest. "He is very nice, and takes a great deal of interest in everything; and then, you know, he is a connection of ours. The Colonel's niece, Mary Chiley——"

"Yes, I know," said Miss Bury. "Poor thing! she looked suffering the last time I saw her. I hope she has found the true consolation to support her, now she has entered into the troubles of life."

"Well, yes, I hope so," said Mrs Chiley, a little doubtfully; "but you know one does not feel the troubles of life very severely at her age; and I don't think I should have called a baby a trouble when I was like her. I never had any, you know, and I used to fret over it a great deal; but the Colonel never liked the noise of children, and I suppose it is all for the best."

"One may always be sure of that," said Miss Bury, in her instructive way. "I suppose the Archdeacon is going soon," she added; "he has been here a long time now. I almost wonder he likes to be so long absent from his parish. Two months, is it not?"

"Oh, no—not quite six weeks," said Mrs Chiley, briskly. "I hope he may be persuaded to stay some time longer. I look upon it as quite a compliment to Carlingford; for, to be sure, he would not stay if he had not some attraction," said the imprudent old woman. And this was precisely what Miss Bury wanted, as any one of acute perceptions might have seen from the first.

"It must be a great responsibility for you," said the Rector's sister, with a sigh, pressing Mrs Chiley's hand. "If it should turn out badly, you know——. Of course, my brother and I don't agree with Mr Beverley on all points—though I am sure I hope he is quite conscientious; but I do feel for you with such a responsibility," said Miss Bury, with a look that made the old lady nervous in spite of herself. Thus, notwithstanding all her sense of the duties of hospitality, and her anxiety about Lucilla's interests, she could not but feel that it would be rather a relief to get so formidable a guest fairly out of the house. It is uncomfortable, it must be allowed, to entertain in your house anybody, particularly a clergyman of whom your Rector does not approve; and there could be no doubt that the Archdeacon was not like the clergymen that Mrs Chiley had been accustomed to. "And he could come back another time," she said to herself, by way of conciliating her own weariness with her visitor's advantage and the interests of Lucilla. But notwithstanding these reflections on Mrs Chiley's part, and notwithstanding the Colonel's less amiable growl, uttered every morning—"Does that parson of yours never mean to go away?" —the Archdeacon showed no intention of budging. It was poor Mrs Chiley who had all the brunt to bear, to exhaust herself in civilities and to be upbraided with "that parson of yours"— whereas he was not in the least her parson, nor even the kind of man she approved of as a clergyman. All this, however, the brave old woman bore with fortitude for Lucilla's sake: certainly it must be Lucilla who kept him in Carlingford—if it were not something else.

Things were in this condition, Mr Cavendish having again disappeared into utter darkness, and Carlingford beginning to enter warmly into the question whether or not Mr Beverley was paying attention to Lucilla, when it happened to Miss Marjoribanks one morning to meet the Archdeacon in a little lane running between Grove Street and Grange Lane. Opening from this lane was a little door in the wall, which admitted to a little garden very bright with flowers of the simplest old-fashioned kinds, with a little house planted at its extremity, which had pretensions to be an old-fashioned and quasi-rural cottage, on the score of being very rickety, uncomfortable, and badly arranged. But it must be a very impracticable erection indeed which does not look tolerable under the bright sunshine on a summer noon, at the end of a pretty garden where children are playing and birds singing, and a woman or two about. Lucilla was standing at the door of this little closed-up hermitage, almost filling up the opening with her crisp summer draperies, and affording only a very partial and tempting glimpse of its flowers and shrubs and whitewashed walls inside; and when Mr Beverley came up to Miss Marjoribanks he felt his curiosity excited. "Is it Armida's garden, or the Elysian fields?" said the Archdeacon; and he made a dead stop before the door, not knowing any more than any other blind mortal what he was going to find inside.

"I don't know anything about Armida," said Miss Marjoribanks; "unfortunately they were all Cambridge in their ways of thinking at Mount Pleasant, and our classics got dreadfully neglected. But you may come in if you like—at least I think you may come in, if you will promise not to frighten the children. I am sure they never saw an Archdeacon in their lives."

"Are there children?" said Mr Beverley, with a doubtful air; for, to tell the truth, he had come to the age at which men think it best to avoid children, unless, indeed, they happen to have a personal interest in them; and he stretched his neck a little to see in over Miss Marjoribanks's head.

"There are a whole lot of children, and a pretty governess," said Lucilla. "It is a school, and I am so much interested in it. I may call it my school, for that matter. I came to know her in the funniest way; but I will tell you that another time. And it was just my luck, as usual. She is so nice, and quite a lady. If you will not say you are an Archdeacon, to frighten the children, I will let you come in."

"You shall call me whatever you like," said Mr Beverley; "when I am with the lady-patroness, what does it matter what I call myself? Let me see how you manage your educational department. I have already bowed before your genius in the other branches of government; but this ought to be more in my own way."

"I don't think you care for visiting schools," said Lucilla. "I know you think it is a bore; but she is so nice, and so nice-looking; I am sure you will be pleased with her. I am quite sure she is a lady, and has seen better days."

"Oh, those dreadful women that have seen better days!" said the Archdeacon; "I think Mrs Chiley has a regiment of them. It is hard to know how to get one's self into sympathy with those faded existences. They fill me with an infinite pity; but then what can one do? If one tries to recall them to the past, it sounds like mockery—and if one speaks of the present, it wounds their feelings. It is a great social difficulty," said Mr Beverley; and he fixed his eyes on the ground and entered meditatively, without looking where he was going, in his Broad-Church way.

"Dear Mrs Chiley is so kind," said Lucilla, who was a little puzzled for the moment, and did not know what to say.

"Mrs Chiley is a good, pure, gentle woman," said the Archdeacon. He spoke in a tone which settled the question, and from which there was no appeal; and no doubt what he said was perfectly true, though it was not a very distinct characterisation. Thus they went in together into the bright little garden, thinking of nothing particular, and loitering as people do who do not know what is coming. There was something that morning in Mr Beverley's tone and manner which struck Lucilla as something more than usual. She was not a young woman to attach undue importance to looks and tones; but the Archdeacon's manner was so softened and mellowed, and his eyes had so much expression in them, and he looked at Lucilla with such marked regard, that it was impossible for her not to recognise that a crisis might be approaching. To be sure, it was not by any means so near as that crisis *manqué* which had so lately passed over her head in respect to Mr Cavendish. But still Miss Marjoribanks could not but remark the signs of a slowly-approaching and most likely more important climax; and as she remarked it, Lucilla naturally by anticipation prepared herself for the coming event that thus threw a shadow upon her. She did not make up her mind to accept Mr Beverley any more than she had made up her mind to accept Mr Cavendish; but she thought it only her duty to him and to herself, and to society in general, to take his claims into full consideration. And no doubt, if these claims had seemed to her sufficiently strong to merit such a reward, Miss Marjoribanks had it in her to marry the Archdeacon, and make him an admirable wife, though she was not at the present moment, so far as she was aware, absolutely what foolish people call in love with him. At the same time, she made herself all the more agreeable to Mr Beverley from her sense of the dawn of tenderness with which he regarded her. And in this way they went up the broad central path which traversed the little garden, neither looking to the left nor the right, but presenting all that appearance of being occupied with each other, which, especially to a female observer, is so easy of interpretation. For, to be sure, the Archdeacon had not the remotest idea into whose house he was going, nor who it was whom he was about to see.

But as it happened, Lucilla's *protégée*, who had seen better days, had just then finished one of her lessons, and sent her little pupils out into the garden. She was preparing for the next little class, when, raising her eyes accidentally, she saw Miss Marjoribanks coming through the garden with the Archdeacon by her side. She was the same person whom Mr Bury had brought to Lucilla with the idea of recommending her to Dr Marjoribanks as a companion and chaperone for his daughter; but since then Mrs Mortimer's appearance had considerably changed. She had grown younger by ten years during the period of comparative comfort and tranquillity which Lucilla's active help and championship had procured for her. Her house, and her garden, and her little scholars, and the bloom on her cheeks, and the filling-up of her worn frame, were all Miss Marjoribanks's doing. In the intervals of her legislative cares Lucilla had run about all over Carlingford searching for pupils, and at the same moment had cut and stitched and arranged, and papered walls, and planted flower-beds, for the feeble creature thus thrown upon her. This was a side of Lucilla's character which certainly she did nothing to hide from the public, but which, at the same time, she never made any fuss about; and it was an endless pleasure to her to find a *protégée* so perfectly content to be "done for," and do as she was told to do. It was thus that the poor faded widow, who was sensitive and had feelings, and forgot herself so far as to faint, or nearly to faint, just at the most unlucky moment possible, when the Rector's character and dignity demanded superior self-control on her part, had found her youth again and her good looks under Lucilla's shadow. When she looked up and saw the two approaching, Mrs Mortimer's first impulse was to smile at the conjunction; but the next moment she had dropped the books out of her hands, and was standing gazing out like a woman in a dream, with the colour all gone out of her cheeks, and even out of her lips, in the surprise of the moment. It was only surprise and a kind of dismay; it was not terror, like that which Mr Cavendish had exhibited at the same apparition. She dropped into her chair without knowing it, and probably would have fainted this time also, if something more urgent than mere "feelings" had not roused her up. As it was, it happened very happily for her that she had thus a little preparation. When she saw that her patroness was leading Mr Beverley up to the door, and that in a minute more he would inevitably be brought to her very side, Mrs Mortimer roused up all her strength. She gathered up her books in her hand without knowing very well what she was doing, and, taking virtue from necessity, went desperately out to meet them. It was Miss Marjoribanks who first saw her, white and tottering, leaning against the trellis of the little porch, and Lucilla could not but give a little cry of alarm and wonder. What kind of man could this be, who thus struck down another victim without even so much as a glance? It was just then that the Archdeacon raised his eyes, and saw standing before him, among the faded roses, the woman whom he had been approaching so indifferently—the faded existence that had seen better days. He saw her, and he stood stock-still, as if it was she who was the basilisk, and the look of pleased interest went out of his face in a moment. In that moment he had become as unconscious of the presence of Lucilla as if he had never in his life softened his voice to her ear, or talked nonsense to please her. His eyes did not seem big enough to take in the figure which stood shrinking and looking at him in the porch. Then he made one long step forward, and took hold of her sleeve—not her hand—as if to convince himself that it was something real he saw. He showed no joy, no satisfaction, nor anything but sheer amaze and wonder, at this unexpected appearance, for he had not had time to prepare himself as she had. "Am I dreaming, or is it you?" he said, in a voice that sounded as different from the voice with which he had been speaking to Lucilla, as if years had elapsed between the two. And it would be vain to describe the amazement and singular sense that the earth had suddenly given way under her feet, with which Miss Marjoribanks stood by and looked on.

CHAPTER XXIII.

Miss Marjoribanks was naturally the first to recover her senses in this emergency. Even she, self-possessed as she was, felt the natural giddiness inseparable from such a strange reversal of the position. But she did not lose her head like the others. She looked at the widow standing white and tremulous in the shadow of the little porch, and on the Archdeacon, whose manly countenance had paled to a corresponding colour. A man does not seize a woman by the sleeve and ask, "Is it *you?*" without some reason for an address so destitute of ordinary courtesy; and Lucilla was sufficiently versed in such matters to know that so rude and startling an accost could be only addressed to some one whose presence set the speaker's heart beating, and quickened the blood in his veins. It was odd, to say the least, after the way in which he had just been speaking to herself; but Miss Marjoribanks, as has been already said, was not the woman to lose her head. She recovered herself with the second breath she drew, and took her natural place. "I can see that you have something to say to each other," said Lucilla. "Mrs Mortimer, ask Mr Beverley to walk in. Never mind me. I want to speak to the little Lakes. I shall come back presently," Miss Marjoribanks added, nodding pleasantly to the Archdeacon—and she went away to the other end of the garden, calling to the children with that self-possession which is the gift only of great minds. But when Lucilla found herself at a safe distance, and saw the Archdeacon stoop to go in under the porch, it cannot be denied that her mind was moved by the sight. It was she who had seen after the putting up of that trellis round that porch, and the arrangement of the Westeria, which had been sprawling all over the front of the house uncared for. If there was any place in the world where she should have been free from such a shock, it certainly should have been here, in this spot, which she had, so to speak, created. Naturally the unfitness of these surroundings to witness a revolution so unlooked-for and disagreeable struck Lucilla. If she had to be again humiliated, and to submit once more to see another preferred to herself, it certainly should have been under other circumstances. When we admit that such a thought did pass through the mind of Miss Marjoribanks, it will prove to all who know her that Lucilla found her position sufficiently aggravating. She had exerted herself for Mrs Mortimer as nobody else in Carlingford would have exerted themselves. She had not only found pupils and a means of living for the widow, which, perhaps, a committee of ladies might have done at the end of a year, had it been put into their hands; but Miss Marjoribanks had done it at once, and had taken charge of that timid and maladroit individual herself, and set her up, and done everything for her. It was Dr Marjoribanks's gardener, under Lucilla's orders, who had arranged and planted the garden, and trained the embowering foliage which had just brushed the Archdeacon's clerical hat as he went in; and in the act of refurnishing her drawing-room, Miss Marjoribanks had managed to procure, without costing anybody anything except a little trouble, as she herself said, many accessories, which gave an air of comfort to the little parlour, in which, no doubt, at that moment, Mr Beverley and Mrs Mortimer were explaining themselves. Lucilla had a great deal too much good sense to upbraid anybody with ingratitude, or even to make any claim upon that slippery quality; but she knew at the same time that the widow was the very last person from whom a new discomfiture should come, and that to enter in under that trellis when he left her was, on the Archdeacon's part, an aggravation of the change in his sentiments which it was difficult to bear.

She walked along the garden path very briskly under the influence of these thoughts, and it was not in nature to do otherwise than snub the children when she joined them. Lucilla was a woman of genius, but she was not faultless; and when she found Ethelinda and Ethelfreda Lake, the two twins, the one with her clean frock all muddy and stained, the other with the front breadth torn right up the middle, it is scarcely to be wondered at if she lost her patience. "You little nasty untidy things!" she said, "I should like to know who you expect is to go mending up and washing every day for you? It will not be Barbara, I am sure," Miss Marjoribanks added, with a fine intonation of scorn, of which the culprits were insensible; and she gave Ethelinda a shake, who was sitting on the wet ground, all muddy with recent watering, and who, besides, was the one who most resembled Barbara. When this temporary ebullition had taken place, Lucilla began gradually to right herself. It was a grand sight, if anybody had been there to witness it, or if anybody could have seen into Miss Marjoribanks's maiden bosom; but the spectacle of a great mind thus recovering its balance is one which can rarely be visible except in its results. While she set the children to rights, and represented to Mrs Mortimer's little servant, who was in the garden furtively on a pretence of cabbages, the extreme folly, and indeed idiocy, of letting them get to the water and make a mess of themselves, Lucilla was in reality coming to herself. Perhaps she spoke with a little more energy than usual; but the offenders were so well aware of their guilt, and so thoroughly satisfied of the justice of the reproof addressed to them, that no other explanation was necessary; and, little by little, Miss Marjoribanks felt herself restored to her natural calm.

"You know I don't like to scold you," she said; "but what would anybody say?—nice clean frocks, that I am sure were put on fresh this morning—and you, Mary Jane——"

"Please, Miss, it was only for a young cabbage. Missis is fond of a bit of vegetable," said the little maid. "I knew *she'd* not say nothing;—and just as I had told 'em all to have done and be good—and nobody knew as *you* was here," said Mary Jane. There was something even in that small and humble testimony to Lucilla's sovereignty which helped on the process which was operating in her mind. She regained bit by bit that serene self-consciousness which places the spirit above the passing vexations of the world. What did it matter what other people might be doing or saying? Was not she still Lucilla Marjoribanks? and when one had said that, one had said all.

"It is time you were all going home to your dinners," said Lucilla; "and I have asked Mrs Mortimer to give you a half-holiday. As for you, you little Linda, you are not fit to be seen; and I am sure if I were your sister I should send you off to bed. Now, get all your hats and things and run away; and if you are not awfully good to-morrow, I shall never ask for another half-holiday again."

Saying which, Miss Marjoribanks herself saw the hats brought out, and the little scholars sent away. She took matters into her own hand with the confidence of a superior nature. "After all the long talk they are having she will not be able for her scholars to-day," Lucilla said magnanimously to herself; and she again made the tour of the garden, inspecting everything, to see that all was in order. With every step that she took, Miss Marjoribanks became more and more herself. As we have already said, it was a grand and inspiring sight; but then, to be sure, as in the former case, her affections, fortunately, were not engaged. She was not in love with the Archdeacon, any more than she had been in love with Mr Cavendish;—though it is true, love is not everything. And to think how he had been looking and talking not much more than half an hour ago, and to reflect that now he had most likely forgotten her very existence, and was explaining himself, and placing that position which would have just suited Lucilla at the feet of the object of her bounty, was enough to have driven a young woman of ordinary mind half out of her senses with disgust and indignation. But, fortunately, Lucilla's mind was not an ordinary one; and every step she took round the garden restored her more and more entirely to herself. Instead of conceiving any jealous dislike to Mrs Mortimer, she had already, as has been stated, exerted herself with her usual benevolence to leave the widow free for the rest of the day. "After all, it is not her fault if she knew him before, or if he was in love with her," Lucilla said to herself. And when she had arrived at this perfectly true and profoundly philosophical conclusion, it may be said that the crisis was at an end.

But then where personal offence and indignation (if the natural shock to Miss Marjoribanks's feelings could be called by such hard names) ended, bewilderment and curiosity began. Who could this Archdeacon be who had frightened the most popular man in Carlingford out of the place, and whose unlooked-for appearance had driven Mrs Mortimer back out of her recovered good looks and cheerfulness into pallor and trembling? It is true that Lucilla knew quite well who he was—the second son of Mr Beverley of Trent Valley, a family as well known as any family in England. Everybody knew all about the Archdeacon: his career from his youth up was as clearly traceable as if he had been killed in a railway accident and had had his memoir published in the 'Times.' There was nothing in the smallest degree secret or mysterious about him; and yet how could it come about that the sight of him should frighten Mr Cavendish out of his senses, and make Mrs Mortimer, who was utterly unconnected with Mr Cavendish, all but faint, as she had done on a former occasion? Was it his mission to go about the world driving people into fits of terror or agitation? To be sure, he was a Broad-Churchman, and not the type of clergyman to which Lucilla in her heart inclined; but still a man may be Broad-Church, and speak a little freely on religious matters, without being a basilisk. As these thoughts went through her mind, Miss Marjoribanks could not help observing that the branches of the pear-tree, which was all that the garden contained in the shape of fruit, had come loose from the wall, and were swaying about greatly to the damage of the half-grown pears,—not to say that it gave a very untidy look to that corner. "I must send Crawford down this evening to fasten it up," Lucilla said to herself, and then went on with what she was thinking; and she made one or two other remarks of the same description in a parenthesis as she made her tour. After all, it is astonishing how many little things go wrong when the man or woman with a hundred eyes is absent for a few days from the helm of affairs. It was nearly a week since Miss Marjoribanks had been round Mrs Mortimer's garden, and in that time the espalier had got detached, some of the verbenas were dead in the borders, and the half of the sticks that propped up the dahlias had fallen, leaving the plants in miserable confusion. Lucilla shook her head over this, as she asked herself what mysterious influence there could be in the Archdeacon. For her own part, she was not in the slightest degree afraid of him, nor could she confess to having felt agitated even when he walked with her into this fated garden; but there could be no doubt of the seriousness of the effect produced by his appearance on the two others. "They have broken half of the props, the little nuisances," Lucilla said to herself, as she pursued her musings. For her large mind was incapable, now that its perfect serenity was happily regained, of confining itself, unless with a very good reason, to one sole subject.

When she had finished her inspection, and saw that nobody had yet appeared at the door, Miss Marjoribanks collected the books which the children had left lying in the summer-house, and put them under cover—for, to tell the truth, it looked a little like rain; and having done this, and looked all round her to see if anything else required her immediate care, Lucilla carried philosophy to its highest practical point by going away, which is, perhaps, a height of good sense which may be thought too much for humanity. It was not too much for Miss Marjoribanks's legislative soul and knowledge of human nature;—and in thus denying herself she was perfectly aware of her advantages, and of the inevitable result. She knew, just as well as if she had already received it, that Mrs Mortimer would write her a little three-cornered note, marked *Private*, as soon as the Archdeacon was gone; and she thought it was highly probable that Mr Beverley himself would come to give some explanation. With this tranquil assurance in her mind, Lucilla turned her face towards Grange Lane. She began to have a kind of conviction too, since this had happened, either that Carlingford would not be raised into a bishopric, or that the Archdeacon at least would not be the first bishop. It was difficult to give any ground for the idea, but it came into her mind with a kind of quiet certainty; and with this conviction, in which she recognised that beautiful self-adjusting balance of compensations which keeps everything right in the world, Lucilla, quite recovered from her shock, had on the whole a pleasant walk home.

As for the two who were shut up together in Mrs Mortimer's parlour, their state of mind was far from partaking of the virtuous peace and serenity which filled Miss Marjoribanks's bosom. It was more than an hour before the Archdeacon went away; and when Mrs Mortimer had a little collected her faculties, the result arrived which had been foreseen by Lucilla. In the first place, terror seized the widow as to what had become of her pupils, whom all this time she had forgotten, and deep was her gratitude when she had ascertained that her protecting genius had sent them away. But with that gratitude came a sudden recollection of the manner in which Mr Beverley and Miss Marjoribanks had been coming together up the garden path, before the mistress of the house showed herself. Mrs Mortimer wrung her hands when she recollected the looks and attitude of the two, and the rumour which had reached her ears that the Archdeacon was paying attention to Miss Marjoribanks. What was she to do?—was her miserable presence here to dispel perhaps the youthful hopes of her benefactress, and make a revolution in Lucilla's prospects? The poor woman felt herself ready to sink into the earth at the thought. She went to the window and looked out disconsolately into the rain —for it had come on to rain, as Lucilla supposed it would— and felt like a creature in a cage, helpless, imprisoned, miserable, not knowing what to do with herself, and the cause of trouble to her best friends. A little house in a garden may look like a little paradise in the sunshine, and yet feel like a dungeon when a poor woman all alone looks out across her flowers in the rain, and sees nothing but the wall that shuts her in, and thinks to herself that she has no refuge nor escape from it—nobody to tell her what to do, nothing but her own feeble powers to support her, and the dreadful idea that she has done harm and can do no good to her only protector. Any reasonable creature would have said, that to be there in her own house, poor enough certainly, but secure, and no longer driven lonely and distressed about the world, was a great matter. But yet, after all, the walls that shut her in, the blast of white, sweeping, downright rain, which seemed to cut her off from any succour outside, and the burden of something on her mind which by herself she was quite unable to bear, was a hard combination; and wringing one's hands, and feeling one's mind ready to give way under a new and unexpected burden, could not advance matters in the slightest degree. She was not strong-minded, as has been already proved; nor, indeed, had she the ordinary amount of indifference to other people, or confidence in herself, which stands in the place of self-control with many people. After she had wrung her hands, and looked out again and again with a vague instinct of perhaps finding some suggestion of comfort outside, Mrs Mortimer relapsed by necessity into the one idea that had been a support to her for so many months past. All that she could do was to consult Lucilla—it might be to wound

Lucilla, for anything she could tell; but when a poor creature is helpless and weak, and has but one friend in the world who is strong, what can she do but apply to her sustainer and guardian? When, after beating about wildly from one point to another, she arrived ultimately, as might have been predicted, and as Miss Marjoribanks had expected from the first, at that conclusion, there remained a further difficulty in respect to the means of communication. Lucilla had settled quite calmly in her own mind that it would be by the medium of a three-cornered note, a matter in which there was no difficulty whatever, for the widow was sufficiently fluent with her pen; but then Lucilla had not thought of Mary Jane, who was the only possible messenger. It was to this point now that Mrs Mortimer's ideas addressed themselves. At that moment the rain poured down fiercer than ever, the bricks of the uncovered wall grew black with the wet, and the Westeria crouched and shivered about the porch as if it wanted to be taken indoors. And then to get wet, and perhaps catch cold, was a thing Mary Jane conscientiously avoided, like the rest of the world; and it was with a sense of alarm even stronger than that excited by the possibility of injuring Lucilla, that Mrs Mortimer very gently and modestly rang her bell.

"I don't think it rains quite so heavily," said the timid experimentalist, feeling her heart beat as she made this doubtful statement. "Have you a pair of goloshes, Mary Jane?"

"No," said the little handmaiden, with precaution; "and, please, if it's for the post, it rains worse nor ever; and I don't think as mother would like——"

"Oh, it is not for the post," said Mrs Mortimer; "it is for Miss Marjoribanks. You can take mine, and then you will not get your feet wet. I go out so very little; you may have them —to keep—Mary Jane. And you can take the big shawl that hangs in the passage, and an umbrella. I don't think it is so heavy as it was."

Mary Jane regarded the rain gloomily from the window; but her reluctance was at an end from the moment she heard that it was to Miss Marjoribanks she was going. To be sure, the distance between the Serenissime Nancy and Thomas, and the other inmates of the Doctor's kitchen, and Mrs Mortimer's little handmaiden, was as great as that which exists between an English duke and the poorest little cadet of a large family among his attendant gentry; but, correspondingly, the merest entrance into that higher world was as great a privilege for Mary Jane, as the Duke's notice would be to the Squire's youngest son. She kept up a momentary show of resistance, but she accepted the goloshes, and even after a moment agreed in her mistress's trembling assertion about the rain. And this was how the three-cornered note got conveyed to its destination in the heaviest of the storm, between three and four o'clock in the afternoon. Mrs Mortimer still sat at her window, wringing her hands from time to time, with her head aching and her heart beating, and a dreadful question in her mind as to what Lucilla would say, or whether perhaps she might reject altogether in her natural indignation the appeal made to her; which was an idea which filled the widow with inexpressible horror. While at the same moment Miss Marjoribanks sat looking for that appeal which she knew was sure to come. The rain had set in by this time with an evident intention of lasting, and even from the windows of Lucilla's drawing-room the prospect of the garden walls and glistening trees was sufficiently doleful. Nobody was likely to call, nothing was doing; and Lucilla, who never caught cold, had not the least fear of wetting her feet. And besides, her curiosity had been rising every moment since her return; and the widow's pathetic appeal, "Come to me, my dearest Lucilla. I have nobody whom I can talk to in the world but you!" had its natural effect upon a mind so feeling. Miss Marjoribanks got up as soon as she had read the note, and changed her dress, and put on a great waterproof cloak. Instead of thinking it a trouble, she was rather exhilarated by the necessity. "Be sure you make your mistress a nice cup of tea as soon as we get there," she said to Mary Jane. "She must want it, I am sure, if she has not had any dinner;" for the little maid had betrayed the fact that Mrs Mortimer could not eat anything, and had sent away her dinner, which was naturally an alarming and wonderful occurrence to Mary Jane. The widow was still sitting at the window when Lucilla appeared tripping across the wet garden in her waterproof cloak, if not a ministering angel, at least a substantial prop and support to the lonely woman who trusted in her, and yet in the present instance feared her. But anything more unlike a disappointed maiden, whose wooer had been taken away from her under her very eyes, could not have been seen. On the contrary, Miss Marjoribanks was radiant, with rain-drops glistening on her hair, and what Mrs Chiley called "a lovely colour." If there was one thing in the world more than another which contented Lucilla, it was to be appealed to and called upon for active service. It did her heart good to take the management of incapable people, and arrange all their affairs for them, and solve all their difficulties. Such an office was more in her way than all the Archdeacons in the world.

"I saw you knew him the moment I looked at you," said Lucilla. "I have seen other people look *like that* when he appeared. Who is he, for goodness' sake? I know quite well, of course, who he is, in the ordinary way; but do tell me what has he done to make people look like that whenever he appears?"

Mrs Mortimer did not directly answer this question—she fixed her mind upon one part of it, like an unreasonable woman, and repeated "Other people?" with a kind of interrogative gasp.

"Oh, it was only a gentleman," said Lucilla, with rapid intelligence; and then there was a little pause. "He has been here for six weeks," Miss Marjoribanks continued: "you must have heard of him; indeed, you would have heard him preach if you had not gone off after these Dissenters. Did you really never know that he was here till to-day?"

"I did not think of him being Archdeacon—he was only a curate when I used to know him," said poor Mrs Mortimer, with a sigh.

"Tell me all about it," said Lucilla, with ingenuous sympathy; and she drew her chair close to that of her friend, and took her hand in a protecting, encouraging way. "You know, whatever you like to say, that it is quite safe with me."

"If you are sure you do not mind," said the poor widow. "Oh, yes, I have heard what people have been saying about him and—and you, Lucilla; and if I had known, I would have shut myself up—I would have gone away for ever and ever—I would——"

"My dear," said Miss Marjoribanks, with a little severity, "I thought you knew me better. If I had been thinking of that sort of thing, I never need have come home at all; and when you know how kind papa has been about the drawing-room and everything. Say what you were going to say, and never think of me."

"Ah, Lucilla, I have had my life," said the trembling woman, whose agitation was coming to a climax—"I have had it, and done with it; and you have been so good to me; and if, after all, I was to stand between you and—and—and—anybody——" But here Mrs Mortimer broke down, and could say no more.

To be sure, she did not faint this time any more than she did on the first occasion when she made Miss Marjoribanks's acquaintance; but Lucilla thought it best, as then, to make her lie down on the sofa, and keep her quite quiet, and hasten Mary Jane with the cup of tea.

"You have been agitated, and you have not eaten anything," said Lucilla. "I am going to stay with you till half-past six, when I must run home for dinner, so we have plenty of time; and as for your life, I don't consider you gone off at all yet, and you are a great deal younger-looking than you were six months ago. I am very glad the Archdeacon did not come until you had got back your looks. It makes such a difference to a man," Miss Marjoribanks added, with that almost imperceptible tone of contempt which she was sometimes known to use when speaking of Their absurd peculiarities. As for Mrs Mortimer, the inference conveyed by these words brought the colour to her pale cheeks.

"It will never come to that," she said, "no more than it did in old days; it never can, Lucilla; and I don't know that it is to be wished. I couldn't help being put out a little when I saw him, you know; but there is one thing, that he never, never will persuade me," said the widow. Lucilla could not but look on in surprise and even consternation, while Mrs Mortimer thus expressed herself. A warm flush animated the pale and somewhat worn face—and a gleam of something that looked absolutely like resolution shone in the yielding woman's mild eyes. Was it possible that even she had one point upon which she could be firm? Miss Marjoribanks stood still, petrified, in the very act of pouring out the tea.

"If it is only one thing, if I were you, I would give in to him," said Lucilla, with a vague sense that this sort of self-assertion must be put a stop to, mingling with her surprise.

"Never," said Mrs Mortimer again, with a still more distinct gleam of resolution. "In the first place, I have no right whatever to anything more than my uncle gave me. He told me himself I was to have no more; and *he* was very, very kind to poor Edward. You don't know all the circumstances, or you would not say so," she cried, with a sob. As for Miss Marjoribanks, if it is possible to imagine her clear spirit altogether lost in bewilderment, it would have been at that moment; but she recovered as soon as she had administered her cup of tea.

"Now tell me all about it," said Lucilla, again sitting down by the sofa; and this time Mrs Mortimer, to whom her excitement had given a little spur and stimulus, did not waste any more time.

"He is my cousin," she said; "not my real cousin, but distant; and I will not deny that, long, long ago—when we were both quite young, you know, Lucilla——"

"Yes, yes, I understand," said Miss Marjoribanks, pressing her hand.

"He was very nice in those days," said Mrs Mortimer, faltering; "that is, I don't mean to say he was not always nice, you know, but only—— I never had either father or mother. I was living with my uncle Garrett—my uncle on the other side; and he thought he should have made me his heiress; but instead of that, he left his money, you know, to *him;* and then he was dreadfully put out, and wanted me to go to law with him and change the will; but I never blamed him, for my part, Lucilla—he knows I never blamed him—and nothing he said would make me give in to go to the law with him——"

"Stop a minute," said Lucilla, "I am not quite sure that I understand. Who was it he wanted you to go to law with? and was it to the Archdeacon the money was left?"

"Oh, Lucilla," said the widow, with momentary exasperation, "you who are so quick and pick up everything, to think you should not understand me when I speak of a thing so important! Of course it was not to Charles Beverley the money was left: if it had been left to him, how could he have wanted me to go to law? It has always been the question between us," said Mrs Mortimer, once more lighting up with exceptional and unwonted energy. "He said I was to indict him for conspiracy; and I declare to you, Lucilla, that he was not to blame. Uncle Garrett might be foolish, but I don't say even that he was foolish: he was so good to him, like a son; and he had no son of his own, and I was only a girl. He never was anything to me," said Mrs Mortimer, wiping her eyes—"never, whatever Charles may choose to say; but if ever I was sure of anything in the world, I am sure that he was not to blame."

Lucilla's head began to whirl; but after her first unsuccessful essay, she was wise enough not to ask any more direct questions. She made all the efforts possible, with ears and eyes intent, to disentangle this web of pronouns, and failing, waited on in the hope that time and patience would throw a little light upon them. "I suppose Mr Beverley thought he was to blame?" she said, when the narrator paused to take breath.

"Is not that what I am saying?" said Mrs Mortimer. "It

was through that it was all broke off. I am sure I don't know whether he has regretted it or not, Lucilla. It is not always very easy to understand a gentleman, you know. After I was married to poor Edward, naturally I never had any more correspondence with him; and to see him to-day without any warning, and to find him just as bent as he was upon making me prosecute, and just as full of bad feeling, and speaking as if there was some reason more than truth and justice why I should be so determined. No, Lucilla," said Mrs Mortimer, raising herself up on the sofa, "it is just the same thing as ever, and the same obstacle as ever, and it never will come to *that*."

"You are agitating yourself," said Miss Marjoribanks; "lie down—there's a dear—and keep quite still, and see whether we cannot make anything better of it. Tell me, what would you go to law with him for?" Lucilla continued, with the natural humility of imperfect comprehension. It was perhaps the first time in her life that such a singular chance had happened to Miss Marjoribanks, as to have a matter explained to her and yet be unable to understand.

"He says he could be indicted for conspiracy, or for having too much influence over him, and making him do what he liked. But he was very good to him, Lucilla, and to my poor Edward; and when I was married to him——"

"Goodness gracious! were you married to him as well?" cried Lucilla, fairly losing the thread and her balance in this confusing circle. Mrs Mortimer grew pale, and rose quite up from the sofa, and went with the air of an insulted woman to seat herself in her usual chair.

"I don't know why you should address me so," she said. "He is nothing to me, and never was. It is an insult to me to think that I must have a personal reason for refusing to do a wicked and unjust thing. I could give up anything," said the widow, losing a little of her dignity, and growing again pathetic —"I would give in in a moment if it was any fancy of mine— you know I would; but when I am sure it would be wicked and unjust——"

"I am sure I am not the person to bid you do anything unjust or wicked," said Lucilla, who, in the utter confusion of her faculties, began to feel offended in her turn.

"Then I beg you will never speak to me of it again!" cried Mrs Mortimer. "How is it possible that either he or you can know the rights of it as I do, who was in the house at the time and saw everything? He may say what he likes, but I know there was no conspiracy; he was just as much surprised as you could be, or Charles, or anybody. Of course it was for his advantage—nobody denies that—but you don't mean to say that a man is to reject everything that is for his advantage?" said the widow, turning eyes of indignant inquiry upon her visitor; and Miss Marjoribanks for once was so utterly perplexed that she did not know how to respond.

"But you said when you were married to him?" said Lucilla, who felt that the tables were turned upon her for the moment. "I am sure I beg your pardon for being so stupid; but whom were you married to?" This was said in the most deprecating tone in the world, but still it irritated Mrs Mortimer, whose mind was all unhinged, and who somehow felt that she was not finding in Miss Marjoribanks the help and support to which her clear and detailed explanation entitled her. Though her head was aching dreadfully, she sat up more upright than ever in her chair.

"I don't think you can mean to insult me, Miss Marjoribanks," said the widow, "after being so kind. Perhaps I have been trying you too much by what I have said; though I am sure I would have given up everything, and gone away anywhere, rather than be the cause of anything unpleasant. You know that it was my poor dear Edward I was married to; you know I have a—a horror," said Mrs Mortimer, faltering, "in general—of second marriages."

"Oh, yes," said Lucilla, "but there are always exceptions, you know; and when people have no children, nor anything—and you that were so young. I always make exceptions, for my part; and if you could only get over this one point," Miss Marjoribanks added, making a dexterous strategical movement. But Mrs Mortimer only shook her head.

"I don't think I am hard to get on with," she said; "but my poor Edward always said one must make a stand somewhere. He used to say I was so easy to be persuaded. He was glad to see I had a point to make a stand on, instead of being disagreeable about it, or thinking he was anything to me. And oh, Lucilla, he was so kind to him," said the widow, with tears in her eyes. "We met him quite by chance, and he was so kind. I will never forget it, if I should live a hundred years. And why should Charles be in such a way? He never did him any harm! If any one was injured, it was me, and I never felt myself injured—neither did Edward. On the contrary, he *always* did him justice, Lucilla," Mrs Mortimer continued, fixing a pathetic look upon her friend. What could Lucilla do? She was burning to take it all in her own hands, and arrange it somehow, and unite the two lovers who had been so long separated; but unless she could understand what the point was on which Mrs Mortimer made her stand, what could she do?

"I never could understand," said the widow, who began to feel her heart sick with the disappointment of that hope which she had fixed in Miss Marjoribanks, "why he should take it so much to heart. Poor Edward never thought of such a thing! and why he should be so set against poor Mr Kavan, and so—— Lucilla! oh, tell me, do you see anything? what do you mean?"

"I want to know who Mr Kavan is?" said Miss Marjoribanks, much startled. She had for the moment forgotten the Archdeacon's discovery and her own suspicions; and the idea of connecting the man who had (apparently) fled from Mr Beverley's presence, with the innocent and helpless woman upon whom the appearance of the Broad-Churchman had so overwhelming an effect, had never hitherto entered her imagination. But this name, which was not the name of anybody she knew, and yet seemed to bear an odd sort of rudimentary relationship to another name, struck her like a sudden blow and brought everything back to her mind. It was a bewildering sort of explanation, if it was an explanation; but still a confused light began to break upon Lucilla's understanding. If this was what it all meant, then there was the widest opening for charitable exertions, and much to be done which only a mind like Miss Marjoribanks's could do.

"That is not his name now," said Mrs Mortimer, "I don't see, if he liked it, why he should not change his name. I am sure a great many people do; but his name was Kavan when he lived with my uncle. I don't remember what it was after, for of course he was always Mr Kavan to me; and Charles Beverley never could bear him. He used to think——but oh, Lucilla, forgive me—oh, forgive me, if it is too much for you!" she added, a moment after, as another idea struck her. "It was not with the idea of—of anything coming of it, you know; it will never come to that—not now;—I don't know if it is to be wished. I am sure he is quite free so far as I am concerned. It was not with that idea I asked for your advice, Lucilla," said the poor woman, in piteous tones. If Miss Marjoribanks had pressed her, and insisted upon knowing what *was* the idea which had moved her friend to ask her advice, Mrs Mortimer would no doubt have found it very hard to reply; but Lucilla had no such cruel intentions; and the widow, notwithstanding her piteous denial of any motive, now that her mind was cleared, and she had caught the comprehension of her auditor, began to regard her with a certain instinct of hope.

As for Miss Marjoribanks, this revelation at once troubled and cleared her mind. If this was the culprit, he *was* a culprit and yet he was innocent; and to heap coals of fire upon his head was in some respects a Christian duty. Her ideas went forward at a bound to a grand finale of reconciliation and universal brotherhood. She saw the tools under her hands, and her very fingers itched to begin. Large and varied as her experience was, she had never yet had any piece of social business on so important a scale to manage, and her eyes sparkled and her heart beat at the idea. Instead of shrinking from interference, her spirits rose at the thought. To vanquish the Archdeacon, to pluck out from the darkness, and rehabilitate and set at his ease the mysterious adventurer, whom, to be sure, *she could not say she knew*—for Lucilla was very careful, even in her own thoughts, not to commit herself on this subject—and to finish off by a glorious and triumphant marriage—not her own, it is true, but of her making, which was more to the purpose,—such was the programme she made out for herself with the speed of lightning, the moment she had laid hold of the clue which guided or seemed to guide her through the labyrinth. It would be too lengthy a matter to go into all her tender cares for the widow's comfort during the rest of her stay, and the pains and delicacy with which she managed to elicit further particulars, and to make out her brief, so to speak, while she cheered up and encouraged the witness. Miss Marjoribanks jumped to the conclusion that "poor Edward" had been, after all, but a temporary tenant of the heart, which was now again free for the reception of the Archdeacon, if he could be got to accept the conditions. When half-past six arrived, and Thomas came for her with the great umbrella, she went off quite resplendent in her waterproof cloak, and utterly indifferent to the rain, leaving Mrs Mortimer worn out, but with a glimmer of hope in her mind. Such was the great work which, without a moment's hesitation, Lucilla took upon her shoulders. She had no more fear of the result than she had of wetting her feet, which was a thing Mrs Mortimer and Thomas were both concerned about. But then Lucilla knew her own resources, and what she was capable of, and proceeded upon her way with that unconscious calm of genius which is always so inexplicable to the ordinary world.

CHAPTER XXIV.

It was the most unlucky moment for the weather to change, being the middle of July, and as near as possible to St Swithin's day; but the season had been so delightful up to that time that nobody in Carlingford at least had any reason to complain. So far as Miss Marjoribanks was concerned, she was rather glad, on the whole, that the next day was wet, and that she could not go out all the morning, nor was likely to be interrupted by visitors. She had all her plans to settle and mature for the great enterprise which she had taken in hand. By this time, so far from feeling any personal interest in the Archdeacon, or considering herself injured by his sudden desertion, that little episode had gone out of Lucilla's mind as completely as if it had never been. In one point, however, Miss Marjoribanks's conviction remained firm; it was impressed upon her mind that Carlingford would not be made into a bishopric, or, if made into a bishopric, that it was not Mr Beverley who would be chosen to occupy the new see. It was one of those instinctive certainties which are not capable of explanation, which was thus borne in upon her spirit, and she could not have felt more sure of it had she seen it under the Queen's own hand and seal. While she went about her usual morning occupations, her mind was full of her great and novel undertaking. Mr Beverley was not a man to be revolutionised in a moment; and many people would have shrunk from the attempt to work in a few days or weeks, with no better arms than those of acquaintance, a change which the influence of love had not been able to do in so many years. But it was not in Lucilla's nature to be daunted by a difficulty so unimportant. There was, thank heaven, some difference between herself and the widow, who, in a strait, could think of nothing better to do, poor soul! than to faint; and Miss Marjoribanks had the advantage of never as yet having been beaten, whereas Mrs Mortimer had undergone numberless defeats.

The hardest matter in the whole business, however, was the identification of the Mr Kavan whom the Archdeacon thought he had seen in Carlingford, and was not afraid to speak of as a clever rascal and adventurer. Mr Beverley had never seen the fellow again, as he had told Lucilla not many days back, and Miss Marjoribanks had been unfeignedly glad to hear it; but now matters had changed. In the course of her reflections, she decided that it would now be best that these two men, if possible, should meet and recognise each other, and that the business should once for all be definitively settled. If all the offence he had committed against society was to have had a large sum of money left him by a childless old man, Lucilla saw no reason why this mysterious culprit should conceal himself; and even if he had taken a little liberty with his name, that was not a crime—his name was his own surely, if anything was his own. At the same time, Miss Marjoribanks took pains to impress upon herself, as it is to be hoped a friendly audience will also have the goodness to do, that she had *no real foundation* for her suspicions as to the identity of this personage, and might turn out to be completely mistaken. He might have made no change whatever on his name; he might be flourishing in some other quarter of England or the world, with all his antecedents perfectly well known, and unconscious of anything to be ashamed about; which, to tell the truth, was, as Lucilla confessed to herself, a much more likely hypothesis than the supposition which had taken such possession of her mind. But then Miss Marjoribanks had a just faith in her instincts, and in those brief but telling pieces of evidence which supported her conclusion. She was thinking over this important branch of the subject with the greatest care and devotion, when, looking out by chance into the rain, she saw the Archdeacon crossing the garden. Perhaps it was just as well that she thus had warning and a moment to prepare for his visit; not that Lucilla was a person to be taken at disadvantage; but still, in a matter so practical and pressing, it was always better to be prepared.

Mr Beverley came in with an air and expression so different from that which he had borne in their intercourse no farther gone than yesterday, that, notwithstanding the corresponding revolution in her own mind, Miss Marjoribanks could not but regard him with mingled admiration and surprise. She judged him as the general world so often judged herself, and gave him credit for skill and courage in assuming such an attitude, when the fact was he was only preoccupied and natural, and did not think of his attitude at all. It did not occur to the Archdeacon that he had sinned towards Lucilla. He thought it right to explain to her his extreme surprise at the sight of Mrs Mortimer, and possibly to make her aware, at the same time, of his grievances, in so far as Mrs Mortimer was concerned; but perhaps Mr Beverley was, on the whole, innocent of those intentions which Mrs Chiley had attributed to him, and which even Lucilla, more clearsighted, had seen dawning in their last interview; for, to be sure, this is one of the questions which the female intellect is apt to judge in a different light from that in which it is regarded by a man. The Archdeacon, accordingly, came in preoccupied, with a cloud on his brow, but without the smallest appearance of penitence or deprecation; by which demeanour he gained, without deserving it, the respect, and to a certain extent the admiration, of Lucilla. His expression was not that of a man repentant, but of a man aggrieved. He had a cloud upon his countenance, and a certain air of offence and temper; and when he sat down, he breathed a short impatient sigh.

"Thank you for receiving me so early," he said. "I called yesterday afternoon, but found you out. You must have had very particular business to take you out in that rain," Mr Beverley continued, with subdued exasperation; for naturally, being a clergyman, he was a little impatient to find, when it was *he* who wanted her, any of his female friends out of the way.

"Yes," said Lucilla, who thought it was best to open her battery boldly and at once. "I was spending the afternoon with poor Mrs Mortimer; poor dear, she is so solitary!" and to meet Mr Beverley's ill-temper, Miss Marjoribanks put on her most heavenly air of sympathy, and rounded her words with a soft sigh, as different from his as a flute is from a trumpet. It was with an exclamation of impatience that the Archdeacon replied.

"*Poor* Mrs Mortimer!" he cried; "I don't know whether you are aware how much her obstinacy has cost me; and herself, I suppose," he added, in a parenthesis. "Not to depreciate your kindness, or the truly human and Christian way in which you have conducted yourself—fancy what my feelings naturally must have been to find her an object of charity—actually of charity! I don't mean to say," said Mr Beverley, controlling himself, "that it is degrading to accept succour when given as from man to man—quite the contrary; but you will excuse me from entering into the general question. She knew perfectly well that if I had known where she was—if she had consented to yield to me on one point—solely on *one* point——"

"And she such an obstinate woman!" said Miss Marjoribanks, with fine scorn. "How could you ever think of such a thing? A woman that never gives in to anybody. If you knew her as well as I do——"

The Archdeacon glanced up with a momentary intense surprise, as if it was within the possibilities that such a change might have taken place in the widow's nature; and then he caught Lucilla's eye, and grew red and more aggrieved than ever.

"Mrs Mortimer happens to be a relative of mine," he said, in his authoritative voice. "I have known her from her youth. I am better instructed in all her affairs than she can possibly be. When I urge her to any step, however much it may be against her inclinations, she ought to know that it can only be for her good. I beg your pardon, Miss Marjoribanks. It will give me great grief to find that you, upon whose superior good sense I have so much calculated, should support her in her folly. I know how much she owes to you——"

"Oh, no, she does not owe me anything," said Lucilla. "It was just my luck, you know. I knew she would turn out to be a lady. I don't want to stand up for her if she is wrong; but I have only heard *her* side. When you tell me about it, I shall be able to form an opinion," Miss Marjoribanks added prudently; "for of course everything has two sides."

"Most things," said Mr Beverley, "but this is precisely one of the things which have not two sides. Nothing except some sort of infatuation or other—but never mind, you shall hear the facts," said the Archdeacon, once more making an effort upon himself. "Her uncle, Mr Garrett, was above eighty. Why Providence should have let him live to such an age to do so much mischief, heaven alone knows. Some different rule seems to exist up *there* about those matters, from what we find to answer on earth," the Broad-Churchman said, with a certain air of disapproval. "He had this young fellow to see him and then to live with him, and took some sort of idiotic fancy to him; and when the will was made, it was found that, with the exception of a small sum to Helen, everything was left to this impostor. No, I can't say I have any patience with her folly. How could any man have two opinions on the subject? He was neither related to him, nor connected with him," cried Mr Beverley, with a momentary inclination, as Lucilla thought, to get aground among the pronouns, as Mrs Mortimer had done. "I do not suspect my cousin," the Archdeacon continued, with an air so severe and indignant that it was evident he was contradicting his own sentiments, "of having any partiality for such a person; but certainly her obstinacy and determination are such——"

"Hush, please," said Lucilla; "you are only laughing when you use such words. Now, tell me one thing, and don't be angry if it is a stupid question—If there was any one that knew her and you, and perhaps him, and was to try—don't you think it might be arranged?"

"By money?" said the Archdeacon; and he smiled one of those disagreeable smiles which youthful writers describe by saying that his lip curled with scorn. "You seem to take me for Mortimer, who could go into that sort of compromise. I suppose he did give them money before—before she was left a widow," said Mr Beverley, grinding his teeth slightly with a savage expression. "No, Miss Marjoribanks. Where everlasting truth and justice are concerned, I do not understand how things can be arranged."

After such a truculent statement, what was the peacemaker to do? She left the fire to blaze out by itself for a minute or two, and then she came down upon the enemy on another wind.

"I am sure I am very sorry," said Lucilla, softly, "to think you should be so fond of her and she so fond of you, and nothing but this standing in the way; and then she is too good for this world, and never thinks of herself. I often think, if anything was to happen to me—and my life is no safer than other people's lives," said Miss Marjoribanks, with a sigh—"what would become of her, poor dear! I am sure, if I knew of any way—— As for obstinate, you know it is not in her to be obstinate. She thinks she is right, and you think you are right; and I suppose neither of you will give in," cried Lucilla. "What is anybody to do?"

"If any one gives in, it should be she," said the Archdeacon. "For my part, I will never stand by and consent to such a robbery—never. In these matters, at least, a man must be a better judge than a woman. If you are her friend you will persuade her of her duty," Mr Beverley added; and he did not show so much as a symptom of yielding. To say that Miss Marjoribanks was not discouraged would be more than the truth; but she was still at the beginning of her forces, and no thought of giving in was in her courageous soul.

"I will tell you what occurs to me," said Lucilla, frankly. "Let us find out something about him. Do you know anything about him? If she were to hear that he was, as you say, an impostor, you know, and a villain?—What is his name?—Where does he live?—Is he a very very wicked man?" said Miss Marjoribanks, and she looked up with that ingenuous look of appeal which was always so touching in her, to the Archdeacon's face.

As for Mr Beverley, in his haste and excitement he gave vent to two very contradictory statements. "She knows all about him. I don't know anything about him," he said, with some heat. "I mean, she knows as much as I do, though she draws such a different conclusion. I am sure I saw him in Carlingford the first day I was here. For anything I can tell, she knows *more* of him than I do," said the Broad-Churchman, with a sudden flash of jealousy and anger. It occurred to Lucilla then for the first time that she had found the grand clue to the whole.

"That would be dreadful," said Miss Marjoribanks, "if she knew him, and was keeping him out of the way till you were gone. I did not think of that. If such a thing should be the case, fond as I am of Mrs Mortimer, I never could go near her any more," said Lucilla, sadly. "Oh, don't say you think so, please. I should have to give her up, and that would be dreadful; for I owe it to papa, when he gives me so much liberty, to be very careful. Oh, Mr Beverley, don't say you think so," cried Lucilla, deeply moved. She put her handkerchief to her eyes, and yet she kept watch upon the Archdeacon through one of the corners. He had got up by this time, and was walking about the room like any other man in trouble. To throw suspicion on the widow, or separate her from so effectual a protector, was the very last thing he had any inclination to do: for, to tell the truth, he made that jealous suggestion only in order to receive an indignant denial, and to be assured that such a thing was impossible. But then Mr Beverley did not know whom he had to deal with, nor that he was not the first man whom Miss Marjoribanks had reduced to his proper place.

"If that was the case," said Lucilla, drying her eyes, "dreadful as it is to think of it—oh, Mr Beverley, if such a thing were the case—it would be far better for her to marry him, and then she would have all the fortune without going to law. If things have gone so far, though it is miserable to think of it, and to believe that she could be so unkind," said Miss Marjoribanks, with a sob, "and so double-minded, and so deceitful to me——"

"In heaven's name what are you thinking of?" said the Archdeacon. He had grown as pale as he was before red, and came to a dead stop in front of Lucilla, and stood lowering and menacing over her. His shadow was so big and strong, and stood so directly between her and the window, that Miss Marjoribanks's heart gave one bound of something like alarm.

"Dear Mr Beverley," said Lucilla, "try and compose yourself. It would be a dreadful trial to me, but I should endeavour to bear it. If we love her, we should, on the contrary, urge her to do it," said the young moralist, with solemnity, "however hard it may be to us. It would be better than—than dreadful concealment and misery—it would be better than knowing and not telling, as you say. Oh, Mr Beverley, if you are sure that is the case, let us both go to her, and beg her to marry him. I could never, never, never see her again," sobbed Lucilla, "but she would be happy; and that would be the end of all."

The Archdeacon, though he was not a weakling, was altogether stunned by this address. He sank into the nearest chair, and drew it closer to Lucilla, and looked perfectly flabby and ghastly in his white tie, with his alarmed countenance. "For the sake of all that is sacred," said Mr Beverley, bending forward towards her, "tell me what foundation you have—tell me all you know."

Now was the critical moment, and Lucilla felt it. If Mrs Chiley, for example, had only advised herself to come in then instead of interrupting people's proposals, and driving a likely suitor to desperation! But such happy chances do not occur at the real crises of life. What she wanted was, naturally, not to explain herself, but to let that arrow rankle in her opponent's heart until it should have served her purpose. All that she said in answer to Mr Beverley's appeal was to hide her face in her handkerchief, which was the only means that occurred to her for the moment of gaining a little time for reflection.

"It is so hard to have such thoughts put into one's head," said Lucilla, "of a person who has been one's friend. And she always looked so nice and so true! I never thought she would deceive any one. I thought she was so transparent, you know. Oh, Mr Beverley, it is so dreadful to be disappointed in one's friends! I wish I had never heard of it—I wish you had never told me. I almost wish, though it is dreadful to say such a thing, that you had never come to Carlingford and found it all out."

"My dear Miss Marjoribanks," said the Archdeacon, solemnly, "I implore you, as the greatest kindness you can do me, to tell me all you know."

"Indeed, I don't know what I know," said Lucilla, partially raising her face out of her handkerchief; "I don't think I know anything, for my part. I always thought if one could rely upon any one, one could rely upon her—for truthfulness, and for yieldingness, and doing what any one asked her. I did think so; and it is perfectly bewildering to think, after all, that she should be obstinate and deceiving, and yet look so different!" said Lucilla. "But if it has come to that, we must be firm, Mr Beverley. If you ask my opinion, I say she should be allowed to marry him. That would solve everything, you know," Miss Marjoribanks added, with sad decision. "She would get all the fortune without going to law, and she would be settled, and off one's mind. That would be my final advice, if everything has happened as you say."

Mr Beverley was driven as nearly out of his senses by this counsel, as it was possible for a man of ordinary self-control and warm temper to be. He got up again and made a stride to and fro, and wiped the moisture from his forehead, which, as Lucilla remarked at the moment, had a Low-Church look, which she would not have expected from him. But, on the other hand, he gave vent to some stifled and unintelligible exclamations which, whatever they might be, were not blessings. Then he came to himself a little, which was what Miss Marjoribanks was most afraid of, and stood over her, large and imposing as before.

"Tell me, for heaven's sake, what you mean!" cried the Archdeacon. "You do not think, surely, that I for a moment meant to imply that Helen would waste a thought upon such a miscreant. Good heavens, marry him! You must be raving. She would as soon think of—going for a soldier," said Mr Beverley, with a hoarse and perfectly unmirthful laugh, "or doing anything else that was mad and unnatural. That is how you women stand up for your friends—always ready to suggest something inconceivably horrible and debasing! Happily you always go too far," he added, once more wiping his forehead. It was a very Low-Church, not to say Dissenterish, sort of thing to do, and it unconsciously reduced her adversary's dignity in Miss Marjoribanks's opinion, besides affording a proof that he was not nearly so much convinced of what he said, as he professed to be, in his secret heart.

"Mr Beverley, I think you forget a little," said Lucilla, with dignity. "I know nobody but yourself who has any suspicions of Mrs Mortimer. If it had been anybody but you, I should have laughed at them. But to return to the question," Miss Marjoribanks added, with calm grace; "I always used to be taught at Mount Pleasant, that feelings had nothing to do with an abstract subject. I don't see, for my part, now you have mentioned it, why she should not marry him. It would arrange the money matter without any trouble; and I have always heard he was very nice," said the bold experimentalist, fixing her eyes calmly upon the Archdeacon's face. "I am sure I should never have thought of it, if it had been left to me; but speaking calmly, I don't see the objections, now it has been proposed. Oh, it is only the bell for luncheon that Thomas is ringing. Is it actually half-past one? and I expect some people," said Lucilla. She got up as she spoke and went to the mirror, and looked at herself with that beautiful simplicity which was one of Miss Marjoribanks's distinguishing features. "When one has been crying it always shows," she said, with a little anxiety. As for Mr Beverley, his state of mind, as the newspapers say, could better be imagined than described.

"I must go away," he said, taking up his hat. "I don't feel capable of meeting strangers after this exciting conversation. Miss Marjoribanks," continued the Archdeacon, taking her hand, and holding it fast over his hat to give emphasis to his address, "at least I can trust to you not to breathe a word to Mrs Mortimer—not a syllable—of the horrible suggestion which has got utterance, I don't know how. I may surely trust to your honour," Mr Beverley said, with emphasis; but by this time Miss Marjoribanks considered it time to bring the crisis to an end.

"I wish you would stay to luncheon," she said; "there are only one or two of my friends. As for *honour*, you know you gentlemen say that we have no sense of honour," said Lucilla, airily; "and to think that two women could be together and not talk of what might perhaps be a marriage——"

At this moment some one rang the door-bell. Lucilla knew perfectly well that it was only the baker, but it could not be expected that the Archdeacon should be similarly initiated into the secrets of the house. He thought, as was natural, that it was the people she expected, and almost wrung her hand as he let it go. "You will let me see you again first," he said, in a tone of entreaty. "Before you see her, you will let me see you again. For heaven's sake don't refuse me," cried Mr Beverley. If anybody had but heard him! as Lucilla said to herself the minute he was gone. And the truth was that Thomas did hear him, who had just opened the door to tell his young mistress that her luncheon was waiting, and whom the Archdeacon did all but knock down-stairs in his sudden and unlooked-for exit. The impression naturally conveyed to Thomas by these words was of the clearest and most distinct description. He was even known to say afterwards, "That he never knew a gentleman as spoke more plain." But Mr Beverley rushed down-stairs, without thinking of Thomas, in a most unenviable frame of mind, into the rain. He was more afraid of meeting Miss Marjoribanks's friends than a man of his size and principles should have been afraid of meeting anybody; but then there is a vast distinction, as everybody is aware, and no one more than the Archdeacon, between physical and moral strength.

As for Lucilla, her tears and anxieties passed off in a miraculous manner as soon as her visitor was gone. She went downstairs and ate her luncheon with the serenest brow and a most agreeable lady-like appetite. And it was not a fib, as may perhaps be supposed, that she was expecting people—for at that hour Miss Marjoribanks always did expect people, who, to be sure, might be kept back by the rain, but whom she was always justified in looking for. Perhaps, on the whole, notwithstanding her warm sense of the duties of hospitality, Lucilla was glad that it rained so heavily, and that nobody came. She had a great deal to think of as she took her maidenly and delicate repast. The first step had been taken, and taken triumphantly. Henceforward, whatever the Archdeacon's illusions might be, he could no longer stand calm upon his eminence, and conclude that it was he, and he alone, who could raise the widow from her lowly estate. Lucilla, it is true, knew that no such idea as that of marrying her uncle's heir would ever present itself to Mrs Mortimer; and that—at least so far as Miss Marjoribanks's information went—such a thought was equally removed from the mind of the personage unknown, whom Mr Beverley denounced as an impostor. But this did not in the least affect the value of the suggestion as an instrument to be used against the Archdeacon, who was big enough to defend himself, and on whose account the young philanthropist had no compunctions. The first step was thus taken, and taken successfully, but it was

only after this that the real difficulties began; and Lucilla knew
no more as yet how she was to find and identify, not to say
assail and vanquish, the other side, the mysterious Mr Kavan,
the man whom the Archdeacon abused and the widow defended,
than even the greatest military genius knows at the commencement of the first campaign how to conduct the second. This
was what she considered so closely as she sat alone in the dull
afternoon. She did not go to Mrs Mortimer, because it was
impossible that every day could be a half-holiday, and because,
on the whole, she judged it best not to subject herself, in the
present undeveloped state of the position, to much questioning;
but she sent her a little note to satisfy her mind, telling her to
keep herself easy, and not to let the Archdeacon bully her, and
to confide in the devotion of her affectionate Lucilla. When
she had thus satisfied the immediate demands of friendship,
Miss Marjoribanks took her work and sat down to reflect.
Nothing could be more exciting than the position in which she
found herself; but the difficulties were only such as stimulated
her genius; and then it was not any selfish advantage, but the
good of her neighbour in its most sublime manifestation—the
good of her neighbour who had injured her, and been insensible
to her attractions, which, according to the world in general, is
the one thing unpardonable to a woman—which Lucilla sought.
And it was not even the scriptural coals of fire she was thinking
of as she pondered her great undertaking in her mind. The
enterprise might not be free from a touch of human vanity, but
it was vanity of a loftier description: the pleasure of exercising
a great faculty, and the natural confidence of genius in its own
powers.

CHAPTER XXV.

The fruit of Lucilla's long and mature reflection was, that, next
morning being fine and all the clouds dispersed, she went out
with her usual firm step and self-possession, and, what was
rather unusual with her, except on necessary occasions of ceremony, knocked at Mrs Woodburn's door.

Mrs Woodburn and Miss Marjoribanks had never, as people
say, taken to each other. They were as different in their ways
as it is possible to imagine. The mimic was a little indolent,

and would not take the trouble to make any exertions for the good of the community, except in the exercise of her peculiar talent, though she had been known, when excited, to go through real fatigue for that; but she had none of the steady force, the persevering energy—or, to sum up all in one word, the genius —of Miss Marjoribanks, who, for her part, recognised the *use* of such an instrument of entertainment as Mrs Woodburn possessed without appreciating it in her own person; for Lucilla had no sense of humour, as she candidly admitted, with that consciousness of her own faults, and slight disposition to consider them virtues, which is common to persons of great endowments. It was accordingly with a slight sense of effort on both sides that they met thus in the familiarity of an early visit, at a moment when people doing their duty to each other in a ceremonial way would not have thought of calling. She was aware that Mrs Woodburn regarded her, even when she kissed her in the most neighbourly and affectionate manner, with a look which seemed to say, "What can she want, coming here so early?" As for Lucilla, she was too wise to pretend that it was a mere visit of regard. She was too wise, and her interlocutor was too clever, and prone to catch every touch of expression, though Miss Marjoribanks flattered herself she had sufficient experience to enable her to dismiss, when there was occasion for it, all expression from her face. But such was not her policy at this moment. When the two faces had touched each other in that loving and sisterly salutation, their owners immediately separated, and regarded each other from two opposite chairs, without decided hostility, it is true, but with the watchful air of two people whom the fates may range on different sides, and whom it behoves to be mutually watchful. And Lucilla thought it the most expedient course, under the circumstances, to begin her investigations at once.

"I have come to make an inquisition," she said; "I may as well confess it at once, for you would find me out if I didn't. Mrs Woodburn, where is Mr Cavendish? I am not going to put up with it any longer. He must be written to, and had back again. The only man that was to be depended upon in Carlingford!" said Lucilla; "and to think he should disappear like this, and never say a word!"

Mrs Woodburn fairly gasped in her companion's face. She could no more tell what this meant, than if she had been a person utterly unacquainted with human motives and ways of working; and, indeed, it was only the tricks of the surface for which she had any real insight. "My brother!" she exclaimed, with something between an impulse of defence and denial, and a quite opposite instinct of confidence. Had he proposed, after all, without telling his sister? Had Lucilla a right to ask the question she uttered so frankly? Had he been prudent for once in his life, and secured this sensible alliance and prop to his position? All these questions rushed at lightning-speed through Mrs Woodburn's mind; but she was not so prompt as Miss Marjoribanks would have been under the circumstances, and all she did was to open her eyes wide, and give a start on her chair, and say, "My brother?" with a voice which trembled, and was half-extinguished by surprise.

"Yes; Mr Cavendish," said Lucilla. "Do tell me his address. There is not a man in Carlingford who is good for anything, now that he is gone. You must see that as well as I do. As for flirting, I have always said he was the only man that knew anything about it. Do tell me where he is, and I will write to him; or, please, send him word for me, that absolutely he must come back. We are all dying for him, you may say."

Mrs Woodburn had recovered a little, and found a moment to think, but her faculties were not so handy, except in her own particular way, as might have been expected from such a clever woman. She could even at that moment have taken off Miss Marjoribanks to the life, but she was in the most profound bewilderment as to what Lucilla could mean; whether she was really laying herself out to "catch" Mr Cavendish, or whether she was merely talking nonsense without any particular meaning; or whether she was feigning indifference by way of getting information; and the stupidest person in Carlingford would have acquitted herself as well as Mrs Woodburn felt able to do in the emergency. "I should think he would rather hear that some of you were willing to live for him," she said, in a tremulous way; finding nothing better come to her lips than the echo of an old compliment, which went against her nature, but yet with an instinct of serving her brother so far as it might be in her power.

"Not me," said Lucilla, frankly. "Some people once thought so, you know; but I can't say I ever thought so. There never will be anything about living or dying between him and me. I hope we know better," said Miss Marjoribanks; "besides, if I were so much as to think of that sort of thing I should feel I was swindling papa. Oh no; I assure you I am quite disinterested. I want him for my Thursdays. Do write, and say he must come home."

"I don't like people to be too disinterested," said Mrs Woodburn; "and I don't think Harry would be at all glad to hear it. I wish he would come back, I am sure. I am always bullying him about it. I thought perhaps some of you young ladies had been unkind to him," said the anxious sister, who had recovered her head, and thought it might be possible to get at the secret, if there was a secret, by means like this.

"No," said Miss Marjoribanks; "*I* have not been unkind to him; and there is nobody else I know of," said the candid Lucilla, "unless poor Barbara; and *she* will never be unkind, you know. I will write him a letter if you will give me his address. Is it true that somebody has left him a great deal of money, and he is going to change his name?"

"His name!" said Mrs Woodburn, with a little cry, like an imprudent woman; and then she recovered herself. "I have not heard of anything of the kind," she said, "and he would be sure to tell me of it; but in Carlingford people know things before they happen. I should be very glad to know that somebody was going to leave him a great deal of money; but I don't know about the name——"

"Oh, I heard it only in a confused sort of way," said Lucilla, "or that he *had* changed his name. I am sure I don't know if it was past or present. Did he ever make any change to be somebody's heir? Oh, I beg your pardon; but you know people do it every day."

Mrs Woodburn had grown quite pale—perhaps because she began to see that there was some method in these questions, perhaps with simple and unreasonable fright at the suggestion. She could not say a word for a moment, so startling was the question; and then there was something in Lucilla's early visit, and in her instant onslaught upon Mr Cavendish, which was alarming. She was so frightened and driven into a corner that she could not tell how to answer. It occurred to her all at once that perhaps Mr Cavendish had opened his heart to Miss Marjoribanks, and given her an inkling of his secret; and what would Lucilla think if she contradicted her brother? Never was a poor woman in a greater difficulty. All her fun and her mimicry collapsed. She no more noticed the peculiarities of Lucilla's look and manner than if she had been an ordinary inhabitant of Grange Lane. "Changed his name?" she faltered, in a blank sort of interrogative way; and in spite of herself faltered and shook, and conveyed to Lucilla the most perfect assurance that what she supposed was true.

"When it is for a great deal of money there is some sense in it; when it is only for a prettier name it is dreadfully stupid. Don't you think so? As if we all could have pretty names!" said Lucilla. "I should like so much to have a talk with Mr Cavendish. I picked up some very very old friends of his the other day—people who used to know him long ago. I am sure he would be interested if he were to know."

"I don't think it could be him," said Mrs Woodburn, with something like the instinct of despair; "I don't remember any very old friends he has; it is so long a time ago——" and then the poor lady stopped short, as if she had something choking her in her throat. "I don't think it could be he."

"Not such a very long time," said Lucilla, in her easy way. "It is dreadful to give him a character for being old. Do write him, please, and tell him about those people. He is sure to be interested if you say it is a lady, and a pretty woman, and a widow," continued Miss Marjoribanks. "She says he was once very kind to her when her poor husband was alive."

Mrs Woodburn recovered herself a little as Lucilla spoke. "It must have been some other Mr Cavendish," she said. "Harry was—so much abroad—so long away from home——" At that moment there was a sound in the house of a heavy step, and Mr Woodburn's whistle became audible in the distance. Then the poor woman, who had a secret, fixed haggard eyes upon Miss Marjoribanks. She dared not say, "Don't speak of this before my husband." She dared not utter a word to awaken suspicion on one side or the other. She knew very well that if Mr Woodburn heard of the existence of any old friends of his brother-in-law, he would insist upon having them produced, and "paying them some attention;" and at the same time Mrs Woodburn could not so far confide in Lucilla as to beg her to keep silent. This was what her brother's poltroonery brought upon the unfortunate woman. And when the emergency came she was not as equal to it as she expected to be. Her talents were not of a nature to do her any good in such a strait. She collapsed entirely, and looked round her in a flutter of fright and despair, as if to find some means of escape.

But this terror all arose from the fact that she did not know Miss Marjoribanks, who was generous as she was strong, and had no intention of going to extremities. Lucilla got up from her chair when she heard Mr Woodburn's whistle coming nearer.

"I hear somebody coming," she said, "and I must not stay, for I have quantities of things to do. Only mind you tell Mr Cavendish I have something quite serious to say to him from his old friend; and from me, please to tell him, that it is *impossible* to get on without him," continued Lucilla, as Mr Woodburn entered the room. "There is not a soul that can flirt or do anything. I should write to him myself if I knew his address."

And then, as was natural, Woodburn, with his usual absurdity, as his wife explained afterwards, struck in with some boisterous *badinage*. As for Mrs Woodburn, in her mingled terror and relief, she was too much excited to know what he said. But when Lucilla, serenely smiling, was gone, the mimic, with her nerves strung to desperation, burst into the wildest comic travesty of Miss Marjoribanks's looks and manners, and her inquiries about Harry, and sent her unsuspicious husband into convulsions of laughter. He laughed until the tears ran down his cheeks—the unconscious simpleton; and all the time his wife could have liked to throw him down and trample on him, or put pins into him, or scratch his beaming, jovial countenance. Perhaps she would have gone into hysterics instead if she had not possessed that other safety-valve, for Mrs Woodburn had not that supreme composure and self-command which belonged to Lucilla's higher organisation. She wrote a long letter that afternoon, and had a dreadful headache all the evening after it, which, considering all things, was to be expected under the circumstances, and was a weak-minded woman's last resource.

No headache, however, disturbed Miss Marjoribanks's beneficent progress. She went home conscious that, if she had not acquired any distinct information, she had at least gained a moral certainty. And besides, she had measured the forces of Mr Cavendish's body-guard, and had found them utterly unequal to any prolonged resistance. All that was wanted was prudence and care, and that good-luck which was as much an endowment in its way as the other qualities by which Lucilla might be said to have secured it. She went home meditating her next step, and with a certain enjoyment in the sense of difficulty and the consciousness of how much skill and power would be required to carry on three different threads of innocent intrigue with the three different persons in the drama, without ever letting the general web get confused, or confounding one strand with another. She had to frighten the Archdeacon with the idea that Mrs Mortimer might marry the impostor, and she had to keep the widow in the profoundest ignorance of this suggestion, and she had to manage and guide the impostor himself, to save his position, and deliver him from his enemies, and make his would-be persecutor for ever harmless. If by chance she should forget herself for a moment, and say to Mr Beverley what she meant for Mr Cavendish, or betray her mode of dealing with either to the third person interested, then farewell to all her hopes. But when all that was required was skill and self-possession and courage, Miss Marjoribanks knew herself too well to be afraid.

She came in with that sense of having done her duty which is so sweet to a well-regulated mind. But it was not to that internal satisfaction alone that Providence limited Lucilla's reward. There are exceptional cases to be found here and there even in this world, in which virtue finds its just acknowledgment, and disinterested well-doing is recompensed as it deserves. While Miss Marjoribanks was still occupied with the arrangement of her plans she was interrupted by a visitor, who entered with a brow clouded by care, and yet exalted by the sense of a charge and dignity which is not afforded to every woman. It was Mrs Centum who thus came to unfold to Lucilla the new event which was about to happen in Carlingford. She had a great deal to say first, as was natural, of the dreadful vexation of such a thing happening in holiday-time when the boys were all at home, and when she did not know what to do.

"But you know, Lucilla, it will be delightful for all you young ladies to have the officers," said Mrs Centum; "it keeps a place lively; though, for my part, I always say in six months there will not be a servant in the house that one can depend upon. It is dreadful for servants—especially young ones, and if they are nice-looking, you know; but it is very nice for the young ladies, and for all the picnics and dances and everything——"

"What officers?" said Lucilla, pricking up her ears—for to tell the truth, the very name of officers in a place like Carlingford, where nobody could flirt but Mr Cavendish, was as water in the desert to Miss Marjoribanks's soul.

"Has not the Doctor told you?" said Mrs Centum—"but, to be sure, very few people know as yet. Mr Centum says it must be all on your account, because you give such nice parties —but of course that is only his fun, you know. However, I suppose somebody has told Lord Palmerston of all those great buildings that were meant for the factories, and of Carlingford being such a healthy place. And so the General is coming to us to-morrow, Lucilla—General Travers, you know, that was in all the papers for something he did in India; Charles used to know him at school. He is quite handsome, and has ever so many medals and things. It is a dreadful addition to one's troubles in holiday-time, you know; but, my dear, I hope you will ask him to your Thursdays, and help us to make Carlingford pleasant to him. It all depends upon him," said Mrs Centum, solemnly;—"if he likes the place, and thinks it will do, and finds nice society—whether it is here or at Hampton that they establish the depot."

"At Hampton!" cried Miss Marjoribanks, naturally excited —"the stupidest, wretchedest little place———"

"That is just what Mr Centum says," said the visitor, with a sigh; " what I am nervous about is the servants, Lucilla; and you know that under-nurse of mine, what a nice steady girl she has always been, and such a comfort—but as soon as the soldiers come it turns their heads. I want you to tell me, if you'll be so very good, Lucilla, how Nancy makes that *paté* that Mr Centum is so fond of. I know it is a good deal to ask; but I am sure you are one to stand by your friends; and if the General should take a dislike to Carlingford through any fault of mine, I never could forgive myself; and I want you to ask him to your Thursdays, Lucilla—there's a dear."

"Dear Mrs Centum," cried Miss Marjoribanks, "papa must call on the General and ask him to dinner: as for my Thursdays, I always say they are not parties; they are only *evenings*," said Lucilla, sweetly, "and not worth a gentleman's while."

"And about the *paté*, Lucilla," said Mrs Centum, anxiously, " I hope you won't think it too much of me to ask;—you are so clever, you know, and so is Nancy: and what with the noise, and the nursery dinners, and all those big boys home from school———"

Mrs Centum fixed her eyes with true solicitude on Lucilla's face. Miss Marjoribanks was magnanimous, but the *paté* in question was one of the greatest triumphs of the Doctor's table. She thought, and with truth, that it *was* a great deal for any one to ask; but then it is true that genius has duties as well as privileges; and to impress upon mediocrity the benefit of loyally following and copying superior intelligence, is of itself a moral effect of the greatest importance. And besides, the woman who at such a moment produced a live General in Carlingford, and held out hopes of officers, was not a woman to be denied.

"I will write it down for you," said Lucilla, graciously, "if you think your cook will understand; or perhaps Nancy might step in and show her how—if I can persuade Nancy. Dear Mrs Centum, I hope you will always feel sure that I am ready to do anything for my friends."

"Oh, thank you, dear," cried the grateful woman; "I knew you were not one to mind; and if Nancy would be so very kind—— I am sure you will like the General," added Mrs Centum, with effusion; "he will live here, you know, if the depot comes, and be such an addition! I said to Charles the moment he told me, That would just be the very thing for Lucilla! And he is quite young-looking, and so nice and pleasant," she added, in the fulness of her enthusiasm and gratitude. As for Miss Marjoribanks, she shook her head, but nevertheless received the assurance with a smile.

"It is not that sort of thing I am thinking of," said Lucilla: "if it had been, I need never have come home; and now, after papa has been so kind about the drawing-room——; but I am always glad to hear of nice new people," said Miss Marjoribanks; "and to meet a man that has been in the world is such a pleasure to papa."

With this benign acknowledgment of the General's merits, Lucilla received Mrs Centum's affectionate leave-takings. To be sure, she knew nothing, and did not occupy herself much at that moment about General Travers. But at the same time Miss Marjoribanks, with her usual piety, recognised the approval of Providence in this new occurrence, and was naturally both encouraged and exhilarated. It is but in rare cases, as has been said, that the reward of virtue is given so promptly, and with such beautiful discrimination: and there are even people in the world who profess to have no faith in any prompt or visible recompense. But Lucilla was not of that new and heretical school. For her own part, she felt it very natural that her exertions for the good of her kind should thus be recognised and acknowledged, and returned to her plans with that sweet and exhilarating sense of moral harmony, which an approving conscience, and an approving heaven, and a sense of blessings earned and goodness recompensed, are so well calculated to give.

CHAPTER XXVI.

Miss Marjoribanks's mind had scarcely subsided out of the first exhilarating sense of a great many things to do, and a truly important mission in hand, when little Rose Lake sought her with that confession of family troubles, and prayer for counsel and aid in the extremity, which opened a new way and mode of working to Lucilla. Rose was proud, poor little soul, not only of her exceptional position, and that of her family, as a family of artists, but also with a constitutional and individual pride as one of the natural conservators of domestic honour, who would rather have died than have heard the Lakes lightly spoken of, or upbraided with debt or indecorum, or any other crime. She had been silent as long as she could about Barbara's shortcomings, jealously concealing them from all the world, and attacking them with a violence which made her big elder sister, who was twice as big and six times as strong as she, tremble before her when they were alone. But little Rose had at length found things come to a point beyond which her experience did not go. Barbara began to have secret meetings with a man whose presence nobody was aware of, and who did not come openly to the house to seek her, and persevered, in spite of all remonstrances, in this clandestine career; and all the prejudices and all the instincts of the young artist rose up against her. A vague presentiment of greater evil behind impelled her to some action, and shame and pride combined at the same time to keep her silent. She could not speak to her father, because the poor man lost his head straightway, and made piteous appeals to her not to make a fuss, and threw the burden back again upon her with a double weight; and besides, he was only a man, though he was her father, and Rose had the pride of a woman in addition to her other pride. In these painful circumstances, it occurred to her to consult Lucilla, who had been, as has been recounted in an early part of this history, a great authority at Mount Pleasant, where her heroic belief in herself led, as was natural, others to believe in her. And then Miss Marjoribanks was one of the people who can keep counsel; and Rose felt, besides, that Lucilla had been injured, and had not revenged herself, and that to put confidence in her would be, to a certain extent, to make up for the offence. All these motives, combined with an intolerable sense of having upon her shoulders a burden greater than she could bear, drove the young artist at last to Grange Lane, where Lucilla, as we have said, was still in the state of mental exhilaration and excitement naturally consequent upon having a very important piece of work in hand.

"I don't know what to do," said Rose; "I made up my mind I never would say a word to any one. It is so strange she should have no proper pride! but then it is dreadful to think, what if anything should come of it! though I am sure I don't know what should come of it; but they might run away, or something; and then people are so fond of talking. I thought for a long time, if I only knew some nice old lady; but then I don't suppose there are any nice old ladies in Carlingford," added the Preraphaelist, with a sigh.

"Oh, you little monster!" cried Lucilla, "there is Mrs Chiley, the dearest old——; but never mind, make haste and tell me all the same."

"Lucilla," said Rose, solemnly, "we are not great people like you; we are not rich, nor able to have all we like, and everybody to visit us; but, all the same, we have our Pride. The honour of a family is just as precious whether people live," said the young artist, with a certain severity, "in Grove Street or in Grange Lane."

This exordium had its natural effect upon Miss Marjoribanks; her imagination leaped forward a long way beyond the reality which her companion talked of so solemnly, and she changed colour a little, as even a woman of her experience might be excused for doing in the presence of something terrible and disastrous so near at hand.

"I wish you would not frighten me," said Lucilla; "I am very sorry for you, you dear little Rose. You are only a baby yourself, and ought not to have any bother. Tell me all about it, there's a dear."

But these soothing tones were too much for Rose's composure. She cried, and her cheeks flushed, and her dewy eyes enlarged and lightened when they had thrown off a little part of their oppression in the form of those hot salt tears. Miss Marjoribanks had never seen her look so pretty, and said so to herself, with a momentary and perfectly disinterested regret that there was "nobody" to see her—a regret which probably changed its character before Rose left the house. But in the mean time Lucilla soothed her and kissed her, and took off her hat and shed her pretty curls off her forehead. These curls were not by any means so strong and vehement in their twist as Miss Marjoribanks's own, but hung loosely and softly with the "sweet neglect" of the poet. "You would look very nice if you would take a little pains," Lucilla said, in her maternal way. "You must wear your hair just so on Thursday; and now tell me all about it—there's a dear."

"Lucilla, *you know*," said Rose, drying her tears, "she has taken to going out in the evening, and I am sure she meets him every night. I can't be a spy on her, whatever she does, and I can't lock her up, you know, or lock the door, or anything like that. I am not her mother," said the poor little sister, pathetically, with a regretful sob. "And then she has taken to making herself *nice* before she goes out. I don't think she ever cared much for being nice—not at home, you know; but now she has pretty collars and gloves and things, and I can't tell where she gets them," cried Rose, her eyes lighting up passionately. "She has no money to spend on such things. Lucilla, I should die if I thought she would accept them from *him*."

"You dear old Rose, you don't know what you are saying," said the experienced Lucilla; "most likely, if she meets a gentleman, she is engaged to him; and They always give people presents, you know. If you would only tell me who it is."

"Lucilla, do not trifle with me," said Rose; "it is much too serious for that—engaged without papa knowing of it, nor me! You know very well that would be no engagement. I sometimes think she is—is—fond of him," said the reverent little maiden, whose voice changed and softened under the influence of that supposition; "and then again I think it is only because he is rich," she went on, with new vehemence. "Oh, Lucilla, if you only knew how dreadful it was to have such thoughts—and there is nobody to take care of her but me! Papa cannot be worried, for that would react upon everything. An artist is not just like other people. It is everybody's duty to leave him undisturbed; and then, you know, he is only a man, and does not understand; and if she won't pay any attention to me when I speak to her, oh, Lucilla, tell me, what can I do?"

"Let me think," said Lucilla, gravely. "You know I can't tell all in a moment. It is Mr Cavendish, I suppose, though you won't say so. Now just wait a moment, and let me think."

"I once thought of going to him," said Rose; "perhaps he might be generous, and go away. An artist can do many things that other people can't do. We have an exceptional position," the Preraphaelist went on, faltering a little, and not feeling quite so sure of the fact on that special occasion. "I thought of going and begging of him, if it was on my knees——"

"My dear," said Lucilla, with great seriousness, "if you did, I think it is most likely he would fall in love with *you*, and that would not mend the matter; and I am sure Barbara would give you poison. I will tell you what we must do. I would not do it for everybody; but you know I was always very fond of you, you dear little Rose. You shall ask me for to-morrow evening to come to tea."

"To come to tea!" echoed poor Rose, in dismay. She had been waiting for Lucilla's advice with a great deal of anxiety; but at the present moment it would be vain to conceal that the proposed expedient seemed to her altogether inadequate for the emergency. The light went out of her face as she opened her eyes wide and fixed them on Lucilla; and for one moment, one desperate moment, Rose was disloyal, and lost faith in the only person who could help her; which, perhaps, under the circumstances, was not a thing to cause much surprise.

"My dear, you may be sure I would not propose it, if I did not feel it was the best thing to do," said Lucilla, with great gravity. "It happens precisely that I want to see Mr Cavendish, and if he is at home he never shows himself, and I have been wondering how I could find him. I shall make him walk home with me," said Miss Marjoribanks, "so you need not be uneasy, Rose, about the trouble I am taking. I am doing it to serve myself as well as you. We shall say eight o'clock, if that is not too late."

"But, Lucilla——" said Rose, with consternation; and then she stopped short, and could not tell what more to say.

"You don't understand it?" said Miss Marjoribanks; "I don't think it was to be expected that you should understand it. A little thing like you has no way of knowing the world. When Barbara knows I am there, she will be sure to bring him to the very door; she will want me to see that he is with her; and you may leave the rest to me," said Lucilla. "For my part, I have something very particular to say to Mr Cavendish. It is my luck," Miss Marjoribanks added, "for I could not think how to get to see him. At eight o'clock to-morrow evening——"

"Yes," said Rose; but perhaps it was still doubtful how far she understood the mode of operations proposed. Lucilla's prompt and facile genius was too much for the young artist, and there was, as she herself would have said, an entire want of "keeping" between her own sense of the position, tragical and desperate as that was, and any state of matters which could be ameliorated by the fact of Miss Marjoribanks coming to tea. It had been Rose's only hope, and now it seemed all at once to fail her; and yet, at the same time, that instinctive faith in Lucilla which came naturally to every one under her influence struggled against reason in Rose's heart. Her red soft lips fell apart with the hurried breath of wonder and doubt; her eyes, still expanded, and clearer than usual after their tears, were fixed upon Lucilla with an appealing questioning look; and it was just at this moment, when Rose was a great deal too much absorbed in her disappointment and surprise, and lingering hope, to take any notice of strange sounds or sights, or of anybody coming, that Thomas all at once opened the door and showed Mrs Centum into the room.

Now it would have mattered very little for Mrs Centum—who, to be sure, knew Lucilla perfectly well, and would never have dreamed for a moment of identifying such a trifling little person as Rose Lake in any way with Miss Marjoribanks; but then Mrs Centum happened at that precise moment to be bringing the new arrival, the important stranger, who had so much in his power—General Travers himself—to be introduced to Lucilla; and it was not the fault either of Rose or the General if it was on the young mistress of the Female School of Design that the warrior's first glance fell. Naturally the conversation had run upon Miss Marjoribanks on the past evening, for Mrs Centum was full of the enthusiasm and excitement incident to that *paté* which Lucilla had so magnanimously enabled her to produce. "Is she pretty?" General Travers had demanded, as was to be expected. "We—ll," Mrs Centum had replied, and made a long pause—"would you call Lucilla pretty, Charles?" and Charles had been equally dubious in his response; for, to be sure, it was a dereliction from Miss Marjoribanks's dignity to call her pretty, which is a trifling sort of qualification. But when the General entered the drawing-room, which might be called the centre of Carlingford, and saw before him that little dewy face, full of clouds and sunshine, uncertain, unquiet, open-eyed, with the red lips apart, and the eyes clear and expanded with recent tears—a face which gave a certain sentiment of freshness and fragrance to the atmosphere like the quiet after a storm—he did not understand what his hosts could mean. "I call her very pretty," he said, under his breath, to his interested and delighted chaperone; and we are surely justified in appealing to the readers of this history, as Lucilla, who was always reasonable, afterwards did to herself, whether it could be justly said, under all the circumstances, that either Rose or the General were to blame?

The little artist got up hurriedly when she awoke to the fact that other visitors had come into the room, but she was not at all interested in General Travers, whom Rose, with the unconscious insolence of youth, classified in her own mind as an elderly gentleman. Not that he was at all an elderly gentleman; but then a man of forty, especially when he is a fine man and adequately developed for his years, has at the first glance no great attraction for an impertinent of seventeen. Rose did not go away without receiving another kiss from Lucilla, and a parting reminder. "To-morrow at eight o'clock; and mind you leave it all to me, and don't worry," said Miss Marjoribanks; and Rose, half ashamed, put on her hat and went away, without so much as remarking the admiration in the stranger's eyes, nor the look of disappointment with which he saw her leave the room. Rose thought no more of him than if he had been a piece of furniture; but as for the General, when he found himself obliged to turn to Lucilla and make himself agreeable, the drawback of having thus had his admiration forestalled and drawn away from its legitimate object was such, that he did not find her at all pretty; which, after all, on a first interview at least, is all They think about, as Miss Marjoribanks herself said.

"We must do all we can to make Carlingford agreeable to the General," said Mrs Centum. "You know how much depends upon it, Lucilla. If we can but make him like the place, only think what an advantage to society—and we have such nice society in Carlingford," said the injudicious woman, who did not know what to say.

"Nothing very particular," said Miss Marjoribanks. "I hope General Travers will like us; but as for the officers, I am not so sure. They are all so light and airy, you know: and to have nothing but flirting men is almost as bad as having nobody that can flirt; which is my position," Lucilla added, with a sigh, "as long as Mr Cavendish is away."

"Lucilla," cried Mrs Centum, a little shocked, "one would think to hear you that you were the greatest coquette possible; and on the contrary she is quite an example to all our young ladies, I assure you, General; and as for flirting——"

"Dear Mrs Centum," said Lucilla, sweetly, "one has always to do one's duty to society. As far as I am concerned, it is quite different. And I don't mean to say that the officers would not be a great acquisition," Miss Marjoribanks continued, with her usual politeness; "but then too many young people are the ruin of society. If we were to run all to dancing and that sort of thing, after all the trouble one has taken——" said Lucilla. Perhaps it was not quite civil; but then it must be admitted, that to see a man look blankly in your face, as if he were saying in his mind, "Then it is only *you*, and not that pretty little thing, that is Miss Marjoribanks!" was about as exasperating a sensation as one is likely to meet with. Lucilla understood perfectly well General Travers's look, and for the moment, instead of making herself agreeable, it was the contrary impulse that moved her. She looked at him, not blankly as he looked at her, but in a calmly considerate way, as she might have looked at Mr Holden the upholsterer, had he proposed a new kind of *tapisserie* to her judgment. "One would be always delighted, of course, to have General Travers," said Miss Marjoribanks, "but I am afraid the officers would not do."

As for Mrs Centum, she was quite incapable of managing such a terrible crisis. She felt it, indeed, a little hard that it should be her man who was defied in this alarming way, while Mr Cavendish and the Archdeacon, the two previous candidates, had both been received so sweetly. To be sure, it was his own fault; but that did not mend matters. She looked from one to the other with a scared look, and grew very red, and untied her bonnet; and then, as none of these evidences of agitation had any effect upon the other parties involved, plunged into the heat of the conflict without considering what she was about to say.

"Lucilla, I am surprised at you," said Mrs Centum, "when you know how you have gone on about Mr Cavendish—when you know what a fuss you have made, and how you have told everybody——"

"By the by, who is Mr Cavendish?" said General Travers, interposing, with that holy horror of a quarrel between women which is common to the inferior half of creation. "I wonder if he is a fellow one used to meet everywhere. One never could get any satisfaction who he belonged to. He never pretended to be one of the Devonshire Cavendishes, you know. I don't know if he had any family at all, or relations, or that sort of thing. In most cases a man gets on just as well without them, in my opinion. I wonder if this fellow you are talking of is he?"

"Oh no," said Mrs Centum. "I hope you will meet him before you leave Carlingford. He has a sister married here; but we have always understood he was one of the Cavendishes. I am sure Mrs Woodburn always gives herself out for somebody," she continued, beginning to let the interesting suspicion enter her mind; for, to be sure, they were about of a standing, and the banker's wife had sometimes felt a little sore at the idea that her neighbour possessed distinctions of family which were denied to herself. "It is true, none of her relations ever come to see her," said Mrs Centum, and she began to forget the General, and Lucilla's reception of him, in this still more interesting subject. It was the first time that the authenticity of the Cavendishes had been attacked in Carlingford; and, to be sure, what is the good of having fine connections if they cannot be produced? While Mrs Centum pondered a suggestion so interesting, Lucilla, on her part, also took advantage of the occasion, and descended from the calm heights of dignity on which she had placed herself. And the General, who was a well-bred man, had got over for the moment the unlucky impression made upon him by the fresh face of little Rose Lake.

"Mr Cavendish is very nice," said Miss Marjoribanks. "I am very fond of all my own relations, but I don't care about other people's. Of course he is one of the Cavendishes. I don't see how he can help it, when that is his name. I should think it was sure to be the same. We should be so obliged to you if you would bring him back to Carlingford. I don't know, I am sure, why he is so obstinate in staying away."

"Perhaps somebody has been unkind to him," said the General, feeling it was expected of him.

"I am sure *I* have not been unkind to him," said Lucilla. "He is such a loss to me. If you are going to do us the pleasure of coming on Thursday—Oh, I am sure we shall feel quite honoured, both papa and I—I will show you how badly off I am. It is not a party in the least, and we don't dance," said Miss Marjoribanks, "that is why I am a little uncertain about the officers. It is one of my principles that too many young people are the ruin of society; but it is hard work sometimes, when one is not properly supported," Lucilla added, with a gentle sigh.

"If I can be of any use," said the amused soldier. "I don't pretend to be able to replace Cavendish, if it is Cavendish; but——"

"No," said Miss Marjoribanks, with resignation, "it is not easy to replace him. He has quite a talent, you know; but I am sure it is very kind of you, and we shall be delighted to have such an acquisition," Lucilla continued, after a pause, with a gracious smile; and then she led her guests down-stairs to luncheon, which was every way satisfactory. As for the General, it cannot be doubted that he had the worst of it in this little encounter, and felt himself by no means such a great personage in Carlingford as his hospitable entertainers had persuaded him he should be. Mrs Centum declared afterwards that she could not form the least idea what Lucilla meant by it, she who was generally so civil to everybody. But it is not necessary to say that Miss Marjoribanks knew perfectly well what she was doing, and felt it imperatively necessary to bring down General Travers to his proper level. Carlingford could exist perfectly well without him and his officers; but Lucilla did not mean that the society she had taken so much pains to form should be condescended to by a mere soldier. And then, after all, she was only human, and it was not to be expected she could pass over the blank look with which her visitor turned to herself, after having by evil fortune cast his eyes upon Rose Lake. At the same time, Miss Marjoribanks, always magnanimous, did not blame Rose, who had no hand whatever in the matter; and if she avenged herself in a lady-like and satisfactory manner, it is not to be supposed that it was simply a sense of offence which actuated Lucilla. She did it, on the contrary, on strictly philosophical principles, having perceived that Mrs Centum was spoiling her General, and that it was absolutely necessary that he should be disabused.

When they left, Mrs Centum was almost afraid to put the question that trembled on her lips. She uttered it at last, faltering, and with a very doubtful expression, for she could not conceal from herself the fact that the General had been snubbed. "How do you like Lucilla?" she said, in the most humble way; and then she turned away her face. She could bear it, whatever it might be. She said to herself that so long as the children were well, and the holidays about over, she could bear anything; and what did it matter to her about the officers?— but at the same time she preferred to avert her face when she received the blow.

"I am sure Miss Marjoribanks is a person for whom I shall always entertain the highest respect," said the General, and he gave a little laugh. "Was that pretty little creature a sister of hers?—or a friend?—or what? I don't know when I have seen anything so pretty," said the unsuspecting man; and then Mrs Centum turned round upon him with a kind of horror.

"*That* Lucilla's sister!—why, she has no sister; I told you so; she is an only child, and will have everything. She will be quite an heiress," cried Mrs Centum, "if the old Doctor were to die; though, I am sure, poor dear man, I hope he will not die. There is no other medical man in the town that one can have the least confidence in, except Dr Rider; and then *he* is so young, and can't have much experience with children. Her sister, indeed! It was little Rose Lake, the drawing-master's daughter," said Mrs Centum, with cruel distinctness. The General only said, "Oh!" but it was in a crestfallen tone; for to be snubbed by one lady, and struck with sudden enthusiasm for another, who, after all, was not a lady to speak of, but only a drawing-master's daughter, was rather hard upon the poor man. Thus it was the soldier, who in ordinary circumstances ought to have been the most successful, who began in the most cruel and uncomfortable way his campaign in Carlingford.

CHAPTER XXVII.

MISS MARJORIBANKS, except for her habitual walk, did not go out much that day. She was too much occupied with what she had in hand. She could not conceive—for Lucilla naturally took a reasonable view of affairs in general, and did not account for the action of any such unknown quantity as love, for example—why Mr Cavendish should conceal himself so carefully from society in Carlingford, and yet run all the risk of meeting Barbara Lake in the evenings. It seemed to Lucilla inconceivable, and yet it was impossible not to believe it. Mr Cavendish, though she had seen him on the very verge of a proposal, did not present himself to her mind in the aspect of a man who would consider the world well lost for any such transitory passion; neither, as was natural, did Barbara Lake appear to Lucilla the least like a person calculated to call forth that sentiment; but nevertheless it must be true, and the only way to account for it was by thinking, after all, what fools *They* were, and what poor judges, and how little to be depended on, when women were concerned. Miss Marjoribanks was determined to lose no more time, but to speak to Mr Cavendish, if it was Mr Cavendish, and she could get the chance, quite plainly of the situation of affairs—to let him know how much she knew, and to spur him up to come forward like a man and brave anything the Archdeacon could do. Had it been any small personal aim that moved Lucilla, no doubt she would have shrunk from such a decided step; but it was, on the contrary, the broadest philanthropical combination of Christian principles, help to the weak and succour to the oppressed, and a little, just a very little, of the equally Evangelical idea of humbling the proud and bringing down the mighty. She was so much occupied with her plans that it was with a little difficulty she roused herself to keep up the conversation with her father at dinner, and be as amusing and agreeable as ordinary; which indeed was more than ordinarily her duty; since Dr Marjoribanks came in, in a fractious and disturbed state of mind, discontented with things in general. The truth was, he had got a letter from Tom Marjoribanks from India, where that unlucky young man had gone. It was all very well and natural and proper to go to India, and Lucilla had felt, indeed, rather satisfied with herself for having helped forward that desirable conclusion, especially after the Doctor had taken pains to explain to her, not knowing that she had any share in it, that it was the very best thing for Tom to do. For it has been already said that Dr Marjoribanks, though he liked Tom, and thought it very odd that Providence should have given the girl to him, and the boy to his incapable sister-in-law, who did not in the least know how to manage him, had no desire to have his nephew for a son-in-law. Going to India was very right and proper, and the best thing to do; for a man might get on *there*, even at the bar, who would have no chance *here;* but after he had made one step in the right direction, it was only to be expected that all sorts of misfortunes should happen to Tom. He was wrecked, which might have been looked for, and he lost his boxes, with the greater part of his outfit, either at that unhappy moment, or in the Desert, or at an after part of his unlucky career; and the object of the letter which Dr Marjoribanks had just received was to get money to make up for his losses. Tom, who was a very good son, did not want to vex his mother, and accordingly it was his uncle whom he applied to, to sell out a portion of the money he had in the Funds. "She would think I was ruined, or that it was my fault, or at least that I meant to spend all my money," wrote Tom, "and you understand, uncle, that it is not my fault." "Confound him! it is never his fault," said Dr Marjoribanks, as if that could possibly be brought against the unfortunate young man as a crime.

"No, papa, it is his luck," said Lucilla; "poor Tom!—but I should not like to take a passage in the same boat with him if I was the other people. Though I am sure he is not a bit to blame."

"I hope he does not mean to go on like this," said the Doctor. "He will soon make ducks and drakes of his five thousand pounds. A young fellow like that ought to mind what he's doing. It is a great deal easier to throw money away than to lay it by."

"Papa, it is his luck," said Miss Marjoribanks; "it is all put into a system in political economy, you know. For my part, I am always the other way. It is very funny before you get used to it; but you know there has to be a balance in everything, and that is how it must be."

"I don't think it at all funny," said Dr Marjoribanks, "unless your good luck and his bad were to be joined together; which is not an expedient I fancy." When he said this the Doctor gave a sharp glance at his daughter, to see if by any chance that might perhaps be what she was thinking of; but naturally the maiden candour and unsuspecting innocence of Lucilla was proof to such glances. She took no notice at all of the implied suspicion. But though it was very absurd for anybody to think that she would have married him, it was not in Miss Marjoribanks's nature to be disloyal to Tom.

"I think he is quite right about his mother, papa," said Lucilla; "she would never understand it, you know; she would think the world was coming to an end. I would not for anything take a passage in the same boat with him, but he is nice in his way, poor fellow! I wonder what he has ever done to have such dreadful luck—but I hope you are going to do what he asks you:" and with this calm expression of her interest Miss Marjoribanks went up-stairs. When the Doctor became thus aware of his daughter's sentiments, it seemed to him that he was more at liberty to be kind to his nephew. He had never been able to divest himself of a little lurking dread, an inherent idea which was so obstinate that it felt like a prophecy, that

P

somehow or other, after costing her father so much, and making such a difference in the house, Lucilla, who on the whole was a dear production, would fall to Tom's share, with all Dr Marjoribanks's other possessions; and the Doctor saw no reason why he should work and lay up money for a boy whom Providence, with a wonderful want of discrimination, had bestowed, not upon him, but upon Mrs John Marjoribanks. However, when that question was settled and done with, his heart began to relent to Tom the unlucky, who, after all, when the son-in-law hypothesis was fully dismissed, was his natural born nephew, and, as Lucilla said, very nice in his way, poor fellow! The Doctor began to write him a letter, and softened more and more with every line he wrote; but as for Lucilla, she had something more immediately important to occupy her up-stairs.

The fact was that Miss Marjoribanks had found a shadowy figure in black in the corner of one of the sofas when she came into the drawing-room—a figure with a veil down, and a large shawl, and a tremulous air. It was very seldom that Mrs Mortimer took courage to visit her young patroness; and to go out at night, except sometimes to Salem Chapel when there was a meeting, and when the timid woman represented to herself that it was her duty, was a thing unknown to her. But yet, nevertheless, it was Mrs Mortimer who sat waiting for Lucilla. They had not met since that momentous interview in which the widow revealed her history to Miss Marjoribanks's sympathetic ears, and the poor woman had been able to bear no longer the solitude of her cottage, and her garden-walls, and her little pupils, and Mary Jane. To know that something was going on outside that concerned her—to hear the waves, as it were, beating round the walls of her prison, and never to have even so much as a peep at them, what they were about, if the tide was beginning to turn, or the wind to change, or the lifeboat to appear—was more than Mrs Mortimer, even with all her training to patience, could put up with; and accordingly she had made a frantic rush out, under cover of night, to see if there was anything to see, and hear if there was anything to hear.

"You don't know how dreadful it is to keep staring at the walls all day and never see any change," said the widow. "It is very stupid and silly, but you know I cannot help it. I get to fancy always that something wonderful must be going on on the other side."

"That is because you don't go out enough," said Lucilla.

"You know how often I have said you should go out once every day; and then you would see that everything outside was very much the same as everything within."

"Oh, Lucilla! don't say so," said Mrs Mortimer; "and besides, *he* has been again, and I could see you had been saying something to him. He spoke as if I understood it all when I did not understand a word of it; and he spoke of him, you know, and was quite solemn, and warned me to think well of it, and not do anything rash—as if I had anything to think about, or was going to do anything! Tell me what you said to him, Lucilla; for I am sure, by the way he spoke, he must have taken him for himself, and perhaps you for me."

"Who did he take for himself, I wonder?" said Lucilla. "As for you and me, dear Mrs Mortimer, we are so different that he could never take us for each other, whatever the circumstances might be."

"Ah, yes, Lucilla! we are different," said the poor widow. "You have all your own people to take care of you, and you are not afraid of anybody; but as for me, I have not a creature in the world who cares what becomes of me." As she made this forlorn statement it was only natural that the poor woman should cry a little. This was no doubt the result of the four garden-walls that closed in so tightly, and the aggravating little pupils; but Miss Marjoribanks felt it was not a state of feeling that could be allowed to go on.

"You ought not to speak like that; I am sure there are a great many people who are interested in you; and you have always Me," said Lucilla, with a certain reproachful tenderness. As for Mrs Mortimer, she raised her head and dried her eyes when Miss Marjoribanks began to speak, and looked at her in a somewhat eager, inquiring way; but when Lucilla uttered those last reassuring words, it is undeniable that the widow's countenance fell a little. She faltered and grew pale again, and only cried the more—perhaps with gratitude, perhaps with disappointment. And when she said, "I am sure you are very kind, Lucilla," which was all the poor soul could utter, it was in a very tremulous undecided voice. The fact that she had always the sympathy and co-operation of such a friend as Miss Marjoribanks, did not seem to have the exhilarating effect upon her that it ought to have had. It did not apparently do any more for her than the similar assurance that Lucilla was coming to tea did for Rose Lake. But then, like every other benefactor of the human race, Miss Marjoribanks was aware that the human mind has its moments of unbelief. It was a discouraging experience to meet with; but she never permitted it seriously to interrupt her exertions for the good of her kind.

"You should not have so poor an opinion of your friends," said Lucilla, who after all was giving only a stone when her suppliant asked for bread. "You know how much interested we all are in you; and for me, anything I can do——"

"Oh, Lucilla, you are very kind; nobody could be kinder," cried Mrs Mortimer, with compunction. "It is very nice to have friends. I do not know what I should do without you, I am sure; but then one cannot live upon one's friends; and then one knows, when they go away," said the widow, with more feeling than distinctness of expression, "that they all go away to something of their own, and pity you or forget you; but you always stay there, and have nothing of your own to go away to. I am not grumbling, but it is hard, Lucilla; and then you are young, and happy, and at home, and I don't think it is possible you can understand."

"My dear," said Miss Marjoribanks, "it is quite easy to understand, and I know exactly what you mean. You want me to tell you all about Mr Beverley, and what I said to him, and what he has in his mind. If he is the something of your own you would like to go away to, I think it is a pity. I am sure he has a temper, and *I* would not marry him for my part. But if you mean *me*, I have nothing to go away to," said Lucilla, with a little scorn. "I should be ashamed not to be enough for myself. When I leave you it is not to enjoy myself, but to think about you and to plan for you; and all that you want to know is about *him!*" said Miss Marjoribanks, piercing through and through the thin armour of her incapable assailant. Naturally all the widow's defences fell before this ruthless response. She cried with a mingled sensation of shame at being found out, and penitence for being so ungrateful, and a certain desolate distress with her own incapacity and want of power to defend herself. It was an acute variety of feminine anguish on the whole. The idea that she, a mature woman, a married woman and widow, who ought to have been done with all these vanities, should have been found out by a young girl to be thinking about *a gentleman*, struck poor Mrs Mortimer with as sharp a sense of shame as if her wistful preoccupation had been a crime. Indeed the chances are, if it had been a crime, she would not have been nearly so much ashamed of it. She hid her face in her hands and blushed down to the very edge of her black dress and up into the glooms of her widow's veil; and all the self-defence she was capable of was a faint "Oh, Lucilla!" a mere appeal of weakness without reason—a virtual throwing of herself in acknowledged guilt at her judge's feet.

"Thomas is coming with the tea," said Miss Marjoribanks. "Come into my room and take off your bonnet. What is the good of worrying yourself when you know I have taken it into my own hands? Spoiling your eyes with crying, and making everybody uncomfortable never does the least good; and, besides, one never knows what harm one might do one's self," said Lucilla, seriously. "I don't think you gone off at all, for my part; but if you don't take proper care—— I shall give you some rose-water, and you will be all right after you have had a cup of tea."

"Oh, no; it will be best to go home. I am such a poor creature now. I am not good for anything. Let me go home, Lucilla," said poor Mrs Mortimer. But Lucilla would not let her go home; and by the time tea was ready, and Dr Marjoribanks had come up-stairs, she had so managed to soothe her visitor's nerves, and console her spirits, that the Doctor himself grew complimentary. He was so civil, in fact, that Lucilla felt slightly startled, and on the whole thought it was as well that the Archdeacon was at hand, and affairs in a promising way; for it was doubtful whether even Miss Marjoribanks's magnanimity could have got over any ridiculous exhibition of interest on the part of her father, who certainly was old enough to know better. Even to see him taking Mrs Mortimer's tea to her and congratulating her upon her improved looks, and felicitating himself and the world in general on the fact that Carlingford agreed with her, was aggravating to his daughter —more aggravating, though it is strange to say so, than even the blank looks of General Travers in the morning, or his transference of the homage intended for herself to little Rose Lake; *that* was no more than a blunder, and Lucilla felt a consolatory conviction that, so far as incivility went, the General had received a very satisfactory set-off. But to see Dr Marjoribanks exerting himself in such an unheard-of way made her open her eyes. If he were still accessible to such influences, nobody could answer for anything that might happen; and the widow was so grateful for his kindness, that at one moment it was all that Lucilla could do to keep her lips shut fast, and restrain herself from a tempting allusion which would have made an end of Mrs Mortimer. It was the first time that Lucilla's *protégée* had ventured to come thus familiarly and uninvited to her friend's house ; and the Doctor, who knew no special reason for the visit, expressed his satisfaction with a warmth which was quite uncalled-for, and hoped that Lucilla might often "have the advantage of her company;" and actually betrayed symptoms of a disposition to "see her home," if Miss Marjoribanks had not already made provision for that emergency. When the visitor had finally departed, under the charge of Thomas and Mary Jane, the father and daughter regarded each other, for the first time, with dubious glances—for, so far as Lucilla was concerned, it was a revelation to her of a new and altogether unsuspected danger ; and the Doctor, for his part, was very conciliatory, and showed a certain consciousness of having committed himself, which made matters twenty times worse.

"Really, Lucilla, your friend is a credit to you," said Dr Marjoribanks. "It was a stroke of talent to pick her up, as you did, and make a woman of her—and a pretty woman, too," he added, incautiously; as if he, at his age, had anything to do with that.

"I am so glad you think so, papa," said Lucilla, in her dutiful way. "I don't think myself that she has gone off at all to speak of. In some lights she might pass for being no older than I am—if she was very well dressed, you know; and it really does not matter what age a woman is if she keeps her looks. I should be very glad to see her nicely married, for my part ; she is one of the people who ought to be married," Miss Marjoribanks continued, with an inflexion of compassionate tolerance in her voice. As for the Doctor, he mistook her as usual, and took her tone of pity and kindly patronising disdain for another instance of his daughter's policy and high art ; whereas the truth was she was quite in earnest, and meant every word she said. And then Dr Marjoribanks's sense of humour was keener than that of Lucilla. After this the conversation flagged slightly, for Miss Marjoribanks had undeniably received a shock. In the midst of her benevolent preoccupation and care for other people, it had suddenly dawned upon her that her own stronghold might be attacked, and the tables turned upon her in the twinkling of an eye. There are days of discouragement in the most triumphant career, and this was one of those uncomfortable moments. Her faith in herself did not fail her for an instant ; but the faith of her natural born subjects —the creatures of her bounty—had visibly failed her. Neither

Rose Lake nor Mrs Mortimer had shown that confidence in Lucilla's genius which experience and loyalty both called upon them to show. When Dr Marjoribanks had gone down-stairs to resume the case which he was writing out for the 'Lancet,' Lucilla passed through one of those moments of sublime despondency which now and then try the spirits of the benefactors of their race. A few tears came to her eyes as she reflected upon this great problem. Without such trials genius would not fully know itself nor be justly aware of its own strength. For no temptation to give up her disinterested exertions had any effect upon the mind of Miss Marjoribanks; and even her sense of pain at the unbelief of her followers was mingled with that pity for their weakness which involves pardon. Even when they wounded her she was sorry for them. It was nature that was in fault, and not the fallible human creatures who had it not in them to believe in the simple force of genius. When Lucilla had shed these few tears over her subjects' weakness and want of faith, she rose up again in new strength from the momentary downfall. It was, as we have said, a sublime moment. The idea of giving them up, and leaving their affairs to their own guidance, never for an instant penetrated into her heroic mind; but she was human, and naturally she felt the prick of ingratitude. When the crisis was over she rose up calmly and lighted her candle, and went to her room with a smile upon her magnanimous lips. As she performed that simple action, Lucilla had lifted up the feeble widow, and taken the family of Lakes, and Mr Cavendish, and even the burly Archdeacon himself, upon her shoulders. They might be ungrateful, or even unaware of all she was doing for them; but they had the supreme claim of Need upon Strength; and Miss Marjoribanks, notwithstanding the wound they had given her, was loyal to that appeal, and to her own consciousness of superior Power.

At the same time, it would not be just to omit all mention of a consolatory recollection which occurred to Lucilla in this moment of her weakness. At such a crisis the mind of genius may be supported by a matter very trifling in itself. Even at the instant when the moisture sprang to her eyes, Miss Marjoribanks said to herself, "Poor Tom!" and felt that the bitterness, to a certain extent, had evaporated out of her tears. He was a long way off, and Lucilla would have thought it madness indeed to connect herself in any way with the fortunes of her unlucky cousin; yet it gave her a certain support to think that, amid all the want of faith she was encountering, Tom believed in her, heart and soul. It was an insignificant matter, so far as any practical result was concerned, if, indeed, anything can be called insignificant which gives strength to a great mind in a moment of discouragement. She said "Poor Tom!" and felt as if for the moment she had something to lean on, and was comforted. We mention this fact rather as a contribution to the history of those phenomena of the human mind, which have as yet escaped the metaphysician, than as an actual circumstance in the life of Miss Marjoribanks. She was a woman of genius, and he only a very simple, unlucky fellow; and yet a sensation of comfort came to Lucilla's heart when she said " Poor Tom!"

CHAPTER XXVIII.

LUCILLA prepared her toilette the next evening, to take tea with the Lakes, with greater care than she would have spent upon a party of much greater pretensions. She was, to be sure, dressed as usual, in the white dress, *high*, which she had brought into fashion in Carlingford; but then that simple evening toilette required many adjuncts which were not necessary on other occasions, seeing that this time she was going to walk to her destination, and had in her mind the four distinct aims of pleasing Rose, of dazzling Barbara, of imposing upon Mr Cavendish, and, finally, of being, as always, in harmony with *herself*. She was as punctual to the hour and minute of her engagement as if she had been a queen; and, indeed, it was with a demeanour as gracious that she entered the little house in Grove Street, where, naturally, there had been also sundry preparations made for her visit. Mr Lake himself, who had postponed his usual walk, and was taking his tea an hour later than usual, received his young visitor with all the suavity natural to him; and as for Barbara, she did the honours with a certain suppressed exultation and air of triumph, which proved to Lucilla that her plan was indeed an inspiration of genius. As for Rose, it would be impossible to describe what were her sensations. Her faith still failed her at that momentous hour. She was sceptical of Lucilla, and naturally of all the world, and regarded everybody with jealous scrutiny and expectation and distrust, as was natural to a young conspirator. She was profoundly excited and curious to know what Miss Marjoribanks meant to do; and at the same time she did not believe in Miss Marjoribanks, and was almost disposed to betray and interfere with her, if such treachery had been possible. It was Rose Lucilla specially came to visit, and yet Rose was the only one who was cool to her, and did not seem fully to appreciate her condescension; but then, happily, Miss Marjoribanks was magnanimous, and at the same time had a purpose to support her, which was much more comprehensive and of larger application than anything that had entered into the mind of Rose Lake.

"I am proud to see you in my house, Miss Marjoribanks," said Mr Lake. "I have always considered your excellent father one of my best friends. I am not able to give my children the same advantages, but I have always brought them up not to have any false pride. We have no wealth; but we have some things which cannot be purchased by wealth," said the drawing-master, with mild grandeur; and he looked round upon the walls of his parlour, which were hung with his own drawings, and where one of Willie's held the place of honour. In all Carlingford there was no other house that enjoyed a similar distinction; and, consequently, it was with a delicious sense of chivalrous deference yet equality that the exceptional man of Grove Street received the young sovereign of Grange Lane.

"I am so glad to come, Mr Lake," said Lucilla. "It is so nice to be among such old friends; and, besides that, you know there never was any voice that suited mine like Barbara's; and that dear old Rose was always my pet at Mount Pleasant. I should have come long ago if anybody had ever asked me," said Miss Marjoribanks. And as for Mr Lake, he was so overpowered by this implied reproach upon his hospitality that he scarcely knew how to reply.

"My dear Miss Marjoribanks, if you have not been asked it has been from no want of—of goodwill," said Mr Lake, anxiously. "I do not know what the girls can have been thinking of. You see Rose's genius takes another line; and Barbara, naturally, has a great many things to think of; but in the future, I hope——"

"Oh, yes; I shall come without being asked," said Lucilla. And when the tea came it was all she could do to keep herself quiet, and remember that she was a visitor, and not take it out of the incapable hands of Barbara, who never gave her father the right amount of sugar in his tea. To tell the truth, Barbara's thoughts were occupied by a very different subject; and even Rose had but little attention to spare for her papa's comforts at that special moment. But Lucilla's larger mind embraced everything. She sat with her very fingers itching to cut the bread-and-butter for him, and give him a cup of tea as he liked it; and asked herself, with indignation, what was the use of that great creature, with her level eyebrows and her crimson bloom, who could not take the trouble to remember that three lumps was what Mr Lake liked. Miss Marjoribanks had never taken tea with him before; but his second cup, had she dispensed it, would have been exactly to his taste—which was a thing Barbara had not learned to make it in all these years. No wonder that a certain sense of contemptuous indignation arose for one moment, even in the calm and impartial bosom of genius. Perhaps Rose would not have done much better; but then Rose was good for something else, which was always a set-off on the other side. Thus it will be seen that Lucilla had a respect for use, even of a kind which in her own person she did not much appreciate, as became a person of a truly enlightened mind; but a creature who was of no earthly good irritated her well-regulated spirit; for, to be sure, the possession of a fine contralto (which is, at the same time, not fine enough to be made use of professionally) is not a matter of sufficient moment in this world to excuse a young woman for not knowing how to give her father a comfortable cup of tea.

It was nearly nine o'clock before Mr Lake went out for his walk, and by that time it was almost dark, and the lamp outside was lighted, which was not far from the door. Lucilla had taken a seat near the window, with the view of witnessing everything; and it cannot be denied that she felt a little excited when Barbara went out of the room after her father, leaving Rose alone with her guest. Miss Marjoribanks's heart gave a beat or two the more in the first minute, though before the next had passed it had fallen into its usual measure. There were no candles as yet in the parlour, and Grove Street —or at least the bit of it which lay before the window, lighted by the lamp outside, and relieved against a little square of bluish-green sky which intervened between Miss Hemmings's house and that of old Mr Wrangle on the opposite side —was very clear to the interested spectator. There was nobody visible but an organ-man, who was grinding a popular melody very dolorously out of his box, in what Rose would have called the middle distance; and beyond, Miss Jane Hemmings looking out of the long staircase window, and three little boys in different attitudes below,—that is, if one did not count a tall figure which, perhaps with the view of listening to the music of the organ, was coming and going in a limited circuit round the light of the lamp.

"How convenient it is to have the lamp so near," said Lucilla. "Oh, don't light any candles, please; it is so nice to sit in the dark. Where is Barbara, I wonder? Let us have some music, and put down that dreadful organ. I hope she has not gone out. And where are you, you sulky little Rose?"

"She has gone up-stairs," said Rose, who began to feel all the enormity of her conduct in thus betraying her sister. "I hate sitting in the dark. I hate being a spy; come in from the window, Lucilla, now you are here——"

"My dear Rose," said Miss Marjoribanks, "I think you forget a little. For my part I do not understand what being a spy means. Barbara knows very well I am here. I should scorn to take an advantage of anybody, for my part. If she does not bring him past the very window, and under my eyes—Ah, yes, that is just what I thought," said Lucilla, with gentle satisfaction. But by this time poor little Rose had roused herself into an innocent fury.

"What is just as you thought?" said Rose, laying an impatient grasp on Miss Marjoribanks's arm. "Come in from the window, Lucilla, this moment—this moment! Oh, me, to think it should be my doing! Oh, Lucilla, don't be so mean and shabby and wretched. I tell you to come in—come in directly! If you do not shut the window, and come and sit here in the corner, I will never, never speak to you again!"

Miss Marjoribanks, as was natural, took no notice of this childish fury. She was sitting just where she had been sitting all the evening, within sight of the street lamp and the organ-grinder, and Miss Jane Hemmings at the staircase window;—just where Barbara had placed her, and where that young woman calculated on finding her, when she made a promenade of triumph up the partially-lighted street by the side of her clandestine suitor. Perhaps Barbara had seen Miss Jane as well, and knew that public opinion was thus watching over her; but at all events she was not at all ashamed of herself, or indignant at being spied upon. On the contrary, it was a kind of apotheosis for Barbara, only second to the grand and crowning triumph which would be accomplished in Carlingford Church under the shadow of that veil of real Brussels, which grew more and more real every day. Thus neither the actors in the drama, nor the principal spectator, were in the smallest degree disturbed by horror or shame or sense of guilt, excepting always the fanciful little Rose, who suffered for everybody; who could have wished that the earth would open and swallow up Barbara and her lover; who could have slaughtered Lucilla on the spot, and given herself over to any kind of torture for her treachery. Naturally nobody paid any sort of attention to Rose. Barbara, for her part, took her admirer's arm in the twilight with a swelling of exultation, which the gaining of the very highest prize in the department of ornamental art could scarcely have conveyed to the bosom of the little artist; and Lucilla put back her small assailant softly with her hand, and smoothed down her ruffled plumes.

"My dear, it is Miss Hemmings that is spying," said Lucilla; "and poor Barbara would be so disappointed if I were to go away from the window. Have patience just a little longer—there's a dear. It is all exactly as I thought."

And then there followed a pause, which was a terrible pause for Rose. The organ-grinder stopped his doleful ditty, and there was scarcely any sound to be heard in the street except the footsteps approaching and retiring, the measured tread of two people occupied with each other, going now more slowly, now more quickly, as the humour seized them, or as their conversation grew in interest; even the sound of their voices came by times to the auditors—Barbara's with an occasional laugh or tone of triumph, and the other deeper, with which Rose had but little acquaintance, but which was perfectly known to Lucilla. All this time, while her companion sat panting in the dark corner, Miss Marjoribanks was looking to the joints of her harness, and feeling the edge of her weapons. For, after all, it was no small enterprise upon which she was going forth. She was going to denounce the faithless knight to his face, and take him out of the hands of the enchantress; but then she herself meant to take him in hand, and show him his true dangers, and vindicate his honour. A more disinterested enterprise was never undertaken by any knight-errant. Yet, at the same time, Lucilla could not help entertaining a certain involuntary contempt for the man who had deserted her own standard to put himself under that of Barbara Lake, and who was being paraded up and down here without knowing it, to gratify the vanity of his new sovereign, and make an exhibition of his weakness. Lucilla would have been more than mortal if she had not felt the difference between her own rule, which would have been all for his good, and the purely egotistical sway of Barbara; and even in her magnanimous mind, it was impossible that pity itself should not be mingled with a certain disdain.

She sat quite still for so long that Barbara grew intoxicated with her triumph. "It is perhaps the last time," Lucilla said to herself, with a movement of compassion; and the breadth of her human sympathy was such that she waited till the very latest moment, and let the deluded young woman have the full enjoyment of her imaginary victory. Then Miss Marjoribanks rose with a certain solemnity, and put on her hat, and gave an unappreciated kiss to Rose, who kept in her corner. "Goodnight; I am going," said Lucilla. The words were simple enough, but yet they rang in Rose's ears like the signal of a conspiracy. When the calm leader of the expedition went forth, sensible of the importance of her mission, but tranquil as great minds always are in a moment of danger, Rose got up too and followed, trembling in every limb. She was capable of having thrown herself upon the spears in her own person in a sudden *élan* of indignation and passion; but she was not capable of waiting till the right moment, and meeting her antagonists in reasonable combat. Miss Marjoribanks went out deliberately, without any unnecessary haste, sweeping into the dusky twilight with her virginal white draperies. It was a very ordinary scene, and yet, even in the midst of her excitement, Rose could not help observing involuntarily its pictorial qualities—if only any painter could have transferred to his canvass the subdued musical hum of surrounding life, the fragrance of the mignonette, and the peaceful stillness of the summer night. The sky shone out green-blue, lambent and wistful, from the vacant space between Miss Hemmings's and Mr Wrangle's, and there were the dusky twilight shadows below, and the yellow gleam of the lamp, and Barbara's exulting triumphant figure, and the white robes of the avenging angel. Rose could not have observed all this if she had not been stilled into a kind of breathless awe by the solemn character of the situation, which struck her as being somehow like one of Millais's pictures. As for the lovers, they had just turned at the moment that Miss Marjoribanks came out, and consequently met her straight in the face, as she stood suave and smiling at the little garden-door.

"It *is* Mr Cavendish," said Lucilla; "I am so glad; I have been hoping and trying to see you for ever so long; and as soon as ever I heard you talking I felt sure it was your voice."

This was the greeting she addressed to Barbara Lake's lover. For his part, he stood before her, growing red and growing pale, struck dumb by the unlooked-for meeting, and with such a sense of being ashamed of himself as never before had entered his mind, though, no doubt, he had done worse actions in his day. Even Barbara had not calculated upon this open encounter; and instead of giving him any assistance, as was a woman's duty in such a case, she only tossed her head, and giggled with an embarrassment which was more pride than shame. As for Mr Cavendish, he would have liked to disappear under the pavement, if it had been possible. For once he and Rose were agreed. If a gulf had opened before him, he would have jumped into it without ever pausing to ask himself why. And yet all the time Miss Marjoribanks was looking as placid as if she had been in her own drawing-room, and expecting his reply to her friendly observations. When he realised that he ought to say something, Mr Cavendish felt that he had as much need to wipe his forehead as ever the Archdeacon had. He turned hot and cold, and felt his mind and his tongue frozen, and could not find a word to say. With a sudden horror he woke up, like one of Comus's revellers, and found himself changed into the likeness of the creature he consorted with. If he had found an ass's head on his shoulders, he could not have felt more startled and horrified than when he heard himself, in the imbecility of the moment, giggle like Barbara, and answer to Lucilla's remark, "Oh! yes, it was my voice."

"I am very sorry to separate you from Barbara," said Miss Marjoribanks; "but she is at home, you know, and I want so much to talk to you. Barbara, good-night; I want Mr Cavendish to walk home with me. Rose, don't stand in the garden and catch cold; thank you, dear, for such a pleasant evening," said Lucilla, pressing another kiss upon her little friend's unwilling cheek. When she had done this, she put out her hand to Barbara, and passed her, sweeping her white garments through the narrow gateway. She took Mr Cavendish's arm as if he had been a young brother come to fetch her. "Let us go round by the chapel," said Miss Marjoribanks, "I have so much to say to you. Be sure to practise for Thursday, Barbara, and bid your papa good-night for me." This was how she carried off Mr Cavendish finally out of Barbara's very fingers, and under her very eyes.

When the two sisters were left standing together at the door, they could do nothing but stare at each other in the extremity of their amazement. Rose, for her part, remained but a moment, and then, feeling by far the guiltiest and most miserable of the whole party, ran up-stairs to her own room and cried as if her heart would break. Barbara, on the contrary, who was past crying, stood still at the door, and watched Lucilla's white dress disappearing on the way to Grange Lane with indescribable emotions. A young woman cannot call the police, or appeal to the crier, when it is her lover whom she has lost: but to see him carried off by the strong hand—to watch him gradually going away and disappearing from her eyes—to hear his steps withdrawing into the distance—was such a trial as few are called upon to bear. She stood and looked after him, and could not believe her eyes. And then it was all so sudden— an affair of a moment. Barbara could not realise how the world had turned round, and this revolution had been effected;—one minute she had been leaning on his arm triumphant, making a show and exhibition of him in the pride of her heart, though he did not know it; and the next was not she standing here watching him with a blank countenance and a despairing heart, while Lucilla had pounced upon him and carried him off in her cruel grasp? The blow was so sudden, that Barbara stood speechless and motionless till the two departing figures had vanished in the darkness. Would he come back again to-morrow, or was he gone for ever and ever? Such were the thoughts of the forsaken maiden, as she stooped paralysed under this sudden change of fortune, at her father's door. If some cruel spectator had thrown into the fire that Brussels veil with which her imagination had so long played, and Barbara had stood heart-struck, watching the filmy tissue dissolve into ashes before her eyes, her sense of sudden anguish could not have been more acute. Yet, after all, Barbara's pangs were nothing to those of Mr Cavendish, as he felt Miss Marjoribanks's light touch on his arm, and felt his doomed feet turn in spite of himself in the most dangerous direction, and became conscious that he was being led, beyond all possibility of resistance, back to Grange Lane and to his fate.

To be sure it was dark, which was one consolation; but it was not dark enough to conceal Lucilla's white dress, nor the well-known form and lineaments of the young monarch of Grange Lane, in whose company nobody could pass unobserved. Mr Cavendish could have faced danger by sea and land with the average amount of courage; but the danger of the walk down the little street, which afterwards led to St Roque's, and up the embowered stillness of Grange Lane, was more than he was equal to. He could not be sure of making a single step by these garden-walls without meeting somebody who knew him — somebody whose curiosity might ruin him in Carlingford; or even without the risk of encountering in the face that arch-enemy, who would not go away, and whose presence had banished him from the place. It may be supposed that, under these terrible circumstances, Mr Cavendish's thoughts of Barbara, who had got him into this scrape, were far from lover-like. He was a man universally popular among ladies, and who owed a great deal of the social consideration which he prized so highly to this fact; and yet the most gentle sentiment in his mind at that moment, was a "Confound these women!" which he breathed to himself, all low and deep, as he went slowly along by Lucilla's side. As for Miss Marjoribanks, her thoughts were of a very much more serious description than anything her unlucky cavalier was thinking of, and a minute or two passed in silence before she could make up her mind to speak.

"I have been thinking a great deal about you lately, and wishing very much to see you," said Lucilla. "Did not Mrs Woodburn tell you?—I think I should have written to you had I known your address."

"And I am sure you would have made me the happiest of men," said the victim, with rueful politeness. "What had I done to deserve such a privilege? But my sister did not tell me; she left me to hear it from your own——"

"Yes," said Miss Marjoribanks, with a certain solemnity, interrupting him; "I have been thinking a great deal—and *hearing* a great deal about you, Mr Cavendish." When she had said this Lucilla sighed, and her sigh found a terrible echo in her hearer's bosom. She knew that he turned green in the darkness as he gave an anxious look at her. But he was too much alarmed to give her an opportunity of studying his face.

"*Hearing* of me," he said, and tried to laugh; "what have my kind friends been saying?" and for one moment the sufferer tried to delude himself that it was some innocent gossip about Barbara which might be circulating in Grange Lane.

"Hush," said Lucilla, "don't laugh, please; for I want to have a very serious talk. I have been hearing about you from some very, very old friends, Mr Cavendish—not anything about *this*, you know," Miss Marjoribanks added, waving her hand in the direction of Grove Street. And then Barbara Lake and everything connected with her vanished like a shadow from the unfortunate man's mind. It was horribly ungrateful on his part, but it was, as Miss Marjoribanks would have said, just what might have been expected, and how They always behave. He had no longer any time or patience for the object which had been giving occupation and interest to his solitude. He woke up in a moment, and gave a passing curse to his folly, and faced the real danger as he best could.

"You must be making a mistake, Miss Marjoribanks," he said, with some bitterness; "it should have been, very, very old enemy. I know who it is. It is that Archdeacon you ladies make such a fuss about. It is he who has been telling lies about me," said Mr Cavendish. He breathed a deep hard breath as he spoke, and the blood came back to his face. Perhaps for the first moment he felt satisfied, and breathed freer after it was over; but at the same time it was very dreadful to him to feel that he was found out, and that henceforward Grange Lane would shut its doors and avert its countenance. "If you take his word for it, I may give in at once," he continued, bitterly. "A parson will say anything; they are as bad as—as women." This the poor man said in his despair, because he did not know what he was saying; for in reality he knew that women had been his best friends, and that he had still a chance, if the judgment was to rest with them.

"You are very ungrateful to say so," said Miss Marjoribanks, "but it is only because you are excited, I suppose. No, Mr Cavendish, it was not the Archdeacon; on the contrary, it was a lady, and she said nothing but good of you," said Lucilla; and then there was a pause. As for Mr Cavendish, it would be altogether impossible to describe the state of his mind. He was like a man suddenly reprieved, but giddy with the shock, and feeling the halter still round his neck, and knowing that he had himself undermined the ground on which he was standing. It was Lucilla who supported him in the shock of the moment, for all his self-command could not keep him from a momentary shiver and stagger when he found that things were not so bad as he thought.

"A lady, and she said nothing but good!" he muttered, under his breath; and then he made an effort to recover himself. "Pardon me, I cannot guess who my unknown friend may be. It is very soothing to one's feelings to be spoken well of by a lady," said Mr Cavendish, and he laughed again in a discordant unsteady way. Lucilla regarded him through all these fluctuations with natural pity, and at the same time with the calmness of a knowledge which was aware of all and had nothing more to discover; and at the end Mr Cavendish perceived her calm, and the absence of wonder and curiosity in her face, and began to perceive that he had something very serious to deal with—more serious even than he had at first supposed.

"I am going to tell you all about it," said Miss Marjoribanks, "but in the mean time wait a minute and let me speak to you. I have something very serious to say."

It was for this they stopped short at the foot of Grange Lane just where the land was already parcelled out for St Roque's. What Lucilla was going to say was too important to be spoken while walking, and she withdrew her hand from Mr Cavendish's arm. They were both so much absorbed that they did not see anybody coming, nor indeed had any attention to spare for external affairs. The blood had deserted Mr Cavendish's face, and he was once more green with anxiety and inquietude. He stood facing her, feeling that the crisis of his fate had come, and not knowing whether it was absolute despair or a faint dawning of hope that possessed him. If he had been the most passionate of lovers, and if she had held in her hands the dreadful alternative between rapture and misery, there could not have been a more rapt and absorbing attention in Mr Cavendish's face.

"I want to tell you, first of all, that you must have confidence in me," said Lucilla; "you—must—have confidence in me. We can do nothing without that. I know everything, Mr Cavendish," Miss Marjoribanks added compassionately—"*everything;* but nobody else knows it. I hope I can arrange everything if it is left in my hands. This is what I wanted to tell you first of all. Before everything, you must have confidence in me."

What Mr Cavendish might have answered to this solemn appeal it would be vain to imagine; for the truth was, he was stopped before he could utter a word. He was stopped and seized by the hand, and greeted with a frankness which was, perhaps, all the more loud and cordial from what appeared to the newcomer the comic character of the situation. "It *is* Cavendish, by Jove!" the intruder exclaimed, waving his hand to some people who were coming on behind him. "I beg a thousand pardons for disturbing you, my dear fellow; but they all talk about you so, that I was determined to make sure it was you. Good heavens, Miss Marjoribanks!" General Travers added, taking off his hat. It was Mr and Mrs Centum who were coming down behind him—she with a light shawl thrown over her head, tempted out by the beauty of the evening; and Lucilla saw in a moment the consequences of this encounter, and how it would be over all Carlingford before to-morrow morning that she and Mr Cavendish were betrothed at the very least. Miss Marjoribanks had all her wits about her, as ever, fortunately for both.

"Yes, it is me," she said, calmly; "I have been taking tea with the Lakes, and I made Mr Cavendish give me his arm home. He did not like being found out, to be sure, but he could not help himself; and we all know about that," Lucilla added, with a smile, taking once more the unfortunate man's arm. "Oh yes, we all know," said Mrs Centum, with a laugh; but yet, notwithstanding, everybody felt sure that it was all Lucilla's cleverness, and that Barbara Lake was a myth and fiction. And it was thus, with Miss Marjoribanks leaning on his arm, and General Travers, in all the warmth of renewed friendship, guarding him on the other side, that Mr Cavendish, whose head was in a whirl of excitement, and who did not know what he was doing, was led back in triumph past Colonel Chiley's very door, where the Archdeacon was lying in wait to crunch his bones, back from all his aberrations into the very heart of Grange Lane.

CHAPTER XXIX.

MR CAVENDISH was led back to his own house that evening by General Travers, whose claim of acquaintance was too decided to be rejected. He never knew very well what passed between the moment when Miss Marjoribanks began to expound to him the urgent necessity that he should confide in her, and the moment in which he found himself in his own house, admitted eagerly by the surprised and anxious servants, and conducted by the energetic soldier. That he had taken leave of Lucilla at her own door, that he had watched her white dress sweep away into the dark garden with a faint sense that it was his only remaining protector who thus left him, and that after that he had smoked a horrible cigar with Mr Centum, and been accompanied home by the old acquaintance who had turned up at so unlucky a moment,—was all that the poor man was aware of. And yet it is to be supposed that on the whole he behaved himself very much like other people, since General Travers had no distinct idea that his company was undesirable, or that his cordial recognition was anything but welcome. The General, indeed, took it as quite natural, under the circumstances, that Cavendish should be a little confused. A man who is no longer a very young man, and has a character to support, does not care to be found mooning with the object of his affections on a summer evening, like a boy of twenty; and General Travers was perfectly aware that he had thus a very good joke against Cavendish. "It is worth a man's while to set up a bachelor establishment in the country," the General said. "By Jove! I wish I could do it. It makes a fellow feel Arcadian, and ready for anything;" and for his own part he was very ready to seize upon his former acquaintance, a man who belonged to his club, and had a chance to know what he was talking about. "As for Charlie Centum," the soldier said, "what between business and matrimony, he has grown the greatest guy imaginable; and I can't go off directly, you know; and then there's always this business about the depot. It's immense luck to find you here, Cavendish," General Travers added, with flattering cordiality; and if poor Mr Cavendish was not grateful, it certainly was not his friend's fault. He led the way into his house with a glum countenance and a sinking heart, though fortunately the latter was not visible. It was a very nice house, fitted up with all that luxury of comfort which a man who has, as Mrs Centum said, "only himself to look to," can afford to collect around him. Mr Cavendish had only himself, and he had made his habitation perfect, though, on the whole, he did not pass a very great deal of his time at home. He had some nice pictures and a good library, though he was not particularly given to the arts; and he had an admirable cellar, as all the gentlemen owned in Carlingford, though, for his own part, he was very moderate in that point, and did not give himself any airs on the subject. Mr Centum, on the contrary, was one of the men who talk about vintages, and raise expectations never to be carried out. And General Travers could not but feel the force of the contrast as he sat deep into the night, and "talked over everything," with the man whom by that time he felt convinced was one of his best friends.

As for Mr Cavendish, it would be very difficult to describe his feelings. He had been knocking about in all sorts of poor places, making clandestine visits to his sister, and hovering round the more than suburban simplicity of Grove Street, and the sense of being once more enveloped and surrounded by all that was pleasant to the eye and comfortable to the outer man was wonderfully consolatory and agreeable. But his mind was in a dreadfully harassed condition all the same. He was preoccupied to the last degree, wondering what Miss Marjoribanks really knew, and how far he had betrayed himself, and to what extent it would be safe, as she herself said, to confide in Lucilla; and at the same time he was obliged to listen to and show a certain interest in the General's stories, and to make now and then a painful effort of mind to recall some of the mutual friends referred to, whose names and persons had in the mean time slipped out of his memory. All the babble of the club, which General Travers felt must be so refreshing to the ears of a rusticated member, fell as flat upon Mr Cavendish, whose mind was full of other matters, as if it had been the merest old woman's gossip, which, to be sure, it slightly resembled in some points. The gallant General made himself so agreeable that he nearly drove the unfortunate man out of his senses, and, when he had exhausted all other means of aggravation, returned with fresh zest to the sentimental circumstances in which, as he supposed, he had found his companion out.

"Very sensible I call it," said General Travers. "To be candid, I don't call her strictly handsome, you know; she's too big for that—and I don't suppose she's of any family to speak of; though perhaps you don't mind that trifling circumstance; but a woman that will dress well and light up well, and knows how to give a man a capital dinner, by Jove! and no doubt has a pretty little bit of money into the bargain—I respect your taste, Cavendish," said the friendly critic, with effusion; and somehow this applause irritated its recipient more than all that had gone before.

"I am sure I am much obliged to you," said Mr Cavendish, "though, unfortunately, I don't merit your approbation. Miss Marjoribanks is a great friend of mine, but she wouldn't have me, and I don't mean to ask her. At the same time, she has very good connections; and that is not the way to talk of a girl of twenty. She is worth a dozen of your fast young ladies," said the sufferer, with some heat. He was not in the least in love with Lucilla, and indeed had a certain dread of her at this present moment; but he could not forget that she had once stood by him in his need—and, besides, he was glad of any subject on which he could contradict his visitor. "I daresay her family is better than either yours or mine. Scotch, you know," said Mr Cavendish, trying to laugh. As for the General, he leaned back on his chair with an indulgent air, and stroked his mustache.

"Beg your pardon—meant no offence," he said. "For my part, I don't see that it matters, if a woman is good-looking and has something, you know. For instance, there was a pretty little thing—a charming little thing—Lake, or something like that——"

"Ah!" said Mr Cavendish. It was a frightful want of self-control; but he had been a long time at full strain, and he could not help it. It did not occur to him, for the moment, that nobody in his senses would have applied the term "little thing" to Barbara; and, after all the slow aggravation that he had been submitting to, the idea of this insolent soldier interfering in Grove Street was beyond his power of endurance. As for the General, the tone of this exclamation was such that he too turned round on his chair, and said, "Yes?" with equally unmistakable meaning, startled, but ready for the emergency, whatever it might be.

Thus the two looked at each other for a second, friends in the ordinary acceptation of the word, and yet, perhaps, on the eve of becoming enemies. Mr Cavendish had, up to that moment, pretty nearly forgotten Barbara Lake. It was a piquant sort of occupation when he had nothing else to do, and when the world, according to his morbid fancy, was on the eve of turning its back upon him—but from the moment when he had said between his teeth "Confound these women!" and had felt the excitement of the approaching crisis, Barbara, and her crimson cheeks, and her level eyebrows, and her contralto, had gone altogether out of his mind. At the same time, it is quite true that a man may feel himself at liberty to forget a woman when other matters of more immediate interest are absorbing his attention, and yet be driven furious by the idea suddenly presented to him that somebody else, who has nothing earthly to do with it, is about to interfere. Mr Cavendish, however, recovered himself while the General sat staring at him, and began to see how ridiculous his defiance was.

"Well?—go on. I did not say anything," he said, and lighted another cigar. Yet he did not face his companion as a friendly listener should, but began to beat measure to an irritating imaginary air on the table, with a certain savage energy by moments, as if he were beating time on the General's head.

"Then why do you stop a fellow short like that?" said General Travers; "I was going to tell you of some one I saw the other day in the house of your—your friend, you know. She was under Miss Marjoribanks's wing, that was how I saw her—and I hope you are not playing the gay deceiver, my friend;—a little thing, round-faced, hazel-eyed—a little soft rosebud sort of creature," said the General, growing eloquent. "By Jove! Cavendish, I hope you don't mean to make yourself disagreeable. These sort of looks, you know——"

"It was Rose, I suppose," said Mr Cavendish, relieved in a moment; and, to tell the truth, he could not help laughing. The more eloquent and angry the General grew, the more amused and contemptuous grew his entertainer. He was so tickled by the position of affairs, that he actually forgot his anxieties for the moment. "No doubt it was Rose," he repeated, and laughed; Rose! what anybody could see in that little dragon! And then the contrast between the soldier, who prided himself on his knowledge of the world, and liked to talk of his family and position, to the annoyance of those who had none, and the amusement of those who happen to possess these valuable qualifications—and the mistress of the Female School of Design, filled Mr Cavendish with amusement: perhaps all the more because he himself was in a similar scrape. As for General Travers, he was as much disposed to be angry as, a moment before, Mr Cavendish had been.

"It might be Rose," he said, "or Lily either, for anything I can tell; but there is nothing laughable in it that I can see. You seem to be perfectly *au courant*, at all events—which I hope is quite satisfactory to Miss Marjoribanks," said the soldier; and then he resumed, after a disagreeable little pause, "they tell me that everybody meets at the Doctor's on Thursdays. I suppose I shall see you there. Thursday, ain't it? tomorrow?" He looked as he spoke, with what seemed to his victim an insulting consciousness, in poor Cavendish's face. But, in reality, the General did not mean to be insulting, and knew nothing whatever of the horrible internal pang which rent his companion when it was thus recalled to him that it *was* tomorrow—a fact which, up to this moment, had not occurred to the unfortunate. To-morrow; and not even to-morrow—to-day— for by this time it was two o'clock in the morning, and the unwelcome intruder was wasting the little time he had for deciding what he should do. Once more his own personal anxieties, which he had put aside for a moment at the sudden dictate of jealousy, surged over everything, and swallowed up all lesser sensations. To-morrow!—and by this time everybody knew that he was in Carlingford, and he could not stay away from the weekly assembly without attracting general attention to himself, and throwing open the flood-gates of suspicion. What was he to do? should he turn his back on the enemy once for all, and run away and break off his connection with Carlingford? or should he dare everything and face the Archdeacon, and put his trust in Lucilla, as that high-minded young woman had invited him to do? With these thoughts in his mind it may be supposed that Mr Cavendish gave but a very mingled attention to the babble of his visitor, who found the wine and the cigars so good, and perhaps had begun to be a little moved out of his ordinary lucidity by their effect.

"You've got a nice little house, Cavendish," said the General, "but it's too small for a married man, my boy. These women are the very deuce for turning a man out of his comfortable quarters. You'll have to go in for boudoirs and those sort of things; and, by George! you'll be an ass if you do, with a snug little box like this to retire into," said the philosophical warrior; and poor Cavendish smiled a ghastly smile, with the strongest inclination all the time to take him by the collar and turn him out of doors. But then he *was* a warrior and a general officer, and a member of the same club, and six feet high—all which particulars, not to speak of the sacred rights of hospitality, made it somewhat difficult to carry this idea out.

"Don't you think Centum will be sitting up for you?" he said, mildly; "it's past two o'clock; and it's Thursday morning," the victim added, with a sigh. The last words were an involuntary utterance of his own despair, but fortunately they struck General Travers's vein of humour, which happened to be lively at the moment, and worked the desired but unexpected result. The General laughed loud and long, and declared that he respected a man who was above-board, and meant to look respectable for Miss Marjoribanks's sake; and then he poured a mighty libation to Lucilla, and took an affectionate leave of her supposed lover. The General made a great commotion in the decorous quiet of Grange Lane when he knocked at Mr Centum's door. Though it was nearly three o'clock in the morning, nothing but his inherent dread of a woman would

have prevented him from knocking up the banker to share his
hilarity; but Mrs Centum, in her night-cap, peaceably asleep as
she was at the moment, daunted the soul of the gallant soldier;
and naturally his recollection was not very perfect next day.
" I had something very funny to tell you; but, by Jove! I forget what it was," General Travers said next morning when he
met his host at breakfast; and thus one bad joke at least was
spared. But Mr Cavendish shut his door upon his departing
guest, without any sense, poor fellow, of having done or said
anything in the least funny. He said, " Thank heaven!" with
a kind of groan of relief when his troublesome visitor was gone.
And then he went back again into his library, where they had
been sitting. Perhaps he had never fully appreciated before
the comfort of everything, the handsome house which he had
enjoyed so long without thinking anything of it, and all the
pleasant luxurious accessories of life. He had been doing without them for a week or two, and he had not liked it; and yet
at that moment it seemed to Mr Cavendish that he could rather
be content to lose them all at a stroke, to make it known in
Carlingford that he was ruined and had lost his fortune, than
that Carlingford should find out that he was not, after all, one
of the Cavendishes, nor the person it took him for. But, alas!
all his fortune could not bring reality to these pretensions, nor
hinder the exposure to which he looked forward with such horror. It is true that he was an adventurer, but he was not a
base one; nor had he done anything dishonourable either to
gain his fortune or to captivate the good opinion of society,
which had become so important to him. But there are actual
crimes that would be sooner forgiven to a man than the folly of
having permitted himself to be considered one of the Cavendishes, and having set his heart on making a figure in that
mild provincial world. Mr Cavendish knew enough of human
nature to know that a duchess or a lord-chamberlain would forgive more readily than Mr and Mrs Centum any such imposition upon them, and intrusion into their exclusive circle. And
then his sister, who could not run away! For her sake it
seemed to him that he had better rush off at once, and sell his
house and furniture and horses, and give up Carlingford. As he
thought of that, all the advantages of Carlingford came upon him
stronger than ever. Perhaps a man who has always been used
to be recognised as one of the members of a local aristocracy,
would not have seen anything half so precious as Mr Cavendish
saw in the fact of being everywhere known and acknowledged

as a constituent part of Grange Lane;—recognised by the county people, and by the poor people, and pointed out as he passed by one and another to any stranger who might happen to be so ignorant as not to know Mr Cavendish. To people who are not used to it, there is a charm in this universal acknowledgment. And then he had more need of it than most men have; and, when Carlingford signed his patent of gentility, and acknowledged and prized him, it did an infinite deal more than it had any intention of doing. To keep its regard and recognition he would have done anything, given up the half or three parts, or even, on emergency, all he had. Perhaps he had an undue confidence in the magnanimity of society, and was too sure that in such a case it would behave with a grandeur worthy of the occasion; but still he was quite right in thinking that it could forgive the loss of his fortune sooner than his real offence. And now it was Thursday morning, the day upon which he must either fight or flee. He too had laughed at Miss Marjoribanks's evenings in his time, and thought of Thursday lightly as Lucilla's day; but there was nothing in the least amusing in the prospect of that assembly now.

When a man has thoughts like these to entertain him, nothing can be more useless than to go to bed, although in ordinary circumstances, at three o'clock in the morning, that is about the only thing one can do. Poor Mr Cavendish, however, was not quite free to act as he thought proper. He had been a long time away from home, and he did not feel himself in a position to shock his servants' feelings with impunity. He went to his room, accordingly, like a martyr, carrying all his difficulties with him, and these unpleasant companions naturally made a night of it when they had him all to themselves. When sheer fatigue and exhaustion procured him a moment's sleep, it was only getting deeper and deeper into trouble; for then it was the Archdeacon who had planted a heavy foot on his neck, or General Travers, who, with still more fatal force, had found out the way to Grove Street. When Mr Cavendish awoke, he said to himself, "Confound these women!" with more fervour than ever; but, at the same time, he swore a mighty oath to himself that he would horsewhip the fellow who ventured to come in his way. Barbara Lake might be no great things, but at least it was to him, and no one else, that she belonged. Such was the complication that afforded him a little outlet for his temper in the midst of the dreadful difficulties of his position, and the question which was constantly renewing itself in his thoughts, as to whether he should go or stay. The idea of presenting himself in the centre of society in Miss Marjoribanks's drawing-room, and being met by the Archdeacon, and held up to public contempt there and then, with all the world looking on, and even Travers, who would carry the narrative out of Carlingford, was something too horrible to be contemplated; and yet how was he to escape? He was still in this state of mind, driven backwards and forwards by every new wind, when the morning came, and when Miss Marjoribanks's note was put into his hand.

For the truth was, that, after long consideration, Lucilla had determined that the matter was one which could not be permitted to stand over. She was of too energetic a temperament to let things linger on in an uncertain way when they could be made an end of, and brought to a conclusion; and then, as nobody can predict what sudden and unexpected turn human affairs may take, it was always possible that, if Miss Marjoribanks did not make an end of the business dramatically, and to the satisfaction of everybody concerned, it might be found some fine day to have resolved itself by means of some one of those illegitimate and incomplete expedients which abound in ordinary life. It was with this view that Miss Marjoribanks took the step of writing to Mr Cavendish. She had written in the sacred retirement of her own maiden chamber, when all the world was still; perhaps at the moment when General Travers was, as he would himself have vulgarly called it, "chaffing" Cavendish about the beautiful and disinterested friendship which united him to the young sovereign of Grange Lane. But naturally such poor raillery was far from the virginal thoughts of Lucilla at that retired and sacred hour; and we may venture to add, that the elevating influence of the maiden's bower in which she composed it, and of that tranquil moment of meditation and solitude, breathed in every line, and gave force to every sentiment of the letter which Mr Cavendish tore open with an excited hand. Perhaps he was too anxious and curious to give it the solemn perusal which it ought to have received.

"MY DEAR MR CAVENDISH,—It was very unlucky that we should have been interrupted this evening at such an important moment, when I had so much to say to you. But I think the best thing I can do is to write, feeling quite sure that when you know all, *you cannot possibly mistake* my motives. Everybody has retired, and I am quite alone, and the silence seems to me full of meaning when I think that the fate of a person for whom

I have so great a regard may be hanging upon it.* I might be
afraid of writing to you so frankly, if I did not feel quite sure
that you would appreciate my intention. Dear Mr Cavendish,
it is not the Archdeacon who has said anything. *He does not
know it is you;* therefore, of course, he could not say anything
directly bearing upon you. But then, you know, if he were to
meet you by hazard, as he is sure to do some day—and for my
part I rather think he is fond of Grove Street—you would be
exposed at once, and everything would be lost, for we all know
the prejudices that exist in Carlingford. I have another plan
of operations to propose to you, which I feel quite sure is for
your good, and also naturally for the good of anybody to whom
you may intend to unite your fortunes. I feel quite sure that
it is far safer to adopt a bold resolution, and to have it over at
once. Come to dinner to-morrow. If you may happen to find
an enemy, you will find also an unlooked-for friend; and, so
far as I am concerned, you *know* that you may calculate on my
support. I do not wonder at your being anxious about it; but
if you will only have full confidence in me and a little in yourself, believe me it will be all over in a night. If there had ever
been anything between you and me, as these stupid people suppose, I might have felt hesitation in writing to you like this;
but when I know a thing to be right, I hope I will never be
afraid to do it. I have been called upon to do many things
that are not common for girls of my age, and perhaps that is
why I made up my mind at once to set this all straight for you.
Once more I repeat, dear Mr Cavendish, have confidence in me.
Come to-morrow evening as if nothing had happened; and take
my word for it that all will go well.—Your friend,

" LUCILLA MARJORIBANKS.

" *P.S.*—If you would like to come and talk it over with me
to-morrow, I shall be at home till twelve o'clock; but unless it
will be a satisfaction to your own mind, it is not necessary for
me, for I have all my plans laid."

It would be quite out of the question to attempt any explanation of Mr Cavendish's feelings when he read this letter. His
utter bewilderment, his terror, his rage, his final helpless sense

* It is only justice to Miss Marjoribanks to say that she was not
addicted to fine writing; but then she was a person who liked to have
everything in keeping, and naturally an emergency such as the present
does not come every day, and requires to be treated accordingly.

that it would be utterly hopeless for him, or half-a-dozen men, to enter the field against this curious complication of unknown friends and open enemies and generous protectors, took away from him the last remnant of courage. He did not know what to do or to think. He swallowed his coffee with a sense of despair, and sent the rest of his breakfast away untasted; thus betraying, without intending it, his emotions to his kitchen. "It stands to reason as there's a cause for it," Mr Cavendish's domestics concluded in committee of the whole house; and surely, if ever man had good reason for not eating his breakfast, it was he. When he had gone over it all again till his head had grown utterly confused and his thoughts were all topsy-turvy, Mr Cavendish took a sudden resolution. He went upstairs and changed his dress with a certain solemnity. He made a toilette more careful than if he were going, as he once had gone, to propose. It was like Nelson going into gala uniform for a battle. And then he went out to discover, if possible, what was coming to him. The difference was, that in this battle no honour, but only a possible salvage of reputation and fortunate escape, was to be gained.

CHAPTER XXX.

IT is possible that some people may think Mr Cavendish's emotions too acute for all the danger to which he was exposed; but no doubt every alarm gets intensified when a man broods on it, and thinks of nothing else for weeks at a time. All that he had to do at the present moment was to walk into Carlingford by the most frequented way, and to go up Grange Lane, where every house was open to him, and where nobody was so great a favourite as he. There were as many chances in his favour that he would not in that friendly neighbourhood encounter his one enemy, as there is for every man who goes into action that the bullet which is predestined to strike somebody will not be directed to him; but then Mr Cavendish had not the excitement of personal conflict, nor the kind of security which is given by sharing a risk with a great many other people. And to see everything smiling and serene around, and yet to know that the most deadly danger may arrive to you at any innocent opening, or round the first street-corner, is a kind of risk which naturally tells upon the nerves more than a more open peril. Mr Cavendish met Dr Marjoribanks, and the Doctor was good enough to stop his brougham and keep him in conversation for five minutes with his back to the foe, if foe there was approaching; and then he met Mrs Chiley, who all but kissed him, and was so glad to see him again, and so pleased that he was in time to make acquaintance with the Archdeacon, and so sure that Lucilla would be quite happy now he had come back. "Perhaps I ought not to say so, but I *know* she has missed you," said the injudicious old lady; and she took both his hands and held the miserable man in a kind of pillory, from whence he gazed with despairing eyes over her shoulder, feeling sure that now was the fatal moment, and that his enemy *must* be coming. But fortune still favoured him, as it happened. He had the presence of mind to say, "I am going to call on Miss Marjoribanks;" and Mrs Chiley dropped his hands on the instant as if they burned her, and patted him on the arm and sent him away. "She is sure to be in just now, and I am so glad; and, my dear, you need not mind me, for I am both your friends," Mrs Chiley said. But when he was delivered from that danger, something still more formidable awaited the unfortunate man. He could not believe his eyes at first, nor conceive it possible that Fate would have such a spite against him; but there was no mistaking the crumpled dress, any more than the straight eyebrows and flashing oblique glances that had already found him out. Of all the horrible chances in the world, it was Barbara—Barbara, who had a right to think he had deserted her on the previous night, and with whom his next interview could not be otherwise than stormy—who thus appeared like a lion in his way. When he saw what awaited him, Mr Cavendish lost courage. His heart sank down into unfathomable depths. He did not know what he could say to her to shorten the inevitable interview, nor how he could escape, nor how hinder her from discovering that it was Lucilla he was going to see; and he had no longer any doubt in his mind that while he was thus engaged the Archdeacon must inevitably appear. If he had had time to think of ordinary subjects, he would have been sufficiently annoyed at the idea of an interview with Barbara in broad daylight on the sacred soil of Grange Lane, where all the world could or might be spectators; but such a merely prudential sentiment was entirely swallowed up to-day in much more urgent considerations. He would have been content just now, in the horror of the moment, to plight his troth to Barbara by way of getting rid of her, and leaving his path clear; but he could not stop her or himself from advancing, and dared not give any vent to the panic which was consuming his soul.

"Oh, I am sure I never thought of seeing you here, Mr Cavendish," said Barbara, with a toss of her head. She would have done a great deal to secure her wavering lover, but she could not be amiable at a moment when she had him at a disadvantage. "Perhaps you are going to see Miss Marjoribanks," said the foolish young woman. To tell the truth, she did not suspect him of any such treachery; but her heart was beating louder than usual, and she had the best position of the two, or thought she had, and chose what she supposed the most aggravating thing to say.

But it is always hard to tell what a man may do when he is in a state of despair. Mr Cavendish looked her in the face with the composure of desperation, though she did not know that. All that he was able to think of was how to get rid of her soonest, and to be able to continue his way. "Yes, I am going to see Miss Marjoribanks," he said, with a face which extremity rendered stolid and impassible. As for poor Barbara, her colour changed in a moment. The very least that she had a right to expect was that he should have asked her pardon, put himself at her feet; and her mingled spite and humiliation and mortification at this response were beyond telling. Her cheeks blazed with sudden rage, her passion was so furious that she actually did what he wanted and stood out of his way, and made him an imperious sign to pass on and leave her. But even then she did not expect to be taken at her word. When Mr Cavendish took off his hat in that heartless way and passed on, Barbara stood aghast, not able to believe her senses. Had he really passed and left her, she who had done so much for him? Had he actually gone over to her adversary before her very eyes? She stood stock-still when he left her, gazing after him, blazing with rage and despite, and scarcely able to keep herself from shrieking out the torrent of reproaches and vituperations that were in her mind. She made no attempt whatever to hide her wrath or jealous curiosity from any eyes that might be there to see; but to be sure she had, as her sister said, no proper pride. If Mr Cavendish had carried out his intentions, the chances are that Barbara, driven desperate, would have rushed after him, and found some means of breaking in upon his interview with Lucilla; but after all this badgering, he had not the courage to carry out his intentions. He looked down the long sunshiny line of Grange Lane with a sickening sense that any of these doors might open at any moment, and his fate rush out upon him. There was not a soul to be seen, but that only made it all the more likely to poor Mr Cavendish's distempered fancy that somebody was coming. He had not even a single thought at leisure to give to Barbara, and never asked himself whether or not she was standing watching him. All his senses and faculties were engaged forecasting what might happen to him before he could reach Dr Marjoribanks's house. He was approaching it from the lower end of Grange Lane, and consequently had everything to risk; and when Mr Centum's door opened, and all the nurses and all the children poured out, the unfortunate man felt his heart jump, and drop again, if possible, lower than ever. It was this that drove him, instead of going on to Lucilla, to take refuge in his sister's house, where the door happened to be open. He rushed in there, and took breath, and was safe for the instant. But Barbara, for her part, watching him, divined none of Mr Cavendish's reasons. Her heart too gave a jump, and her wrath cooled down miraculously. No doubt it was a little impatience at being questioned which had made him answer as he did. He had not gone to Lucilla—he had not deserted her standard, who had always met him halfway, and done so much for him. Barbara calmed down as she saw him enter at Mrs Woodburn's door. After having thus witnessed his safe exit, she felt at liberty to go back and return to her own affairs, and prepare her toilette for the evening; for it moved her very little less than Mr Cavendish to know that it was Thursday, and that there was no telling what might happen that night.

As for the hero of all this commotion, he went and buried himself in Mrs Woodburn's back drawing-room, and threw himself on the sofa in the dark corner, and wiped his forehead like the Archdeacon. It was not his fault if events had overwhelmed him. If he had not met in succession Dr Marjoribanks and Mrs Chiley and Barbara, he would have gone right to Lucilla without stopping to question himself further—but he could not bear all this accumulation. Panic had seized upon him, and this panic wrought more effectually than all argument. It was so terrible to live under such a shadow, that he felt it must be put an end to. If only he were left at rest for this moment, he felt that he could make up his mind to take the perilous leap at night, and dare everything. "It can't be worse than ruin," he said to himself, and tried not to think that for his sister it might be something even worse than ruin. But the first thing of all was to get a little rest in the mean time, and hide himself, and forget the nightmare that was seated on his shoulders. When Mrs Woodburn came to him in haste, and saw his careful dress and pale looks, she was frightened for the moment. She thought it possible for one second that despair had driven him out of his wits, and that there might be, for anything she could tell, a little bottle of prussic acid in his waistcoat pocket. That was her first idea, and her second was that he was going to carry out at last his most wise and laudable resolution of proposing to Miss Marjoribanks, and that it was this—naturally a serious and hazardous enterprise—which made him look so pale.

"Harry, if you are going to Lucilla——!" said Mrs Woodburn; "wait and rest yourself a little, and I will get you a glass of wine. Keep still; there's some Tokay," said the anxious sister. "Don't you go and worry yourself. You shall see nobody. I'll bring it you with my own hand."

"Oh, confound the Tokay!" said Mr Cavendish. "I know what Woodburn's Tokay is—if that mattered. Look here, I want to speak to you. I *was* going to Lucilla, but I'm not up to it. Oh, not in the way you think! Don't be a fool like everybody. I tell you she wouldn't have me, and I won't ask her. Read this, which is much more to the purpose," Mr Cavendish added, taking out Miss Marjoribanks's letter. He watched her while she read it, with that sense of contempt and superiority which a man naturally feels who has advanced much beyond the point in any special matter at which his interlocutor is still stationary. He even smiled at her cry of horror and amazement, and found the agitation she showed ridiculous. "Don't make a row about it," he said, regaining his colour as his sister lost hers. "It's all right. I can't ask Lucilla Marjoribanks to have me after that, but I mean to put my trust in her, as she says. I was going to ask her to explain; but after all, on thinking of it, I don't see the good of explanations," said Mr Cavendish, with lofty tranquillity. "The fact is, she is right, Nelly, and, stand or fall, we'll have it out to-night."

But Mrs Woodburn was scarcely in a condition to reply, much less to give any advice. "Oh, good heavens! what does she know?" cried the trembling woman. "What do you suppose she can know? She gave me a dreadful fright, coming and asking about you and your name. And then she never was a great friend of mine—and if she should say anything to Woodburn! Oh, Harry, go away, go away, and don't face her. You know you slighted her, and she is laying a snare for us. Oh, Harry, go away! She can't do you much harm, but she could ruin me, and any little peace I have! Woodburn would never—never forgive—he would be frantic, you know. It has always been he that made a fuss about the Cavendishes—and, good heavens! to be in a girl's power, and she one that you have slighted, Harry! Oh, for heaven's sake, for pity's sake, if you care anything for me——"

"Hold your tongue, Nelly," said Mr Cavendish. "Don't make a row. What on earth is the use of heaven's-saking? I tell you I am going to make an end of it. If I were to run away now, it would turn up again at some other corner, and some other moment. Give me a pen and a bit of paper. I will write a note, and say I am coming. I don't want any explanations. If it's all a mistake, so much the better; but I'm going to face it out to-night."

It was some time before Mrs Woodburn recovered her senses; but in the mean time her brother wrote Lucilla his note, and in sight of his sister's agitation felt himself perfectly composed and serene and manful. It even made him complaisant to feel the difference that there was, when the emergency really arrived at last, between his own manly calm and her womanish panic. But then it was for herself that she was afraid, lest her husband should find out that she was not one of the Cavendishes. "You must have been giving yourself airs on the subject," Mr Cavendish said, as he fastened up his note. "I never was so foolish as that, for my part;" and naturally the more he admired his own steadiness and courage, the steadier and more courageous he grew—or at least so he felt for the moment, with her terror before his eyes.

"If you do go," said Mrs Woodburn at last, "oh, Harry, for goodness' sake, mind that you deny *everything*. If you confess to anything, it will all be proved against you; don't allow a single thing that's said to you. It is a mistaken identity, you know—that is what it is; there was a case in the papers just the other day. Oh, Harry, for heaven's sake don't be weak!—deny everything; you don't know anything about it—you don't know what they mean—you can't understand——"

"It is I that have to do it, Nelly," said Mr Cavendish, more and more tranquil and superior. "You must let me do it my way;" and he was very kind and reassuring to her in his composure. This was how things ought to be; and it was astonishing how much he gained in his own mind and estimation by Mrs Woodburn's panic. Being the stronger vessel, he was of course superior to all that. But somehow when he had got back to his own house again, and had no longer the spectacle of his sister's terror before him, the courage began to ooze out of Mr Cavendish's finger-points; he tried hard to stimulate himself up to the same point, and to regain that lofty and assured position; but as the evening approached, matters grew rather worse than better. He did not turn and flee, because flight, in the present alarmed and touchy state of public opinion, would have equally been destruction; and nobody could answer for it how far, if he failed to obey her, Miss Marjoribanks's discretion might go. And thus the eventful evening fell, and the sun went down, which was to Mr Cavendish as if it might be the last sun he should ever (metaphorically) see—while, in the mean time, all the other people dressed for dinner as if nothing was going to happen, and as if it was merely a Thursday like other Thursdays, which was coming to Grange Lane.

CHAPTER XXXI.

LUCILLA waited till twelve o'clock, as she had said, for Mr Cavendish's visit; and so mingled are human sentiments, even in the mind of a person of genius, that there is no doubt she was at once a little disappointed, and that Mr Cavendish gained largely in her estimation by not coming. Her pity began to be mingled by a certain respect, of which, to tell the truth, he was not worthy; but then Miss Marjoribanks did not know that it was circumstances, and not self-regard, or any sense of dignity, that had kept him back. With the truest consideration, it was in the dining-room that Lucilla had placed herself to await his visit; for she had made up her mind that he should not be disturbed *this time* by any untimely morning caller. But as she sat at the window and looked out upon the garden, and was tantalised by fifty successive ringings of the bell, none of which heralded her expected visitor, a gentler sentiment gradually grew in Lucilla's mind. Perhaps it would not be just to call it positively regret; but yet she could not help a kind of impression that if the Archdeacon had never come to Carlingford, and if Mr Cavendish had never been so weak as to be drawn aside by Barbara Lake, and if everything had gone as might have been expected from first appearances—that, on the whole, it might have been well. After all, he had a great many good qualities. He had yielded to panic for the moment, but (so far as Lucilla knew) he was now girding up his loins to meet the emergency in a creditable way; and if, as has been just said, nothing had come in the way—if there had been no Archdeacon, no Mrs Mortimer, no Barbara—if Mr Chiltern had died, as was to have been expected, and Mr Cavendish been elected for Carlingford—then Lucilla could not help a momentary sense that the arrangement altogether might have been a not undesirable one. Now, of course, all that was at an end. By dexterous management the crisis might be tided over, and the worst avoided; but Lucilla became regretfully conscious that now no fate higher than Barbara was possible for the unfortunate man who might once, and with hope, have aspired to herself. It was very sad, but there was no help for it. A certain tenderness of compassion entered Miss Marjoribanks's bosom as she realised this change. It would be hard if a woman did not pity a man thus shut out by hard fate from any possibility of ever becoming the companion of her existence—a man who, on the whole, had many capabilities, yet whose highest fortune in life could not mount above Barbara Lake!

This thought filled Lucilla's heart with gentle regret. It was sad, but it was inevitable; and when Mr Cavendish's note was brought to her, in which he said simply, and very briefly, that though not sure whether he understood the meaning of her letter, he should certainly do himself the pleasure of accepting as usual her kind invitation, Miss Marjoribanks's regret grew more and more profound. Such a man, who had been capable of appreciating herself, to think that, having known her, he should decline upon Barbara! The pity was entirely disinterested, for nobody knew better than Lucilla that, under the circumstances, no other arrangement was possible. He might marry the drawing-master's daughter, but Miss Marjoribanks was too well aware of her duty to her friends, and to her position in society, to have given her consent to his marriage with anybody's daughter in Grange Lane. But still it was a pity—nobody could say that it was not a pity—a man so visibly capable of better things.

Lucilla, however, could not afford to waste her morning in

unprofitable regrets. An evening so critical and conclusive had to be provided for in many different ways. Among other things, she had to invite, or rather command, the presence of a guest whom, to tell the truth, she had no particular desire to see. The Archdeacon was only a man when all was said, and might change his mind like other men; and to bring Mrs Mortimer to Grange Lane in the evening, looking interesting, as, to be sure, she could look by times, after that unpleasant exhibition of Dr Marjoribanks's feelings, was naturally a trial to Lucilla. Mr Beverley had drawn back once before, and that when Mrs Mortimer was young, and no doubt a great deal more attractive than at present; and now that she was a widow, forlorn and faded, it would be no wonder if he were to draw back, especially, as Lucilla acknowledged to herself, when he saw the ancient object of his affections in her own society, and among all the fresh young faces of Grange Lane: and if the Archdeacon should draw back, and leave the field open, and perhaps the Doctor, who ought to know better, should step in—when she had got so far, Lucilla rose up and shook out her draperies, as if by way of shaking off the disagreeable idea. "At all events I have to do my duty," she said to herself. And thus it was with that last and most exquisite refinement of welldoing, the thought that she might possibly be going to harm herself in benefiting others, that Miss Marjoribanks heroically put on her hat, and issued forth in the dinner-hour of the little pupils, to invite her last and most important guest.

This period of suspense had not been by any means a happy or comfortable period for Mrs Mortimer. The poor widow was living in a constant expectation of something happening, whereas her only true policy was to have made up her mind that nothing would ever happen, and shaped herself accordingly to her life. Instead of eating her dinner as she ought to have done at that hour of leisure, and fortifying herself for the weary afternoon's work, she was sitting as usual at the window when Miss Marjoribanks came to the door. And if it was a tedious business looking out of the window when the rain was drenching the four walls of the garden and breaking down the flowers, and reducing all the poor little shrubs to abject misery, it could not be said to be much more cheerful in the sunshine, when pleasant sounds came in over that enclosure —voices and footsteps of people who might be called alive, while this solitary woman was buried, and had nothing to do with life. Such a fate may be accepted when people make up their minds to it; but when, so far from making up one's mind, one fixes one's thoughts upon the life outside, and fancies that every moment the call may come, and one may find one's place again in the active world, the tedium grows more and more insupportable. As for Lucilla, naturally she could not see any reason why Mrs Mortimer should sit at the window—why she could not content herself, and eat her dinner instead.

"There are a great many people in Carlingford who have not nearly such a pleasant look-out," Lucilla said; "for my part I think it is a very pretty garden. The Westeria has grown quite nice, and there is a little of everything," said Miss Marjoribanks; and, so far as that went, she was no doubt the best judge, having done it all herself.

"Oh, yes, it is very pretty; and I am sure I am very grateful to Providence for giving me such a home," said the widow; but she sighed, poor soul, as she said it: for, to tell the truth, though she was not so young as she once was, it takes some people a long time to find out that they themselves are growing old, and have done with life. And then outside, in that existence which she could hear but could not see, there was one figure which was wonderfully interesting to poor Mrs Mortimer; which is a complication which has a remarkable effect on the question of content or discontent.

"You ought to take a walk every day," said Miss Marjoribanks, "that is what is the matter with you; but, in the mean time, there is something else I want you to do. This is Thursday, you know, and I have always some people on Thursday. It is not a party—it is only an Evening—and no dress to speak of. Your black silk will look quite nice, and be all that is necessary. Black is very becoming to some people," said Lucilla, reflectively. She looked at Mrs Mortimer with her head a little on one side, and saw in a moment, with the rapid glance of genius, just what she wanted. "And some lace for your head," Miss Marjoribanks added. "I don't think you have gone off at all, and I am sure you will look very nice. It is at nine o'clock."

"This evening, Lucilla!" said Mrs Mortimer, faintly; "but you know I never go out—I am not fit for society. Oh, don't ask me, please! Since poor Edward died——"

"Yes," said Lucilla, "it must have been a great loss, I am sure; though I can't say I mind going into a room alone, as some people do; but you know you can avoid that, if you like, by coming early. Come at eight, and there will be nobody in the drawing-room, and you can choose your own corner. Put it quite back—at the back of your head," said Miss Marjoribanks, with a little anxiety. "I could show you how if I had the lace. I do so want you to look nice. Oh, never mind the fashion. When one has a style of one's own, it is always twenty times better. Put it as you used to wear it before you were married; and then, with that nice black silk——"

"Oh, Lucilla, don't ask me," said the widow. "I shall not know how to talk, nor look, nor anything; and then I know nobody; and then——"

"My dear, you have always *me*," said Lucilla, with tender reproach. "I am so sorry I can't stop any longer. I leave it quite to your own taste about the lace. And you will find people you know, you may be quite sure of that. Remember, not later than nine o'clock; and come at eight if you don't like to come into the room by yourself. Good-bye now. I want you to look very nice to-night," Miss Marjoribanks added, giving her friend an affectionate kiss; "you must, for my sake."

"But, Lucilla——" cried Mrs Mortimer.

It was vain to make any further protest, however, for Lucilla was gone, having, in the first place, communicated her requirements to Mary Jane, who was not likely to forget, nor to let her mistress be late. "And mind she is *nice*," said Miss Marjoribanks, emphatically, as she went out at the door. It was necessary she should be nice; without that the intended *situation* which Lucilla was preparing—the grand finale of her exertions—would fall flat, and probably fail of its effect. For this it was necessary that the widow should look not only pretty, but interesting, and a little pathetic, and all that a widow should look when first dragged back into society. Miss Marjoribanks gave a momentary sigh as she emerged from the garden door, and could not but feel conscious that in all this she might be preparing the most dread discomfiture and downfall for herself. Even if it passed over as it ought to do, and nobody was charmed but the Archdeacon, who was the right person to be charmed, Lucilla felt that after this she never could have that entire confidence in her father which she had had up to this moment. The incipient sentiment Dr Marjoribanks had exhibited was one that struck at the roots of all faith in him as a father; and every person of sensibility will at once perceive how painful such a suggestion must have been to the mind of a young woman so entirely devoted as was Miss Marjoribanks to the consolation and comfort of her dear papa.

Lucilla was not allowed to spend the rest of this momentous afternoon in maturing her plans, as might have been necessary to a lesser intelligence; and when the refreshing moment came at which she could have her cup of tea before preparing for the fatigues of the evening, it was Mrs Chiley who came to assist at that ceremony. The old lady came in with an important air, and gave Lucilla a long, lingering kiss, as old ladies sometimes do when they particularly mean it. "My dear, I am not going to stay a moment, but I thought you might have something to tell me," the kind old woman said, arranging herself in her chair with the satisfaction of a listener who expects to be confided in. As for Lucilla, who had no clue to Mrs Chiley's special curiosity, and who had a good many things on her mind just at that moment which she rather preferred not to talk about, she was for once struck with veritable astonishment, and did not know what to say.

"Dear Mrs Chiley, what should I have to tell you?" said Miss Marjoribanks. "You know very well where I should go the very first moment if anything happened;" and by way of staving off more particular questions, she took her old friend a cup of tea.

"Yes, my dear, I hope so," said Mrs Chiley, but at the same time her disappointment was evident. "It is very nice, thank you—your tea is always nice, Lucilla—but it was not that I was thinking of. I can't understand how it is, I am sure. I saw him to-day with my own eyes, and could not help seeing how anxious he was looking! I hope, I do hope, you have not been so cruel as to refuse him, Lucilla—and all for something that is not his fault, poor fellow, or that could be explained, you may be sure."

Miss Marjoribanks grew more and more surprised as she listened. She put away the kettle without filling the teapot, and left her own cup standing untasted, and went and sat down on the stool by Mrs Chiley's feet. "Tell me whom I have refused this time, for I don't know anything about it," said Lucilla; and then her visitor burst forth.

"It must be all that creature's fault! He told me he was coming here; and to tell the truth, I stood and watched him, for you know how interested I am, my dear; and then a little while after he met *that* Barbara. Oh, Lucilla, why were you ever so foolish as to have her here? I told you how it would end when you brought those artist people about your house. They are all a set of adventurers!" cried Mrs Chiley. "I saw them meet, and I was so disgusted that I did not know what I was doing; but he passed her as nicely as possible. Just a civil word, you know, and then he was past. Just as I would have done myself; for it is always best not to be uncivil to anybody. I could see her standing as if she had been struck with lightning; and naturally, Lucilla, I never thought anything else than that he had come here, and that all was right between you. Oh, my dear, I hope you are sure you have not refused him," Mrs Chiley said, piteously; "anyhow, Lucilla, you need not mind telling *me*. I may be sorry, but I will not blame you, my dear."

"I have not refused anybody," said Lucilla, with a modest innocence that it was a pleasure to see; "but dear Mrs Chiley," she continued, raising her drooping eyelids, "I think you make a mistake about Mr Cavendish. My own opinion is that Barbara would make him a very nice wife. Oh, please, don't be angry! I don't mean to say, you know, that I think her quite what one would call *nice*—for one's self. But then the gentlemen have such strange ways of thinking. Many a girl whom we could not put up with is quite popular with Them," said Miss Marjoribanks, with a certain mild wonder at the inexplicable creatures whom she thus condescended to discuss. "I suppose they have a different standard, you know; and for my part, I would advise Mr Cavendish to marry Barbara. I think it is the best thing he could do."

"Lucilla!" cried Mrs Chiley, almost with a shriek of horror. She thought, as was perhaps natural, that there was some pique in what her young companion said; not doing Miss Marjoribanks justice—as indeed few people did—for that perfect truthfulness which it was Lucilla's luck always to be able to maintain. Mrs Chiley thought it was her young friend's maidenly pride and determination not to take up the part of a woman slighted or jilted. "You may refuse him, my dear, if your heart is not with him," said the old lady; "but I would not be so hard upon him as that, poor fellow. You may say what you please, but I always will think him nice, Lucilla. I know I ought to be on the Archdeacon's side," said Mrs Chiley, putting her handkerchief to her eyes; "but I am an old woman, and I like my old friends best. Oh, Lucilla, it is not kind of you to keep up appearances with me. I wish you would give way a little. It would do you good, my darling; and you know I might be both your grandmothers, Lucilla," she cried, putting her arm round her favourite. As for Miss Marjoribanks, she gave her old friend a close embrace, which was the only thing that even her genius could suggest to do.

"I have always *you*," said Lucilla, with touching eloquence; and then she freed herself a little from Mrs Chiley's arms. "I don't say, perhaps, that everybody will receive her; but I mean to make an effort, for my part; and I shall certainly tell Mr Cavendish so if he ever speaks of it to me. As for Mr Beverley, he is going to be married too. Did not you hear? He told me all about it himself one day," said Miss Marjoribanks; "and I will ask him to-night if I may not tell you who the lady is. It is quite a little romance, and I hope we shall have two marriages, and it will make it quite gay for the winter. When you know all about it," Lucilla added, tenderly, by way of breaking the shock, "I am sure you will be pleased."

But instead of being pleased, Mrs Chiley was speechless for the moment. Her fresh old cheeks grew ashy with dismay and horror. "The Archdeacon too!" she cried, gasping for breath. "Oh, Lucilla, my dear!—and you?" Then the kind old lady held Miss Marjoribanks fast, and sobbed over her in the despair of the moment. To think, after all the pains that had been taken, and all the hopes and all the speculations, that neither the one nor the other was coming to anything! "If it should be that General, after all—and I cannot abide him," sobbed Lucilla's anxious friend. But Miss Marjoribanks's genius carried her through this trial, as well as through all the others which she had yet encountered on her way.

"Dear Mrs Chiley!" said Lucilla, "it is so good of you to care; but if it had been *that* I was thinking of, I need never have come home at all, you know; and my object in life is just what it has always been, to be a comfort to papa."

Upon which Mrs Chiley kissed her young friend once more with lingering meaning. "My dear, I don't know what They mean," she said, with indignation; "everybody knows men are great fools where women are concerned—but I never knew what idiots they were till now; and you are too good for them, my darling!" said Mrs Chiley, with indignant tenderness. Perhaps Miss Marjoribanks was in some respects of the same way of thinking. She conducted her sympathetic friend to the garden door, when it came to be time for everybody to go and dress, with a certain pathetic elevation in her own person, which was not out of accord with Mrs Chiley's virtuous wrath. To have Mrs Mortimer and Barbara Lake preferred to her did not wound Lucilla's pride—one can be wounded in that way only by one's equals. She thought of it with a certain mild pity and charitable contempt. Both these two men had had the chance of having *her*, and this was how they had chosen! And there can be little wonder if Miss Marjoribanks's compassion for them was mingled with a little friendly and condescending disdain.

It was, however, an ease to Lucilla's mind that she had let Mrs Chiley know, and was so far free to work out her plans without any fear of misconception. And on the whole, her old friend's tender indignation was not disagreeable to her. Thus it was, without any interval of repose to speak of, that her lofty energies went on unwearied to overrule and guide the crisis which was to decide so many people's fate.

CHAPTER XXXII.

DR MARJORIBANKS was not a man to take very much notice of trivial external changes; and he knew Lucilla and her constitution, and, being a medical man, was not perhaps so liable to parental anxieties as an unprofessional father might have been; but even he was a little struck by Miss Marjoribanks's appearance when he came into the drawing-room. He said, "You are flushed, Lucilla? is anything going to happen?" with the calmness of a man who knew there was not much the matter—but yet he did observe that her colour was not exactly what it always was. "I am quite well, papa, thank you," said Lucilla, which, to be sure, was a fact the Doctor had never doubted; and then the people began to come in, and there was no more to be said.

But there could be no doubt that Lucilla had more colour than usual. Her pulse was quite steady, and her heart going on at its ordinary rate; but her admirable circulation was nevertheless so far affected, that the ordinary rose-tints of her complexion were all deepened. It was not so distinctly an improvement as it would have been had she been habitually pale; but still the flush was moderate, and did Miss Marjoribanks no harm. And then it was a larger party than usual. The Centums were there, who were General Travers's chaperons, and so were the Woodburns, and of course Mrs Chiley, which made up the number of ladies beyond what was general at Dr Marjoribanks's table. Lucilla received all her guests with the sweetest smiles and all her ordinary ease and self-possession, but at the same time her mind was not free from some excitement. She was on the eve of a crisis which would be the greatest failure or the greatest success of her public life, and naturally she anticipated it with a certain emotion.

Mr Cavendish, for his part, had sufficient sense to come very early, and to get into a dark corner and keep himself out of the way; for though he was screwed up to the emergency, his self-possession was nothing to that of Lucilla. But on the whole, it was perhaps Mrs Woodburn who suffered the most. Her heightened colour was more conspicuous than that of Miss Marjoribanks, because as a general rule she was pale. She was pale, almost white, and had dark eyes and dark hair, and possessed precisely all the accessories which make a sudden change of complexion remarkable; and the effect this evening was so evident that even her husband admired her for a moment, and then stopped short to inquire, "By George! had she begun to paint?" to which question Mrs Woodburn naturally replied only by an indignant shrug of her white shoulders and aversion of her head. She would not have been sorry, perhaps, for this night only, if he had believed that it was rouge, and not emotion. Of all the people at Dr Marjoribanks's table, she perhaps was the only one really to be pitied. Even Mr Cavendish, if vanquished, would at the most receive only the recompense of his deeds, and could go away and begin over again somewhere else, or bury himself in the great depths of general society, where nobody would be the wiser; but as for his sister, she could not go away. The first result for her would be to give the master to whom she belonged, and for whom she had, with some affection, a great deal of not unnatural contempt, a cruel and overwhelming power over her; and she knew, poor soul, that he was not at all too generous or delicate to make use of such a power. In such a case she would be bound to the rock, like a kind of hapless Andromeda, to be pecked at by all the birds and blown at by all the winds, not to speak of the devouring monster from whom no hero could ever deliver her; and with all these horrible consequences before her eyes, she had to sit still and look on and do nothing, to see all the hidden meaning of every look and movement without appearing to see it, to maintain ordinary conversation when her ear was strained to the uttermost to hear words of fate on which her whole future depended. No wonder her colour was high; and she could not go into a corner, as Mr Cavendish did, nor keep silent, nor withdraw herself from observation. Neither her pulse nor her heart would have borne the scrutiny to which Miss Marjoribanks's calm organs might have been subjected with perfect security; and the chances are, if the Doctor had by any hazard put his finger on her wrist when he shook hands with her, that instead of handing her over to General Travers to be taken down to dinner, he would have, on the contrary, sent her off to bed.

Fortunately by this time the year was declining, and that happy season had returned in which people once more begin to dine by artificial light; and at the same time it was not absolutely dark in the drawing-room, so that Lucilla had not, as she said, thought it necessary to have the candles lighted. "If there should happen to be a mistake as to who is to take down who, it will only be all the more amusing," said Miss Marjoribanks, "so long as you do not go off and leave *me*." This was addressed to the Archdeacon, to whom Lucilla was very particular in her attentions at that moment. Mrs Chiley, who was looking on with a great sense of depression, could not help wondering why—"When she knows he is engaged and everything settled," the old lady said to herself, with natural indignation. For her part, she did not see what right a man had to introduce himself thus under false pretences into the confiding bosom of society—when he was as bad as married, or even indeed worse. She was ruffled, and she did not think it worth while to conceal that she was so; for there are limits to human patience, and a visitor who stays six weeks ought at least to have confidence in his entertainers. Mrs Chiley for once in her life could have boxed Lucilla's ears for her uncalled-for civility. "I think it very strange that it is not the General who takes her downstairs," she said to Mrs Centum. "It is all very well to have a respect for clergymen; but after being here so often, and the General quite a stranger—I am surprised at Lucilla," said the indiscreet old lady. As for Mrs Centum, she felt the neglect, but she had too much proper pride to own that her man was not receiving due attention. "It is not the first time General Travers has been here," she said, reserving the question; and so in the uncertain light, when nobody was sure who was his neighbour, the procession filed down-stairs.

To enter the dining-room, all brilliant and shining as it was, radiant with light and flowers and crystal and silver, and everything that makes a dinner-table pretty to look upon, was, as Mrs Centum said, "quite a contrast." A close observer might have remarked, as Mrs Woodburn and Lucilla took their places, that both of them, instead of that flush which had been so noticeable a short time before, had become quite pale. It was the moment of trial. Poor Mr Cavendish, in his excitement, had taken just the place he ought not to have taken, immediately under the lamp at the centre of the table. During the moment when the unsuspecting Archdeacon said grace with his eyes decorously cast down, Miss Marjoribanks owned the ordinary weakness of humanity so much as to drop her fan and her handkerchief, and even the napkin which was arranged in a symmetrical pyramid on her plate. Such a sign of human feebleness could but endear her to everybody who was aware of the momentous character of the crisis. When these were all happily recovered and everybody seated, Lucilla kept her eyes fixed upon the Archdeacon's face. It was, as we have said, a terrible moment. When he raised his head and looked round him, naturally Mr Beverley's eyes went direct to the mark like an arrow; he looked, and he saw at the centre of the table, surrounded by every kind of regard and consideration, full in the light of the lamp, his favourite adventurer, the impostor whom he had denounced the first time he took his place by Miss Marjoribanks's side. The Archdeacon rose to his feet in the excitement of the discovery; he put his hand over his eyes as if to clear them. He said, "Good God!" loud out, with an accent of horror which paralysed the two people lower down than himself. As for Miss Marjoribanks, she was not paralysed—she who had not lost a single glance of his eyes or movement of his large person. Lucilla rose to the height of the position. She put her hand upon his arm sharply, and with a certain energy. "Mr Beverley, Thomas is behind you with the soup," said Miss Marjoribanks. The Archdeacon turned round to see what it was, conscious that somebody had spoken to him, but as indifferent to his companion and to civility as he was to Thomas and the soup. "What?" he said, hoarsely, interrupting his scrutiny for the moment. But when he had met Miss Marjoribanks's eye the Archdeacon sat down. Lucilla did not liberate him for a moment from that gaze. She fixed her eyes upon his eyes, and looked at him as people only look when they mean something. "If you tell me what surprised you so much, perhaps I can explain," said Miss Marjoribanks. She spoke so that nobody could hear but himself; and in the mean time General Travers at her left hand was making himself excessively agreeable to Mrs Woodburn, and no doubt occupying all her attention; and Lucilla never turned her eyes for a moment from the Archdeacon's face.

"I beg your pardon," said Mr Beverley. "I was confounded by what I saw. Good heavens! it is not possible I can deceive myself. I understand your alarm. I am not going to make a disturbance and break up your party. I can wait," the Archdeacon said, drawing a rapid forcible breath. "Miss Marjoribanks, do you know who that man is?"

"Oh yes," said Lucilla, softening into a smile. "Perfectly, I assure you. He is one of papa's guests, and very much respected in Carlingford; and he is one of my—very particular friends," Miss Marjoribanks added. She laughed as she spoke, a kind of laugh which is only appropriate to one subject, and which is as good, any day, as a confession; and the flush was so obliging as to return at that moment to her ingenuous countenance. "We have known each other a long time," Lucilla went on after that pretty pause; and then she raised her confiding eyes, which had been cast down, once more to the Archdeacon's face. "You can't think how nice he is, Mr Beverley," said Miss Marjoribanks. She clasped her hands together, just for a moment, as she did so, with an eloquent meaning which it was impossible to mistake. The Archdeacon, for his part, gazed at her like a man in a dream. Whether it was true—or whether he was being made a fool of more completely than ever man before was—or whether he was the victim of an optical or some other kind of delusion,—the poor man could not tell. He was utterly stricken dumb, and did not know what to say. He accepted the soup humbly, which Thomas set before him, though it was a white soup—an effeminate dish, which went utterly in the face of his principles. And then he looked at the innocent young creature at his side in that flutter of happy confusion. It was a terrible position for the Broad-Churchman. After such a tacit confession he could not spring from his seat and hurl the impostor out of the room, as in the first place he had a mind to do. On the contrary, it was with a voice trembling with emotion that he spoke.

"My dear Miss Marjoribanks," said the Archdeacon, "I am struck dumb by what you tell me. Good heavens! that it should have come to this; and yet I should be neglecting my duty if I kept silent. You do not—you cannot know who he is."

"Oh yes," said Lucilla, with another little laugh—"*everything*—and how he used to know Mrs Mortimer, and all about it. He has no secrets from me," said Miss Marjoribanks. She caught Mr Cavendish's eye at the moment, who was casting a stealthy glance in her direction, and who looked cowed and silenced and unquiet to the most miserable degree; and she gave him a little reassuring nod, which the Archdeacon watched with an inward groan. What was he to do? He could not publicly expose the man who had just received this mark of confidence from his young hostess, who knew everything. Perhaps it was one of the greatest trials of Christian patience and fortitude which the Archdeacon, who was not great, as he himself would have said, in the passive virtues, had undergone in all the course of his life. He was so utterly subdued and confounded that he ate his soup, and never found out what kind of soup it was. That is, he consumed it in large spoonfuls without being aware, by way of occupying his energies and filling up the time.

"You cannot mean it," he said, after a pause. "You must be imperfectly informed. At least let me talk to your father. You must hear all the rights of the story. If you will let me speak half-a-dozen words to—to that person, Miss Marjoribanks, I am sure he will leave the place; he will give up any claim——"

"Oh yes, please talk to him," said Miss Marjoribanks, "it will be so nice to see you friends. Nothing would make me so happy. You know I have heard all about it from you and from Mrs Mortimer already, so I am sure there cannot be much more to tell; and as for papa, he is very fond of Mr Cavendish," said Lucilla, with an imperceptible elevation of her voice.

"Is it *he* whom you call Mr Cavendish?" said the Archdeacon. He too had raised his voice without knowing it, and several people looked up, who were not at the moment engaged in active conversation of their own. The owner of that name, for his part, also turned his face towards the upper end of the table. He was sick of the suspense and continued endurance, and by this time was ready to rush upon his fate.

"Did any one call me?" he said; and there was a little pause, and the company in general fixed its regard upon those three people with a sense that something remarkable was going on among them, though it could not tell what or why.

"The Archdeacon wants to make your acquaintance," said Miss Marjoribanks. "Mr Cavendish—Mr Beverley. There, you know each other; and when we are gone you can talk to each other if you like," Lucilla added; "but in the mean time *you* are too far off, and *I* want the Archdeacon. He is *so* much liked in Carlingford," she continued, lowering her voice. "You can't think how glad we are to have him back again. I am sure if you only knew him better——" said Miss Marjoribanks. As for the Archdeacon, words could not give any idea of the state of his mind. He ate his dinner sternly after that, and did not look at anything but his plate. He consumed the most exquisite *plats*, the tenderest wings of chicken and morsels of *paté*, as if they had been his personal enemies. For, to tell the truth, he felt the tables altogether turned upon him, and was confounded, and did not know what it could mean.

It was the General who took up Mr Beverley's abandoned place in the conversation. The gallant soldier talked for two with the best will in the world. He talked of Cavendish, and all the pleasant hours they had spent together, and what a good fellow he was, and how much the men in the club would be amused to hear of his domesticity. It was a kind of talk very natural to a man who found himself placed at table between his friend's sister, and, as he supposed, his friend's future bride. And naturally the Archdeacon got all the benefit. As for Lucilla, she received it with the most perfect grace in the world, and saw all the delicate points of the General's wit, and appreciated him so thoroughly, that he felt half inclined to envy Cavendish. "By Jove! he is the luckiest fellow I know," General Travers said; and probably it was the charms of his intelligent and animated conversation that kept the ladies so long at table. Mrs Chiley, for her part, did not know what to make of it. She said afterwards that she kept looking at Lucilla until she was really quite ashamed; and though she was at the other end of the table, she could see that the poor dear did not enjoy her dinner. It happened, too, that when they did move at last, the drawing-room was fuller than usual. Everybody had come that evening—Sir John, and some others of the county people, who only came now and then, and without any exception *everybody* in Carlingford. And Lucilla certainly was not herself for the first half-hour. She kept close to the door, and regarded the staircase with an anxious countenance. When she was herself at the helm of affairs, there was a certain security that everything would go on tolerably—but nobody could tell what a set of men left to themselves might or might not do. This was the most dreadful moment of the evening. Mrs Mortimer was in the drawing-room, hidden away under the curtains of a window, knowing nobody, speaking to nobody, and in a state of mind to commit suicide with pleasure; but Miss Marjoribanks, though she had cajoled her into that martyrdom, took no notice of Mrs Mortimer. She was civil, it is true, to her other guests, but there could not be a doubt that Lucilla was horribly preoccupied, and in a state of mind quite unusual to her. "I am sure she is not well," Mrs Chiley said, who was watching her from afar. "I saw that she did not eat any dinner"—and the kind old lady got up slowly and extricated herself from the crowd, and put herself in motion as best she could, to go to her young friend's aid.

It was at this moment that Lucilla turned round radiant upon the observant assembly. The change occurred in less than a moment, so suddenly that nobody saw the actual point of revolution. Miss Marjoribanks turned round upon the company and took Mr Cavendish's arm, who had just come upstairs. "There is a very, very old friend of yours in the corner who wants to see you," said Lucilla; and she led him across the room as a conqueror might have led a captive. She took him through the crowd, to whom she dispensed on every side her most gracious glances. "I am coming directly," Miss Marjoribanks said—for naturally she was called on all sides. What most people remarked at this moment was, that the Archdeacon, who had also come in with the other gentlemen, was standing very sullen and lowering at the door, watching that triumphal progress. And it certainly was not Lucilla's fault if Mrs Chiley and Lady Richmond, and a few other ladies, were thus led to form a false idea of the state of affairs. "I suppose it is all right between them at last," Lady Richmond said, not thinking that Barbara Lake was standing by and heard her. According to appearances, it was all perfectly right between them. Miss Marjoribanks, triumphant, led Mr Cavendish all the length of the room to the corner where the widow sat among the curtains, and the Archdeacon looked on with a visible passion, and jealous rage, which were highly improper in a clergyman, but yet which were exciting to see. And this was how the little drama was to conclude, according to Lady Richmond and Mrs Chiley, who, on the whole, were satisfied with the conclusion. But, naturally, there were other people to be consulted. There was Mr Beverley, whom Miss Marjoribanks held in leash, but who was not yet subdued; and there was Dr Marjoribanks, who began to feel a little curiosity about his daughter's movements, and did not make them out; and there was Barbara Lake, who had begun to blaze like a tempest with her crimson cheeks and black bold eyes. But by this time Lucilla was herself again, and felt the reins in her hands. When she had deposited Mr Cavendish in safety, she faced round upon the malcontents and upon the observers, and on the world in general. Now that her mind was at rest and everything under her own inspection, she felt herself ready and able for all.

CHAPTER XXXIII.

The Archdeacon stood before the fireplace with Dr Marjoribanks and a host of other gentlemen. Mr Beverley's countenance was covered with clouds and darkness. He stood, not with the careless ease of a man amusing himself, but drawn up to his full height and breadth, a formidably muscular Christian, in a state of repression and restraint, which it was painful, and at the same time pleasing, to see. The Berserker madness was upon him; and yet such are the restraints of society, that a young woman's eye was enough to keep him down—Lucilla's eye, and the presence of a certain number of other frivolous creatures in white muslin, and of some old women, as he irreverently called them, who were less pleasant, but not more imposing. He was an Archdeacon, and a leading man of his party, whose name alone would have conferred importance upon any "movement," and whom his bishop himself—not to speak of the clergy whom he charged in his visitation addresses like a regiment of cavalry —stood a little in awe of. Yet such are the beneficial restraints of society, that he dared not follow his natural impulses, nor even do what he felt to be his duty, for fear of Miss Marjoribanks, which was about the highest testimony to the value of social influence that could be given. At the same time, it was but natural that under such circumstances the Archdeacon should feel a certain savage wrath at the bond that confined him, and be more indignant than usual at the false and tyrannical conventionalism called society. And it was at this moment, of all times in the world, that General Travers, like a half-educated brute as (according to Mr Beverley's ideas) he was, took the liberty of calling his attention to what the soldier called "a lot of pretty girls." "And everything admirably got up, by Jove!" he added; not having the remotest idea what effect so simple an observation might produce.

"Yes, it is admirably got up," said the Archdeacon, with a snarl of concealed ferocity. "You never said anything more profoundly true. It is all got up, the women, and the decorations, and the gaiety, and all this specious seeming. And these are creatures made in the image of God!" said the Broad-Churchman—" the future wives and mothers of England. It is enough to make the devils laugh and the angels weep!"

It may be supposed that everybody was stricken with utter amazement by this unlooked-for remark. Dr Marjoribanks, for his part, took a pinch of snuff, which, as a general rule, he only did at consultations, or in the face of a difficulty; and as for the unlucky soldier who had called it forth, there can be no doubt that a certain terror filled his manly bosom, for he naturally felt as if he must have said something extraordinary to call forth such a response.

"I never was accused before of saying anything profoundly true," the General said, and he grew pale. "I didn't mean it, I'm sure, if that is any justification. Where has Cavendish vanished to, I wonder?" the soldier added, looking round him, scared and nervous—for it was evident that his only policy was to escape from society in which he was thus liable to commit himself without knowing how.

"Female education is a monstrous mistake," said Mr Beverley—"always has been, and, so far as I can see, always will be. Why should we do our best to make our women idiots? They are bad enough by nature. Instead of counterbalancing their native frivolity by some real instruction——good heavens!" The critic paused. It was not that his emotions were too much for him; it was because the crowd opened a moment, and afforded him a glimpse of a figure in black silk, with the lace for which Miss Marjoribanks had stipulated falling softly over a head which had not quite lost its youthful grace. He gave a glance round him to see if the coast was clear. Lucilla was out of the way at the other end of the room, and he was free. He made but one stride through the unconscious assembly which he had been criticising so severely, and all but knocked down little Rose Lake, who was not looking at the Archdeacon, though she stood straight in his way. He might have stepped over her head without knowing it, so much was he moved. All the gay crowd gave way before him with a cry and flutter; and Lucilla, for her part, was out of the way!

But there are moments when to be out of the way is the highest proof of genius. Miss Marjoribanks had just had a cup of tea brought her, of which she had great need, and her face was turned in the other direction, but yet she was aware that the Archdeacon had passed like a Berserker through those ranks which were not the ranks of his enemies. She felt without seeing it that the "wind of his going" agitated his own large coat-tails and heavy locks, and made a perfect hurricane among the white muslin. Lucilla's heart beat quicker, and she put down her tea, though she had so much need of it. She could not swallow the cordial at such a moment of excitement. But she never once turned her head, nor left off her conversation, nor betrayed the anxiety she felt. Up to this time she had managed everything herself, which was comparatively easy; but she felt by instinct that now was the moment to make a high effort and leave things alone. And it may be added that nothing but an inherent sense of doing the right thing under the circumstances could have inspired Miss Marjoribanks to the crowning achievement of keeping out of the way.

When Mr Beverley arrived in front of the two people who were seated together in the recess of the window, he made no assault upon them, as his manner might have suggested. On the contrary, he placed himself in front of them, with his back to the company, creating thus a most effectual moral and physical barrier between the little nook where his own private vengeance and fate were about to be enacted, and the conventional world which he had just been denouncing. The Archdeacon shut the two culprits off from all succour, and looked down upon them, casting them into profound shade. "I don't know what combination of circumstances has produced this meeting," he said, "but the time was ripe for it, and I am glad it has happened," and it was with dry lips and the calmness of passion that he spoke.

Mrs Mortimer gave a little cry of terror, but her companion, for his part, sat quite dumb and immovable. The moment had arrived at last, and perhaps he too was glad it had come. He sat still, expecting to see the earth crumble under his feet, expecting to hear the humble name he had once borne proclaimed aloud, and to hear ridicule and shame poured upon the impostor who had called himself one of the Cavendishes. But it was no use struggling any longer. He did not even raise his eyes, but sat still, waiting for the thunderbolt to fall.

But to tell the truth, the Archdeacon, though a torrent of words came rushing to his lips, felt at a difficulty how to begin. "I don't understand how it is that I find you here with the man who has ruined your prospects," he said, with a slight incoherence; and then he changed the direction of his attack.

"But it is you with whom I have to do," he said; "you, sir, who venture to introduce yourself into society with—with your victim by your side. Do you not understand that compassion is impossible in such a case, and that it is my duty to expose you? You have told some plausible story here, I suppose; but nothing can stand against the facts. It is my duty to inform Dr Marjoribanks that it is a criminal who has stolen into his house and his confidence—that it is a conspirator who has ventured to approach his daughter—that it is——"

"A criminal? a conspirator?" said Mr Cavendish, and he looked in his accuser's face with an amazement which, notwithstanding his rage, struck the Archdeacon. If he had called him an impostor, the culprit would have quailed and made no reply. But the exaggeration saved him. After that first look of surprise, he rose to his feet and confronted the avenger, who saw he had made a blunder without knowing what it was. "You must be under some strange mistake," he said. "What do you accuse me of? I know nothing about crime and conspiracy. Either you are strangely mistaken, or you have forgotten what the words mean."

"They are words which I mean to prove," said the Archdeacon; but there can be no doubt that his certainty was diminished by the surprise with which his accusation was received. It checked his first heat, and it was with a slightly artificial excitement that he went on, trying to work himself up again to the same point. "You who worked yourself into a wretched old man's confidence, and robbed an unoffending woman," said Mr Beverley; and then in spite of himself he stopped short; for it was easier to say such things to a woman, who contradicted without giving much reason, than to a man who, with an air of the utmost astonishment, stood regarding his accuser in the face.

"These are very extraordinary accusations," said Mr Cavendish. "Have you ever considered whether you had any proof to support them?" He was not angry to speak of, because he had been entirely taken by surprise, and because at the same time he was unspeakably relieved, and felt that the real danger, the danger which he had so much dreaded, was past and over. He recovered all his coolness from the moment he found out that it was not a venial imposition practised upon society, but a social crime of the ugliest character, of which he was accused. He was innocent, and he could be tranquil on that score. "As for robbing Mrs Mortimer," he added, with a little impatience, "she knows, on the contrary, that I have always been most anxious and ready to befriend her——"

"To befriend——Her!" cried the Archdeacon, restored to all his first impetuosity. He could not swear, because it was against his cloth and his principles; but he said, "Good heavens!" in a tone which would have perfectly become a much less mild expletive. "It is better we should understand each other thoroughly," he said. "I am not in a humour for trifling. I consider it is *her* fortune which enables you to make an appearance here. It is *her* money you are living upon, and which gives you position, and makes you presume as—as you are doing—upon my forbearance. Do you think it possible that I can pass over all this and let you keep what is not yours? If you choose to give up everything, and retire from Carlingford, and withdraw all your pretensions——. It is not my part," said Mr Beverley, with solemnity, taking breath, "to deal harshly with a penitent sinner. It is my duty, as a clergyman, to offer you at least a place of repentance. After *that*——"

But he was interrupted once more. Mrs Mortimer made her faint voice heard in a remonstrance. "Oh, Charles, I always told you—I had no right to anything!" cried the terrified widow; but that was not what stopped the Archdeacon. It was because his adversary laughed that he stopped short. No doubt it was the metallic laugh of a man in great agitation, but still Mr Beverley's ear was not fine enough at that moment to discriminate. He paused as a man naturally pauses at the sound of ridicule, still furious, yet abashed, and half conscious of a ludicrous aspect to his passion—and turned his full face to his antagonist, and stood at bay.

"It is a modest request, certainly," Mr Cavendish said. "Give up all I have and all I am, and perhaps you will forgive me! You must think me a fool to make such a proposal; but look here," said the accused, energetically; "I will tell you the true state of affairs, if for once you will listen. I do it, not for my sake, nor for your sake, but for the sake of—of the women involved," he added hastily; and it was well for him that, instead of looking at the shrinking widow beside him as he said so, his eye had been caught by the eager eye of his sister, who was watching from her corner. With that stimulus he went on, calming himself down, and somehow subduing and imposing upon the angry man by the mere act of encountering him fairly and openly. "I will tell you what are the actual circumstances, and you can see the will itself if you will take the trouble," said the defendant, with a nervous moderation and self-restraint, in which there was also a certain thrill of indignation. "The old man you speak of might have left his money to a more worthy person than myself, but he never meant to leave it to his grand-niece; and she knew that. She was neither his companion nor his nurse There was nothing between them but a few drops of blood. For my part, I gave him——but, to be sure, it would not interest you to know how I spent my youth. You came upon the scene like—a man in a passion," Mr Cavendish said, with an abrupt laugh, which this time was more feeble, and proved that his composure was giving way, "and misjudged everything, as was natural. You are doing the same again, or trying to do it. But you are a clergyman, and when you insult a man——"

"I am ready to give him satisfaction," said the Broad-Churchman, hotly; and then he made a pause, and that sense of ridicule which is latent in every Englishman's mind, came to the Archdeacon's aid. He began to feel ashamed of himself, and at the same time his eye caught his own reflection in a mirror, and the clerical coat which contrasted so grotesquely with his offer of "satisfaction." Mr Beverley started a little, and changed his tone. "This has lasted long enough," he said, in his abrupt imperious way. "*This* is not the place nor the time for such a discussion. We shall meet elsewhere," the Archdeacon added, austerely, with a significance which it is impossible to describe. His air and his words were full of severe and hostile meaning, and yet he did not know what he meant any more than Mr Cavendish did, who took him at his word, and retired, and made an end of the interview. Whatever the Archdeacon meant, it was his adversary who was the victor. *He* went off, threading his way through the curious spectators with a sense of relief that almost went the length of ecstasy. He might have been walking on his head for anything he knew. His senses were all lost and swallowed up in the overwhelming and incredible consciousness of safety. Where were they to meet elsewhere? With pistols in a corner of Carlingford Common, or perhaps with their fists alone, as Mr Beverley was Broad-Church? When a man has been near ruin and has escaped by a hairbreadth, he may be permitted to be out of his wits for a few minutes afterwards. And the idea of fighting a duel with a dignitary of the Church so tickled Mr Cavendish, that he had not the prudence to keep it to himself. "You will stand by me if he calls me out?" he said to General Travers as he passed; and the air of utter consternation with which the warrior regarded him, drove Mr Cavendish into such agonies of laughter, that he had to retire to the landing-place and suffocate himself to subdue it. If any man had said to him that he was hysterical, the chances are that it was he who would have called that man out, or at least knocked him down. But he had to steal down-stairs afterwards and apply to Thomas for a cordial more potent than tea; for naturally, when a man has been hanging over an abyss for ever so long, it is no great wonder if he loses his head and balance when he suddenly finds himself standing on firm ground, and feels that he has escaped.

As for the Archdeacon, when the other was gone, he sat down silently on his abandoned chair. He was one of the men who take pride in seeing both sides of a question; and to tell the truth, he was always very candid about disputed points in theology, and ready to entertain everybody's objection; but it was a different thing when the matter was a matter of fact. He put down his face into his hands, and tried to think whether it was possible that what he had just heard might be the true state of the case. To be sure, the widow who was seated half-fainting by his side had given him the same account often enough, but somehow it was more effective from the lips of a man who confronted him than from the mild and weeping woman whom he loved better than anything else in the world, but whose opinion on any earthly (or heavenly) subject had not the weight of a straw upon him. He tried to take that view of it; and then it occurred to him that nothing was more ludicrous and miserable than the position of a man who goes to law without adequate reason, or without proof to maintain his cause. Such a horrible divergence from everything that was just and right might be, as that the well-known and highly-esteemed Archdeacon Beverley might be held up for the amusement and edification of the country in a 'Times' leader, which was a martyrdom the Archdeacon would have rather liked than otherwise in a worthy cause, but not for a wretched private business connected with money. He sighed as he pondered, feeling, as so many have felt, the difficulties which attend a good man's progress in this life—how that which is just is not always that which is expedient, and how the righteous have to submit to many inconveniences in order that the adversary may have no occasion to blaspheme. In this state of mind a man naturally softens towards a tender and wistful sympathiser close at hand. He sighed once more heavily, and lifted his head, and took into his own a soft pale hand which was visible near him among the folds of black silk.

"So you too have been brought into it, Helen," the Archdeacon said, pathetically; "I did not expect to see you here."

"It was Lucilla," said Mrs Mortimer, timidly; "it was not any wish of mine. Oh, Charles! if you would let me speak. If you will but forget all this, and think no more about it; and I will do my best to make you a——" Here the poor woman stopped short all at once. What she meant to have said was, that she would make him a good wife, which nature and truth and the circumstances all prompted her to say—as the only possible solution to the puzzle. But when she had got so far, the poor widow stopped, blushing and tingling all over, with a sense of shame, more overwhelming than if she had done a wicked action. It was nothing but pure honesty and affection that prompted her to speak; and yet, if it had been the vilest sentiment in human nature, she would not have been so utterly ashamed. "That was not what I meant to say!" she cried, with sharp and sudden wretchedness; and was not the least ashamed of telling a downright lie instead.

But, to tell the truth, the Archdeacon was paying no particular attention. He had never loved any other woman; but he was a little indifferent as to what innocent nonsense she might please to say. So that her confusion and misery, and even the half offer of herself which occasioned these feelings, were lost upon him. He kept her hand and caressed it in the midst of his own thoughts, as if it was a child's head he was patting. "My poor Helen," he said, coming back to her when he found she had stopped speaking, "I don't see why you should not come, if this sort of thing is any pleasure to you; but afterwards——" he said, reflectively. He went to that sort of thing often himself, and rather liked it, and did not think of any afterwards; but perhaps the case of a weak woman was different, or perhaps it was only that he happened to be after his downfall in a pathetic and reflective state of mind.

"Afterwards?" said Mrs Mortimer. She did not take the word in any religious or philosophical, but in its merest matter-of-fact meaning, and she was sadly hurt and wounded to see that he had not even noticed what she said, much as she had been ashamed of saying it. She drew away her hand with a quick movement of despite and mortification, which filled Mr Beverley with surprise. "Afterwards I shall go back to my little house and my school, and shut myself in, and never, never come back again, you may be sure," said the widow, with a rush of tears to her eyes. Why they did not fall, or how she kept herself from fainting—she who fainted so easily—she never, on reviewing the circumstances, could tell; and Miss Marjoribanks always attributed it to the fact that *she* was absent, and there was no eau-de-cologne on the table. But whatever the cause might be, Mrs Mortimer did not faint; and perhaps there never was anything so like despair and bitterness as at that moment in her mild little feminine soul.

"Never come back again?" said the Archdeacon, rousing up a little; and then he put out his large hand and took back the other, as if it had been a pencil or a book that he had lost. All this, let it be known, was well in the shadow, and could not be seen by the world in general to teach the young people a bad lesson. "Why should not you come back? I am going away too," said Mr Beverley; and he stopped short, and resisted the effort his prisoner made to withdraw. Oddly enough at that moment his Rectory rose suddenly before him as in a vision— his Rectory, all handsome and sombre, without a soul in it, room after room uninhabited, and not a sound to be heard, except that of his own foot or his servant's. It was curious what connection there could be between that and the garden, with its four walls, and the tiny cottage covered with Westeria. Such as it was, it moved the Archdeacon to a singular, and, considering the place and moment, rather indecorous proceeding. Instead of contenting himself with the resisting hand, he drew the widow's arm within his as they sat together. "I'll tell you what we must do, Helen," he said, confidentially—"we must go back to Basing together, you and I. I don't see the good of leaving you by yourself here. You can make what alterations you like when you get to the Rectory; and I shall let that— that person alone, if you wish it, with his ill-gotten gear. He will never come to any good," said the Archdeacon, with some satisfaction; and then he added in a parenthesis, as if she had expressed some ridiculous doubt on the subject, "Of course I mean that we should be married before we go away." It was in this rapid and summary manner that the whole business was settled. Naturally his companion had nothing to say against such a reasonable arrangement. She had never contradicted him in her life about anything but one thing; and that being set aside, there was no possible reason why she should begin now.

CHAPTER XXXIV.

This was how the crisis came to an end, which had been of so much interest to the parties immediately affected. Mrs Woodburn had one of her nervous attacks next morning, and was very ill, and alarmed Dr Marjoribanks ; but at her very worst moment the incorrigible mimic convulsed her anxious medical adviser and all her attendants by a sudden adoption of the character of Mrs Mortimer, whom she must have made a careful study of the previous night. "Tell him to tell him to go down-stairs," cried the half-dead patient; "I want to speak to him, and he is not to hear ;—if he were not so thoughtless, he would offer him some lunch at least," Mrs Woodburn said, pathetically, with closed eyes and a face as pale as death. "She never did anything better in her life," Dr Marjoribanks said afterwards ; and Mr Woodburn, who was fond of his wife in his way, and had been crying over her, burst into such an explosion of laughter that all the servants were scandalised. And the patient improved from that moment. She was perfectly well and in the fullest force a week afterwards, when she came to see Lucilla, who had also been slightly indisposed for a day or two. When Thomas had shut the door, and the two were quite alone, Mrs Woodburn hugged Miss Marjoribanks with a fervour which up to that moment she had never exhibited. "It was only necessary that we should get into full sympathy with each other as human creatures," she said, lifting her finger like the Archdeacon ; and for all the rest of that autumn and winter Mrs Woodburn kept society in Carlingford in a state of inextinguishable laughter. The odd thing was that Miss Marjoribanks, who had been one of her favourite characters, disappeared almost entirely from her repertory. Not quite altogether, because there were moments of supreme temptation which the mimic could not resist ; but as a general rule Lucilla was the only woman in Carlingford who escaped the universal critic. No sort of acknowledgment passed between them of the obligations one had to the other, and, what was still more remarkable, no discussion of the terrible evening when Lucilla had held the Archdeacon with her eye, and prevented the volcano from exploding. Perhaps Mrs Woodburn, for her part, would have been pleased to have had such an explanation, but Miss Marjoribanks knew better. She knew it was best not to enter upon confidences which neither could ever forget, and which might prevent them meeting with ease in the midst of the little world which knew nothing about it. What Lucilla knew, she knew, and could keep to herself; but she felt at the same time that it was best to have no expansions on the subject. She kept it all to herself, and made the arrangements for Mrs Mortimer's marriage, and took charge of everything. Everybody said that nothing could be more perfect than the bride's toilette, which was as nice as could be, and yet not like a *real* bride after all; a difference which was only proper under the circumstances; for she was married in lavender, poor soul, as was to be expected. "You have not gone off the least bit in the world, and it is quite a pleasure to see you," Lucilla said, as she kissed her *that* morning—and naturally all Carlingford knew that it was owing to her goodness that the widow had been taken care of and provided for, and saved up for the Archdeacon. Miss Marjoribanks, in short, presided over the ceremony as if she had been Mrs Mortimer's mother, and superintended the wedding breakfast, and made herself agreeable to everybody. And in the mean time, before the marriage took place, most people in Carlingford availed themselves of the opportunity of calling on Mrs Mortimer. "If she should happen to be the future bishop's lady, and none of us ever to have taken any notice of her," somebody said, with natural dismay. Lucilla did not discourage the practical result of this suggestion, but she felt an instinctive certainty in her mind that *now* Mr Beverley would never be bishop of Carlingford, and indeed that the chances were Carlingford would never be elevated into a bishopric at all.

It was not until after the marriage that Mr Cavendish went away. To be sure, he was not absolutely present at the ceremony, but there can be no doubt that the magnificent *parure* which Mrs Mortimer received the evening before her marriage, "from an old friend," which made everybody's mouth water, and which she herself contemplated with mingled admiration and dismay, was sent by Mr Cavendish. "Do you think it could be from *him;* or only from him?" the bride said, bewildered and bewildering. "I am sure he might have known I never should require anything so splendid." But Lucilla, for her part, had no doubt whatever on the subject; and the perfect good taste of the offering made Miss Marjoribanks sigh, thinking once more how much that was admirable was wasted by the fatal obstacle which prevented Mr Cavendish from aspiring to anybody higher than Barbara Lake. As for the Archdeacon, he too found it very easy to satisfy his mind as to the donor of the emeralds. He put them away from him severely, and did not condescend to throw a second glance at their deceitful splendour. "Women are curiously constituted," said Mr Beverley, who was still at the height of superiority, though he was a bridegroom. "I suppose those sort of things give them pleasure—things which neither satisfy the body nor delight the soul."

"If it had been something to eat, would it have pleased you better?" said Lucilla, moved for once in her life to be impertinent, like an ordinary girl. For really when a man showed himself so idiotic as to despise a beautiful set of emeralds, it went beyond even the well-known tolerance and compassionate good-humour with which Miss Marjoribanks regarded the vagaries of "the gentlemen." There is a limit in all things, and this was going too far.

"I said, to satisfy the body, Miss Marjoribanks," said the Archdeacon, "which is an office very temporarily and inadequately performed by something to eat. I prefer the welfare of my fellow-creatures to a few glittering stones—even when they are round Her neck," Mr Beverley added, with a little concession to the circumstances. "Jewellery is robbery in a great town where there is always so much to be done, and so little means of doing it; to secure health to the people, and education——"

"Yes," said Miss Marjoribanks, who knew in her heart that the Archdeacon was afraid of her. "It is so nice of you not to say any of those dreadful sanitary words—and I am sure you could make something very nasty and disagreeable with that diamond of yours. It is a beautiful diamond; if I were Helen I should make you give it me," said Lucilla, sweetly; and the Archdeacon was so much frightened by the threat that he turned his ring instinctively, and quenched the glitter of the diamond in his closed hand.

"It was a present," he said, hastily, and went away to seek some better occupation than tilting with the womankind, who naturally had possession of the bride's little house and everything in it at that interesting moment. It was the last evening of Lucilla's reign, and she was disposed to take the full good of it. And though Mrs Mortimer's *trousseau* was modest, and not, as Lydia Brown repeated, like that of a *real* bride, it was still voluminous enough to fill the room to overflowing, where it was all being sorted and packed under Miss Marjoribanks's eye.

"It is a very nice diamond indeed," said Lucilla; "if I were you I should certainly make him give it to me—rings are no good to a gentleman. They never have nice hands, you know—though indeed when they have nice hands," said Miss Marjoribanks, reflectively, "it is a great deal worse, for they keep always thrusting them under your very eyes. It is curious why they should be so vain. They talk of women!" Lucilla added, with natural derision; "but, my dear, if I were you I would make him give it me; a nice diamond is always a nice thing to have."

"Lucilla," said the widow, "I am sure I don't know how to thank you for all you have done for me; but, dear, if you please, I would not talk like that! The gentlemen laugh, but I am sure they don't like it all the same;" for indeed the bride thought it her duty, having won the prize in her own person, to point out to her young friend how, to attain the same end, she ought to behave.

Miss Marjoribanks did not laugh, for her sense of humour, as has been said, was not strong, but she kissed her friend with protecting tenderness. "My dear, if that had been what I was thinking of I need never have come home," said Lucilla; and her superiority was so calm and serene, that Mrs Mortimer felt entirely ashamed of herself for making the suggestion. The widow was simple-minded, and, like most other women, it gratified her to believe that here and there, as in Miss Marjoribanks's case, there existed one who was utterly indifferent to the gentlemen, and did not care whether they were pleased or not; which restored a little the balance of the world to the widow-bride, who felt with shame that she cared a great deal, and was quite incapable of such virtue. As for Lucilla herself, she was not at that moment in conscious enjoyment of the strength of mind for which her friend gave her credit. On the contrary, she could not help a certain sense of surprised depression as she superintended the packing of the boxes. The man had had it in his power to propose to her, and he was going to be married to Mrs Mortimer! It was not that Lucilla was wounded or disappointed, but that she felt it as a wonderful proof of the imperfection and weakness of human nature. Even in the nineteenth century, which has learnt so much, such a thing was possible! It filled her with a gentle sadness as she had the things put in, and saw the emeralds safely deposited in their resting-place. Not that she cared for the Archdeacon, who had thus disposed of himself; but still it was a curious fact that such a thing could be.

Altogether it must be admitted that at this special moment Miss Marjoribanks occupied a difficult position. She had given the Archdeacon to understand that Mr Cavendish was a "*very* particular friend;" and even when the danger was past, Lucilla scorned to acknowledge her pious prevarications. During all this interval she continued so gracious to him that everybody was puzzled, and Mrs Woodburn even insisted on her brother, after all, making his proposal, which would be better late than never.

"I am sure she is fond of you," said the softened mimic, "and that sort of thing doesn't matter to a woman as it does to a man;" for it has been already said that Mrs Woodburn, notwithstanding her knack of external discrimination, had very little real knowledge of character. And even at moments, Mr Cavendish himself, who ought to have known better, was half-tempted to believe that Lucilla meant it. The effect upon Dr Marjoribanks was still more decided. He thought he saw in his daughter the indications of that weakness which is sometimes so surprising in women, and it disturbed the Doctor's serenity; and he actually tried to snub Lucilla on sundry occasions, with that wonderful fatuity which is common to men.

"I hope when this marriage is over people will recover their senses. I hear of nothing else," Dr Marjoribanks said one day at dessert, when they were alone. He took some chestnuts as he spoke, and burned his fingers, which did not improve his temper. "That sort of rubbish, I suppose, is much more interesting than attending to your natural duties," the Doctor added, morosely, which was not a kind of address which Miss Marjoribanks was used to hear.

"Dear papa," said Lucilla, "if I attended to my duties ever so much I could not keep you from burning your fingers. There are some things that people *must* do for themselves," the dutiful daughter added, with a sigh. Nobody could doubt who knew Lucilla that she would have gladly taken the world on her shoulders, and saved everybody from those little misadventures; but how could she help it if people absolutely would not take care of themselves?

The Doctor smiled grimly, but he was not satisfied. He was, on the contrary, furious in a quiet way. "I don't need at this time of day to be told how clever you are, Lucilla," said her father; "and I thought you had been superior to the ordinary folly of women——"

"Papa, for heaven's sake!" cried Miss Marjoribanks. She

was really alarmed this time, and she did not hesitate to let it be apparent. " I do not mean to say that I always do precisely what I ought to do," said Lucilla; " nobody does that I know of; but I am sure I never did anything to deserve *that*. I never was superior, and I hope I never shall be; and I know I never pretended to it," she said, with natural horror; for the accusation, as everybody will perceive, was hard to bear.

The Doctor laughed again, but with increased severity. " We understand all that," he said. " I am not in the secret of your actions, Lucilla. I don't know what you intend, or how far you mean to go. The only thing I know is that I see that young fellow Cavendish a great deal oftener in the house and about it than I care to see him; and I have had occasion to say the same thing before. I know nothing about his means," said Dr Marjoribanks; " his property may be in the Funds, but I think it a great deal more likely that he speculates. I have worked hard for my money, and I don't mean it to go in that way, Lucilla. I repeat, I am not in the secret of your proceedings——"

" Dear papa! as if there was any secret," said Lucilla, fixing her candid eyes upon her father's face. " I might pretend I did not understand you if there was anything in what you say, but I never go upon false pretences when I can help it. I am very fond of Mr Cavendish," she continued, regretfully, after a pause. " There is nobody in Carlingford that is so nice; but I don't see whom he can marry except Barbara Lake." Miss Marjoribanks would have scorned to conceal the unfeigned regret which filled her mind when she uttered these words. " I am dreadfully sorry, but I don't see anything that can be done for him," she said, and sighed once more. As for the Doctor, he forgot all about his chestnuts, and sat and stared at her, thinking in his ignorance that it was a piece of acting, and not knowing whether to be angry or to yield to the amusement which began to rise in his breast.

" He may marry half-a-dozen Barbara Lakes," said Dr Marjoribanks, " and I don't see what reason we should have to interfere: so long as he doesn't want to marry you——"

" That would be impossible, papa," said Lucilla, with pensive gravity. " I am sure I am very, very sorry. She has a very nice voice, but a man can't marry a voice, you know; and if there was anything that I could do—— I am not sure that he ever wished for *that* either," Miss Marjoribanks added, with her usual candour. " It is odd, but for all that it is true."

T

For it was a moment of emotion, and she could not help giving utterance to the surprise with which this consideration naturally filled her mind.

"What is odd, and what is true?" said Dr Marjoribanks, growing more and more bewildered. But Lucilla only put aside her plate and got up from her chair.

"Not any more wine, thank you," she said. "I know you don't want me any more, and I have so much to do. I hope you will let me invite Barbara here when they are married, and pay her a little attention; for nobody likes her in Grange Lane, and it would be so hard upon *him*. The more I think of it, the more sorry I am," said Lucilla; "he deserved better, papa; but as for me, everybody knows what is my object in life."

Thus Miss Marjoribanks left the table, leaving her father in a singular state of satisfaction and surprise. He did not believe a word of what she had been saying, with that curious perversity common to the people who surrounded Lucilla, and which arose not so much from doubt of her veracity as from sheer excess of confidence in her powers. He thought she had foiled him in a masterly manner, and that she was only, as people say, amusing herself, and had no serious intentions; and he laughed quietly to himself when she left him, in the satisfaction of finding there was nothing in it. Miss Marjoribanks, for her part, went on tranquilly with the arrangements for the marriage; one by one she was disembarrassing herself from the complications which had grown round her during the first year of her reign in Carlingford; and now only the last links of the difficulty remained to be unrolled.

The explanation she had with Mr Cavendish himself was in every way more interesting. It happened pretty late one evening, when Lucilla was returning with her maid from the widow's little cottage, which was so soon to be deserted. She was just at that moment thinking of the Westeria which had grown so nicely, and of all the trouble she had taken with the garden. Nobody could tell who might come into it now, after she had done so much for it; and Miss Marjoribanks could not but have a momentary sense that, on the whole, it was a little ungrateful on the part of Mrs Mortimer, when everybody had taken such pains to make her comfortable. At this moment, indeed, Lucilla was slightly given to moralising, though with her usual wisdom she kept her meditations to herself. She was thinking with a momentary vexation of all the plants that had been put into the beds, and of so much time and trouble lost—when Mr

Cavendish came up to her. It was a cold evening, and there was nothing in common between this walk and the walk they had taken together from Grove Street to Grange Lane on an earlier occasion. But this time, so far from being reluctant to accompany her, Mr Cavendish came to her side eagerly. The maid retired a little behind, and then the two found themselves in that most perfect of all positions for mutual confidence—a street not too crowded and noisy, all shrouded in the darkness, and yet twinkling with the friendly lights of an autumn evening. Nothing could have been more perfect than their isolation from the surrounding world, if they thought proper to isolate themselves; and yet it was always there to be taken refuge in if the confidence should receive a check, or the mind of the chance companions change.

"I have been trying to catch a glimpse of you for a long time," said Mr Cavendish, after they had talked a little in the ordinary way, as everybody was doing in Grange Lane, about the two people henceforward to be known in Carlingford as "the Beverleys." "But you are always so busy serving everybody. And I have a great deal to say to you that I don't know how to say."

"Then don't say it, please," said Lucilla. "It is a great deal better not. It might be funny, you know; but I am not disposed to be funny to-night. I am very glad about Mrs Mortimer, to be sure, that she is to be settled so nicely, and that they are going to be married at last. But, after all, when one thinks of it, it is a little vexatious. Just when her house was all put to rights, and the garden looking so pretty, and the school promising so well," said Lucilla; and there was a certain aggrieved tone in her voice.

"And it is you who have done everything for her, as for all the rest of us," said Mr Cavendish, though he could not help laughing a little; and then he paused, and his voice softened in the darkness by Lucilla's side. "Do not let us talk of Mrs Mortimer," he said. "I sometimes have something just on my lips to say, and I do not know whether I dare say it. Miss Marjoribanks——"

And here he came to a pause. He was fluttered and frightened, which was what she, and not he, ought to have been. And at the bottom of his heart he did not wish to say it, which gave far more force to his hesitation than simply a doubt whether he might dare. Perhaps Lucilla's heart fluttered too, with a sense that the moment which once would not have been an unwelcome moment, had at last arrived. Her heart, it is true, was not *very* particularly engaged; but still she was sensible of all Mr Cavendish's capacities, and was "very fond" of him, as she said; and her exertions on his behalf had produced their natural effect, and moved her affections a little. She made an involuntary pause for the hundredth part of a minute, and reckoned it all up again, and asked herself whether it were possible. There was something, in the first place, becoming and suitable in the idea that she, who was the only person who knew his secret, should take him and it together and make the best of them. And Lucilla had the consciousness that she could indeed make a great deal of Mr Cavendish. Nobody had ever crossed her path of whom so much could be made; and as for any further danger of his real origin and position being found out and exposed to the world, Miss Marjoribanks was capable of smiling at that when the defence would be in her own hands. She might yet accept him, and have him elected member for Carlingford, and carry him triumphantly through all his difficulties. For a small part—nay, even for the half of a minute—Lucilla paused, and made a rapid review of the circumstances, and reconsidered her decision. Perhaps if Mr Cavendish had been really in earnest, that which was only a vague possibility might have become, in another minute, a fact and real. It was about the first time that her heart had found anything to say in the matter; and the fact was that it actually fluttered in her reasonable bosom, and experienced a certain *malaise* which was quite new to her. Was it possible that she could be in love with Mr Cavendish? or was it merely the excitement of a final decision which made that unusual commotion far away down at the bottom of Lucilla's heart.

However that might be, Miss Marjoribanks triumphed over her momentary weakness. She saw the possibility, and at the same moment she saw that it could not be; and while Mr Cavendish hesitated, she, who was always prompt and ready, made up her mind.

"I don't know what I have done in particular, either for her or the rest of you," she said, ignoring the other part of her companion's faltering address, "except to help to amuse you; but I am going to do something very serious, and I hope you will show you are grateful, as you say—though I don't know what you have to be grateful about—by paying great attention to me. Mr Cavendish, I am going to give you good advice," said Lucilla; and, notwithstanding her courage, she too faltered a little, and felt that it was rather a serious piece of business that she had taken in hand.

"Advice?" Mr Cavendish said, like an echo of her voice; but that was all he found time to say.

"We are such old friends, that I know you won't be vexed," said Lucilla; "and then we understand each other. It is so nice when two people understand each other; they can say quantities of things that strangers cannot say. Mr Cavendish, you and Barbara are in love," said Lucilla, making a slight pause, and looking in his face.

"Miss Marjoribanks!" cried the assaulted man, in the extremity of his amazement and horror. As for Lucilla, she came a little closer to him, and shook her head in a maternal, semi-reproving way.

"Don't say you are not," said Miss Marjoribanks; "you never could deceive *me*—not in anything like that. I saw it almost as soon as you met. They are not rich, you know, but they are very nice. Mr Lake and Rose," said Lucilla, with admirable prudence, keeping off the difficult subject of Barbara herself, "are the two very nicest people I know; and everybody says that Willie is dreadfully clever. I hope you will soon be married, and that you will be very happy," she continued, with an effort. It was a bold thing to say, and Lucilla's throat even contracted a little, as if to prevent the words from getting utterance; but then she was not a person, when she knew a thing was right, to hesitate about doing it; and in Miss Marjoribanks's mind duty went before all, as has already been on several occasions said.

After this a horrible silence fell upon the two—a silence which, like darkness, could be felt. The thunderbolt fell upon the victim's unprotected head without any warning. The idea that Lucilla would talk to him about Barbara Lake was the very last that could have entered Mr Cavendish's mind. He was speechless with rage and mortification. He took it for an insult inflicted upon him in cold blood, doing Lucilla as much injustice as the other people who took the candid expression of her sentiments for a piece of acting. He was a gentleman notwithstanding his doubtful origin, and civilised down to his very finger-tips; but he would have liked to have knocked Miss Marjoribanks down, though she was a woman. And yet, as she was a woman, he dared not for his life make any demonstration of his fury. He walked along by her side down into the respectable solitude of Grange Lane, passing through a bright bit of George Street, and seeing askance, by the light from the shop windows, his adviser walking beside him, with the satisfaction of a good conscience in her face. This awful silence lasted until they reached Dr Marjoribanks's door.

"Thank you for coming with me so far," said Lucilla, holding out her hand. "I suppose I must not ask you to come in, though papa would be delighted to see you. I am afraid you are very angry with me," Miss Marjoribanks added, with a touch of pathos; "but you may be sure I would always stand by *you;* and I said it because I thought it was for the best."

"On the contrary, I am much obliged to you," said Mr Cavendish, with quiet fury, "and deeply touched by the interest you take in my happiness. You may be sure I shall always be grateful for it; and for the offer of your support," said the ungrateful man, with the most truculent meaning. As for Miss Marjoribanks, she pressed quite kindly the hurried hand with which he touched hers, and went in, still saying, "Good-night." She had done her duty, whatever might come of it. He rushed home, furious; but she went to a little worsted-work with a mind at peace with itself and all men. She was gentler than usual even to the maids, who always found Miss Marjoribanks a good mistress—but she felt a little sad in the solitude of her genius. For it is true that to be wiser and more enlightened than one's neighbours is in most cases a weariness to the flesh. She had made a sacrifice, and nobody appreciated it. Instead of choosing a position which pleased her imagination, and suited her energies, and did not go against her heart, Lucilla, moved by the wisest discretion, had decided, not without regret, to give it up. She had sacrificed her own inclination, and a sphere in which her abilities would have had the fullest scope, to what she believed to be the general good; and instead of having the heroism acknowledged, she was misunderstood and rewarded with ingratitude. When Miss Marjoribanks found herself alone in the solitude of her drawing-room, and in the still greater solitude, as we have said, of her genius, she felt a little sad, as was natural. But at the same moment there came into Lucilla's mind a name, a humble name, which has been often pronounced in the pages of this history, and it gave her once more a certain consolation. A sympathetic presence seemed to diffuse itself about her in her loneliness. There are moments when the faith of a very humble individual may save a great soul from discouragement; and the consciousness of being believed in once more came with the sweetest and most salutary effect upon Lucilla's heart.

CHAPTER XXXV.

It was the very day after the marriage, and two or three days after this conversation, that Mr Cavendish left Carlingford. He went to spend the winter in Italy, which had long been "a dream" of his, as he explained to some of the young ladies— most of whom had the same "dream," without the enviable power of carrying it out. He made very brief and formal adieux to Lucilla, to the extreme amazement of all the surrounding world, and then disappeared, leaving—just at that moment after the excitement of the marriage was over, when Grange Lane stood most in need of somebody to rouse its drooping spirits—a wonderful blank behind him. Lucilla said much less about her feelings on this occasion than she was in the habit of doing, but there could be no doubt that she felt it, and felt it acutely. And the worst of it was, that it was she who was universally blamed for the sudden and unexplained departure of the most popular man in Carlingford. Some people thought he had gone away to escape from the necessity of proposing to her; and some of more friendly and charitable disposition believed with Mrs Chiley that Lucilla had refused him; and some, who were mostly outsiders and of a humble class, were of opinion that Miss Marjoribanks had exercised all her influence to send Mr Cavendish out of the way of Barbara Lake. It was with this impression that Rose made her way one of those foggy autumn mornings through the fallen leaves with which the garden was carpeted, to see if any explanation was to be got from Lucilla. The art-inspectors from Malborough House had just paid their annual visit to Carlingford, and had found the Female School of Design in a condition which, as they said in their report, "warranted the warmest encomiums," and Rose had also won a prize for her veil in the exhibition at Kensington of ornamental art. These were triumphs which would have made the little artist overwhelmingly happy, if they had not been neutralised by other circumstances; but as it was, they only aggravated the difficulties of the position in which she found herself. She came to Lucilla in a bonnet—a circumstance which of itself was solemn and ominous; for generally that portentous article of dress, which was home-made, and did not consist with cheerful dispositions, was reserved by Rose for going to church; and her soft cheeks were pale, and the hazel eyes more dewy than usual, though it was rain, and not dew, that had been falling from them during those last painful days.

"I am ashamed to ask you such a question," said Rose; "but I want you to tell me, Lucilla, if you know why Mr Cavendish has gone away. She will not come and ask you herself, or rather I would not let her come; for she is so passionate, one does not know what she might not do. You have behaved a little strange, Lucilla," said the straightforward Rose. "If he cared for her, and she cared for him, you had no right to come and take him away."

"My dear, I did not take him away," said Miss Marjoribanks. "I had to talk to him about some—business; that was all. It is disgraceful of Barbara to bother you about it, who are only a baby and oughtn't to know anything——"

"Lucilla!" cried Rose, with flashing eyes, "I am seventeen, and I will not put up with it any longer. It is all your fault. What right had you to come and drag us to your great parties? We are not as rich as you, nor as fine, but we have a rank of our own," cried the little artist. "You have a great deal more money, but we have some things that money cannot buy. You made Barbara come and sing, and put things into her head; and you made me come, though I did not want to. Why did you ask *us* to your parties, Lucilla? It is all your fault!"

Lucilla was in a subdued state of mind, as may have been perceived, and answered quite meekly. "I don't know why you should all turn against me like this," she said, more sadly than surprised. "It is unkind of you to say it was my fault. I did not expect it from you; and when I have so many vexations——" Miss Marjoribanks added. She sat down as she spoke, after being repulsed by Rose, with an air of depression which was quite unusual to her; for to be blamed and misunderstood on all sides was hard for one who was always working in the service of her fellow-creatures, and doing everything for the best.

As for Rose, her heart smote her on the instant. "Have *you* vexations, Lucilla?" she said, in her innocence. It was the first time such an idea had entered into her mind.

"I don't think I have anything else," said Lucilla; though

even as she said it she began to recover her spirits. "I do all I can for my friends, and they are never pleased; and when anything goes wrong it is always my fault."

"Perhaps if you were not to do so much——" Rose began to say, for she was in her way a wise little woman; but her heart smote her again, and she restrained the truism, and then after a little pause she resumed her actual business. "I am ashamed to ask you, but do you know where Mr Cavendish is, Lucilla?" said Rose. "She is breaking her heart because he has gone away."

"Did he never go to say good-bye nor anything?" asked Miss Marjoribanks. She was sorry, for it was quite the contrary of the advice she had given, but still it would be wrong to deny that Mr Cavendish rose higher in Lucilla's opinion when she heard it. "I don't know any more than everybody knows. He has gone to Italy, but he will come back, and I suppose she can wait," Miss Marjoribanks added, with perhaps a touch of contempt. "For my part, I don't think she will break her heart."

"It is because you do not know her," said Rose, with some indignation—for at seventeen a broken heart comes natural. "Oh, Lucilla, it is dreadful, and I don't know what to do!" cried the little artist, changing her tone. "I am a selfish wretch, but I cannot help it. It is as good as putting an end to my Career; and just after my design has been so successful—and when papa was so proud—and when I thought I might have been a help. It is dreadful to think of one's self when her heart is breaking; but I shall have to give up everything; and I—I can't help feeling it, Lucilla," cried Rose, with a sudden outburst of tears.

All this was sufficiently unintelligible to Miss Marjoribanks, who was not the least in anxiety about Barbara's breaking heart. "Tell me what is the matter, and perhaps we can do something," said Lucilla, forgetting how little her past exertions had been appreciated; and Rose, with equal inconsistency, dried her tears at the sound of Miss Marjoribanks's reassuring voice.

"I know I am a wretch to be thinking of myself," she said. "She cannot be expected to stay and sacrifice herself for us, after all she has suffered. She has made up her mind and advertised in the 'Times,' and nothing can change it now. She is going out for a governess, Lucilla."

"Going for a—what?" said Miss Marjoribanks, who could not believe her ears.

"For a governess," said Rose, calmly; for though she had been partly brought up at Mount Pleasant, she had not the elevated idea of an instructress of youth which might have been expected from a pupil of that establishment. "She has advertised in the 'Times,'" Rose added, with quiet despair, "with no objections to travel. I would do anything in the world for Barbara, but one can't help thinking of one's self sometimes, and there is an end of my Career." When she had said this she brushed the last tear off her eyelashes, and sat straight up, a little martyr and heroic victim to duty. "Her eye, though fixed on empty space, beamed keen with honour;" but still there was a certain desperation in the composure with which Rose regarded, after the first outburst, the abandonment of all her hopes.

"She is a selfish thing," said Lucilla, indignantly; "she always was a selfish thing. I should like to know what she can teach anybody? If I were you and your papa, I certainly would not let her go away. I don't see any reason in the world why you should give in to her and let her stop your—your Career, you know; why should you? I would not give in to her for one moment, if I were your papa and you."

"Why should I?" said Rose; "because there is nobody else to do anything, Lucilla. Fleda and Dreda are such two little things; and there are all the boys to think of, and poor papa. It is of no use asking why. If I don't do it, there will be nobody to do it," said Rose, with big tears coming to her eyes. Her Career was dear to her heart, and those two tears welled up from the depths; but then there would be nobody else to do it —a consideration which continually filters out the people who are good for anything out of the muddy current of the ordinary world.

"And your pretty drawings, and the veil, and the School of Design!" cried Lucilla. "You dear little Rose, don't cry. It never can be permitted, you know. She cannot teach anything, and nobody will have her. She is a selfish thing, though she is your sister; and if I were your papa and you——"

"It would be no good," said Rose. "She will go, whatever anybody may say. *She* does not care," said the little martyr, and the two big tears fell, making two big round blotches upon the strings of that bonnet which Lucilla had difficulty in keeping her hands off. But when she had thus expressed her feelings, Rose relented over her sister. "She has suffered so much here; how can any one ask her to sacrifice herself to us?" said the young artist mournfully. "And I am quite happy," said Rose—"quite happy; it makes all the difference. It is her *heart*, you know, Lucilla; and it is only my Career."

And this time the tears were dashed away by an indignant little hand. Barbara's heart, if she had such an organ, had never in its existence cost such bitter drops. But as for Lucilla, what could she do? She could only repeat, "If I was your papa and you," with a melancholy sense that she was here balked and could do no more. For even the aid of Miss Marjoribanks was as nothing against dead selfishness and folly, the two most invincible forces in the world. Instead of taking the business into her own hands, and carrying it through triumphantly as she had hitherto been in the habit of doing, Lucilla could only minister to the sufferer, and keep up her courage, and mourn over the Career thus put in danger. Barbara's advertisement was in the newspapers, and her foolish mind was made up; and the hope that nobody would have her was a forlorn hope, for somebody always does have the incapable people, as Miss Marjoribanks was well aware. And the contralto had been of some use in Grange Lane and a little in Grove Street, and it would be difficult, either in the one sphere or the other, to find any one to fill her place. It was thus amid universal demolition that Christmas approached, and Miss Marjoribanks ended the first portion of her eventful career.

CHAPTER XXXVI.

ONE fytte of Lucilla's history is here ended, and another is to be told. We have recorded her beginning in all the fulness of youthful confidence and undaunted trust in her own resources; and have done our best to show that in the course of organising society Miss Marjoribanks, like all other benefactors of their kind, had many sacrifices to make, and had to undergo the mortification of finding out that many of her most able efforts turned to other people's profit and went directly against herself. She began the second period of her career with, to some certain extent, that sense of failure which is inevitable to every high intelligence after a little intercourse with the world. She had succeeded in a great many things, but yet she had not succeeded in all; and she had found out that the most powerful exertions in behalf of friends not only fail to procure their gratitude, but sometimes convert them into enemies, and do actual harm; which is a discovery which can only be made by those who devote themselves, as Miss Marjoribanks had done, to the good of the human species. She had done everything for the best, and yet it had not always turned out for the best; and even the people who had been most ready to appeal to her for assistance in their need, had proved the readiest to accuse her when something disagreeable happened, and to say " It was your fault." In the second stage of her progress Miss Marjoribanks found herself, with a great responsibility upon her shoulders, with nearly the entire social organisation of Carlingford depending upon her; and, at the same time, with her means of providing for the wants of her subjects sensibly diminished, and her confidence in the resources of the future impaired to an equal degree. One thing was sure, that she had taken the work upon her shoulders, and that she was not the woman to draw back, whatever the difficulties might be. She did not bate a jot of her courage, though the early buoyancy of hope had departed, never to return. It is true that she was not so joyful and triumphant a figure as when she conquered Nancy, and won over Dr Marjoribanks, and electrified Mr Holden by choosing curtains which suited her complexion; but with her diminished hopes and increased experience and unabated courage, no doubt Miss Marjoribanks presented a still nobler and more imposing aspect to everybody who had an eye for moral grandeur, though it would be difficult to tell how many of such worthy spectators existed in Grange Lane.

There was, as our readers are aware, another subject also on which Lucilla had found her position altered. It was quite true that, had she been thinking of *that*, she never need have come home at all; and that, in accepting new furniture for the drawing-room, she had to a certain extent pledged herself not to marry immediately, but to stay at home and be a comfort to her dear papa. This is so delicate a question that it is difficult to treat it with the freedom necessary for a full development of a not unusual state of mind. Most people are capable of falling in love only once or twice, or at the most a very few times, in their life; and disappointed and heart-broken suitors are not so commonly to be met with as perhaps could be wished. But at the same time, there can be little doubt that the chief way in which society is supposed to signify its approval and admiration and enthusiasm for a lady, is by making dozens of proposals to her, as may be ascertained from all the best-informed sources. When a woman is a great beauty, or is very brilliant and graceful, or even is only agreeable and amusing, the ordinary idea is, that the floating men of society, in number less or more according to the lady's merits, propose to her, though she may not perhaps accept any of them. In proportion as her qualities rise towards the sublime, these victims are supposed to increase; and perhaps, to tell the truth, no woman feels herself set at her true value until some poor man, or set of men, have put, as people say, their happiness into her hands. It is, as we have said, a delicate subject to discuss; for the truth is, that this well-known and thoroughly established reward of female excellence had not fallen to Miss Marjoribanks's lot. There was Tom, to be sure, but Tom did not count. And as for the other men who had been presented to Lucilla as eligible candidates for her regard, none of them had given her this proof of their admiration. The year had passed away, and society had laid no tribute of this description upon Lucilla's shrine. The Archdeacon had married Mrs Mortimer instead, and Mr Cavendish had been led away by Barbara Lake! After such an experience nothing but the inherent sweetness and wholesome tone of Miss Marjoribanks's character could have kept her from that cynicism and disbelief in humanity which is so often the result of knowledge of the world. As for Lucilla, she smiled as she thought of it, not cynically, but with a sweetly melancholy smile. What she said to herself was, Poor men! they had had the two ways set before them, and they had not chosen the best. It made her sad to have this proof of the imperfection of human nature thrust upon her, but it did not turn her sweet into bitter, as might have been the case with a more ordinary mind. Notwithstanding that this universal reward, which in other cases is, as everybody knows, given so indiscriminately, and with such liberality, had altogether failed in her case, Lucilla still resumed her way with a beautiful constancy, and went forward in the face of fate undaunted and with a smile.

It was thus she began the second period of her career. Up to this moment there had never been a time in which it was not said in Carlingford that some one was paying attention to Miss Marjoribanks; but at present no one was paying attention to her. There were other marriages going on around her, and other preliminaries of marriage, but nobody had proposed to Lucilla. Affairs were in this state when she took up her burden again boldly, and set out anew upon her way. It was a proof of magnanimity and philanthropy which nobody could have asked from her, if Lucilla had not been actuated by higher motives than those that sway the common crowd. Without any assistance but that of her own genius—without the stimulating applause of admirers, such as a woman in such circumstances has a right to calculate upon—with no sympathising soul to fall back upon, and nothing but a dull level of ordinary people before her,—Miss Marjoribanks, undaunted, put on her harness and resumed her course. The difficulties she had met only made her more friendly, more tender, to those who were weaker than herself, and whom evil fortune had disabled in the way. When Barbara Lake got her situation, and went out for a governess, and Rose's fears were realised, and she had with bitter tears to relinquish her Career, Lucilla went and sat whole afternoons with the little artist, and gave her the handiest assistance, and taught her a great many things which she never could have learned at the School of Design. And the effect of this self-abnegation was, that Lucilla bore General Travers's decision, and gave up all hope of the officers, with a stout-heartedness which nobody could have looked for, and did not hesitate to face her position boldly, and to erect her standard, and to begin her new campaign unaided and unappreciated as she was. People who know no better may go away upon marriage-tours, or they may fly off to foreign travel, or go out as governesses, when all things do not go just as they wish. But as for Miss Marjoribanks, she stood bravely at her post, and scorned to flinch or run away. Thus commenced, amid mists of discouragement, and in an entire absence of all that was calculated to stimulate and exhilarate, the second grand period of Lucilla's life.

CHAPTER XXXVII.

It would be vain to follow Lucilla in detail through her consistent and admirable career; nor is it necessary to say that she went on steadily in face of all her discouragements, with that mixture of success and failure which comes natural to all human affairs. The singular thing about it was, that the years passed on, and that she was permitted by the world in general to fulfil her own promise and prophecy about remaining ten years at home to be a comfort to her dear papa. She had been nineteen when she began her career, and she was nine-and-twenty when that little episode occurred with young Dr Rider, before he was married to his present wife. There would have been nothing in the least unsuitable in a marriage between Dr Rider and Miss Marjoribanks, though people who were the best informed never thought either of them had any serious meaning; but, of course, the general public, having had Lucilla for a long time before their eyes, naturally added on seven or eight years to her age, and concluded her to be a great deal older than the young doctor, though everybody allowed that it would have been a most advantageous match for him in every possible point of view. But, however, it did not come to anything, no more than a great many other nibbles of the same kind did. The period arrived at which Lucilla had thought she might perhaps have begun to go off in her looks, but still there was no immediate appearance of any change of name or condition on her part. Many people quite congratulated themselves on the fact, as it was impossible to imagine what might be the social condition of Grange Lane without Miss Marjoribanks; but it is doubtful whether Lucilla congratulated herself. She was very comfortable, no doubt, in every way, and met with little opposition to speak of, and had things a great deal more in her own hands than she might have had, had there been a husband in the case to satisfy; but notwithstanding, she had come to an age when most people have husbands, and when an independent position in the world becomes necessary to self-respect. To be sure, Lucilla *was* independent; but then—there is a difference, as everybody knows.

And Miss Marjoribanks could not but feel that the world had not shown that appreciation of her, to which, in her earlier days, she looked forward with so little fear. The ten years, as they had really gone by, were very different from the ten years she had looked forward to, when, in the triumph of her youth, she named that period as the time when she might probably begin to go off, and would be disposed to marry. By this time the drawing-room carpets and curtains had faded a little, and Lucilla had found out that the delicate pale green which suited her complexion was not to call a profitable colour; and nobody could have thought or said that to marry at this period would be in the least degree to swindle the Doctor. Thus the moment had arrived to which she looked forward, but the man had not arrived with it. Ten years had passed, during which she had been at the head of society in Grange Lane, and a great comfort to her dear papa; and now, if there remained another development for Lucilla's character, it was about time that it should begin to show itself. But at the same time, the main element necessary for that new development did not seem at present likely to be found in Grange Lane.

Unless, indeed, it might happen to be found in the person of Mr Ashburton, who was so often in Carlingford that he might be said to form a part of society there. It was he who was related to the Richmonds, who were a family much respected in the county. He had been at the bar, and even begun to distinguish himself, before old Miss Penrhyn died and left him the Firs. He had begun to distinguish himself, but he had not, it appeared, gone so far as to prevent him from coming down to his new property and settling upon it, and taking his place as a local notability. He was not a man who could be expected to care for evening parties in a provincial town; but he never refused to dine with Dr Marjoribanks, and was generally popular up-stairs, where he always paid a little attention to Lucilla, though nothing very marked and noticeable. Mr Ashburton was not like Mr Cavendish, for instance (if anybody remembered Mr Cavendish), a man whose money might be in the Funds, but who more probably speculated. Everybody knew everything about him, which was an ease to the public mind. The Firs was as well known as Carlingford steeple, and how much it was worth a-year, and everything about it; and so was the proprietor's pedigree, which could be traced to a semi-mythical personage known as old Penrhyn, whose daughter was Sir John Richmond's grandmother. The Firs, it is true, had descended in the female line, but still it is something to know where a man comes from, even on one side.

Mr Ashburton made himself very agreeable in the neighbourhood, and was never above enlightening anybody on a point of law. He used to say that it was kind to give him something to do, which was an opinion endorsed practically by a great many people. It is true that some of his neighbours wondered much to see his patience, and could not make out why he chose to rusticate at the Firs at his age, and with his abilities. But either he never heard these wonderings, or at least he never took any notice of them. He lived as if he liked it, and settled down, and presented to all men an aspect of serene contentment with his sphere. And it would be difficult to say what suggestion or association it was which brought him all of a sudden into Miss Marjoribanks's head, one day, when, seeing a little commotion in Masters's shop, she went in to hear what it was about. The cause of the commotion was an event which had been long expected, and which, indeed, ten years before, had been looked on as a possible thing to happen any day. The wonder was, not that old Mr Chiltern should die, but that he should have lived so long. The ladies in Masters's cried, "Poor dear old man!" and said to each other that however long it might have been expected, a death always seemed sudden at the last. But, to tell the truth, the stir made by this death was rather pleasant than sad. People thought, not of the career which was ended, but of the one which must now begin, and of the excitement of an election, which was agreeable to look forward to. As for Lucilla, when she too had heard the news, and had gone upon her way, it would be vain to assert that a regretful recollection of the time when Mr Cavendish was thought a likely man to succeed Mr Chiltern did not occur to her. But when Miss Marjoribanks had dismissed that transitory thought, Mr Ashburton suddenly came into her head by one of those intuitions which have such an effect upon the mind that receives them. Lucilla was not of very marked political opinions, and perhaps was not quite aware what Mr Ashburton's views were on the Irish Church question, or upon parliamentary reform; but she said after, that it came into her mind in a moment, like a flash of lightning, that he was the man. The idea was so new and so striking, that she turned back and went, in the excitement of the moment, to suggest it to Mrs Chiley, and see what her old friend and the Colonel would say. Of course, if such a thing was practicable, there was no time to lose. She turned round quickly, according to her prompt nature; and such was her absorbed interest in the idea of Mr Ashburton, that she did not know until she had almost done it, that she was walking straight into her hero's arms.

"Oh, Mr Ashburton!" said Lucilla, with a little scream, "is it you? My mind was quite full of you. I could not see you for thinking. Do come back with me, for I have something very particular to say——"

"To me?" said Mr Ashburton, looking at her with a smile and a sudden look of interest; for it is always slightly exciting to the most philosophical mortal to know that somebody else's mind is full of him. "What you have said already is so flattering——"

"I did not mean anything absurd," said Miss Marjoribanks.

"Don't talk any nonsense, please. Mr Ashburton, do you know that old Mr Chiltern is dead?"

Lucilla put the question solemnly, and her companion grew a little red as he looked at her. "It is not my fault," he said, though he still smiled; and then he grew redder and redder, though he ought to have been above showing such signs of emotion; and looked at her curiously, as if he would seize what she was going to say out of her eyes or her lips before it was said.

"It is not anything to laugh about," said Lucilla. "He was a very nice old man; but he is dead, and somebody else must be Member for Carlingford: that was why I told you that my mind was full of you. I am not in the least superstitious," said Miss Marjoribanks, solemnly; "but when I stood there—there, just in front of Mr Holden's—you came into my mind like a flash of lightning. I was not thinking of you in the least, and you came into my mind like—like Minerva, you know. If it was not an intimation, I don't know what it was. And that was why I ran against you, and did not see you were there. Mr Ashburton, it is you who must be the man," said Lucilla. It was not a thing to speak lightly about, and for her part she spoke very solemnly; and as for Mr Ashburton, his face flushed deeper and deeper. He stood quite still in the excitement of the moment, as if she had given him a blow.

"Miss Marjoribanks, I don't know how to answer you," he cried; and then he put out his hand in an agitated way and grasped her hand. "You are the only creature in Carlingford, man or woman, that has divined me," he said, in a trembling voice. It was a little public at the top of Grange Lane, where people were liable to pass at every moment; but still Miss Marjoribanks accepted the pressure of the hand, which, to be sure, had nothing whatever to do with love-making. She was more shy of such demonstrations than she had been in her confident youth, knowing that in most cases they never came to anything, and at the same time that the spectators kept a vivid recollection of them; but still, in the excitement of the moment, Miss Marjoribanks accepted and returned in a womanly way the pressure of Mr Ashburton's hand.

"Come in and let us talk it over," Lucilla said, feeling that no time was to be lost. It was a conference very different from that which, had Mr Chiltern been so well advised as to die ten years before, might have been held in Dr Marjoribanks's drawing-room over his successor's prospects; but at the same time there was something satisfactory to the personal sentiments of both in the way in which this conversation had come about. When Lucilla took off her hat and sat down to give him all her attention, Mr Ashburton could not but feel the flattering character of the interest she was taking in him. She was a woman, and young (comparatively speaking), and was by no means without admirers, and unquestionably took the lead in society; and to be divined by such a person was perhaps, on the whole, sweeter to the heart of the aspirant than if Colonel Chiley had found out his secret, or Dr Marjoribanks, or even the Rector: and Lucilla for her part had all that natural pleasure in being the first to embrace a new interest which was natural under the circumstances. "Let us talk it all over," she said, giving Mr Ashburton a chair near her own. "If I believed in spirit-rapping, you know, I should be sure that was what it meant. I was not thinking of you in the least, and all at once, like a flash of lightning—Mr Ashburton, sit down and tell me—what is the first thing that must be done?"

"If I could ask you to be on my committee, that would be the first thing to be done," said Mr Ashburton, "but unfortunately I can't do that. Let me tell you in the first place how very much I am obliged——"

"Don't say that, please," said Miss Marjoribanks, with her usual good sense, "for I have done nothing. But papa can be on the committee, and old Colonel Chiley, who is such a one for politics; and of course Sir John—that will be a very good beginning; and after that——"

"My dear Miss Marjoribanks," Mr Ashburton said, with a smile, and a little hesitation, "Sir John takes exactly the other side in politics; and I am afraid the Doctor and the Colonel are not of the same way of thinking; and then my opinions——"

"If they are not of the same way of thinking we must make them," said Lucilla; "after having such an intimation, I am not going to be put off for a trifle; and besides, what does it matter about opinions? I am sure I have heard you all saying over and over that the thing was to have a good *man*. Don't go and make speeches about opinions. If you begin with that, there is no end to it," said Miss Marjoribanks. "I know what you gentlemen are. But if you just say distinctly that you are the best man——"

"It would be an odd thing to say for one's self," said Mr Ashburton, and he laughed; but, to tell the truth, he was not a man of very quick understanding, and at the first outset of the thing he did not understand Lucilla; and he was a little—just a very little—disappointed. She had divined him, which was a wonderful proof of her genius; but yet at the bottom she was only an ignorant woman after all.

"I see it all quite clear what to do," said Miss Marjoribanks. "You must have the Colonel and Sir John, and everybody. I would not pay the least attention to Tories or Whigs, or anything of the sort. For my part I don't see any difference. All that has to be said about it is simply that you are the right man. Papa might object to one thing and the Colonel might object to another, and then if Sir John, as you say, is of quite another way of thinking—— But you are the man for Carlingford all the same; and none of them can say a word against that," said Lucilla, with energy. She stopped short, with her colour rising and her eyes brightening. She felt herself inspired, which was a new sensation, and very pleasant; and then the idea of such a coming struggle was sweet to Miss Marjoribanks, and the conviction burst upon her that she was striking out a perfectly new and original line.

As for her candidate, he smiled, and hesitated, and paid her pretty little compliments for a few minutes longer, and said it was very good of her to interest herself in his fortunes. All which Lucilla listened to with great impatience, feeling that it had nothing to do with the matter in hand. But then after these few minutes had elapsed the meaning of his fair adviser, as he called her, began to dawn upon Mr Ashburton's mind. He began to prick up his mental ears, so to speak, and see that it was not womanish ignorance, but an actual suggestion. For, after all, so long as he was the Man for Carlingford, all the rest was of little importance. He took something out of his pocket, which was his address to the constituency of Carlingford (for being anxious on the subject, he had heard of Mr Chiltern's death an hour or two before anybody else), and choke-full of political sentiments. In it he described to the electors what he would do if they sent him to Parliament, as carefully as if their election could make him Prime Minister at least; and naturally a man does not like to sacrifice such a confession of faith. "I should like to read it to you," he said, spreading it out with affectionate care: but Lucilla had already arranged her plans, and knew better than that.

"If you were to read it to me," said Miss Marjoribanks, "I should be sure to be convinced that you were quite right, and to go in with you for everything; and then I should be no good, you know. If it were to drive papa and Sir John and the Colonel all to their own ways of thinking, we never should make any progress. I would never mind about anybody's ways of thinking, if I were you. After all," said Lucilla, with fine satire, of which she was unconscious, " what does it matter what people think? I suppose when it comes to doing anything, the Whigs and the Tories are just the same. Mr Ashburton, it is the Man that is wanted," said Miss Marjoribanks, with all the warmth of sudden conviction. She felt a little like Joan of Arc as she spoke. When an army has the aid of a sacred maiden to bring inspiration to its counsels, the idea of going on in the old formal way is no longer to be tolerated. And such was the force of Lucilla's conviction, that Mr Ashburton, though he felt a little affronted, and could not but look with fond and compunctious regret upon his address, yet began more and more to feel that there was justice in what she said.

"I will think over what you say," he said, rather stiffly, and put up his address—for it was natural, when he had done her such an honour as to offer to read it to her, that he should be affronted by her refusal. It was a bold experiment on Lucilla's part, but then she was carried out of herself at the moment by the singular flash of inspiration. "I will think over what you say," Mr Ashburton continued; "and if my judgment approves—— At all events I shall not issue *this* till I have thought it all over. I am sure I am extremely obliged to you for your interest." And here he stopped short, and looked as if he were going to get up and go away, which would have spoiled all.

"You are going to stop to lunch," said Lucilla; "somebody is sure to come in. And you know you must not lose any opportunity of seeing people. I am so glad to-night is Thursday. Tell me just one thing, Mr Ashburton, before any one comes. There is one thing that is really important, and must be fixed upon. If we were to make any mistake, you know——"

"What?" said the candidate, eagerly—"about Reform? I have expressed myself very clearly——"

Lucilla smiled compassionately, and with the gentlest tolerance, at this wild suggestion. "I was not thinking of Reform," she said, with that meekness which people assume when it is of no use being impatient. "I was thinking what your colours were to be. I would not have anything to do with the old colours, for my part—they would be as bad as opinions, you know. You may laugh, but I am quite in earnest," said

Miss Marjoribanks. As for Mr Ashburton, he did not begin to laugh until he had fixed upon her that gaze of utter amazement and doubt with which on many similar occasions ordinary people had regarded Lucilla—thinking she was joking, or acting, or doing something quite different from the severe sincerity which was her leading principle. She was so used to it, that she waited with perfect patience till her companion's explosion of amusement was over. He was thinking to himself what a fool she was, or what a fool he was to think of taking a woman into his counsels, or what curious unintelligible creatures women were, made up of sense and folly; and all the time he laughed, which was a relief to his feelings. Miss Marjoribanks laughed a little too, to keep him in countenance, for she was always the soul of good-nature; and then she repeated, "Now you must tell me what our colours are to be——"

"I am sure I don't know anything about colours," said the candidate, "any more than you do about opinions. I think they are equally unimportant, to say the least. I shall adopt the colours of my fair counsellor," Mr Ashburton added, laughing, and making a mock-bow to her, and getting his hat as he did so—for he had naturally calmed down a little from the first enthusiasm with which he had hailed the woman who divined him, and he did not mean to stay.

"Blue and yellow are the old colours," said Lucilla, thoughtfully, "and you are the new man, you know, and we must not meddle with these antiquated things. Do you think this would do?" As she spoke she took up a handful of ribbons which were lying by, and put them up to her face with an air of serious deliberation which once more disturbed Mr Ashburton's gravity. And yet, when a young woman who is not at all bad-looking puts up a rustling, gleaming knot of ribbons to her hair and asks a man's opinion of the same, the man must be a philosopher or a wretch indeed who does not give a glance to see the effect. The candidate for Carlingford looked and approached, and even, in the temptation of the moment, took some of the long streamers in his hand. And he began to think Miss Marjoribanks was very clever, and the most amusing companion he had met with for a long time. And her interest in him touched his heart; and, after all, it is no drawback to a woman to be absurd by moments. His voice grew quite soft and caressing as he took the end of ribbon into his hand.

"If they are your colours they shall be mine," he said, with a sense of patronage and protection which was very delightful;

and the two were still talking and laughing over the silken link thus formed between them, when the people came in whom Lucilla was expecting to lunch, and who were naturally full of Mr Chiltern's death, which, poor old man! was so sudden at the last. Mr Ashburton stayed, though he had not intended it, and made himself very pleasant. And Lucilla took no pains to conceal her opinion that the thing was neither to consider Whigs nor Tories, but a good *Man*. And Major Brown, who had come with his daughters, echoed this sentiment so warmly that Mr Ashburton was entirely convinced of the justice of Miss Marjoribanks's ideas. "We can't have a tip-topper, you know," Major Brown said, who was not very refined in his expressions; "and what I should like to see is a man that knows the place, and would look after Carlingford. That's what we're all looking for." Mr Ashburton did not declare himself to Major Brown, but he dashed off his new address ten minutes after he had taken leave of Miss Marjoribanks, and put the other one in the fire like a Christian, and telegraphed for his agent to town. Lucilla, for her part, made an effort equally great and uncompromising. She took the ribbon Mr Ashburton had played with, and cut it up into cockades of all descriptions. It was an early moment, but still there was no time to be lost in a matter of such importance. And she wore one on her breast and one in her hair when Mr Ashburton's address was published, and all the world was discussing the new candidate.

"Of course they are his colours—that is why I wear them," said Lucilla. "I shall always think there was something very strange in it. Just after I had heard of poor old Mr Chiltern's death, as I was passing Holden's—when I was not in the least thinking of him—he came into my mind like a flash of lightning, you know. If I had been very intimate with poor old Mr Chiltern, or if I believed in spirit-rapping, I should think *that* was it. He came into my head without my even thinking of him, all in a moment, with his very hat on and his umbrella, like Minerva—wasn't it Minerva?" said Miss Marjoribanks. And she took up Mr Ashburton's cause openly, and unfurled his standard, and did not even ask her father's opinion. "Papa knows about politics, but he has not had an intimation, as I have," said Lucilla. And, naturally, she threw all the younger portion of Grange Lane, which was acquainted with Mr Ashburton, and looked forward eagerly to a little excitement, and liked the idea of wearing a violet-and-green cockade, into a flutter of excitement. Among these rash young people there were even a few individuals who took Lucilla's word for it, and knew that Mr Ashburton was very *nice*, and did not see that anything more was necessary. To be sure, these enthusiasts were chiefly women, and in no cases had votes; but Miss Marjoribanks, with instinctive correctness of judgment, decided that there were more things to be thought of than the electors. And she had the satisfaction of seeing with her own eyes and hearing with her own ears the success of that suggestion of her genius. Carlingford had rarely been more excited by any public event than it was by the address of the new candidate, who was in the field before anybody else, and who had the boldness to come before them without uttering any political creed. "The enlightened electors of Carlingford do not demand, like other less educated constituencies, a system of political doctrines cut and dry, or a representative bound to give up his own judgment, and act according to arbitrary promises," said the daring candidate: "what they want is an honest man, resolved to do his duty by his country, his borough, and his constituency; and it is this idea alone which has induced me to solicit your suffrages." This was what Mr Ashburton said in his address, though at that moment he had still his other address in his pocket, in which he had entered at some length into his distinctive personal views. It was thus that an independent candidate, unconnected with party, took the field in Carlingford, with Miss Marjoribanks, like another Joan of Arc, wearing a knot of ribbons, violet and green, in her hair, to inspire and lead him on.

CHAPTER XXXVIII.

LIFE with most people is little more than a succession of high and low tides. There are times when the stream runs low, and when there is nothing to be seen but the dull sandbanks, or even mudbanks, for months, or even years together; and then all at once the waters swell, and come rushing twice a-day like the sea, carrying life and movement with them. Miss Marjoribanks had been subject to the *eaux mortes* for a long time: but now the spring-tides had rushed back. A day or two after Mr Ashburton had been revealed to her as the predestined member, something occurred, not in itself exciting, but which was not without its ultimate weight upon the course of affairs. It was the day when aunt Jemima was expected in Grange Lane. She was aunt Jemima to Lucilla; but the Doctor called her Mrs John, and was never known to address her by any more familiar title. She was, as she herself described it, a widow lady, and wore the dress of her order, and was the mother of Tom Marjoribanks. She was not a frequent visitor at Carlingford, for she and her brother-in-law had various points on which they were not of accord. The Doctor, for his part, could not but feel perennially injured that the boy had fallen to the lot of Mrs John, while he had only a girl—even though that girl was Lucilla; and aunt Jemima could not forgive him for the rude way in which he treated her health, which was so delicate, and his want of sympathy for many other people who were delicate too. Even when she arrived, and was being entertained with the usual cup of tea, fears of her brother-in-law's robustness and unsympathetic ways had begun to overpower her. "I hope your papa does not ask too much from you, Lucilla," she said, as she sat in her easy-chair, and took her tea by the fire in the cozy room which had been prepared for her. "I hope he does not make you do too much, for I am sure you are not strong, my dear. Your poor mamma, you know——" and Mrs John looked with a certain pathos at her niece, as though she saw signs of evil in Lucilla's fresh complexion and substantial frame.

"I am pretty well, thank you, aunt Jemima," said Miss Marjoribanks; "and papa lets me do pretty much what I like: I am too old now, you know, to be told what to do."

"Don't call yourself old, my dear," said aunt Jemima, with a passing gleam of worldly wisdom—"one gets old quite soon enough. Are you subject to headaches, Lucilla, or pains in the limbs? Your poor mamma——"

"Dear aunt Jemima, I am as well as ever I can be," said Miss Marjoribanks. "Tell me when you heard from Tom, and what he is doing. Let me see, it is ten years since he went away. I used to write to him, but he did not answer my letters—not as he ought, you know. I suppose he has found friends among the Calcutta ladies," said Lucilla, with a slight but not unapparent sigh.

"He never says anything to me about Calcutta ladies," said Tom's mother; "to tell the truth, I always thought before he went away that he was fond of *you*—I must have been mistaken, as he never said anything; and *that* was very fortunate at all events."

"I am sure I am very thankful he was not fond of me," said Lucilla, with a little natural irritation, "for I never could have returned it. But I should like to know why that was so fortunate. I can't see that it would have been such a very bad thing for him, for my part."

"Yes, my dear," said aunt Jemima, placidly, "it would have been a very bad thing; for you know, Lucilla, though you get on very nicely here, you never could have done for a poor man's wife."

Miss Marjoribanks's bosom swelled when she heard these words—it swelled with that profound sense of being unappreciated and misunderstood, which is one of the hardest trials in the way of genius; but naturally she was not going to let her aunt see her mortification. "I don't mean to be any man's wife just now," she said, making a gulp of it—"I am too busy electioneering; we are going to have a new member in dear old Mr Chiltern's place. Perhaps he will come in this evening to talk things over, and you shall see him," Lucilla added, graciously. She was a little excited about the candidate, as was not unnatural—more excited, perhaps, than she would have been ten years ago, when life was young; and then it was not to be expected that she could be pleased with aunt Jemima for thinking it was so fortunate; though even that touch of wounded pride did not lead Miss Marjoribanks to glorify herself by betraying Tom.

"My brother-in-law used to be a dreadful Radical," said aunt Jemima; "I hope it is not one of those revolutionary men; I have seen your poor uncle sit up arguing with him till I thought they never would be done. If that is the kind of thing, I hope you will not associate yourself with it, Lucilla. Your papa should have more sense than to let you. It does not do a young woman any good. I should never have permitted it if you had been *my* daughter," added Mrs John, with a little heat—for, to tell the truth, she too felt a slight vexation on her part that the Doctor had the girl—even though not for twenty girls would she have given up Tom.

Miss Marjoribanks looked upon the weak woman who thus ventured to address her with indescribable feelings; but after all she was not so much angry as amused and compassionate. She could not help thinking to herself, if she had been Mrs John's daughter, how perfectly docile aunt Jemima would have been by this time, and how little she would have really ventured to interfere. "It would have been very nice," she said, with a meditative realisation of the possibility—"though it is very odd to think how one could have been one's own cousin—I should have taken very good care of you, I am sure."

"You would have done no such thing," said Mrs John; "you would have gone off and married; I know how girls do. You have not married now, because you have been too comfortable, Lucilla. You have had everything your own way, and all that you wanted, without any of the bother. It is very strange how differently people's lots are ordered. I was married at seventeen—and I am sure I have not known what it was to have a day's health——"

"Dear aunt Jemima!" said her affectionate niece, kissing her, "but papa shall see if he cannot give you something, and we will take such care of you while you are here."

Mrs John was softened in spite of herself; but still she shook her head. "It is very nice of you to say so, my dear," she said, "and it's pleasant to feel that one has somebody belonging to one; but I have not much confidence in your papa. He never understood my complaints. I used to be very sorry for your poor mamma. He never showed that sympathy—but I did not mean to blame him to you, Lucilla. I am sure he is a very good father to you."

"He has been a perfect old angel," said Miss Marjoribanks; and then the conversation came to a pause, as it was time to dress for dinner. Mrs John Marjoribanks had a very nice room, and everything that was adapted to make her comfortable; but she too had something to think of when the door closed upon Lucilla, and she was left with her maid and her hot water and her black velvet gown. Perhaps it was a little inconsistent to wear a black velvet gown with her widow's cap; it was a question which she had long debated in her mind before she resigned herself to the temptation—but then it always looked so well, and was so very profitable! and Mrs John felt that it was incumbent upon her to keep up a respectable appearance for Tom's sake. Tom was very much in her mind at that moment, as indeed he always was; for though it was a long time ago, she could not get the idea out of her head that he must have said something to Lucilla before he went off to India; and he had a way of asking about his cousin in his letters; and though she would have done anything to secure her boy's happiness, and was on the whole rather fond of her niece, yet the idea of the objections her brother-in-law would have to such a match, excited to the uttermost the smouldering pride which existed in aunt Jemima's heart. He was better off, and had always been better off, than her poor John—and he had robust health and an awful scorn of the coddling, to which, as he said, she had subjected his brother; and he had money enough to keep *his* child luxuriously, and make her the leader of Carlingford society, while *her* poor boy had to go to India and put himself in the way of all kinds of unknown diseases and troubles. Mrs John was profoundly anxious to promote her son's happiness, and would gladly have given every penny she had to get him married to Lucilla, "if that was what he wanted," as she justly said; but to have her brother-in-law object to him, and suggest that he was not good enough, was the one thing she could not bear. She was thinking about this, and whether Tom really had not said anything, and whether Lucilla cared for him, and what amid all these perplexities she should do, while she dressed for dinner; and, at the same time, she felt her palpitation worse than usual, and knew Dr Marjoribanks would smile his grim smile if she complained, so that her visit to Grange Lane, though Lucilla meant to take such care of her, was not altogether unmingled delight to Mrs John.

But, nevertheless, Dr Marjoribanks's dinner-table was always a cheerful sight, even when it was only a dinner-party of three; for then naturally they used the round table, and were as snug as possible. Lucilla wore her knot of green and violet ribbons on her white dress, to her aunt's great amazement, and the Doctor had all the air of a man who had been out in the world all day and returned in the evening with something to tell— which is a thing which gives great animation to a family party. Mrs John Marjoribanks had been out of all that sort of thing for a long time. She had been living quite alone in a widowed forlorn way, and had half forgotten how pleasant it was to have somebody coming in with a breath of fresh air about him and the day's budget of news—and it had an animating effect upon her, even though she was not fond of her brother-in-law. Dr Marjoribanks inquired about Tom in the most fatherly way, and what he was about, and how things were looking for him, and whether he intended to come home. "Much better not," the Doctor said,—"I should certainly advise him not, if he asked me. He has got over all the worst of it, and now is his time to do something worth while."

"Tom is not one to think merely of worldly advantages," said his mother, with a fine instinct of opposition. "I don't think he would care to waste all the best part of his life making money.

I'd rather see him come home and be happy, for my part, even if he were not so rich——"

"If all men were happy that came home," said the Doctor, and then he gave a rather grim chuckle. "Somebody has come home that you did not reckon on, Lucilla. I am sorry to spoil sport; but I don't see how you are to get out of it. There is another address on the walls to-day besides that one of yours——"

"Oh, I hope there will be six addresses!" cried Miss Marjoribanks; "if we had it all our own way it would be no fun;—a Tory, and a Whig, and a—did you say Radical, aunt Jemima? And then, what is a Conservative?" asked Lucilla, though certainly she had a very much better notion of political matters than aunt Jemima had, to say the least.

"I wonder how you can encourage any poor man to go into Parliament," said Mrs John; "so trying for the health as it must be, and an end to everything like domestic life. If it was my Tom, I would almost rather he stayed in India. He looks strong, but there is never any confidence to be put in young men looking strong. Oh, I know you do not agree with me, Doctor; but I have had sad reason for my way of thinking," said the poor lady. As for the Doctor, he did not accept the challenge thus thrown to him. Tom Marjoribanks was not the foremost figure in the world in his eyes, as the absent wanderer was in that of his mother; and he had not yet unburdened himself of what he had to say.

"I am not saying anything in favour of going into Parliament," said the Doctor. "I'd sooner be a bargeman on the canal, if it was me. I am only telling Lucilla what she has before her. I don't know when I have been more surprised. Of course you were not looking for *that*," said Dr Marjoribanks. He had kept back until the things were taken off the table, for he had a benevolent disinclination to spoil anybody's dinner. Now, when all the serious part of the meal was over, he tossed the 'Carlingford Gazette' across the table, folded so that she could not miss what he wanted her to see. Lucilla took it up lightly between her finger and thumb; for the Carlingford papers were inky and badly printed, and soiled a lady's hand. She took it up delicately without either alarm or surprise, knowing very well that the Blues and the Yellows were not likely without a struggle to give up to the new standard, which was violet and green. But what she saw on that inky broadsheet overwhelmed in an instant Miss Marjoribanks's self-possession. She turned pale, though her complexion was, if possible, fresher than ever; and even shivered in her chair, though her nerves were so steady. Could it be a trick to thwart and startle her? or could it be true? She lifted her eyes to her father with a look of horror-stricken inquiry, but all that she met in return was a certain air of amusement and triumph, which struck her at the tenderest point. He was not sorry nor sympathetic, nor did he care at all for the sudden shock she had sustained. On the contrary, he was laughing within himself at the utterly unexpected complication. It was cruel, but it was salutary, and restored her self-command in a moment. She might have given way under kindness, but this look of satisfaction over her discomfiture brought Lucilla to herself.

"Yes, I thought you would be surprised," said Dr Marjoribanks, dryly; and he took his first glass of claret with a slow relish and enjoyment, which roused every sentiment of self-respect and spark of temper existing in his daughter's mind. "If you had kept your own place it would not have mattered; but I don't see how you are to get out of it. You see young ladies should let these sort of things alone, Lucilla." This was all the feeling he showed for her in her unexpected dilemma. Miss Marjoribanks's heart gave one throb, which made the green and violet ribbons jump and thrill; and then she came to herself, and recognised, as she had so often done before, that she had to fight her way by herself, and had nobody to look to. Such a thought is dreary enough sometimes, and there are minds that sink under it; but at other times it is like the touch of the mother earth which gave the giant back his strength; and Lucilla was of the latter class of intelligence. When she saw the triumph with which her embarrassment was received, and that she had no sympathy nor aid to look for, she recovered herself as if by magic. Let what would come in the way, nothing could alter her certainty that Mr Ashburton was the man for Carlingford; and that determination not to be beaten, which is the soul of British valour, sprang up in an instant in Miss Marjoribanks's mind. There was not even the alternative of victory or Westminster Abbey for Lucilla. If she was ever to hold up her head again, or have any real respect for herself, she must win. All this passed through her head in the one bewildering moment, while her father's words were still making her ears tingle, and *that name*, printed in big inky letters, seemed to flutter in all the air round her. It was hard to believe the intelligence thus conveyed, and harder still to go on

in the face of old friendships and the traditions of her youth;
but still duty was dearer than tradition, and it was now a necessity to fight the battle to the last, and at all risks to win.

"Thank you all the same, papa, for bringing me the paper,"
said Lucilla. "It would have been a great deal worse if I had
not known of it before I saw him. I am sure I am very glad
for one thing. He can't be married or dead, as people used to
say. I am quite ashamed to keep you so long down-stairs,
aunt Jemima, when I know you must be longing for a cup of
tea—but it is somebody come back whom nobody expected.
Tell him I shall be *so* glad to see him, papa; though I have no
reason to be glad, for he was one of my *young* friends, you
know, and he is sure to think I have gone off." As she spoke,
Lucilla turned aunt Jemima, to whom she had given her arm,
quite round, that she might look into the great glass over the
mantelpiece: "I don't think I *am* quite so much gone off as I
expected to be," said Miss Marjoribanks, with candid impartiality; "though of course he will think me stouter—but it does
not make any difference about Mr Ashburton being the right
man for Carlingford." She said the words with a certain solemnity, and turned Mrs John, who was so much surprised as to
be speechless, round again, and led her up-stairs. It was as if
they were walking in a procession of those martyrs and renouncers of self, who build up the foundations of society; and
it would not be too much to say that under her present circumstances, and in the excitement of this singular and unexpected
event, such was the painful but sublime consciousness which
animated Lucilla's breast.

As for Dr Marjoribanks, his triumph was taken out of him by
that spectacle. He closed the door after the ladies had gone,
and came back to his easy-chair by the side of the fire, and
could not but feel that he had had the worst of it. It was
actually Mr Cavendish who had come home, and whose address
to the electors of Carlingford, dated from Dover on his return
to England, the Doctor had just put into his daughter's hand.
But wonderful and unlooked-for as was the event, Lucilla,
though taken unawares, had not given in, nor shown any signs
of weakness. And the effect upon her father of her last utterance and confession was such that he took up the paper again
and read both addresses, which were printed side by side. In
other days Mr Cavendish had been the chosen candidate of
Grange Lane; and the views which he expressed (and he expressed his views very freely) were precisely those of Dr Mar-

joribanks. Yet when the Doctor turned to Mr Ashburton's expression of his conviction that he was the right man for Carlingford, it cannot be denied that the force of that simple statement had a wonderful effect upon his mind—an effect all the greater, perhaps, in comparison with the political exposition made by the other unexpected candidate. The Doctor's meditations possibly took a slumbrous tone from the place and the moment at which he pursued them; for the fact was that the words he had just been hearing ran in his head all through the reading of the two addresses. Mr Cavendish would think Lucilla had gone off; but yet she had not gone off so much as might have been expected, and Mr Ashburton was the man for Carlingford. Dr Marjoribanks laughed quietly by himself in his easy-chair, and then went back to Mr Cavendish's opinions; and ended again, without knowing it, in a kind of odd incipient agreement with Lucilla. The new candidate was right in politics; but, after all, Mr Ashburton was a more satisfactory sort of person. He was a man whom people knew everything about, and a descendant of old Penrhyn, and had the Firs, and lived in it, and spent about so much money every year honestly in the face of the world. When a man conducts himself n this way, his neighbours can afford to be less exacting as to his political opinions. This comparison went on in the Doctor's thoughts until the distinction between the two grew confused and faint in that ruddy and genial glow of firelight and lamplight and personal wellbeing which is apt to engross a man's mind after he has come in out of the air, as people say, and has eaten a good dinner, and feels himself comfortable; and at last all that remained in Dr Marjoribanks's mind was that Mr Cavendish would think Lucilla had gone off, though she had not gone off nearly so much as might have been expected; at which he laughed with an odd sound, which roused him, and might have induced some people to think he had been sleeping—if, indeed, anybody had been near to hear.

But this news was naturally much more serious to Miss Marjoribanks when she got up-stairs, and had time to think of it. She would not have been human if she had heard without emotion of the return of the man whom she had once dreamed of as member for Carlingford, with the addition of other dreams which had not been altogether without their sweetness. He had returned now and then for a few days, but Lucilla knew that he had never held up his head in Grange Lane since the day when she advised him to marry Barbara Lake. And now when he had bethought himself of his old ambition, had he possibly bethought himself of other hopes as well? And the horrible thing was, that she had pledged herself to another, and put her seal upon it that Mr Ashburton was the man for Carlingford! It may be supposed that, with such a complication in her mind, Miss Marjoribanks was very little capable of supporting aunt Jemima's questions as to what it was about, and who was Mr Cavendish, and why was his return of consequence to Lucilla? Mrs John was considerably alarmed and startled, and began to think in earnest that Tom was fond of his cousin, and would never forgive his mother for letting Lucilla perhaps marry some one else, and settle down before her very eyes.

"If it is a very particular friend, I can understand it," Mrs John said, with a little asperity; but that was after she had made a great many attempts, which were only partially successful, to find it all out.

"Dear aunt Jemima," said Lucilla, "we are all particular friends in Carlingford—society is so limited, you know;—and Mr Cavendish has been a very long time away. He used to be of such use to me, and I am so fond of him," Miss Marjoribanks said, with a sigh; and it may be supposed that Mrs John's curiosity was not lessened by such a response.

"If you are engaged to any one, Lucilla, I must say I think I ought to have been told," said Tom's mother, with natural indignation. "Though I ought not to blame *you* for it, perhaps. It is a sad thing when a girl is deprived of a mother's care; but still I am your nearest relation——"

"My dear aunt, it is something about the election," said Miss Marjoribanks. "How could I be engaged to a man who has been away ten years?"

"Tom has been away ten years," said Mrs John, impetuously; and then she blushed, though she was past the age of blushing, and made haste to cover her imprudence. "I don't see what you can have to do with the election," she said, with suspicion, but some justice; "and I don't feel, Lucilla, as if you were telling me all."

"I have the favours to make, aunt Jemima," said Lucilla—"green and violet. You used to be so clever at making bows, and I hope you will help me;—papa, you know, will have to be on Mr Ashburton's committee," Miss Marjoribanks added; and then, in spite of herself, a sigh of doubt and anxiety escaped her bosom. It was easy to say that "papa would be on Mr Ashburton's committee, you know," but nobody had known that

x

Mr Cavendish was coming to drive everything topsy-turvy; and Lucilla, though she professed to know only who was the man for Carlingford, had at the same time sufficient political information to be aware that the sentiments propounded in Mr Cavendish's address were also Dr Marjoribanks's sentiments; and she did not know the tricks which some green-and-violet spirit in the dining-room was playing with the Doctor's fancy. Perhaps it might turn out to be Mr Cavendish's committee which her father would be on; and after she had pledged herself that the other was the man for Carlingford! Lucilla felt that she could not be disloyal and go back from her word, neither could she forget the intimation which had so plainly indicated to her that Mr Ashburton was the man; and yet, at the same time, she could not but sigh as she thought of Mr Cavendish. Perhaps he had grown coarse, as men do at that age, just as Lucilla herself was conscious that he would find her stouter. Perhaps he had ceased to flirt, or be of any particular use of an evening; possibly even he might have forgotten Miss Marjoribanks—but naturally that was a thing that seemed unlikely to Lucilla. And oh! if he had but come a little earlier, or for ever stayed away!

But while all these thoughts were going through her mind, her fingers were still busy with the violet-and-green cockades which aunt Jemima, after making sure that Mr Ashburton was not a Radical, had begun to help her with. And they sat and talked about Mrs John's breathing, which was so bad, and about her headaches, while Lucilla by snatches discussed the situation in her mind. Perhaps, on the whole, embarrassment and perplexity are a kind of natural accompaniment to life and movement; and it is better to be driven out of your senses with thinking which of two things you ought to do than to do nothing whatever, and be utterly uninteresting to all the world. This at least was how Lucilla reasoned to herself in her dilemma; and while she reasoned she used up yard upon yard of her green ribbon (for naturally the violet bore but a small proportion to the green). Whatever she might have to do or to suffer—however her thoughts might be disturbed or her heart distracted—it is unnecessary to add that it was impossible to Lucilla either to betray or to yield.

CHAPTER XXXIX.

It was a very good thing for Lucilla that Mrs John was so much of an invalid, notwithstanding that the Doctor made little of her complaints. All that Dr Marjoribanks said was—with that remnant of Scotch which was often perceptible in his speech —that her illnesses were a fine thing to occupy her, and he did not know what she would do without them—a manner of speaking which naturally lessened his daughter's anxiety, though her sympathetic care and solicitude were undiminished. And no doubt, when she had been once assured that there was nothing dangerous in her aunt's case, it was a relief to Miss Marjoribanks at the present juncture that Mrs John got up late and always breakfasted in her own room. Lucilla went into that sanctuary after she had given her father his breakfast, and heard all about the palpitation and the bad night aunt Jemima had passed; and then when she had consoled her suffering relative by the reflection that one never sleeps well the first night or two, Miss Marjoribanks was at liberty to go forth and attend a little to her own affairs, which stood so much in need of being attended to. She had had no further talk with the Doctor on the subject, but she had read over Mr Cavendish's address, and could not help seeing that it went dead against her candidate; neither could Lucilla remain altogether unaffected by the expression of feeling in respect to "a place in which I have spent so many pleasant years, and which has so many claims on my affections," and the touching haste with which the exile had rushed back as soon as he heard of the old member's death. If it touched Miss Marjoribanks, who was already pledged to support another interest, what might it not do to the gentlemen in Grange Lane who were not pledged, and who had a friendship for Mr Cavendish? This was the alarming thought that had disturbed her sleep all night, and returned to her mind with her first awakening; and when she had really her time to herself, and the fresh morning hours before her, Lucilla began, as everybody ought to do, by going to the very root and foundation, and asking herself what, beyond all secondary considerations, it was *right* to do. To change from one side to the other and go back from her word was a thing abhorrent to her; but still Miss Marjoribanks was aware that there are certain circumstances in which honesty and truth themselves demand what in most cases is considered an untruthful and dishonest proceeding.

Thus in order to come to a right decision, and with a sense of the duty she owed to her country which would have shamed half the electors in England, not to say Carlingford, Lucilla, who naturally had no vote, read the two addresses of the two candidates, and addressed herself candidly and impartially to the rights of the subject. Mr Cavendish was disposed, as we have said, to be pathetic and sentimental, and to speak of the claims the borough had upon his affections, and the eagerness with which he had rushed home at the earliest possible moment to present himself to them. If poor old Mr Chiltern had been King Bomba, or a gloomy Oriental tyrant, keeping all possible reformers and successors banished from his dominions, the new candidate could not have spoken with more pathos. It was a sort of thing which tells among the imaginative part of the community, or so, at least, most people think; and Miss Marjoribanks was moved by it for the first moment; but then her enlightened mind asserted its rights. She said to herself that Mr Cavendish might have come home at any hour, by any steamboat; that Calais and Boulogne, and even Dieppe, were as open to him as if he had been an actual refugee, and that consequently there was nothing particular to be pathetic about. And then, if the town had such claims on his affections, why had he stayed so long away? These two rationalistic questions dispersed the first *attendrissement* which had begun to steal over Lucilla's mind. When she came to this conclusion, her difficulties cleared away. She had no reason to go back from her engagements and reject that intimation which had so impressed it on her that Mr Ashburton was the man. It was a sacrifice which ancient truth and friendship did not demand, for verity was not in the document she had just been reading, and that appeal to sentiment was nothing more than what is generally called humbug. "He might have been living here all the time," Lucilla said to herself; "he might have had much stronger claims upon our affections; if he had wanted, he might have come back ages ago, and not let people struggle on alone." When this view of the subject occurred to her, Lucilla felt more indignation than sympathy. And then, as Dr Marjoribanks had done, she turned to the calm utterance of her own candidate— the man who was the only man for Carlingford—and that sweet sense of having given sound counsel, and of having at last met with some one capable of carrying it out, which makes up for so many failures, came like balm to Lucilla's bosom. There was nothing more necessary; the commotion in her mind calmed down, and the tranquillity of undisturbed conviction came in its place. And it was with this sense of certainty that she put on her bonnet and issued forth, though it snowed a little, and was a very wintry day, on Mr Ashburton's behalf, to try her fortune in Grange Lane.

She went to Mrs Chiley's, who was now very old, poor old lady! and feeble, and did not like to leave her sofa. Not but what she could leave the sofa, she said to her friends, but at that time of the year, and at her time of life, it was comfortable. The sofa was wheeled to the side of the fire, and Mrs Chiley reclined upon it, covered with knitted rugs of the brightest colours, which her young friends all worked for her. The last one arrived was what used to be called an Affghanistan blanket, done in stripes of all sorts of pretty tints, which was a present from Mrs Beverley. "Her work, she says, Lucilla," said the old lady; "but we know what sort of soft dawdling woman she is, and it must have been the Archdeacon's nieces, you know." But still it had the place of honour at present, covering Mrs Chiley's feet, and affording something to talk about when any one came in. And by her side was a little table upon which stood one China rose, in a glass of water—a pale rose, almost as pale as her soft old cheeks, and chilled like them by the approaching frost. And the fire burned with an officious cheerfulness at her elbow, as if it thought nothing of such accidental circumstances as winter and old age. To be sure this was a reflection which never came into Mrs Chiley's head, who was, on the contrary, very thankful for the fire, and said it was like a companion. "And I often think, my dear, how do the poor people get on, especially if they are old and sick, they have no fires to keep them cheerful in this dreadful weather," the kind old lady would say. She did say so now when Lucilla came in, glowing with cold and her rapid walk, and with a flake or two of snow slowly melting on her sealskin cloak. Perhaps it was not a sentiment the Colonel agreed with, for he gave a humph and a little hoist of his shoulders, as if in protest, being himself a good deal limited in his movements, and not liking to own it, by the wintry torpor within his big old frame, and the wintry weather outside.

"Come and tell us all the news, Lucilla, my darling," Mrs Chiley said, as she drew down her young friend's glowing face to her own, and gave her one of her lingering kisses; "I felt sure you would come and tell us everything. I said it would not be like Lucilla if she didn't. We know nothing but *the fact*, you know—not another word. Make haste and tell us everything, my dear."

"But I don't know anything," said Miss Marjoribanks. "Of course you mean about Mr Cavendish. I saw it in the papers, like everybody else, but I don't know anything more."

And then Mrs Chiley's countenance fell. She was not very strong, poor old lady, and she could have cried, as she said afterwards. "Ah, well, I suppose there is not time," she said, after a little pause; "I suppose he has not got here from Dover yet—one always forgets the distance. I calculated it all over last night, and I thought he would get home by the eleven train; but these trains are never to be calculated upon, you know, my dear. I *am* a little disappointed, Lucilla. Poor dear! to think how he must have rushed home the first moment —I could have cried when I read that address."

"I don't see why any one should cry," said Lucilla. "I think he makes a great deal too much of that; he might have come ever so many years ago if he had liked. Poor Mr Chiltern did not banish him, poor old man!—he might have been here for years."

Upon which the Colonel himself drew a little nearer, and poked the fire. "I am glad to see you are so sensible, Lucilla," he said. "It's the first rational word I have heard on the subject. *She* thinks he's a kind of saint and martyr; a silly young fellow that runs off among a set of Frenchmen because he can't get everything his own way—and then he expects that we are all to go into transports of joy, and give him our votes," Colonel Chiley added, smashing a great piece of coal with the poker, with a blow full of energy, yet showing a slight unsteadiness in it, which sent a host of blazing splinters into the hearth. He was a man who wore very well, but he was not so steady as he once was, and nowadays was apt, by some tremulous movement, to neutralise the strength which he had left.

Mrs Chiley, for her part, was apt to be made very nervous by her husband's proceedings. She was possessed by a terror that the splinters some day would jump out of the hearth on to the carpet and fly into the corners, "and perhaps burn us all up in our beds," as she said. She gave a little start among her cushions, and stooped down to look over the floor. "He will never learn that he is old," she said in Lucilla's ear, who instantly came to her side to see what she wanted; and thus the two old people kept watch upon each other, and noted, with a curious mixture of vexation and sympathy, each other's declining strength.

"For my part, I would give him all my votes, if I had a hundred," said Mrs Chiley; "and so will you, too, when you hear the rights of it. Lucilla, my dear, tell him—I hope *you* are not going to forsake old friends."

"No," said Miss Marjoribanks—but she spoke with a gravity and hesitation which did not fail to reach Mrs Chiley's ear— "I hope I shall never desert my old friends; but I think all the same that it is Mr Ashburton who is the right man for Carlingford," she said, slowly. She said it with reluctance, for she knew it would shock her audience, but, at the same time, she did not shrink from her duty; and the moment had now arrived when Lucilla felt concealment was impossible, and that the truth must be said.

As for Mrs Chiley, she was so distressed that the tears came to her eyes; and even the Colonel laughed, and did not understand it. Colonel Chiley, though he was by no means as yet on Mr Cavendish's side, was not any more capable than his neighbours of understanding Miss Marjoribanks's single-minded devotion to what was just and right; and why she should transfer her support to Ashburton, who was not a ladies' man, nor, in the Colonel's opinion, a marrying man, nor anything at all attractive, now that the other had come back romantic and repentant to throw his honours at her feet, was beyond his power of explanation. He contented himself with saying "humph;" but his wife was not so easily satisfied. She took Lucilla by the hand and poured forth a flood of remonstrances and prayers.

"I do not understand you, Lucilla," said Mrs Chiley. "He whom we know so little about—whom, I am sure, you have no reason to care for. And where could you find anybody nicer than Mr Cavendish?—and he to have such faith in us, and to come rushing back as soon as he was able. I am sure you have not taken everything into consideration, Lucilla. He might not perhaps do exactly as could have been wished, before he went away; but he was young and he was led astray; and I do think you were a little hard upon him, my dear; but I have always said I never knew anybody nicer than Mr Cavendish. And what possible reason you can have to care about that other man——"

"It was like a special Intimation," said Lucilla, with solemnity. "I don't see how I could neglect it, for my part. The day the news came about poor old Mr Chiltern's death I was out, you know, and heard it; and just at one spot upon the pavement, opposite Mr Holden's, it came into my mind like a flash of lightning that Mr Ashburton was the man. I don't care in the least for him, and I had not been thinking of him, or anything. It came into my head all in a moment. If I had been very intimate with poor dear old Mr Chiltern, or if I believed in spirit-rapping, I should think it was a message from *him*."

Lucilla spoke with great gravity, but she did not impress her audience, who were people of sceptical minds. Mrs Chiley, for her part, was almost angry, and could scarcely forgive Lucilla for having made her give grave attention to such a piece of nonsense. "If it *had* been him," she said, with some wrath, "I don't see how having been dead for a few hours should make his advice worth having. It never was good for anything when he was alive. And you don't believe in spirit-rapping, I *hope*. I wonder how you can talk such nonsense," the old lady said severely. And Colonel Chiley, who had been a little curious too, laughed and coughed over the joke; for the two old people were of the old school, and of a very unbelieving frame of mind.

"I knew you would laugh," said Miss Marjoribanks, "but I cannot help it. If it had been impressed upon *your* mind like that, you would have been different. And, of course, I like Mr Cavendish much the best. I am so glad I have no vote," said Lucilla; "it does not matter to anybody what I think; but if I had anything to do with it, you know I could not stand up for Mr Cavendish, even though I am fond of him, when I felt sure that Mr Ashburton is the man for Carlingford—nobody could ask me to do that."

There followed a pause upon this declaration; for Miss Marjoribanks, though she had no vote, was a person of undoubted influence, and such a conviction on her part was not to be laughed at. Even Colonel Chiley, who was undecided in his own mind, was moved by it a little. "What does the Doctor think?" he asked. "Ashburton doesn't say a word about his principles that I can see; and the other, you know——"

"Dear Colonel Chiley," cried Lucilla, "he is not going to be Prime Minister; and I have always heard you say, as long as I can remember, that it was not opinions, you know, but a good *man* that people wanted. I have heard people talking politics for hours, and I always remember you saying that, and thinking it was the only sensible thing that was said; but, of course, I don't understand politics," Lucilla added, with humility. As for the Colonel, he took up the poker, perhaps to hide a little pleasant confusion, and again drew near the fire.

"By George! I believe Lucilla is in the right," he said, with a certain agreeable consciousness. Perhaps he did not quite recollect at what moment of his life he had originated that sentiment, but he thought he could recollect having said it; and it was with the view of carrying off the bashfulness of genius, and not because the coals had any need of it, that he took up the poker—a proceeding which was always regarded with alarm and suspicion by his wife.

"The fire is very nice," said Mrs Chiley. "I hate to have the fire poked when it does not want it. Lucilla, if you make him go over to *that* Mr Ashburton's side, you will have a great deal to answer for, and I will never forgive you. My dear, you must be dreaming—a man that is as dry as a stick, and not one-hundredth nor one-thousandth part so nice——"

"I shan't say another word," said Lucilla; "I shan't stay any longer, for I can't help it, and you would be angry with me. People can't help what they believe, you know. There is poor little Oswald Brown, who has doubts, and can't go into the Church, and will ruin all his prospects, and nobody can help it——"

"If I were his mother I should help it!" cried Mrs Chiley. "I promise you he should not talk of his doubts to me! A bit of a lad; and what is good enough for all the bishops, and everybody in their senses, is not good enough for him! If that is the kind of example you are going to follow, Lucilla——"

"Dear Mrs Chiley," said Miss Marjoribanks, "everybody knows what my Church principles are; and perhaps you will come round to think with me; but I am not going to say any more about it now. I am so glad your rheumatism is better this morning; but you must wrap up well, for it is so cold, oh, so cold, out of doors!"

When Lucilla had thus dismissed the subject, she came to her old friend's side and bent over her in her sealskin cloak, to say good-bye. Mrs Chiley took her by both hands as she thus stood with her back to the old Colonel, and drew her down close, and looked searchingly into her eyes. "If you have any *particular* reason, Lucilla, you ought to tell me—that would make such a difference," said the old lady. "I always tell you everything," said Miss Marjoribanks with evasive fondness, as she kissed the soft old withered cheek; and naturally, with the Colonel behind, who was standing up before the fire shadowing over them both, and quite unaware of this little whispered episode, it would have been impossible to say more had there been ever so much to say. But it had been a close encounter in its way, and Lucilla was rather glad to get off without any further damage. She did not feel quite successful as she went out; but still she had left a very wholesome commotion behind her; for Colonel Chiley could not but feel that the sentiment which she had quoted from himself was a very just sentiment. "By George! Lucilla was in the right of it," he said again, after she was gone; and in fact went through a process very similar to that which had modified the sentiments of Dr Marjoribanks on the previous night. Mr Cavendish was a young fellow who had rushed off among a set of Frenchmen because Lucilla Marjoribanks would not have him, or because he could not marry Barbara Lake in addition, or at least somehow because he failed of having his own way. It was all very well for him to come back and make a commotion, and be sentimental about it. But what if, after all, Ashburton, who had the Firs, and lived there, and spent his money like a Christian, was the man for Carlingford? The Colonel's mind still wavered and veered about; yet it had received an impulse which was by no means unworthy of consideration.

As for Mrs Chiley, she laid back her head upon her pillows and painfully questioned with herself whether Lucilla could have any *particular* reason for taking Mr Ashburton's part so warmly. She thought with justice that Miss Marjoribanks was looking brighter and better, and had more of her old animation than she had shown for a long time—which arose from the simple fact that she had something in hand, though the old lady thought it might have a more touching and delicate motive. If *that* was the case, it would make a great difference. Mrs Chiley was no longer able to go out in the evening, and had to be dependent on other people's observation for a knowledge of what happened —and she was wounded by a sense that her young friend had not been appreciated as her worth deserved. If Mr Ashburton had the sense to see what was for his own advantage, it would be a frightful thing, as Mrs Chiley said to herself, if Lucilla's friends should fly in his face. And though it was a hard trial to give up Mr Cavendish, still if anything of the kind had happened—— Thus it will be evident that Lucilla's visit, though it was not a long one, nor the least in the world an argumentative visit, was not without its fruit.

She went up Grange Lane again cheerful and warm in her sealskin coat. It was a thing that suited her remarkably well, and corresponded with her character, and everybody knows how comfortable they are. The snow-flakes fell softly, one at a time, and melted away to nothing upon her sleeves and her shoulders without leaving any trace—and Lucilla, with the chill air blowing in her face, and those feathery messengers in the air, could not but feel that her walk and the general readiness which she felt to face all kinds of objections and difficulties, and to make a sacrifice of her own feelings, had in them a certain magnanimous and heroic element. For after all she had no *particular* reason, as Mrs Chiley said. Mr Ashburton was a dry man, and of very little use in a social point of view, and had never paid her any attention to speak of, nor at all put himself forth as a candidate for her favour. If he had done so, she would not have felt that thrill of utter disinterestedness which kept her as warm within as her sealskin did without.

There was not a soul to be seen in Grange Lane at that moment in the snow, which came on faster and faster, but one of Mr Wentworth's (who at that time was new in St Roque's) grey sisters, and another lady who was coming down, as quickly as Lucilla was going up, by the long line of garden-walls. The gentlemen were either at business or at their club, or keeping themselves snug indoors; and it was only these devoted women who braved the elements outside. The figure in the grey cloak was occupied simply with the poor people, and that is not our present business; but the other two were otherwise inspired. Mr Cavendish, who had lately arrived, had not been able to make up his mind to face the weather; but his sister was of a different way of thinking. She was not of half the capacity of Lucilla, but still she felt that something ought to be done, and that there was not a moment to be lost. When she saw it was Miss Marjoribanks that was advancing to meet her, a momentary chill came over Mrs Woodburn. She was thinking so much of her own errand that she could not but jump at the idea that nothing less important could have induced Lucilla to be out of doors on such a day; and her heart beat loud as the two drew near each other. Was it an unexpected and generous auxiliary, or was it a foe accomplished and formidable? For one thing, she was not coming out of Mr Centum's, where Mrs Woodburn herself was going, which at least was a relief. As they came nearer, the two ladies instinctively looked to their weapons. They had met already in many a little passage of arms, but nothing like this had ever occurred to them before. If they were to work in union, Mrs Woodburn felt that they would carry all before them; and if not, then it must be a struggle unto the death.

"Is it really you, Lucilla?" she said; "I could not believe my eyes. What can have brought you out of doors on such a day? You that have everything your own way, and no call to exert yourself——"

"I have been to see Mrs Chiley," said Lucilla, sweetly; "when the weather is bad she sees nobody, and she is always so pleased to have me. Her rheumatism is not so bad, thank you—though I am sure if this weather should last——"

"You would see Mrs Beverley's blanket," said Mrs Woodburn, who was a little nervous, though perhaps that might only be the cold; "but we know what sort of woman she is, and it must have been the Archdeacon's nieces, my dear. Do turn back with me a moment, Lucilla; or I shall go with you. I want to speak to you. Of course you have heard of Harry's coming home?"

"I saw it in the papers," said Miss Marjoribanks, whose perfect serenity offered a curious contrast to her companion's agitation. "I am sure I shall be very glad to see him again. I hope he will come to dinner on Thursday as he used to do. It will be quite nice to see him in his old place."

"Yes," said Mrs Woodburn; "but that was not what I was thinking of. You know you used always to say he ought to be in Parliament; and he has always kept thinking of it since he went away—and thinking, I am sure, that it would please you," said the poor woman, faltering; for Lucilla listened with a smile that was quite unresponsive, and did not change countenance in the least, even at this tender suggestion. "He has come home with that object now, you know, now that poor old Mr Chiltern is dead; and I hope you are going to help us, Lucilla," said Mrs Woodburn. Her voice quite vibrated with agitation as she made this hurried, perhaps injudicious, appeal, thinking within herself at the same moment what would Harry say if he knew that she was thus committing him. As for Lucilla, she received it all with the same tranquillity, as if she expected it, and was quite prepared for everything that her assailant had to say.

"I am sure I wish I had a vote," said Lucilla; "but I have no vote, and what can a girl do? I am so sorry I don't understand about politics. If we were going in for that sort of thing, I don't know what there would be left for the gentlemen to do."

"You have influence, which is a great deal better than a vote," said Mrs Woodburn; "and they all say there is nobody like a lady for electioneering—and a young lady above all; and then you know Harry so well, and can always draw him out to the best advantage. I never thought he looked so nice, or showed his talents so much, as when he was with you," said the eager advocate. She was only wrapped in a shawl herself, and when she looked at Lucilla's sealskin coat, and saw how rosy and comfortable she looked, and how serene and immovable, poor Mrs Woodburn was struck with a pang of envy. If Miss Marjoribanks had married ten years ago, it might have been she now who would have had to stand trembling with anxiety and eagerness among the falling snow, knowing sundry reasons why Mr Cavendish should be disposed to go into Parliament more substantial than that of gratifying a young lady, and feeling how much depended on her ability to secure support for him. This, as it happened, had fallen to his sister's share instead, and Lucilla stood opposite to her looking at her, attentive and polite, and unresponsive. If Harry had only not been such a fool ten years ago! for Mrs Woodburn began to think now with aunt Jemima, that Lucilla did not marry because she was too comfortable, and, without any of the bother, could have everything her own way.

"It is so cold," said Miss Marjoribanks, "and I do think it is coming on to snow very fast. I don't think it is good to stand talking. Do come in to lunch, and then we can have a long chat; for I am sure nobody else will venture out to-day."

"I wish I could come," said Mrs Woodburn, "but I have to go down to Mary Centum's, and hear all about her last new housemaid, you know. I don't know what servants are made of, for my part. They will go out in their caps and talk to the young men, you know, in a night that is enough to give any one their death," the mimic added, with a feeble exercise of her gift which it was sad to see. "But Harry will be sure to come to call the first time he goes out, and you *will* not forget what I have said to you, Lucilla?" and with this Mrs Woodburn took her young friend's hand and looked in her face with a pathetic emphasis which it would be impossible to describe.

"Oh no, certainly not," said Miss Marjoribanks, with cheerful certainty; and then they kissed each other in the midst of the falling snow. Mrs Woodburn's face was cold, but Lucilla's cheek was warm and blooming, as only a clear conscience and a sealskin cloak could have made it; and then they went their several ways through the wintry solitude. Ah, if Harry had only not been such a fool ten years ago! Mrs Woodburn was not an enthusiastic young wife, but knew very well that marriage had its drawbacks, and had come to an age at which she could appreciate the comfort of having her own way without any of the bother. She gave a furtive glance after Lucilla, and could not but acknowledge to herself that it would be very foolish of Miss Marjoribanks to marry, and forfeit all her advantages, and take somebody else's anxieties upon her shoulders, and never have any money except what she asked from her husband. Mrs Chiley, to be sure, who was more experienced than Mrs Woodburn, and might have been her grandmother, took a different view of the subject; but this was what the middle-aged married woman felt, who had, as may be said, two men to carry on her shoulders, as she went anxiously down Grange Lane to conciliate Mrs Centum, wrapping her shawl about her, and feeling the light snow melt beneath her feet, and the cold and discomfort go to her heart. She had her husband to keep in good-humour, and her brother to keep up and keep to the mark, and to do what she could to remedy in public the effects of his indolent Continental habits, and carry, if it was possible, the election for him—all with the horrid sense upon her mind that if at any time the dinner should be a little less cared for than usual, or the children more noisy, Woodburn would go on like a savage. Under such circumstances, the poor woman, amid her cares, may be excused if she looked back a little wistfully at Lucilla going home all comfortable and independent and light-hearted, with no cares, nor anybody to go on at her, in her sealskin coat.

This was how Lucilla commenced that effective but decorous advocacy which did Mr Ashburton so much good in Carlingford. She did not pretend to understand about politics, or to care particularly about Reform or the Income-tax; but she expressed with quiet solemnity her conviction that it was not opinions but a good man that was wanted; that it was not a prime minister they were going to elect, and that Mr Ashburton was the man for Carlingford. "By George! Lucilla is in the right of it!" Colonel Chiley said; "that was always my opinion;" and the people in Grange Lane soon began to echo the Colonel's sentiments, which were so sound and so just.

As for Miss Marjoribanks, nobody had any occasion to "go on" about any neglect on her part of her household duties. Dr Marjoribanks's dinners were always excellent, and it was now, as ever, a privilege to be admitted to his table; and nothing could be more exemplary than the care Lucilla took of aunt

Jemima, who had always such bad nights. Even on this snowy afternoon she went in from her more important cares with a complexion freshened by the cold, and coaxed Mrs John into eating something, and made her as comfortable as possible at the drawing-room fireside.

"Now, tell me all about Tom," Lucilla said, when she had got her work, and settled herself comfortably for a quiet afternoon—for the snow had come on heavier than ever, and unless it might be a sister of charity, or such another sister not of charity, as Lucilla had already encountered, nobody was like to stir abroad or to disturb the two ladies in their work and their talk. Lucilla had some very interesting worsted-work in hand; and the drawing-room never looked more cozy, with somebody to talk to inside, and the wintry world and driving snow without. And such an invitation as Miss Marjoribanks had just given lifted aunt Jemima into a paradise of content. She took Lucilla at her word, and told her, as may be supposed, *all* about Tom, including many things which she was quite acquainted with and knew by heart; and at the same time there was a something implied all through, but never obtrusively set forth, which was not displeasing to the auditor. Miss Marjoribanks listened with affectionate satisfaction, and asked a great many questions, and supplied a great many reminiscences, and entered quite into the spirit of the conversation, and the two spent a very pleasant afternoon together,—so pleasant that Mrs John felt quite annoyed at the reflection that it must come to an end like everything else that is good, and that she must get herself once more into her velvet gown and dine with her brother-in-law. If Providence had only given her the girl instead of the Doctor, who would no doubt have got on quite well without any children! but then, to be sure, if Lucilla had been hers to start with, she never could have married Tom.

For this was the extravagant hope which had already begun to blossom in his mother's breast. To be sure, a woman might marry Tom who was too comfortable at home to think of marrying just anybody who might make her an offer. But it was not easy to tell how Lucilla herself felt on this subject. Her complexion was so bright with her walk, her sensations so agreeable after that warm, cheerful, pleasant afternoon, her position so entirely everything that was to be desired, and her mind so nobly conscious of being useful to her kind and country, that, even without any additional argument, Miss Marjoribanks had her reward, and was happy. Perhaps a touch more exquisite might still come in to round the full proportions of content. But, to tell the truth, Lucilla was so well off that it was not necessary to invent any romantic source of happiness to account for the light of well-being and satisfaction that shone in her eyes.

CHAPTER XL.

The result of Miss Marjoribanks's wise precaution and reticence was that Sir John Richmond and the Doctor and Colonel Chiley were all on Mr Ashburton's committee. They might not agree with his principles; but then when a man does not state any very distinct principles, it is difficult for any one, however well disposed, to disagree with him; and the fact that he was the man for Carlingford was so indisputable, that nobody attempted to go into the minor matters. "Mr Ashburton is a gentleman known to us all," Sir John said, with great effect, in his nomination speech; and it was a sentence which went to the hearts of his audience. The other candidate had been a long time from home, and it was longer still since anybody in Carlingford could be said to have benefited by his residence there. He had had all his things down from town, as Mr Holden, the upholsterer, pithily remarked—and that made a great difference to start with. As for Mr Ashburton, though it is true nobody knew what he thought about Reform or the Income-tax, everybody knew that he lived at the Firs, and was supplied in a creditable way by George Street tradesmen. There was no mystery whatever about him. People knew how much he had a-year, and how much he paid for everything, and the way in which his accounts were kept, and all about him. Even when he had his wine direct from the growers (for naturally his own county could not supply the actual liquor), it was put in Carlingford bottles, and people knew the kinds he had, and how much, and a hundred agreeable details. And then "he was a gentleman as was always ready to give his advice," as some of the people said. All this furnished an immense body of evidence in his favour, and made Sir John's remark eloquent. And then Carlingford, as a general rule, did not care the least in the world about Reform. There were a few people who had once done so, and it was remarked in Grove Street that Mr Tozer had once been in a dreadful state of mind about it. But he was quite tranquil on the subject now, and so was the community in general. And what was really wanted, as Lucilla's genius had seen at a glance, was not this or that opinion, but a good man.

But at the same time it would be vain to deny that Miss Marjoribanks looked forward to a possible visit from Mr Cavendish with a certain amount of anxiety. She was not frightened, for she knew her own powers; but she was a little excited and stimulated by the idea that he might come in at any minute, bringing back a crowd of recollections with him; and it was a perpetual wonder to her how he would take the inevitable difference—whether he would accept it as natural, or put on the airs of an injured man. Lucilla did not go out the two afternoons after her meeting with Mrs Woodburn, partly that she might not miss him if he called—for it was better to have it over; but Mr Cavendish did not come on either of these days. After that, of course, she did not wait for him any longer. But on the third or fourth day, when she was in Miss Brown's photographing room (the eldest Miss Brown was not married, and was a mother to the younger girls, and always enthusiastic about sitters), Mr Ashburton called about business, and Thomas came to fetch Miss Marjoribanks. She was sitting with the greatest good-nature for half-a-dozen pictures, knowing in her secret heart all the time that she would look a perfect fright, and that all Carlingford would see her grinning with imbecile amiability out of the hazy background of Miss Brown's *cartes*. Lucilla knew this, and had hitherto avoided the process with success; but now she gave in; and as the Major was there, of course they talked of the coming election, which, indeed, at present was almost the only topic of conversation in Grange Lane.

"Of course you are on Mr Ashburton's committee," said Lucilla; "you must be, or going to be, after what you said the other day at lunch——"

"What did I say?" asked Major Brown, with an air of dismay; for, to tell the truth, his heart inclined a little towards poor Mr Cavendish, who was an old neighbour, and to whom Major Brown could not but think the Marjoribanks and others had behaved rather cruelly. But then in these electioneering matters one never knows what one may have done to compromise one's self without meaning it; and the Major was a little anxious to find out what he had said.

"Dear Major Brown," said Lucilla, seriously, "I am so sorry if you did not mean it. I am sure it was that as much as anything that influenced Mr Ashburton. He was turning it all over in his mind, you know, and was afraid the people he most esteemed in Carlingford would not agree with him, and did not know what to do; and then you said, What did it matter about opinions, if it was a good man?—that was what decided him," said Miss Marjoribanks, with sad yet gentle reproachfulness. "I am so sorry if you did not mean what you said——"

"Good heavens! I don't remember saying anything of the sort," said Major Brown. "I—I am sure I never thought of influencing anybody. It is true enough about a good man, you know; but if I had imagined for an instant that any one was paying attention—— By George! it was you that said it, Lucilla—I remember now."

"Please don't make fun of me," said Miss Marjoribanks; "as if anybody cared what *I* say about politics. But I know that was what decided poor Mr Ashburton. Indeed, he told me so; and when he finds you did not mean anything——"

"But, good heavens!—I—I did mean something," cried the accused, with dismay. And he grew quite inarticulate in his confusion, and red in the face, and lost his head altogether, while Lucilla sat calmly looking on with that air of virtue at once severe and indulgent, which pities, and blames, and hopes that perhaps there is not so much harm done as might have been expected. This was the position of affairs when Thomas came to say that Miss Marjoribanks was wanted, as she had told him to do when her candidate came; for, to be sure, it was only next door. It was terrible to hear the soft sigh she gave when she shook hands with Major Brown. "I hope he will not feel it so much as I think; but I should be afraid to tell him," said Lucilla; and she went away, leaving the good man in a state of bewilderment and embarrassment and doubt, which would have been much more unpleasant if he had not felt so flattered at the same time. "I never meant to influence anybody, I am sure," he said, with a comical mixture of complacence and dismay, when Lucilla was gone. "I have always said, papa, that you don't think enough of the weight people give to your opinion," Miss Brown replied, as she gave the final bath to her negatives; and they both left off work with a certain glow of comforted *amour propre*, and the most benevolent sentiments towards Mr Ashburton, who, to tell the truth, until he got his lesson from Miss Marjoribanks, had never once thought about the opinion of Major Brown.

He was sitting with aunt Jemima when Lucilla came in, and

talking to her in a steady sort of a way. Nothing could have made Mr Ashburton socially attractive, but still there are many people to whom this steady sort of talk is more agreeable than brilliancy. When a man is brilliant there is always a doubt in some minds whether he is trustworthy, or sincere, or to be relied upon; but an ordinary common-sense sort of talker is free from such suspicion. Mr Ashburton was very sorry to hear that Mrs John Marjoribanks had bad nights, and suggested that it might be nervous, and hoped that the air of Carlingford would do her good, and was very glad to hear that her son was getting on so well in India; and aunt Jemima could not help approving of him, and feeling that he was a person of substance and reflection, and not one of those fly-away young men who turn girls' heads, and never mean anything. Lucilla herself gained something in Mrs John's eyes from Mr Ashburton's high opinion; but at the same time it was quite clear that he was not thinking of anything sentimental, but was quite occupied about his election, as a man of sense should be. Lucilla came in with a fine bloom on her cheeks, but still with a shade of that sadness which had had so great an effect upon Major Brown. She had taken off her hat before she came in, and dropped into her chair with an air of languor and fatigue which was quite unusual to her. "It makes such a difference in life when one has something on one's mind," said Lucilla, and she sighed, as was but natural; for though that did not affect the energy of her proceedings, she knew and remembered at moments of discouragement how seldom one's most disinterested exertions are appreciated at the end.

"You want your lunch, my dear," said Mrs John.

"Perhaps I do," said Miss Marjoribanks, with a mournful affectionate smile. "I have been sitting to Maria Brown. She has taken six, and I am sure they are every one more hideous than the other; and they will go all over England, you know, for the Browns have hosts of people belonging to them; and everybody will say, 'So *that* is Miss Marjoribanks.' I don't think I am vain to speak of," said Lucilla, "but that sort of thing goes to one's heart."

"These amateurs are terrible people," said Mr Ashburton, in his steady way; "and photographs are a regular nuisance. For my part——"

"Don't say that," said Miss Marjoribanks. "I know what you are going to say; and you *must* sit to her, please. I have said already she must do one of you; and I will tell you presently about the Major. But wait and talk to aunt Jemima a little, for I am so tired," said Lucilla. She was lying back negligently in her seat, with that air of languor which so many young ladies excel in, but which was for her a novel indulgence. Her hand hung over the arm of her chair as if there was no longer any force in it. Her head fell back, her eyes were half closed; it was a moment of abandonment to her sensations, such as a high-principled young woman like Miss Marjoribanks seldom gives way to. But Lucilla went into it conscientiously, as into everything she did, that she might regain her strength for the necessary duties that were before her.

And it was at this moment that Thomas appeared at the door with a suspicion of a grin appearing at the corners of his sober mouth, and announced Mr Cavendish, who came in before an ordinary woman would have had time to open her eyes. This was the moment he had chosen for his first visit; and yet it was not he who had chosen it, but fate, who seemed to have in this respect a spite against Lucilla. It was not only the embarrassing presence of his rival, but the fact that neither of the two people in the room knew or had ever seen Mr Cavendish, that put a climax to the horror of the situation. She alone knew him, and had to take upon herself to present and introduce him, and bridge over for him the long interval of absence, and all this with the sense of being in the enemy's interest, and to a certain extent false to Mr Cavendish! Lucilla rose at once, but she was not a woman to make pretences. She did not throw off all in a moment her fatigue, and dash into spasmodic action. She held out her hand silently to Mr Cavendish, with a look which spoke only affectionate satisfaction in a friend's return. She did not even speak at all for the first moment, but contented herself with a look, which indeed, if he had been younger and less preoccupied, would no doubt have touched his very heart.

"So you have really come back," she said. "I am so glad! after all that people said about your being married and dead and ever so many stupid things. Oh! don't look at me, please. It doesn't matter with a gentleman, but I know as well as if you had told me that you think me dreadfully gone off——"

"*I* entertain such a profane idea!" said Mr Cavendish; but he was considerably embarrassed, and he was a great deal stouter, and altogether different from what he used to be, and he had not the light hand of his youth for a compliment. And then he sat down on the chair Thomas had given him; and he looked uncomfortable, to say the least of it; and he was getting large in dimensions and a little red in the face, and had by no means the air of thinking that it didn't matter for a gentleman. As for Miss Marjoribanks, it would be impossible to say what mists of illusion dropped away from her mind at the sight of him. Even while she smiled upon the new-comer, she could not but ask herself, with momentary dismay—Had *she* really gone off as much in the same time?

"I have been looking for you," Miss Marjoribanks resumed; "I waited in for you Tuesday and Wednesday, and it is so odd you should have come just at this minute. Aunt Jemima, this is Mr Cavendish, whom you have heard so much about—and don't go, please, Mr Ashburton—you two must know each other. You will be hearing of each other constantly; and I suppose you will have to shake hands or something on the hustings—so it will be much the best to begin it here."

But the two candidates did not shake hands: they bowed to each other in an alarming way, which did not promise much for their future brotherliness; and then they both stood bolt upright and stared at Miss Marjoribanks, who had relapsed, in the pleasantest way in the world, into her easy-chair.

"Now, please sit down and talk a little," said Lucilla; "I am so proud of having you both together. There never has been anybody in the world that I have missed so much as *you* —you knew that when you went away, but you didn't mind. Mr Ashburton is very nice, but he is of no use to speak of in an evening," said Miss Marjoribanks, turning a reflective glance upon her own candidate with a certain sadness; and then they both laughed as if it was a joke; but it was no joke, as one of them at least must have known.

"Lucilla," said Mrs John, with consternation, "I never heard anybody talk as you do; I am sure Mr Ashburton is the very best of society, and as for Mr Cavendish——"

"Dear aunt Jemima," said Lucilla, "would you mind ringing the bell? I have been sitting to Maria Brown, and I am almost fainting. I wish you gentlemen would sit to her; it would please her, and it would not do *you* much harm; and then for your constituents, you know——"

"I hope you don't wish me to look like one of Maria Brown's photographs to *my* constituents," said Mr Cavendish; "but then I am happy to say they all know me pretty well." This was said with a slight touch of gentlemanly spite, if there is such a thing; for, after all, he *was* an old power in Carlingford, though he had been so long away.

"Yes," said Lucilla, reflectively, "but you are a little changed since then; a little perhaps—just a little—stouter, and——"

"Gone off?" said Mr Cavendish, with a laugh; but he felt horribly disconcerted all the same, and savage with Miss Marjoribanks, and could not think why "that fellow" did not go away. What had *he* to do in Lucilla's drawing-room? what did he mean by sitting down again and talking in that measured way to the old lady, as if all the ordinary rules of good breeding did not point out to him that he should have gone away and left the field clear?

"Oh, you know it does not matter for a gentleman," said Lucilla; and then she turned to Mr Ashburton—"I am sure the Major wants to see you, and he thinks that it was he who put it into your head to stand. He was here that day at lunch, you know, and it was something he said——"

"Quite true," said Mr Ashburton in his business way. "I shall go to see him at once. Thank you for telling me of it, Miss Marjoribanks; I shall go as soon as I leave here."

And then Mr Cavendish laughed. "This is what I call interesting," he said. "I hope Mr Ashburton sees the fun; but it is trying to an old friend to hear of *that* day at lunch, you know. I remember when these sort of allusions used to be pleasant enough; but when one has been banished for a thousand years——"

"Yes," said Lucilla, "one leaves all that behind, you know —one leaves ever so many things behind. I wish we could always be twenty, for my part. I always said, you know, that I should be gone off in ten years."

"Was it the only fib you ever told that you repeat it so?" said Mr Cavendish; and it was with this pretty speech that he took her down-stairs to the well-remembered luncheon. "But you *have* gone off in some things when you have to do with a prig like that," he said in her ear, as they went down together, "and cast off old friends. It was a thing a fellow did not expect of *you.*"

"I never cast off old friends," said Miss Marjoribanks. "We shall look for you on Thursday, you know, all the same. Must you go, Mr Ashburton? when lunch is on the table? But then, to be sure, you will be in time at the Browns'," said Lucilla, sweetly, and she gave the one rival her hand while she held the arm of the other, at the door of the dining-room, in which Mr Ashburton had gallantly deposited aunt Jemima before saying good-bye. They were both looking a little black, though the gloom was moderate in Mr Ashburton's case; but as for Lucilla, she stood between them a picture of angelic sweetness and goodness, giving a certain measure of her sympathy to both—Woman the Reconciler, by the side of those other characters of Inspirer and Consoler, of which the world has heard. The two inferior creatures scowled with politeness at each other, but Miss Marjoribanks smiled upon them both. Such was the way in which she overcame the difficulties of the meeting. Mr Ashburton went away a little annoyed, but still understanding his instructions, and ready to act upon them in that business-like way he had; and Mr Cavendish remained, faintly reassured, in the midst of his soreness and mortification, by at least having the field to himself and seeing the last (for the present) of his antagonist—which was a kind of victory in its way.

"I thought I knew you better than to think you ever would have anything to do with *that* sort of thing," said Mr Cavendish. "There are people, you know, whom I could have imagined—but a prig like that." He became indeed quite violent, as aunt Jemima said afterwards, and met with that lady's decided disapproval, as may be supposed.

"Mr Ashburton is very well bred and agreeable," Mrs John said, with emphasis. "I wish all the young men I see nowadays were as nice."

"Young men!" said Mr Cavendish. "Is that what people call young nowadays? And he must be insane, you know, or he would never dream of representing a town without saying a single word about his principles. I daresay he thinks it is original," said the unhappy man. He thought he was pointing out his rival's weakness to Lucilla, and he went on with energy—"I know you better than to think you can like that milk-and-water sort of thing."

"Oh, I don't pretend to know anything about politics," said Lucilla. "I hear you gentlemen talk, but I never pretend to understand. If we were not to leave you *that* all to yourselves, I don't know what you could find to do," Miss Marjoribanks added compassionately; and as she spoke she looked so like the Lucilla of old, who had schemed and plotted for Mr Cavendish, that he could not believe in her desertion in his heart.

"That is a delusion like the going off," he said. "I can't believe you have gone over to the enemy. When I remember how I have been roving about all those ten years, and how different it might have been, and whose fault it all was——"

This Mr Cavendish said in a low voice, but it did not the

less horrify aunt Jemima, who felt prepared for any atrocity after it. She would have withdrawn, in justice to her own sense of propriety; but then she thought it was not impossible that he might propose to Lucilla on the spot, or take her hand or something, and for propriety's sake she stayed.

"Yes," said Lucilla—and her heart did for one little moment give a faint thump against her breast. She could not help thinking what a difference it might have made to him, poor fellow, had he been under her lawful and righteous sway these ten years. But as she looked at him, it became more and more apparent to Miss Marjoribanks that Mr Cavendish *had* gone off, whatever she herself might have done. The outlines of his fine figure had changed considerably, and his face was a little red, and he had the look of a man whose circumstances, spiritual and temporal, would not quite bear a rigid examination. As she looked at him her pity became tinged by a certain shade of resentment, to think that after all it was his own fault. She could not, notwithstanding her natural frankness of expression, say to him—" You foolish soul, why didn't you marry me somehow, and make a man of yourself?" Lucilla carried honesty very far, but she could not go as far as that. " Yes," she said, turning her eyes upon him with a sort of abstract sympathy, and then she added softly—" Have you ever seen Her again?" with a lowering of her voice.

This interesting question, which utterly bewildered aunt Jemima, drove Mr Cavendish wild with rage. Mrs John said afterwards that she felt a shiver go through her as he took up the carving-knife, though it was only to cut some cold beef. He grew white all at once, and pressed his lips tightly together, and fixed his eyes on the wall straight before him. "I did not think, after what I once said to you, Miss Marjoribanks, that you would continue to insult my judgment in that way," he said, with a chill which fell upon the whole table, and took the life out of everything, and dimmed the very fire in the chimney. And after that the conversation was of a sufficiently ordinary description until they went back again into the drawing-room, by which time Mr Cavendish seemed to have concluded that it was best to pocket the affront.

"I am going to begin my canvass to-morrow," he said. "I have not seen anybody yet. I have nobody but my sister to take *me* in hand, you know. There was once a time when it might have been different"—and he gave Lucilla a look which she thought on the whole it was best to meet.

"Yes," said Miss Marjoribanks, with cruel distinctness, "there was a time when you were the most popular man in Grange Lane—everybody was fond of you. I remember it as if it had been yesterday," said Lucilla, with a sigh.

"You don't give a man much encouragement, by Jove!" said the unlucky candidate. "You remember it like yesterday! It may be vanity, but I flatter myself I shall still be found the most popular man in Grange Lane."

Miss Marjoribanks sighed again, but she did not say anything. On the contrary she turned to aunt Jemima, who kept in the background an alarmed and alert spectator, to consult her about a shade of wool; and just then Mr Cavendish, looking out of the window, saw Major Brown conducting his rival through his garden, and shaking hands with him cordially at the door. This was more than the patience of the other candidate could bear. A sudden resolution, hot and angry, as are the resolutions of men who feel themselves to have a failing cause, came into his mind. He had been badgered and baited to such an extent (as he thought) that he had not time to consider if it was wise or not. He, too, had sat to Maria Brown, and commanded once the warmest admiration of the household. He thought he would put it to the test, and see if after all his popularity was only a thing to be remembered like yesterday; —and it was with this intention that he bade a hurried good-bye to Lucilla, and, rushing out, threw himself at once upon the troubled waves of society, which had once been as smooth as glass to the most popular man in Grange Lane.

CHAPTER XLI.

Mr Cavendish thought he had been an object of admiration to Maria Brown, as we have said. He thought of it with a little middle-aged complacency, and a confidence that this vague sentiment would stand the test he was about to apply to it, which did honour to the freshness of his heart. With this idea it was Miss Brown he asked for as he knocked at the Major's door; and he found them both in the drawing-room, Maria with gloves on to hide the honourable stains of her photography, which made her comparatively useless when she was out of her "studio"—and her father walking about in a state of excitement, which was, indeed, what Mr Cavendish expected. The two exchanged a guilty look when they saw who their visitor was. They looked as people might well look who had been caught in the fact and did not know how to get over it. They came forward, both of them, with a cowardly cordiality and eagerness to welcome him—"How very good of you to come to see us so soon!" Miss Brown said, and fluttered and looked at her father, and could not tell what more to say. And then a dead pause fell upon them—such a pause as not unfrequently falls upon people who have got through their mutual greetings almost with an excess of cordiality. They stopped short all at once, and looked at each other, and smiled, and made a fatal conscious effort to talk of something. "It is so good of you to come so soon," Miss Brown repeated; "perhaps you have been to see Lucilla," and then she stopped again, slightly tremulous, and turned an appealing gaze to her papa.

"I have come to see *you*," said Mr Cavendish, plucking up all his courage. "I have been a long time gone, you know, but I have not forgotten Carlingford; and you must forgive me for saying that I was very glad to hear I might still come to see— Miss Brown. As for Lydia?" said the candidate, looking about him with a smile.

"Ah, Lydia," said her sister, with a sigh—"her eldest is eight, Mr Cavendish. We don't see her so often as we should like—marriage makes such a difference. Of course it is quite natural she should be all for her own family now."

"Quite natural," said Mr Cavendish, and then he turned to the Major. "I don't think there are quite so many public changes as I expected to see. The old Rector always holds out, and the old Colonel; and you have not done much that I can see about the new paving. You know what I have come home about, Major; and I am sure I can count upon you to support me," the candidate said, with a great deal more confidence than he felt in his voice.

Major Brown cleared his throat; his heart was moved by the familiar voice, and he could not conceal his embarrassment. "I hope nothing will ever occur," he said, "to make any difference in the friendly feelings—I am sure I shall be very glad to welcome you back permanently to Carlingford. You may always rest assured of that," and he held out his hand. But he grew red as he thought of his treachery, and Maria, who was quaking over it, did not even try to say a word to help him—and as for

Mr Cavendish, he took up his position on the arm of the sofa, as he used to do. But he had a slim youthful figure when he used to do it, and now the attitude was one which revealed a certain dawning rotundity, very different, as Maria afterwards said, from one's idea of Mr Cavendish. He was not aware of it himself, but as these two people looked, their simultaneous thought was how much he had changed.

"Thank you, you are very kind," said Mr Cavendish. "I have been a little lazy, I am afraid, since I came here; but I expect my agent down to-night, and then, I hope, you'll come over to my place and have a talk with Woodburn and Centum and the rest about it. I am a poor tactician, for my part. You shall contrive what is best to be done, and I'll carry it out. I suppose I may expect almost to walk over," he said. It was the confidence of despair that moved him. The more he saw that his cause was lost, the more he would make it out that he was sure to win—which is not an unusual state of mind.

"I—I don't know, I am sure," said poor Major Brown. "To tell the truth, I—though I can safely say my sympathies are always with you, Cavendish—I—have been so unfortunate as to commit myself, you know. It was quite involuntary, I am sure, for I never thought my casual expression of opinion likely to have any weight——"

"Papa never will perceive the weight that is attached to his opinion," said Miss Brown.

"I was not thinking of it in the least, Maria," said the modest Major; "but the fact is, it seems to have been *that* that decided Ashburton to stand; and after drawing a man in to such a thing, the least one can do is to back him out in it. Nobody had an idea then, you know, that you were coming back, my dear fellow. I assure you, if I had known——"

"But even if you had known, you know you never meant it, papa," said Maria. And Mr Cavendish sat on the arm of the sofa, and put his hands deep into his pockets, and dropped his upper lip, and knit his eyebrows a little, and listened to the anxious people excusing themselves. He did not make any answer one way or another. He was terribly mortified and disappointed, and it went against his pride to make any further remonstrances. When they had done, he got down off his seat and took his right hand out of his pocket and offered it to Miss Brown, who, putting her own into it, poor soul! with the remembrance of her ancient allegiance, was like to cry.

"Well," he said, "if that is the case, I suppose I need not

bother you any longer. You'll give me your good wishes all the same. I used to hear of Ashburton sometimes, but I never had the least idea he was so popular. And to tell the truth, I don't think he's any great things to brag of—though I suppose it's not to be expected *I* should appreciate his qualities," Mr Cavendish added, with a laugh. As for Miss Brown, it was all she could do to keep from crying as he went away. She said she could see, by the way he left the drawing-room, that he was a stricken deer; and yet, notwithstanding this sympathetic feeling, she could not but acknowledge, when Miss Marjoribanks mentioned it, that, to have been such a handsome man, he was inconceivably gone off.

Mr Cavendish went up Grange Lane with his hands in his pockets, and tried to think that he did not care; but he did care all the same, and was very bitter in his mind over the failure of friends and the vanity of expectations. The last time he had walked past those garden-walls he had thought himself sure of the support of Carlingford, and the personal esteem of all the people in all the houses he was passing. It was after the Archdeacon had broken down in his case against the man whom he called an adventurer, and when Mr Cavendish felt all the sweetness of being a member of an oligarchy, and entitled to the sympathy and support of his order. Now he went along the same path with his hat over his ears and his hands in his pockets, and rage and pain in his heart. Whose fault was it that his friends had deserted him and Carlingford knew him no more? He might as well have asked whose fault it was that he was getting stout and red in the face, and had not the same grace of figure nor ease of mind as he used to have? He had come very near to settling down and becoming a man of domestic respectability in this quiet place, and he had just escaped in time, and had laughed over it since, and imagined himself, with much glee, an old fogie looking after a lot of children. But the fact is that men do become old fogies even when they have no children to look after, and lose their figure and their elasticity just as soon, and perhaps a little sooner, in the midst of what is called life than in any milder scene of enjoyment. And it would have been very handy just now to have been sure of his election without paying much for it. He had been living fast, and spending a great deal of money, and this, after all, was the only real ambition he had ever had; and he had thought within himself that if he won he would change his mode of life, and turn over a new leaf, and become all at once a different man. When a man has made such a resolution, and feels not only that a mere success but a moral reformation depends upon his victory, he may be permitted to consider that he has a right to win; and it may be divined what his state of mind was when he had made the discovery that even his old friends did not see his election to be of any such importance as he did, and could think of a miserable little bit of self-importance or gratified vanity more than of his interests— even the women who had once been so kind to him! He had just got so far in his thoughts when he met Mr Centum, who stared for a moment, and then burst into one of his great laughs as he greeted him. "Good Lord! Cavendish, is this you? I never expected to see you like that!" the banker said, in his coarse way. "You're stouter than I am, old fellow; and such an Adonis as you used to be!" Mr Cavendish had to bear all this without giving way to his feelings, or even showing them any more than he could help it. Nobody would spare him that imbecile suggestion as to how things used to be. To be growing stouter than Centum without Centum's excuse of being a well-to-do householder and father of a family, and respectable man from whom stoutness was expected, was very bitter to him; but he had to gulp it down, and recollect that Centum was as yet the only influential supporter, except his brother-in-law, whom he had in Carlingford.

"What have you been doing with yourself since you came that nobody has seen you?" said Mr Centum. "If you are to do any good here, you know, we shall have to look alive."

"I have been ill," said the unfortunate candidate, with a little natural loss of temper. "You would not have a man to trudge about at this time of year in all weathers when he is ill."

"I would not be ill again, if I were you, till it's all over," said Mr Centum. "We shall have to fight every inch of our ground; and I tell you that fellow Ashburton knows what he's about—he goes at everything in a steady sort of way. He's not brilliant, you know, but he's sure——"

"Brilliant!" said Mr Cavendish, "I should think not. It is Lucilla Marjoribanks who is putting him up to it. You know she had an old grudge at me."

"Oh, nonsense about Lucilla," said Mr Centum. "I can tell you Ashburton is not at all a contemptible adversary. He is going to work in the cunningest way—not a woman's sort of thing; and he's not a ladies' man like you," the banker added, with a laugh. "But I am afraid you can't go in for that sort of thing as you used to do, Cavendish. You should marry, and settle, and become a steady member of society, now you've grown so stout." This was the kind of way in which he was addressed even by his own supporter, who uttered another great laugh as he went off upon his busy way. It was a sort of thing Mr Cavendish was not used to, and he felt it accordingly. To be sure he knew that he was ten years older, and that there were several things which he could not do with the same facility as in his youth. But he had saved up Carlingford in his imagination as a spot in which he would always be young, and where nobody should find out the difference; and instead of that, it was precisely in Carlingford that he was fated to hear how changed he was, with a frankness which only old friends would have been justified in using. As for Lucilla Marjoribanks, she was rather better looking than otherwise, and absolutely had not gone off. It did not occur to Mr Cavendish that this might be because Lucilla at present was not still so old as he had been ten years ago, in the period which he now considered his youth. He was rather disposed, on the contrary, to take a moral view, and to consider that it was her feminine incapacity for going too far, which had kept years and amusements from having their due effect upon Miss Marjoribanks. And, poor fellow, he *had* gone too far. He had not been as careful in his life as he might have been had he stayed at Carlingford; and now he was paying the penalty. Such was the edifying state of mind which he had come to when he reached the top of Grove Street. And there a waft of soft recollections came across his mind. In the absence of all sympathy he could not help turning back to the thought of the enchantress of old who used to sing to him, and listen to him, and storm at him. Probably he would have ended by strolling along the familiar street, and canvassing for Mr Lake's vote, which would have done him no good in Carlingford, but just then Dr Marjoribanks stopped in his brougham. The Doctor was looking very strange that morning, though nobody had particularly remarked it—perhaps because he smoothed his countenance when he was out of the brougham, which was his refuge when he had anything to think about. But he stopped suddenly to speak to Mr Cavendish, and perhaps he had not time to perform that ceremony. He looked dark and cloudy, and constrained, and as if he forced himself to speak; which, to be sure, under the circumstances, was not so very strange.

"I am very glad to see you," the Doctor said, "though you were a day too late, you know. Why didn't you give us warning before we all went and committed ourselves? If we had known that you were coming——"

"Ah, that's what old Brown said," said Mr Cavendish, with a slight shrug of his shoulders; which was imprudent, for the Major was not so old as the Doctor, and besides was a much less important man in Grange Lane.

"So you have been to see old Brown," said Dr Marjoribanks, in his dry way. "He always was a great admirer of yours. I can't wish you luck, you know, for if you win we lose——"

"Oh, I don't want you to wish me luck. I don't suppose there can be much comparison between my chance and that of a new man whom nobody ever heard of in my time," said the candidate for Carlingford. "I thought you Scotchmen, Doctor, always liked to be on the winning side."

"We've a way of making our side the winning side," said Dr Marjoribanks, grimly, for he was touchy where his nationality was concerned. "Health all right, I hope?" he added, looking at Mr Cavendish with that critical medical glance which shows that a verbal response is quite unnecessary. This time there was in the look a certain insinuation of doubt on the subject, which was not pleasant. "You are getting stout, I see," Dr Marjoribanks added—not laughing, but as if that too was poor Mr Cavendish's fault.

"Yes, I'm very well," he answered, curtly; but the truth was that he did not feel sure that he was quite well after he had seen the critical look in Dr Marjoribanks's eye.

"You young men always go too fast," said the Doctor, with a strange little smile; but the term at least was consolatory; and after that Dr Marjoribanks quite changed his tone. "Have you heard Woodburn talking of that great crash in town?" he said—"that India house, you know—I suppose it's quite true?"

"Quite true," said Mr Cavendish, promptly, and somehow he felt a pleasure in saying it. "I got all the particulars to-day in one of my letters—and lots of private people involved, which is always the way with these old houses," he added, with a mixture of curiosity and malice—"widows, and all sorts of superannuated folks."

"It's a great pity," said the Doctor: "I knew old Lichfield once, the chief partner—I am very sorry to hear it's true;" and then the two shook hands, and the brougham drove on. As for Mr Cavendish, he made up his mind at once that the Doctor was involved, and was not sorry, and felt that it was a sort of judicial recompense for his desertion of his friends. And he went home to tell his sister of it, who shared in his sentiments. And then it was not worth while going out any more that day—for the electioneering agent, who knew all about it, was not coming till the last train. "I suppose I shall have to work when he is here," Mr Cavendish said. And in the mean time he threw himself into an easy-chair. Perhaps that was why he was getting so stout.

And in the mean time the Doctor went on visiting his patients. When he came back to his brougham between his visits, and went bowling along in that comfortable way, along the familiar roads, there was a certain glumness upon his face. He was not a demonstrative man, but when he was alone you could tell by certain lines about the well-worn cordage of his countenance whether all was right with the Doctor; and it was easy to see just at this moment that all was not right with him. But he did not say anything about it when he got home; on the contrary, he was just as usual, and told his daughter all about his encounter with Mr Cavendish. "A man at his time of life has no right to get fat—it's a sort of thing I don't like to see. And he'll never be a ladies' man no more, Lucilla," said the Doctor, with a gleam of humour in his eye.

"He is exactly like George the Fourth, papa," said Miss Marjoribanks; and the Doctor laughed as he sat down to dinner. If he had anything on his mind he bore it like a hero, and gave no sign; but then, as Mrs John very truly remarked, when a man does not disclose his annoyances they always tell more upon him in the end.

CHAPTER XLII.

THERE were a great many reasons why this should be a critical period in Miss Marjoribanks's life. For one thing, it was the limit she had always proposed to herself for her term of young-ladyhood; and naturally, as she outgrew the age for them, she felt disposed to put away childish things. To have the control of society in her hands was a great thing; but still the mere means, without any end, was not worth Lucilla's while—and her Thursdays were almost a bore to her in her present stage of development. They occurred every week, to be sure, as usual;

but the machinery was all perfect, and went on by itself, and it was not in the nature of things that such a light adjunct of existence should satisfy Lucilla, as she opened out into the ripeness of her thirtieth year. It was this that made Mr Ashburton so interesting to her, and his election a matter into which she entered so warmly, for she had come to an age at which she might have gone into Parliament herself had there been no disqualification of sex, and when it was almost a necessity for her to make some use of her social influence. Miss Marjoribanks had her own ideas in respect to charity, and never went upon ladies' committees, nor took any further share than what was proper and necessary in parish work; and when a woman has an active mind, and still does not care for parish work, it is a little hard for her to find a "sphere." And Lucilla, though she said nothing about a sphere, was still more or less in that condition of mind which has been so often and so fully described to the British public—when the ripe female intelligence, not having the natural resource of a nursery and a husband to manage, turns inwards, and begins to "make a protest" against the existing order of society, and to call the world to account for giving it no due occupation—and to consume itself. She was not the woman to make protests, nor to claim for herself the doubtful honours of a false position; but she felt all the same that at her age she had outlived the occupations that were sufficient for her youth. To be sure, there were still the dinners to attend to, a branch of human affairs worthy of the weightiest consideration, and she had a house of her own, as much as if she had been half-a-dozen times married; but still there are instincts which go even beyond dinners, and Lucilla had become conscious that her capabilities were greater than her work. She was a Power in Carlingford, and she knew it; but still there is little good in the existence of a Power unless it can be made use of for some worthy end.

She was coming up Grange Lane rather late one evening, pondering upon these things—thinking within herself compassionately of poor Mr Cavendish, a little in the same way as he had been thinking of her, but from the opposite point of view. For Lucilla could not but see the antithesis of their position, and how he was the foolish apprentice who had chosen his own way and was coming to a bad end, while she was the steady one about to ride by in her Lord Mayor's coach. And Miss Marjoribanks was thinking at the same time of the other candidate, whose canvass was going on so successfully; and that, after the election and all the excitement was over, she would feel a blank. There could be no doubt she would feel a blank—and Lucilla did not see how the blank was to be filled up as she looked into the future; for, as has been said, parish work was not much in her way, and for a woman who feels that she is a Power, there are so few other outlets. She was a little disheartened as she thought it all over. Gleams of possibility, it is true, crossed her mind, such as that of marrying the member for Carlingford, for instance, and thus beginning a new and more important career; but she was too experienced a woman not to be aware by this time, that possibilities which did not depend upon herself alone had better not be calculated upon. And there did occur to her, among other things, the idea of making a great Experiment which could be carried out only by a woman of genius—of marrying a poor man, and affording to Carlingford and England an example which might influence unborn generations. Such were the thoughts that were passing through her mind when, to her great surprise, she came up to her father, walking up Grange Lane over the dirty remains of the snow—for there was a great deal of snow that year. It was so strange a sight to see Dr Marjoribanks walking that at the first glance Lucilla was startled, and thought something was the matter; but, of course, it all arose from a perfectly natural and explainable cause.

"I have been down to see Mrs Chiley," said the Doctor; "she has her rheumatism very bad again; and the horse has been so long out that I thought I would walk home. I think the old lady is a little upset about Cavendish, Lucilla. He was always a pet of hers."

"Dear Mrs Chiley! she is not very bad, I hope?" said Miss Marjoribanks.

"Oh no, she is not very bad," said the Doctor, in a dreary tone. "The poor old machine is just about breaking up, that is all. We can cobble it this once, but next time perhaps——"

"Don't talk in such a disheartening way, papa," said Lucilla. "I am sure she is not so very old."

"We're all pretty old, for that matter," said the Doctor; "we can't run on for ever, you know. If you had been a boy like that stupid fellow Tom, you might have carried on my practice, Lucilla—and even extended it, I shouldn't wonder," Dr Marjoribanks added, with a little grunt, as who should say *that* is the way of the world.

"But I am not a boy," said Lucilla, mildly; "and even if I

had been, you know, I might have chosen another profession. Tom never had any turn for medicine that I ever heard of——"

"I hope you know pretty well about all the turns he ever had with that old——woman," said the Doctor, pulling himself up sharply, "always at your ear. I suppose she never talks of anything else. But I hope you have too much sense for that sort of thing, Lucilla. Tom will never be anything but a poor man if he were to live a hundred years."

"Perhaps not, papa," said Lucilla, with a little sigh. The Doctor knew nothing about the great social experiment which it had entered into Miss Marjoribanks's mind to make for the regeneration of her contemporaries and the good of society, or possibly he might not have distinguished Tom by that particular title. Was it he, perhaps, who was destined to be the hero of a domestic drama embodying the best principles of that Moral Philosophy which Lucilla had studied with such success at Mount Pleasant? She did not ask herself the question, for things had not as yet come to that point, but it gleamed upon her mind as by a side-light.

"I don't know how you would get on if you were poor," said the Doctor. "I don't think that would suit you. You would make somebody a capital wife, I can say that for you, Lucilla, that had plenty of money and a liberal disposition like yourself. But poverty is another sort of thing, I can tell you. Luckily you're old enough to have got over all the love-in-a-cottage ideas—if you ever had them," Dr Marjoribanks added. He was a worldly man himself, and he thought his daughter a worldly woman; and yet, though he thoroughly approved of it, he still despised Lucilla a little for her prudence, which is a paradoxical state of mind not very unusual in the world.

"I don't think I ever had them," said Lucilla—"not that kind of poverty. I know what a cottage means; it means a wretched man, always about the house with his feet in slippers, you know—what poor dear Mr Cavendish would come to if he was poor——"

The Doctor laughed, though he had not seemed up to this moment much disposed for laughing. "So that is all your opinion of Cavendish," he said; "and I don't think you are far wrong either; and yet that was a young fellow that might have done better," Dr Marjoribanks said reflectively, perhaps not without a slight prick of conscience that he had forsaken an old friend.

"Yes," said Lucilla, with a certain solemnity—"but you

know, papa, if a man will not when he may——" And she sighed, though the Doctor, who had not been thinking of Mr Cavendish's prospects in that light, laughed once more; but it was a sharp sort of sudden laugh without much heart in it. He had most likely other things of more importance in his mind.

"Well, there have been a great many off and on since that time," he said, smiling rather grimly. "It is time you were thinking about it seriously, Lucilla. I am not so sure about some things as I once was, and I'd rather like to see you well settled before—— It's a kind of prejudice a man has," the Doctor said abruptly, which, whatever he might mean by it, was a dismal sort of speech to make.

"Before what, papa?" asked Lucilla, with a little alarm.

"Tut—before long, to be sure," he said, impatiently. "Ashburton would not be at all amiss if he liked it and you liked it; but it's no use making any suggestions about those things. So long as you don't marry a fool——" Dr Marjoribanks said, with energy. "I know—that is, of course, I've *seen* what that is; you can't expect to get perfection, as you might have looked for perhaps at twenty; but I advise you to marry, Lucilla. I don't think you are cut out for a single woman, for my part."

"I don't see the good of single women," said Lucilla, "unless they are awfully rich; and I don't suppose I shall ever be awfully rich. But, papa, so long as I can be a comfort to you——"

"Yes," said the Doctor, with that tone which Lucilla could remember fifteen years ago, when she made the same magnanimous suggestion, "but I can't live for ever, you know. It would be a pity to sacrifice yourself to me, and then perhaps next morning find that it was a useless sacrifice. It very often happens like that when self-devotion is carried too far. You've behaved very well, and shown a great deal of good sense, Lucilla—more than I gave you credit for when you commenced —I may say that; and if there was to be any change, for instance——"

"What change?" said Lucilla, not without some anxiety; for it was an odd way of talking, to say the least of it; but the Doctor had come to a pause, and did not seem disposed to resume.

"It is not so pleasant as I thought walking over this snow," he said; "I can't give *that* up, that I can see. And there's more snow in the air if I'm any judge of the weather. There—

go in—go in; don't wait for me;—but mind you make haste and dress, for I want my dinner. I may have to go down to Mrs Chiley again to-night."

It was an odd way of talking, and it was odd to break off like this; but then, to be sure, there was no occasion for any more conversation, since they had just arrived at their own door. It made Lucilla uneasy for the moment, but while she was dressing she managed to explain it to herself, and to think, after all, it was only natural that her papa should have seen a little into the movement and commotion of her thoughts; and then poor dear old Mrs Chiley being so ill, who was one of his own set, so to speak. He was quite cheerful later in the evening, and enjoyed his dinner, and was even more civil than usual to Mrs John. And though he did not come up to tea, he made his appearance afterwards with a flake of new-fallen snow still upon his rusty grey whiskers. He had gone to see his patient again, notwithstanding the silent storm outside. And his countenance was a little overcast this time, no doubt by the late walk, and the serious state Mrs Chiley was in, and his encounter with the snow.

"Oh yes, she is better," he said. "I knew she would do this time. People at our time of life don't go off in that accidental kind of way. When a woman has been so long used to living, it takes her a time to get into the way of dying. She might be a long time thinking about it yet, if all goes well——"

"Papa, don't speak like that!" said Lucilla. "Dying! I can't bear to think of such a thing. She is not so very old."

"Such things will happen whether you can bear to think of them or not," said the Doctor. "I said you would go down and see her to-morrow. We've all held out a long time—the lot of us. I don't like to think of the first gap myself, but somebody must make a beginning, you know."

"The Chileys were always older than you," said Mrs John. "I remember in poor Mrs Marjoribanks's time:—they were quite elderly then, and you were just beginning. When my Tom was a baby——"

"We were always of the same set," said the Doctor, interrupting her without hesitation. "Lucilla, they say Cavendish has got hold of the Rector. He has made believe to be penitent, you know. That is cleverer than anything you could have done. And if he can't be won back again it will be serious, the Colonel says. You are to try if you can suggest anything. It seems," said the Doctor, with mingled amusement and satire, and a kind of gratification, "that Ashburton has great confidence in you."

"It must have been the agent," said Lucilla. "I don't think any of the rest of them are equal to that. I don't see, if that is the case, how we are to win him back. If Mr Ashburton had ever done anything very wicked, perhaps——"

"You are safe to say *he* is not penitent anyhow," said Dr Marjoribanks, and he took his candle and went away with a smile. But either Mr Ashburton's good opinion of Lucilla, or some other notion, had touched the Doctor. He was not a man who said much at any time, but when he bade her good-night, his hand drooped upon Lucilla's shoulder, and he patted it softly, as he might have patted the head of a child. It was not much, but still it was a good deal from him. To feel the lingering touch of her father's hand caressing her, even in so mild a way, was something quite surprising and strange to Miss Marjoribanks. She looked up at him almost with alarm, but he was just then turning away with his candle in his hand. And he seemed to have laid aside his gloom, and even smiled to himself as he went up-stairs. "If *she* had been the boy instead of that young ass," he said to himself. He could not have explained why he was more than ordinarily hard just then upon the innocent, far-distant Tom, who was unlucky, it is true, but not exactly an ass, after all. But somehow it struck the Doctor more than ever how great a loss it was to society and to herself that Lucilla was not "the boy." She could have continued, and perhaps extended, the practice, whereas just now it was quite possible that she might drop down into worsted-work and tea-parties like any other single woman—while Tom, who had carried off the family honours, and was "the boy" in this limited and unfruitful generation, was never likely to do anything to speak of, and would be a poor man if he were to live for a hundred years. Perhaps there was something else behind that made the Doctor's brow contract a little as he crossed the threshold of his chamber, into which, no more than into the recesses of his heart, no one ever penetrated; but it was the lighter idea of that comparison, which had no actual pain in it, but only a kind of humorous discontent, which was the last articulate thought in his mind as he went to his room and closed his door with a little sharpness, as he always did, upon the outside world.

Aunt Jemima, for her part, lingered a little with Lucilla downstairs. "My dear, I don't think my brother-in-law looks well tonight. I don't think Carlingford is so healthy as it is said to be.

If I were you, Lucilla, I would try and get your papa to take something," said Mrs John, with anxiety, "before he goes to bed."

"Dear aunt Jemima, he never takes anything. You forget he is a doctor," said Miss Marjoribanks. "It always puts him out when he has to go out in the evening; and he is sad about Mrs Chiley, though he would not say so." But nevertheless Lucilla knocked at his door when she went up-stairs. And the Doctor, though he did not open, growled within with a voice which reassured his dutiful daughter. "What should I want, do you think, but to be left quiet?" the Doctor said. And even Mrs John, who had waited at his door, with her candle in her hand, to hear the result, shrank within at the sound and was seen no more. And Miss Marjoribanks, too, went to her rest, with more than one subject of thought which kept her awake. In the first place, the Rector was popular in his way, and if he chose to call all his forces to rally round a penitent, there was no saying what might come of it; and then Lucilla could not help going back in the most illogical manner to her father's caress, and wondering what was the meaning of it. Meantime the snow fell heavily outside, and wrapped everything in a soft and secret whiteness. And amid the whiteness and darkness, the lamp burned steadily outside at the garden-gate, which pointed out the Doctor's door amid all the closed houses and dark garden-walls in Grange Lane—a kind of visible succour and help always at hand for those who were suffering. And though Dr Marjoribanks was not like a young man making a practice, but had perfect command of Carlingford, and was one of the richest men in it, it was well known in the town that the very poorest, if in extremity, in the depths of the wildest night that ever blew, would not seek help there in vain. The bell that had roused him when he was young, still hung near him in the silence of his closed-up house when he was old, and still could make him spring up, all self-possessed and ready, when the enemy Death had to be fought with. But that night the snow cushioned the wire outside, and even made white cornices and columns about the steady lamp, and the Doctor slept within, and no one disturbed him; for except Mrs Chiley and a few chronic patients, there was nothing particularly amiss in Carlingford, and then it was Dr Rider whom all the new people went to, the people who lived in the innumerable new houses at the other end of Carlingford, and had no hallowing tradition of the superior authority of Grange Lane.

CHAPTER XLIII.

The talk of this evening might not have been considered of any importance to speak of, but for the extraordinary and most unlooked-for event which startled all Carlingford next morning. Nobody could believe that it was true. Dr Marjoribanks's patients waited for him, and declared to their nurses that it was all a made-up story, and that he would come and prove that he was not dead. How could he be dead? He had been as well as he ever was that last evening. He had gone down Grange Lane in the snow, to see the poor old lady who was now sobbing in her bed, and saying it was all a mistake, and that it was she who ought to have died. But all those protestations were of no avail against the cold and stony fact which had frightened Thomas out of his senses, when he went to call the Doctor. He had died in the night without calling or disturbing anybody. He must have felt faint, it seemed, for he had got up and taken a little brandy, the remains of which still stood on the table by his bedside; but that was all that anybody could tell about it. They brought Dr Rider, of course; but all that he could do was to examine the strong, still frame—old, and yet not old enough to be weakly, or to explain such sudden extinction—which had ceased its human functions. And then the news swept over Carlingford like a breath of wind, though there was no wind even on that silent snowy day to carry the matter. Dr Marjoribanks was dead. It put the election out of people's heads, and even their own affairs for the time being; for had he not known all about the greater part of them—seen them come into the world and kept them in it—and put himself always in the breach when the pale Death approached that way? He had never made very much boast of his friendliness or been large in sympathetic expressions, but yet he had never flinched at any time, or deserted his patients for any consideration. Carlingford was sorry, profoundly sorry, with that true sorrow which is not so much for the person mourned as for the mourner's self, who feels a sense of something lost. The people said to themselves, Whom could they ever find who would know their constitutions so well, and who was to take care of So-and-so if he had another attack? To be sure Dr Rider was at hand, who felt a little agitated about it, and was conscious of the wonderful opening, and was very ready to answer, " I am here;" but a young doctor is different from an old one, and a living man all in commonplace health and comfort is not to be compared with a dead one, on the morning at least of his sudden ending. Thank heaven, when a life is ended there is always that hour or two remaining to set straight the defective balances, and do a hasty late justice to the dead, before the wave sweeps on over him and washes out the traces of his steps, and lets in the common crowd to make their thoroughfare over the grave.

"It cannot be the Doctor," Mrs Chiley said, sobbing in her bed, "or else it has been in mistake for me. He was always a healthy man, and never had anything the matter with him—and a great deal younger than we are, you know. If anything has happened to him it must have been in mistake for me," said the poor old lady, and she was so hysterical that they had to send for Dr Rider, and she was thus the first to begin to build the new world on the foundations of the old, little as she meant it. But for the moment everything was paralysed in Grange Lane, and canvassing came to a standstill, and nothing was discussed but Dr Marjoribanks—how he was dead, though nobody could or would believe it; and how Lucilla would be left, and who her trustees were, and how the place could ever get used to the want of him, or would ever look like itself again without his familiar presence. It was by way of relieving their minds from the horror of the idea, that the good people rushed into consultations what Lucilla would do. It took their minds a little off the ghastly imagination of that dark room with the snow on the window, and the late moonlight trying to get into the darkness, and the white rigid face inside, as he was said to have been found. It could not but make a terrible change to her—indeed, through her it could not but make a great change to everybody. The Doctor's house would, of course, be shut up, which had been the most hospitable house in Carlingford, and things would drop into the unsatisfactory state they used to be in before Miss Marjoribanks's time, and there would no longer be anybody to organise society. Such were the ideas the ladies of Grange Lane relapsed into by way of delivering themselves from the pain of their first realisation of what had happened. It would make a great change. Even the election and its anticipated joys could not but change character in some respects at least, and there would be nobody to make the best of them; and then the question was, What would Lucilla do? Would she have strength to "make an effort," as some people suggested; or would she feel not only her grief, but her downfall, and that she was now only a single woman, and sink into a private life, as some others were inclined to believe?

Inside the house, naturally, the state of affairs was sad enough. Lucilla, notwithstanding the many other things she had had to occupy her mind, was fond of her father, and the shock overwhelmed her for the moment. Though she was not the kind of woman to torture herself with thinking of things that she might have done, still at the first moment the idea that she ought not to have left him alone—that she should have sat up and watched or taken some extraordinary unusual precaution—was not to be driven away from her mind. The reign of reason was eclipsed in her as it often is in such an emergency. She said it was her fault in the first horror. "When I saw how he was looking, and how he was talking, I should never have left him," said Lucilla, which indeed was a very natural thing to say, but would have been an utterly impossible one to carry out, as she saw when she came to think of it. But she could not think of it just then. She did not think at all that first long snowy, troubled day, but went about the house, on the bedroom floor, wringing her hands like a creature distracted. "If I had only sat up," she said; and then she would recall the touch of his hand on her shoulder, which she seemed still to be feeling, and cry out, like all the rest of the world, that it could not be true. But, to be sure, that was a state of feeling that could not last long. There are events for which something higher than accident must be held accountable, were one ever so ready to take the burden of affairs on one's own shoulders; and Lucilla knew, when she came to herself, that if she had watched ever so long or so closely, that could have had no effect upon the matter. After a while the bewildering sense of her own changed position began to come upon her, and roused her up into that feverish and unnatural activity of thought which, in some minds, is the inevitable reaction after the unaccustomed curb and shock of grief. When she had got used to that dreadful certainty about her father, and had suddenly come with a leap to the knowledge that she was not to blame, and could not help it, and that though *he* was gone, *she* remained, it is no censure upon Lucilla to say that her head became immediately full of a horror and confusion of thoughts, an involuntary stir and bustle of plans and projects, which she did all she could to put down, but which would return and overwhelm her whether she chose it or not. She could not help asking herself what her new position was, thinking it over, so strangely free and new and unlimited as it seemed. And it must be recollected that Miss Marjoribanks was a woman of very active mind and great energies, too old to take up a girl's fancy that all was over because she had encountered a natural grief on her passage, and too young not to see a long future still before her. She kept her room, as was to be expected, and saw nobody, and only moved the household and superintended the arrangements in a muffled way through Thomas, who was an old servant, and knew "the ways" of the house; but notwithstanding her seclusion and her honest sorrow, and her perfect observance of all the ordinary restraints of the moment, it would be wrong to omit all mention of this feverish bustle of thinking which came into Lucilla's mind in her solitude. Of all that she had to bear, it was the thing that vexed and irritated and distressed her the most—as if, she said to herself indignantly, she ought to have been able to think of anything! And the chances are that Lucilla, for sheer duty's sake, would have said, if anybody had asked, that of course she had not thought of anything as yet; without being aware that the mere shock, and horror, and profound commotion had a great deal more to do than anything else in producing that fluttering crowd of busy, vexatious speculations which had come, without any will of hers, into her heart.

It looked a dreadful change in one way as she looked at it without wishing to look at it in the solitude of her own room, where the blinds were all down, and the snow sometimes came with a little thump against the window, and where it was so dark that it was a comfort when night came, and the lamp could be lighted. So far as Carlingford was concerned, it would be almost as bad for Miss Marjoribanks as if she were her father's widow instead of his daughter. To keep up a position of social importance in a single woman's house, unless, as she had herself lightly said so short a time since, she were awfully rich, would be next to impossible. All that gave importance to the centre of society—the hospitable table, the open house—had come to an end with the Doctor. Things could no more be as they had once been, in that respect at least. She might stay in the house, and keep up to the furthest extent possible to her its old traditions; but even to the utmost limit to which Lucilla could think it right to go it could never be the same. This consciousness kept gleaming upon her as she sat in the dull daylight behind the closed blinds, with articles of mourning piled about everywhere, and the grey dimness getting into her very eyes, and her mind distressed by the consciousness that she ought to have been unable to think; and the sadness of the prospect altogether was enough to stir up a reaction, in spite of herself, in Miss Marjoribanks's mind.

And on the other side she would no doubt be very well off, and could go wherever she liked, and had no limit, except what was right and proper and becoming, to what she might please to do. She might go abroad if she liked, which perhaps is the first idea of the modern English mind when anything happens to it, and settle wherever she pleased, and arrange her mode of existence as seemed good in her own eyes. She would be an heiress in a moderate way, and aunt Jemima was by this time absolutely at her disposal, and could be taken anywhere; and at Lucilla's age it was quite impossible to predict what might not happen to a woman in such a position. When these fairer possibilities gleamed into Lucilla's mind, it would be difficult to describe the anger and self-disgust with which she reproached herself—for perhaps it was the first time that she had consciously failed in maintaining a state of mind becoming the occasion; and though nobody but herself knew of it, the pain of the accusation was acute and bitter. But how could Miss Marjoribanks help it?— the mind travels so much quicker than anything else, and goes so far, and makes its expeditions in such subtle, stealthy ways. She might begin by thinking of her dear papa, and yet before she could dry her eyes might be off in the midst of one of these bewildering speculations. For everything was certain now so far as he was concerned; and everything was so uncertain, and full of such unknown issues, for herself. Thus the dark days before the funeral passed by—and everybody was very kind. Dr Marjoribanks was one of the props of the place, and all Carlingford bestirred itself to do him the final honours; and all her friends conspired how to save Lucilla from all possible trouble, and help her over the trial; and to see how much he was respected was the greatest of all possible comforts to her, as she said.

Thus it was that among the changes that everybody looked for, there occurred all at once this change which was entirely unexpected, and put everything else out of mind for the moment. For to tell the truth, Dr Marjoribanks was one of the men who, according to external appearance, need never have died. There was nothing about him that wanted to be set right, no sort of loss, or failure, or misunderstanding, so far as anybody could see. An existence in which he could have his friends to dinner every week, and a good house, and good wine, and a very good table, and nothing particular to put him out of his way, seemed in fact the very ideal of the best life for the Doctor. There was nothing in him that seemed to demand anything better, and it was confusing to try to follow him into that which, no doubt, must be in all its fundamentals a very different kind of world. He was a just man and a good man in his way, and had been kind to many people in his lifetime—but still he did not seem to have that need of another rectifying, completer existence which most men have. There seemed no reason why he should die—a man who was so well contented with this lower region in which many of us fare badly, and where so few of us are contented. This was a fact which exercised a very confusing influence, even when they themselves were not aware of it, on many people's minds. It was hard to think of him under any other circumstances, or identify him with angels and spirits—which feeling on the whole made the regret for him a more poignant sort of regret.

And they buried him with the greatest signs of respect. People from twenty miles off sent their carriages, and all the George Street people shut their shops, and there was very little business done all day. Mr Cavendish and Mr Ashburton walked side by side at the funeral, which was an affecting sight to see; and if anything more could have been done to show their respect which was not done, the corporation of Carlingford would have been sorry for it. And the snow still lay deep in all the corners, though it had been trampled down all about the Doctor's house, where the lamp was not lighted now of nights; for what was the use of lighting the lamp, which was a kind of lighthouse in its way, and meant to point out succour and safety for the neighbours, when the physician himself was lying beyond all hope of succour or aid? And all the Grange Lane people retired in a sympathetic, awe-stricken way, and decided, or at least the ladies did, to see Lucilla next day, if she was able to see them, and to find out whether she was going to make an effort, or what she meant to do. And Mrs Chiley was so much better that she was able to be up a little in the evening, though she scarcely could forgive herself, and still could not help thinking that it was she who had really been sent for, and that the Doctor had been taken in mistake. And as for Lucilla, she sat in her room and cried, and thought of her father's hand upon her shoulder—that last unusual caress which was more touching to think of than a world of words. He had been fond of her and proud of her, and at the last moment he had showed it. And by times she seemed to feel again that lingering touch, and cried as if her heart would break: and yet, for all that, she could not keep her thoughts steady, nor prevent them from wandering to all kinds of profane out-of-door matters, and to considerations of the future, and estimates of her own position. It wounded her sadly to feel herself in such an inappropriate state of mind, but she could not help it; and then the want of natural light and air oppressed her sorely, and she longed for the evening, which felt a little more natural, and thought that at last she might have a long talk with aunt Jemima, who was a kind of refuge in her present loneliness, and gave her a means of escape at the same time from all this bustle and commotion of unbecoming thoughts.

This was enough surely for any one to have to encounter at one time; but that very night another rumour began to murmur through Carlingford—a rumour more bewildering, more incredible still, than that of the Doctor's death, which the town had been obliged to confirm and acknowledge, and put its seal to. When the thing was first mentioned, everybody (who could find it in their heart to laugh) laughed loud in the face of the first narrator with mingled scepticism and indignation. They asked him what he meant by it, and ridiculed and scoffed at him to his face. "Lucilla will be the richest woman in Grange Lane," people said; "everybody in Carlingford knows that." But after this statement had been made, the town began to listen. It was obliged to listen, for other witnesses came in to confirm the story. It never might have been found out while the Doctor lived, for he had a great practice, and made a great deal of money; but now that he was dead, nothing could be hid. He was dead, and he had made an elaborate will, which was all as just and righteous as a will could be; but after the will was read, it was found out that everything named in it had disappeared like a bubble. Instead of being the richest, Dr Marjoribanks was one of the poorest men in Carlingford, when he shut his door behind him on that snowy night. It was a revelation which took the town perfectly by storm, and startled everybody out of their senses. Lucilla's plans, which she thought so wicked, went out all of a sudden, in a certain dull amaze and dismay, to which no words could give any expression. Such was the second inconceivable reverse of fortune which happened to Miss Marjoribanks, more unexpected, more incomprehensible still than the other, in the very midst of her most important activities and hopes.

CHAPTER XLIV.

WHEN the first whisper of the way in which she was—as people say—"left," reached Lucilla, her first feeling was incredulity. It was conveyed to her by aunt Jemima, who came to her in her room after the funeral with a face blanched with dismay. Miss Marjoribanks took it for grief; and, though she did not look for so much feeling from Mrs John, was pleased and comforted that her aunt should really lament her poor papa. It was a compliment which, in the softened and sorrowful state of Lucilla's mind, went to her heart. Aunt Jemima came up and kissed her in a hasty excited way, which showed genuine and spontaneous emotion, and was not like the solemn pomp with which sympathising friends generally embrace a mourner; and then she made Lucilla sit down by the fire and held her hands. "My poor child," said aunt Jemima—"my poor, dear, sacrificed child! you know, Lucilla, how fond I am of you, and you can always come to me——"

"Thank you, dear aunt Jemima," said Miss Marjoribanks, though she was a little puzzled. "You are the only relative I have, and I knew you would not forsake me. What should I do without you at such a time? I am sure it is what dear papa would have wished——"

"Lucilla," cried Mrs John, impulsively, "I know it is natural you should cry for your father; but when you know all,—you that never knew what it was to be without money—that never were straitened even, or obliged to give up things, like most other young women. Oh, my dear, they said I was to prepare you, but how can I prepare you? I feel as if I never could forgive my brother-in-law; that he should bring you up like this, and then——"

"What is it?" said Miss Marjoribanks, drying her tears. "If it is anything new, tell me, but don't speak so of—of—— What is it? say it right out."

"Lucilla," said aunt Jemima, solemnly, "you think you have a great deal of courage, and now is your time to show it. He has left you without a farthing—he that was always thought to be so rich. It is quite true what I am saying. He has gone and died and left nothing, Lucilla. Now I have told you; and oh, my poor, dear, injured child," cried Mrs John, with fervour, "as long as I have a home there will be room in it for you."

But Lucilla put her aunt away softly when she was about to fall upon her neck. Miss Marjoribanks was struck dumb; her heart seemed to stop beating for the moment. "It is quite impossible—it cannot be true," she said, and gave a gasp to recover her breath. Then Mrs John came down upon her with facts, proving it to be true—showing how Dr Marjoribanks's money was invested, and how it had been lost. She made a terrible muddle of it, no doubt, but Lucilla was not very clear about business details any more than her aunt, and she did not move nor say a word while the long, involved, endless narrative went on. She kept saying it was impossible in her heart for half of the time, and then she crept nearer the fire and shivered, and said nothing even to herself, and did not even seem to listen, but knew that it must be true. It would be vain to attempt to say that it was not a terrible blow to Lucilla; her strength was weakened already by grief and solitude and want of food, for she could not find it in her heart to go on eating her ordinary meals as if nothing had happened; and all of a sudden she felt the cold seize her, and drew closer and closer to the fire. The thoughts which she had been thinking in spite of herself, and for which she had so greatly condemned herself, went out with a sudden distinctness, as if it had been a lamp going out and leaving the room in darkness, and a sudden sense of utter gloom and cold and bewildering uncertainty came over Lucilla. When she lifted her eyes from the fire, into which she had been gazing, it almost surprised her to find herself still in this warm room where there was every appliance for comfort, and where her entire wardrobe of new mourning—everything, as aunt Jemima said, that a woman could desire—was piled up on the bed. It was impossible that she could be a penniless creature, left on her own resources, without father or supporter or revenue; and yet—good heavens! could it be true?

"If it is true, aunt Jemima," said Lucilla, "I must try to bear it; but my poor head feels all queer. I'd rather not think any more about it to-night."

"How can you help thinking about it, Lucilla?" cried Mrs John. "I can think of nothing else; and I am not so much concerned as you."

Upon which Lucilla rose and kissed aunt Jemima, though her head was all confused and she had noises in her ears. "I don't think we are much like each other, you know," she said. "Did you hear how Mrs Chiley was? I am sure she will be very sorry;" and with that Miss Marjoribanks softened, and felt a little comforted, and cried again—not for the money, but for her father. "If you are going down-stairs, I think I will come down to tea, aunt Jemima," she said. But after Mrs John had gone away full of wonder at her philosophy, Lucilla drew close to the fire again and took her head between her hands and tried to think what it meant. Could it be true? Instead of the heiress, in a good position, who could go abroad or anywhere, and do anything she liked, was it possible that she was only a penniless single woman with nobody to look to, and nothing to live on? Such an extraordinary incomprehensible revolution might well make any one feel giddy. The solid house and the comfortable room, and her own sober brain, which was not in the way of being put off its balance, seemed to turn round and round as she looked into the fire. Lucilla was not one to throw the blame upon her father, as Mrs John had done. On the contrary she was sorry, profoundly sorry for him, and made such a picture to herself of what his feelings must have been, when he went into his room that night and knew that all his hard-earned fortune was gone, that it made her weep the deepest tears for him that she had yet shed. "Poor papa!" she said to herself; and as she was not much given to employing her imagination in this way, and realising the feeling of others, the effect was all the greater now. If he had but told her, and put off a share of the burden from his own shoulders on to hers who could have borne it! but the Doctor had never done justice to Lucilla's qualities. This, amid her general sense of confusion and dizziness and insecurity, was the only clear thought that struck Miss Marjoribanks; and that it was very cold and must be freezing outside; and how did the poor people manage who had not all her present advantages? She tried to put away this revelation from her, as she had said to aunt Jemima, and keep it for a little at arm's length, and get a night's rest in the mean time, and so be able to bring a clear head to the contemplation of it to-morrow, which was the most judicious thing to do. But when the mind has been stimulated by such a shock, Solomon himself, one would suppose, could scarcely, however clearly he might perceive what was best, take the judicious passive way. When Lucilla got up from where she was crouching before the fire, she felt so giddy that she could scarcely stand. Her head was all queer, as she had said, and she had a singing in her ears. She herself seemed to have changed along with her position. An hour or two before, she could have answered for her own steadiness and self-possession in almost any circumstances, but now the blood seemed to be running a race in her veins, and the strangest noises hummed in her ears. She felt ashamed of her weakness, but she could not help it; and then she was weak with grief and excitement and comparative fasting, which told for something, probably, in her inability to bear so unlooked-for a blow.

But Miss Marjoribanks thought it was best to go down to the drawing-room for tea, as she had said. To see everything just as it had been, utterly indifferent and unconscious of what had happened, made her cry, and relieved her giddiness by reviving her grief; and then the next minute a bewildering wonder seized her as to what would become of this drawing-room, the scene of her triumphs—who would live in it, and whom the things would go to—which made her sick, and brought back the singing in her ears. But on the whole she took tea very quietly with aunt Jemima, who kept breaking into continual snatches of lamentation, but was always checked by Lucilla's composed looks. If she had not heard this extraordinary news, which made the world turn round with her, Miss Marjoribanks would have felt that soft hush of exhaustion and grief subdued which, when the grief is not too urgent, comes after all is over; and even now she felt a certain comfort in the warm firelight and the change out of her own room—where she had been living shut up, with the blinds down, and the black dresses everywhere about, for so many dreary days.

John Brown, who had charge of Dr Marjoribanks's affairs, came next day and explained everything to Lucilla. The lawyer had had one short interview with his client after the news came, and Dr Marjoribanks had borne it like a man. His face had changed a little, and he had sat down, which he was not in the habit of doing, and drawn a kind of shivering long breath; and then he had said, "Poor Lucilla!" to himself. This was all Mr Brown could say about the effect the shock had on the Doctor. And there was something in this very scanty information which gave Lucilla a new pang of sorrow and consolation. "And he patted me on the shoulder that last night," she said, with tender tears; and felt she had never loved her father so well in all her life—which is one of the sweeter uses of death which many must have experienced, but which belonged to a more exquisite and penetrating kind of emotion than was common to Lucilla.

"I thought he looked a little broken when he went out," said Mr Brown, "but full of pluck and spirit, as he always was. 'I am making a good deal of money, and I *may* live long enough to lay by a little still,' were the last words he said to me. I remember he put a kind of emphasis on the *may*. Perhaps he knew he was not so strong as he looked. He was a good man, Miss Marjoribanks, and there is nobody that has not some kind thing to tell of him," said the lawyer, with a certain moisture in his eyes; for there was nobody in Carlingford who did not miss the old Doctor, and John Brown was very tender-hearted in his way.

"But nobody can know what a good father he was," said Lucilla, with a sob; and she meant it with all her heart, thinking chiefly of his hand on her shoulder that last night, and of the "Poor Lucilla!" in John Brown's office; though, after all, perhaps, it was not chiefly as a tender father that Dr Marjoribanks shone, though he gave his daughter all she wanted or asked for. Her grief was so true, and so little tinctured by any of that indignation over the unexpected loss, which aunt Jemima had not been able to conceal, that John Brown was quite touched, and felt his heart warm to Lucilla. He explained it all very fully to her when she was composed enough to understand him; and as he went through all the details the giddiness came back, and once more Miss Marjoribanks felt the world running round, and heard his statement through the noises in her ears. All this settled down, however, into a certain distinctness as John Brown, who was very clear-headed and good at making a concise statement, went on; and gradually the gyrations became slower and slower, and the great universe became solid once more, and held to its moorings under Lucilla's feet, and she ceased to hear that supernatural hum and buzz. The vague shadows of chaos and ruin dispersed, and through them she saw once more the real aspect of things. She was not quite penniless. There was the house, which was a very good house, and some little corners and scraps of money in the Funds, which were Lucilla's very own, and could not be lost; and last of all there was the business—the best practice in Carlingford, and entire command of Grange Lane.

"But what does that matter?" said Lucilla; "if poor papa had retired indeed, as I used to beg him to do, and parted with it—— But everybody has begun to send for Dr Rider already," she said, in an aggrieved voice; and then for the first time John Brown remembered, to his confusion, that there was once said to be "something between" Miss Marjoribanks and Dr Rider; which complicated the affair in the most uncomfortable way.

"Yes," he said, "and of course that would make it much more difficult to bring in another man; but Rider is a very honourable young fellow, Miss Marjoribanks——"

"He is not so very young," said Lucilla. "He is quite as old as I am, though no one ever would think so. I am sure he is honourable, but what has that to do with it? And I do think Mrs Chiley might have done without—anybody else: for a day or two, considering when it was——"

And here she stopped to cry, unreasonably, but yet very naturally; for it did feel hard that in the house to which Dr Marjoribanks's last visit had been paid, another doctor should have been called in next day.

"What I meant to say," said John Brown, "was, that Dr Rider, though he is not rich, and could not pay a large sum of money down, would be very glad to make some arrangement. He is very anxious about it, and he seemed himself to think that if you knew his circumstances you would not be disinclined to—— But as I did not at all know——"

Lucilla caught, as it were, and met, and forced to face her, her informant's embarrassed, hesitating look. "You say this," said Miss Marjoribanks, "because people used to say there was something between us, and you think I may have some feeling about it. But there never was anything between us. Anybody with a quarter of an eye could have seen that he was going out of his senses about that little Australian girl. And I am rather fond of men that are in love—it shows they have some good in them. But it is dreadful to talk of such things now," said Lucilla, with a sigh of self-reproach. "If Dr Rider has any arrangement to propose, I should like to give him the preference, please. You see they have begun to send for him already in Grange Lane."

"I will do whatever you think proper," said John Brown, who was rather scared, and very much impressed by Miss Marjoribanks's candour. Dr Rider had been the first love of Mr Brown's own wife, and the lawyer had a curious kind of satisfaction in thinking that this silly young fellow had thus lost two admirable women, and that probably the little Australian was equally inferior to Miss Marjoribanks and Mrs Brown. He ought to have been grateful that Dr Rider had left the latter lady to his own superior discrimination—and so he was; and yet it gave him a certain odd satisfaction to think that the Doctor was not so happy as he might have been. He went away fully warranted to receive Dr Rider's proposition, and even, to a certain extent, to decide upon it—and Lucilla threw herself back in her chair in the silent drawing-room, from which aunt Jemima had discreetly withdrawn, and began to think over the reality of her position as she now saw it for the first time.

The sense of bewildering revolution and change was over; for, strangely enough, the greater a change is the more easily the mind, after the first shock, accepts and gets accustomed to it. It was over, and the world felt steady once more under Lucilla's feet, and she sat down, not precisely amid the ruins of her happiness, but still in the presence of many an imagination overthrown, to look at her real position. It was not, after all, utter poverty, misery, and destitution, as at the first glance she had believed. According to what John Brown had said, and a rapid calculation which Lucilla had herself made in passing, something approaching two hundred a-year would be left to her —just a small single woman's revenue, as she thought to herself. Two hundred a-year! All at once there came into Miss Marjoribanks's mind a sudden vision of the two Miss Ravenswoods, who had lived in that pretty set of rooms over Elsworthy's shop, facing into Grange Lane, and who had kept a lady's maid, and asked the best people in the place to tea, upon a very similar income, and how their achievements had been held up to everybody as a model of what genteel economy could do. She thought of them, and her heart sank within her; for it was not in Lucilla's nature to live without a sphere, nor to disjoin herself from her fellow-creatures, nor to give up entirely the sovereign position she had held for so many years. Whatever she might ultimately do, it was clear that, in the mean time, she could not make up her mind to any such giving up of the battle as that. And then there was the house. She might let it to the Riders, and add probably another hundred a-year to her income; for though it was an excellent house, and worth more than a hundred a-year, still there was no competition for houses in Grange Lane, and the new Doctor was the only probable tenant. And, to tell the truth, though Lucilla was very reasonable, it went to her heart at the present moment to think

of letting the house to the new Doctor, and having the patients
come as usual, and the lamp lighted as of old, and nothing
changed except the central figure of all. She ought to have
been above such sentimental ideas when a whole hundred pounds
a-year was in question; but she was not, which of itself was a
strange phenomenon. If she could have made up her mind to
that, there were a great many things that she might have done.
She might still have gone abroad, and to some extent taken a
limited share in what was going on in some section of English
society on the Continent. Or she might have gone to one of
the mild centres of a similar kind of life in England. But such
a prospect did not offer many attractions to Miss Marjoribanks.
If she had been rich, it would have been different. Thus there
gradually dawned upon her the germ of the plan she ultimately
adopted, and which was the only one that commended itself to
her feelings. Going away was expensive and troublesome at
the best; and even at Elsworthy's, if she could have made up
her mind to such an expedient, she would have been charged a
pound a-week for the rooms alone, not to speak of all kinds of
extras, and never having the satisfaction of feeling yourself in
your own place. Under all the circumstances, it was impressed
upon Lucilla's mind that her natural course was to stay still
where she was, and make no change. Why should she make
any change? The house was her own, and did not cost anything,
and if Nancy would but stand by her and one good maid——
It was a venture; but still Lucilla felt as if she might be equal
to it. Though she was no mathematician, Miss Marjoribanks
was very clever at mental arithmetic in a practical sort of way.
She put down lines upon lines of figures in her head while she
sat musing in her chair, and worked them out with wonderful
skill and speed and accuracy. And the more she thought of it,
the more it seemed to her that this was the thing to do. Why
should she retreat and leave her native soil and the neighbourhood of all her friends because she was poor and in trouble?
Lucilla was not ashamed of being poor—nor even frightened by
it, now that she understood what it was—any more than she
would have been frightened, after the first shock, had her
poverty even been much more absolute. She was standing
alone at this moment as upon a little island of as yet undisturbed seclusion and calm, and she knew very well that outside
a perfect sea of good advice would surge round her as soon as
she was visible. In these circumstances Lucilla took by instinct
the only wise course: she made up her mind there and then

with a perfect unanimity which is seldom to be gained when counsellors are admitted. And what she decided upon, as was to be expected from her character, was not to fly from her misfortune and the scene of it, but to confront fate and take up her lawful burden and stay still in her own house. It was the wisest and the easiest, and at the same time the most heroic course to adopt, and she knew beforehand that it was one which would be approved of by nobody. All this Lucilla steadily faced and considered and made up her mind to while she sat alone; although silence and solitude and desolation seemed to have suddenly come in and taken possession all around her of the once gay and brilliant room.

She had just made her final decision when she was rejoined by her aunt, who, everybody said, was at this trying moment like a mother to Lucilla. Yet aunt Jemima, too, had changed a little since her brother-in-law's death. She was very fond of Miss Marjoribanks, and meant every word she had said about giving her a home, and still meant it. But she did not feel so certain now as she had done about Tom's love for his cousin, nor at all anxious to have him come home just at this moment; and for another thing, she had got a way of prowling about the house and looking at the furniture in a speculative, auctioneering sort of way. "It must be all sold, of course," aunt Jemima had said to herself, "and I may as well look what things would suit me; there is a little chiffonier that I have always wanted for my drawing-room, and Lucilla would like to see a few of the old things about her, poor dear." With this idea Mrs John gave herself a great deal of unnecessary fatigue, and gave much offence to the servants by making pilgrimages all over the house, turning up at the most unlikely places and poking about in the least frequented rooms. It was a perfectly virtuous and even amiable thing to do, for it was better, as she reasoned, that they should go to her than to a stranger, and it would be nice for Lucilla to feel that she had some of the old things about her; but then such delicate motives are seldom appreciated by the homely critics down-stairs.

It was with something of this same air that she came into the drawing-room, where Lucilla was. She could not help laying her hand in a suggestive sort of a way on a small table which she had to pass, as if she were saying to herself (as indeed she was saying), "The veneer has been broken off at that side, and the foot is mended; it will bring very little; and yet it looks well when you don't look too close." Such were the ideas with which aunt Jemima's mind was filled. But yet she came forward with a great deal of sympathy and curiosity, and forgot about the furniture in presence of her afflicted niece.

"Did he tell you anything, Lucilla?" said Mrs John; "of course he must have told you something—but anything satisfactory, I mean."

"I don't know if you can call it satisfactory," said Lucilla, with a sudden rush of softer thoughts; "but it was a comfort to hear it. He told me something about dear papa, aunt Jemima. After he had heard of *that*, you know—all that he said was, Poor Lucilla! And don't you remember how he put his hand on my shoulder that last night? I am so—so—glad he did it," sobbed Miss Marjoribanks. It may be supposed it was an abrupt transition from her calculations; but after all it was only a different branch of the same subject; and Lucilla in all her life had never before shed such poignant and tender tears.

"He might well say, Poor Lucilla!" said Mrs John— "brought up as you have been, my dear; and did not you hear anything more important?—I mean, more important in a worldly point of view," aunt Jemima added, correcting herself; "of course, it must be the greatest comfort to hear something about your poor papa."

And then Lucilla unfolded John Brown's further particulars to her surprised hearer. Mrs John lived upon a smallish income herself, and she was not so contemptuous of the two hundred a-year. "And the house," she said—"the house would bring you in another hundred, Lucilla. The Riders, I am sure, would take it directly, and perhaps a great part of the furniture too. Three hundred would not be so bad for a single woman. Did you say anything about the furniture, my dear?" aunt Jemima added, half regretfully, for she did feel that she would be sorry to lose that chiffonier.

"I think I shall stay in the house," said Lucilla; "you may think it silly, aunt Jemima, but I was born in it, and——"

"Stay in the house!" Mrs John said, with a gasp. She did not think it silly, but simple madness, and so she told her niece. If Lucilla could not make up her mind to Elsworthy's, there was Brighton and Bath and Cheltenham, and a hundred other places where a single woman might be very comfortable on three hundred a-year. And to lose a third part of her income for a piece of sentiment was so utterly unlike any conception aunt Jemima had ever formed of her niece. It *was* unlike Miss

Marjoribanks; but there are times of life when even the most reasonable people are inconsistent. Lucilla, though she felt it was open to grave criticism, felt only more confirmed in her resolution by her aunt's remarks. She heard a voice aunt Jemima could not hear, and that voice said, Stay!

CHAPTER XLV.

It must be allowed that Lucilla's decision caused very general surprise in Carlingford, where people had been disposed to think that she would be rather glad, now that things were so changed, to get away. To be sure it was not known for some time; but everybody's idea was that, being thus left alone in the world, and in circumstances so reduced, Miss Marjoribanks naturally would go to live with somebody. Perhaps with her aunt, who had something, though she was not rich; perhaps, after a little, to visit about among her friends, of whom she had so many. Nobody doubted that Lucilla would abdicate at once, and a certain uneasy, yet delicious, sense of freedom had already stolen into the hearts of some of the ladies in Grange Lane. They lamented, it is true, the state of chaos into which everything would fall, and the dreadful loss Miss Marjoribanks would be to society; but still, freedom is a noble thing, and Lucilla's subjects contemplated their emancipation with a certain guilty delight. It was, at the same time, a most fertile subject of discussion in Carlingford, and gave rise to all those lively speculations and consultations, and oft-renewed comparing of notes, which take the place of bets in the feminine community. The Carlingford ladies as good as betted upon Lucilla, whether she would go with her aunt, or pay Mrs Beverley a visit at the Deanery, or retire to Mount Pleasant for a little, where those good old Miss Blounts were so fond of her. Each of these opinions had its backers, if it is not profane to say so; and the discussion which of them Miss Marjoribanks would choose waxed very warm. It almost put the election out of people's heads; and indeed the election had been sadly damaged in interest and social importance by the sad and most unexpected event which had just happened in Grange Lane.

But when the fact was really known, it would be difficult to describe the sense of guilt and horror which filled many innocent bosoms. The bound of freedom had been premature—liberty and equality had not come yet, notwithstanding that too early unwise *élan* of republican satisfaction. It was true that she was in deep mourning, and that for a year, at least, society must be left to its own devices; and it was true, also, that she was poor—which might naturally be supposed a damper upon her energies—but, at the same time, Carlingford knew its Lucilla. As long as she remained in Grange Lane, even though retired and in crape, the constitutional monarch was still present among her subjects; and nobody could usurp her place or show that utter indifference to her regulations which some revolutionaries had dreamed of. Such an idea would have gone direct in the face of the British Constitution, and the sense of the community would have been dead against it. But everybody who had speculated upon her proceedings disapproved of Lucilla in her most unlooked-for resolution. Some could not think how she could bear it, staying on there when everything was so changed; and some said it was a weakness they could never have believed to exist in her; and some—for there are spiteful people everywhere—breathed the names of Cavendish and Ashburton, the rival candidates, and hinted that Miss Marjoribanks had something in her mind to justify her lingering. If Lucilla had not been supported by a conscious sense of rectitude, she must have broken down before this universal disapprobation. Not a soul in the world except one supported her in her resolution, and that was perhaps, of all others, the one least likely to be able to judge.

And it was not for want of opportunity to go elsewhere. Aunt Jemima, as has been seen, did not lose an instant in offering the shelter of her house to her niece; and Mrs Beverley wrote the longest, kindest, most incoherent letter, begging her dear Lucilla to come to her immediately for a long visit, and adding, that though she had to go out a good deal into society, she needn't mind, for that everything she could think of would be done to make her comfortable; to which Dr Beverley himself, who was now a dean, added an equally kind postscript, begging Miss Marjoribanks to make her home at the Deanery "until she saw how things were to be." "He would have found me a place, perhaps," Lucilla said, when she folded up the letter—and this was a terrible mode of expression to the genteel ears of Mrs John.

"I wish you would not use such words, my dear," said aunt

Jemima; "even if you had been as poor as you thought, my house would always have been a home for you. Thank heaven I have enough for both; you never needed to have thought, under any circumstances, of taking a—a situation. It is a thing I could never have consented to,"—which was a very handsome thing of aunt Jemima to say.

"Thank you, aunt," said Lucilla, but she sighed; for, though it was very kind, what was Miss Marjoribanks to have done with herself in such a dowager establishment? And then Colonel Chiley came in, who had also his proposal to make.

"*She* sent me," the Colonel said; "it's been a sad business for us all, Lucilla; I don't know when I have felt anything more; and as for her, you know, she has never held up her head since——"

"Dear Mrs Chiley!" Miss Marjoribanks said, unable to resist the old affection; "and yet I heard she had sent for Dr Rider directly," Lucilla added. She knew it was quite natural, and perhaps quite necessary, but then it did seem hard that his own friends should be the first to replace her dear papa.

"It was I did that," said the Colonel. "What was a man to do? I was horribly cut up, but I could not stand and see her making herself worse; and I said you had too much sense to mind——"

"So I ought," said Lucilla, with penitence, "but when I remembered where he was last, the very last place——"

It was hard upon the Colonel to stand by and see a woman cry. It was a thing he could never stand, as he had always said to his wife. He took the poker, which was his favourite resource, and made one of his tremendous dashes at the fire, to give Lucilla time to recover herself, and then he turned to aunt Jemima, who sat pensively by—

"*She* sent me," said the Colonel, who did not think his wife needed any other name—"not that I would not have come of my own accord; we want Lucilla to go to us, you see. I don't know what plans she may have been making, but we're both very fond of her—she knows that. I think, if you have not settled upon anything, the best that Lucilla can do is to come to us. She'll be the same as at home, and always somebody to look after her——"

The old Colonel was standing before the fire, wavering a little on his long unsteady old legs, and looking wonderfully well preserved, and old and feeble; and Lucilla, though she was in mourning, was so full of life and force in her way. It was a curious sort of protection to offer her, and yet it was real protection, and love and succour, though, heaven knows! it might not perhaps last out the year.

"I am sure, Colonel Chiley, it is a very kind offer," said aunt Jemima, "and I would have been thankful if she could have made up her mind to go with me. But I must say she has taken a very queer notion into her head—a thing I should never have expected from Lucilla—she says she will stay here."

"Here?—ah—eh—what does she mean by here?" said the Colonel.

"*Here*, Colonel Chiley, in this great big melancholy house. I have been thinking about it, and talking about it till my head goes round and round. Unless she were to take Inmates," said aunt Jemima, in a resigned and doleful voice. As for the Colonel he was petrified, and for a long time had not a word to say.

"*Here!*—By Jove, I think she must have lost her senses," said the old soldier. "Why, Lucilla, I—I thought—wasn't there something about the money being lost? You couldn't keep up this house under a—fifteen hundred a-year at least; the Doctor spent a mint of money;—you must be going out of your senses. And to have all the sick people coming, and the bell ringing of nights. Bless my soul! it would kill anybody," said Colonel Chiley. "Put on your bonnet, and come out with me; shutting her up here, and letting her cry, and so forth—I don't say it ain't natural—I'm terribly cut up myself whenever I think of it; but it's been too much for her head," said the Colonel, with anxiety and consternation mingling in his face.

"Unless she were to take Inmates, you know," said aunt Jemima, in a sepulchral voice. There was something in the word that seemed to carry out to a point of reality much beyond anything he had dreamt of, the suggestion Colonel Chiley had just made.

"Inmates! Lord bless my soul! what do you mean, ma'am?" said the old soldier. "Lucilla, put on your bonnet directly, and come and have a little fresh air. She'll soon be an inmate herself if we leave her here," the Colonel said. They were all very sad and grave, and yet it was a droll scene; and then the old hero offered Lucilla his arm, and led her to the door. "You'll find me in the hall as soon as you are ready," he said, in tones half gruff, half tender, and was glad to go down-stairs, though it was cold, and put on his greatcoat with the aid of Thomas, and stand warming the tips of his boots at the hall fire. As for Lucilla, she obeyed him without a word; and it was with his unsteady but kind old arm to lean upon that she first saw how the familiar world looked through the mist of this strange change that had come over it, and through the blackness of her crape veil.

But though she succeeded in satisfying her friends that she had made up her mind, she did not secure their approval. There were so many objections to her plan. "If you had been rich even, I don't think I should have approved of it, Lucilla," Mrs Chiley said, with tears; "and I think we could have made you happy here." So the good old lady spoke, looking round her pretty room, which was so warm and cheery and bright, and where the Colonel, neat and precise as if he had come out of a box, was standing, poking the fire. It looked all very solid and substantial, and yet it was as unstable as any gossamer that the careless passenger might brush away. The two good people were so old that they had forgotten to remember they were old. But neither did Lucilla think of that. This was really what she thought and partly said—

"I am in my own house, that wants no expense nor changing, and Nancy is getting old, and does not mind standing by me. And it is not so much trouble after all keeping everything nice when there is no gentleman coming in, and nothing else to do. And, besides, I don't mean to be Lucilla Marjoribanks for ever and ever." This was the general scope, without going into all the details, of what Lucilla said.

But, at the same time, though she was so happy as not to be disturbed in her decision, or made uncomfortable, either by lamentation or remonstrance, and had no doubt in her mind that she was doing right, it was disagreeable to Miss Marjoribanks to go thus in the face of all her friends. She went home by herself, and the house did look dreary from the outside. It was just as it had always been, for none of the servants were dismissed as yet, nor any external change made; but still a look as if it had fallen asleep—a look as if it too had died somehow, and only pretended to be a house and home—was apparent, in the aspect of the place; and when the servants were gone, and nobody remained except Lucilla and her faithful Nancy, and a young maid—which must be the furthest limit of Miss Marjoribanks's household, and difficult enough to maintain upon two hundred a-year—what would it look like? This thought was more discouraging than any remonstrances; and it was with a heavy heart that Lucilla re-entered her solitary house. She told Thomas to follow her up-stairs; and when she sank, tired, into a chair, and put up her veil before commencing to speak to him, it was all she could do to keep from crying. The depressing influences of this sad week had told so much on her, that she was quite fatigued by her walk to see Mrs Chiley; and Thomas, too, knew why he had been called, and stood in a formal manner before her, with his hands crossed, against the closed door. When she put back her thick black veil, the last climax of painful change came upon Miss Marjoribanks. She did not feel as if she were Lucilla; so discouraged and depressed and pale, and tired with her walk as she was, with all sorts of projects and plans so quenched out of her; almost if she had been charged with being somebody else, the imputation was one which she could not have denied.

"Thomas," she said, faintly, "I think I ought to speak to you myself about all that has happened—we are such old friends, and you have been such a good kind servant. You know I shan't be able to keep up——"

"And sorry we all was, Miss, to hear it," said Thomas, when Lucilla's utterance failed. "I am sure there never was a better master, though particular; and for a comfortabler house——"

"If I had been as poor papa expected to leave me," said Miss Marjoribanks, after a little pause, "everything would have gone on as usual: but after your long service here, and so many people as know you, Thomas, you will have no difficulty in getting as good a place; and you know that anything I can say——"

"Thank you, Miss," said Thomas; and then he made a pause. "It was not exactly that as I was thinking of; I've set my heart, this many a day, on a little business. If you would be so kind as to speak a word for me to the gentlemen as has the licensing. There ain't nobody as knows better how——"

"What kind of a business, Thomas?" said Lucilla, who cheered up a little in ready interest, and would have been very glad if she could have taken a little business too.

"Well, Miss, a kind of a quiet—public-house, if I don't make too bold to name it," said Thomas, with a deprecating air—" not one of them drinking-places, Miss, as, I know, ladies can't abide; but many a man, as is a very decent man, wants his pint o' beer now and again, and their little sort of clubs of a night as well as the gentlefolks; and it's my opinion, Miss, as it's a man's dooty to see as that sort of thing don't go too far, and yet as his fellow-creatures has their bit of pleasure," said Thomas, who naturally took the defensive side.

"I am sure you are quite right," said Lucilla, cheering up more and more, and instinctively, with her old statesmanlike breadth of view, throwing a rapid glance upon the subject to see what capabilities there might be in it; "and I hope you will try always to exercise a good influence—What is all that noise and shouting out of doors?"

"It's one of the candidates, Miss," said Thomas, "as is addressing of the bargemen at the top o' Prickett's Lane."

"Ah!" said Lucilla; and a deep sigh escaped from her bosom. "But you cannot do anything of that kind, you know, Thomas, without a wife."

"Yes, Miss," said Thomas, with great confusion and embarrassment; "that was just what I was going to say. Me and Betsy——"

"Betsy!" said Lucilla, with dismay; for it had been Betsy she had specially fixed upon as the handy, willing, cheerful maid who, when there was no gentleman coming in, and little else to do, might keep even this big house in order. She sighed; but it was not in her power, even if she had desired it, to put any restriction upon Betsy's wishes. And it was not without a momentary envy that she received the intelligence. It was life the housemaid was about to enter on—active life of her own, with an object and meaning—clogged by Thomas, no doubt, who did not appear to Lucilla as the bright spot in the picture —but still independent life; whereas her mistress knew of nothing particularly interesting in her own uncertain future. She was roused from her momentary meditation by the distant shouts which came from the top of Prickett's Lane, and sighed again, without knowing it, as she spoke.

"It's a pity you had not got your—little inn," said Lucilla, for the sake of euphony, "six months or a year ago, for then you might have voted for Mr Ashburton, Thomas. I had forgotten about the election until now."

"Not as that needn't stand in the way, Miss," said Thomas, eagerly; "there's Betsy's brother as has it now, and he ain't made up his mind about his vote; and if he know'd as it would be any comfort to you——"

"Of course it will be a comfort to me!" said Miss Marjoribanks; and she got up from her chair with a sense that she was still not altogether useless in the world. "Go and speak to him directly, Thomas; and here's one of Mr Ashburton's colours that I made up myself; and tell him that there can be no doubt *he* is the man for Carlingford; and send up Nancy to me. And I hope Betsy and you will be very happy," said Lucilla. She had been dreadfully down, but the rebound was all the more grateful. "I am not done with yet, and, thank heaven! there must always be something to do," she said to herself when she was alone. And she threw off her shawl, and began to make the drawing-room look like itself; not that it was not perfectly in order, and as neat as a room could be; but still the neatness savoured of Betsy, and not of Lucilla. Miss Marjoribanks, in five minutes, made it look like that cosy empire of hospitality and kindness and talk and wit, and everything pleasant, that it used to be; and then, when she had finished, she sat down and had a good cry, which did not do her any harm.

Then Nancy appeared, disturbed in her preparations for dinner, and with her arms wrapped in her apron, looking glum and defiant. Hers was not the resigned and resourceful preparation for her fate which had appeared in Thomas. She came in, and put the door ajar, and leant her back against the sharp edge. She might be sent off like the rest, if that was Miss Lucilla's meaning—her that had been in the house off and on for more than thirty years; but if it was so, at least she would not give up without unfolding a bit of her mind.

"Come in," said Lucilla, drying her eyes—"come in and shut the door; you had better come and sit down here, Nancy, for I have a great deal to say, and I want to speak to you as a friend."

Nancy shut the door, but she thought to herself that she knew what all this meant, and made but a very little movement into the room, looking more forbidding than ever. "Thank you all the same, Miss Lucilla, but I ain't too old to stand," she said; and stood firm to meet the shock, with her arms folded under her apron, thinking in her heart that it was about one of the almshouses, her horror and hope, that her young mistress was going to speak.

"Nancy," said Lucilla, "I want to tell you what I am going to do. I have to make up my mind for myself now. They all go against me, and one says I should do this and another says I should do that; but I don't think anybody knows me so well as you do. Don't stand at the door. I want to consult you as a friend. I want to ask you a question, and you must answer as if you were before a judge—I have such confidence in *you*."

Nancy's distrust and defiance gave way a little before this appeal. She came a step nearer, and let the apron drop from her folded arms. "What is it, Miss Lucilla?—though I ain't pretending to be one to advise," she said, building a kind of intrenchment round her with the nearest chairs.

"You know how things are changed," said Lucilla, "and that I can't stay here as I used to do. People think I should go and live with somebody; but *I* think, you know—if I was one of those ladies that have a faithful old servant to stand by them, and never to grumble nor make a fuss, nor go back on the past, nor go in for expensive dishes—one that wouldn't mind cooking a chop or making a cup of tea, if that was all we could afford— why, I think, Nancy——"

But Nancy could not hear any more. She made a little rush forward, with a kind of convulsive chuckling that was half sobbing and half laughter. "And me here!" cried Dr Marjoribanks's famous cook, who had spent a fortune on her gravy-beef alone, and was one of the most expensive people in Carlingford—"me as has done for you all your days! me as would —if it was but a roast potato!" cried the devoted woman. She was in such a state of hysterical flutter and excitement that Lucilla had to take her almost into her arms and put the old woman into a chair and bring her to, which was an occupation quite in Miss Marjoribanks's way.

"But I shall only have two hundred a-year," said Lucilla. "Now don't be rash; there will have to be a maid to keep things tidy, and that is every farthing I shall have. You used to spend as much in gravy-beef," said Miss Marjoribanks, with a sigh.

"Oh, Miss Lucilla, let bygones be bygones," said Nancy, with tears. "If I did, it wasn't without many a little something for them as was too poor to buy it for themselves—for I never was one as boiled the senses out of a bit of meat; and when a gentleman is well-to-do, and hasn't got no occasion to count every penny—— The Doctor, I will say for him, was never one as asked too many questions. Give him a good dinner on his own table, and he wasn't the gentleman as grudged a bit of broken meat for the poor folks. He did a deal of good as you nor no one never know'd of, Miss Lucilla," said Nancy, with a sob.

And then his daughter and his faithful old servant cried a little in company over Dr Marjoribanks's vacant place. What could a man have more? Nobody was made altogether desolate by his death, nor was any heart broken, but they wept for him honestly, though the old woman felt happy in her sorrow. And Lucilla, on her knees before the fire, told Nancy of that exclamation the Doctor had made in John Brown's office, and how he had put his hand on her shoulder that last night. "All he said was, Poor Lucilla!" sobbed Miss Marjoribanks; "he never thought of himself nor all his money that he had worked so hard for;" and once more that touch of something more exquisite than was usual to her went sharply down into Lucilla's heart and brought up tenderer and deeper tears.

She felt all the better for it after, and was even a little cheerful in the evening, and like herself; and thus it will be seen that one person in Carlingford—not, it is true, a popular oracle, but of powerful influence and first-rate importance in a practical point of view—gave the heartiest approbation to Miss Marjoribanks's scheme for her new life.

CHAPTER XLVI.

LUCILLA'S calculations were fully justified by the result. Twenty times in a day she recognised the wisdom of her own early decision, which was made while she was still by herself, and before anybody had come in to advise her. If she had left it over until the time when, though much shaken, she was understood to be able to see her friends, it is just possible that the whirlwind of popular opinion which raged about her might have exercised a distracting influence even upon Miss Marjoribanks's clear head and steady judgment. For even now, though they saw her in her own house, in her mourning, people would not believe that it was true, and that Lucilla actually intended to make "no change;" and all that tide of good advice which had been flowing through Carlingford ever since the Doctor's death in the form of opinion, now rushed in upon her, notwithstanding that all the world knew that she had made up her mind. "Everybody says you are going to stay on, but we do hope it is not true, Lucilla," her friends said, in many voices. "It is dreadful for us to lose you, but you never *could* bear it, dear." And this was repeated so often that if Miss Marjoribanks had been weak-minded, she must have ended by believing not only that it was more than she was equal to, but more than she ought to be equal to—which was a more touching argument still.

"You are excited now," Miss Brown said, who had a great deal of experience in family troubles; "one always is at such a time; but when things have settled down in their ordinary way, then you will find it is more than you can bear. I think it is always best to make a change. If you were to travel a little, you know——"

"But, my dear, I am poor," said Lucilla.

"It doesn't require so much money when you know how to set about it," said her adviser; "and there are so many people who would be glad to have you, Lucilla! And then you might settle a little at Caen or Tours, or some of those nice places, where there is such capital English society, and everything so cheap; or, if you thought your health required it, at Pau or Nice, you know. You are looking quite pale, and I don't think you were ever very strong in the chest, Lucilla; and everything is *so* different on the Continent—one feels it the moment one crosses the Channel; there is something different in the very air."

"It smells different, I know," said Lucilla, meekly; and then the conversation was interrupted by that afternoon cup of tea, which Nancy could not be got to think was an extravagance, and around which, to tell the truth, the Grange Lane ladies began to resume their habit of gathering—though Miss Marjoribanks, of course, was still quite unequal to society—as in the old times.

"And unless it is for a very short time, Lucilla," Mrs Centum said, who had joined them, "you never can keep it up, you know. *I* could not pretend to afford Nancy, for my part; and when a cook is extravagant she may promise as faithfully as you please, and make good resolutions, and all that; but when it is in her, Lucilla—I am sure one or two receipts she has given me have been quite ridiculous. You don't like to give in, I know, but you'll be driven to give in; and if she does not get you into debt as well, you will be very lucky. I know what it is. With my family, you know, a week of Nancy would make an end of me."

"And the worst of all is," said Lady Richmond, who had driven in expressly to add her mite to the treasure of precious counsel, of which Miss Marjoribanks was making so little use, "that I am sure Lucilla is over-estimating her strength. She will find after that she is not equal to it, you know; all the associations—and the people coming at night to ask for the Doctor—and—and all that. I know it would kill *me*."

"Dear Lady Richmond," said Lucilla, making a desperate stand, and setting, as it were, her back against a rock, "don't you think I can bear it best here where you are all so kind to me; and where everybody was so fond of—of *him ?* You can't think what a comfort it is to me," said Lucilla, with a sob, "to see all the hatbands upon the gentlemen's hats."

And then there was a pause, for this was an argument against which nobody could find anything to say.

"For my part, I think the only thing she can do is to take Inmates," said aunt Jemima. "If I were obliged to leave she would be so very lonely. I have known ladies do it who were in a very good position, and it made no difference; people visited them all the same. She could say, 'In consequence of changes in the family,' or 'A lady who has a larger house than she requires;' which I am sure is quite true. It goes to one's heart to think of all these bedrooms, and only one lady to sleep in them all—when so many people are so hampered for want of room. Or she might say, 'For the sake of society;' for, I am sure, if I should have to go away——"

"But I hope you are not going away. It would be so sad for Lucilla to be left alone," said Lady Richmond, who took a serious view of everything, "at such a time."

"Oh, no!" aunt Jemima said, faltering a little; and then a pink blush, which seemed strangely uncalled for in such a mild little tea-party, came over her mature countenance; "but then one can never tell what may happen. I might have other duties—my son might make a call upon my time. Not that I know of anything at present," she added, hurriedly, "but I never can bind myself on account of Tom——"

And then she caught Lucilla's eye, and grew more confused than ever. What could she have to be confused about? If Tom did make a call upon her time, whatever that might mean, there was nothing in it to call a blush upon his mother's face. And the fact was, that a letter had come from Tom a day or two before, of which, contrary to all her usual habits, aunt Jemima had taken no notice to Lucilla. These were things which would have roused Miss Marjoribanks's curiosity if she had been able to think about anything, as she said. But her visitors were taking their cup of tea all the time, in a melancholy, half-sympathetic, half-disapproving way, and they could not be expected to see anything particularly interesting in aunt Jemima's blush.

And then Rose Lake came in from Grove Street, who was rather an unusual visitor, and whose appearance, though they were all very kind and gracious to her, rather put the others to flight; for nobody had ever quite forgotten or forgiven Barbara's brief entrance into society and flirtation with Mr Cavendish, which might be said to have been the beginning of all that happened to him in Grange Lane. As for Mrs Centum, she took her leave directly, and pressed Lucilla's hand, and could not help saying in her ear that she hoped *the other* was not coming back to Carlingford to throw herself in poor Mr Cavendish's way. "It would do him so much harm," Mrs Centum said, anxiously; "but oh! I forgot, Lucilla, you are on the other side."

"I am on no side *now*," said Miss Marjoribanks, with plaintive meaning; "and Barbara was as old as I am, you know, and she must have gone off."

"I have no doubt she has gone off," said Mrs Centum, with righteous indignation. "As old as you, Lucilla! She must be ten years older at least; and such a shocking style of looks—if men were not so infatuated! And you have not gone off at all, my poor dear," she added, with all the warmth of friendship. And then they were joined at the door by the county lady, who was the next to go away.

"My dear, I hope you will be guided for the best," Lady Richmond said as she went away; but she gave a deep sigh as she kissed Lucilla, and looked as if she had very little faith in the efficacy of her own wish. Maria Brown had withdrawn to another part of the drawing-room with aunt Jemima, so that Lucilla was, so to speak, left alone with Rose. And Rose, too, had come with the intention of giving advice.

"I hear you are going to stay, Lucilla," she said, "and I did not think I would be doing my duty if I did not tell you what was in my mind. *I* can't do any good to anybody, you know; but you who are so clever, and have so much in your power——"

"I am poor now," said Miss Marjoribanks; "and as for being clever, I don't know about that. I never was clever about drawing or Art, like you."

"Oh, like me," said poor little Rose, whose Career had been sacrificed ten years ago, and who was a little misanthropical now, and did not believe even in Schools of Design; "I am not so sure about the moral influence of Art as I used to be—except High Art, to be sure; but we never have any High Art down here. And oh, Lucilla! the poor people *do* want something done for them. If I was as clever as you, with a great house all to myself like this, and well off, and with plenty of influence, and no ties——" said Rose, with energetic emphasis. She made a pause there, and she was so much in earnest that the tears came into her eyes. "I would make it a House of Mercy, Lucilla! I would show all these poor creatures how to live and how to manage, if I was as clever as you; and teach them and their children, and look after them, and be a mother to them!" said Rose; and here she stopped short, altogether overcome by her own magnificent conception of what her friend could or might do.

Aunt Jemima and Miss Brown, who had drawn near out of curiosity, stared at Rose as if they thought she had gone mad; but Lucilla, who was of a larger mind and more enlightened ideas, neither laughed nor looked horrified. She did not make a very distinct answer, it is true, but she was very kind to her new adviser, and made her a fresh cup of tea, and even consented, though in an ambiguous way, to the principle she had just enunciated. "If you won't be affronted, my dear," Lucilla said, "I do not think that Art could do very much in Carlingford; and I am sure any little thing that I may be of use for——" But she did not commit herself any further, and Rose too found the result of her visit unsatisfactory, and went home disappointed in Lucilla. This was how the afternoon passed; and at the end of such a day it may well be imagined how Miss Marjoribanks congratulated herself on having made up her mind before the public, so to speak, were admitted. For Rose was followed by the Rector, who, though he did not propose in so many words a House of Mercy, made no secret of his conviction that parish-work was the only thing that could be of any service to Lucilla; and that, in short, such was the inevitable and providential destination of a woman who had "no ties." Indeed, to hear Mr Bury, a stranger would have been disposed to believe that Dr Marjoribanks had been, as he said, "removed," and his fortune swept away, all in order to indicate to Lucilla the proper sphere for her energies. In the face of all this it will be seen how entirely Miss Marjoribanks's wisdom in making her decision by herself before her advisers broke in upon her, was justified. She could now set her back against her rock, and face her assailants, as Fitz-James did.

> "Come one, come all, this rock shall fly
> From its firm base as soon as I,"

might have been her utterance; but she was not in a defiant mood. She kissed all her counsellors that day (except, of course, the Rector), and heard them out with the sweetest patience; and then she thought to herself how much better it was that she had made up her mind to take her own way.

Notwithstanding, all this commotion of public opinion about her made a certain impression upon Miss Marjoribanks's mind. It was not unpleasant to feel that, for this moment at least, she was the centre of the thoughts of the community, and that almost everybody in Carlingford had taken the trouble to frame an ideal existence for her, according as he or she regarded life. It is so seldom that any one has it in his power, consciously and evidently, to regulate his life for himself, and make it whatever he wants it to be. And then, at the same time, the best that she could make of it would, after all, be something very limited and unsatisfactory. In her musings on this subject, Lucilla could not but go back a great many times to that last conversation she had with her father, when she walked up Grange Lane with him that night over the thawed and muddy snow. The Doctor had said she was not cut out for a single woman; and Lucilla, with candour, yet a certain philosophical speculativeness, had allowed that she was not—unless, indeed, she could be very rich. If she had been very rich, the prospect would no doubt have been, to a certain extent, different. And then, oddly enough, it was Rose Lake's suggestion which came after this to Lucilla's mind. She did not smile at it as some people might expect she would. One thing was quite sure, that she had no intention of sinking into a nobody, and giving up all power of acting upon her fellow-creatures; and she could not help being conscious of the fact that she was able to be of much use to her fellow-creatures. If it had been Maria Brown, for instance, who had been concerned, the whole question would have been one of utter unimportance, except to the heroine herself; but it was different in Miss Marjoribanks's case. The House of Mercy was not a thing to be taken into any serious consideration; but still there was something in the idea which Lucilla could not dismiss carelessly as her friends could. She had no vocation, such as the foundress of such an establishment ought to have, nor did she see her way to the abandonment of all projects for herself, and that utter devotion to the cause of humanity which would be involved in it; but yet, when a woman happens to be full of energy and spirit, and determined that whatever she may be she shall certainly not be a nonentity, her position is one that demands thought. She was very capable of serving her fellow-creatures, and very willing and well disposed to serve them; and yet she was not inclined to give herself up entirely to them, nor to relinquish her personal prospects—vague though these might be. It was a tough problem, and one which might have caused a most unusual disturbance in Lucilla's well-regulated mind, had not she remembered all at once what deep mourning she was in, and that at present no sort of action, either of one kind or another, could be expected of her. There was no need for making a final decision, either about the parish-work, or about taking Inmates, as aunt Jemima proposed, or about any other single suggestion which had been offered to her; no more than there was any necessity for asking what her cousin Tom's last letter had been about, or why his mother looked so guilty and embarrassed when she spoke of him. Grief has its privileges and exemptions, like other great principles of life; and the recollection that she could not at present be expected to be able to think about anything, filled Lucilla's mind with the most soothing sense of consolation and refreshing calm.

And then other events occurred to occupy her friends; the election for one thing began to grow a little exciting, and took away some of the superfluous energy of Grange Lane. Mr Ashburton had carried all before him at first; but since the Rector had come into the field, the balance had changed a little. Mr Bury was very Low-Church; and from the moment at which he was persuaded that Mr Cavendish was a great penitent, the question as to which was the Man for Carlingford had been solved in his mind in the most satisfactory way. A man who intrenched himself in mere respectability and trusted in his own good character, and considered himself to have a clear conscience, and to have done his duty, had no chance against a repentant sinner. Mr Cavendish, perhaps, had not done his duty quite so well; but then he was penitent, and everything was expressed in that word. The Rector was by no means contemptible, either as an adversary or a supporter—and the worst of it was that, in embracing Mr Cavendish's claims, he could scarcely help speaking of Mr Ashburton as if he was in a very bad way. And feeling began to rise rather high in Carlingford. If anything could have deepened the intensity of Miss Marjoribanks's grief, it would have been to know that all this was going on, and that affairs might go badly with her candidate, while she was shut up, and could give no aid. It was hard upon her, and it was hard upon the candidates themselves— one of whom had thus become generally disapproved of, without, so far as he knew, doing anything to deserve it; while the other occupied the still more painful character of being on his promotion—a repentant man, with a character to keep up. It was no wonder that Mrs Centum grew pale at the very idea of such a creature as Barbara Lake throwing herself in poor Mr Cavendish's way. A wrong step one way or other—a relapse into the ways of wickedness—might undo in a moment all that it had cost so much trouble to do. And the advantage of the Rector's support was thus grievously counterbalanced by what might be called the uncertainty of it—especially as Mr Cavendish was not, as his committee lamented secretly among themselves, a man of strong will or business habits, in whom implicit confidence could be placed. He might get restive, and throw the Rector over just at the critical moment; or he might relapse into his lazy Continental habits, and give up churchgoing and other good practices. But still, up to this moment, he had shown very tolerable perseverance; and Mr Bury's influence thrown into his scale had equalised matters very much, and made the contest very exciting. All this Lucilla heard, not from Mr Cavendish, but from her own candidate, who had taken to calling in a steady sort of way. He never went into any effusions of sympathy, for he was not that kind of man; but he would shake hands with her, and say that people must submit to the decrees of Providence; and then he would speak of the election and of his chances. Sometimes Mr Ashburton was despondent, and then Lucilla cheered him up; and sometimes he had very good hopes.

"I am very glad you are to be here," he said on one of these occasions. "It would have been a great loss to me if you had gone away. I shall never forget our talk about it here *that* day, and how you were the first person that found me out."

"It was not any cleverness of mine," said Lucilla. . "It came into my mind all in a moment, like spirit-rapping, you know. It seems so strange to talk of that *now;* there have been such changes since then—it looks like years."

"Yes," said Mr Ashburton, in his steady way. "There is nothing that really makes time look so long; but we must all bow to these dispensations, my dear Miss Marjoribanks. I would not speak of the election, but that I thought it might amuse you. The writs are out now, you know, and it takes place on Monday week."

Upon which Miss Marjoribanks smiled upon Mr Ashburton, and held out her hands to him with a gesture and look which said more than words. "You know you will have *all* my best wishes," she said; and the candidate was much moved—more moved than at such a moment he had thought it possible to be.

"If I succeed, I know whom I shall thank the most," he said, fervently; and then, as this was a climax, and it would have been a kind of bathos to plunge into ordinary details after it, Mr Ashburton got up, still holding Lucilla's hand, and clasped it almost tenderly as he said good-bye. She looked very well in her mourning, though she had not expected to do so; for black was not Lucilla's style. And the fact was, that instead of having gone off, as she herself said, Miss Marjoribanks looked better than ever she did, and was even embellished by the natural tears which still shone by times in her eyes. Mr Ashburton went out in a kind of bewilderment after this interview, and forgot his overcoat in the hall, and had to come back for it, which was a confusing circumstance; and then he went on his way with a gentle excitement which was not unpleasant. "Would she, I wonder?" he said to himself, as he went up Grange Lane. Perhaps he was only asking himself whether Lucilla would or could be present along with Lady Richmond and her family at the window of the Blue Boar on the great day; but if that was it, the idea had a certain brightening and quickening influence upon his face and his movements. The doubt he had on the subject, whatever it was, was not a discouraging, but a piquant, stimulating, exciting doubt. He had all but proposed the question to his committee when he went in among them, which would have filled these gentlemen with wonder and dismay. But though he did not do that, he carried it home with him, as he trotted back to the Firs to dinner. Mr Ashburton took a walk through his own house that evening, and examined all its capabilities—with no particular motive, as he was at pains to explain to his housekeeper; and again he said to himself, "Would she, I wonder?" before he retired for the night; which was no doubt an unusual sort of iteration for so sensible a man, and one so fully occupied with the most important affairs, to make.

As for Lucilla, she was not in the way of asking herself any questions at that moment. She was letting things take their course, and not interfering; and consequently, nothing that happened could be said to be her fault. She carried this principle so far, that even when aunt Jemima was herself led to open the subject, in a hesitating way, Miss Marjoribanks never even asked a single question about Tom's last letter. She was in mourning, and that was enough for her. As for appearing at the window of the Blue Boar with Lady Richmond, if that was what Mr Ashburton was curious about, he might have saved himself the trouble of any speculations on the subject. For though Miss Marjoribanks would be very anxious about the election, she would indeed have been ashamed of herself could her feelings have permitted her to appear anywhere in public so soon. Thus, while Mr Ashburton occupied himself much with the question which had taken possession of his mind, Lucilla took a good book, which seemed the best reading for her in her circumstances, and when she had looked after all her straitened affairs in the morning, sat down sweetly in the afternoon quiet of her retirement and seclusion, and let things take their way.

CHAPTER XLVII.

As the election approached, it became gradually the one absorbing object of interest in Carlingford. The contest was so equal that everybody took a certain share in it, and became excited as the decisive moment drew nigh. Most of the people in Grange Lane were for Mr Ashburton, but then the Rector, who was a host in himself, was for Mr Cavendish; and the coquetting of the Dissenting interest, which was sometimes drawn towards the liberal sentiments of the former candidate, but sometimes could not help reflecting that Mr Ashburton "dealt" in George Street; and the fluctuations of the bargemen, who were, many of them, freemen, and a very difficult part of the population, excited the most vivid interest. Young Mr Wentworth, who had but lately come to Carlingford, had already begun to acquire a great influence at Wharfside, where most of the bargees lived, and the steady ones would no doubt have been largely swayed by him had his inclinations been the same as the Rector's; but Mr Wentworth, perversely enough, had conceived that intuitive repugnance for Mr Cavendish which a high-principled and not very tolerant young man often feels for the middle-aged individual who still conceives himself to have some right to be called young, and whose antecedents are not entirely beyond suspicion. Mr Wentworth's disinclination (and he was a man rather apt to take his own way) lay like a great boulder across the stream of the Rector's enthusiasm, and unquestionably interrupted it a little. Both the candidates and both the committees had accordingly work enough to do up to the last moment. Mr Cavendish all at once became a connoisseur in hams, and gave a magnificent order in the most complimentary way to Tozer, who received it with a broad smile, and "booked" it, as he said. "It ain't ham he's awanting," the butterman said, not without amusement; for Tozer was well to do, and, except that he felt the honour of a mark of confidence, was not to be moved one way or another by one order. "If he dealt regular, it might be different. Them's the sort of folks as a man feels drawn to," said the true philosopher. Mr Ashburton, on the other side, did not make the impression which his friends thought he ought to have made in Prickett's Lane; but at least nobody could say that he did not stick very close to his work. He went at it like a man night and day, and neglected no means of carrying it to a successful issue; whereas, as Mr Centum and Mr Woodburn mourned in secret to each other, Cavendish required perpetual egging on. He did not like to get up in the morning, and get early to his work. It went against all his habits—as if his habits mattered in the face of so great an emergency; and in the afternoon it was hard to prevent him from lounging into some of his haunts, which were utterly out of the way of business. He would stay in Masters's for an hour at a time, though he knew Mr Wentworth, who was Masters's great patron, did not care for him, and that his favour for such a Tractarian sort of place was bitter to the Rector. Anything for a little idleness and waste of time, poor Mr Centum said, who was two stone lighter on the eve of the election than when the canvass began. Such a contrast would make any man angry. Mr Cavendish was goaded into more activity as the decisive moment approached, and performed what seemed to himself unparalleled feats. But it was only two days before the moment of fate when the accident happened to him which brought such dismay to all his supporters. Our own opinion is, that it did not materially affect the issue of the contest one way or other; but that was the reverse of the feeling which prevailed in Grange Lane.

It was just two days before the election, and all seemed going on sufficiently well. Mr Cavendish had been meeting a Dissenting committee, and it was on leaving them that he found himself at the corner of Grove Street, where, under ordinary circumstances, he had no occasion to be. At a later period he was rather fond of saying that it was not of his own motion that he was there at all, but only in obedience to the committee, which ordered him about like a nigger. The spring afternoon was darkening, and the Dissenters (almost wholly unimpressed by his arguments, and remarking more strongly than ever where Mr Ashburton "dealt," and how thoroughly everybody knew all about him) had all dispersed. It was but natural, when Mr Cavendish came to the corner of Grove Street, where, in other days, he had played a very different part, that certain softening influences should take possession of his soul. "What a voice she had, by Jove!" he said to himself; "very different from that shrill pipe of Lucilla's." To tell the truth, if there was one person in Carlingford whom he felt a resentment against, it was Lucilla. She had never done him any harm to speak of, and once she had unquestionably done him a great deal of good. But, on the other hand, it was she who first showed herself candidly conscious that he had grown stout, and who all along had supported and encouraged his rival. It was possible, no doubt, that this might be pique; and, mixed with his anger for her sins against him, Mr Cavendish had, at the same time, a counterbalancing sense that there still remained to him in his life one supereminently wise thing that he still could do—and that was, to go down Grange Lane instantly to the Doctor's silenced house, and go down on his knees, or do any other absurdity that might be necessary to make Lucilla marry him; after which act he would henceforward be, pecuniarily and otherwise (notwithstanding that she was poor), a saved man. It did not occur to him that Lucilla would never have married him, even had he gone down on his knees; but perhaps that would be too much to ask any man to believe of any woman; and his feeling that this was the right thing to do, rather strengthened than otherwise the revolt of his heart against Lucilla. It was twilight, as we have said, and he had done a hard day's work, and there was still an hour before dinner which he seemed to have a right to dispose of in his own way; and he did hesitate at the corner of Grove Street, laying himself open, as it were, to any temptation that might offer itself. Temptations come, as a general rule, when they are sought; and thus, on the very eve of the election, a grievous accident happened to Mr Cavendish. It might have happened at any time, to be sure, but this was the most inopportune moment possible, and it came accordingly now.

For as he made that pause, some one passed him whom he could not but look after with a certain interest. She went past him with a whisk, as if she too was not without reminiscences. It was not such a figure as a romantic young man would be attracted by on such a sudden meeting, and it was not attraction but recollection that moved Mr Cavendish. It was the figure of a large woman in a large shawl, not very gracefully put on, and making her look very square about the shoulders and bunchy at the neck; and the robe that was whisked past him was that peculiar kind of faded silk gown which looks and rustles like tin, or some other thin metallic substance. He made that momentary pause at the street corner, and then he went on slowly, not following her, to be sure, but merely, as he said to himself, pursuing his own course; for it was just as easy to get into Grange Lane by the farther end as by this end. He went along very slowly, and the lady before him walked quickly, even with something like a bounce of excitement, and went in at Mr Lake's door long before Mr Cavendish had reached it. When he came up on a level with the parlour window, which was partially open though the evening was so cold, Mr Cavendish positively started, notwithstanding the old associations which had been rising in his mind; for there was pouring forth from the half-open window such a volume of melody as had not been heard for years in Grove Street. Perhaps the voice had lost some of its freshness, but in the surprise of the moment the hearer was not critical; and its volume and force seemed even greater than before.

It has been already mentioned in this history that a contralto had a special charm for Mr Cavendish. He was so struck that he stood stock-still for the moment, not knowing what to make of it; and then he wavered for another moment, with a sudden sense that the old allegorical crisis had occurred to him, and that Pleasure, in a magnificent gush of song, wooed him on one side, while Duty, with still small voice, called him at the other. He stood still, he wavered—for fifty seconds perhaps the issue was uncertain, and the victim was still within reach of salvation; but the result in such a case depends very much upon whether a man really likes doing his duty, which is by no means an invariable necessity. Mr Cavendish had in the abstract no sort of desire to do his unless when he could not help it, and consequently his resistance to temptation was very feeble. He was standing knocking at Mr Lake's door before half the thoughts appropriate to the occasion had got through his mind, and found himself sitting on the little sofa in Mr Lake's parlour as he used to do ten years ago, before he could explain to himself how he came there. It was all, surely, a kind of enchantment altogether. He was there—he who had been so long away from Carlingford—he who had been so deeply offended by hearing his name seriously coupled with that of Barbara Lake—he who ought to have been anywhere in the world rather than here upon the eve of his election, when all the world was keeping watch over his conduct. And it was Barbara who sat at the piano singing—singing one of the same songs, as if she had spent the entire interval in that occupation, and never had done anything else all these years. The sensation was so strange that Mr Cavendish may be excused for feeling a little uncertainty as to whether or not he was dreaming, which made him unable to answer himself the graver question whether or not he was doing what he ought to do. He did not seem to be able to make out whether it was now or ten years ago—whether he was a young man free to amuse himself, or a man who was getting stout, and upon whom the eyes of an anxious constituency were fixed. And then, after being so virtuous for a length of time, a forbidden pleasure was sweet.

Mr Cavendish's ideas, however, gradually arranged themselves as he sat in the corner of the little haircloth sofa, and began to take in the differences as well as the bewildering resemblances of the present and past. Barbara, like himself, had changed. She did not insult him, as Lucilla had done, by fresh looks and mischievous candour about "going off." Barbara *had* gone off, like himself, and, like himself, did not mean to acknowledge it. She had expanded all over, as was natural to a contralto. Her eyes were blacker and more brilliant in a way, but they were eyes which owned an indescribable amount of usage; and her cheeks, too, wore the deep roses of old, deepened and fixed by wear and tear. Instead of feeling ashamed of himself in her presence, as he had done in Lucilla's, Mr Cavendish felt somehow consoled and justified and sympathetic. "Poor soul!" he said to himself, as he sat by while she was singing. She, too, had been in the wars, and had not come out scatheless. She did not reproach him, nor commiserate him, nor look at him with that mixture of wonder and tolerance and pity which other people had manifested. She did not even remark that he had grown stout. He was not a man fallen,

fallen, fallen from his high estate, to Barbara. She herself had fallen from the pinnacles of youth, and Mr Cavendish was still a great man in her eyes. She sang for him as she had sung ten years ago, and received him with a flutter of suppressed delight, and in her satisfaction was full of excitement. The hard-worked candidate sank deeper and deeper into the corner of the sofa and listened to the music, and felt it very soothing and pleasant, for everybody had united in goading him on rather than petting him for the last month or two of his life.

"Now tell me something about yourself," he said, when the song was over, and Barbara had turned round, as she used to do in old times, on her music-stool; "I hear you have been away, like me."

"Not like you," said Barbara, "for you went because you pleased, and I went——"

"Why did you go?" asked Mr Cavendish.

"Because I could not stay here any longer," said Barbara, with her old vehemence; "because I was talked about, and looked down upon, and—— Well, never mind, that's all over now; and I am sure I am very glad to see you, Mr Cavendish, as a *friend*."

And with that something like a tear came into her eye. She had been knocked about a good deal in the world, and though she had not learned much, still she had learned that she was young no longer, and could not indulge in the caprices of that past condition of existence. Mr Cavendish, for his part, could not but smile at this intimation that he was to be received as a friend, and consequently need not have any fear of Barbara's fascinations,—as if a woman of her age, worn and gone off as she was, could be supposed dangerous; but still he was touched by her tone.

"We were once very good friends, Barbara," said the inconsistent man; "we have lost sight of each other for a long time, as people do in this world; but we were once very good friends."

"Yes," she said, with a slight touch of annoyance in her voice; "but since we have lost sight of each other for so long, I don't see why you should call me Barbara. It would be much more becoming to say Miss Lake."

Mr Cavendish was amused, and he was touched and flattered. Most people had been rather forbearing to him since he came back, putting up with him for old friendship's sake, or supporting his cause as that of a reformed man, and giving him, on the whole, a sort of patronising humiliating countenance; and to find somebody in whose eyes he was still the paladin of old times, *the* Mr Cavendish whom people in Grange Lane were proud of, was balm to his wounded soul.

"I don't know how I am to learn to say Miss Lake—when you are just as good to me as ever, and sing as you have just been doing," he said. "I suppose you say so because you find me so changed?"

Upon which Barbara lifted her black eyes and looked at him as she had scarcely done before. The eyes were as bright as ever, and they were softened a little for the moment out of the stare that seemed to have grown habitual to them; and her crimson cheeks glowed as of old; and though she was untidy, and looked worn, and like a creature much buffeted about by wind and waves, she was still what connoisseurs in that article call a fine woman. She looked full at Mr Cavendish, and then she cast down her eyes, as if the sight was too much for her. "I don't see any difference," she said, with a certain tremor in her voice; for he was a man of whom, in the days of her youth, she had been fond in her way.

And naturally Mr Cavendish was more touched than ever. He took her hand, and called her Barbara again without any reproof; and he saw that she trembled, and that his presence here made to the full as great an impression as he had ever done in his palmiest days. Perhaps a greater impression; for their old commerce had been stormy, and interrupted by many a hurricane; and Barbara then had, or thought she might have, many strings to her bow, and did not believe that there was only one Mr Cavendish in the world. Now all that was changed; and if this old hope should revive again, it would not be allowed to die away for any gratification of temper. Mr Cavendish did not remember ever to have seen her tremble before, and he too was fond of her in his way.

This curious revival did not come to anything of deeper importance, for of course just then Rose came in from her household affairs, and Mr Lake to tea; and the candidate recollected that it was time for dinner. But father and sister also gave him, in their different ways, a rather flattering reception. Mr Lake had already pledged him his vote, and was full of interest as to how things were going on, and enthusiastic for his success; and Rose scowled upon him as of old, as on a dangerous character, whose comings and goings could not be seen without apprehension; which was an unexpected pleasure to a man who had been startled to find how very little commotion his presence made in Grange Lane. He pressed Barbara's hand as he went away, and went to his dinner with a heart which certainly beat lighter, and a more pleasant sense of returning self-confidence, than he had felt for a long time. When he was coming out of the house, as a matter of course, he met with the chief of his Dissenting supporters, accompanied (for Mr Bury, as has been said, was very Low-Church, and loved, wherever he could do it, to work in unison with his Dissenting brethren) by the Rector's churchwarden, both of whom stopped with a curiously critical air to speak to the Candidate, who had to be every man's friend for the time being. The look in their eyes sent an icy chill through and through him, but still the forbidden pleasure had been sweet. As he walked home, he could not help thinking it over, and going back ten years, and feeling a little doubtful about it, whether it was then or now. And as he mused, Miss Marjoribanks, whom he could not help continually connecting and contrasting with the other, appeared to him as a kind of jealous Queen Eleanor, who had a right to him, and could take possession at any time, should she choose to make the effort; while Barbara was a Rosamond, dilapidated indeed, but always ready to receive and console him in her bower. This was the kind of unconscious sentiment he had in his mind, feeling sure, as he mused, that Lucilla would be very glad to marry him, and that it would be very wise on his part to ask her, and was a thing which might still probably come to pass. Of course he could not see into Miss Marjoribanks's mind, which had travelled such a long way beyond him. He gave a glance up at the windows, as he passed her door, and felt a kind of disagreeable satisfaction in seeing how diminished the lights were in the once-radiant house. And Lucilla was so fond of a great deal of light! but she could not afford now to spend as much money upon wax as a Continental church might do. Mr Cavendish had so odd a sense of Lucilla's power over him, that it gave him a certain pleasure to think of the coming down of her pride and diminution of her lights.

But the fact was, that not more than ten minutes after he had passed her door with this reflection, Lucilla, sitting with her good book on the table and her work in her hand, in the room which was not so well lighted as it used to be, heard that Mr Cavendish had been met with coming out of Mr Lake's, and that Barbara had been singing to him, and that there was no telling what might have happened. "A man ain't the man for Carlingford as takes up with that sort," Thomas said, indignantly, who had come to pay his former mistress a visit, and to assure her of his brother-in-law's vote. He was a little more free-spoken than of old, being now set up, and an independent householder, and calling no man master; and he was naturally indignant at an occurrence which, regarded in the light of past events, was an insult not only to Carlingford, but to Lucilla. Miss Marjoribanks was evidently startled by the news. She looked up quickly as if she had been about to speak, and then stopped herself and turned her back upon Thomas, and poked the fire in a most energetic way. She had even taken the hearth-brush in her hand to make all tidy after this onslaught, but that was a thing that went to Thomas's heart.

"I couldn't stand by and see it, Miss Lucilla," said Thomas; "it don't feel natural;" and there was actually a kind of moisture in his eye as he took that domestic implement out of her hand. Mr Cavendish pitied Lucilla for having less light than of old, and Thomas for being reduced so low as to sweep her own hearth. But Lucilla was very far from pitying her own case. She had been making an effort over herself, and she had come out of it triumphant; after reading so many good books, it is not to be wondered at if she felt herself a changed and softened and elevated character. She had the means in her hands of doing her candidate's rival a deadly mischief, and yet, for old friendship's sake, Lucilla made up her mind to forbear.

"I will give it you, Thomas," she said, with dignity, holding the hearth-brush, which was in such circumstances elevated into something sublime, "if you will promise, never, until after the election—never to say a word about Mr Cavendish and Miss Lake. It was quite right to tell me, and you are very kind about the hearth; but you must promise never to say a syllable about it, not even to Nancy, until the election is over; or I will never give it you, nor ask you to do a single thing for me again."

Thomas was so much struck with this address that he said "Good Lord!" in sheer amazement; and then he made the necessary vow, and took the hearth-brush out of Lucilla's hand.

"No doubt he was asking for Mr Lake's vote," said Miss Marjoribanks. "They say everybody is making great exertions, and you know they are both my friends. I ought to be pleased whoever wins. But it is impressed on my mind that Mr Ashburton will be the man," Lucilla added, with a little solemnity, "and, Thomas, we must give them fair-play."

It would be vain to assert that Thomas understood this

romantic generosity, but he was taken by surprise, and had relinquished his own liberty in the matter, and had nothing further to say. Indeed he had so little to say down-stairs, that Nancy, who was longing for a little gossip, insulted and reviled him, and declared that since he took up with *that* Betsy there never was a sensible word to be got out of him. And all the time the poor man was burning with this bit of news. Many a man has bartered his free-will before under the influence of female wiles, or so at least history would have us believe; but few have done it for so poor a compensation as that hearth-brush. Thomas withdrew sore at heart, longing for the election to be over, and kept his word like an honest man; but notwithstanding, before the evening was over, the fatal news was spreading like fire to every house in Grange Lane.

CHAPTER XLVIII.

It is probable that Mr Cavendish considered the indulgence above recorded all the more excusable in that it was Saturday night. The nomination was to take place on Monday, and if a man was not to be supposed to be done with his work on the Saturday evening, when could he be expected to have a moment of repose? He had thought as he went home—for naturally, while putting himself so skilfully in the way of temptation, such questions had not entered into his mind—that the fact of to-morrow being Sunday would effectually neutralise any harm he could have been supposed to have done by a visit so simple and natural, and that neither his sister nor his committee, the two powers of which he stood in a certain awe, could so much as hear of it until the election was over, and all decided for good or for evil. This had been a comfort to his mind, but it was the very falsest and most deceitful consolation. That intervening Sunday was a severer calamity for Mr Cavendish than half-a-dozen ordinary days. The general excitement had risen so high, and all the chances on both sides had been so often discussed and debated, that something new was as water in the desert to the thirsting constituency. The story was all through Grange Lane that very night, but Carlingford itself, from St Roque's to the wilderness of the North End, tingled with it next morning. It is true, the Rector made no special allusion to it in his sermon, though the tone of all his services was so sad, and his own fine countenance looked so melancholy, that Mr Bury's devoted followers could all see that he had something on his mind. But Mr Tufton at Salem Chapel was not so reticent. He was a man quite famous for his extempore gifts, and who rather liked to preach about any very recent public event, which it was evident to all his hearers could not have found place in a "prepared" discourse; and his sermon that morning was upon wickedness in high places, upon men who sought the confidence of their fellows only to betray it, and offered to the poor man a hand red with his sister's (metaphorical) blood.

But it would be wrong to say that this was the general tone of public opinion in Grove Street; most people, on the contrary, thought of Mr Cavendish not as a wolf thirsting for the lamb's blood, but rather himself as a kind of lamb caught in the thicket, and about to be offered up in sacrifice. Such was the impression of a great many influential persons who had been wavering hitherto, and inclining on the whole to Mr Cavendish's liberal principles and supposed Low-Church views. A man whose hand is red metaphorically with your sister's blood is no doubt a highly objectionable personage; but it is doubtful whether, under the circumstances, an enlightened constituency might not consider the man who had given a perfectly unstained hand to so thoroughly unsatisfactory a sister as more objectionable still; and the indignation of Grange Lane at Barbara's reappearance was nothing to the fury of George Street, and even of Wharfside, where the bargees began to scoff openly. Society had nothing worse to say than to quote Mrs Chiley, and assert that "these artist people were all adventurers;" and then Grange Lane in general could not forget that it "had met" Barbara, nor dismiss from its consideration her black eyes, her level brows, and her magnificent contralto; whereas in the other region the idea of the Member for Carlingford marrying "that sort!" cast all the world into temporary delirium. It was a still more deadly offence to the small people than to the great. And the exceptional standing which poor Mr Lake and his daughter Rose used to lay claim to—the "rank of their own" which they possessed as artists—was a pretension much more disagreeable to the shopkeepers than to society in general. Thus in every sense Mr Cavendish had done the very worst for himself by his ill-timed indulgence; and his guilt was about the same with most of his critics whether he meant perfectly well and innocently, or entertained the most guilty intentions ever conceived by man.

And all his misfortunes were increased by the fact that the intervening day was a Sunday. Barbara Lake herself, who did not know what people were saying, and who, if she had known, would not have cared, came to church, as was natural, in the morning; and, under pretence that the family pew was full, had the assurance, as people remarked, to come to the middle aisle, in that same silk dress which rustled like tin, and made more demonstration than the richest draperies. The pew-opener disapproved of her as much as everybody else did, but she could not turn the intruder out; and though Barbara had a long time to wait, and was curiously inspected by all the eyes near her while she did so, the end was that she got a seat in her rustling silk not very far from where Lucilla sat in deep mourning, a model of every righteous observance. As for poor Barbara, she too was very exemplary in church. She meant nobody any harm, poor soul. She could not help the flashing of those big black eyes, to which the level line above them gave such a curious appearance of obliqueness—nor was it to be expected that she should deny herself the use of her advantages, or omit to "take the second" in all the canticles with such melodious liquid tones as made everybody stop and look round. She had a perfect right to do it; indeed it was her duty, as it is everybody's duty, to aid to the best of their ability in the church-music of their parish, which was what Lucilla Marjoribanks persisted in saying in answer to all objections. But the effect was great in the congregation, and even the Rector himself was seen to change colour as his eye fell upon the unlucky young woman. Mr Cavendish, for his part, knew her voice the moment he heard it, and gave a little start, and received such a look from his sister, who was standing by him, as turned him to stone. Mrs Woodburn looked at him, and so did her husband, and Mr Centum turned a solemnly inquiring reproachful gaze upon him from the other side of the aisle. "Oh, Harry, you will kill me with vexation! why, for goodness' sake, did you let her come?" his sister whispered when they had all sat down again. "Good heavens! how could I help it?" cried poor Mr Cavendish, almost loud enough to be heard. And then by the slight, almost imperceptible, hum around him, he felt that not only his sister and his committee, but the Rector and all Carlingford, had their eyes upon him, and was thankful to look up the lesson, poor man, and bury his face in it. It was a hard punishment for the indiscretion of an hour.

But perhaps of all the people concerned it was the Rector who was the most to be pitied. He had staked his honour upon Mr Cavendish's repentance, and here was he going back publicly to wallow in the mire—and it was Sunday, when such a worldly subject ought not to be permitted to enter a good man's mind, much less to be discussed and acted upon as it ought to be if anything was to be done; for there was little more than this sacred day remaining in which to undo the mischief which a too great confidence in human nature had wrought. And then, to tell the truth, the Rector did not know how to turn back. It would have been hard, very hard, to have told all the people who confided in him that he had never had any stronger evidence for Mr Cavendish's repentance than he now had for his backsliding; and to give in, and let the other side have it all their own way, and throw over the candidate with whom he had identified himself, was as painful to Mr Bury as if, instead of being very Low-Church, he had been the most muscular of Christians. Being in this state of mind, it may be supposed that his sister's mild wonder and trembling speculations at lunch, when they were alone together, were well qualified to raise some sparks of that old Adam, who, though well kept under, still existed in the Rector's, as in most other human breasts.

"But, dear Edward, I would not quite condemn him," Miss Bury said. "He has been the cause of a good deal of remark, you know, and the poor girl has been talked about. He may think it is his duty to make her amends. For anything we can tell, he may have the most honourable intentions——"

"Oh, bother his honourable intentions!" said the Rector. Such an exclamation from him was as bad as the most dreadful oath from an ordinary man, and very nearly made Miss Bury drop from her chair in amazement. Things must have gone very far indeed when the Rector himself disregarded all proprieties and the sacredness of the day in such a wildly-daring fashion. For, to tell the truth, in his secret heart Mr Bury was himself a little of the way of thinking of the people in Grove Street. Strictly speaking, if a man has done anything to make a young woman be talked about, every well-principled person ought to desire that he should make her amends; but at the same time, at such a crisis there was little consolation in the fact that the candidate one was supporting and doing daily battle for had honourable intentions in respect to Barbara Lake. If it had been Rose Lake, it would still have been a blow; but Rose was unspeakably respectable, and nobody could have said a syllable on the subject: while Barbara, who came to church in a tin gown, and rustled up the middle aisle in it, attracting all eyes, and took such a second in the canticles that she overwhelmed the choir itself—Barbara, who had made people talk at Lucilla's parties, and had been ten years away, wandering over the face of the earth, nobody could tell where—governessing, singing, play-acting, perhaps, for anything that anybody could tell! A clergyman, it is true, dared not have said such a thing, and Mr Bury's remorse would have been bitter could he have really believed himself capable even of thinking it; but still it is certain that the unconscious, unexpressed idea in his mind was, that the honourable intentions were the worst of it—that a candidate might be a fool, or even an unrepentant sinner, and after all it would be chiefly his own concern; but that so much as to dream of making Barbara Lake the Member's wife, was the deepest insult that could be offered to Carlingford. The Rector carried his burden silently all day, and scarcely opened his lips, as all his sympathetic following remarked; but before he went to bed he made a singular statement, the complete accuracy of which an impartial observer might be disposed to doubt, but which Mr Bury uttered with profound sincerity, and with a sigh of self-compassion. "*Now* I understand Lucilla Marjoribanks," was what the good man said, and he all but puffed out the candle he had just lighted, with that sigh.

Lucilla, however, in her own person took no part in it at all, one way or other. She shook hands very kindly with Barbara, and hoped she would come and see her, and made it clearly apparent that *she* at least bore no malice. "I am very glad I told Thomas to say nothing about it," she said to aunt Jemima, who, however, did not know the circumstances, and was very little the wiser, as may be supposed.

And then the two ladies walked home together, and Miss Marjoribanks devoted herself to her good books. It was almost the first moment of repose that Lucilla had ever had in her busy life, and it was a repose not only permitted but enjoined. Society, which had all along expected so much from her, expected now that she should not find herself able for any exertion; and Miss Marjoribanks responded nobly, as she had always done, to the requirements of society. To a mind less perfectly regulated, the fact that the election which had been so interesting to her was now about, as may be said, to take place without her, would have been of itself a severe trial; and the sweet composure with which she bore it was not one of the least remarkable phenomena of the present crisis. But the fact was that this Sunday was on the whole an oppressive day. Mr Ashburton came in for a moment, it is true, between services; but he himself, though generally so steady, was unsettled and agitated. He had been bearing the excitement well until this last almost incredible accident occurred, which made it possible that he might not only win, but win by a large majority. "The Dissenters have all held out till now, and would not pledge themselves," he said to Lucilla, actually with a tremble in his voice; and then he told her about Mr Tufton's sermon and the wickedness in high places, and the hand imbrued metaphorically in his sister's blood.

"I wonder how he could say so," said Lucilla, with indignation. "It is just like those Dissenters. What harm was there in going to see her? I heard of it last night, but even for your interest I would never have spread such mere gossip as that."

"No—certainly it is mere gossip," said Mr Ashburton; "but it will do him a great deal of harm all the same;" and then once more he got restless and abstracted. "I suppose it is of no use asking you if you would join Lady Richmond's party at the Blue Boar? You could have a window almost to yourself, you know, and would be quite quiet."

Lucilla shook her head, and the movement was more expressive than words. "I did not think you would," said Mr Ashburton; and then he took her hand, and his looks too became full of meaning. "Then I must say adieu," he said—"adieu until it is all over. I shall not have a moment that I can call my own—this will be an eventful week for me."

"You mean an eventful day," said Lucilla; for Mr Ashburton was not such a novice as to be afraid of the appearance he would have to make at the nomination. He did not contradict her, but he pressed her hand with a look which was equivalent to kissing it, though he was not romantic enough to go quite that length. When he was gone, Miss Marjoribanks could not but wonder a little what he could mean by looking forward to an eventful week. For her own part, she could not but feel that after so much excitement things would feel rather flat for the rest of the week, and that it was almost wrong to have an election on a Tuesday. Could it be that Mr Ashburton had some other contest or candidateship in store for himself which he had not told her about? Such a thing was quite possible; but what had Lucilla in her mourning to do with worldly contingencies? She went back to her seat in the corner of the sofa and her book of sermons, and read fifty pages before tea-time; she knew how much, because she had put a mark in her book when Mr Ashburton came in. Marks are very necessary things generally in sermon-books; and Lucilla could not but feel pleased to think that since her visitor went away she had got over so much ground.

To compare Carlingford to a volcano that night (and indeed all the next day, which was the day of nomination) would be a stale similitude; and yet in some respects it was like a volcano. It was not the same kind of excitement which arises in a town where politics run very high—if there are any towns nowadays in such a state of unsophisticated nature. Neither was it a place where simple corruption could carry the day; for the freemen of Wharfside were, after all, but a small portion of the population. It was in reality a quite ideal sort of contest—a contest for the best man, such as would have pleased the purest-minded philosopher. It was the man most fit to represent Carlingford for whom everybody was looking, not a man to be baited about parish-rates and Reform Bills and the Irish Church; —a man who lived in or near the town, and "dealt regular" at all the best shops; a man who would not disgrace his constituency by any unlawful or injudicious sort of love-making— who would attend to the town's interests and subscribe to its charities, and take the lead in a general way. This was what Carlingford was looking for, as Miss Marjoribanks, with that intuitive rapidity which was characteristic of her genius, had at once remarked; and when everybody went home from church and chapel, though it was Sunday, the whole town thrilled and throbbed with this great question. People might have found it possible to condone a sin or wink at a mere backsliding; but there were few so bigoted in their faith as to believe that the man who was capable of marrying Barbara Lake could ever be the man for Carlingford; and thus it was that Mr Cavendish, who had been flourishing like a green bay-tree, withered away, as it were, in a moment, and the place that had known him knew him no more.

The hustings were erected at that central spot, just under the windows of the Blue Boar, where Grange Lane and George Street meet, the most central point in Carlingford. It was so near that Lucilla could hear the shouts and the music and all the divers noises of the election, but could not, even when she went into the very corner of the window and strained her eyes to the utmost, see what was going on, which was a very trying position. We will not linger upon the proceedings or excitement of Monday, when the nomination and the speeches were made, and when the show of hands was certainly thought to be in Mr Cavendish's favour. But it was the next day that was the real trial. Lady Richmond and her party drove past at a very early hour, and looked up at Miss Marjoribanks's windows, and congratulated themselves that they were so early, and that poor dear Lucilla would not have the additional pain of seeing them go past. But Lucilla did see them, though, with her usual good sense, she kept behind the blind. She never did anything absurd in the way of early rising on ordinary occasions; but this morning it was impossible to restrain a certain excitement, and though it did her no good, still she got up an hour earlier than usual, and listened to the music, and heard the cabs rattling about, and could not help it if her heart beat quicker. It was perhaps a more important crisis for Miss Marjoribanks than for any other person, save one, in Carlingford; for of course it would be foolish to attempt to assert that she did not understand by this time what Mr Ashburton meant; and it may be imagined how hard it was upon Lucilla to be thus, as it were, in the very outside row of the assembly—to hear all the distant shouts and sounds, everything that was noisy and inarticulate, and conveyed no meaning, and to be out of reach of all that could really inform her as to what was going on.

She saw from her window the cabs rushing past, now with her own violet-and-green colours, now with the blue-and-yellow. And sometimes it seemed to Lucilla that the blue-and-yellow predominated, and that the carriages which mounted the hostile standard carried voters in larger numbers and more enthusiastic condition. The first load of bargemen that came up Grange Lane from the further end of Wharfside were all Blues; and when a spectator is thus held on the very edge of the event in a suspense which grows every moment more intolerable, especially when he or she is disposed to believe that things in general go on all the worse for his or her absence, it is no wonder if that spectator becomes nervous, and sees all the dangers at their darkest. What if, after all, old liking and friendship had prevailed over that beautiful optimism which Lucilla had done so much to instil into the minds of her townsfolk? What if something more mercenary and less elevating than the ideal search for the best man, in which she had hoped Carlingford was engaged, should have swayed the popular mind to the other side? All these painful questions went through Lucilla's mind as the day crept on; and her suspense was much aggravated by aunt Jemima, who took no real interest in the election, but who kept saying every ten minutes—"I wonder how the poll is going on—I wonder what that is they are shouting—is it 'Ashburton for ever!' or 'Cavendish for ever!' Lucilla? Your ears should be sharper than mine; but I think it is Cavendish." Lucilla thought so too, and her heart quaked within her, and she went and squeezed herself into the corner of the window, to try whether it was not possible to catch a glimpse of the field of battle; and her perseverance was finally rewarded by the sight of the extremity of the wooden planks which formed the polling-booth; but there was little satisfaction to be got out of that. And then the continual dropping of aunt Jemima's questions drove her wild. "My dear aunt," she said at last, "I can see nothing and hear nothing, and you know as much about what is going on as I do"—which, it will be acknowledged, was not an answer such as one would have expected from Lucilla's perfect temper and wonderful self-control.

The election went on with all its usual commotion while Miss Marjoribanks watched and waited. Mr Cavendish's committee brought their supporters very well up in the morning—no doubt by way of making sure of them, as somebody suggested on the other side; and for some time Mrs Woodburn's party at Masters's windows (which Masters had given rather reluctantly, by way of pleasing the Rector) looked in better spirits and less anxious than Lady Richmond's party, which was at the Blue Boar. Towards noon Mr Cavendish himself went up to his female supporters with the bulletin of the poll—the same bulletin which Mr Ashburton had just sent down to Lucilla. These were the numbers; and they made Masters's triumphant, while silence and anxiety fell upon the Blue Boar:—

Cavendish,	283
Ashburton,	275

When Miss Marjoribanks received this disastrous intelligence, she put the note in her pocket without saying a word to aunt Jemima, and left her window, and went back to her worsted-work; but as for Mrs Woodburn, she gave her brother a hug, and laughed, and cried, and believed in it, like a silly woman as she was.

"It is something quite unlooked-for, and which I never could have calculated upon," she said, thrusting her hand into an imaginary waistcoat with Mr Ashburton's very look and tone, which was beyond measure amusing to all the party. They laughed so long, and were so gay, that Lady Richmond solemnly levelled her opera-glass at them with the air of a woman who was used to elections, but knew how such *parvenus* have their heads turned by a prominent position. "That woman is taking some of us off," she said; "but if it is me, I can bear it. There is nothing so vulgar as that sort of thing, and I hope you never encourage it in your presence, my dears."

Just at that moment, however, an incident occurred which took up the attention of the ladies at the windows, and eclipsed even the interest of the election. Poor Barbara Lake was interested, too, to know if her friend would win. She was not entertaining any particular hopes or plans about him. Years and hard experiences had humbled Barbara. The Brussels veil which she used to dream of had faded as much from her memory as poor Rose's Honiton design, for which she had got the prize. At the present moment, instead of nourishing the ambitious designs which everybody laid to her charge, she would have been content with the very innocent privilege of talking a little to her next employers about Mr Cavendish, the member for Carlingford, and his visits to her father's house. But at the same time, she had once been fond of him, and she took a great interest in him, and was very anxious that he should win. And she was in the habit, like so many other women, of finding out, as far as she could, what was going on, and going to see everything that there might be to see. She had brought one of her young brothers with her, whose anxiety to see the fun was quite as great as her own; and she was arrayed in the tin dress—her best available garment—which was made long, according to the fashion, and which, as Barbara scorned to tuck it up, was continually getting trodden on, and talked about, and reviled at, on that crowded pavement. The two parties of ladies saw, and even it might be said heard, the sweep of the metallic garment, which was undergoing such rough usage, and which was her best, poor soul. Lady Richmond had alighted from her carriage carefully tucked up, though there were only a few steps to make, and there was no *lady* in Carlingford who would have swept "a good gown" over the stones in such a way; but then poor Barbara was not precisely a lady, and thought it right to look as if it did not matter. She went up to read the numbers of the poll —in the sight of everybody; and she clasped her hands together with ecstatic satisfaction as she read ; and young Carmine, her brother, dashed into the midst of the fray, and shouted "Cavendish for ever! hurrah for Cavendish!" and could scarcely be drawn back again to take his sister home. Even when she withdrew, she did not go home, but went slowly up and down Grange Lane with her rustling train behind her, with the intention of coming back for further information. Lady Richmond and Mrs Woodburn both lost all thought of the election as they watched; and lo! when their wandering thoughts came back again, the tide had turned.

The tide had turned. Whether it was Barbara, or whether it was fate, or whether it was the deadly unanimity of those Dissenters, who, after all their wavering, had at last decided for the man who "dealt" in George Street—no one could tell; but by two o'clock Mr Ashburton was so far ahead that he felt himself justified in sending another bulletin to Lucilla—so far that there was no reasonable hope of the opposite candidate ever making up his lost ground. Mrs Woodburn was not a woman to be content when reasonable hope was over—she clung to the last possibility desperately, with a pertinacity beyond all reason, and swore in her heart that it was Barbara that had done it, and cursed her with her best energies; which, however, as these are not melodramatic days, was a thing which did the culprit no possible harm. When Barbara herself came back from her promenade in Grange Lane, and saw the altered numbers, she again clasped her hands together for a moment, and looked as if she were going to faint; and it was at that moment that Mr Cavendish's eyes fell upon her, as ill fortune would have it. They were all looking at him as if it was his fault; and the sight of that sympathetic face was consoling to the defeated candidate. He took off his hat before everybody; probably, as his sister afterwards said, he would have gone and offered her his arm had he been near enough. How could anybody wonder, after that, that things had gone against him, and that, notwithstanding all his advantages, he was the loser in the fight?

As for Lucilla, she had gone back to her worsted-work when she got Mr Ashburton's first note, in which his rival's name stood above his own. She looked quite composed, and aunt Jemima went on teasing with her senseless questions. But Miss Marjoribanks put up with it all; though the lingering progress of these hours from one o'clock to four, the sound of cabs furiously driven by, the distant shouts, the hum of indefinite din that filled the air, exciting every moment a keener curiosity, and giving no satisfaction or information, would have been enough to have driven a less large intelligence out of its wits. Lucilla bore it, doing as much as she could of her worsted-work, and saying nothing to nobody, except, indeed, an occasional word to aunt Jemima, who would have an answer. She was not walking about Grange Lane repeating a kind of prayer for the success of her candidate, as Barbara Lake was doing; but perhaps, on the whole, Barbara had the easiest time of it at that moment of uncertainty. When the next report came, Lucilla's fingers trembled as she opened it, so great was her emotion; but after that she recovered herself as if by magic. She grew pale, and then gave a kind of sob, and then a kind of laugh, and finally put her worsted-work back into her basket, and threw Mr Ashburton's note into the fire.

"It is all right," said Lucilla. "Mr Ashburton is a hundred ahead, and they can never make up that. I am so sorry for poor Mr Cavendish. If he only had not been so imprudent on Saturday night!"

"I am sure I don't understand you," said aunt Jemima. "After being so anxious about one candidate, how can you be so sorry for the other? I suppose you did not want them both to win?"

"Yes, I think that *was* what I wanted," said Lucilla, drying her eyes; and then she awoke to the practical exigencies of the position. "There will be quantities of people coming to have a cup of tea, and I must speak to Nancy," she said, and went down-stairs with a cheerful heart. It might be said to be as good as decided, so far as regarded Mr Ashburton; and when it came for her final judgment, what was it that she ought to say?

It was very well that Miss Marjoribanks's unfailing foresight led her to speak to Nancy; for the fact was, that after four o'clock, when the polling was over, everybody came in to tea. All Lady Richmond's party came, as a matter of course, and Mr Ashburton himself, for a few minutes, bearing meekly his new honours; and so many more people besides, that but for knowing it was a special occasion, and that "our gentleman" was elected, Nancy's mind never could have borne the strain. And the tea that was used was something frightful. As for aunt Jemima, who had just then a good many thoughts of her own to occupy her, and did not care so much as the rest for all the chatter that was going on, nor for all those details about poor Barbara and Mr Cavendish's looks, which Lucilla received with such interest, she could not but make a calculation in passing as to this new item of fashionable expenditure into which her niece was plunging so wildly. To be sure, it was an occasion that never might occur again, and everybody was so excited as to forget even that Lucilla was in mourning, and that such a number of people in the house so soon might be more than she could bear. And she was excited herself, and forgot that she was not able for it. But still aunt Jemima, sitting by, could not help thinking, that even five-o'clock teas of good quality and unlimited amount would very soon prove to be impracticable upon two hundred a-year.

CHAPTER XLIX.

Mr Ashburton, it may be supposed, had but little time to think on that eventful evening; and yet he was thinking all the way home, as he drove back in the chilly spring night to his own house. If his further course of action had been made in any way to depend upon the events of this day, it was now settled beyond all further uncertainty; and though he was not a man in his first youth, nor a likely subject for a romantic passion, still he was a little excited by the position in which he found himself. Miss Marjoribanks had been his inspiring genius, and had interested herself in his success in the warmest and fullest way; and if ever a woman was made for a certain position, Lucilla was made to be the wife of the Member for Carlingford. Long long ago, at the very beginning of her career, when it was of Mr Cavendish that everybody was thinking, the ideal fitness of this position had struck everybody. Circumstances had changed since then, and Mr Cavendish had fallen, and a worthier hero had been placed in his stead; but though the person was changed, the circumstances remained unaltered. Natural fitness was indeed so apparent, that many people would have been disposed to say that it was Lucilla's duty to accept Mr Ashburton, even independent of the fact that he was perfectly eligible in every other respect.

But with all this the new Member for Carlingford was not able to assure himself that there had been anything particular in Lucilla's manner to himself. With her as with Carlingford, it was pure optimism. He was the best man, and her quick intelligence had defined it sooner than anybody else had done. Whether there was anything more in it, Mr Ashburton could not tell. His own impression was, that she would accept him; but if she did not, he would have no right to complain of "encouragement," or to think himself jilted. This was what he was thinking as he drove home; but at the same time he was very far from being in a desponding state of mind. He felt very nearly as sure that Lucilla would be his wife, as if they were already standing before the Rector in Carlingford Church. He had just won one victory, which naturally made him feel more confident of winning another; and even without entertaining any over-exalted opinion of himself, it was evident that, under all the circumstances, a woman of thirty, with two hundred a-year, would be a fool to reject such an offer. And Lucilla was the very furthest in the world from being a fool. It was in every respect the beginning of a new world to Mr Ashburton, and it would have been out of nature had he not been a little excited. After the quiet life he had led at the Firs, biding his time, he had now to look forward to a busy and important existence, half of it spent amid the commotion and ceaseless stir of town. A new career, a wife, a new position, the most important in his district—it was not much wonder if Mr Ashburton felt a little excited. He was fatigued at the same time, too much fatigued to be disposed for sleep; and all these united influences swayed him to a state of mind very much unlike his ordinary sensible calm. All his excitement culminated so in thoughts of Lucilla, that the new Member felt himself truly a lover; and late as the hour was, he took up a candle and once more made a survey all alone of his solitary house.

Nothing could look more dismal than the dark rooms, where there was neither light nor fire—the great desert drawing-room, for example, which stood unchanged as it had been in the days of his grandaunts, the good old ladies who had bequeathed the Firs to Mr Ashburton. He had made no change in it, and scarcely ever used it, keeping to his library and dining-room, with the possibility, no doubt, always before him of preparing it in due course of time for his wife. That moment had now arrived, and in his excitement he went into the desolate room with his candle, which just made the darkness visible, and tried to see the dusky curtains and faded carpet, and the indescribable fossil air which everything had. There were the odd little spider-legged stands, upon which the Miss Penrhyns had placed their work-boxes, and the old sofas on which they had sat, and the floods of old tapestry-work with which they had decorated their favourite sitting-room. The sight of it chilled the Member for Carlingford, and made him sad. He tried to turn his thoughts to the time when this same room should be fitted up to suit Lucilla's complexion, and should be gay with light and with her presence. He did all he could to realise the moment when, with a mistress so active and energetic, the whole place would change its aspect, and glow forth resplendent into the twilight of the county, a central point for all. Perhaps it was his fatigue which gained upon him just at this moment, and repulsed all livelier thoughts; but the fact is, that however willing Lucilla might turn out to be, her image was coy, and would not come. The more Mr Ashburton tried to think of her as in possession here, the more the grim images of the two old Miss Penrhyns walked out of the darkness and asserted their prior claims. They even seemed to have got into the library before him when he went back, though there his fire was burning, and his lamp. After that there was nothing left for a man to do, even though he had been that day elected Member for Carlingford, but to yield to the weakness of an ordinary mortal, and go to bed.

Thoughts very different, but even more disturbing, were going on at the same time in Grange Lane. Poor Mr Cavendish, for one thing —upbraided by everybody's looks, and even by some people's words—feeling himself condemned, censured, and despised on all sides—smarting under his sister's wild reproaches and her husband's blunt commentary thereupon,—had slunk away from their society after dinner, not seeing *now* why he should bear it any longer. "By Jove! if it had only been for *her* sake, you might have left over your philandering for another night," Mr Woodburn had said, in his coarse way; and it was all Mr Cavendish could do to refrain from saying that one time and another he had done quite enough for *her* sake, but he did not see any reason why he should put up with it any longer. He strolled out of doors, though the town was still in commotion, and could not but think of the sympathetic countenance which had paled to-day at sight of the numbers of the poll. She, by heaven! might have had reason to find fault with him, and she had never done so; *she* had never perceived that he was stout, or changed from old times. As he entertained these thoughts, his steps going down Grange Lane gradually quickened, but he did not say to himself where he was going. He went a very roundabout way, as if he did not mean it, as far as St Roque's, and then up by the lane to the far-off desert extremity of Grove Street. It was simply to walk off his excitement and disappointment, and free himself from criticism for that evening at least; but as he walked he could not help thinking that Barbara, if she were well dressed, would still be a fine woman, that her voice was magnificent in its way, and that about Naples, perhaps, or the baths of Lucca, or in Germany, or the south of France, a man might be able to get on well enough with such a companion, where society was not so exacting or stiff-starched as in England. And the end was, that the feet of the defeated candidate carried him, ere ever he was aware, with some kind of independent volition of their own, to Mr Lake's door—and it may be here said once for all, that this visit was decisive of Mr Cavendish's fate.

This will not be regarded as anything but a digression by such of Lucilla's friends as may be solicitous to know what she was making up her mind to under the circumstances; but the truth is that Lucilla's historian cannot, any more than Miss Marjoribanks herself could, refrain from a certain regret over Mr Cavendish. That was what he came to, poor man! after all his experiences; a man who was capable of so much better things—a man even who, if he had made a right use of his opportunities, might once have had as good a chance as any other of marrying Lucilla herself. If there ever was an instance of chances thrown away and lost opportunities, surely here was that lamentable example. And thus, poor man! all his hopes and all his chances came to an end.

As for Miss Marjoribanks herself, it would be vain to say that this was not a very exciting moment for her. If there ever could be said to be a time when she temporarily lost the entire sway and control of herself and her feelings, it would be at this crisis. She went about all that evening like a woman in a dream. For the first time in her life she not only did not know what she would do, but she did not know what she wanted to do. There could now be no mistaking what Mr Ashburton's intentions were. Up to a very recent time Lucilla had been able to take refuge in her mourning, and conclude that she had no present occasion to disturb herself. But now that calm was over. She could not conceal from herself that it was in her power by a word to reap all the advantages of the election, and to step at once into the only position which she had ever felt might be superior to her own in Carlingford. At last this great testimonial of female merit was to be laid at her feet. A man thoroughly eligible in every way—moderately rich, well connected, able to restore to her all, and more than all, the advantages which she had lost at her father's death—a man, above all, who was Member for Carlingford, was going to offer himself to her acceptance, and put his happiness in her hands; and while she was so well aware of this, she was not at all so well aware what answer she would make him. Lucilla's mind was in such a commotion as she sat over her embroidery, that she thought it strange indeed that it did not show, and could not understand how aunt Jemima could sit there so quietly opposite her, as if nothing was the matter. But, to tell the truth, there was a good deal the matter with aunt Jemima too, which was perhaps the reason why she saw no signs of her companion's agitation. Mrs John Marjoribanks had not been able any more than her niece to shut her eyes to Mr Ashburton's evident meaning; and now that matters were visibly coming to a crisis, a sudden panic and horror had seized her. What would Tom say? If she stood by and saw the prize snapped up under her very eyes, what account could she give to her son of her stewardship? How could she explain her silence as to all *his* wishes and intentions, her absolute avoidance of his name in all her conversations with Lucilla? While Miss Marjoribanks marvelled that the emotion in her breast could be invisible, and at aunt Jemima's insensibility, the bosom of that good woman was throbbing with equal excitement. Sometimes each made an indifferent remark, and panted after it as if she had given utterance to the most exhausting emotions; but so great was the preoccupation of both that neither observed how it was faring with the other.

But perhaps, on the whole, it was aunt Jemima that suffered the most; for her there was nothing flattering, nothing gratifying, no prospect of change or increased happiness, or any of the splendours of imagination involved. All that could happen to her would be the displeasure of her son and his disappointment; and it might be her fault, she who could have consented to be chopped up in little pieces, if that would have done Tom any good; but who, notwithstanding, was not anxious for him to marry his cousin, now that her father's fortune was all lost and she had but two hundred a-year. They had a silent cup of tea together at eight o'clock, after that noisy exciting one at five, which had been shared by half Carlingford, as aunt Jemima thought. The buzz of that impromptu assembly, in which everybody talked at the same moment, and nobody listened, except perhaps Lucilla, had all died away into utter stillness; but the excitement had not died away; *that* had only risen to a white heat, silent and consuming, as the two ladies sat over their tea.

"Do you expect Mr Ashburton to-morrow, Lucilla?" aunt Jemima said, after a long pause.

"Mr Ashburton?" said Lucilla, with a slight start; and, to tell the truth, she was glad to employ that childish expedient to gain a little time, and consider what she should say. "Indeed I don't know if he will have time to come. Most likely there will be a great deal to do."

"If he does come," said Mrs John, with a sigh—"or *when* he does come, I ought to say, for you know very well he *will* come, Lucilla—I suppose there is no doubt that he will have something very particular to say."

"I am sure I don't know, aunt Jemima," said Miss Marjoribanks; but she never raised her eyes from her work, as she would have done in any other case. "Now that the election is over, you know——"

"I hope, my dear, I have been long enough in the world to know all about that," aunt Jemima said, severely, "and what it means when young ladies take such interest in elections;" and then some such feeling as the dog had in the manger—a jealousy of those who sought the gift though she herself did not want it—came over Mrs John, and at the same time a sudden desire to clear her conscience and make a stand for Tom. She did it suddenly, and went further than she meant to go; but then she never dreamt it would have the least effect. "I would not say anything to disturb your mind, Lucilla, if you have made up your mind; but when you receive your new friends, you might think of other people who perhaps have been fond of you before you ever saw them, or heard their very name."

She was frightened at it herself before the words were out of her mouth, and the effect it had upon Miss Marjoribanks was wonderful. She threw her embroidery away, and looked Tom's mother keenly in the face. "I don't think you know anybody who is fond of me, aunt Jemima," she said; "I don't suppose anybody is fond of me. Do you?" said Lucilla. But by that time aunt Jemima had got thoroughly frightened, both at herself and her companion, and had nothing more to say.

"I am sure all these people to-day have been too much for you," she said. "I wonder what they could all be thinking

of, for my part, flocking in upon you like that, so soon after——
I thought it was very indelicate of Lady Richmond. And Lucilla, my dear, your nerves are quite affected, and I am sure you ought to go to bed."

Upon which Miss Marjoribanks recovered herself in a moment, and folded up her worsted-work. "I do feel tired," she said, sweetly, "and perhaps it *was* too much. I think I will take your advice, aunt Jemima. The excitement keeps one up for the moment, and then it tells after. I suppose the best thing is to go to bed."

"Much the best, my dear," aunt Jemima said, giving Lucilla a kiss; but she did not take her own advice. She took a long time to think it all over, and sat up by the side of the decaying fire until it was midnight—an hour at which a female establishment like this should surely have been all shut up and at rest. And Lucilla did very much the same thing, wondering greatly what her aunt could tell her if she had a mind, and having the greatest inclination in the world to break into her chamber, and see, at any risk, what was in Tom's last letter. If she could have seen that, it might have thrown some light on the problem Lucilla was discussing, or given her some guidance through her difficulties. It was just then that Mr Ashburton was inviting her image into the fossil drawing-room, and finding nothing but the grim shades of the Miss Penrhyns answer to his call. Perhaps this was because Lucilla's image at that moment was called upon more potently from another quarter in a more familiar voice.

But after this exhausting day and late sitting-up, everybody was late in the morning, at least in Grange Lane. Miss Marjoribanks had slept little all night, and she was not in a more settled state of mind when the day returned which probably would bring the matter to a speedy decision. Her mind was like a country held by two armies, one of which by turns swept the other into a corner, but only to be driven back in its turn. After the unaccountable stupidity of the general public—after all the Cavendishes, Beverleys, and Riders who had once had it in their power to distinguish themselves by at least making her an offer, and who had not done it—here at last, in all good faith, honesty, and promptitude, had appeared a man superior to them all—a man whom she would have no reason to be ashamed of in any particular, sensible like herself, public-spirited like herself—a man whose pursuits she could enter into fully, who had a perfectly ideal position to offer her, and in whose person, indeed, all sorts of desirable qualities seemed to meet. Miss Marjoribanks, when she considered all this, and thought over all their recent intercourse, and the terms of friendship into which the election had brought them, felt, as any other sensible person would have felt, that there was only one answer which could be given to such a man. If she neglected or played with his devotion, then certainly she never would deserve to have another such possibility afforded to her, and merited nothing better than to live and die a single woman on two hundred a-year. But then, on the other hand, there would rush forth a crowd of quick-coming and fantastic suggestions which took away Lucilla's breath, and made her heart beat loud. What if there might be "other people" who had been fond of her before she ever heard Mr Ashburton's name? What if there might be some one in the world who was ready, not to offer her his hand and fortune in a reasonable way, as Mr Ashburton no doubt would, but to throw himself all in a heap at her feet, and make the greatest fool of himself possible for her sake? Miss Marjoribanks had been the very soul of good sense all her days, but now her ruling quality seemed to forsake her. And yet she could not consent to yield herself up to pure unreason without a struggle. She fought manfully, womanfully, against the weakness which hitherto must have been lying hidden in some out-of-the-way corner in her heart. Probably if Mr Ashburton had asked her all at once amid the excitement of the election, or at any other unpremeditated moment, Lucilla would have been saved all this self-torment; but it is hard upon a woman to have a proposal hanging over her head by a hair, as it were, and to look forward to it without any uncertainty or mystery, and have full time to make up her mind. And there was no accounting for the curious force and vividness with which that strange idea about "other people," upon which aunt Jemima would throw no light, had come into Lucilla's head.

She was still in the same frightful chaos of uncertainty when Mr Ashburton was shown into the drawing-room. She had not even heard him ring, and was thus deprived of the one possible moment of coming to a decision before she faced and confronted her fate. Miss Marjoribanks's heart gave a great jump, and then she recovered herself, and rose up without faltering, and shook hands with him. She was all alone, for aunt Jemima had not found herself equal to facing the emergency; and there was not the least possibility of evading or postponing, or in any way running away from it now. Lucilla sat down again upon her sofa where she had been sitting, and composed herself with a certain despairing tranquillity, and trusted in Providence. She had thrown herself on other occasions, though never at an equally important crisis, upon the inspiration of the moment, and she felt it would not forsake her now.

"I should be sorry the election was over," said Mr Ashburton, who was naturally a little agitated too, "if I thought its privileges were over, and you would not let me come—— I shall always think I owe my success to you; and I would thank you for being so kind—so very kind to me, if——"

"Oh dear, no; pray don't say so," cried Lucilla. "I only felt sure that you were the best man—the only man—for Carlingford."

"I wish I might but prove the best man for something else," said the candidate, nervously; and then he cleared his throat. "I would say you had been kind if I did not hope—if I was not so very anxious that you should be something more than kind. It may be vain of me, but I think we could get on together. I think I could understand you, and do you justice—— Lucilla! what is the matter? Good heavens! is it possible that I have taken you quite by surprise?"

What caused this question was, that Miss Marjoribanks had all at once changed colour, and given a great start, and put her hand to her breast, where her heart had taken such a leap that she felt it in her throat. But it was not because of what Mr Ashburton was saying; it was because of one of the very commonest sounds of everyday existence—a cab driving down Grange Lane; but then it was a cab driving in such a way that you could have sworn there was somebody in it in a terrible hurry, and who had just arrived by the twelve o'clock train.

"Oh no, no," said Miss Marjoribanks; "I know you have always done me more than justice, Mr Ashburton, and so have all my friends; and I am sure we always will get on well together. I wish you joy with all my heart, and I wish you every happiness; and I always thought up to this very last moment——"

Lucilla stopped again, and once more put her hand to her breast. Her heart gave another jump, and, if such a thing were possible to a heart, went off from its mistress altogether, and rushed down-stairs bodily to see who was coming. Yet, with all her agitation, she had still enough self-control to lift an appealing look—a look which threw herself upon his mercy, and implored his forbearance—to Mr Ashburton's face.

As for the Member for Carlingford, he was confounded, and could not tell what to make of it. What was it she had thought up to the very last moment? Was this a refusal, or was she only putting off his claim, or was it something altogether independent of him and his intentions that agitated Lucilla to such an unusual extent? While he sat in his confusion trying to make it out, the most startling sound interrupted the interview. The old disused bell that had so often called Dr Marjoribanks up at night, and which hung near the door of the old Doctor's room, just over the drawing-room, began to peal through the silence, as if rung by a hand too impatient to notice what it was with which it made its summons.

"Papa's bell!" Miss Marjoribanks cried, with a little shriek; and she got up trembling, and then dropped upon her seat again, and in her agitated state burst into tears. And Mr Ashburton felt that, under these most extraordinary circumstances, even so sensible a woman as Lucilla might be justified in fainting, embarrassing and uncomfortable as that would be.

"I will go and see what it means," he said, with still half the air of a man who had a right to go and see, and was, as it were, almost in his own house. As he turned round, the door bell pealed wildly below in correction of the mistake. It was evident that somebody wanted admission who had not a moment to lose, and who was in the habit of pulling wildly at whatever came in his way. Mr Ashburton went out of the room to see who it was, a little amused and a little alarmed, but much annoyed at bottom, as was only natural, at such an interruption. He did not very well know whether he was accepted or rejected; but it was equally his duty in either case to put a stop to the ringing of that ghostly bell. He went away, meaning to return immediately and have it out and know his fate. And Lucilla, whose heart had come back, having fully ascertained who it was, and was now choking her with its beating, was left to await the new event and the new-comer alone.

CHAPTER L.

MR ASHBURTON went away from Lucilla's side, thinking to come back again, and clear everything up; but he did not come back. Though he heard nothing, and saw nothing, that could

throw any distinct light on the state of her mind, yet instinct
came to his aid, it is to be supposed, in the matter. He did not
return: and Lucilla sat on her sofa with her hands clasped together to support her, and her heart leaping in her very mouth.
She was in a perfect frenzy of suspense, listening with her whole
heart and soul; but that did not prevent the same crowd of
thoughts which had been persecuting her for twenty-four hours
from keeping up their wild career as before. What reason had
she to suppose that "any one" had arrived? Who could arrive in that accidental way, without a word of warning? And
what possible excuse had she to offer to herself for sending the
new member for Carlingford—a man so excellent and honourable and eligible—away? The minutes, or rather the seconds,
passed over Miss Marjoribanks like hours, as she sat thus waiting, not daring to stir lest the slightest movement might keep
from her ears some sound from below, till at last the interval
seemed so long that her heart began to sink, and her excitement
to fail. It could not be any one—if it had been any one, something more must have come of it before now. It must have
been Lydia Richmond coming to see her sister next door, or
somebody connected with the election, or——

When she got as far as this, Lucilla's heart suddenly mounted
up again with a spring into her ears. She heard neither words
nor voice, but she heard something which had as great an effect
upon her as either could have had. On the landing half-way
up the stairs, there had stood in Dr Marjoribanks's house from
time immemorial a little old-fashioned table, with a large china
bowl upon it, in which the cards of visitors were placed. It was
a great bowl, and it was always full, and anybody rushing up-
stairs in a reckless way might easily upset table and cards and
all in their progress. This was what happened while Lucilla
sat listening. There was a rumble, a crash, and a sound as of
falling leaves, and it made her heart, as we have said, jump into
her ears. "It is the table and all the cards," said Lucilla—and
in that moment her composure came back to her as by a miracle.
She unclasped her hands, which she had been holding pressed
painfully together by way of supporting herself, and she gave a
long sigh of unutterable relief, and her whirl of thought stopped and cleared up with an instantaneous rapidity. Everything seemed to be explained by that sound; and there never
was a greater change upon the looks and feelings of any one
in this world than that which passed upon the looks and feelings of Lucilla, in the interval between the drawing-up of that

cab and the rush of Tom Marjoribanks at the drawing-room door.

For after the commotion on the staircase Lucilla had no further doubt on the subject. She even had the strength to get up to meet him, and hold out her hands to him by way of welcome—but found herself, before she knew how, in the arms of a man with a beard, who was so much changed in his own person that he ventured to kiss her, which was a thing Tom Marjoribanks, though her cousin, had never dared to do before. He kissed her—such was his audacity; and then he held her at arm's length to have a good look at her; and then, according to all appearance, would have repeated his first salutation, but that Lucilla had come to herself, and took the reins at once into her hand.

"Tom!" she said, "of course it is you; nobody else would have been so impertinent. When did you come? Where did you come from? Who could ever have thought of your appearing like this, in such an altogether unexpected——?"

"Unexpected!" said Tom, with an astonished air. "But I suppose you had other things to think of. Ah, Lucilla, I could not write to you. I felt I ought to be beside you, trying if there was not something I could do. My mother told you, of course; but I could not trust myself to write to *you*."

Then Lucilla saw it all, and that aunt Jemima had meant to do Mr Ashburton a good turn. And she was not grateful to her aunt, however kind her intentions might have been. But Tom was holding her hand, and looking into her face while this thought passed through her mind, and Miss Marjoribanks was not the woman, under any circumstances, to make dispeace.

"I am sure I am very glad," said Lucilla. "I would say you were changed, but only of course that would make you think how I am changed; and though one knows one has gone off——"

"I never saw you look so nice all your life," cried Tom, energetically; and he took hold of both her hands, and looked into her face more and more. To be sure he had a kind of right, being her cousin, and newly returned after so long an absence; but it was embarrassing all the same.

"Oh, Tom, don't say so," cried Lucilla; "if you but knew how different the house is, and everything so altered—and dear papa!"

It was natural, and indeed it was only proper, that Miss Marjoribanks should cry—which she did abundantly, partly for grief, and partly because of the flutter of agitation, and something like joy, in which she was, and which, considering that she had always frankly owned that she was fond of Tom, was quite natural too. She cried with honest abandonment, and did not take much notice what her cousin was doing to comfort her, though indeed he applied himself to that benevolent office in the most anxious way.

"Don't cry, Lucilla," he said, "I can't bear it. It don't look natural to see you cry. My poor uncle was an old man, and you were always the best daughter in the world——"

"Oh, Tom! sometimes I don't think so," sobbed Lucilla; "sometimes I think if I had sat up that last night—— And you don't know how good he was. It was me he was thinking of, and never himself. When he heard the money was lost, all that he said was, Poor Lucilla! You rang his bell though it is the night-bell, and nobody ever touches it now; I knew it could be nobody but you; and to see you again brings up everything so distinctly. Oh, Tom! he was always very fond of you."

"Lucilla," said Tom Marjoribanks, "you know I always had a great regard for my uncle. But it was not for him I came back. He was never half so fond of me as I am of you. You know that as well as I do. There never was a time that I would not have gone to the other end of the world if you had told me; and I have done it as near as possible. I went to India because you sent me away. And I have come back——"

"You have not come back only for an hour, I hope," said Miss Marjoribanks, with momentary impatience; "you are not obliged to talk of everything all in a moment—and when one has not even got over one's surprise at seeing you. When *did* you come back? When did you have anything to eat? You want your breakfast or your lunch or something; and, Tom! the idea of sitting here talking to me, and talking nonsense, when you have not seen your mother. She is in her own room, you unnatural boy—the blue room, next to what used to be yours. To think aunt Jemima should be in the house, and you should sit here talking nonsense to me!"

"This minute," said Tom, apologetically; but he drew his chair in front of Miss Marjoribanks, so that she could not get away. "I have come back to stay as long as you will let me," he said; "don't go away yet. Look here, Lucilla—if you had married, I would have tried to bear it; but as long as you are not married, I can't help feeling as if there might be a chance for me yet. And that is why I have come home. I met somebody coming down-stairs."

"Tom," said Miss Marjoribanks, "it is dreadful to see that you have come back just as tiresome as ever. I always said I would not marry for ten years. If you mean to think I have never had any opportunities——"

"Lucilla," said Tom, and there was decision in his eye, "somebody came down-stairs as I came in. I want to know whether it is to be him or me!"

"Him—or you!" said Lucilla, in dismay. Blunderer as he was, he had gone direct to the very heart of the question, and it was impossible not to tremble a little in the presence of such straightforward clearsightedness. Miss Marjoribanks had risen up to make her escape as soon as it should be possible, but she was so much struck by Tom's unlooked-for perspicuity that she sat down again in her consternation. "I think you are going out of your mind," she said. "What do you know about the gentleman who went down-stairs? I am not such a wonderful beauty, nor such a witch, that everybody who sees me should want to—to marry me. Don't talk any more nonsense, but let me go and get you something to eat."

"They would if they were of my way of thinking," said the persistent Tom. "Lucilla, you shan't go. This is what I have come home for. You may as well know at once, and then there can be no mistake about it. My poor uncle is gone, and you can't be left by yourself in the world. Will you have him or me?"

"I am not going to be tyrannised over like this," said Lucilla, with indignation, again rising, though he still held her hands. "You talk as if you had just come for a call, and had everything to say in a moment. When a man comes off a long journey, it is his breakfast he wants, and not a——not anything else that I know of. Go up to your mother, and let me go."

"Will you have him or me?" repeated Tom. It was not wisdom, it was instinct, that made him thus hold fast by his text; and as for Lucilla, nothing but the softened state in which she was, nothing but the fact that it was Tom Marjoribanks who had been ten years away, and was always ridiculous, could have kept her from putting down at once such an attempt to coerce her. But the truth was, that Miss Marjoribanks did not feel her own mistress at that moment, and perhaps that was why he had the audacity to repeat, "Will you have him or me?"

Then Lucilla found herself fairly driven to bay. "Tom!" she said, with a solemnity that overwhelmed him for the moment, for he thought at first, with natural panic, that it was himself who was being rejected, "I would not have *him* if he were to go down on his knees. I know he is very nice and very agreeable, and the best man—— And I am sure I ought to do it," said Miss Marjoribanks, with a mournful sense of her own weakness; "and everybody will expect it of me; but I am not going to have him, and I never meant it, whatever you or anybody may say."

When Lucilla had made this decisive utterance she turned away with a certain melancholy majesty to go and see after lunch—for he had loosed her hand and fallen back in consternation, thinking for the moment that it was all over. Miss Marjoribanks sighed, and turned round, not thinking of Tom, who was safe enough, but with a natural regret for the Member for Carlingford, who now, poor man, was as much out of the question as if he had been dead and buried. But before she reached the door Tom had recovered himself. He went up to her in his ridiculous way without the slightest regard either for the repast she was so anxious to prepare for him, or for his mother's feelings, or indeed for anything else in the world, except the one thing which had brought him, as he said, home.

"Then, Lucilla, after all, it is to be me," he said, taking her to him, and arresting her progress as if she had been a baby; and though he had such a beard, and was twice as big and strong as he used to be, there were big tears in the great fellow's eyes. "It is to be me after all," said Tom, looking at her in a way that startled Lucilla. "Say it is to be me!"

Miss Marjoribanks had come through many a social crisis with dignity and composure. She had never yet been known to fail in an emergency. She had managed Mr Cavendish, and, up to the last moment, Mr Ashburton, and all the intervening candidates for her favour, with perfect self-control and command of the situation. Perhaps it was because, as she had herself said, her feelings had never been engaged. But now, when it was only Tom—he whom, once upon a time, she had dismissed with affectionate composure, and given such excellent advice to, and regarded in so motherly a way—all Lucilla's powers seemed to fail her. It is hard to have to wind up with such a confession after having so long entertained a confidence in Lucilla which nothing seemed likely to impair. She broke down just at the moment when she had most need to have all her wits about her.

Perhaps it was her past agitation which had been too much for her. Perhaps it was the tears in Tom Marjoribanks's eyes. But the fact was that Lucilla relinquished her superior position for the time being, and suffered him to make any assertion he pleased, and was so weak as to cry, for the second time, too— which, of all things in the world, was surely the last thing to have been expected of Miss Marjoribanks at the moment which decided her fate.

Lucilla cried, and acquiesced, and thought of her father and of the Member for Carlingford, and gave to each a tear and a regret; and she did not even take the trouble to answer any question, or to think who it was she was leaning on. It was to be Tom after all—after all the archdeacons, doctors, generals, members of Parliament—after the ten years and more in which she had not gone off—after the poor old Doctor's grudge against the nephew whom he did not wish to inherit his wealth, and aunt Jemima's quiet wiles, and attempt to disappoint her boy. Fate and honest love had been waiting all the time till their moment came; and now it was not even necessary to say anything about it. The fact was so clear that it did not require stating. It was to be Tom after all.

To do him justice, Tom behaved at this moment, in which affairs were left in his hands, as if he had been training for it all his life. Perhaps it was the first time in which he had done anything absolutely without a blunder. He had wasted no time, and no words, and left no room for consideration, or for that natural relenting towards his rival which was inevitable as soon as Mr Ashburton was off the field. He had insisted, and he had perceived that there was but one alternative for Lucilla. Now that all was over, he took her back to her seat, and comforted her, and made no offensive demonstrations of triumph. "It is to be me after all!" he repeated; and it was utterly impossible to add anything to the eloquent brevity of this succinct statement of the case.

"Tom," said Miss Marjoribanks, when she had a little recovered, "if it is to be you, that is no reason why you should be so unnatural. Go up directly and see your mother. What will aunt Jemima think of me if she knows I have let you stay talking nonsense here?"

"Yes, Lucilla—this moment," said Tom; but all the same he showed not the slightest inclination to go away. He did not quite believe in it as yet, and could not help feeling as if, should he venture to leave her, the whole fabric of his incredible good fortune must dissolve and melt away. As for Lucilla, her self-possession gradually came back to her when the crisis was over, and she felt that her involuntary abdication had lasted long enough, and that it was full time to take the management of affairs back into her own hands.

"You shall go *now*," she said, drying her eyes, "or else you cannot stay here. I thought of letting you stay in the house, as aunt Jemima is with me; but if you do not mean to go and tell your mother, I will tell Nancy to send your things up to the Blue Boar. Ring the bell, please; if you will not ring the bell, I can do it myself, Tom. You may say what you like, but I know you are famishing; and aunt Jemima is in the blue room, next door to——oh, here is Nancy. It is Mr Tom, who has come home," said Lucilla, hastily, not without a rising colour; for it was hard to explain why, when his mother was in the blue room all this time, he should have stayed here.

"Yes, Miss Lucilla—so I heard," said Nancy, dropping a doubtful curtsy. And then only Tom was persuaded, and bethought himself of his natural duty, and rushed up-stairs. He seized Nancy's hand, and shook it violently, as he passed her, to her great consternation. The moment of his supremacy was over. It was to be Tom after all; but Lucilla had recovered her self-possession, and taken the helm in her hand again, and Tom was master of the situation no more.

"Yes, it is Mr Tom," said Lucilla, shaking her head with something between a smile and a sigh. "It could be nobody but him that would ring *that* bell, and upset all the cards. I hope he has not broken dear papa's punch-bowl that he used to be so fond of. He must have something to eat, Nancy, though he is such an awkward boy."

"I don't see nothing like a boy in him," said Nancy; "he's big and stout, and one o' them awful beards. There's been a deal of changes since he went away; but if he's new comed off that terrible long journey, it is but natural, as you say, Miss Lucilla, that he should want something to eat."

And then Miss Marjoribanks made various suggestions, which were received still doubtfully by her prime minister. Nancy, to tell the truth, did not like the turn things were taking. Lucilla's maiden household had been on the whole getting along very comfortably, and there was no telling how long it might have lasted without any new revolution. To be sure, Mr Ashburton had looked dangerous, but Nancy had seen a great many dangers of that kind blow over, and was not easily alarmed. Mr Tom, however, was a very different person; and Nancy was sufficiently penetrating to see that something had happened. Therefore she received very coldly Lucilla's suggestions about lunch. "It ain't like the old times," she said at last, "when there was always something as one could put to the fire in a hurry;" and Nancy stood turning round the handle of the door in her hand, and contemplating the changed state of affairs with a sigh.

"That would be all very true if you were like anybody else," said Lucilla; "but I hope you would not like to send Mr Tom off to the Blue Boar. After all, perhaps it is better to have a—a gentleman in the house. I know you always used to think so. They are a great deal of trouble; but—for some things, you know——" said Lucilla; "and then Mr Tom is not just like other people; and whatever happens, Nancy, you are an old dear, and it shall never make any difference between you and me."

When she had said these words, Lucilla gave her faithful servant a hug, and sent her off to look after Tom Marjoribanks's meal; and then she herself went half-way down-stairs and picked up the cards that were still scattered about the landing, and found with satisfaction that the Doctor's old punchbowl was not broken. All Tom's things were lying below in the hall—heaps of queer Indian-looking baggage—tossed down anyhow in a corner, as if the owner had been in much too great a hurry to think of any secondary circumstances. "And it was there he met poor Mr Ashburton," said Lucilla to herself, with a certain pathos. There it was indeed that the encounter had taken place. They had seen each other but for a moment, but that moment had been enough to send the Member for Carlingford away dejected, and to impress upon Tom's mind the alternative that it was either to be "him or me." Miss Marjoribanks contemplated the spot with a certain tender sentimental interest, as any gentle moralist might look at a field of battle. What feelings must have been in the minds of the two as they met and looked at each other! What a dread sense of disappointment on the one side; what sharp stimulation on the other! Thus Lucilla stood and looked down from her own landing upon the scene of that encounter, full of pensive interest. And now it was all over, and Mr Ashburton had passed away as completely as Mr Chiltern, who was in his grave, poor man; or Mr Cavendish, who was going to marry Barbara Lake. The thought of so

2 E

sudden a revolution made Lucilla giddy as she went thoughtfully up-stairs. Poor Mr Ashburton! It hardly seemed real even to Miss Marjoribanks when she sat down again in the drawing-room, and confessed to herself that, after all, it was to be Tom.

But when he came down-stairs again with his mother, Lucilla was quite herself, and had got over all her weakness. Aunt Jemima, for her part, was in a very agitated state of mind. Tom had come too soon or Mr Ashburton too late, and all the fruits of her little bit of treachery were accordingly lost, and, at the same time, the treachery itself remained, revealed at least to one person in the very clearest light. It did not seem possible to aunt Jemima that Lucilla would not tell. If she had not done it now, in the excitement of the moment, at least it would come out some time when she was least expecting it, and her son's esteem and confidence would be lost. Therefore it was with a very blank countenance that Mrs John Marjoribanks came down-stairs. She dared not say a word, and she had to kiss her niece, and take her to her maternal bosom, Tom looking on all the while; but she gave Lucilla a look that was pitiful to see. And when Tom finally was dismissed to his room, to open his trunks and show the things he had brought home, aunt Jemima drew near her future daughter with wistful guiltiness. There was no comfort to her in the thought of the India shawl, which her son had gone to find. Any day, any hour, Lucilla might tell; and if the unlucky mother were put on her defence, what could she say?

"Lucilla," said the guilty woman, under her breath, "I am sure you think it very strange. I don't attempt to deceive *you*. I can't tell you how thankful and glad I am that it has all ended so well ; but you know, Lucilla, in the first place, I did not know what your feelings were; and I thought, perhaps, that if anything would tell, it would be a surprise, and then——"

"Did you, aunt Jemima?" said Miss Marjoribanks, with gentle wonder. "I thought you had been thinking of Mr Ashburton, for my part."

"And so I was, Lucilla," said the poor lady, with great relief and eagerness. "I thought he was coming forward, and of course he would have been a far better match than my Tom. I had to think for you both, my dear. And then I never knew what your feelings were, nor if you would care ; and then it was not as if there had been a day fixed——"

"Dear aunt Jemima," said Miss Marjoribanks, "if you are pleased now, what does it matter? but I do hope you are pleased now?"

And Mrs John took her niece into her arms again, this time with better will, and cried. "I am as happy as ever I can be," said the inconsistent mother. "I always knew you were fond of each other, Lucilla; before you knew it yourselves, I saw what would come of it. But my poor brother-in-law—— And you will make my boy happy, and never turn him against his mother," cried the repentant sinner. Lucilla was not the woman to resist such an appeal. Mrs John had meant truly enough towards her in other ways, if not in this way; and Miss Marjoribanks was fond of her aunt, and it ended in a kiss of peace freely bestowed, and a vow of protection and guidance from the strong to the weak, though the last was only uttered in the protectress's liberal heart.

CHAPTER LI.

When Miss Marjoribanks had time to consider the prospect which had thus so suddenly opened before her, it also had its difficulties, like everything else in the world. Her marriage now could not be the straightforward business it might have been had it been Mr Ashburton instead of Tom. In that case she would have gone to an established house and life—to take her place in the one and her share in the other, and to find the greater part of her surroundings and duties already fixed for her, which was a thing that would have very greatly simplified the matter. But Tom, who had dashed home from India at full speed as soon as he heard of his uncle's death, had left his profession behind him at Calcutta, and had nothing to do in England, and was probably too old to resume his (non) practice at the bar, even if he had been in the least disposed to do so; while, at the same time, an idle man—a man to be found everlastingly at home—would have been insupportable to Lucilla. Miss Marjoribanks might feel disposed (for everybody's good) to assume the sovereign authority in her own house, but to marry anybody that would be merely an appendage to her was a thing not to be thought of; and as soon as the first preliminaries were arranged her active mind sprang up with redoubled vigour from the maze in which it had been. Her intelligence had suspended, so to speak, all its ordinary operations for twenty-four hours at least, while it was busy investigating the purely personal question: from the moment when the Member for Carlingford was finally elected until Tom Marjoribanks rang the night-bell at the old Doctor's door, Lucilla's thoughts had been in that state of over-stimulation and absorption which is almost as bad as having no power of thought at all. But as soon as the pressure was removed—as soon as it was all over, and the decision made, and no further question was possible—then Miss Marjoribanks's active mind sprang up with renewed energy. For it was not only a new beginning, but everything had to be settled and arranged.

Her mind was full of it while her hands were busy putting away all the Indian presents which Tom had brought—presents which were chronological in their character, and which he had begun to accumulate from the very beginning of his exile. It could not but be touching to Lucilla to see how he had thought of her for all these years; but her mind being, as everybody is aware, of a nobly practical kind, her thoughts, instead of dallying with these tokens of the past, went forward with serious solicitude into the future. The marriage could not take place until the year was out; and there was, accordingly, time to arrange everything, and to settle all the necessary preliminaries to a point as near perfection as is possible to merely human details. Tom, no doubt, was very urgent and pressing, and would have precipitated everything, and had the whole business concluded to-morrow, if he could have had his way. But the fact was that, having once given in to him in the memorable way which we have already recorded, Lucilla did not now, so far as the final arrangements were concerned, make much account of Tom's wishes. Heaven be praised, there was one of the two who knew what was right and proper, and was not to be moved from the correct path by any absurd representations. Miss Marjoribanks was revolving all these important questions when she laid her hand by chance, as people say, upon the 'Carlingford Gazette,' all damp and inky, which had just been laid upon the library table. It contained, of course, all the news of the election, but Lucilla was too well acquainted with that beforehand to think of condescending to derive her information from a newspaper. She looked at the advertisements with an eye which saw all that was there without pausing upon anything in particular. She saw the usual notice about Marmalade Oranges, and the announcement that young Mr Vincent, who after that made himself so well known in Carlingford, was to preach the next Sunday in Salem Chapel, and all the other important novelties in the place; but naturally she took but a moderate amount of interest in such details as these.

Suddenly, however, Lucilla's eye, which, if it could ever be said to be vacant, had been regarding vacantly the list of advertisements, kindled up, and all its usual energy and intelligence came back to it. Her thoughtful face woke up as from a dream. Her head, which had been drooping in pensive meditation, grew erect—her whole figure expanded. She clasped her hands together, as if in the fervour of the moment, nobody else being present, she could not refrain from shaking hands with herself, and giving vent to a self-congratulation. "It is a special providence," said Lucilla to herself, with her usual piety; and then she folded up the paper in a little square, with the announcement in the middle which had struck her so much, and placed it where Tom could not fail to see it when he came in, and went up-stairs with a new and definite direction given to her thoughts. That was how it must be! Lucilla, for her part, felt no difficulty in discerning the leadings of Providence, and she could not but appreciate the readiness with which her desires were attended to, and the prompt clearing-up of her difficulties. There are people whose inclinations Providence does not seem to superintend with such painstaking watchfulness; but then, no doubt, that must be their own fault.

And when Tom came in, they had what aunt Jemima called "one of their discussions" about their future life, although the only thing in it worthy consideration, so far as Tom was concerned, seemed to be the time when they should be married, which occupied at present all that hero's faculties. "Everything else will arrange itself after, you know," he said, with calm confidence. "Time enough for all the rest. The thing is, Lucilla, to decide when you will leave off those formalities, and let It be. Why shouldn't it be now? Do you think my uncle would wish to keep us unhappy all for an idea?"

"My dear Tom, I am not in the least unhappy," said Lucilla, interrupting him sweetly, "nor you either, unless you tell dreadful stories; and as for poor dear papa," Miss Marjoribanks added, with a sigh, "if we were to do exactly as *he* wished, I don't think It would ever be. If you were not so foolish, you would not oblige me to say such things. Tom, let us leave off talking nonsense—the thing that we both want is something to do."

"That is what *I* want," said Tom, quickly; "but as for you, Lucilla, you shall do nothing but enjoy yourself and take care of yourself. The idea of *you* wanting something to do!"

Miss Marjoribanks regarded her betrothed with mild and affectionate contempt as he thus delivered himself of his foolish sentiments. "It is of no use trying to make him understand," she said, with an air of resignation. "Do you know that I have always been doing something, and responsible for something, all my life?"

"Yes, my poor darling," said Tom, "I know; but now you are in my hands I mean to take care of you, Lucilla; you shall have no more anxiety or trouble. What is the good of a man if he can't save the woman he is fond of from all that?" cried the honest fellow—and Lucilla could not but cast a despairing glance round her, as if appealing to heaven and earth. What was to be done with a man who had so little understanding of her, and of himself, and of the eternal fitness of things?

"My dear Tom," she said once more, mildly, "we may have lost some money, but we are very well off, and Providence has been very kind to us. And there are a great many poor people in the world who are not so well off. I have always tried to be of some use to my fellow-creatures," said Lucilla, "and I don't mean, whatever you may say, to give it up now."

"My dearest Lucilla, if it was the poor you were thinking of——! I might have known it was something different from my stupid notions," cried Tom. This kind of adoration was new to Lucilla, notwithstanding her many experiences. And he thought it so good of her to condescend to be good, that she could not help thinking a little better of herself than ordinary, though that, perhaps, was not absolutely needful; and then she proceeded with the elucidation of her views.

"I have been of some use to my fellow-creatures in my way," said Miss Marjoribanks, modestly, "but it has been hard work, and people are not always grateful, you know. And then things are a good deal changed in Carlingford. A woman may devote herself to putting some life into society, and give up years of her time, and—and even her opportunities and all that, and do a great deal of good; but yet if she is put aside for a moment, there is an end of it. I have been doing the best I could for Carlingford for ten years," said Lucilla, with a little natural sadness, "and if any one were to examine into it, where is it all now? They have only got into the way of looking to me; and I do believe if you were to go up and down from Elsworthy's to St Roque's, though you might find people at dinner here and there, you would not find a shadow of what could really be called society in all Grange Lane!"

Lucilla paused, for naturally her feelings were moved; and while Tom bent over her with tender and respectful devotion, it was not to be wondered at if Miss Marjoribanks, in the emotion of her heart, should wipe away a tear.

"After working at it for ten years!" said Lucilla; "and now, since poor papa died, who was always full of discrimination—— This is what will come of it, Tom," she added, solemnly—"they will go back to their old ridiculous parties, as if they had never seen anything better; and they will all break up into little cliques, and make their awful morning calls and freeze one another to death. That will be the end of it all, after one has slaved like a—like a woman in a mill," said the disappointed reformer, "and given up ten years."

"My poor darling!" cried Tom, who would have liked to go and challenge Carlingford for being so insensible to his Lucilla's devotion and cherishing maternal care.

"But if it had been the poor," said Miss Marjoribanks, recovering her spirits a little, "they could not help being the better for what one did for them. They might continue to be as stupid as ever, and ungrateful, and all that; but if they were warm and comfortable, instead of cold and hungry, it would always make a difference. Tom, I will tell you what you will do if you want to please me. You will take all our money and realise it, you know, whatever that means, and go off directly, as fast as the train can carry you, and buy an estate."

"An estate!" cried Tom, in consternation; and the magnitude of the word was such, and Lucilla was so entirely in earnest, that he jumped from his chair and gazed at her as if constrained, notwithstanding his amazement, to rush off instantly and obey.

"I did not mean just this moment," said Lucilla; "sit down, and we can talk it all over, Tom. You know it would be something for you to do; you cannot just go living on like this at your age; you could improve the land, you know, and do all that sort of thing, and the people you could leave to me."

"But Lucilla," said Tom, recovering a little from his consternation, "it is not so easy buying an estate. I mean all that I have to be settled upon you, in case of anything happening.

Land may be a safe enough investment; but, you know, very often, Lucilla—the fact is, it doesn't pay."

"*We* could make it pay," said Miss Marjoribanks, with a benevolent smile, "and besides there are estates and estates. I don't want you to go and throw away your money. It was in the 'Carlingford Gazette' this morning, and I can't help feeling it was a special providence. Of course you never looked at it in the paper, though I marked it for you. Tom, it is Marchbank that I want you to buy. You know how papa used to talk of it. He used to say it was just a nice little property that a gentleman could manage. If he had been spared," said Lucilla, putting her handkerchief to her eyes, "and these wicked dreadful people had not failed, nor nothing happened, I know he would have bought it himself. Dear papa! and he would have given it to me; and most likely, so far as one can tell, it would have come to you at the last, and you would have been Marjoribanks of Marchbank, like our great-great-grandpapa; and that is what I want you to do."

Lucilla's proposition, as it thus unfolded itself, took away Tom Marjoribanks's breath, for notwithstanding that it came from a (young) lady, and was confused by some slightly unintelligible conditions about doing good to one's fellow-creatures, it was not a trifling or romantic suggestion. Tom, too, could remember Marchbank, and his uncle's interest in it, and the careful way in which he explained to the ignorant that this was the correct pronunciation of his own name. While Lucilla made her concluding address, Tom seemed to see himself a little fellow, with his eyes and his ears very wide open, trotting about with small steps after the Doctor, as he went over the red brick house and neglected gardens at Marchbank: it was only to be let then, and had passed through many hands, and was in miserable case, both lands and house. But neither the lands nor the house were bad of themselves, and Tom was, like Lucilla, perfectly well aware that something might be made of them.

This idea gave a new direction to his thoughts. Though he had been brought up to the bar, he had never been a lover of town, and was in reality, like so many young Englishmen, better qualified to be something in the shape of a country gentleman than for any other profession in the world; and he had left his profession behind, and was in most urgent want of something to do. He did not give in at once with a lover's abject submission, but thought it over for twenty-four hours at all his spare moments,—when he was smoking his evening cigar in the garden, and studying the light in his lady's window, and when he ought to have been asleep, and again in the morning when he sallied forth, before Miss Marjoribanks's blinds were drawn up or the house had fairly awoke. He was not a man of brilliant ability, but he had that sure and steady eye for the real secret of a position which must have been revealed to every competent critic by the wonderful clearsightedness with which he saw, and the wise persistence with which he held to the necessity of an immediate choice between himself and Mr Ashburton. He had seen that there was but one alternative, and he had suffered no delay nor divergence from the question in hand. And it was this same quality which had helped him to the very pretty addition to his small patrimony which he had meant to settle on Lucilla, and which would now make the acquisition of Marchbank an easy thing enough. And though Tom had looked wise on the subject of investment in land, it was a kind of investment in every way agreeable to him. Thus Lucilla's arrow went straight to the mark—straighter even than she had expected; for besides all the other and more substantial considerations, there was to Tom's mind a sweet sense of poetic justice in the thought that, after his poor uncle's failure, who had never thought him good enough for Lucilla, it should be he and no other who would give this coveted possession to his cousin. Had Marchbank been in the market in Dr Marjoribanks's time, it was, as Lucilla herself said, his money that would have bought it; but in such a case, so far as the Doctor was concerned, there would have been little chance for Tom. Now all that was changed, and it was in Tom's hands that the wealth of the family lay. It was he who was the head, and could alone carry out what Lucilla's more original genius suggested. If the Doctor could but have seen it, he who had formed plans so very different—but perhaps by that time Dr Marjoribanks had found out that Providence after all had not been so ill-advised as he once thought in committing to his care such a creative intelligence as that of Lucilla, and withholding from him "the boy."

As for Miss Marjoribanks, after she had made up her mind and stated her conviction, she gave herself no further trouble on the subject, but took it for granted, with that true wisdom which is unfortunately so rare among women. She did not talk about it overmuch, or display any feverish anxiety about Marchbank, but left her suggestion to work, and had faith in Tom. At the same time, the tranquillising sense of now knowing, to a certain extent, what lay before her came into Lucilla's mind. It would be a new sphere, but a sphere in which she would find herself at home. Still near enough to Carlingford to keep a watchful eye upon society and give it the benefit of her experience, and yet at the same time translated into a new world, where her influence might be of untold advantage, as Lucilla modestly said, to her fellow-creatures. There was a village not far from the gates at Marchbank, where every kind of village nuisance was to be found. There are people who are very tragical about village nuisances, and there are other people who assail them with loathing, as a duty forced upon their consciences; but Lucilla was neither of the one way of thinking nor of the other. It gave her the liveliest satisfaction to think of all the disorder and disarray of the Marchbank village. Her fingers itched to be at it—to set all the crooked things straight, and clean away the rubbish, and set everything, as she said, on a sound foundation. If it had been a model village, with prize flower-gardens and clean as Arcadia, the thought of it would not have given Miss Marjoribanks half so much pleasure. The recollection of all the wretched hovels and miserable cottages exhilarated her heart.

"They may be as stupid and ungrateful as they like," she said to herself, "but to be warm and comfortable instead of cold and hungry always makes a difference." Perhaps it was not the highest motive possible, and it might be more satisfactory to some people to think of Lucilla as actuated by lofty sentiments of philanthropy; but to persons acquainted with Miss Marjoribanks's character, her biographer would scorn to make any pretence. What would be the good of a spirit full of boundless activity and benevolent impulses if there was nobody to help?—what would be the use of self-devotion if the race in general stood in no need of charitable ministrations? Lucilla had been of use to her fellow-creatures all her life; and though she was about to relinquish one branch of usefulness, that was not to say that she should be prevented from entering into another. The state of the Marchbank village did her good to the very bottom of her soul. It justified her to herself for her choice of Tom, which, but for this chance of doing good, might perhaps have had the air of a merely selfish personal preference. Now she could regard it in a loftier light, and the thought was sweet to Lucilla; for such a beautiful way of helping her neighbour would no doubt have been to a certain extent impracticable amid the many occupations of the Member's wife.

Perhaps the most difficult thing in Miss Marjoribanks's way at this otherwise satisfactory moment was the difficulty she found in persuading society, first of the reality, and then of the justice, of the step she had taken. Most of them, to tell the truth, had forgotten all about Tom Marjoribanks. It is true that when Lucilla's intentions and prospects were discussed in Grange Lane, as they had been so often, it was not uncommon for people to say, "There was once a cousin, you know;" but nobody had ever given very much heed to the suggestion. When Lucilla went to tell Mrs Chiley of what had happened, she was but inadequately prepared for the surprise with which her intelligence was received. For it all seemed natural enough to Miss Marjoribanks. She had gone on very steadily for a long time, without thinking particularly about anybody, and disposed to accept the most eligible and satisfactory person who happened to present himself; but all the time there had been a warm corner in her heart for Tom. And then the eligible person had not come, and she had been worried and wearied, and had had her losses, like most other people. And it had always been pleasant to remember that there was one man in the world who, if she but held out a finger to him—— But then the people in Grange Lane were not capable of discrimination on such a delicate subject, and had never, as was to be expected, had the smallest insight into Lucilla's heart.

"You have something to tell me, Lucilla?" said old Mrs Chiley. "You need not say no, for I can see it in your eyes. And how lucky it is the Colonel is out, and we can have it all to ourselves! Come here and sit by me, and tell me all—every word."

"Dear Mrs Chiley," said Lucilla, "you can always see what one means before one says a word. And it has all happened so suddenly; but the very first thing I thought of doing was to come and tell you."

Mrs Chiley gave her young friend, who was leaning over her, a hug, which was the only answer which could be made to so touching a speech, and drew Lucilla down upon a low chair that had been placed by the side of her sofa. She kept Miss Marjoribanks's hand in her own, and caressed it, and looked at her with satisfaction in every line of her face. After waiting so long, and having so many disappointments, everything was going to turn out so entirely as it ought to do at last.

"I think I know what you are going to tell me, my dear," said Mrs Chiley; "and I am so pleased, Lucilla. I only wonder you did not give me a hint from the very first. You remember I asked you when you came here that snowy evening. I was a hard-hearted old woman, and I daresay you were very vexed; but I am so glad to think that the Colonel never stood out against him, but gave his consent that very day."

This was the moment, if there ever was such a moment, when Lucilla lost courage. Mrs Chiley was so entirely confident as to what was coming, and it was something so different that was really coming; and it was hard upon Miss Marjoribanks to feel that she was about to disappoint everybody's expectations. She had to clear her throat before she spoke—she who was generally so ready for every emergency; and she could not help feeling for the moment as if she was a young girl who had run away with somebody, and deceived all her anxious friends.

"Dear Mrs Chiley, I am afraid I am not going to say what you expected," said Lucilla. "I am very comfortable and happy, and I think it's for the best; and I am so anxious that you should like him; but it is not the person you are thinking of. It is——"

Here the old lady, to Lucilla's surprise, rose up upon her pillows and threw her arms round her, and kissed her over again, and fell a-crying. "I always said how generous you were, Lucilla," cried Mrs Chiley. "I knew it from the first. I was always fond of him, you know; and now that he has been beaten, poor dear, and disappointed, you've gone and made it up to him! Lucilla, other people may say what they like, but it is just what I always expected of you!"

This unlooked-for burst of enthusiasm took Lucilla entirely by surprise. She could not say in reply that Mr Cavendish did not want her to make it up to him; but the fact that this was the only alternative which occurred to Mrs Chiley filled Miss Marjoribanks with a sense of something like positive guilt. She had deceived everybody, and raised false expectations, and how was she to explain herself? It was with humility and embarrassment that she spoke.

"I don't know what you will say when you hear who it really is," she said. "He has been fond of me all this time, though he has been so far away. He went to India because I sent him, and he came back as soon as ever he heard about— what had happened. And what could I do? I could not be so ungrateful or so hard-hearted *again*, as to send him away?"

"Lucilla, who is it?" said Mrs Chiley, growing pale—for she generally had a little wintry bloom on her cheek, like the China roses she was so fond of. "Don't keep me like this in suspense."

"Dear Mrs Chiley," said Lucilla, with the brevity of excitement, "I don't see what other person in the world it could be but my cousin Tom."

Poor Mrs Chiley started, so that the sofa and Lucilla's chair and the very room shook. She said herself afterwards that she felt as if somebody had discharged a pistol into her breast. She was so shocked and startled that she threw off all her coverings and the Affghanistan blanket Mrs Beverley had sent, and put her tottering feeble old feet to the floor; and then she took her young friend solemnly by both her hands.

"Oh, Lucilla, my poor dear!" she cried, "you have gone and done it without thinking what you were doing. You have taken it into your head that it was all over, and that there was nothing more to look for. And you are only nine-and-twenty, Lucilla; and many a girl marries very well—better than common—long after she's nine-and-twenty; and I know for a fact —oh! my poor dear child, I know for a *certain* fact!—that Mr Ashburton was coming forward. He as good as said it to Lady Richmond, Lucilla. He as good as said, as soon as the election was over—and now you have gone and got impatient, and thrown yourself away!"

Miss Marjoribanks was quite carried away for the moment by this flood of sorrowful eloquence. She was silenced, and had nothing to answer, and accepted it as in some respect the just penalty for the disappointment she was causing to everybody. She let Mrs Chiley say out her say, and then she restored the old lady to her sofa, and made her comfortable, and covered her up with all her wraps and blankets. Though she ran on in a feeble strain, all the time weeping and lamenting, Lucilla took no notice. She wrapped her old friend up, and put her pillows just as she liked them, and sat down again on the low chair; and by that time the poor old lady had sunk into a faint sob of vexation and disappointment, and had given her remonstrances up.

"Now, I will tell you all about it," said Miss Marjoribanks. "I knew you would be surprised; and if it would be any comfort to you, dear Mrs Chiley, to know that Mr Ashburton *did*——"

"And you refused him, Lucilla?" Mrs Chiley asked, with horror in her face.

"Ought I to have accepted him when there was somebody I liked better?" said Lucilla, with the force of conscious virtue, "and you used always to say just the contrary. One great thing that supported me was, that *you* would be sure to understand. I did not know it at the time," said Miss Marjoribanks, with sweet confidence and simplicity, "but I see it all now. Why it never came to anything before, you know, was, that I never could in my heart have accepted anybody but Tom."

Mrs Chiley turned round with an unaffected surprise, which was not unmingled with awe. Up to this moment she had been under the impression that it was the blindness, and folly, and stupidity of the gentlemen which had kept it from ever coming to anything. It was altogether a new light that broke upon her now, confusing, though on the whole satisfactory; but for the moment she was struck dumb, and had no answer to make.

"I never knew it myself until—quite lately," said Miss Marjoribanks, with confidential tenderness, "and I don't think I could tell it to any one but you. Dear Mrs Chiley, you have always taken such an interest in me! I sent him away, you know, and thought I was only fond of him because he was my cousin. And then there were all the others, and some of them were very nice; but always when it came to the point—— And it never came into my head that Tom was at the bottom of it all—never till the other day."

Mrs Chiley was still so much confounded by this unexpected revelation that it was some time before she could find her voice; and even now the light penetrated slowly into her mind, and it was only by degrees that she accepted the new fact thus presented to her faith—that it was not the gentlemen who were to blame—that it was all Lucilla's or rather Tom Marjoribanks's fault.

"And Mr Ashburton, Lucilla?" she asked, faintly.

"I am very sorry," said Miss Marjoribanks, "very, very sorry; but I don't think I can blame myself that I gave him encouragement, you know. I may have been foolish at other times, but I am sure I was very careful with him. It was all the election that was to blame. I spoke very frankly to him," Lucilla added, "for I knew he was a man to do me justice; and it will always be a comfort to me to think that we had our—our explanation, you know, before I knew it was Tom."

"Well, Lucilla, it is a great change," said Mrs Chiley, who could not reconcile herself to the new condition of affairs. "I don't mean to pretend that I can make up my mind to it all at once. It seems so strange that you should have been setting your heart on some one all these ten years, and never saying a word; I wonder how you could do it. And when people were always in the hopes that you would marry at home, as it were, and settle in Carlingford. I am sure your poor dear papa would be as much astonished as anybody. And I suppose now he will take you away to Devonshire, where his mother lives, and we shall never see you any more." And once more Mrs Chiley gave a little sob. "The Firs would almost have been as good as Grange Lane," she said, "and the Member for Carlingford, Lucilla!"

As for Miss Marjoribanks, she knelt down by the side of the sofa and took her old friend, as well as the blankets and pillows would permit, into her arms.

"Dear Mrs Chiley, we are going to buy Marchbank and settle," said Lucilla, weeping a little for company. "You could not think I would ever go far away from you. And as for being Member for Carlingford, there are Members for counties too," Miss Marjoribanks said in her excitement. It was a revelation which came out unawares, and which she never intended to utter; but it threw a gleam of light over the new world of ambition and progress which was opened to Lucilla's far-seeing vision; and Mrs Chiley could not but yield to the spell of mingled awe and sympathy which thrilled through her as she listened. It was not to be supposed that what Lucilla did was done upon mere unthinking impulse; and when she thought of Marchbank, there arose in Mrs Chiley's mind "the slow beginnings of content."

"But, Lucilla," the old lady said with solemnity, as she gave her a last kiss of reconciliation and peace, "if all Grange Lane had taken their oaths to it, I never could have believed, had you not told me, that, after all, it was to be Tom!"

CHAPTER THE LAST.

THIS was the hardest personal encounter which Miss Marjoribanks was subjected to; but when the news circulated in Grange Lane there was first a dead pause of incredulity and amazement, and then such a commotion as could be compared to nothing except a sudden squall at sea. People who had been going peaceably on their way at one moment, thinking of nothing, were to be seen the next buffeted by the wind of Rumour and tossed about on the waves of Astonishment. To speak less metaphorically (but there are moments of emotion so overwhelming and unprecedented that they can be dealt with only in the language of metaphor), every household in Grange Lane, and at least half of the humbler houses in Grove Street, and a large proportion of the other dwellings in Carlingford, were nearly as much agitated about Lucilla's marriage as if it had been a daughter of their own. Now that he was recalled to their minds in such a startling way, people began to recollect with greater and greater distinctness that "there was once a cousin, you know," and to remember him in his youth, and even in his boyhood, when he had been much in Carlingford. And by degrees the Grange Lane people came to see that they knew a great deal about Tom, and to remind each other of the abrupt end of his last visit, and of his going to India immediately after, and of many a little circumstance in Lucilla's looks and general demeanour which this *dénouement* seemed to make plain.

Lady Richmond, though she was a little annoyed about Mr Ashburton's disappointment, decided at once that it was best to ignore that altogether, and was quite glad to think that she had always said there must be somebody. "She bore up a great deal too well against all her little disappointments," she said, when discussing the matter. "When a girl does that, one may be always sure there is somebody behind—and you know I always said, when she was not just talking or busy, that there was a preoccupation in Lucilla's eye." This was a speech which Mrs Woodburn, as might have been expected, made a great deal of—but, notwithstanding, it had its effect in Grange Lane. Going back upon their recollections, most people were able to verify the fact that Miss Marjoribanks had borne her little disappointments very well, and that there was sometimes a preoccupation in her eye. The first was beyond dispute; and as for the second, it was a thing which did not require a very great stretch of imagination to suppose—and the unexpected sensation of finding at last a distinct bit of romance to round off Lucilla's history, was pleasant to most people. If she had married Mr Ashburton, it would have been (so far as anything connected with Miss Marjoribanks could be) a commonplace conclusion. But now she had upset everybody's theories, and made an altogether original and unlooked-for ending for herself, which was a thing to have been expected from Lucilla, though nobody could have foreseen the special turn which her originality would take.

And nothing could have come in more appropriately after the

election, when people felt the blank of ordinary existence just beginning to settle down upon them again. It kept all Carlingford in conversation for a longer time than might be supposed in these busy days; for there was not only the fact itself, but what *they* were to do, and where they were to go, to be discussed. And then Tom himself began to be visible about Grange Lane; and he had heaps of Indian things among his baggage, and recollected so affectionately the people he used to know, and dispensed his curiosities with such a liberal hand, that the heart of Carlingford was touched. He had a way of miscalculating distances, as has been said, and exercised some kind of magnetic influence upon all the little tables and unsteady articles of furniture, which somehow seemed to fall if he but looked at them. But, on the other hand, John Brown, who had in hand the sale of Marchbank, found him the most straightforward and clear-headed of clients. The two had all the preliminaries arranged before any other intending purchaser had time to turn the matter over in his mind. And Tom had the old brick house full of workmen before anybody knew it was his. When the summer had fairly commenced he went over and lived there, and saw to everything, and went so far as to fit up the drawing-room with the same well-remembered tint of pale-green which had been found ten years ago to suit so well with Lucilla's complexion. It was perhaps a little hazardous to repeat the experiment, for green, as everybody knows, is a very trying colour; but it was a most touching and triumphant proof that to Tom, at least, Lucilla was as young as ever, and had not even begun to go off. It was Mr Holden who supplied everything, and he was naturally proud of the trust thus reposed in him, and formed the very highest opinion of his customer; and it was probably from his enthusiasm on this subject that might be traced the commencement of that singular revolution of sentiment in Grange Lane, which suddenly woke up all in an instant without knowing how, to recognise the existence of Mr Marjoribanks, and to forget the undue familiarity which had ventured upon the name of Tom.

When Lucilla went over in the most proper and decorous way, under the charge of aunt Jemima, to see her future home, the sight of the village at Marchbank was sweet to her eyes. That it was not by any means sweet to any other sense, did but enhance Miss Marjoribanks's satisfaction. "A year after this!" she said to herself, and her bosom swelled; for to realise clearly how much she had it in her power to do for her fellow-creatures was indeed a pleasure. It occupied her a great deal more than the gardens did, which Tom was arranging so carefully; or even than the kitchen, which she inspected for the information of Nancy; for at that time the drawing-room was not fitted up. Lucilla's eyes went over the moral wilderness with the practical glance of a statesman, and, at the same time, the sanguine enthusiasm of a philanthropist. She saw of what it was capable, and already, in imagination, the desert blossomed like a rose before her beneficent steps, and the sweet sense of well-doing rose in her breast. And then to see Tom at Marchbank was to see his qualities. He was not a man of original mind, nor one who would be likely to take a bold initiative. Considering all the circumstances, that was a gift which was scarcely to be wished for; but he had a perfect genius for carrying out a suggestion, which, it need scarcely be added, was a faculty that, considering the good fortune which Providence had so long reserved for him, made his character as near perfect as humanity permits. Lucilla felt, indeed, as she drove away, that approbation of Providence which a well-regulated mind, in possession of most things which it desires, might be expected to feel. Other delusive fancies *had* one time and another swept across her horizon; but after all there could be no doubt that only thus could she have been fitly mated, and full development afforded to all the resources of her spirit. As the carriage passed the Firs she sighed and put down her veil with a natural sentiment; but still she felt it was for the best. The Member for Carlingford must be a busy man, occupied about his own affairs, and with little leisure for doing good to his fellow-creatures except in a parliamentary way. "And there are members for counties as well," Lucilla, in the depths of her soul, said to herself. Then there rose up before her a vision of a parish saved, a village reformed, a county reorganised, and a triumphant election at the end, the recompense and crown of all, which should put the government of the country itself, to a certain extent, into competent hands. This was the celestial vision which floated before Miss Marjoribanks's eyes as she drove into Carlingford, and recollected, notwithstanding occasional moments of discouragement, the successful work she had done, and the good she had achieved in her native town. It was but the natural culmination of her career that transferred her from the town to the county, and held out to her the glorious task of serving her generation in a twofold way, among the poor and among the rich. If a momentary sigh for Grange Lane, which was about to lose her, breathed from her lips, it was sweetened by a smile of satisfaction for the county which was about to gain her. The lighter preface of life was past, and Lucilla had the comfort of feeling that its course had been full of benefit to her fellow-creatures; and now a larger sphere opened before her feet, and Miss Marjoribanks felt that the arrangements of Providence were on the whole full of discrimination, and that all was for the best, and she had not lived in vain.

This being the case, perhaps it is not necessary to go much further into detail. Mr Ashburton never said anything about his disappointment, as might have been expected. When he did mention that eventful day at all, he said that he had happened accidentally to be calling on Miss Marjoribanks the day her cousin came home, and saw at once the state of affairs; and he sent her a very nice present when she was married. After all, it was not her fault. If Providence had ordained that it was to be Tom, how could Lucilla fly in the face of such an ordinance? and, at the same time, there was to both parties the consoling reflection, that whatever might happen to them as individuals, the best man had been chosen for Carlingford, which was an abiding benefit to all concerned.

Under all the circumstances, it was to be looked for that Miss Marjoribanks's spirits should improve even in her mourning, and that the tenacity with which she clung to her father's house should yield to the changed state of affairs. This was so much the case that Lucilla took heart to show Mrs Rider all over it, and to point out all the conveniences to her, and even, with a sigh, to call her attention to the bell which hung over the Doctor's bedroom door. "It breaks my heart to hear it," Miss Marjoribanks said; "but still Dr Rider will find it a great convenience." It was a very nice house; and so the new Doctor's wife, who had not been used to anything so spacious, was very willing to say; and instead of feeling any grudge against the man who was thus in every respect to take her father's place, so sweet are the softening influences of time and personal wellbeing, that Lucilla, who was always so good-natured, made many little arrangements for their comfort, and even *left the carpets*, which was a thing nobody could have expected of her, and which aunt Jemima did not scruple to condemn. "They are all fitted," Lucilla said, "and if they were taken up they would be spoiled; and besides, we could have no use for them at Marchbank." It was a very kind thing to do, and simplified matters very much for the Riders, who were not rich. But aunt Jemima, in the background, could not but pull Lucilla's sleeve, and mutter indistinct remarks about a valuation, which nobody paid any particular attention to at the moment, as there were so many things much more important to think of and to do.

And the presents that came pouring in from every quarter were enough to have made up for twenty carpets. Lucilla got testimonials, so to speak, from every side, and all Carlingford interested itself, as has been said, in all the details of the marriage, as if it had been a daughter of its own. "And yet it is odd to think that, after all, I never shall be anything but Lucilla Marjoribanks!" she said, in the midst of all her triumphs, with a certain pensiveness. If there could be any name that would have suited her better, or is surrounded by more touching associations, we leave it to her other friends to find out; for at the moment of taking leave of her, there is something consoling to our own mind in the thought that Lucilla can now suffer no change of name. As she was in the first freshness of her youthful daring when she rose like the sun upon the chaos of society in Carlingford, so is she now as she goes forth into the County to carry light and progress there. And in this reflection there is surely comfort for the few remaining malcontents, whom not even his own excellent qualities, and Lucilla's happiness, can reconcile to the fact, that after all it was Tom.

THE END.

www.ingramcontent.com/pod-product-compliance
Lightning Source LLC
Chambersburg PA
CBHW032010300426
44117CB00008B/971